ROBERT MITCHUM

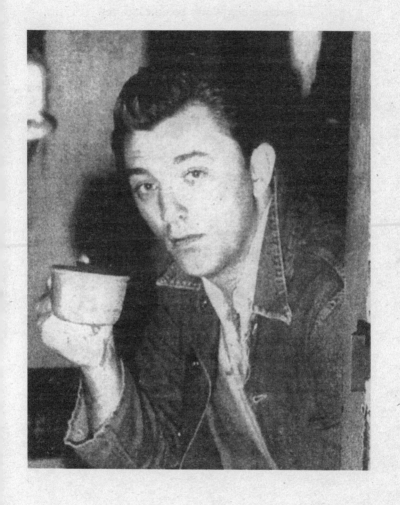

ROBERT MITCHUM
"Baby, I Don't Care"

LEE SERVER

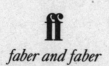

faber and faber

First published in the United States in 2001
by St Martin's Press
175 Fifth Avenue, New York, NY 10010

First published in the United Kingdom in 2001
by Faber and Faber Limited
3 Queen Square London WC1N 3AU

This paperback edition first published in 2002

Typeset by Faber and Faber in Minion
Printed in England by Mackays of Chatham plc, Chatham, Kent

Lee Server is hereby identified as author of this
work in accordance with Section 77 of the Copyright,
Designs and Patents Act 1988

A CIP record for this book
is available from the British Library

ISBN 0–571–21010–4

2 4 6 8 10 9 7 5 3

For
ELIZABETH SERVER
and
TERRI HARDIN

Contents

Jeez, it just struck me—wouldn't it be fun to be a real movie star and get to act like one? "A round for the house, waiter!" Get shitfaced snockered. Wow! Just like Robert Mitchum. That'd be somethin', friends—that'd be something else.

Actor Peter Boyle

*

Warring, boy! Warring together! Left hand and right hand! Hate and Love! Good and Evil! But wait. Hot dog! Old Devil's a-losin' . . . He's a-slippin', boy!

Davis Grubb, *The Night of the Hunter*

Introduction

What do you want, my life story? I told everything I know to the Los Angeles Police Department.

He liked to call himself the oldest whore in town. Just show me that Hollywood green, he would say, I'll play anything: midgets, Chinese washerwomen. An ideal role? Dad, you got to be kidding. Maybe Camille: lie on a couch and cough for twenty reels. Making movies was an economic expedient; pride didn't enter into it. Never forget, he would say, one of the biggest stars in the world was Rin Tin Tin, and she was a four-legged bitch. There were those who enjoyed the attention, Robert Mitchum understood. If they weren't movie stars they would be languishing in custody for exposing themselves in the park. He selected his jobs according to the number of days off. Made a hundred and twenty pictures altogether, forty of them in the same raincoat. Maybe it was a hundred and twenty-five. Hard to keep count. He'd seen very few of the things himself. They didn't pay you to watch 'em. And it was always a pain in the ass to find parking.

Robert Mitchum came from Bridgeport, Connecticut, a town that once elected P. T. Barnum as mayor, and he made his mark in Hollywood, California, the place—a reporter once wrote—he hated with all the venom of someone who owed it everything he had. He was raised in an atmosphere of dislocation and unconventionality, in a family of de facto gypsies uprooted by loss and lack of wherewithal, a kind of test case for the national upheaval to come. The Great Depression further shaped him, a teenager wandering through a landscape of despair and violence. On the road he tangled with cops and grifters, saw corpses and hungry children, grew up before his time. He toured the country by thumb and freight train. He was a hobo, a bum, signature epithets to which he pridefully clung long after he had hopped his last freight. He liked to say, maybe even believed, through all the years of fame and riches, the mansions and sports cars, the dinners with kings and presidents, that he was only here "between trains."

In the 1940s, the bum became a movie actor, first an unshaven bad guy, soon a hero, of a sort. He had a different, curious presence on screen, nothing like it before. The big, muscular physique pegged him for tough guys and outdoor parts, cowboys and soldiers. But the attitude (wry, ambivalent), the style (indolent, soft-spoken), had none of the usual vitality and aggression of the standard-issue male star. He smoldered, had that opiated, heavy-lidded look, had an almost feminine languor, moved only as much as necessary and then with a measured, sinuous grace. He seemed to withdraw from the camera where others would try to attack it. But maybe this was some kind of trick because you found yourself watching him much more closely, afraid you would miss something, a gesture, a mumbled line, a ruffled eyebrow. His acting belonged to no school, no real tradition. He formed his screen characters from a mental storehouse of observational and experiential data and a musical approach to pace and intonation and the spatial relationship of performer to camera. His aura of brooding bemusement and simmering violence found a perfect home in the thriving—yet unnamed—genre of shadows and cynicism and ambiguity now called film noir. *Out of the Past. Crossfire. His Kind of Woman. Angel Face.* He became the movies' outside man, without roots or ties, beyond the bounds of polite society, ever suspicious to the upholders of the law. He made other types of pictures, too, respectable productions, classics fit for the academy, but most of his jobs would be on the cinematic equivalent of the wrong side of the tracks: action

movies, movies with fistfights and bullet wounds, movies about disreputable men and sultry, suspect females. Many years he labored at
RKO for the man he called the Phantom, Howard Hughes, and
Hughes's idea of production values was a girl in a tight sweater.
"Gorilla pictures," Mitchum called them. "I've never done a movie
with guns," a nervous actress said to him on her first day. Mitchum
said, "I've never done one without."

In the 1950s, he abandoned the dying studio system for a more
congenial independence. Widescreen and color and exotic locations
were the thing now. The movies became a "magic carpet" for a guy
with a terminal case of wanderlust. The ex-hobo and would-be soldier-of-fortune took the grand tour at producers' expense, paid daydreams that had him sailing on the Caribbean, grappling with
Swedish starlets in Paris, smuggling moonshine through the Smokey
Mountains, winning revolutions in Old Mexico. He picked his own
pictures now, sometimes produced them. *Bandido! Cape Fear.*
Heaven Knows, Mr. Allison. Night of the Hunter. The Sundowners.
Thunder Road. He made wonderful entertainments and singular
masterpieces and hack jobs of an astonishing banality. Critics had a
love-hate relationship with the star, more often hate, calling him a
sleepwalker, just going through the motions, when awake.
Distinguished associates, Charles Laughton, John Huston, dis-
agreed, thinking him one of the best actors the movies had ever
known, perhaps even the best, a man who ought to have done
Shakespeare's tragedies—with his power and brilliance he could
have been the era's greatest Lear or Macbeth. Mitchum, finding self-
promotion lacking in cool, came down on the side of the critics. "I
have two acting styles," he liked to say. "With and without a horse."

Most Hollywood stars were to some degree exponents of a
personality-based method in which acting was *being,* the characters
predominantly animated by the individual actor's own personality
and perspective (if any). With Mitchum, self-image and screen
image seemed to bleed together with a particular compatibility.
Personal experience and philosophical viewpoint were the life-giv-
ing forces behind those characterizations of disillusion, detachment,
disdain for authority and convention, behind the hooded, haunted

gaze of somebody who had seen things at their worst and knew there was more of the same on its way. The matching of real and reel would come to seem remarkably seamless at times, news reports and film reviews almost interchangeable in their delineations of a brawling, womanizing tough guy, ever at odds with the powers that be, on-screen and off-screen a succession of fistfights, felonies, jail cells, beautiful dames. Art left off and life began, or the other way around, some jazz like that. Hollywood's Bad Boy, the press called him. Lurid headlines charted an unusual lifestyle: "Mitchum in Brawl—G.I. Hospitalized," "Bare Starlet Puts Mitchum in Doghouse," "Narcotic Arrest Smashes Film Career," "Bob Mitchum Due in Court on Flee Rap," "3 Teenage Girls Tell Police: Robert Mitchum Hit Us," "Robert Mitchum, the Nude Who Came to Dinner." In 1948, a drug scandal and subsequent prison term should have finished him in pictures, would have been the finish of another, holier actor, but with Mitchum, the shock, the aftereffects among the ticket buyers—the "great unwashed" he called them—were ultimately softened by prior expectation.

He scoffed at this shallow public persona, the hell-raiser, the lout, the outlaw, even as he supplied new tales of anarchy, fresh outbursts of iconoclasm to every cub reporter in line for an interview. In fact, the popular image revealed only the surface of a more complicated, mostly hidden reality, leaving unexamined the man Mitchum's contradictions and unpredictabilities, his secret selves—Mitchum the poet, the autodidact, the lyric philosopher, the left-wing firebrand, far-right crank, depressed loner, harried husband. A man of many parts, few people ever saw or claimed to know how all the pieces came together, not even those who knew him best. "My family is baffled. My close acquaintances—that's four people—keep asking me where I am, who I am. . . ."

"No. . . . Oh, no," said a long-time professional confidante, "you'll never understand that. I don't know that anyone ever did."

He was a movie star for more than half a century, staying at the job longer than almost anybody, career ebbing and flowing, counted out more than once and then coming back big as ever. *El Dorado.*

Ryan's Daughter. The Friends of Eddie Coyle. Farewell, My Lovely. The Winds of War. The colossal presence, the often brilliant performances, were delivered, as always, without visible fuss. It was a job of work, movie acting, he always said, like plumbing or fixing a car, only with more makeup. His celestial place in the scheme of things cinematic became all the more apparent as the golden age talent pool faded into the sunset. "He's the only Gary Cooper still alive," said the *Winds* producer. People knew what it meant. They didn't make 'em like that anymore. Mitchum was one of a kind and the last of the breed. His stature, his legend, grew even as the jobs he took became unworthy and threadbare. "You don't get to do better," he liked to say, "you only get to do more." Shambling into his seventies, he remained, whatever the crummy project, the movies' supreme outsider, great sad-eyed adventurer, bitterly funny pessimist.

> Reporter: "Mr. Mitchum, do you think you will
>   become a cult hero, say, in the 1990s, like Bogart in
>   the 1960s?"
> Mitchum: "What year is it now, Jack?"

In an era when movie actors cried like schoolgirls if you gave them an award or whined to caring talk-show hostesses if they took too many drugs, Mitchum's mythic presence, an image of beatific stoicism, grace under fire, wry unflappability in the face of life's ever-threatening absurdities, looked all the more majestic and ineffably cool. In the end, when the doctors came and tried to tell him how he had to live his life so as not to die, they found the patient would not cooperate but had bought into the myth himself, as if it were real.

Part one

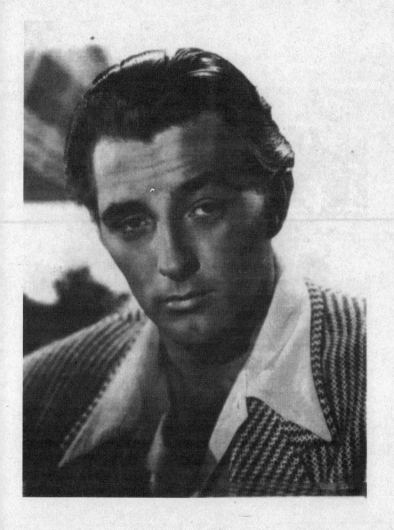

CHAPTER ONE

The Ferret-Faced Kid

His father was A tough son of a bitch, he would say proudly.

The blood of early Scots-Irish settlers and American Indians ran in the veins of James Thomas Mitchum. He hailed from the town of Lane in eastern South Carolina, a small, slim young man with a lean, handsome face and sly, expressive dark eyes. People who knew him remembered a man of much charm and humor, physically strong out of all proportion to his slender frame. He liked a good fight. His fierceness was legendary among those who gathered together to pass around a bottle. The wildness that came with the drinking, people ascribed, as per the prejudicial thinking of the time, to his Indian heritage. Indians, even half-breeds, everybody knew, were drawn to liquor even though the stuff made them lose their minds. Only a fool would challenge Jimmy Mitchum to a fight, but there were always fools to be found in the backcountry of South Carolina as in every other part of the world. When he was seventeen—the first son would speak of this—he was said to have killed a man in a brawl in a place called Hellhole Swamp.

He went into the service, leaving the rural South for the first time in his life. A private in the U.S. Army, he came to be stationed in Connecticut, and it was there, in the port of New London, that the young man met a girl, a pretty, sad-faced Norwegian immigrant named Ann Harriet Gunderson. She was the daughter of a sea captain. Gustav Olaf Gunderson of Christiania, broad-shouldered, barrel-chested, nearly three hundred pounds, had sailed the merciless waters of the North Atlantic and the Barents Sea far above the Arctic Circle. Among the ocean fishermen of Norway there were weird tales told about this giant, powerful man. Once, long ago, a ship he skippered had gone down in a terrible storm. The captain and four crewmen had escaped on a lifeboat, but only Gunderson was still aboard when a rescue ship found him weeks later, looking little the worse for his ordeal. A court of inquiry said that questions remained unanswered. A lurid rumor followed Gunderson—that he had survived by consuming the flesh of his own shipmates.

The captain had a wife, Petrine, a tiny but strong-willed woman, a refined and learned mate for the tough sea rover. Without help for much of each year while Gustav roamed the world, it was Petrine who brought up their three children: son, Charles, daughters Gertrude and Ann Harriet. From the time she was a little girl, Mrs. Gunderson daydreamed of a life on the stage, and she would nurture in her kids a great appreciation of music and books and paintings, a love of art, of beautiful things. Petrine's girls sang, played musical instruments, drew, and painted. And son, Charlie, too, built like his father and like him to become a merchant sailor, loved music and performing and as a boy hoped to grow up to be a song-and-dance man.

Early in the new century the Gunderson family joined the great wave of European migrants crossing the ocean to America. They settled among their fellow "squareheads" in coastal Connecticut, first in New London and then in Bridgeport, a thriving manufacturing center along Long Island Sound at the mouth of the Pequonnock River, a short rail journey north of New York City. In the new homeland the Gundersons resumed a life not so different from what it had been in Norway. Papa returned to the sea, a merchant sailor, gone for weeks and months at a time, and Petrine was left to run the house and raise the family. Young Ann Harriett knew no English when she arrived at Ellis Island, but she had a good mind and studied hard and graduated from high school with honors. One weekend, not long after graduation, she went with her sister to the annual regatta in New London, and there, in her prettiest summer dress, she met a young man. Jimmy Mitchum was handsome and funny and strong. She fell in love. It was the inescapable impulse of the genteel, intelligent Gunderson women to fall for strong, simple men. Sister Gertrude was the same—she had found her own beau, an itinerant wrestler from Quebec.

In the spring of 1913, twenty-year-old Ann and twenty-two-year-old James were wed, and in July of the following year the couple had their first child, a girl they named Annette. The young family lived a life of no special concern. They were happy. Jimmy was a restless, vital character but without any particular ambition in life. He moved them all down to South Carolina for a time, but soon they were back in Bridgeport, living in the big East End house at 476 Logan Street. Sister Gertrude by now had married her own peripatetic scrapper, Wilfred Jean Tetreault. Her new husband had not been able to make a living as a wrestler, and he had not been able to do much else, but Gertie adored him. Jim and Bill became pals, roistering comrades in the watering holes of Connecticut. The pair had a standing challenge at every tavern—they would take on any three comers, any time, any place. Sometimes, when there were no challengers, they went ahead and found them anyway.

On August 6, 1917, at the house in Bridgeport, Ann gave birth to her second child, a blond-haired, hazel-eyed boy. Baptized by the minister from the Newfield Methodist Church, the boy was named Robert Charles Durman Mitchum. He was a taciturn baby—unsmiling in all family photos—and with somber, torpid eyes that attracted much comment. He fell on his head as a small child, and a doctor told the mother her boy showed signs of brain damage. "You can see it in the eyes," the doctor said. "No, that's the way they've always been," said Ann.

Soon the young Mrs. Mitchum was expecting again. "One day when my mother was pregnant with John," Robert would recall in years ahead, "she was on a trolley car and this conductor was harassing her, pushing her to the rear, and my father picked him up and threw him right through the window, jumped out after him and stomped his brains out. He had to leave town."

James Mitchum took his family and returned to the South. They settled in Charleston and he found a job in the port at the military railhead. The end of World War I and the return of personnel and equipment from Europe had put a considerable strain on these transportation centers. There was unending activity in the navy yard where James Mitchum did wearying labor, coupling and uncoupling and helping to shunt the steady streams of heavy freight cars. It was dangerous work. Hardly a day went by without a man mangling a foot or breaking a finger or an arm disentangling those big wooden cars, wrestling the heavy metal couplings with their slivers like tiny daggers that entered the flesh even through thick gloves. Many times, heading off for work, Jimmy Mitchum would tell his wife, "One of these days, Annie, they're going to bring me home in a box."

One February night in 1919, at the Charleston navy yard, Mitchum was standing on a track siding between two boxcars, completing the manual operation of disconnecting one from the other. He had shouted the all clear to a brakeman who had signaled the engineer to haul away. There was no explanation for what happened next. Mixed signals, mechanical error, stupidity. No one would ever be held accountable. It was simply a tragic mistake, an inevitability when men worked among giant, inexorable machines. The train engine started, the boxcar jerked to life. Jimmy Mitchum thought it was pulling forward as expected and he glanced away. But the engine was in reverse and the cars suddenly rolled back. A foot to the left or right and another moment to realize what had happened and there might have been space and time to escape the impact of one car rolling against another. Instead he stood there, caught directly between the solid iron couplers, taking the full weight on flesh and bone. His skeleton shattered. His insides burst and their hematic content exploded from mouth and nose and eyes. The brakeman screamed for help, and men in the yard rushed over to drag him clear, and they carried him indoors and someone went for a doctor, and someone else went to find the injured man's wife. He was still alive when she got there. Ann cradled the broken form in her arms and, weeping on his bloodstained body, she held him like that for some time after he was gone.

A widow at twenty-five. Two children, another on the way. In compensation for her husband's death, the government awarded Mrs. Mitchum an eighteen-dollar-a-month pension. Ann stayed for a time in Jim's hometown of Lane, then, uncomfortable among the small town strangers, gathered her possessions and kids and returned to her own family in Connecticut. The baby was not yet two years old, but he had perceived the sadness all around him. On the train ride north he was inconsolable, cried all the time, mother and sister would remember. He had been just old enough to feel the imprint of his father's presence and then to feel his absence, and he would carry a sense of loss and abandonment into childhood and beyond.

Ann nursed her grief through the spring and summer. On September 6 the widow gave birth to a boy she named John Newman Mitchum.

She began her life again. Family members did what they could to help out. Some relatives offered more than Ann desired. "Uncle Bill Tetreault, the wrestler, Gertrude's monster," Annette recalled, "he was not a scholar and a gentleman. He made passes at Mother, always putting his hands on her. She told him to stop. We all told him to stop. One time she emptied a full coffee-pot with grounds all over his head. That stopped him for then, but he came back and started with the hands on her again. Once she grabbed up a big wad of flypaper and plastered it onto his balding head."

The simpleminded chauvinism of the day painted a widow with much of the same scarlet color attached to a divorcée. A single woman who had experienced sexual relations—the fact of it alone was enough to provoke certain men. Finding a new husband seemed a good idea. She met a man, a jaunty New York Irishman named Bill Clancy. He worked as a newspaper reporter, though as Robert would recall it, the man had other pursuits. He remembered Clancy and some tough guys meeting in the kitchen after midnight, muffled voices. Bootleggers, said Bob. It was a growth industry in any port in those Prohibition days. One way or another the man was not unacquainted with the illegal liquor. On his good days he was a funny, happy fellow with a talent for writing lighthearted and sentimental verse, but he was a drunkard, and the drink turned him angry and violent. One night he went berserk, tearing their house apart and then turning his rage on Ann. "One of my earliest remembrances," wrote John Mitchum, "was coming home with Bob to a dark and empty house, its windows broken out, its doors shattered. Neighbors talked in subdued whispers of Clancy's attempt to kill Mother, who had fled for her life."

They never saw their new stepfather again.

This was Ann's last attempt to create for her children anything like a traditional family environment. From now on tradition was out the window. They were all—mother and kids—just going to have to make it up as they went along.

There was in Ann Gunderson Mitchum Clancy an instinctually unconventional, almost bohemian outlook on life that had lurked beneath the surface of the proper Scandinavian lady. She was intellectually curious, spiritually adventurous. She devoured books, magazines and—it would be a trait Robert would inherit—retained everything with a near photographic memory. She carried the family's genetic predisposition toward the arts, was a talented representational painter, self-taught musician, could read and play music, read and wrote poetry. She encouraged the same love of art and literature in her children. "When she came across poetry that captured her," said Robert, "she would show it to me and read it in cadence. We had a lot of books, a library, and I had the run of it. She really was a great woman."

She was a free thinker, not rebellious but a natural, quiet iconoclast. In a time when conservative narrow-mindedness was the norm and bigotry a commonplace, Ann was independent, nonjudgmental, without racial or ethnic prejudice. She paid at best lip service to the Protestant Church of her forebears. Years later, with typical unconventionality, she—along with her daughters—would become a devoted follower of an Asian-based faith some labeled a mystic sect. An unusual woman. She would raise unusual children.

Robert's independent streak seemed fixed from the cradle. When he was four he walked out the front door of the house and past the front gate and kept going. It took most of the day to find him. He had walked to the edge of town. A woman brought him over to a policeman who took him home. Ann was frantic. Tears in her eyes, she held him and begged him not to do it again. He had just wanted to see what was out there, Robert would recollect.

Sometimes it seemed to Ann that Robert, and then John, too, when he could crawl out of the crib, were just magnets for trouble and disaster. Other mothers' children got scraped knees or bumps on the head. Bob and Jack were always coming home half-murdered. One day, seven-year-old Robert took his little brother with him for a stroll down busy Stratford Avenue. John ran straight before the wheels of a speeding vehicle, his body thrown sideways directly into the path of a second car. As a horrified crowd gathered and an ambulance rushed the unconscious boy to the hospital, Robert turned and ran home to report the news.

"Where is your brother?" asked Ann.

"He's been run over by two cars . . . but I don't think he's dead yet."

John's head had been nearly twisted off. His jaw had to be reset and wired into position and a steel plate inserted above the neck at the back of his skull.

One evening, middle of a Connecticut winter, the boys sat with some neighborhood kids on the Bridgeport dock. Bob lost his balance and fell into the icy waters, nearly drowning. A Portuguese fisherman came almost too late, dragging the boy out on a wooden pike. Convulsing with cold, the water on his face and clothing turning to ice, Robert staggered home. His mother found him coated in a layer of frost like a snowman. His skin underneath was blue. He became inflamed with fever. His chest swelled up till he could barely breathe. The doctor said he had pleurisy, and the boy lay in bed for weeks.

When the youngest was old enough to go to school, Ann went out and got a job, first assisting in a photographer's shop and then as a linotypist in the composing room of the local newspaper, the *Bridgeport Post*. With no father and his mother often not home, John stuck ever closer to his older brother. "They were like twins, inseparable," remembered sister Annette. "A real team, and together they would march out the door, off to get into mischief, as boys will do. I can still see them coming down the street after one of their adventures, all scuffed up, one pants leg up, one down."

Robert was a different person at home with his mother, quiet, a reader from the age of four, devouring books by the hundreds. Mother and sister never did know the other boy who grew up and got into fights and talked all the four-letter words. All their lives, when Bob became famous and they would read the articles in the newspapers, they would never quite recognize the person being written about. "This uncouth ruffian, the one in the papers," said his sister, "that was not him! He was a brilliant person, very self-conscious and with an extremely painful shyness."

It was clearly Ann's secret desire that her children might become artists, as she had once dreamed of becoming. "She nurtured it in all of us," Annette would remember. "She gave us music and books and pictures to look at. She inspired us to think great thoughts, to express ourselves, to dream wonderful dreams." Robert as a child pored over illustrated storybooks and magazines, sometimes drawing his own words and pictures on the blank pages and spaces, continuing the adventures in the books. Doris Dickerson, a young girl whose family later came to live in that Logan Street house, would remember finding some of these books left behind, with their handmade additions, scenes of adventure and travel. In one, on the inside cover, was a bright drawing in colored pencil, a self-portrait: a boy with cowboy hat, six-guns and boots, astride a horse, and below in red block letters the words "THIS IS ME, BOB MITCHUM."

Sister Annette, a beautiful little girl with a head of golden curls, as the oldest child was the first to pursue her artistic impulses in a public sphere. She danced and sang on the street and in the park, whenever the urge took her. A man told her she should be on the stage. "I went to Mother and stomped my foot and said I wouldn't eat my dinner if I couldn't go on the stage. I didn't know what a stage was.

Mother told me. She said if that was the case she would send me to get dancing lessons. And she did, and she could hardly afford it. The teachers I went to had a vaudeville act in the season. A song-and-dance act. They liked me and eventually, when I was thirteen, fourteen, I went on the road with them and did my own dance act."

Robert expressed his creativity primarily in words, by the time he was six and seven spending much of his spare time penciling couplets and rhymes and short stories. He wrote things on little pieces of paper, saving some and tossing others to the floor and under the bed. He created his own newspaper he called *The Gold Streak,* writing short news items interspersed with poems and limericks. Ann took notice of these writings and, pleased and excited, began collecting them, prowling the bedroom for the discarded works as well. One piece of verse she found folded into a tight square holding up a window. She went to her mother: "My son's a writer!" One day she put a sheaf of Bob's verse together and brought it down to the newspaper. There was a children's department at the *Post,* a page for the young ones appearing every Saturday. The editor of this page was known as Uncle Dudley. Uncle Dudley was an Englishman, a former soldier in the British army named Hugh Cunningham Morris, a dapper middle-aged man with a formal bearing and a thickly plummy accent. Ann told him about her wonderful son and showed him the poems. The Englishman listened and looked, charmed by the young mother, finding her sweetly feminine yet very dignified and self-effacing in the way of the shy Scandinavians. He was so taken by the lovely Norwegian widow that it is probable he would have been kindly disposed toward Bob Mitchum's poems had they been written in drool. But the things Morris saw as he scanned the penciled sheets were dashed good for a little beggar in short pants. He read "The Holy Star" and "Waiting for Dawn" and something called "War Poem" in which the little tyke "caught the grim spirit of the horrors of the battle." Morris told Ann he would like to publish some of her boy's creations and would run as well a brief profile about the lad and his devoted mom. The page ran, with the selection of poems and the sympathetic story and a photo of Robert in overcoat and cap intently scribbling on a pad. Overnight Ann's boy became Bridgeport's most famous, certainly youngest, poet— the "male Nathalia Crane," they called him, after a then famous nine-year-old girl who toured the nation reading her work in a little pinafore. Teachers at the McKinley Grammar School fawned over the youthful literary wonder. People would point at him in the street after the story came out; strangers would come up and want to shake his hand. Robert did not enjoy the public exposure. "He hated people to know how sensitive and vulnerable he was," said his sister. "He didn't express himself because he wanted attention or money. Bob wrote for the same reason that you breathe in and out." He read a book by H. G. Wells and began to wish that, like the character in the story, he could take a drug that would make him invisible.

Ann was delighted by the newspaper story and so grateful to the man who was Uncle Dudley that she asked him to the house for dinner. "He was a beautiful, wonderful man," said Annette Mitchum. "And we hoped that he and mother would see much more of each other."

The newspaper man hoped so too. Ann's admirer was *Major* Hugh Cunningham Morris, from Landsend, England, late of His Majesty's, slipped into America across the Canadian border. A character seemingly sired by Talbot Mundy out of Rudyard Kipling, Morris had roamed the world, fought in colonial uprisings in strange-sounding countries (young Winston Churchill had been a comrade in the Boer War). His body had sustained the wear and tear of shrapnel wounds, stabbings by irate natives, imprisonment, explosion, shipwreck. His health was far from tip-top, his glory days were behind him now, and he had been just scraping by in the world the last few years. But still a man of great pluck and charm. Sister Annette adored him at once and hoped he would stick around, but the boys were more ambivalent. They treated him as an interloper, paying little interest or respect.

With an ally at the paper putting in a good word, Ann was able to get a better job there, moving over to the editorial department as a proofreader. As Annette had hoped, Mother and Major Morris became quite devoted to one another. They strolled about Bridgeport side by side and he spent much time at the house, though no more than was decent. He understood the boys' initial resentment and applied his great store of charm toward winning them over. He would sit among them after dinner and tell some well-worn stories—they made Annie roll her eyes with embarrassment, some of them, but he did it to tickle the lads. There was the time in Egypt, for instance, leading the Camel Corps back to headquarters after a long, dangerous mission, with the commanding officer and the troops lined up to greet him. He'd stopped his weary mount directly before his nibs the CO and the bloody beast had picked that moment to unload his ballast of water, and the Major had to sit there aloft in the saddle while below him the camel sprayed the commander and forced up a cloud of dust all over the officers and men.

Once Morris arranged to take Robert up in an airplane—his first flight, in goggles and leather helmet, sitting in the tiny open portal behind the Major as they buzzed the farmhouses and skimmed along the riverbank. It was a thrilling adventure but Robert kept his enthusiasm under control. "I'm afraid we kids didn't give this one much of a break for a long time," he would recall.

The brothers remained undisciplined, prone to finding trouble whenever they left the house. It was a boyhood, said Robert, "of broken windows and bloody noses." One of their pals ended up getting an eye shot out with a BB-gun blast. Another time they were playing behind the local ice cream factory when John started a bonfire that swept to the building and burned it to the ground. People stopped chucking Bob under the chin and calling him the new Nathalia Crane. In their East End neighborhood, said John, they came to be known as "them ornery Mitchum boys." They were tough little urchins roaming the streets of Bridgeport. Both of them—just like their father—enjoyed using their fists. Robert was rail thin, with bony arms, but he wasn't afraid of anyone. There was a miserable satisfaction in giving a beating to some of those kids who had things that Robert didn't have. He could understand what that was about years later, looking back. He was jealous of boys whose dads were coming home after work, whose dads carried them on their shoulders or threw a baseball to them or took them fishing.

Papa Gunderson had put a down payment on a farm property in rural Delaware, and it was decided that Petrine (as John would remember it, his grandmother had been dissatisfied with her life in Connecticut and often talked of returning to Norway) along with daughter Gertrude, her husband, and their three children would move out there and try to make a go of it. Bob and Jack learned that they would be going, too. The boys' frequent delinquency and their behavior toward Major Morris doubtless influenced Ann's decision to pack them off with the relatives while she stayed behind in Bridgeport. Ann promised to write and visit them as soon as she could, but it was hard for Robert not to see what she was doing as a second parental abandonment. It only increased his inherent feelings of aloneness and a growing desire to become self-reliant.

In the 1920s, the region of the Gunderson farm in the small mid-Atlantic state was still largely unchanged since the nineteenth-century. There were expanses of virgin forest, horses remained a primary means of transportation and mechanical power, and telephones, radios, and various modern conveniences were not yet commonplace items as they were in Bridgeport. The farm was twenty acres or so of wooded and cultivated land, with an old clapboard main house, a tiny barn, peach and apple trees, forest. They kept a cow for milk and butter, a few chickens provided eggs on a good day, a swayback horse pulled a harrow. Oil lamps gave them light. Water came from a hand pump adjacent to the kitchen door. A sometimes muddy path led across the yard to the outhouse. In the winter the outhouse door would freeze shut and you had to go get a hammer and spike or else go squat in the frozen woods.

Life began at dawn. Uncle Bill, eagerly and for the first time in his life assuming an executive role, banged through the halls yelling, "Rise and shine!" and rousting them all out to begin the day's chores. The kids—the Mitchums and Louise, Patty, and Gil

Tetreault—milked the cow, fed chickens, gathered and chopped firewood. Bill was a taskmaster and at times a brutal disciplinarian. Once, Annette recalled, eight-year-old Louise did not jump to when her father barked an order and he knocked her clear across the room. But Bill never touched the Mitchum boys, John would remember. It was part of a sentimental vow he had made to the memory of their father. Their cousins would look on with envy as Jack and his brother often got away with murder.

Robert's life on the farm was a new and exotic adventure. He liked being around the animals, picking fruit off trees, and wielding an ax to chop firewood. He could go swimming in a wooded pond or hike to Jones Beach on Delaware Bay and swim and fish and catch soft-shell crabs (they would bring them back in a sack for Aunt Gertrude to fry). He liked to tramp the woods, walking beyond the pathways into the deep overgrown wilderness so far from any sign or sound of people that he could pretend he had gone all the way to darkest Africa or the jungles of South America. At night in his bunk with the white light of the moon coming through the bedroom window, the dead silence of the farm freed his mind of distractions and he would conjure things from his imagination, images and stories. Some nights he would lie in bed and write rhymes in his head, jotting them down by the moonlight if he thought it worth the effort. In the night, in his bed, he would sometimes hear the keening whistle of a freight train hurtling by somewhere in the distance and he would imagine himself on board, on his way to strange places he had read about in books and dreamed of one day visiting.

John would write that Delaware taught them "about bigotry and red-neck perverseness." The local toughs would come to harass the new city kids but soon found that Robert and Jack were hardly the Connecticut Buster Browns they had imagined. "Bob and I had to fight constantly . . . [but] the country boys fought with no style or grace. Their swings, although prodigious, were not exactly championship style." Robert's dangly arms were skinny as toothpicks but he fought with a cold-blooded decisiveness that managed to send most of the yokel attackers running in retreat.

When school opened in the autumn, the brothers hiked a dirt path to the main road and boarded the school bus to Felton High. Seventy years later, surviving schoolmates remembered young Bob Mitchum, skinny, very smart, and from the start bound and determined to get up to something.

"He was so thin then, you couldn't believe how big he got as a man," said seventh-grade classmate Margaret Smith. "His hair was kind of blond, and the face was just all bones, very narrow. They said he was part Indian and he looked like it with very high cheekbones. He was not handsome then! His little brother was the good-looking one." Robert agreed—"I looked like a goddamned little ferret . . . my head was one big cowlick."

"Skinny. Long skinny arms, bony face," said Virginia Trice, another Felton schoolgirl. "And that prominent dimple in his chin—that was not something everybody had back then."

"Nice, friendly, nothing uppish about him—of course his family had no money," Emma Warner recalled. "The boys never had anything."

"He wore old clothes, must have been secondhand," said Smith. "They hung off him. A big man's belt that was too big."

"He was a character," said Warner. "Always looking to get into trouble. He was bright. Didn't have to study. I guess that's how come he had time to get into stuff."

"The thing about Bob Mitchum," said Margaret Smith, "he was very, very intelligent. He knew more than the teachers, and he wasn't afraid to stand up and contradict them. And the teachers didn't know what to say, because he would turn out to be right. They just looked embarrassed. He'd stand up and explain the way it should be. He was so advanced—makes our teachers sound kind of dumb, don't it? He was the smartest one in the class that was for sure. But the strange thing is he never took any books home. I never saw him take a book home in his life and yet he knew everything. He was so advanced that it sort of disrupted the class."

"Personally, I thought an awful lot of him," Virginia Trice would say about the boy who became a movie star. "I always got along with him. Most of the kids liked him and . . . I think . . . even some of the teachers liked him because he had a good personality. A very bright fellow, didn't have to work at school like some of the rest of us. But he was . . . ever' once in a while a little mischievous."

"He put thumb tacks on our seats," said Smith. "And when you wore a sash he would tie you to the chair, him and some other boys liked to do that."

"He and another boy went down to the brook close to the school," said Trice, "and they caught hop toads and put 'em in the inkwells that were sunken into the desk. And once in a while you would hear someone scream because a frog would hop out of the inkwell at 'em."

"Our classroom in seventh grade was a long, narrow room," said Warner. "There were just two rows of desks, and the teacher, Miss Robbins, was sitting up on her desk at the front of the classroom. And Robert was in the back and threw an eraser that was just full of chalk dust and hit the teacher in the face and she fell off the desk. Why'd he do it? I don't know. I didn't know that he didn't like her. Everybody just screamed and were so upset and the principal had to come in and fan her and straighten her up, and they took him away to the principal's office. Suspended him, I guess."

"There were some little kids and he stole their marbles. . . ."

"He had firecrackers one day at the school. . . ."

". . . wrote a bad word on the blackboard, letters about a foot tall."

"Somethin' happened . . . no, I will not tell you or anybody else about what he did that time."

*

The smartest kid in the school and the biggest mischief maker. It was a combination that puzzled and infuriated the faculty at the Felton school. The whip-smart boys had always been the apple polishers, the disciplined, the ambitious. Everyone, even the slow ones, wanted good grades, compliments, encouragement; but Robert, said his classmates, seemed indifferent to official approval. He was good at math, at history, at English, but it all seemed like yesterday's news to him, the way he acted. "He musta been bored," said one of the girls, remembering seventy years ago. "He acted like it was all kind of boring to him," said another.

At Felton Robert found a pal. Another outsider, another discipline problem. His name was Manuel Barque. He came from New York City with his brother, Louis. The Barques were what were known as "home boys," orphans or troubled youths resettled by an agency that arranged to place them on small family farms where they were boarded and cared for to a lesser or greater degree in exchange for their labor. There were some who knew Robert in school who thought he was a home boy, too, because he never spoke of his parents, and no one knew his people, and he had that same attitude—independent, a bit of a grudge against the authorities, didn't care what people thought of him. Charlie and Annie Welch raised the Barque boys. They were good people, kind, not like some of the sponsors of the home boys who just looked on them as free labor, unpaid farmhands. Louis was older and more reserved, and Mr. Welch liked him; the boy would go to Sunday school and to the little Methodist Church. Mrs. Welch was a good Christian woman, but Manuel was her pet, and Manuel was full of the devil, though Mrs. Welch liked to say that most of the trouble he got into was the fault of that boy Bob Mitchum.

Manuel Barque and Robert Mitchum shared a disdain for the teachers and especially for the principal. Felton had some good teachers, some OK teachers, and some Manuel and Bob thought were bastards, but they did not discriminate one from the other. Mr. McFadden, the music teacher, Mr. Severson, manual training, Mr. Glackin, science, Miss Robbins, Mrs. Greeley. Manuel and Robert hated them all. But their great enemy, their nemesis, was Mr. Petry, the principal. A short, chubby man, fierce, he brooked no nonsense. Everyone had to toe the line in his school. Bad boys got a stern lecture with a wagging finger in the face, and if they were really bad he would take a switch to them and whip them on the buttocks and the back. He roamed the halls—if he caught you where you weren't supposed to be, he would grab you hard on the ear or pinch you on the soft part of the shoulder just below the neck and march you to his office. He gave Robert the shoulder pinch treatment one time and Robert backhanded him in the face and ran down the hallway and out the door. Petry got him into his office and went at him with the whip, threatening to expel him.

Manuel and Robert plotted their escape from school. They talked about stealing a boat somewhere out on the bay and sailing off to a life of adventure. One morning a group of the kids were milling around by the service station across from the school. People bought candy and sodas there and hung around before the nine o'clock bell rang. Manuel and Robert said they weren't going to school; they were running away. They were going to go up to Connecticut to see Robert's mom, maybe get some money and things, and then head off for Canada and become trappers, or maybe down to Florida and live on the beach and fish. Margaret Smith remembered standing there with them that morning. "They'd gotten off the bus and just decided they weren't going in to school any more. The bell rang and everybody headed into the building but them. Me and another girl looked back and saw them across the road. And they weren't there long before they got into a big truck that was stopped there and drove off with them. This other girl and I were dumbfounded. Children didn't do that kind of thing then, hitchhiking. There was some ruckus when it became known they were missing. We didn't have the communication you have today, so it took some time for everyone to get alerted and to have the police looking for them. I don't know if they thought they were kidnapped or what. I knew they went hitchhiking, ran away from school, but I didn't say a word. I was pretty lively when I went to school and we didn't squeal on each other."

They were found a day later. Cold and hungry, they had begged for food and a woman had called the sheriff. Mr. Welch and the school bus driver, Mr. Moore, drove up the thirty miles or so and brought them back. Uncle Bill, who had a soft spot for Bob that did not extend to his own children, just sadly ordered the boy up to his room. Grandmother Petrine came in later, red-eyed, and reluctant-ly administered a brief whipping.

Manuel's Mrs. Welch tried her best to keep him away from the

Mitchum boy. She rued the day they ever met and was never so happy as on the day Robert moved out of Delaware. Bob wrote to Manuel after he left, according to people who knew them, even after he became a movie star, and Mrs. Welch would not tell Manuel but would take the letters and burn them.

In the summer and on holidays, the missing members of the Gunderson and Mitchum clan came to visit. Ann would arrive for a stay, along with Annette, now a veteran in show business after her seasons on the vaudeville circuit dancing in an act put together by her Bridgeport dancing teachers. Grandfather Gunderson—the kids called him "Big Daddy"—would return from months at sea and frolic with the young ones and carouse with the local farmers. He liked to dazzle the children with shows of his incredible strength; and once, during a Fourth of July gathering, he slipped under a hay-wagon holding half-a-dozen occupants and with his powerful shoulders and back muscles lifted the wagon from beneath and top-pled it sideways. Then one time he arrived at the farm less than his usual boistrous self, and the adults became very subdued as well. The doctor in Bridgeport had told Captain Gunderson that he had an advanced cancer in his stomach, and Big Daddy had come to say good-bye to everyone. He returned to Connecticut, and a few weeks later he was dead.

One morning Ann showed up with Major Morris in tow and announced to all that they were now husband and wife. Bob and John scratched their chins. The Major rooted around Woodside with his usual affable, oblivious manner, his heavy British accent all but incomprehensible to the local dirt farmers of whom he inquired about the possibility of riding in their next big fox hunt. A year later Ann arrived from Bridgeport heavy with child. She gave birth to a girl they named Carol Morris, and mother and baby remained on the farm for a time with Grandmother Petrine to care for them while the Major stayed behind at the newspaper, writing obituaries.

Robert's days at the Felton school were numbered. The abrupt disruption of his formal studies was nigh, the result of a culminating act of antiauthoritarianism, an act that in those more innocent times was considered unthinkably outrageous. The whole incident would forever remain a legend among the classmates of Felton High School, a tale told and retold—though more often whispered—from those hallowed halls to every corner of Delaware, from one generation to another. As legends will, some details have faded or become confused with the passage of time, but all who speak of it agree to the general turn of events. There was Bob Mitchum, there was a hat, and there was something unexpected inside the hat.

"Well," said one who had been there, after some reluctance and with a degree of laughing embarrassment, "Bob . . . or somebody . . . did a number two . . . he just . . . well, what they said . . . he shit in the teacher's hat."

Other survivors confirmed or elaborated the tale.

"Sir, it was the hat belonging to Mr. McFadden."

"Mr. McFadden, he was the music teacher, a nice-looking, crippled gentleman, had a limp. . . . Why him I can't say, maybe he was too serious for some of the boys, I don't know."

"I don't know whose hat it was," said another, "but it was a very nice man's hat and they shouldn't have done that to it."

"The hat situation . . . they said he did it. . . . I don't know."

"I only heard tell of it later, but they said he stood on the teacher's desk and did it."

"They found it in Mr. Petry's chair."

"In the girls' locker room . . ."

"In my opinion the other boys put him up to a lot of things, and he would be the one [to] just go ahead and do it. He was the one always took the rap for 'em anyway."

"Either him or Manuel did it, I think. And they was proud of it."

Rightly or wrongly accused, Mitchum would take the fall for the shit-in-the-hat caper. Petry had him brought into the outer office and formally expelled him, then escorted the boy out the front door. Bob left without looking back. There were some things you just didn't dignify with a protest. He walked the entire long route back to Woodside, a nearly six-mile hike. Under grilling he confessed to his family what had happened and to them declared his innocence of the charge. Uncle Bill rode to the school to talk things over with the principal and see about setting things right. Petry told him what he thought of the little fiend he called a nephew, and Uncle Bill was soon illustrating some of his favorite wrestling holds. The secretary screamed, faculty members came running, and with an honor guard that included the beefy football coach, Tetreault was shown the exit.

Robert wrote a letter to his mother in Bridgeport: "Petry is a coward, preying on a child. Some day I am coming back and so help me I am going to ruin him as he ruined me if he is still alive. But I suppose it will be just his luck to be dead."*

*

They had always lived close to the bone on the Woodside farm. Uncle Bill tried to make a commercial success of the place, but his attempts to market crops—grapes, peaches, Christmas trees—had never added up to anything. They could barely be described as self-sufficient. And now, with no more support from Big Daddy Gunderson, it had become a hand-to-mouth existence. The boys wondered why their mother's new husband back in Bridgeport didn't make a better effort to support them. Later, more forgiving, Robert would say, "We couldn't understand that he was full of shrapnel and couldn't work hard enough to keep us all together as a family unit." Instead they turned to the only member of the extended Mitchum clan who showed any propensity for solvency.

*Mitchum would on occasion absurdly claim to have been voted Felton's class valedictorian (and his equally trouble-making pal Manuel Barque honored as salutatorian!)—and say that he had set fire to the school instead and left town the day before graduation, a case of wishful daydreaming, though some journalists have printed the claim as fact. In 1976 the Felton school board, hoping to have the now-famous film star appear at their bicentennial celebration, wrote to him in Los Angeles and offered as enticement the high school diploma he had never earned. Mitchum did not return to Felton, but the diploma was forwarded to him nonetheless.

Annette had begun to enjoy a degree of success as a performer. She toured on one of the East Coast vaudeville circuits for a time, part of an all-female troupe known as the Six Yankee Doodles. She was still just a girl, not long in her teens, but she had matured with all her experiences working on the road. In Washington she met a boy in the U.S. Navy named Ernie Longaker—a sailor like Big Daddy, a man in uniform like Daddy Jimmy—and she married him. Annette continued to work while Ernie went to sea. She appeared on the stage in Philadelphia and then in the chorus of a variety show in New York City. She had an apartment there, and soon she was sharing it with her peripatetic mother, two brothers, and baby Carol.

Annette believed the family had a strain of Gypsy blood on her mother's side. None of them ever worried much about putting down roots or where next month's rent was coming from. "They were an unusual family," said Reva Frederick, who knew them all later in California. "They were not a warm family; I did not see a lot of emotion or physical closeness that you might see in other families. Robert was certainly not *family oriented* in the way some people are. But the women had this interesting matriarchal point of view; I don't think they expected much from the men in the family, never expected them to be the bread-winner. Ann thought the best bet was that everybody should live together in the same place, everybody welcome. And whoever was working, I guess, chipped in and the rest took a piece of it. If you didn't want to work that didn't seem to bother Ann, and if you did then you could spread it around to those that didn't. As I say, it was an interesting point of view."

They lived now in a cold-water flat in Hell's Kitchen, a tough slum on the West Side, midtown, crowded with poor Irish, Italians, and other immigrant groups but only blocks away from the thriving, star-laden center of American show business—Broadway. There were five, sometimes six—when Annette's Ernie was around—in the small place on Fifty-sixth Street. And then one more—the Major had lost his increasingly tentative position at the *Bridgeport Post*. He gathered up his few belongings—his medals, his snapshots from Mesopotamia, his yellowed letter from Winston Churchill—and took the train to New York, squeezing into the apartment with his wife, daughter and step-children.*

It was a tough, violent neighborhood and the local teens, many of them belonging to ethnic gangs, made the farm boys in Delaware look like daisies. There were threats on every block, fights to be fought or to be only very carefully avoided—if you were ever pegged as a chicken, you were a dead man. Robert showed what he was made of early on when he stepped in to save his brother from a beating, and then the entire gang descended. They "butchered" him, said his sister, but the gang members left so much of their own blood, so many of their own teeth on the Manhattan asphalt that few ever looked for a second opportunity to teach the Mitchum boys a lesson. Early on, Robert dropped the Felton twang he had picked up that characterized him as a bumpkin in New York. One of his talents was mimickry, imitating the voices and accents of the people he met. Within a month or so he was talking like a Ninth Avenue mick.

Robert had to go back to school, state law. He enrolled in Haaren High on Fifty-ninth Street. Haaren was no Felton High School. There were all kinds of ornery characters in attendance; some of them looked old enough to have graduated—or been expelled—years ago, blue-jawed characters with their dirty boots up on the desk. Mitchum managed to hold up his end in a tough crowd. Here, as in Felton, he showed little but contempt for figures of authority, and he was sent home more than once for bad behavior. One time he tossed a firecracker into a tuba during a school concert, right in the middle of the "Poet and Peasant" Overture. And to think the bandleader had earlier encouraged him to join the band and let him take home a saxophone to practice on. His mother learned how to play it herself and then coached him at night. He picked it up fast, as he did so many things, but got bored and dropped it. Years later, in

*The house on Logan Street where Robert spent his early childhood had been sold for three thousand dollars, all of it going to unpaid levies and the mortgage company. The family that purchased the place found it in very poor condition and without a furnace or water heater. The rooms contained items abandoned by the Mitchums—pieces of furniture, a oiuja board, and numerous sketches and paintings by Ann and others that a surviving member of the new owner's family described as "very lovely."

Hollywood, he would sometimes happen upon a sax on a set or at a party and wow people with his unexpected proficiency.

Robert preferred to do his learning in private, on his own terms. He discovered the palacelike library at Fifth and Forty-second and would stay until closing in the cavernous reading rooms with a stack of books before him—novels, histories, anthropological studies, poetry, biographies. He and his brother loved to explore the city's museums, returning again and again to the Museum of Natural History especially, imaginations set afire by the exhibits depicting ancient Indian camps, knights in armor, Egyptian mummies, bejeweled swords and daggers. The vivid glimpses of exotic peoples and locales primed a growing wanderlust.

New York offered young Bob another sort of education, heretofore neglected. He and John slept in the kitchen. The original, much larger apartment had been turned into two residences, crudely partitioned with a slab of plywood running next to the kitchen door. At night, with the lights out, the cracks and wormholes in the wood gave them glimpses of the neighboring apartment, rented out to a couple of gin-swilling NYU students. One night there were strange sounds coming through the wall that brought the Mitchum brothers crawling from their cots to investigate. The college boys had company, pickups from a local speak, bootleg hooch was flowing, and soon the quartet were out of their clothes and rolling around in orgiastic celebration while Bob and Jack watched the show from the other side, bumping heads against the cracks. It was like a Tijuana Bible come to life, the boys thought, most informative.

Robert had never had much truck with girls, and they didn't seem to like him, all skin and bones, indented chin, face like a damn ferret. In any case, rural Delaware was a prim, God-fearing place and had been unlikely to offer much in the way of sensual inducements. New York was another story altogether. In addition to the eye-opening antics seen through the plywood wall, Robert came in close contact with many beautiful and relatively godless women from Annette's growing circle of Broadway acquaintances, some of them stopping by the apartment for a late night coffee after long hours on the stage. One of these lovelies, friendly and high-spirited, was a stripper currently employed at Minsky's Burlesque. Feeling sympathy for Annie's skinny brother when he expressed his dream of someday getting to see such an interesting-sounding show, the young woman arranged to sneak him in one night as her underaged guest. He stood by the backstage door at a prearranged time until out slipped his lovely liaison wearing a long, fur coat, in which she enveloped him and stealthily escorted him into the theater. Fresh from her own appearance on the stage, the lady had nothing on beneath the fur. Robert struggled to keep his balance while bathed in the heat of her luscious femininity. It was a fever-inducing experience, as was the show itself, glimpsed from a discreet nook in the wings. His subsequent inclination toward a showbiz career Robert would blame on this epochal viewing. "Any boyhood visions of growing up to be a policeman or fireman collapsed right there," he later confessed. He would return to the burlesque house on a number of occasions during his Manhattan sojourn, becoming friendly with several of the show's star performers, and it was there—he claimed when anyone had the temerity to inquire—it was there, backstage at Minsky's, between the lissome thighs of a sympathetic stripteaser, that he would surrender whatever technically remained of his innocence.

It was only with the family's arrival in New York that Robert began to comprehend the terrible circumstances into which the country had been plunged. In the time since the stock market crash of 1929, the enormous economic downturn had rapidly dismantled great chunks of the social infrastructure across America, upsetting the lives of mllions. Everywhere now was mounting unemployment, dislocation, despair. A city as powerful as New York continued to function much as before, the streets and subways still crowded with gainfully employed citizenry; but the nightmarish effects of the Great Depression had become a citywide specter visible on every block. Mitchum would never forget the haunted-looking beggars skulking around Tmes Square, the cardboard shanties under the bridges and in empty lots, the shivering men lined up in the snow outside a church soup kitchen, waiting hours sometimes for a cup of hot broth and a small hunk of bread. And there were worse things to see: the ones who didn't survive the hardship, dead from starvation or disease or fear, the bodies lying where they fell until the city could collect them like the day's trash. "You'd find 'em under the subway steps," Mitchum remembered, "huddled up and gone."

His family hung on, barely. They moved to another apartment uptown in the West Nineties, but the rent still came due each month. Ann had to stay home to take care of baby Carol, while the rest did whatever they could to bring in some money. On arrival from Bridgeport, the Major had made the rounds of the Manhattan newspapers and magazines looking for a position, without success. His roster of claimed talents included a clever way with cards, and now and then he would hear of a game going on somewhere and scrounge up fifty cents or so and try and make it grow. Once he actually came back with ten dollars for the kitty. For a time Jack worked as a delivery boy at a market, taking big boxes of groceries to the elegant apartment houses on Central Park South. The temptation to remove some mouthwatering item or two from the deliveries was always mitigated by the fear of losing the job and the dimes that it earned him. They scratched by, hand to mouth. One night the family dinner consisted of a bag of roasted walnuts one of the boys had stolen from a vendor. Robert found a job jerking sodas at the drugstore of the Astor Hotel on Broadway. He worked for twelve hours on Christmas Day 1931, so the boss treated him to a dinner on the house, a feast it seemed at the time, with his stomach always empty—a hamburger and a chocolate soda.

At fourteen he left home.

"You read these stories that Bob ran away," said his sister, recalling the events of sixty-seven years earlier. "He didn't run away. Mother packed his things for him! Like many great minds, artists and visionaries, and Bob was a little bit of all of that, he was curious, wanted to see everything. He had to get out and explore the world. He read everything, and when he learned about interesting things and places, he became so eager to go see them. He'd read a story about the Okefenokee Swamp, or this or that, and he'd say, 'I've just got to go see what that looks like.' Mother used to read us a little poem, I don't know who wrote it, and it mentions the 'great wide wonderful world, so beautifully dressed,' and Bob just couldn't wait to go out and see it."

Mitchum would remember it in less idealistic terms. "I was a poor kid and a lot of trouble. I never got along too well anywhere. Fifth wheel kind of thing . . .

"I got tired of gnawing on chicken necks and hit the road.

"I guess my ambition was . . . to be a bum."

He had daydreamed about tramps and hoboes the way other boys did about cowboys and airplane daredevils. They were the last great American adventurers, knights of the open road and all that jazz. It was a life Robert had read about, hungrily devoured, in alluring stories and books by Jack London and Jim Tully and others who wrote of train-hopping vagabonds in a world of thrills, danger, and absolute freedom. Tully, in particular, was a kind of private god to Mitchum. The "hobo author," as he was called, a two-fisted intellectual, proud nihilist, hard-boiled stylist, Tully wrote of social outcasts and bottom-rungers, tramps, prizefighters, carnies, orphans. Mitchum read his *Beggars of Life,* a memoir of Tully's days as a "road kid"—a young drifter—read it again and again till the type was stained and smeared with dirty fingerprints and pages fell loose from the binding.

*

In the early '30s, history conspired to create a hobo subculture the likes of which Jim Tully could never have imagined in his footloose days. With the Depression spreading across the land, plaguelike, an economic Black Death, hundreds of thousands of jobless and destitute Americans began to leave their homes and families and wander the country in search of work, food, survival. They left in cars, like Steinbeck's Joads, in trembling jalopies stuffed with their every possession; they tramped and hitchhiked; and in ever-increasing numbers they rode the trains, illegally hopping the freights that crisscrossed every part of the country. Most of the hoboes on the road were adult males, but as the Depression continued into a second and third year, conditions growing worse, families unable to cope and schools being shut down, hordes of children became a part of this desperate, aimless migration as well. There were an estimated 250,000 youths—the so-called wild boys of the road—riding the rails at the height of the Depression.

Crowds of a hundred and more would gather to catch a single freight train, a ragtag army swarming onto the cars as they rolled down the track. Outside rail yards they built encampments, "hobo jungles" they were called, and a few had grown to the size of small towns. Some communities were taking drastic, even violent measures to drive off the scourge of the wandering unemployed. Some among the nation's wealthy and reactionary feared their anarchic ranks would become an organized revolutionary force, hoboes rising up to attack the banks and factories en masse and topple Herbert Hoover's government.

On a morning in 1932, fourteen-year-old Robert Mitchum hopped aboard a freight train heading south.

CHAPTER TWO

Boxcar to the Promised Land

There were times, he would remember, lying on his back on an open flatcar on a warm summer night and staring at the stars overhead, when he would feel blissfully happy and free. And then there were the other times. Evenings with the cold wind whipping through his bones. Staring out from an open boxcar through the windows of passing houses, imagining he saw the families inside gathered together at the dinner table or huddled around a Christmas tree, times when he would be filled with loneliness and trying not to cry. One time he was riding a reefer, a refrigerator car, into Idaho Falls in the dead of winter. What he was doing in that part of the world he couldn't say, had probably hopped the wrong freight or something. It was ten below zero outside. Shivering, teeth chattering. Nothing to eat for twenty-four hours except a can of unthawed peaches found trackside. He had an old newspaper and stuffed the pages inside his pants for warmth. A hobo crouching nearby had started a little campfire in the car. A spark touched the newspaper sticking out of the leg of Robert's pants and it went up in flames. He awoke with his legs on fire. The hobo helped him tear his burning pants off. It was the only pair he had, too. When you were standing with no pants on under a streetlamp in Idaho in the middle of winter, trying to find some frozen clothes to steal off a clothesline and then trying to thaw them out in a depot campfire without burning those up, too—well, Mitchum liked to say, after that things could only get better.

In the beginning he wandered the country with no timetable, many times with no destination clearly in mind, just enjoying the

ride and the view provided by a "sidecar Pullman," the thrill of finding himself in places he had previously known only in pictures, in
books. Chicago. The Big Santee. The Mississippi. The Blue Ridge
Mountains. Down in the Carolinas to see the land his father had
come from. The real hoboes—a term meant to describe only those
migrants who traveled in search of work—called people like Robert
"scenery bums," young punks who rode the trains just looking for
adventure. Some of those job-seeking hoboes knew the schedules
and destinations of the freights in a given territory better than a
damn conductor, but scenery bums like Bob often didn't care where
a train was going. There was a special excitement in hopping a
freight to an unknown destination, leaving it up to fate. Would
tomorrow drop you in New Orleans or West Virginia? Every month
or so he would make his way to an appointed place where his mother would be able to write to him, care of the general post office.
Often as not his mother had sent him something, a clean shirt,
money, a tin of candies. Sometimes, out of nowhere, he would be
sitting on the steps outside the post office and he would read her
note and start tearing up. He was far from home and only fourteen
years old, no matter how much he tried to deny it.

The denizens of the road, of the rails, were a kind of society unto
themselves, with their own customs, their own laws and lingo.
Mitchum relished becoming part of this world of outsiders. These
were his people, he liked to say, the ones who didn't fit in. In the
hobo jungles, the improvised transient centers that grew up around
the jumping-off points on the tracks, he would sit around the camp-
fires and the garbage can grills and listen like a disciple to the huddled veterans telling their tales of brushes with death on the trains,
violent run-ins with some notorious railroad bull, and other adventures, some bloodcurdling and some hilarious, Robert listening to
the tales while he ate from his tin cup of beans or mulligan stew procured for a few pennies' donation or by chipping in a couple of scav-
enged vegetables. Some of those guys were amazing storytellers and
could hold a crowd in their palm as they wove a wild tale that was
half memory and half nonsense; they could make the crowd roar

with laughter at a funny windup or leave them blubbering if it was a sad story and had anything to do with a mother or a devoted dog.

It was an education. Every day he had to learn something new to survive. He learned how to catch and cook a squirrel, how to tell directions from the stars at night, how to repair socks, how to fight a man coming at you with a length of chain. He had long been a rather emancipated boy, and the road made him even more grown-up before his time. He had already, at fourteen, developed a taste for alcohol and its effects, sneaking off with many a bottle of his grandmother's fruit wines back at the farm, but liquor was scarce on the road. Sometimes, in a jungle or in a boxcar with some other bums, a bottle of moonshine made the rounds, but it usually cost you. There was, however, another substance available to down-and-outers on the road looking for a buzz, and it was free for the taking. Marijuana grew wild in many parts of the country and was often found in great thriving clumps along the railroad tracks. "Back then it was the poor man's whiskey," Mitchum said. Those who knew what they were looking for could weed it out and stuff their pockets full before hopping a freight. You rolled it in a page of newspaper and lit it up. It was a pleasant way to get through a long ride, sometimes having to sit all night in pitch-black darkness and in cold. Robert liked it maybe even more than booze. He liked the way it seemed to slow things down, allowed the mind to wrestle with a thought at greater leisure, to ponder more deeply. He liked the way it made a joke heard sound funnier and a girl look prettier. It relaxed you, it felt good, it was sexually stimulating. He couldn't believe the Lucky Strike people hadn't already cornered the market on the stuff. As he traveled the country he became a connoisseur of the weed, came to know its botanical history, its strengths and strains. After much practice, he claimed to be able to taste the regional characteristics in any sampling—Georgia hemp from Louisiana shitweed from California Red, and so on—at a single toke, blindfolded. In later years, he would collect seeds of the best stuff he found, and he would find a place in the yard or driveway where he lived and raise his own crop.

He always liked to stay ahead a few dollars, but sometimes he found himself down to his last nickel, and sometimes he found himself without a cent to his name. He would roll into a new town, hungry, and hope to find a breadline with a free meal; or he would roam a neighborhood and knock on back doors and ask if they could spare some food, usually offering to do chores in exchange. If a man was home, he usually found something for you to do, like chop some firewood or wash his car; if it was just the housewife, she seldom asked for anything but that you complimented her cooking, which he always did. In some places the bums who came before you left coded chalk marks or scratches on the curb or the fence post telling you which houses were generous and which ones to avoid at all cost. Sometimes he panhandled on the streets, but that was likely to bring on the fuzz anywhere but in the big cities. Sometimes when he was really starving and had no place to go, he would turn himself in to the local police station, say he was making his way back home and had no place to sleep. If they had any sympathy, the cops would put you in a cell overnight, give you some of their grub, and in the morning make you sweep up the jailhouse for your keep.

He took jobs when they presented themselves. He was a dishwasher in Ohio, a fruit picker in Georgia, a ditchdigger someplace else. He always said he was older than he was when asked, and nobody ever asked for any proof. In Pennsylvania he landed in an old coal town in the hills and was taken in by a sweet, middle-aged widow lady. She gave him a room and food and told him she would find some good honest work for him and sent him to the local coal mine where her brother gave him a job. "I went down into the pit with a sledge hammer," Mitchum recalled, "and took one look around that cramped hole and almost went out of my mind. Claustrophobia. The only thing that kept me down there was a 250 pound Polish foreman who waved a twenty pound hammer at my head and said, 'You no quit!' So I no quit. But I was so sick I couldn't eat. . . . At night I'd just stand around on the street and watch the miners making passes at the girls. I lasted long enough to pay the lady who was so nice to me and then I cut out again."

The drifter's world into which he had thrown himself was dangerous and unforgiving. An al fresco ride on a train was fraught with
peril. You could easily be set on fire or have your eyes burned out by
live cinders blowing back from the engine. The train might hit a
steep downhill pass so fast that you would be tossed off like a rag
doll, or the freight you were sitting on in a gondola could shift suddenly and slide you out into space, or sitting in an open boxcar with
legs dangling out the way many kids liked to do could leave you with
your limbs ripped open by a signal post or crushed by the sudden
entrance into a narrow tunnel. Many people, especially the young
ones, routinely fell under the wheels while trying to board a train or
fell to their deaths moving between moving cars or walking a roof
walk. If the train itself didn't kill or maim you, the employees of the
railroad made a try at it. There were conductors and railway bulls
who took their oath of office so seriously or had such a mean streak
that they would do anything they could, including murder, to keep
the bums from riding. In the jungles, 'boes were always updating
each other on what yards and what trains to avoid because of tough
security or a sadist wielding a monkey wrench or a hammer.

Catch a safe ride and avoid the vicious railroad workers and there
were always your fellow bums to worry about. Most hoboes were
ordinary decent people down on their luck, but infesting their ranks
were many predators—thieves and rapists and psychos—and even
the ordinary joes could turn vicious when things became bad
enough. There were people riding the rails who would stab you to
death for two nickels you kept in your shoe. In the dark of a boxcar
at night while people tried to sleep, there was always somebody slipping up to try and pick a pocket or steal a bindle. And if they weren't
after your goods they were trying for a feel of your privates. These
things often led to a scuffle, somebody pulling a shiv and somebody
else leaking blood. Once Robert saw a fight in a rolling open box that
resolved itself with one man shoving the other out of the car and the
guy falling splat on his head on a cement wall.

Everywhere he went, Mitchum saw terrible evidence of what desperation and hopelessness could do to human beings. Suicides were
common around hobo jungles and rail yards. One time he followed

a crowd to see them taking down a man who'd hung himself underneath a rail overpass. Another time a man riding in a boxcar with him slit his wrists during the night. Mitchum saw, too, the things people did to keep living: the young boys who took it up the ass for a cup of food, the man in a jungle in Kentucky prostituting his daughter for ten cents a throw, a blanket spread out on the dirt, forty or fifty men lined up, the girl no more than twelve.

As the numbers of the wandering disenfranchised increased with each year of the Depression, many communities across the country began to take measures against them. Police and sheriff's departments and private security posses increased in number, given a mandate to make shiftless visitors unwelcome. One time Mitchum remembered coming into a depot with a trainload of hoboes and being met by a vigilante group armed with shotguns and pitchforks, making sure no one on that freight set foot in their town.

"Mother would get letters from Bob," said Annette Mitchum. "He would tell her how he was doing, when he might be coming back their way for a visit. He would tell her where she could reach him next, and she would try to put a few dollars aside for him and send it to that town, and he could go there and get it when he arrived. And Robert had asked her to send it to him in Savannah, Georgia. He was going there to pick up his money when they arrested him."

He came into Savannah on a freight with about seventeen other kids, as he remembered it. "I was cold and hungry. So I dropped off to get something to eat. This big fuzz grabbed me. 'For what?' I asked. He grinned. 'Vagrancy. We don't like Yankee bums around here.'" Mitchum told him he had money and he was about to pick up some more. "He just belted me with his club and ran me in . . . a dangerous and suspicious character with no visible means of support." It was the common charge in those days. "They were always locking you up for poverty."

After a few days in the Savannah cooler, young Robert was marched before a magistrate to plead his case. By now, said Mitchum, they were trying to add a shoe store burglary to the charges. It looked like it would go through for awhile, a minimum of five years behind bars. But the robbery turned out to have occurred while the accused was already under lock and key. At that revelation some people in the courtroom snickered and maybe Mitchum smirked or something.

The judge said, "The vagrancy charge still goes, anyway. Seven days with the County. Take him outta here."

He was taken to the Chatham County Camp No. 1, located in the middle of some hades called Pipemaker Swamp. The mosquitoes were as big as your fist and the swamp rats the size of dogs. It was a chain gang. You wore a metal clamp around your ankles through which they ran a heavy chain connecting you in lines of five prisoners to a chain. At dawn they marched you into a truck and took you to work at hard labor repairing the roads outside Savannah. The sheriff's department rented its charges to the city for a small profit. It was nothing unusual for those times. Mitchum had heard that in Texas they sold you outright to labor camps, and what became of you after that was none of their concern.

"It wasn't particularly hard to take. I got fed, you know. I guess it was depressing. The first night, I slept on the floor and the guy next to me was dyin' of a tubercular hemorrhage."

The clamp on his leg had been fastened too tight and bit through his flesh. A pustulant ulceration developed. Nobody gave a damn. Every prisoner there was hurt or sick with something. He calculated that there were at least four different virulent diseases making the rounds among his fellow miscreants. Nobody gave a shit. They weren't running a hospital there, a guard told a guy lagging back, coughing up his insides. There was work to be done. One of the other prisoners told Robert that sometimes if the state needed the labor they would extend your sentence, just make up some infraction and give you another thirty days. Assessing these factors, Mitchum saw no future in chain gang road repair. He got the lowdown on running away. In fact, it was a cinch to take off when you were out on the work detail. The new road bordered the swamp and the trees, and they took the chains off your legs while you worked. They would shoot at you and maybe chase you for a while, but after that nobody would spend sixty cents to try and catch you. They'd just go out and round up someone to take your place. That was all there was to an escape attempt: you either got away or you got a bullet. Out on the highway one of the captains in charge of the work detail was an older man named Captain Fry. He had jaundice, maybe hepatitis: his flesh was the color of margarine, and flecks of bile floated across his eyeballs. He would sit on a camp chair with a .30-.30 rifle on his lap, muttering to himself in the sun. "I don' know what he sees through them eyes," a fellow prisoner told Robert, "but I know he blowed a man's head off last month." Still, Mitchum thought the jaundiced captain was the best bet, and one afternoon after the sun had dropped behind the trees and the captain was sitting and distracted with chatting to himself, Mitchum turned and ran into the woods. He heard a rifle crack and thought he felt the bullet whizzing alongside his ear. He heard voices shouting and someone blowing a whistle and another rifle shot, and then he was in the thick of the woods and he was gone.

He hitchhiked out of Georgia and up to Baltimore, living for some days in an abandoned house with a gang of derelict youths trying to make a living from dog-napping, snatching the family pooches from wealthy neighborhoods and then returning them when a reward was posted. An infection in his ankle had spread to most of his lower leg. It was swollen and purple and hurt like hell. He covered the open sores with a bandage made from rags, and each time he unwrapped it to take a look it had added a few more colors and pustules. He began to think he might have been bitten by a poisonous snake back in the swamp and wondered if there was an antidote available. He lay on the floor of the old house while his new pals were out stealing dogs. His leg throbbed and he tried to keep from crying. He wrote some lines on the back of a postcard that he intended to mail to his mother: "Trouble lies in sullen pools along the road I've taken. . . ."

After some days and the leg getting only worse, he decided to try and get home. The folks were back in Delaware now, though not at the farm. He hitched his way north, though with his pants leg torn open and his calf covered in wet red bandages not many people wanted to give him a lift. At last in Pennsylvania a doctor picked him up and after looking over the leg and giving Robert some pain pills drove him all the way to his mother's address in the town of Rising Sun. Bob was white-faced and delirious when they carried him in, John would remember, and his leg looked like a festering tree stump. The doctor told Ann that the swollen, infected limb was full of poison and it would end up killing him if it continued to spread. "If you love your son," the doctor said, "the best thing is to get him to the hospital and get that leg taken off."

Ann wouldn't do it. She hated to see Bob suffering, but she couldn't drag him down to some charity ward and let them saw off his leg. Grabbing up a basket, she set off into the woods that began just behind the house. She was gone for hours, carefully picking out leaves and wild herbs, filling the basket, coming home scratched and mud-spattered. From the dampened and dirty ingredients she made a poultice and applied it to the wounded leg. "She made another and another," said Annette, "for two days, constantly changing the dressing and drawing the poisons out. And knowing Mother, she probably never slept the whole time. And in the end the poison had been all drained and the fever and swelling began to go down. And my brother kept his leg."

In Robert's absence, the Mitchum clan's sojourn in New York had come to an end. There was little work on Broadway these days, and Annette had gone to join her husband, now transferred to Long Beach, California. Left to depend on themselves, the Major and his family were unable to meet even their minimal expenses in Manhattan and soon abandoned the city to live again with Grandmother Petrine and the Tetreaults in rural Delaware. Things were hardly better there. The farm had gone under, and now everyone lived together in an improvised apartment on the ground floor of a fundamentalist church in the tiny community of Rising Sun. Uncle Bill took whatever odd jobs he could find to put food on the table, but resources were stretched thin even before the arrival of Ann and her brood, men, women, and children crammed one on top of the other in the tiny set of rooms. It was worse than the chain gang, Robert thought, but for now there was no place else to go.

His bad leg had become so raw and weak that it would take a month and more to heal. He hated being confined to the sorry, over-crowded apartment, and when Uncle Bill carved out a crutch for him to hobble around on, he eagerly went off in search of whatever excitement a hobbling fifteen-year-old boy could find in Rising Sun and environs. Jack was a young man now, strong and handsome. Away from his brother's shadow, in recent months he had begun to come into his own, doing well as a student at Caesar Rodney High in nearby Camden. He was an athlete, a good student, a popular boy with new pals and a string of girlfriends. Briefly—and for the last time—the hierarchy was reversed, the older brother tagging along with the younger. Robert sat on the sidelines, watched his brother play football, met his buddies. Jack had female friends now, too. One girl he knew was a pretty and slender brunette with dark eyes, a sweet and soft-spoken thirteen-year-old by the name of Dorothy Spence. They had met at school that autumn and were just getting to know each other. They had walked and talked together and shared a soda or two. Not exactly dates or intimate encounters like those with some other local girls he knew, a few of whom had gone behind the corn shed with him and kissed and played games, but it wasn't for lack of interest on Jack's part. "My heart was hers," he said of Dottie Spence, and he had every intention of getting to know her better as the season progressed. And then, one afternoon at Voshal's Mill Pond outside Camden, a swimming hole and hangout for the local schoolkids, he made the mistake of introducing her to brother Bob.

To be perfectly honest, Dorothy would say in the years ahead, when asked to recall that momentous first encounter, she hadn't liked him. He was a smart aleck, he cursed, he told rude stories, he was rather scrawny and odd-looking, like an overgrown urchin in his baggy old clothes, and hopping about on a poorly made crutch. She was friendly and polite and took his teasing good-naturedly because she did like his better-behaved brother, but once Dorothy Spence left the boys for home that afternoon, she didn't give Jack Mitchum's older sibling another thought.

Robert, by grand contrast, experienced an immediate and

profound attraction to his brother's dark-eyed, soft-spoken female friend, though typically he disguised his feelings behind a veil of wisecracking indifference. He returned to Rising Sun that day in a state of anxious excitement, moonstruck. All evening he could think of nothing but the girl by the pond, and that night in bed, crouched over one of Jack's school composition books, he scribbled poetry in a Byronic frenzy, a strange outburst of passionate feeling for a person he had known for one afternoon. "All my lonely life I've loved you lovely stranger," the boy wrote that night.

How to account for such sudden and, as it would prove, unwavering commitment to a largely unknown object of desire? "Love at first sight—ever hear of it?" said his sister. "Real love is always mysterious. Who are we to try and understand it?" Robert's own recorded assessment was bluntly deterministic and even more to the point: "She was it," he said. "And that was that."

All that remained was for someone to tell Dorothy about it.

Robert pursued her all that autumn and winter. He would find his way to Caesar Rodney in the afternoons and wait to see her come out of school, and on Saturdays he would take the bus or hike three miles out to the Spence family home in Camden. He would drag John along for company (at first miffed at the woman-stealing antics of his "rapscallion" brother, Jack soon recognized the singular nature of Bob's pursuit). They would sit on the curb outside the Spence place and wait for Dottie to come out and join them, and then Jack the chaperone would sit there bored stiff and twiddling his thumbs while the other two whispered and giggled in each other's ears.

It was flattering to be the object of such great interest. Boys Dottie's age were not ordinarily so serious or so romantic. The more she saw of Bob Mitchum, the more she came to revise her initial low opinion of him. Indeed, she came to realize that Bob was a most unusual and exceptional young man, funny and kind and intelligent. He was a poet, of all things, who knew the most beautiful, strange words, and an orator who could recite Shakespeare by heart. He was a colorful and worldly person, too, only a couple of years older than she was, but he had traveled all over and done exciting things, and though his stories of New York City and riding freights and going to jail were often shocking and embarrassing to hear, they were terribly impressive. Robert made everyone else she knew in Delaware look awfully dull by comparison.

He was a little too colorful for some, including her parents, hard-working, middle-class folks who ran a general store in the town and who were not thrilled at their daughter's friendship with a once and future hobo (they were understandably prevented from hearing of his criminal conviction and time spent on the chain gang). Not by nature a rebellious child, Dorothy hated to disappoint or distress her mother and dad. But she did not stop seeing the boy, and her feelings for him continued to improve until one Saturday night on a double date with his cousin Gilbert and another girl, riding around in Gilbert's car, talking and laughing, an absolutely ordinary Saturday night she would remember forever only because it was the night she knew for certain that she was in love.

She was just thirteen years old, Robert would say in her defense, the age when young girls fall for derelicts.

He worked for a while as an apprentice mechanic in a local garage. Then, in the summer of 1933, not yet sixteen and lying about his age, he became one of the first volunteers for the Civilian Conservation Corps, an employment program created by newly elected Pres. Franklin Roosevelt. An innovative attempt to create jobs for some among the millions left unemployed by the Depression, FDR's CCC put young men to work on federal land projects and emergency relief assignments, simple physical jobs mostly, paying thirty dollars a month. Robert was assigned with a few hundred other enlistees to a tideland reclamation project and spent several months toting trees and shoveling dirt for ten hours each day. It was not much different from the chain gang, really. They didn't even let you keep your wages, sending all but five bucks per month directly home to your family. The months of steady, hard labor became a transformative experience—by the end of that first tour of duty in Roosevelt's "tree army" Robert had lost the skinny frame of his youth, returning home a strikingly powerful physical specimen with thick-muscled arms and broad shoulders.

The Mitchum-Morris-Tetreault-Gunderson clan had a new plan for survival. Annette's dispatches from Long Beach had painted a rosy and tempting picture of a Garden of Eden by the Pacific. It was easy, warm, abundant, everything that Rising Sun was not. With another Delaware winter ahead and no end to their hopeless, raffish condition in sight, it was decided to pull up stakes once more and move out to blessed-sounding California.

The family prepared for an autumn hegira, pooling their resources to buy an old flivver for the long ride west. Robert decided to head out before them, bumming his way to California, and Jack excitedly accepted his invitation to come along. Bob and Dottie had been going steady for months, and his restless nature was well known to her by now.

"I'll be back for you," Robert said. "I don't know how long it will take. But I'll be back."

Ann packed the bindles for her two boys, with going-away presents of new socks and handkerchiefs. They left Delaware in July with a friend Robert had made in the CCC, Carroll Davis, an Alabama boy returning home. In the New York City produce market they hooked up with a trucker headed for Florida, and with some hiking and another hitched ride made their way to Davis's hometown outside Birmingham, where the Mitchum boys spent a few days feeding on southern hospitality. Well rested and with their bellies full, Bob and Jack bid farewell to Carroll and his family and moved along, heading down the road with their thumbs out. Rides proved hard to come by on the southern byways that summer, and the boys found themselves on a most circuitous route to California. A sedan carrying three raucous mountaineers picked them up, then took them far off course on a bruising sidetrack that began with the purchase of three jugs of moonshine from a backwoods still. Generously the roving mountaineers shared the white lightnin' with the two young hitchhikers, Bob and Jack availing themselves till their eyes clouded over. The events of the next few days became a blur of festive and life-threatening behavior. One night in a hillside motor court the brothers were stirred from a drunken stupor by the sound of gunfire. The mountaineers had gotten into a regular Hatfield and McCoy contretemps with some other gang of hillbillies, and soon there were pistols and shotguns roaring from either side of the court. Bob and Jack crouched under a bed as window glass shattered and wood splinters flew through the air. They would look up through their fingers and catch glimpses of their drunken driver happily shooting at the unseen assailants. Eventually there was a ceasefire or a lull in the action, everyone scrambled into the sedan, and they tore out of there and didn't look back. The trip ended in a mountain settlement straight out of *L'il Abner*, old ladies smoking corncob pipes, goats in the road, young beauties bursting out of dresses made from ripped flour sacks. There was more moonshine on tap. Jack would remember them waking up this time in a muddy pen being poked at by curious razorback hogs.

They decided that hopping trains might be less dangerous after all; and with Robert teaching Jack the ropes on the fly, they caught a freight that took them as far as New Orleans. That night in a hobo jungle Bob got the word on a train heading west the next morning, and at dawn they placed themselves at the far end of the rail yard as the cars began slowly rolling out. They stood at the edge of the track and Bob looked down the line, waiting for the car he wanted to ride. There was a water tank beside them with a hose dangling free, and Jack decided to grab a last, long drink. The next thing he knew, a railroad bull appeared out of nowhere with a revolver aiming at his chest and barked at him not to move an inch.

Robert was already on board, and he leaned out from the blinds at the back end of the moving car, shouting, "Run! Come on! He won't shoot!"

Jack started, balked, looked at the .38 staring at him, and decided that the railroad cop knew a little more about whether he would or wouldn't shoot than did brother Bob. And so the train rolled on, picking up speed and carrying Robert out of sight, and Jack put his hands behind his back as instructed and followed the man with the gun along the siding to the station.

Bob Mitchum crossed the California border on an empty boxcar beneath a bleaching afternoon sun. Out of the desert and through the valley, the freight approached LA by nightfall. The other bums had warned him to get off before the final stop. If the bulls caught you there, they said, you were marched straight to the delousing pen at Lincoln Heights and locked up for a week. Robert decided to take his chances anyway and rode straight into the Alameda Street yards. With his worldly goods in the knotted bindle flung over his shoulder, he climbed down from the freight car and stood for the first time in the city of Los Angeles.

He skulked in the shadows looking out for police and walked along the twelve-foot wire fence that ran down the yard as far as the eye could see. He walked along until he heard the sounds of voices, muffled laughter, and a guitar. A quartet of Mexicans was sitting in near darkness on the ground beneath a signal tower. There was a guy strumming and another quietly singing along in Spanish while a big jug of red wine was sampled and passed from one to the other. They greeted him and offered up the jug and a patch of ground. One man pointed at Robert's face.

"*Tu eres Indio*," the Mexican said.

Somebody lit up a joint and passed that around, too. In fragments of English they told him about a place down the road where he could get a free hot meal, and later the man who had been singing showed him an opening in the fence where he could reach the street and pointed him toward the Midnight Mission. Robert was impressed. He had never seen anything like it—a reception committee for the bums. "*This was the place*," he would remember saying to himself on that fateful first night in California. "*The Promised Land.*"

The mission fed him a dinner of chicken with gravy and mashed potatoes, and when he was done—it being too late to start out for his sister's place—they gave him a voucher for a bed at the Panama Hotel, not much better than a flophouse really, in the middle of skid row, rummies and old prostitutes in the lobby. They gave him a cot in a tiny cubicle, and in the morning he found the Pacific Electric's

Red Car that took him all the way to Long Beach for a dime. Arriving at Annette's and her husband Ernie's bungalow a few blocks from the ocean, Robert stretched himself out on the living room sofa and didn't move again for the better part of a week.

There was no sign of Jack Mitchum for another ten days. After the cops got the drop on him back in Louisiana, Jack was confined for a while and then escorted to the county line with a stern suggestion that he never come back. He continued on his way west, but all alone now, did not have an easy time of it. Catching the wrong train more than once, he went as far out of his way as the Arizona-Mexico border and then, riding a freight straight into Los Angeles like his brother but without Robert's good luck, was rounded up with a group of hoboes and forced to spend three days in the holding tank. Worn to the marrow by his adventure, Jack could barely stand by the time he reached Annette's Long Beach bungalow. She told him that Bob was down the hall in the tub, and Jack went back to find him luxuriating in a bubble bath, his head sticking out of the suds as he smoked a cigarette and read a detective magazine. Jack stood wavering in the doorway, expecting some show of enthusiasm for his deathless appearance.

"That laconic fart looked up at me blandly and asked, 'What kept you?'"

After all Robert had seen of Depression-ravaged America, Long Beach seemed an earthly paradise. Bright cloudless skies, warm ocean breezes, rolling blue- and-silver-waves crashing on a golden beach. There was a boardwalk with a midway called the Pike, filled with smiling families and sailors in crisp, white uniforms and beautiful girls in brightly colored dresses. You could ride a merry-go-round and buy fresh-spun pink cotton candy. There were palm trees and happy people and no smog. Long Beach was a seaport, built on offshore oil and maritime commerce; and there was a dark underbelly to the place as in any port town, with seedy dives and clip joint dance halls, a lively corps of hookers and male hustlers to service the visiting navy boys and merchant seamen, and the Chicago mob running gambling boats two miles offshore. But all anyone who lived in

Long Beach in the 1930s would ever remember, looking back, was a gentle, happy town, fun and easygoing, where anybody could walk anywhere they wanted and feel safe, day or night, hot dogs were a nickel, hamburgers were a dime, and the sun never stopped shining.

"Bob had himself a great time in Long Beach," remembered Anthony Caruso, a teenager then, who met Robert Mitchum that summer and would remain a friend for more than sixty years to come. "He looked at that beach and the girls lying around in bathing suits, and he knew that was for him. He became a beach rat, Bob did. He was a good-looking kid, a great-looking kid. God, he had muscles and shoulders that wouldn't stop. He walked up and down the beach and flexed his muscles. And the girls there just fell for him. I went to Long Beach Poly High and so did Bob's brother, John, but Bob was kind of a dropout kid. He wasn't interested in studies or sports or any of that stuff. Just a beach bum. But a great guy and a lot of fun."

Robert became part of a coterie of amiable lowlifes who spent their time together in the penny arcades or sprawled on the boardwalk and the sand ogling girls and making mischief. His new best friend and Long Beach mentor was a character named Elmer Ellsworth Jones, a reform school graduate, émigré from Wilkes-Barre, Pennsylvania, who lived in a bachelor hovel next to the post office. "Jonesy" had extraordinary reserves of self-assurance, would challenge giants to a fight though he was small of stature, and had women coming in and out of his apartment at all hours though he was quite homely to behold. Jones and crew, John Mitchum would write, "cut a swath through the town like a thresher shark in a school of herring." It was mostly hijinks and seduction the guys indulged in, but criminal behavior was not out of the question for some of them. When the circumstances proved irresistable, Robert recalled, he and some pals would roll drunks for their wallets.

In the last days of summer, the family arrived from Delaware. Everyone moved into the small frame house at 314 Wisconsin Street. The place belonged to a man named Emmet Sullivan, a cousin of Ed Sullivan, the New York columnist and future television host. He was the perfect landlord for the East Coast emigrants, reluctant to press his case when the rent became overdue. They would greet him like a long lost uncle when he arrived to collect: Annette or little Carol would sing for him, the Major would recite some tale of the Boer War. Once he had nearly gotten out the door with a six-dollar down payment when Bob convinced him to let him bet it on a sure thing at the racetrack.

Anthony Caruso visited the Mitchum brothers at Wisconsin Street. He remembered, "It was a pretty crappy place. The blankets were dirty, the beds were never made. I don't think anybody ever slept on sheets. It was a very happy-go-lucky family. Believe me, it was very bohemian. The two boys, Bob and John, did pretty much whatever the hell they wanted to. Their mother was a strong woman, you know, really was, but she didn't try to control either one of the boys in any way."

As the need arose, and if the sunshine did not prove too enticing, Robert would take whatever work became available, dishwasher, floor sweeper, truck loader. In the winter of 1935–36, he went on the road again, heading east with the ultimate goal of visiting Dorothy. After some weeks he reached Ohio and looked up an acquaintance from Long Beach, recently returned to his wealthy family in Toledo. "Bob called me one day out of the blue," Frederick Fast told reporter Bill Davidson. "I went downtown and picked him up at a center the city ran for boys on the bum. He lived with us during that winter. My father gave him a job operating a punch press at the factory he owned. Bob hated it and he soon got fired. I remember he used to infuriate my father, a conservative gentleman, because he'd come downstairs wearing shoes but no socks. The temperature might be below zero, but Bob was on a kick then where he didn't like socks and just wouldn't wear them."

He moved on in the spring, eager to see his girl. By this time Dorothy had left her parents' home and was living in Philadelphia, had a job as a secretary in an insurance company. She was no kid anymore but an alluring young woman, wearing sophisticated frocks, hair prettily coiffed in the big city beauty parlor. Robert had to scare off a few potential suitors now. He told her she had to hold on, trust him, they would get married one day soon when he'd made his fortune or something.

"Stick with me, kid," he said, "and you'll be farting through silk."

Robert returned to the West Coast, back to the life of a beach rat. He slept at the Wisconsin Street house or at Elmer Jones's digs or wherever a night's adventure landed him. When the wanderlust took hold again he would pick up and leave, be gone for a few weeks or months at a time. He reenlisted with the CCC and worked in the forests outside Chino, California. He won some amateur boxing matches on fight nights at the camp. With the might of his shoulders and heavy hands, victory came easily enough most times—one good shot and the other guy went flying and out for the count. For a couple of months he followed the semipro boxing circuit around central Cal and Nevada, picking up twenty-five dollars or so in prize money each time he knocked someone on his ass. He had a forty-six-inch chest and a beautiful sloping right hook, and promoters wondered if they might be looking at a new star. Robert enjoyed himself and didn't get a scratch until one night he was matched against a fierce middleweight with arms so long that when he leaned back his elbows touched the ground. The man slapped him with an unexpected left and Mitchum's head spun around.

"Did I hurt you, baby?" the man said.

Robert, breathing through his mouth, said, "Yes."

The man laughed, said, "That's what we're here for."

The next punch sent Mitchum down in a cloud of blood. The bridge of his nose brutally broken in two places and the lens of an eye damaged, Robert promptly retired from the ring.

At Long Beach and other ports along the California coast, he worked occasionally as a stevedore, loading and unloading the liners and freighters that steamed in from around the world. The longshoremen were among the most politicized of American labor groups, with tough left-wing union leaders in a perpetual war with the employers. Robert attended meetings and listened to fire-and-brimstone speeches by guest revolutionaries. He was not much of a joiner, but he had seen enough injustice and capitalist opportunism in his travels to listen with sympathy to these political preachers, and for a time in this period he considered his own politics to be "conditional communist." He would sometimes even claim to have been a card-carrying CP member and to have written a few speeches for some of the "rabble-rousers." These experiences contributed to a stage play he would write some years later concerning the well-known (and much hated) Harry Bridges, an Australian émigré union leader and Communist whom U.S. authorities fought long and hard to expel. *Fellow Traveler* satirically dramatized Bridges's deportation by steamship and his imagined fate, castaway on a South Pacific island, organizing a tribe of cannibals.

There was a local theater group in Long Beach called the Players Guild, a privately funded community endeavor dedicated to bringing the city an annual series of professional-quality dramatic productions, both originals and Broadway hits. The guild had been around for years and did not attract much attention, but that began to change in the winter of 1936–37, following the arrival of a new artistic supervisor named Elias Day, a veteran actor and director, not a famous figure exactly but a respected theatrical talent with imposing credits who had worked in some capacity with every theatrical notable since the turn of the century. Sister Annette, after a period restricted to housewifery and having a child (a boy, Tony), had been looking to return to show business, and the good things she had heard about the Players Guild and the talents of Mr. Day led her to become a member. She helped out with a couple of the productions and saw Day in action. Annette had long believed that Robert was a natural performer like the rest of them, but he was too shy to express himself in a public forum and ranked acting very low among his artistic compulsions. Only once had she gotten a chance to make him do something before a crowd. There had been some sort of talent contest sponsored by an oil company, and she had practically dragged him up there to sing a rendition of "Would You?" And hadn't her instincts been proved correct! She had been delighted to see her brother's suave, assured stage presence and the way the girls in the audience reacted to him, spontaneously swooning the way girls were supposed to have done when Sinatra came along years later. But when they had talked about it since then, Bob stubbornly continued to show no interest in such public display. He could recite Shakespeare by the page, but the idea of jumping around on a stage tugging on your hair and pretending to be a character somebody made up seemed to him a rather sissified and embarrassing endeavor. Annette didn't give up. She knew Bob's little games, the way he tried to hide his real feelings behind a layer of disinterest and ridicule. He just had to be pushed, Annette thought.

She'd gotten a copy of the play that would be the guild's next production, *Rebound* by Donald Ogden Stewart. She had read it and given it to her mother, and both agreed that the part of Johnnie Cole would be just perfect for the reluctant Robert. "The trick was how to get him to try for it," Annette remembered. "That night, we waited until Jack was out of the house, and Mother said, 'Bob, there's a reading at the playhouse. Can you drive us down?' And Bob said, 'Sure, I'll take you down.' That got him into the playhouse they used, inside the old Union Pacific Depot. Bob walked us in, and we sat him down on the aisle, and I sat behind him. And they came to the role that Mom and I thought belonged to Bob. And the secretary called, 'Is there anybody wants to read for the part of Johnnie Cole?' When she said that, I heard Bob take a breath. He stopped breathing. You see, Bob and I had ESP since we were born. I kid you not. Mother had it, too. Before either of us would say anything, the other would know what it was. And he knew what I was thinking when the secretary spoke. And the dame looked around and said it again, 'Is there anybody wants to read for this part?' And Bob sat there frozen, not making a sound. And then I took my right thumb and pushed it against his back real hard until he jumped from the seat and they all looked up at him from the director's table. And they saw him and they got him to read the part and the rest is history. I like to say to people that right here on this hand is the thumb that made a star!"

Elias and his wife and assistant, Oranne Truitt Day, saw the attractive, broad-shouldered young man lurch into view, and one or the other called for him to come down. Casting a withering look at his sister, Robert walked to the director's table and introduced himself, took up the pages they wanted to hear, glanced at the words, and then barely took another look—the photographic recall that would one day wow them on assorted movie sets—as he began reciting/acting in a resonant baritone voice. The two at the director's table looked at each other, whispered for a moment, then Mr. Day told Robert when to show up for the first rehearsal.

The guild's players were local people of all ages and backgrounds. Most were amateurs on a lark, though there were some who had professional aspirations and dreamed of a future on the stage, even a few who nurtured fantasies of breaking into the movies that were made practically in their backyard (though even in Long Beach everyone thought of Hollywood as an unreal and unreachable place and much farther away than the hour-long ride on the Red Car). Robert was among those actors in the group who had no aspirations beyond having a merry time. But with his previous attempts at self-expression confined to the writing pad and the recesses of his mind, this initial participation in a group artistic effort would prove to be a revealing and liberating experience. "One of the most enjoyable and satisfying encounters of my life," he would write of it some years later, in a brief memoir prepared for the Los Angeles Parole Board apropos a felony conviction. "For the first time I had the acquaintance of young people who shared my ideas and reflections, and though most of us were threadbare poor, we enjoyed the counsel of our mentors and forgot our fears of the future."

Margie Reagan, then forty years old and a participant in guild productions since 1930, would remember Bob Mitchum exuding something like star power from his first day as an actor at the Long Beach Depot Theater, an enormous attractiveness that was not confined to the stage. "Everybody wanted to be around him. Especially the girls—the actresses and script girls. They were crazy about him, and he sometimes took his pick after the show. One wink from Bob and that was it. He had that look. They never turned him down."

As he did in so many creative endeavors, Robert took to acting with a natural, instinctive ability. Almost at once Elias Day let it be

known that in Mitchum he believed he had found a raw talent with
enormous potential, and he lavished on the young man a great deal
of individual attention, something, in his stay at the guild, he would
do with only one other new performer, an actress named Laraine
Johnson. (Renaming herself Laraine Day in his honor, she would
become a leading movie star of the 1940s and eventually a Mitchum
costar; Johnson/Day knew Robert from the guild though they did
not work together on the stage; she would recall him as being "very
odd.") But if Day had his favorites, no one in the company was
neglected. The small, intense man worked closely with each cast
member, advising and guiding them through even the briefest
walk-ons. "He wanted everybody to be as good as they could be,"
said Margie Reagan. "He really helped you. There were directors
who might just take you through it and try and make it smooth. But
Elias Day was really interested in making you act. He would talk to
you about the character you were playing and what the motivation
was so you could understand why you said what you said.
Sometimes he almost went too far, yelling if he got upset, and stopping you to fix something even when you were in final rehearsal. He
was almost more of a great *coach* than a great director. But he was
wonderful."

Rebound, a Broadway hit in 1929, was a Molnarian romantic
comedy with a few somber thought pills scattered among the bons
mots. Mitchum's was a supporting part—Annette had not wanted
to push things *too* far—though playwright Stewart would call it the
most difficult part in the play. The character Johnnie Coles is an
urbane gigolo who attempts to seduce the married heroine. There
were a few good lines, some titillating stage business, and a brief
emotional breakdown scene. A very nice showcase for any twenty
year old's acting debut. The production opened on the night of
August 11, 1937, to an audience of locals, guild subscribers, the players' family members, and the Long Beach newspaper critics.
Mitchum walked onto the stage so assured and effective it was as
though he had roamed the boards for years. But the whole company
was good that opening night, a couple of missed cues and such but
otherwise a thoroughly professional-looking, sophisticated job. The

local reviews were uniformly positive, and the *Press-Telegram*'s Jane Ahlswede made special mention of the performance by the "outstanding . . . Bob Mitchum."

Annette had been right. Brother Bob was a natural. Tremendous presence, everyone who was there said so. Robert took the plaudits, smirked, and went on his way. He wasn't the sort to run through the streets declaring he'd found his calling in life. It had been fun; it had put him into close contact with many friendly and attractive women. Perhaps he would do it again sometime, if he felt like it.

That second appearance on stage came in the following spring of 1938. By then Elias Day was dead. His widow, Oranne, opted to continue with the guild; and a friend from the New York stage, Larry Johns, had come west to help her, bringing with him a license to produce the first regional theater version of Kaufman-Ferber's Broadway hit, *Stage Door*. Robert dropped by the Depot and met with the new director, and Larry Johns cast him in the small but showy role of Keith, an egotistical playwright. Johns, like Day before him, recognized Mitchum's ability at once. After the first readthrough he knew that the young man had what it took to become a first-rate actor. "He was just born to it," said the director. Margie Reagan recalled, "Bob became one of Mr. Johns's pets. He saw in Bob something special and wanted to bring out his talent." Oranne Day shared in the excitement over Mitchum's potential. Her own production of the high school comedy *Life Begins at Sixteen*, performed twice in May 1938, would be Robert's first opportunity to play a leading role. Pleased with her faith in him, Bob invited Mrs. Day to come and meet the family for dinner at the bungalow on Wisconsin Street. When she arrived at the appointed time, Bob was nowhere to be seen. Admitted to the house, she waited while one by one the other members of the household drifted through to the kitchen, took their food and ate it anywhere, then wandered off again. One boy, she would remember, came along carrying a halfdozen snakes on his person (presumably Jack, lately an amateur herpetologist). No one asked who she was or who had invited her. It was a clan of eccentrics straight out of *You Can't Take It with You,* Oranne told them back at the guild. And Robert never did show up.

In July he took another featured role—in hindsight the most significant role of his brief career in the theater: Duke Mantee in Robert Sherwood's *The Petrified Forest,* the gangster character that had made Humphrey Bogart famous a few years back. For the first time Mitchum performed a part that anticipated his cinematic persona to come: a gun-toting tough guy, laconic, cynical, deadpan funny. Robert's friend Anthony Caruso, by then trying to build his own career as an actor working with the Federal Theater Company in Hollywood, was visiting his family in Long Beach. *The Petrified Forest* was being performed that weekend and Caruso went. There on stage in a major part, to Caruso's amusement, was his beach rat pal Bob Mitchum. "I thought, God, this kid is great! He gave a performance as Mantee that was absolutely fantastic."

Day and Johns were generously eager to shepherd Robert to the next level of what they believed could be a marvelous acting career. They invited Hollywood talent agents and other industry folk to the shows, and any who actually showed up they tried to put in touch with their boy. But Mitchum resisted these favors, didn't really want to be an actor, he complained. If anything—and he wasn't sure there was anything—he wanted to write. As if trying to prove his lack of dedication, he skipped out on some performances, once calling the theater shortly before the curtain went up to say he had taken a trip up to the mountains and couldn't make it back. "He never explained or apologized to Mr. Johns," said Margie Reagan. "Apologizing was hardly Bob's way."

Still, his work in the theater had been inspirational. Reading play scripts, taking them apart and seeing how they were put together, he became intrigued by the form and began to write his own pieces for the stage. Oranne Day was encouraging here, too, and got him to submit to the Players Guild some one-act plays, among them a fantasy for children called *Smiler's Dragon,* presented at the Depot in a single performance on February 28, 1939. He worked on full-length works as well, including *Fellow Traveler,* which he sent to agents and theater companies around the country, without any takers, though he would claim to have received a long letter of praise and encouragement from Eugene O'Neill no less. Through the years Mitchum would occasionally make reference to this unknown work, his most elaborate written creation, recalling it with pride or, depending on the hour of the night, ridicule (e.g., "just a piece of shit written by a left-handed retarded child in crayon").

Sister Annette (now devoted to resuming her career after her marriage to the navy man dissolved) began getting work as a singer and piano player in Long Beach and then in some of the better nightspots in LA, and Bob happily volunteered to become Annie's creative consultant and "special lyric" writer. Annette liked to do more than merely tinkle the keys and sing the latest hits. She wanted to give her audience a textured act that mingled music with intimate conversation, verse, anecdote. Robert first provided her with an opening recitative, some clever and charming lines with which to greet the crowd. He soon began crafting whole songs and spoken or sung verses for her to perform. It was material of the sort that was then properly labeled "sophisticated," full of high-priced vocabulary, inside cracks, and a knowing attitude toward things like sex. He was so fertile with this stuff that he had new material for her every night. Robert hung out at the clubs all night, at the bar, or back in the dressing room with his sister. At the end of her last show, they would repair to an all-night coffee shop where they would sit and schmooze with the other cabaret and club performers, singers and musicians and comedians who appeared on the boulevards and in side street dives and hot spots throughout Los Angeles. Before long he was writing material for some of them as well, his clients including such denizens of the nightclub as Belle Barth and a transvestite performer named Rae Bourbon. For ten or twenty dollars per piece, he would write them a song, or satiric new lyrics to a hit tune, or sentimental interlude patter, whatever was needed. Much of it was risqué stuff, packed with off-color implications and double entendres, going as far as the law or a club's management would allow. Mitchum would laughingly recall, "Some were so blue I blush to remember 'em."

On one occasion Robert composed a serious dramatic oration, a commissioned piece for the vaudeville comedian Benny Rubin. Titled "The Refugee," it was a florid plea for universal brotherhood, with the climactic declamation, "Hear me, brother, hear me say, I was *born a refugee!*" Rubin performed it in blackface to an accompanying symphonic arrangement of "America the Beautiful," in an all-star benefit show at Earl Carroll's theater-restaurant in Hollywood. After fifty years in showbiz, Rubin would remember it as his "biggest success. With the finish, cheering shrilled over the heavy applause and I took many bows." Mitchum took fifty bucks.

It all flowed with ease from the young man's pen, and he could sit in a booth and scribble a job from start to finish while surrounded by people yakking and drinking their coffee. Perhaps a hundred or more pieces were created in this way, written, handed over, and forgotten. Sixty years later the remnants of Mitchum's "cabaret" work would be preserved mostly in the remarkable memory of Robert's sister, still able to recite by heart examples of his witty and erudite compositions, full as they are of intricate and unexpected rhymes and wordplay that would not have shamed a Coward or Porter—all the more amazing in that they were the work of a twenty-one-year-old sometime stevedore.

Tony Caruso had an apartment in a run-down building on Highland Avenue just above Hollywood Boulevard. He rented the top floor, three bedrooms and a bath. "I was the fair-haired boy in the Federal Theater. I was trying to get into the movies, work on radio, anything. But there wasn't much money around, so I rented space in the apartment to anybody that needed a place to sleep. And I would get enough guys in there, charge 'em ten bucks a month or so, and then I didn't have to pay any rent myself. We called it El Rancho Broke-O 'cause everybody was broke.

"One day Bob showed up in town and asked if I could give him a bunk. So I became his landlady and found a bed for him and he moved in for a month or two; I don't know how long he stayed. Every time I saw Bob he was up to something different, and this time he was gonna be a writer. And he tried. I'd be in the room with him while he was trying to work something out, scripts or stories he was hoping he could sell somewhere. Radio was big then, and he thought that he might write for some of the radio shows or somethin'. He was trying to find a way to make a buck in show business. We all were. But none of us knew how. We didn't know shit from Shinola."

El Rancho Broke-O: It was like a very poor man's Garden of Allah, an affable roost and halfway house for aspiring or out-of-work movie actors and other Hollywood characters. Tenants floating in and out included Don DeFore, future film and television star, and Pierce Lyden, perennial bad guy in low budget Westerns. Mitchum would sit among them with his steel Underwood and try and type out something he could sell, pulp stories for the magazines or some dialogue sample that might get him an interview at one of the radio stations or movie studios. He would often wander down the block to Rose's Bookstore, a hangout for local writers. He'd sit in the back room with the scenarists and pulp hacks drinking jug wine, and he'd hope for some practical advice; but all he ever heard were obscene cracks about venal publishers and moronic producers. One of the writers he met was a rising star of private eye fiction, Raymond Chandler, author of *The Big Sleep* and *Farewell, My Lovely*. "I wasn't sure what to make of him," Mitchum would recall. "I thought he affected a British accent, and he was always wearing white gloves . . . a nice guy, but distant, suspicious of everybody."

As Caruso remembered it, the El Rancho gang would be off looking for work during the day and then at night roam down Hollywood Boulevard and hit the joints. They'd go see Wingy Manone in some joint. The Nat "King" Cole Trio played on Vine Street and you could go in there and listen for twenty-five cents a drink. And not everybody always paid for their drinks. Mitchum loved the music and he made the rounds every night. He was a devotee of the cool white-and-black small combos and piano players that performed around the boulevard, Cole and Harry the Hipster and Slim "Flat Foot Floogie" Gaillard. He admired the language of the hip musicians, and before long he'd made their jive idioms his own (an everlasting devotion, he would still be speaking that '30s and '40s jazz slang on his deathbed). "Bob soaked up life in those days, you know?" said Tony Caruso. "He liked everything. He took it all in. He liked to live hard. He liked to drink hard. Women. You name it."

One day Mitchum packed up and left El Rancho Broke-O. "The writing didn't work out, I guess. He didn't write anything worth a damn. And then he took off and I wished him well. And the next thing I knew about Bob Mitchum he was in a picture."

When Annette began getting steady gigs and tired of the long commute from Long Beach, she took an apartment in Los Angeles and Robert moved in for a while. They had such a close relationship—a mutual mind-reading act after all—that as two single people living together in the small apartment, his sister would recall, some people in Hollywood had "weird" ideas about them. Robert was a poor choice of roommate in any case, always avoiding his small share of the chores, never cleaning up whatever mess he left behind him. But he was soon moving along. One of the characters from Annette's nightclub crowd, celebrity astrologist Carroll Righter, had on occasion paid Bob to punch up his lecture act. Generally impressed by the young man's talent and his striking physique, Righter offered him a job as his secretary-chauffeur for an upcoming lecture and chart-reading tour of the tony winter resorts of Florida. The salary was not bad, there was a plush Cadillac for the driving, and the trip might allow him a chance to see "his girl," Dorothy, presumably waiting with eternal patience for his next visit.

They set off for Florida in January 1940. The long ride went without incident until they reached Louisiana and a sudden storm washed over them. The car slid out of control, leaped off the edge of the bridge they were approaching, and plowed into swampy water. Mitchum sprang through the window and scrambled to safety, but Righter had been hit in the neck by the portable typewriter stowed on the back shelf and he lay on the floor, stunned. The car looked as if it could slide underwater at any moment, but Mitchum stomped back into the muck, forced the door open, and dragged Righter clear.

"*You saved me,*" the astrologist sputtered. "*You risked your life to save mine.*"

"What did you want me to do, read a magazine?" Mitchum said.

A truck driver stopped and came down to help pull Righter to solid ground and then took them to the nearest town. The fire department towed the Cadillac out of the bayou, and the boys at the gas station got it running and cleaned it up, but the fabric-covered seats had gotten so wet that they oozed like a dirty sponge for the rest of the drive. They had to sit on old newspapers and torn cardboard boxes to keep their pants dry. "It's like I'm back ridin' on a fucking freight train," Mitchum complained.

They got to Florida, setting up shop in beachside hotels among the vacationing elite in Saint Petersburg, Naples, and Palm Beach. Robert was expected to drum up business for the lectures among the lounging dowagers and divorcées. "We charged a dollar admission for people wanting to find out what was giving with the stars. After the old guy gave his spiel, I'd pitch the women into having a horoscope reading."

The tour had not quite concluded when Mitchum went to Righter and told him he was quitting to go north to find his fiancée and get married. Righter asked him if he knew Dorothy's birthday. Robert told it to him.

Carroll Righter stared back silently, then slowly, ruefully turned his eyes to the ceiling and shook his head.

"A *Taurus* . . . dear boy . . . no . . . no . . . no. . . ."

Dorothy Spence's parents, her friends, almost anyone who could catch her ear, had told her to forget him. He was a bum, and even if he wasn't a bum he was gone now, had a new life in California. It was like waiting for a ghost. She wouldn't listen, didn't care what anyone said about him. She knew Bob's faults and she didn't care. They loved each other and that was that, and to heck with what they all thought. She was working at the insurance company in Philadelphia when he arrived—it was the middle of March—freezing cold in his Palm Beach finery, ice cream suit and panama hat. He told her he had won some money in a crap game and they were going to get hitched. Right away. Didn't want them waiting for her family to get involved and try and talk her out of it. Dottie, looking shaken, went to her office and told them she was going to need some time off. Her coworkers passed the hat and gave her a hundred dollars as a wedding present. A friend named Charlie Thompson agreed to be best man, and the three of them drove to Dover, Delaware, for a marriage license and then combed the town for a ring and a nice dress for Dorothy to get married in.

"Robert found a plain gold band," Dorothy would remember, "but then came the problem of measuring my finger. He and Charlie solved the problem by borrowing the jeweler's sample scale and going out to look for me. They'd forgotten the name of the store I'd gone into, so they simply wandered up and down the main street. At last I saw them through the window, so I pulled on the gown and ran into the street. We measured my finger on the sidewalk, and I tore back into the shop before they could get the idea that I'd run off with their dress."

On the evening of March 16, 1940, they got into Thompson's car and drove out to the home of a Methodist minister. "He led us into the living room," said Dorothy, "and I remember the temperature seemed somewhere below zero. So we adjourned to the kitchen where there was warmth, plus a rather strong smell of cabbage."

The old minister buttoned up his frock coat while his wife abandoned the stove and removed her apron. "Do you want the old service or the new one?" the minister asked.

Dorothy said, "The old one."

It sounded more romantic.

The next day the newlyweds bought two tickets for California and boarded the Greyhound bus.

With Annette making a living in LA, the Morrises decided they, too, had had enough of Long Beach. They found a small house for rent at 954 Palm Avenue in West Hollywood and they all moved in, the Major and Ann, Carol, Jack, Annette, and Tony. When Bob telegraphed to say he was bringing home a brand-new wife, they wondered where they were going to put the couple. Out in the backyard was a chicken shack that had been built by the previous tenants—

there were still a few feathers lying around—and it looked big enough to fit a bed and things, so the family decided it could be Bob and Dorothy's honeymoon cottage. "We got the Lysol and the scrub brushes and cleaned out the chicken coop," said Annette. "We got out all the smells and dressed it up so it was beautiful. Made a nice little bungalow out of it. And that was where Bob and Dot first lived until he made some loot and they could get their own place."

For a time they thrived on the narcotic aftereffects of their long anticipated union. That couldn't last. Robert, like one who has only belatedly read the fine print on a contract, bristled to learn that society imposed certain constrictions on the married man: for instance, you were supposed to spend all your time around this one broad. And Dorothy, who'd thought Bob's writing for nightclub performers sounded rather glamorous when he told her about it on the Greyhound bus, soon came to realize that it did not provide anything like a steady salary and often kept him out on the town till dawn with a lot of odd characters, including women. She was happy, no doubt; they had waited so long, and no one had thought it would ever happen, and now she had his ring on her finger. But it had to be a strain . . . nights lying in bed alone in the chicken-coop bungalow.

The house on Palm, overcrowded already with the permanent residents, was forever filled with friends of the family, musicians and actors and aspiring playwrights and little-theater directors and astrologers and mystics, eccentrics of every stripe, characters like no one Dorothy had ever met in Delaware—her husband excepted, of course. She got along with everybody, but the new Mrs. Mitchum was down-to-earth, not head-in-the-clouds, and there were recurring if indirect suggestions that she was not living up to the family's bohemian standard.

Robert was lured back into acting, taking one of the leads in a nonpaying little-theater production of a play by Claire Parrish called *Maid in the Ozarks*. A response to the great Broadway success of *Tobacco Road*, it had a similar rustic setting and required the entire cast to speak in ersatz hillbilly twangs. Playing one of the concupiscent Ozarkians was a very young blonde actress named Gloria Grahame, who would work with Robert many times in the years ahead in the movies, though such success was not then even a dream for either of them. Hanging around the cast, John Mitchum was introduced to Gloria's older sister, Joy, they began seeing each other, and the two were married by the end of the year.

Bob would most likely have continued on with his haphazard and penurious creative pursuits if not for the fact that Dorothy learned she was pregnant. He had up to now cleverly avoided most of the trappings of responsibility, but the threat of fatherhood, and perhaps Dorothy's pronounced reluctance to bring a child into the world without a dime to their names and while living in a converted chicken coop, would give Mitchum pause. He had to pull himself up by the lapels and face the fact that the time had come at last to stop fooling around, making castles in the air, and go find some tangible occupation with a regular paycheck at the end of every week. In his mind, some small, very distant voice he was not familiar with told him that if you were a guy who had gone and gotten himself married and there was a child and—according to the radio—a war coming on, then what you did was you got yourself a lunch box and went to work.

Hitler was raging across Europe, and storm clouds hovered over the United States. The defense industry had rapidly expanded with the growing likelihood of U.S. participation in the conflict, and the armament and aircraft factories of Southern California were now operating on round-the-clock schedules. Jobs were plentiful, and Mitchum quickly found a position as a sheet metal worker at the Lockheed Aircraft plant in Burbank. The base pay was $29.11 a week, though you could easily average a take-home of $42 with regular overtime hours. He was assigned to the graveyard shift, from midnight to morning, six nights a week. He was given a visor and a lead skirt. He was given a rubber apron.

It was the beginning of the worst year of his life.

Work in the plant was noisy and dangerous and something of a grift.

"We were making a lot of obsolete airplanes (old Lockheed Hudsons) that we sold to the British, and they didn't want 'em, but they were stuck with the contract. I didn't like the whole idea of it." He was a shaper operator. He fed sheets of metal into a machine. The machine went *screeeeeechunkchunkscreeeeee*, ear-piercing metallic sounds, with knives sticking out all over it, spinning around at 26,000 revolutions per minute, throwing out streams of red-hot metal. To Robert it looked like something dreamed up by Edgar Allan Poe. He would stand before it with a kind of hypnotized horror, waiting for his fingers to get lopped off and shaped and bloody sparks to fly out. When somebody's machine malfunctioned, you held your breath. Blades would come loose and shoot across the floor. One time Mitchum saw a knife come loose and slice right through the wall of the building. It finally landed somewhere in Glendale, he believed. Many of the workers were Oklahoma farm boys out of Steinbeck, innocent fellows right off the horse-drawn plow. The Okies would write home with wonder, said Mitchum, "Hoowee, you ort to see this here machine!" They'd be scratching themselves and forget what they were doing and the next thing you knew they had lost an arm.

Before the Lockheed job, Robert had made a commitment to another play. His farewell appearance, he figured. Now he had to rehearse and act and do the godawful job and wait for his kid to arrive all at the same time. It was a production of *The Lower Depths* by Maxim Gorky, directed by a Russian named Mike Stanislavsky and performed at the tiny La Cienega Theatre. Robert played his part in imitation of blustery character actor Gregory Ratoff. It was a shoddy enterprise. They'd be on the stage acting and all the lights would go out. It would be somebody in the dressing room plugging in a hot plate to warm up his blintzes. Sometimes the actors had to raise their voices to be heard over the arguments going on backstage. Robert was at the theater on March 8, 1941, when Dorothy went into labor. He rushed to the hospital in full makeup, a Russian peasant pacing the waiting room with the other expectant fathers. That night Dorothy Mitchum gave birth to their first child, a boy. He would be named James in honor of Bob's long-gone father.

Robert's partner at the Lockheed plant was a young, red-haired Irishman from the Valley named Jim Dougherty. "It started out that I would run the shaper and Bob was making the setups," Dougherty recalled. "And then they put him on a shaper of his own. His machine you pushed by hand because the parts were smaller. There were sparks everywhere. They weren't actually sparks, they were pieces of aluminum, and he got so he could direct them in any direction. And if the boss walked in there and Bob didn't want him in there he would just send those sparks at him. We got along. We kidded each other. I'd throw a rag in his machine and it would crack just like a whip. He'd jump right up on the bench, yelling, 'Don't do that; don't do that!'

"Bob was a good guy," said Dougherty. "Somebody you liked to know. Very easygoing. And a fantastic storyteller. During the lunch break he would always have a new one. About boxing. And riding the rails. They sounded like tall tales but we all enjoyed them."

Dougherty's girlfriend and soon-to-be wife was a fifteen-year-old beauty named Norma Jean Baker. In years to come, when Norma Jean had become a very famous actress named Marilyn Monroe, Mitchum liked to recall a warm social friendship with the child bride and future star. But these were more of Bob's "tall tales," according to Jim Dougherty. "Yeah, I'd hear him on television saying how back then we all went dancing and saw Frank Sinatra and all this. It didn't hurt anybody if he wanted to say it, but Bob never did meet Norma Jean when I was married to her. The closest he came was to eat some of her sandwiches. He never had any lunch to bring to work, and I'd give him one of Norma Jean's, tuna salad or bologna. And I'd tell her my buddy didn't have anything to eat and she started putting in an extra sandwich or two for Bob."

On December 7 the Japanese attacked Pearl Harbor and America found itself at war. Many of the young men at the plant went into the service, Jim Dougherty included. "Bob didn't get in," said Dougherty. "He said they wouldn't take him in the military because he had false teeth. That's what he told me."

Production at Lockheed naturally increased with the war on. Now it was no longer a matter of workers hoping for some overtime. Everybody worked extra hours, like it or not. Some days when they got behind schedule or someone didn't show, they were forced to work a full second shift: sixteen hours or more grinding metal in that hellish din. There was a foreman Robert despised, one of those hectoring types who liked to poke a pencil in your face. Robert gave him the hot sparks treatment. They got into a fight and he picked up something and threw it in the foreman's face. They hauled him down to the office. They told him they believed he was crazy, certifiable. He waited to be fired and sent home. They gave him a three-cent raise. It was wartime. You couldn't get fired. The aircraft factory was doing work vital to the war effort and jobs were frozen. You couldn't even quit. He might as well be in prison, Mitchum thought.

At home things were no less tense. Within the family there was much dissatisfaction over Robert's abandonment of his artistic pursuits, with antagonism directed at Dorothy for supposedly turning free-spirited Bob into a conventional wage slave. Mitchum felt increasingly uncomfortable, he recalled, "in light of my mother's and sister's accusative conviction that my wife was somehow responsible for what they regarded as 'enforced labor.'"

Things came to a head early in 1942. He didn't sleep anymore. He was disoriented all the time now, didn't know whether it was morning or night, and was beset by hallucinations. "I'd think it was afternoon. I'd get up, take a shower, go to the kitchen and discover I'd been asleep for a hot twenty minutes. I hadn't slept for a year."

One morning he came out of the plant at 8 A.M. heading for the trolley that took him home to West Hollywood. The trolley came, and he remembered not being able to read the number on the front of the car. Somebody had to tell him what it was, he just couldn't make it out. He sat in his seat on the ride home and looked out at the strangely clouded streets. He would hold his palm up to his face and try and make it come into focus. He made his way to the house and found a chair to sit in and told Dorothy that his vision was not at all as it should be. "I suppose she was a little alarmed, yeah. I was, naturally, because I had a lot of responsibility and I didn't know how I was going to handle it. I mean, I couldn't do anything for anyone if I couldn't see."

His sight did not return, and Dorothy took him to see a doctor. The doctor sent him to the hospital in Glendale, where Robert's eyes were examined by an ocular specialist named Seymour Dudley.

"There's nothing wrong with you physically," Dr. Dudley told him.

"Hey man, I'm blind!" Mitchum said.

It was, said the specialist, a psychologically induced affliction. Stress, exhaustion, hatred of his job.

"What can I do?"

"Get some sleep. Quit your job."

"They don't let you quit. There's a war on. I'm frozen."

"We can get you out," the doctor said.

"My family will starve," Mitchum said.

"It's lose the job or lose your mind," the doctor said.

He had tried to be a straight citizen; no one could say he hadn't tried. And it had gotten him a nice nervous breakdown in return. So that would have to be the last time for anything like that. He had fourteen dollars saved up. Dorothy went out and got a secretarial job. Robert's eyesight returned to normal after some days away from Lockheed. His mother said, "Why don't you try getting work in the pictures? You'd be a marvelous picture actor."

There was an agent he had met back when he was working in a play downtown. What the hell was the guy's name? Bob wondered. He had been very appreciative at the time, given him a business card and everything. He remembered it: Paul Wilkins. Mitchum looked him up and they got together. Wilkins was a third-string agent with no stars in his stable but a few character players whose commissions kept him solvent. He knew Mitchum could act. The boy was big and masculine, a little raw looking, more a cowboy type than a matinee idol. With his broken nose and ditchdigger's shoulders, nobody was going to mistake him for Fredric March. Mitchum said that all he wanted was some work that paid him enough to feed his family. Wilkins told Robert they would give it a shot. He would try and set up some interviews and keep an ear open for anything that might fit Bob's type.

In the following weeks Wilkins carted the hopeful movie player around to some small-time producers' offices and had him pose for a few publicity pictures, but they didn't arouse any interest. Unsure if the agent would ever find him anything, Mitchum tried an end run with a friend from the Players Guild and registered for screen extra work. But even this mundane employment, standing around in crowd scenes, seemed to require an inside track. While he waited for something to happen he took a part-time job selling shoes on the weekend at a shop on Wilshire Boulevard. It was clownish work, on your knees wrestling with strangers' feet, you were supposed to push the old shoes nobody wanted and make people believe the wrong size fit them perfectly. The salesmen lived for female customers who forgot to put on their underpants.

Toward the end of May 1942, Paul Wilkins called Robert to say that he'd gotten him an interview with Harry Sherman's outfit. "Pop" Sherman was an independent producer of B Westerns, most notably the long-running Hopalong Cassidy series with Bill Boyd. Wilkins told him to wear a clean suit and tie. Robert had just the one suit at the moment, borrowed from somebody. It wasn't all that clean, and the tear in the crotch of the trousers had been repaired with a strip of black adhesive.

The offices of Harry Sherman Productions were in the California Studios on Gower Street. When Mitchum got there he was ushered into an executive office occupied by the head man himself and several harried assistants. Introductions were brusquely made. Sherman and the assistants huddled over photographs and a résumé Wilkins had supplied. They looked down at his pictures; they looked up at him in the flesh. They got him to say a few random lines; and when they heard his basso voice, one of them told him he'd have to raise his pitch a little for the sake of the microphones.

"You'll vibrate. Sound like a gorilla."

"He looks kinda mean around the eyes," Pop Sherman said approvingly.

An assistant took Mitchum back the way he had come.

"What now?" he said.

The assistant said, "Don't shave."

He went to find Dottie at her job and told her she had to come out and celebrate.

"Guess what, your husband is going to be a movie actress."

They went to a drugstore on LaBrea and shared an ice cream soda. When the bill came, he hunted for change in the pockets of his borrowed suit.

Part two

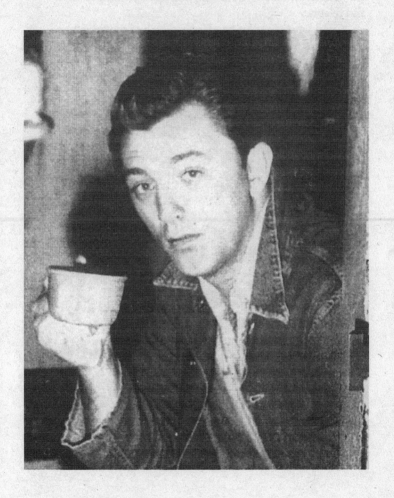

CHAPTER THREE

In a Dead Man's Hat

On the first day of June, with the sun barely clearing the eastern hills, Tony Caruso's friend and sometime roommate Pierce Lyden was sitting on a bench in the Los Angeles bus station clutching a ticket to Bakersfield when he looked up to see a bewhiskered Robert Mitchum coming across the waiting room. With a five-day growth on his chin and a battered cardboard suitcase in his hand, the fella looked like a refugee from skid row.

Pierce Lyden said, "What the heck are *you* doin' here?"

Bob told him, "I got an agent and he got me a movie job! I'm off to Kernville on a Hopalong."

"No kidding. Join the crowd, pardner. That's where I'm going."

Bob said he didn't know one thing about the job. Was he supposed to bring his own makeup or his own horse or what? He didn't know what his part was, but he told Pierce what Pop Sherman had said about his eyes lookin' mean, and Pierce said that sounded like a bad guy part. Mitchum said he didn't know if he'd be playing a young girl or a Chinaman, but for a hundred bucks a week he was ready to do it. Then somebody announced the bus for Bakersfield and the two men climbed aboard the Greyhound and headed north.

The Hopalong Cassidy series, seven years old in 1942, was an industry phenomenon, lucrative, respected, and influential. The title character originated in the popular novels of Clarence E. Mulford, a New York civil servant before he turned to writing some of the more authentic and entertaining tales of cowboy fiction, adventures of a gimpy, middle-aged drifter and trail boss. In February 1935,

Mulford signed a contract granting the movie rights to his novels to Harry Sherman and a couple of partners in the newly formed Prudential Studios Corporation in return for the payment of $2,500 for each Cassidy movie put into production, with a whopping $250 due in advance. Sherman was clearly not looking to do typical Western shoot-'em-ups in the Tom Mix, Ken Maynard tradition. His first choice to play Cassidy was James Gleason, the scrawny fifty-ish Bowery Irishman who more typically portrayed cabdrivers and fight managers. Gleason dropped out after a money squabble, and Pop went looking for another Hopalong, setttling on a more conventional-looking lead in William Boyd. The tall, fair-haired, thirty-eight-year-old Hollywood veteran was in the silent years a favorite of D. W. Griffith and C. B. DeMille (who cast him as Simon of Cyrene in *King of Kings*) and, with his pleasant, Oklahoma-tinged voice, a busy minor star in the talkies. In the early 1930s, a foolish case of mistaken identity hurt his career when the newspapers confused him with another performer of the same name, a theater favorite, William "Stage" Boyd, who had gotten caught up in a vice scandal. Bill Boyd began to hit the bottle. When Pop Sherman went out to Boyd's Malibu home to offer him the Cassidy series, the actor was sprawled on the beach, sleeping off a two-day drunk. Sherman signed him anyway, at a salary of thirty thousand dollars for six pictures, with the proviso that Boyd give up liquor. To Sherman's surprise, the actor would take an active and creative interest in his portrayal, demanding among other things that his Hoppy never resort to excessive violence and that his dialogue always be grammatically correct. Boyd's characterization of Cassidy as a figure of good-humored compassion and avuncular authority was unique among cowboy heroes, while his distinctive look—the blue-black costuming, the tall-in-the-saddle posture astride a magnificent white steed—remains one of the immortal iconic images of the genre. From the beginning, the Hoppys were considered among the very best of B Westerns. They were well produced, with generally above-average scripts, solid direction, and good acting. Pop Sherman tried to find the best talents his restricted budgets could afford. He broke in many a tyro actor, screenwriter, and cinematographer who would go on to bigger things. And he would resurrect the careers of seasoned directors and others whose big things were all behind them. That was pretty much how it was when you hired onto a Hopalong Cassidy picture: you were either on your way up or on your way out.

Mitchum and Pierce Lyden climbed off the bus in Bakersfield and transferred to the "stage"—a bone-rattling, clapboard truck—that took them up to Kernville, a tiny mountain enclave on the fast-flowing Kern River with scenic vistas in every direction, weathered old buildings, and its own Western movie street at the eastern end of town. The chamber of commerce did a brisk business in making the manufactured ghost town available to Hollywood characters like Harry Sherman for a daily or weekly fee.

It was past noon when they arrived. The sun was shining, the air tasted cold and clean. Taking up his cardboard suitcase, Mitchum crossed over to the entrance of the Mountain Inn where a bunch of cowboys were gathered on the open wooden porch. He greeted them with a big friendly smile, determined to make a good impression, but the cowboys only stared back with long faces. One of the bunch at last offered a spiritless greeting and said he would take Mitchum over to the wardrobe tent.

They went along the dusty Kernville street and Mitchum asked, "What's wrong with everybody?"

"Did you know Charlie Murphy?" the guy asked.

"Nope. I don't know anybody."

"Well, Charlie Murphy's just got hisself killed."

Another cowboy player and stuntman, he'd been driving a four-up, a stagecoach drawn by four horses, and was having trouble controlling the rig when he hit a bump, lost his seating, and fell forward into the horses, under the horses, under the wagon, one wheel rolling over him, crunching his skull. He'd been driven off to the hospital in Bakersfield, but from the way he'd looked, everybody figured he was a goner. Filming was shut down for the afternoon as a show of respect. Everybody had liked old Charlie, even if he didn't know jack shit about driving a four-up.

Mitchum was introduced to the costumer, Earl Moser, who suited him from the racks and bins of cowpoke gear—boots, jeans, chaps, denim shirt.

"What's your hat size?" Moser asked.

"Seven and a quarter."

Earl placed a well-used Stetson on top of the pile of clothes. Mitchum picked it up and found the rim all sort of crusty and stained. Moser saw him picking at it and took a look. "Oh. Yeah. This one belonged to ole Charlie. That was a real shame what happened to him." He took out a kerchief and cleaned off some of the gore or whatever it was and handed the thing back.

"And that is how I started out in pictures," Mitchum would tell it through the years to come. "In a dead man's hat."

He met his fellow players. There was Bill Boyd, Hoppy himself, friendly but aloof; the good-natured Scotsman Andy Clyde, who played Hoppy's rubber-legged comic sidekick, California; and the third regular, Jay Kirby, doing the male ingenue role. There was crotchety Russell Simpson, one of those character men you saw in a thousand movies without ever knowing their names. And George Reeves, a young hero type with baby-smooth skin and chiseled features on a Charles Atlas figure. He was going to play a Mexican peon in the movie. Bob had seen him in *Gone With the Wind,* one of the Tarlton twins chewing the fat with Scarlett O'Hara. A big break like that, and here he was, three, four years later, happy with day work on a Hopalong. Mitchum wondered where that left him with his broken-nosed mug, unshaven cheeks looking like a squirrel's ass.

Most of the men gathered in Kernville were riding extras and stuntmen, and even if they had to speak some lines from time to time, few of them thought of themselves as actors. They were part of the Gower Gulch posse, a kind of *Legion Étrangère* of dispossessed cowhands come to Hollywood to scratch out a living, mostly in Poverty Row oaters. Some of them were veterans of the last big cattle drives, some were ex-rodeo tramps, some listed more regrettable experiences on their résumés. "Real cowboys and some outlaws," Mitchum recalled. "The last fading few of the ex-train robbers who used to work silent pictures." A tough bunch, they spent their down time drinking, gambling, and brawling. And they loved telling stories. They were barely literate, some of them, but they were champion storytellers; and Mitchum enjoyed their nightly swapping of tales of Texas stampedes and Hollywood Boulevard bar fights, playing poker with Wyatt Earp or screwing Louise Brooks. Some of those stories had been told so many times the teller could not remember if it had happened to him or to somebody else. Ever adaptable, Mitchum fell right in with them, sitting around at night drinking rotgut and matching their bull with his own ripe brand. The authenticity of the cowboys did much to assuage the vestigial embarrassment he continued to feel about making faces for his pay. With this rowdy bunch doing it, the job couldn't be all that unmanly. They helped him in another way: his observational skills went to work collecting their personal tics and speech patterns and lingo. The look and manner of some of those roughneck, laconic cowboys would inform various Western and tough guy characterizations Mitchum would create in the years ahead.

When an assistant director asked him how well he rode, Bob told him no problem there, he'd grown up with horses on his grandfather's farm. Then it came time to saddle up. Pierce Lyden: "He told me about all the riding he did as a kid, but it didn't look to me like he'd ever seen a horse before let alone could ride one." Mitchum's assigned pony quickly threw him to the dirt. He brushed himself off and tried again, with the same result. Cowboys rode by, glancing down at the new guy sprawled on his ass. Mitchum said to the horse, "Listen you son-of-a-bitch, I need this job, so it's you or me." The horse threw him again. Years later Bill Boyd told Bob's brother, John, how he'd seen Bob haul back and slug the animal—"a right hand that made it roll its eyes backward."

"He had guts," said Lyden. "He just hung in there." Later, actor Cliff Parkinson offered a bit of advice, and Bob found that it actually worked and was a lot easier on the knuckles: "Just *look* like you can ride, kid." Mitchum's confidence was bolstered when he learned that Hoppy himself hated horses and could barely ride even after

more than two dozen Westerns. Anything above a straightaway can-
ter required the services of Boyd's double and stuntman, Ted Wells
(a star himself in the 1920s in the old Pawnee Bill Jr. series, now
reduced to galloping in long shots).

Filming got under way on *Border Patrol*. The unusual story line was
the work of another of Pop Sherman's discoveries, twenty-seven-
year-old Michael Wilson, the future scripter of *A Place in the Sun*
and *The Bridge on the River Kwai*, and in the '50s one of the prominent victims of the Hollywood blacklist. *Border Patrol* found Hoppy,
California, and Johnny busting up the slave-labor operation of frontier despot Orestes Krebs, whose outlaw minions kidnapped
Mexicans and put them to work in his silver mine (here was one of
those "subversive" plot lines the witch-hunters of the House Un-
American Activities Committee later decried, lefty Wilson trying to
turn Saturday matinee kids against capitalism). Mitchum was to
play the role of Quinn, a man wanted for robbery in three states and
a stranger to soap and razor. He met the director, Lesley Selander, a
brisk, no-nonsense guy who'd been doing Hopalongs for five years
now. If Mitchum was waiting to discuss the part and the nuances of
performance with Selander, he would be waiting a very long time.
An efficient craftsman who would work on almost nothing but B
Westerns for his entire fifty-year career, Selander had trained with
Woody "One Take" Van Dyke on Buck Jones silents, and like that
master he was known for keeping a breakneck pace both on the
screen and on the set. He didn't waste time, and he didn't like two-
bit day players wasting time either. There wasn't going to be any of
that Elias Day–style direction here, searching for motivation and
understanding of the character. You were a shitheel trying to kill
Hoppy; that was all there was to understand. And the motivation
was the paycheck.

The first images of Robert Mitchum recorded by a motion picture camera appear in the opening scene of the sixty-one-minute-
long *Border Patrol*. He is barely distinguishable in a few hundred
frames of dusty, wide-angle action. Chasing a sombreroed Mexican,
Mitchum rides toward the camera with another bad guy. They both

raise their guns, but Mitchum's doesn't seem to work and he stares down at it instead. It looks like a flub and would certainly have warranted a second take on another production, but Selander lived with it. The Mexican is shot dead, and Cassidy and pals come running. Mitchum gets a brief close-up and his very first line of dialogue, perfectly enunciated and delivered in a sonorous baritone:

"Come on, let's get out of here!"

Les Selander called, "Cut!" and as Mitchum later put it, "My fortune was made."

The actor's celluloid debut contained several moments of awkwardness—a wandering gaze in a group shot, some odd tiptoeing in his wardrobe department cowboy boots—but an undeniable screen presence was visible from the get-go. There, in embryonic form to be sure, was the characteristic Mitchum style, the slow, deliberate motions confidently mapping out his piece of screen space, the precisely judged gesture and body language, the caustic, sardonic attitude projected through the heavy-lidded, sleepily sensual eyes that would soon garner so much attention. Transcending—if just slightly—the underwritten part, he gave to this utility bad guy a distinguishing air of smoldering menace.

In the absence of direction, Mitchum relied on intuition and observation of his fellow performers to help him make the leap from theatrical to screen acting. He no doubt learned much from the working methods of Bill Boyd, a decent actor who made everything he did on screen look natural. Boyd was a scrupulous underplayer, moving with a calm precision and speaking in a firm, matter-of-fact tone, seldom raising his voice. A seemingly generous performer, he never tried to hog the camera, crying for close-ups or upstaging the other actors. And yet on screen he never lost his dominating presence—the others had to shout, growl, or gesticulate to stay even with him. Mitchum, who would become one of the foremost exponents and masters of this style of calculated underplaying, came to see how the mechanics of filmmaking made ludicrous the grand gestures and projected speech necessary in the live theater but made possible, through the magnifying powers of lens and microphone, the creation of intimate, believable characterizations built out of gesture, intonation, even silence. In time he would learn, too, of the camera's occult powers, its peculiar and inexplicable ability, under the right circumstances and with a compatible human subject, to read an actor's thoughts.

*

The company worked a long day. If there was still sun anywhere in the sky, the camera kept turning. One time Mitchum watched as Andy Clyde was positioned in the only area of sunlight left at the end of the day, a spot with a big muddy ditch next to it. "Clyde fell right into the ditch. He stood up, brushing the mud and glop off him, and said, with dignity, 'This isn't the *theatre!*'"

Working nonstop, and with only six reels to fill (approximately one hour of screen time), they shot *Border Patrol* in a week. The next film in the series, titled *Hoppy Serves a Writ,* went into production before the dust had settled on the last one. The unit packed up its camera and lights, costumes and six-shooters, and left Kernville for the the desert wastes and big boulders around Lone Pine. Mitchum went with them. For efficiency's sake, Sherman tried to maintain a repertory company for the series, using many of the same personnel from film to film if they didn't drop out for better-paying or more comfortable work elsewhere or for drunkenness that held up a production. Evidently, Sherman had been pleased with his new addition to the Cassidy troupe. Mitchum would end up doing seven Hoppys in that 1942–43 season. Only Bill Boyd and Andy Clyde appeared in as many. Lesley Selander would direct all but three of the seven. Two were guided by Frenchman George Archainbaud, once a big name at RKO, and one, *The Leather Burners,* by Joseph E. Henabery, a forgotten name from silent picture days. Bill Boyd would tell Mitchum about Henabery one night after the director had gone to bed. He was a former actor who played Abe Lincoln in Griffith's *Birth of a Nation,* then became a major director in silents, putting Rudolph Valentino through his paces and living in a Beverly Hills palazzo. But that was then, and Henabery was working as a machine operator at Lockheed when Sherman hired him to call the shots on *Leather Burners*.

"That's how it can be in this business, Bob," Hoppy told him. "One day you're on top and the next you're in the gutter. And there's plenty of folks just waitin' to scrape their boot off on ya."

The Leather Burners was memorable among the Cassidys for its bizarre climax, featuring a cattle stampede inside a mine shaft. It was Joseph Henabery's last picture.

In six of Mitchum's seven Hoppys he would be cast as various sorts of desperado; in just one, *Bar 20*, as an ambivalent good guy, clean-shaved in a three-piece suit, playing leading lady Dustine Farnum's insufferable fiancé. With each succeeding job the Sherman people gave him more screen time, and with each his self-confidence and understanding of the medium would increase. The Hoppys were Mitchum's film school and a formative and lasting influence on the career to come. The way they made those B Westerns, no frills, no pretense, just-get-it-done, strict egalitarianism—everybody swallowed the same dust, ate the same chow, used the same honey wagon—this would remain in Robert Mitchum's mind the ideal, the most comfortable and least embarrassing way of making movies, an approach he would try to encourage no matter how far from those innocent and threadbare productions his career would take him. In the decades ahead he would sometimes find himself in rarefied branches of the cinema, in sometimes opulent and spectacular circumstances, earning a paycheck that would cover the budget for an entire season of Hopalong Cassidys, clutching at the world's most famous women, reciting the words of distinguished authors, and listening to the direction of erudite artists and pretentious fools, and through it all he would act unwaveringly as though he were still making a seven-day oater back in Kernville.

"I was very pleased to work on the Hoppys," Mitchum would say. "Supper on the ground, free lunch, a hundred dollars a week, and all the horse manure you could carry home."

So now he was in the movie business. If Mitchum felt any great revelation in his first experience as a film actor, felt any profound sense of his calling in life, he kept it to himself. The workaday atmosphere, the long hours, and his sore ass conspired to eliminate any notions of romance and glamour he could have brought to the job. Rolling around in the dirt in Kernville and soaking with sweat in Lone Pine was not the movie business the ladies in the beauty parlors read about in *Photoplay* and *Modern Screen*. He had no illusions about that now. It was just something he could do, maybe better than most of the "mean-faced" cowboys he'd been working with, but that wasn't saying much. He wasn't looking for more. You got to work in the fresh air, it took you out of the house, and it sure as hell beat selling shoes. Fifty years later, when asked what he liked about the acting business, he would give pretty much the same answer.

He returned to Los Angeles after his initial sojourn in Hopalong country. The bills had not stopped coming while he was away, and even with Pop Sherman's dough in his pocket, things were still very tight around the two households. Paul Wilkins wanted to talk about a game plan for the actor's career, but Mitchum told him that right now he wanted to do anything that paid. He couldn't think about the proper "buildup" with milk and diapers to be paid for. Wilkins sent him to interviews and casting calls all over town. Sources list Mitchum appearing in a lost Max Factor–produced short subject about makeup techniques, and he took a featured part in another short, one produced by Walter Wanger for the California Board of Health. Titled *The Silent Enemy*, it dealt with the delicate topic of venereal disease. No, this was not the Hollywood they read about in *Modern Screen*. It was nearly the end of summer before Wilkins got him another job in a real movie, a quickie musical called *Follow the Band*, a nine-day wonder at Universal. This would be Mitchum's first job behind the walls of a big studio. Eddie Quillan was top-billed as a shoeless hick who discovers the ecstatic pleasures of swing music. It was a glorified vaudeville show really, featuring an assortment of minor big bands and nightclub acts like Hilo Hattie. Mitchum's small role as Quillan's pal Tate Winters garnered his first mention in a movie review when the picture eventually crawled into release. *Variety* listed him among those providing "standard support." Mitchum had made a stronger impression on his castmates with his raunchy stories and uninhibited style. Frank "Junior" Coghlan recalled the morning Mitchum came to work boasting of terrifying a cute waitress, proposing to "hang her from a chandelier and go *up* on her!"

Wilkins at last found a job for Mitchum with some prestige, a bit in an A picture and at Metro-Goldwyn-Mayer, the most distinguished of all Hollywood studios. *The Human Comedy* was one of Metro's big pictures for the year, Academy Award–type stuff. A tragicomic look at home front life in a small town, sticky humanism from the pen of William Saroyan, the film was being directed by Clarence Brown—no less than Garbo's favorite director—and starred Mickey Rooney, Frank Morgan, and Van Johnson, with enough supporting parts to populate two or three small towns. Along with a couple of other new faces, Barry Sullivan and Don DeFore (another former tenant at El Rancho Broke-O), Mitchum played a soldier on leave, flirting with the local girls, among them a young Donna Reed. Shooting was painfully slow and complicated. Clarence Brown and his massive crew took as long with one scene as Selander took to make an entire Hoppy. The lighting for a new camera setup might take half a day while the company sat around and waited. Mitchum's finished scene, anyway, was a good one, with a brief but charming and sexy appearance. His potential was apparent, but nobody at Metro seemed to notice. Mitchum went back to Bs: the Westerns *Beyond the Last Frontier* with Eddie Dew and *The Lone Star Trail* with a thick-around-the-waist Johnny Mack Brown, and an odd campus-set spy film, *We've Never Been Licked* (a title Mitchum savored as a double entendre). The jobs lasted from a day to a week or so and ranged from brief bits to featured parts.

He got a role as a hoodlum in a Laurel and Hardy picture shooting at Fox. *The Dancing Masters* was one of the team's last features. The picture was not very funny, and shooting it was not much fun. Mitchum recalled, "Off camera Oliver Hardy . . . had phlebitis, or something like that, and he was not at all happy. And Stan was sort of dazed and just sat in the corner. . . . It was not my place or privilege to engage in conversations with Mr. Laurel or Mr. Hardy, but they were not antic performers off-stage."

Early in 1943, Dorothy learned that she was pregnant again. Deciding they needed more space than the tiny chicken coop provided and wanting to be settled by the time the baby came, Bob went looking for a new place. Brother Jack was away in the service, and the Major was somewhere at sea in the merchant marine. Robert was the only man in the family now, and his mother hoped he would stay within reach. Just down the road, at 1922 North Palm, he found a small, two-bedroom frame house for rent. The owner wanted fifty dollars a month, within their budget but no bargain, with the wood rotting and the paint flaking to the touch and so snug you could touch the back windows from the front door. They took the place. Bob called it his "shanty." Dorothy, perhaps, would have liked an address farther from the shadow of Bob's other family—the undercurrents of tension between wife and in-laws continued—but she wanted to go on working for as long as possible. Bob was away long hours some weeks, and it was after all good to have Ann and Annette around to take care of Josh.

Sister Annette had returned to performing and landed a longterm gig at a small club called the Villa Riviera. While working there one night she met a soldier who, out of the blue, began calling her "Julie." Always alert to the presence of mystic forces, Annette recalled a numerologist once recommending that she change her name to one with five letters. So she did, calling herself Julie forever after. The soldier who did the renaming promised to come back and marry her—"They all proposed marriage before they shipped out," she recalled ruefully—but he was killed at sea.

Having managed to stay out of the service himself, her brother Robert had begun to reap a professional benefit from the war: every studio needed its own platoons of young soldiers for the scores of war movies now in production. In uniform, brawny Bob Mitchum made an imposing-looking fighter for American victory. Throughout 1943 he moved from one branch of the service to another, battling Japanese or Germans, depending on the day of the week. He played a GI in *Cry Havoc* (dying in the arms of nurse Ella Raines), a sailor in *Minesweeper,* and a Canadian version of same in *Corvette K-225,* a Marine Raider in the brutal *Gung Ho!,* an Air Corps sergeant in *Aerial Gunner,* a commando in *Doughboys in Ireland.*

In the summer Dorothy gave up her office job and stayed home with Josh and the baby on the way. Bob was making enough to take care of the bills and pay many of his mother's expenses as well. He was gone now more days than not, off at dawn to one studio or another and back very late if at all. On October 16 Dottie gave birth to a second son. They called him Christopher.

Nineteen forty-three drew to a close. By December he had appeared in nineteen feature films. To the public he was still a face in the crowd. And if any members of an audience had been struck by his screen presence in one of those nineteen films, they had a slim chance of connecting it to a name—he was unlikely to be billed in the posters and seldom mentioned in the more detailed cast list scrolled at the end of a feature. He had garnered no press beyond a few passing mentions by reviewers; and without studio backing an unestablished performer did not get publicity in the fan magazines or the gossip columns. Wilkins certainly did not have the juice to promote that kind of attention for an unknown. But there were those within the movie industry who made it their business to keep an eye open for interesting new faces that wandered onto the screen, no matter how briefly; and by the end of 1943—Mitchum's first full year in the business—some of these people had begun to take notice of the big, broad-shouldered actor with the smoldering, masculine good looks. William Pine and William Thomas, the low-budget producing team known as "The Two Dollar Bills," had hired Mitchum for a pair of back-to-back programmers, *Aerial Gunner* and *Minesweeper,* paying him seventy-five dollars a day. The team released through Paramount, and when their liaison at the studio got a look at Mitchum in *Minesweeper,* he was struck at once by the actor's incipient star quality and advised them to sign him up quick.

Thomas didn't even remember the nobody's name, but he knew a lucrative-sounding tip when he heard one. By the time the producer found his way to Paul Wilkins, the agent gave him the brush-off, telling Dollar Bill they had better offers in the works, one from Columbia, one of the majors, where Mitchum was working in an execrable Kenny Baker musical, *Doughboys in Ireland*. Harry Cohn had watched some dailies for *Doughboys*, noticed the newcomer, and now dangled a studio contract worth $350 per week. Jeff Donnell, the voluptuous leading lady in the film, already under contract at the studio, extolled the virtues of a steady paycheck and the nurturing of a home studio. With his family to think about, she advised that Bob accept the offer. He didn't. Something better would come along. Or wouldn't. Donnell told biographer George Eells, "He had this quality—I'm me and this is it. And whatever happens, I don't give a damn."

At Metro, director-producer Mervyn LeRoy was preparing to shoot *Thirty Seconds Over Tokyo*, a dramatization of the April 1942 American bombing of the Japanese capital. Set to star Spencer Tracy, Van Johnson, and Robert Walker, it was a gigantic production with a shooting schedule of over three months, a prestigious credit and a potential gravy train for a freelance player like Mitchum. Wilkins nagged LeRoy for a meeting with his boy Bob. LeRoy tested him. He tested him again—Mitchum would claim thirty times. "You're either the best actor I've ever seen or the worst." Finally he gave in, casting Wilkins's brawny client for the role of Bob Gray, a real-life character, one of Jimmy Doolittle's fearless pilots. This gig had big time written all over it, a top-of-the-line MGM movie, with Mitchum working beside Metro's most distinguished employee, Tracy, and the popular bobby-soxer favorites Johnson and Walker.

LeRoy wanted authentic backgrounds and lots of military hardware and arranged to shoot much of the film at the Naval Air Station in Pensacola, Florida, the actual training ground of the Doolittle Tokyo Raiders. The government saw this dramatization of the symbolically important raid—America's audacious response to Pearl

Harbor, dumping a few thousand bombs in the emperor's front yard—as welcome propaganda for the war effort and offered LeRoy full cooperation. The actual war was ignored for a time in favor of MGM's imitation mission, and Gen. Hap Arnold and Doolittle himself were assigned to the production as technical advisers. Shooting the aerial scenes, LeRoy got to play with as many as fifty B-29 bombers at a time. While the hapless Arnold stood by, the director, using a radio phone to speak directly to the pilots, would send the great armada circling aimlessly in the skies as he looked for a photogenic cloud formation.

Bob and much of the cast and crew arrived by train from California and transferred to Egland Field where they were housed in the utilitarian barracks. They took their meals from the mess line, showered communally, shat in the immodest group latrines, and basically enjoyed all the movie actor perks of the average enlisted man. This was Mitchum's greatest opportunity to date, Paul Wilkins had informed him repeatedly, a shot at a contract with MGM—a studio that made nothing but A pictures—but though his work on film was excellent, he showed no interest in making a similarly good impression off camera. Like the other actors, Robert grew more bored and restless with each passing week they were on location. Great amounts of alcohol were consumed and things got very rowdy at times. There were late night parties, fights, various hijinks, Mitchum earning a reputation for dropping his pants in front of officers and other dignified types. For recreation he began screwing around with the bosomy secretary of a visiting Metro executive. The exec got wind of it, but the secretary wouldn't reveal her lover's identity, so the whole company had to stand on the drill field and listen to a lecture about the price of moral turpitude and the desecration of the good name of MGM. The fake soldiers and the real ones clashed, sometimes violently. "Lookit the Hollywood fags!" the actors would hear as they went about the field. One night a brutal fight broke out in the barracks. Mitchum claimed he stepped in to stop a drunken sergeant from abusing Robert Walker. Actor Steve Brodie would recall, "Mitch . . . grabbed the son of a bitch and they went fifty feet to the front doors." The door burst from its hinges and the pair

tumbled down six steps onto the concrete walkway. Mitchum in a
fury pulled the sergeant up by his stripes and began pounding him.
It took three men to pull them apart.

The *Tokyo* company returned to California eventually and
resumed filming at the Culver City studio. Mitchum ordinarily
took public transportation to work and bummed a ride home at
night, but this proved impractical for getting out to Culver on time
so he invested a hundred bucks in an ancient Chrysler. He parked
it in the studio lot, but one of MGM's suits was repulsed at the
sight of the old rustbucket in among the shining movie star sports
cars and executive sedans and had someone track down the owner
and order him to park it on the street in the future. Mitchum
responded with what would become a characteristic reaction to
official disciplinarians, an act of passive-aggressive protest: he left
the Chrysler at home and arrived at the studio hours late. LeRoy
reamed him out. Mitchum, with seeming indifference, explained
the situation. "Oh, Christ. Forget it," LeRoy said. "Park where you
want, just be here on time."

Working with Spencer Tracy gave Mitchum his first opportunity
to make a close study of one of the certified great actors in the business. A complicated character in real life, a craggy, florid-faced
Irishman bloated from drink and tortured by assorted demons, on
film Tracy's characters projected an almost serene dignity and
humane, good-humored authority. His acting was scaled for maximum truthfulness, and he achieved the most powerful effects
through the most seemingly economical of methods. Tracy was the
sort of actor Mitchum could admire without embarrassment, a natural actor without the preening, painted-face vanity of so many
other stars. Through the years Mitchum would endorse the simple
philosophy of Tracy and Humphrey Bogart, "Learn your lines and
don't bump into the furniture."

Mitchum made a more intimate study of another Metro star.
During the *Tokyo* filming on the lot, he became friendly with Lucille
Ball. They shared a few laughs in the commissary and met up for
cocktails after work. The beautiful redheaded actress was unhappy

with husband Desi Arnaz's philandering and liked to give it back to him from time to time. She and Mitchum had a brief fling.

Fidelity was not one of Robert's virtues—he would never be particularly good at avoiding pleasure of any sort if it was offered. He was not an aggressive lothario, but his looks and charisma drew women to him without much effort on his part. It had been that way for some time, and things had only gotten easier within the free-spirited Hollywood community. In the studio environment especially he was surrounded by females—starlets, secretaries, wardrobe girls—many of them young, single, and frisky.

As Wilkins—and presumably Mitchum—had hoped, Metro considered putting the fledgling actor under contract. Trying to gauge his potential, the studio sent him to a session with its revered in-house acting coach, Lillian Burns. She was believed to have near mystical powers when it came to discerning a young performer's strengths and weaknesses and how to access the one and eliminate the other. Janet Leigh was among the stars who considered Burns a "mentor," and less talented actresses like Lana Turner were said to have achieved whatever believability they had on screen due to Burns's tutelage. Burns was shown some of the *Thirty Seconds Over Tokyo* rushes and then met with Mitchum in her office. She said, "They want me to do some scenes with you. To work with you. I'm not going to do anything with you."

Burns later recalled the meeting for Janet Leigh. "Lillian said that she had seen this animal, sensual magnetism," said Leigh, "and this great natural talent. She told me Bob was ready to do whatever was asked of him, but she said, *'Do exactly what you've been doing.'* She saw it immediately."

In the course of production, Mervyn LeRoy had come to the conclusion that Bob Mitchum was not after all the worst actor he had ever seen. Directing him in a strong bit played with Van Johnson on the deck of an aircraft carrier, LeRoy "sensed that he had something special." After Mitchum became a star, Leroy liked to say that he had discovered him, ignoring the actor's nineteen previous credits. But certainly LeRoy would have a crucial role to play in the next stage of Mitchum's fast-developing career. Frank Ross, Jean Arthur's producer husband, was just then planning a film version of Lloyd Douglas's thick, religioso adventure novel, *The Robe*. Mervyn LeRoy expected to direct it and was preparing to join Ross over at the RKO studio as soon as he finished with the endless *Thirty Seconds*. Mulling over the major roles in *The Robe*, LeRoy had a casting inspiration: Bob Mitchum would be perfect for the important part of Demetrius, the epic's muscular slave turned feisty Christian. LeRoy and Ross conferred, then talked to Ben Piazza, head of talent at RKO, recommending they sign their boy up for the planned production.

Mitchum went to a meeting at RKO headquarters in Hollywood. Piazza, primed by LeRoy, liked what he saw. He sent the actor on to see some of the staff producers. Most were impressed by the young man with the sleepy eyes and the deep voice. But not everybody. There were concerns about his jagged nose, his size, his deep voice. Mitchum recalled waiting outside one supervisor's office after an interview while the men inside discussed him. "But he looks like a monster!" he heard one of them say.

When the vote was tallied, Piazza sent for Paul Wilkins and told him that RKO was considering signing his client to a long-term contract, and what did he think about that?

It was then, in May of 1944, that Mitchum received his notice to report for military induction. Two and a half years since Pearl Harbor, and the war raged on. This was the real war, not the one in Culver City or the Valley. After two and a half years of casualties, the need for fresh blood was greater than ever, and many men who had avoided going into uniform for one reason or another—fatherhood, physical impairments, mental problems—were finding that the U.S. Army could use them after all. Mitchum had never shown much interest in the war. It had always gotten along just fine without him. Brother John was a more "gung ho" personality, a sentimentalist and patriot. And the Major . . . well, Bob's stepfather would have parachuted into Berlin and kicked Hitler's ass personally if someone had sported him the airfare. But Robert was a professional againster and sceptic, and the regimentation and authoritarianism of military life could not have seemed like his cup of tea. Lockheed had been bad enough. Bios by studio flacks would state that Mitchum had tried to enlist many times and was rejected, but Bob himself never endorsed such claims. Of his entry into the service he said, "When they took me away, I still had the porch rail under my fingernails."

As it happened, the army didn't want him—for now. He was processed and then excused until the next quota call. Later in the year, a regulation exemption of fathers further postponed his induction. RKO now had a firm offer on the table for his services, a seven-year contract. Feeling that the time had come to grab onto a little security, Mitchum told Wilkins to negotiate a deal. With someone of Wilkins's low stature in the business, this typically meant bending over and taking whatever the studio chose to offer. It was a typical long-term studio contract filled with corporate-friendly loopholes, including one-way renewal options that gave RKO the right to get rid of him after every twenty-six weeks and a "morals clause" that allowed for his instant dismissal in the event of any embarrassing or scandalous behavior. All creative decisions were to be ceded to the studio, and any lack of cooperation by the employee could result in suspension without pay. Standard Hollywood-style indentured servitude. The contract called for an initial salary of $350 per week with incremental pay raises after each renewal, topping out at $2,000 per in the seventh and final year. It was good pay by 1940s standards, though there were many weeks during his time as an itinerant screen actor when he had made more money.

An unexpected vote of confidence in Mitchum's prospects was cast by David O. Selznick, distinguished independent producer and high roller. Selznick agreed to buy a piece of the contract for his Vanguard Films, giving him periodic exclusive rights to the actor's services. The contract was signed on May 25, 1944, and went into effect seven days later.

In the meantime, Mitchum was making a one-week wonder at Monogram Pictures. Earlier in the year he had done a small part in a low-budget movie called *Johnny Doesn't Live Here Anymore,* a cheapie retread of the Jean Arthur comedy *The More the Merrier,* about romance blooming amid the wartime housing shortage. It was the work of a new team of penny-ante producers calling themselves the King Brothers. Mitchum had made an impression, and when the Kings were ready to film a suspense story called *Love from a Stranger* they offered him a lead role.

According to associates, the brothers King (nee Kosinski) had been slot-machine distributors among other things before they exited Chicago for Hollywood and the movies. Maurice and Frank King proved to be perspicacious filmmakers, with a real eye for exciting new talent, the kind that could be had for a price (they later gave regular under-the-table employment to the best of the blacklisted screenwriters when those writers were perforce more affordable). Early on they established a close relationship with writer Philip Yordan, one of the movies' great hustler creators in the Ben Hecht tradition, then at the outset of a long career. Yordan recalled to Pat McGilligan, "Frank was like a 300-pound Chinaman. Always a big cigar in his mouth and his drawer full of Hershey bars, a couple hundred Hershey bars. . . . Maurie had been a prize fighter and would always have black coffee, but he was heavy, too." Over at Columbia the Kings had viewed an unreleased feature called *The Whistler*, an atmospheric B mystery full of clever directorial touches imitative of Alfred Hitchcock, the work of a hundred-dollar-a-week contract director named William Castle. They arranged to borrow him from Harry Cohn for a 500 percent markup. Castle went over to Monogram's tiny, red brick studio, met Maurice, Frank, and apprenticing little brother, Hymie, and Phil Yordan, who was asleep on a couch at the time. Yordan was roused, and he and Castle spitballed a story line.

"Let's do a murder mystery—something frightening," Castle said.

"That's a good idea. . . . How about a guy that wakes up and finds his wife murdered in bed?"

"I saw that picture last night."

"I must have, too."

They talked out something else: a small-town girl, she marries a guy she barely knows, a glove salesman, there's a mad strangler on the loose, wears gloves, the bride fears it's her husband. The cops close in. Her life's in danger. The husband is about to be arrested. And then for the climax comes the big switch.

"What switch?" asked Yordan.

"How the hell do I know?" said Castle.

The screenwriter had a habit of subcontracting his assignments, finding "surrogates" to write a first-draft script, and then touching it up or rewriting the whole thing from scratch as needed. He gave the murder plot to a guy named Dennis Cooper, an aspiring novelist who worked as a clerk at a Pickwick bookshop. Cooper wrote a draft, and Yordan revised it, keeping in mind that the film had to be shot in seven days at a cost of fifty thousand dollars or under.

The Kings cast the story's three main parts with care. To play Millie, the naive newlywed, they borrowed—from David Selznick— twenty-two-year-old Kim Hunter, who had made her screen debut the previous year in a similar role in Val Lewton's *The Seventh Victim* (the Kings and Castle no doubt had Lewton's acclaimed series of subtle microbudget shockers much on their minds for this project). The part of the husband suspected of murder was given to Dean Jagger, a homely, middle-aged second lead in mostly A movies, good at conveying both square-headed sincerity and weakness of charac- ter. And tapped for the role of Fred, the plot's switcheroo, the trav- eling salesman and old boyfriend who helps Millie in her crisis until he is revealed to be the actual killer, the Kings went to the young actor they had used in *Johnny Doesn't Live Here*, Robert Mitchum. It was, by the standards of his usual acting jobs, a complex part that called for shifting displays of charm, devotion, and stolidity before climaxing with a showstopping crazy act.

Not the typical churn-'em-out B movie hack, William Castle was ambitious and self-conscious, a devotee of Orson Welles and Alfred Hitchcock, and he clearly intended to make more of *Love from a Stranger* (soon retitled *When Strangers Marry*) than fifty grand and seven days should have allowed. Kim Hunter recalled, "Bill Castle rounded us up and said, 'Would you mind terribly rehearsing for a week before we go to the studio?' For free, of course, because this was all such a low budget. 'And you can't tell the King Brothers.' And we all said, 'Oh, God, yes, we'd love to rehearse.' So we went over to Bill's small apartment in Hollywood and we got to work out the scenes and talk about the characters and everything we needed to prepare. Bob Mitchum was good. He gave Bill whatever he asked for. I didn't have enough experience myself to know if someone was terribly talented or had what it took to become a star, though he was very handsome. But Bob was an actor, a true actor. And he was a joy to work with.

"Thank God we had rehearsals because when we did go over to Monogram to start shooting there was no time to think. You moved from scene to scene. You just did it. But Bill Castle was marvelous, and because of those days in Bill's apartment we knew what we were doing. It was a very tight schedule. The studio was so small and I think everything we did was on just one stage."

There was one element of discord as the filming went on. According to Kim Hunter, the Kings were eager to sign Mitchum to a multifilm contract. When Bob told them he wasn't interested, "they tried to *convince* him. He'd be sitting down, waiting for his next scene or something, and suddenly he would be surrounded, one side and the other, by chaps he swore had guns, and they were trying to talk him into signing. I know Bob was very glad when the film was over with because he was still alive! And believe me, we were all eager to get out of there, but Bob in particular was relieved."

When Strangers Marry would turn out to be a little miracle of efficient creativity, transcending the restrictions and expectations of a Poverty Row cheapie by means of an intense, surprise-laden script, expressive direction, fluid camera work, and a superb portrayal of vulnerability and aching disappointment by young Kim Hunter. Mitchum, less skilled than she at this time, is occasionally wooden but overall an effectively ambiguous presence as the spurned but still loyal boyfriend. Underacting all the way, even his climactic descent into madness is kept low on the over-the-top meter. William Castle's Hitchcock infatuation is evident in emulations like the shock cut between a screaming woman discovering a body and a whistling locomotive (a direct steal from *The 39 Steps*) and an impudent Hitchcockian cameo (Castle seen in a framed photograph given to the police). The film's more significant association is with a genre still developing and unnamed in 1944. Critics in postwar Paris created the term *film noir* to describe what they saw as a new wave of similarly gloomy and pessimistic Hollywood mysteries and crime dramas. These black films were dark in tone, cynical and violent, and dark in their visual style, awash in shadow and half-light. They evoked a world of danger, paranoia, and corruption, of moral and psychological dislocation. The settings were largely urban and nocturnal, an artificial warren of tenements, alleyways, saloons, cheap hotels, police stations, and greasy spoon diners. In film noir, heroes and heroines were not the pure and noble creatures of Hollywood tradition but ran the gamut of maladjustment, from alienation to criminal insanity.

Released in the first full year of the noir cycle, 1944—the year of *Double Indemnity, Phantom Lady,* and *Murder, My Sweet*—*When Strangers Marry,* in its brief six reels, managed to include a full complement of noir themes and motifs: sexual obsession, the wrong man, betrayal, hallucination, a manhunt, a shadow-haunted soundstage Manhattan (and one classic scene for the anthologies: Kim Hunter alone in a hotel room lit only by a garish neon sign, gripped by a mounting sense of dread). It was Mitchum's debut in a genre with which he would be more strongly identified than any other actor. Here was the first embryonic version of Mitchum's noir outsider and, too, the first of his gallery of lethal psychopaths.

On release, the Kings' economical thriller was acclaimed by those critics who were actually willing to look at a lowly Monogram Pictures release. James Agee, in *The Nation,* wrote: "I have seldom for years now seen one hour so energetically and sensibly used." Its reputation would continue to grow through the years, culminating in historian Don Miller's unequivocal assessment of *When Strangers Marry* as "the finest B film ever made."

Shooting on the King Brothers production had ended on June 3, overlapping by two days the start of Bob's RKO contract. On June 5 he crossed the threshhold of his new home at 780 Gower Street.

RKO had been created at an oyster bar luncheon in the autumn of 1928, a merger of FBO (Film Booking Offices), a minor movie studio belonging to Joseph Kennedy; David Sarnoff's Radio Corporation of America; and the Keith-Albee-Orpheum circuit of vaudeville theaters. Headquarters would be FBO's lot between Gower and Melrose, directly adjacent to Paramount Pictures, on a plot of land previously owned by a Hollywood cemetary. Trade-named "Radio Pictures" for its RCA connection and recurring use of broadcast stars, with a logo of a beeping radio tower, RKO began releasing features in 1929, assuming a place beside Fox, MGM, Warner Bros., Columbia, Paramount, and Universal as one of the so-called majors of the sound era (Columbia and Universal, in the beginning, considered somewhat less major than the rest). Through the years the studio would have its share of popular successes and award winners, producing some of the greatest works of Hollywood's golden age—*King Kong, The Informer, Little Women,* the Astaire-Rogers musicals, *Gunga Din, Citizen Kane.* But RKO had never achieved the strong profile of the industry's front-runners, hamstrung by lack of a clear identity (something comparable to Warner's blue-collar aesthetic or MGM's mix of glamour and icon-ic stars like Garbo and Gable) and a revolving-door policy for its production heads. With no presiding mogul-for-life, no Thalberg, Zanuck, or Cohn to set the course, RKO had lurched through the years from one interim regime to another, each with its own guiding principles and often questionable inspirations. After teetering on the brink of oblivion during the tenure of the artistically ambitious George J. Schaefer (patron of Orson Welles's Mercury Productions among other bad business decisions), RKO in 1942 had begun a pol-icy of "entertainment, not genius" as dictated by new production chief Charles Koerner. Koerner's dedication to lowest-common-denominator commercial projects—a slate of musicals, comedies, Westerns, and horrors—brought the studio back from the brink, and RKO was posting record profits by the time Robert Mitchum signed on the dotted line in May 1944.

Nothing the actor saw in his first days at the studio did anything to make him believe he was out of his depth. He was introduced around, met supervisors who struck him as semiliterate at best and fellow "starlets" one step above retarded, floating around on clouds of their own self-satisfaction. "They had forty stock actors under contract at the time," he recalled. "They were all six feet tall with lifts and padding. They all came in, chucked the producer's secretary under the chin, and said, 'Hon, did you get the script?' Then they drove their Cadillacs to the Mocambo. I figured—these cats were *working*? I should own the joint!"

Production plans on *The Robe* had stalled.* Instead of the biblical epic, Mitchum's initial assignment was something considerably less prestigious: *Girl Rush,* a musical comedy Western starring the studio's woebegone would-be Abbott and Costello team of Alan Carney and Wally Brown, with female leads Frances Langford and Vera Vague, the full-faced girl singer and the fluty-voiced comedienne fitting the movie around their performances on Bob Hope's weekly radio show. The knockabout plot involved gold rush claim jumping and mail-order brides and included a long sequence with most of the male cast members in drag. Four songs had been composed to order: "When I'm Walking Arm in Arm with Jim," "Annabella's Bustle," "Rainbow Valley," and "If Mother Could Only See Us Now," a score worthy of a Carney and Brown vehicle.

Mitchum's first scene came some twenty-two minutes after his fifth-place billing in the opening credits. He'd looked good on film before, but the RKO stylists had gone to work, and his appearance here was startlingly photogenic: rising up from a crowded dinner table, a pompadoured Superman in buckskin, huge shoulders and inflated chest above an impossibly slim waist, hands poised on studded, sexily low-slung gun belt. "I'm a regular faggot's dream," he mumbled at the preview. The film proved to be a good showcase for RKO's new contract player. Mitchum exuded a maximum of masculine charisma throughout, did charming love scenes with Frances Langford, displayed a breezy sense of humor, and maintained his cool aplomb even in a bonnet and gingham dress.

---

*After several aborted attempts, Frank Ross would make *The Robe* at Fox in 1953, with Victor Mature in the part of Demetrius.

Studio execs decided they were not happy with the name "Robert Mitchum." A memo was sent to the actor: he would henceforth be known as "Robert Marshall."

Mitchum responded: "Screw that."

Someone from the studio told Paul Wilkins to explain to his client how things worked: he was their property now, they knew their business, and he ought to have the sense to defer to their judgment in these matters.

Mitchum had agreed to have his broken nose touched up for the sake of future fame and riches, but the request to change his name struck him as a more personal affront. Mitchum said, "I'm not changing it." His father had given him that name. What the fuck. Forget it. He told Wilkins to tear up the contract for all he cared.

The agent pleaded his case to the studio. Bob had already gotten featured billing with his given name. He was already getting recognized, receiving fan mail. Bob was no ordinary actor, the agent said, and thus should have a name "as different as his personality." Wilkins wrote to Ben Piazza, "I have observed that the main reason for changing a name is to try to build someone up who hasn't made good under their previous name. This is certainly not Mitchum's case. He desires to cooperate in every way possible, but . . . we request that he be known on the screen as Robert Mitchum."

It was an arbitrary move on the studio's part. After all, it wasn't as if they were contending with Spangler Arlington Brugh or Marion Morrison, the birth names of Robert Taylor and John Wayne respectively. But the studio did not like to back down too easily and told Wilkins to let his boy think about it for a few days.

One afternoon Bob and Dorothy had lunch together in the studio commissary. They met the English actress Jill Esmond, former wife of Laurence Olivier. Mitchum voiced his current complaint, and Esmond told them that years ago the studio had tried the same thing with her ex-husband, wanted to call him "Larry Olson" or some such.

Just then the producer pushing for the name change passed by their table. "Hello, Bob. Hello, Mrs. Marshall."

"Mrs. *Mitchum*," Dorothy said firmly.

"Oh, you'll get used to it," he said with a chuckle and went on his way.

"Who was that?" Jill asked.

Bob savored each syllable of a name the producer did deem screenworthy: "Herman . . . Schlom."

Tim Holt had gone into the service, and RKO decided that Robert Mitchum—yes, he could keep his own damn name (Bob would claim that the frustrated producer bestowed the rejected name on his first son, Marshall Schlom, instead)—was going to step into Holt's boots as their new B Western star. In July he went to work on a remake, the second remake, of an old Zane Grey title, *Nevada*. Just over twenty-four months after his first job in front of a movie camera, as a grizzled heavy trading bullets with old Hoppy, Mitchum was to play a starring role, the white-hatted hero, in his own low-budget oater.

The new version of *Nevada*, like the two previous, had little in common with the popular novelist's original story, Norman Houston taking credit for the plot-heavy script centered around the discovery of the Comstock Lode. Assigned to direct was Edward Killy. This "feisty little Irishman" (per Robert Wise) was an RKO veteran who had worked his way up from assistant jobs to B unit director and was now in the process of working his way back down again. As a director of actors, Killy made Les Selander look like George Cukor.

Mitchum's part, stoic hero Jim Lacy, like Hopalong Cassidy, rode with two saddle pals, to be played by a likable young actor named Richard Martin as the guitar-strumming Chico Rafferty and by perpetual ornery sidekick Guinn "Big Boy" Williams. There were also two leading ladies for Mitchum to smile at (though this demure horse opera allowed no hint of romance with either of them): Nancy Gates as the innocent daughter of a miner and glamorous blonde Anne Jeffreys as a worldly saloon operator.

"I was assigned to it, and I went, 'No, not another Western!'" Anne Jeffreys recalled. "But they told me this was from a Zane Grey book. And that was what they thought was most important: Zane

Grey. But they did say that Bob Mitchum was doing it, and he was good, and they wanted to build him up with this one. There was a mystique about Mitchum, even then, you know. You heard these stories that he had been a hobo and been to jail and all that. But then I saw him giving an interview to a reporter one time, and he said that he had been born with a silver spoon in his mouth, from a very wealthy family. You didn't know what to believe."

Nevada took Mitchum back to Lone Pine for ten days of location shooting. Back to the Dow Hotel and the Bucket of Blood Saloon. Long days filming in the scorching temperatures of midsummer on the alkali desert beyond Lone Pine proved to be sheer hell for cast and crew. "I remember that the cowboys—when it really got over-bearing out there on that desert," Mitchum said, "they'd gallop by the camera and sprinkle a handful of sand into it. Well, that's about a two hour delay while they'd clean that camera up. We'd go and fall in the shade of a cactus."

Nevada castmates remembered Bob as a quiet man and some-thing of a loner during this stay at the rugged location. "At the end of every day's shooting," actress Margie Stewart told *Western Clippings* magazine, "Anne Jeffreys and the rest would meet in the bar where our star was always found slumped down on a bar stool with his hat pulled way over his face. We would say, 'There's our handsome leading man.' No comment from Bob."

"He was a great guy," said Richard Martin. "I got along with him—every one of us did—but he was controversial. If you *didn't* like Bob Mitchum, you just didn't like him. He wasn't going to change himself in any way to fit what anybody else might expect of him."

Anne Jeffreys discovered that the brawny cowboy actor had a brain. "He was very intelligent, carried on these very deep conversa-tions. His looks didn't call for that! He used to quote poetry. Very deep. *I* thought it was deep. . . . It was lovely. He was charming, and a lot of laughs, and very charismatic. One night after shooting we had dinner and Mitch said, 'Let's walk some of this off.' I said, 'OK,' and we took a stroll along the little road that ran through the town, unpaved, just talking and walking. We reached the end of the town, and the road ran along and out of sight. There was a glorious full moon in the sky that night. I said, 'I wonder where this road goes?' And Mitch said, 'I have no idea, but it must be someplace beautiful.' And so we walked on, and the road took us right into the city dump."

*

The *Nevada* company returned to the studio for another two weeks of filming interiors. If Bob was supposed to be a star now, it was almost entirely theoretical. An unproven lead in a B Western, even a Zane Grey Western, apparently didn't rate many perquisites in the RKO hierarchy. For the first couple of months they had him putting his belongings and change of clothes in one of the lockers near the public toilets. It was not much bigger than the one he'd had at Lockheed. Space was at a premium on the Gower Street lot, and you were expected to do your washing up at home. Dismissed at the end of shooting one late afternoon, coated in grime and various effluents, Mitchum went out on the lawn in the open courtyard below the executive offices, stripped down, and started showering with a garden hose. Somebody alerted Ed Killy to this spectacle and he came rushing over.

"What in the hell do you think you're doing?"

"I've got no place to take a shower," Mitchum said. "I can't put my clothes on over all this crap!"

Killy clutched his scalp. "For Jesus sake put your pants on!"

Then he dragged Mitchum to the producer's office and threw a fit. "This is the fucking star of the picture, mister, and he hasn't got a place to change his goddamn underwear!"

The studio arranged to provide Bob with a small dressing room.

Pleased with what they were seeing in the *Nevada* dailies, Herman Schlom and Sid Rogell scheduled another Zane Grey remake for Mitchum, to begin production as soon as a shooting script could be readied. *West of the Pecos* reassembled much of the *Nevada* personnel, including Ed Killy, Norman Houston, and cinematographer

Harry Wilde, with actor Richard Martin reprising his role as Chico, the Irish-Mexican sidekick (the option on his seventy-five-dollar-a-week contract having been picked up). And once again location shooting would be done in and around Lone Pine. So much for the similarities. The style of the film was quite different from its strait-laced predecessor. Essentially comic in tone, *Pecos* devoted a great deal of its running time to a Sylvia Scarlett-ish subplot involving costar Barbara Hale disguised as a young cowboy and the merry fall-out therefrom as she travels across the frontier with Bob, an oblivious gunslinger. In one scene, Mitchum pulls "cowboy" Barbara onto his lap while rolling a cigarette from tobacco pouch and papers and teaching "him" how to lick it closed. The cross-dressing frolic gets even more curious when straight man Mitchum throws open his bedroll and invites his transvestite trailmate to join him under the covers, spoon fashion.

"Nothin' like company on a cold night," says Mitchum. "Come on, kid, get in."

"I want to sleep alone," says the "boy."

"Oh no you don't. Come on, get in and cuddle. . . ."

Mitchum was increasingly confident in front of the camera, the good-humored performance in *West of the Pecos* a sizable improvement over his work in *Nevada*. As the earlier film's earnest hero he seemed interchangeable with any number of deadpan B picture cowboy stars. In *Pecos* he began to reveal the lurking possibilities. He was charming, slyly funny, coolly laid back—a rather *hip* horse opera star. His improved riding skills were also evident, notably in a full gallop one-hand-on-the-reins running insert.

The studio execs were pleased with what they saw in both *Nevada* and *West of the Pecos*. Mitchum's rugged good looks were really coming across—there were fewer cracks about him resembling a beached shark. RKO foresaw a long line of Zane Grey horse operas in the new boy's future.

Mitchum, who had originally come to the studio after Mervyn LeRoy's big talk about megabudget productions like *The Robe*, let it be known that he was eager to do something that didn't require the use of a saddle. The King Brothers tried to borrow him for the title role in their next film, *Dillinger*, but the studio's Ben Piazza told them that the part and the project were too unsavory for their rising star. The role went to Lawrence Tierney, and the picture made a fortune. Mitchum lobbied for the part of Sonja Henie's hockey player love interest in a romance called *It's a Pleasure*. Producer David Lewis tested him and decided that Mitchum dwarfed the dainty skater. Lewis went with the shorter Michael O'Shea. Mitchum sulked. Wilkins told him to relax, something good would come. There was plenty of time. For now, why didn't he try and enjoy being the new Tim Holt?

Throughout the summer and fall of 1944, independent producer Lester Cowan and director William Wellman were preparing to make a film, *The Story of G.I. Joe*, based on the work of Pulitzer Prize–winning war correspondent Ernie Pyle. For Wellman—"Wild Bill" of legend, a tough-talking, whip-cracking Hollywood character and director of classics like *Wings*, *The Public Enemy*, *Nothing Sacred*, and *The Ox-Box Incident*—G.I. Joe had become one of those rare projects that grabbed him by the balls, a personal obsession. Wellman's filmography included classics and clunkers, but he was determined to get this one right, putting the truth and poetry of Pyle's writing on celluloid. Wanting to avoid movie star glamour at all costs, Wellman had been looking for new faces to populate his cinematic Company C, Eighteenth Infantry. He would claim that he didn't even know Mitchum was in the business when he saw the man for the first time and, in signature Wild Bill style, accosted him in front of the Brown Derby restaurant on Hollywood Boulevard.

"What's your name, bub? Mine's Wellman."

"Bob Mitchum. And the purpose of your inquiry?"

"I make pictures. What do you do for a living?"

"That, Dad, is a matter of opinion."

One day some months before, Lester Cowan had arrived at William Wellman's Beverly Hills house. Unknown producers didn't usually show up unannounced on the Wellman doorstep, the director told

him, and even if he knew him he would certainly never let a
producer come inside. Cowan said to listen, that he was going to
make a great movie about the American foot soldier, the best thing
of its kind, from the Ernie Pyle stories, and Wellman was the only
man who could direct it.

Wild Bill had been a pilot in the French Foreign Legion's
Lafayette Flying Corps during World War I, a colorful experience he
never got tired of invoking. Wellman told Cowan, "You're talking to
an old broken-down old flier. . . . I hate the goddamn infantry and I
don't want to have anything to do with them and please thank Mr.
Pyle, but not for me."

A few days later, Lester Cowan had Pyle himself call the director
and try and make him change his mind. Pyle told him of the great
need for such a picture and what it would mean to all the kids fighting for his and Wellman's country. The director reluctantly agreed
to visit with Pyle at his home in Albuquerque. The writer who had
been traipsing around the European war fronts turned out to be a
frail, gray-haired, middle-aged man. Pyle's home life was modest
and lonesome. His wife stayed in her room and drank. Ernie slept in
the garage. Wellman settled into the guest room, uncertain what he
was doing there. He had yet to read a word of Pyle's writings, and
with nothing to do that night but listen to the clink of Mrs. Pyle's ice
cubes, he cracked open Ernie's latest, called *Brave Men*. He read the
dedication:

> *In solemn salute to those thousands of our comrades—great, brave
> men that they were—for whom there will be no homecoming, ever.*

Oh, Jeez, Wild Bill thought. He sat in bed turning pages till dawn,
reading Ernie's tenderly etched sketches of ordinary soldiers as they
lived and died in the great conflict overseas. By morning Wellman
was making plans to shoot the picture.

Pyle's deal with Lester Cowan included certain informal guarantees.
He wanted no phony love interest added to the story, and the actor
playing Pyle himself had to look "anemic" and "weigh in the neighborhood of 112 pounds." Without actually putting them on a scale,

the producer first considered Fred Astaire for the part and then settled on Burgess Meredith. A screenplay was manufactured by the
triumvirate of Leopold Atlas, Philip Stevenson, and Guy Endore
(the latter best known as the author of the fiendish novel *The
Werewolf of Paris, not* a Pulitzer Prize winner). Then Wellman
brought Pyle to Hollywood for a polishing job. "We worked together day after day and it gradually became a great shooting script.
Cruel, factual, unaffected, genuine, and with a heart as big as
Ernie's."

There was no plot and no hero in any conventional Hollywood
sense, and no villain—only an inexorable but virtually unseen
enemy. Next to Pyle, the white-haired observer of the young
Americans' struggle, the most prominent character was that of
Charlie Company's empathetic commanding officer, Lt. Bill
Walker, based like many of the characters on a real person. Wellman
was still looking for somebody to play Walker only a matter of
weeks before filming, when he and his assistant director, Robert
Aldrich, ran into Mitchum on Hollywood Boulevard. He took
Mitchum over to Lester Cowan's office and conducted a bantering
interrogation.

"What kind of parts have you done?"

"For two years I've been supporting horses—or vice versa."

"You mean to tell me you haven't been knocking 'em dead on
Broadway? How tall are you?"

"Six foot or so, I guess."

"You guess? Don't you know? Every goddamn midget that comes
in here says he's six feet tall. Alan Ladd is six feet three. What's the
matter with your nose?"

"Nothing. It serves the purpose—I breathe through it."

Coincidence can sometimes look like destiny: in 1928, Wellman had
directed the film version of Jim Tully's *Beggars of Life,* one of
Robert's favorite books; in 1933, he had directed *Wild Boys of the
Road,* about the Depression "road kids," and that one could have
been Robert's own story. Cowan got RKO's permission to test
Mitchum for *G.I. Joe.* Wellman told him they would do the long

scene between Pyle and Walker, near the end of the script. In the scene, the correspondent comes to see the lieutenant in his tent while he is writing yet another letter to the mother of a soldier killed in battle. Walker, in conversation, reflects on the dreadful job at hand and the waste and absurdity of war. It was the most concentrated and emotional scene Mitchum had ever attempted in the movies.

Clearly aware that this was a big break, the only opportunity at hand to climb out of the B picture ghetto, Mitchum spent all the time he had preparing for the audition, speaking the lines, pondering his approach. He didn't know much about the war really. He didn't know anybody to talk to who had been involved. But Julie did. She had met hundreds of GIs while doing her nightclub act around California. Sometimes the places would be packed with nothing but men in uniform. Robert talked to her about the veterans she had met, and Julie told him how she would never see gung ho happy warriors the way you saw them in the movies. The ones who had been in the thick of it, she said, came back withdrawn, exhausted. They had faced down death or seen it get their buddies, and they were sad-faced and depressed, many of them.

They shot the test with no frills, a couple of fill lights aimed on a tiny stage with a Western wagonwheel for a prop. Wellman gave few suggestions. He wanted to see what the wise guy might come up with on his own. So Mitchum played the scene as he thought it would work, speaking the sad lines with a low key, weary anguish. There was a long silence when it was over. Wellman couldn't speak, forgot to say, "Cut." He was even more knocked out later when he screened the footage. "I saw something so wonderful, so completely compelling," he said, "that I was mad at myself for not having built the set so that I could have the test be the actual scene that came out in the picture. He was fantastic."

Mitchum would say, "I think he was surprised I remembered most of the words, that's all."

Cowan went to RKO and made a deal. The loan-out called for a payment of $800 a week for six weeks and second-place billing.

Mitchum would receive only his regular $350 weekly salary, and the studio pocketed the profit.

Production got under way in November. Cowan had arranged with the army to obtain the services of more than a hundred active-duty soldiers, most of them veterans of the North African and Italian campaigns depicted in the film. The director planned to use only these actual combat troops as extras and for all uniformed bit parts. "I made actors out of them," Wellman said, "and then all the actors had to live with them, drill with them, and learn to be like them." Actors carried eighty-pound packs all day long and dined on the dreaded K rations. Wellman was pursuing a physical and psychological realism for *G.I. Joe* that would have made von Stroheim proud. Filming began in the Mojave, filling in for coastal Algeria, then moved to rented space at the Selznick studio in Culver City. Old standing sets were ruthlessly reduced to smoking ruins, the cathedral town built for DeMille's 1928 silent *The Godless Girl* turned into ravaged San Vittorio, where Charlie Company cleans out a nest of invisible snipers. For the long, central sequence of the men trapped interminably in the valley below a fortified monastery, shot on cramped interiors, Wellman had his designers create an ultrarealistic wasteland of rain and muck and cold. The director's son, William Wellman, Jr., visited his father during the filming and recalled the uncomfortable conditions. "Even for a kid it was no fun to be there, and the actors were all stuck in it all day long. Muddy, wet, a terrible mess to have to work in. My father wanted it to be 'war is hell' and it was."

Eagerly escaping this misery when shooting concluded for the day, Mitchum would head for the nearest tavern, usually accompanied by a number of his fellow "GIs." Bearded, faces usually still coated in grime, they made quite a spectacle at whatever bars would have them. The distinguished star of the film, Burgess "Buzz" Meredith, turned out to have a powerful thirst. Meredith didn't see much in Mitchum's acting at the time—only realizing how strongly the younger man was coming across when he saw the finished film—but found him to be a very agreeable drinking companion, and they closed down many a bar together. "Bob was a swinger—and I was a swinger in those days—we did a lot of funning around outside the set," Meredith recalled. The fun ended abruptly when his pregnant wife, Paulette Goddard, lost the baby they had both wanted so much. Meredith always remembered how Mitchum helped him through this crisis, "talked to me and tried to help as best he could and I appreciated his kindness."

Filming on *G.I. Joe* continued into the new year: 1945. New sequences were added as they went along. The episodic nature of the script allowed Wellman to improvise whole sequences and to expand the roles of actors whose work pleased him, as in the case of his Sergeant Warnicki, played by ex-boxer Freddie Steele.

Wellman was a colorful dynamo on his sets, twitching and grabbing his arthritic arms, shouting insults, goosing and screaming at the actors and crew members, an ebullient version of Brian Donlevy's sadistic commandant in *Beau Geste*, Wild Bill's 1939 love song to his beloved Foreign Legion. When he took former middleweight boxing champion Freddie Steele through his big scene as dim-witted Sergeant Warnicki gone mad with battle fatigue, Steele felt like he was back in the ring.

"Once we did that scene," Steele said. "No good. Twice we did it. It stinks. So, we rest and do it again. Wellman says nix. Don't I understand? We do it again. He blows up and swears. By this time I'm getting tired and I'm getting sore. We do it again. He gets sarcastic. We do it again and he blows his top. 'You slaphappy so-and-so. Maybe you shouldn't have had that last fight!' That's nothing to say to a fighter, see? If I didn't have to do the scene again, I'd have socked him one. We did it again and that Wellman kisses me and says, 'That's what I wanted.'

"That so-and-so is a wonderful guy. . . ."

Mitchum required none of Wellman's theatrics to get him through the part of Bill Walker. As with the screen test, the director needed only to give him the encouragement and the space to show what he could do. The result was a performance that was like nothing

Mitchum had ever done on film before. His Lieutenant Walker lived and breathed, the humanity and psychic pain of the soldier palpable things, not screenwriters' constructs. It was a small part—*G.I. Joe* was an ensemble piece, and not even Meredith's Ernie Pyle got to dominate the screen for long—but Mitchum's one good scene was the emotional and philosophical core of the film. In a virtual soliloquy, his worn-down lieutenant struggles with little success to find some meaning in all the death and destruction surrounding him, his face a haunted mask of resignation and despair. An intimate and tender scene, its impact increases in retrospect as it serves as Lieutenant Walker's last testament. His eventual—it feels inevitable—death in combat occurs offscreen. The body is brought down from the battlefield in the mountains, gracelessly strapped to the back of a mule. Wellman staged a Calvary of shattering sadness: the soldiers of Charlie Company straggling up to pay their last respects to their beloved lieutenant (now a captain), touching his hand or his cheek, muttering their farewells ("I sure am sorry, sir . . ."), the seasoned warriors turned childlike in their bereavement.

The Story of G.I. Joe contains no flag-waving, no self-righteousness. War is presented in humanistic terms as a dangerous and unbearable endeavor that will more than likely destroy you. One by one the characters in *G.I. Joe* lose their lives or, in the case of Sergeant Warnicki, their minds. Having little connection to the countless propaganda films that preceded it, *G.I. Joe* was a movie that offered the armed services "no recruitment value." Young boys would not be rushing to join up upon seeing this one. It was purely and simply an antiwar film, a daring approach by Wellman and Cowan with the war still very much in progress at the time of shooting. It was, though, the film that great numbers of veterans would ultimately say came closest to the truth of their experience in World War II. One of those vets, Gen. Dwight Eisenhower, would call it the greatest war film he had ever seen.

No, the real war was not over yet. Wellman's hundred-plus U.S.

Army extras were returned to combat duty. "Oh, those poor guys," the director would say. "Every one who was in that picture went into the last battle they had—the last one, you know, Okinawa—and most of them never came back."

Ernie Pyle, too, would die in the Pacific, killed by a sniper, never seeing the film Wild Bill had made for him.

When Mitchum returned to the fold at RKO it was business as usual. He had earned the praise of big names in the business—Mervyn LeRoy, William Wellman. *Thirty Seconds Over Tokyo* had been a huge hit, *When Strangers Marry* a sleeper of the year, and there was already a good buzz surrounding the unfinished *G.I. Joe*. But at RKO they continued to see Bob in a Stetson and spurs. Preparations were made for the next Zane Grey Western, *Wanderer of the Wasteland*, once more assigned to producer Schlom, writer Houston, and director Killy. A winning team—*Nevada* had been well received by audiences. *West of the Pecos*, waiting for release, looked good, too. Mitchum might even be better than Tim Holt.

But *Wanderer* never got made, not with Bob Mitchum.

It wasn't easy being the only man around Palm Avenue. The women of the two neighboring Mitchum households had become rivals for his attention. Dorothy quite logically believed that his first responsibility was to his wife and kids, but his mother and sister remained a major presence in Bob's life, and there were lingering resentments if he seemed to favor the bonds of matrimony over those of blood relations, or vice versa. Bob just wanted to bounce his kids on his knees and be left the hell alone. These home front tensions, possible anxieties over the future, plus a great deal of alcohol, all contributed to the unfortunate events of April 6.

Both Dorothy and baby Christopher were ill that night. Dorothy was laid up in bed and relatives had come to help. In the court document he later filed, Mitchum said that he had been out to obtain a prescription for the sick child. "I called my wife . . . and my sister answered the phone. She refused to allow me to talk to my wife, and hung up the receiver. There followed several attempts, all of which had the same result. . . ." Calling one last time, Mitchum said he was coming home and would "demand an accounting." When Mitchum arrived at the house, two sheriff's deputies were waiting for him.

"What the hell is this?" Mitchum growled, as their flashlights shone in his face.

"Hold it right there, mister," said one of the deputies.

"Stand still and keep your hands at your sides," said the other one.

"We're investigating a reported disturbance here."

"You been threatening anybody, fella?"

"This is my place," Mitchum told them, "and I'm going in to see my wife and kids!" Fucking cops, keeping a man out of his own house!

"You just stay where you are, mister, until we tell you different."

"How much you had to drink tonight?"

Mitchum hovered before the porch steps, nursing his grievance, while the deputies talked to someone through the screen door. No one wanted to press any charges. It was all a misunderstanding probably. The deputies decided to have a few last words with Mitchum before they went away and led him down to the curb by the squad car. But Bob wasn't in a mood to hear anymore of their shit, and in a burst of alcohol-fueled impulsivity he now demanded they arrest him. Take it all the way if they dared. Did these dirty cops think they could come up on a man's own porch and hassle him for no reason? He clawed open the door of the cop car.

"Let's go downtown right now, motherfuckers!"

Exactly who struck the first blow would be a fact lost in the heat of the moment. In some accounts Mitchum would recall that he'd put a fist into one cop's face and broken his nose, and things turned a little ugly after that. Or else he recollected that it was the deputies who got things rolling—jamming him into the squad car with a hard swing of a billy club to the ribs. He felt an arched bone in his chest crack, and he curled over to protect himself and kicked the guy in the balls at the same time; and maybe then came the nose-breaking punch, and the club came down on his shoulders and his spine, and the other deputy, blood pouring down his chin, stomped him with his boot, hit him with his gun butt until he collapsed, caught between the curb and the open back door of the cop car; and the two men began raining down blows, sticking a gun barrel against his skull while they cuffed him and locked him in the backseat. He was booked at the sheriff's substation on Fairfax Avenue and taken to a jail cell, where he had a well-earned snooze.

In the morning Mitchum conferred with a studio-sent lawyer. The attorney thought sure they would get a slap on the wrist. Maybe finish up the weekend in jail and pay a small fine. But Judge Cecil Holland wasn't in a wrist-slapping frame of mind that day. The judge handed him 180 days. "Hundred and eighty . . . no way I can make that," Mitchum said. In those days of war it was not unusual for the court to offer certain miscreants a patriotic alternative to jail time, and after some consideration this is what Judge Holland did. Mitchum would be allowed to go into the armed services, in return for which his sentence would be rescinded. In Mitchum's most colorful account of the event, it was the two deputies who had beaten him who took him to the enlistment center, in handcuffs.

One way or another, he was in the army now.

CHAPTER FOUR

The Man with the Immoral Face

It was life imitating art—he still had some of the *G.I. Joe* mud in his scalp from Wellman's Company C. But this time there were no lieutenant's stripes on his sleeve. He was just another grunt, meat on the hoof for the noble war effort. "I told them I was homosexual and they said, 'Prove it!' But I couldn't find a willing partner. Then they said, 'Bend over!' And I said, 'I can't—my back.' And they said, 'Ah-ha! IA! Infantry!'" At the Los Angeles induction center he was loaded into a bus with a half a hundred other recruits, many of them rosy-cheeked teenagers ten years his junior, and taken to Camp Roberts for basic training. It was round-the-clock commotion. That first night, he crawled from his bunk at three in the morning, looked out the barracks window, and saw a noisy close-order drill in progress. He turned back around to see the platoon sergeant standing in the doorway.

"Leaving or just coming in?"

"What the hell's the difference?" the sergeant said.

At Camp Roberts they taught him how to salute a superior, how to shoot a rifle, how to clean and assemble the same, how to stab a canvas dummy with a bayonet, and mostly how to walk for miles with a full pack and not be heard to complain about it. Most of it was familiar stuff—he had played similar scenes a dozen times for the cameras. Two weeks after his arrival he was given special leave to return to LA and shoot a day of retakes on *G.I. Joe*. Even before they learned of this special treatment some of the guys at the camp tried to razz him about his acting career—more of that "Hollywood faggot" stuff he'd gotten while shooting *Thirty Seconds Over Tokyo*—

but most of his barracks mates—unripe kids just torn from their
mama's arms—were respectfully starry-eyed and mainly wanted to
know whether he had ever banged any of their favorite actresses. "I
worked mostly with donkeys and brood mares," he would say. "But
some of them were pretty damn attractive."

On May 8 Germany surrendered to the Allied forces now sweeping
through their country. The war in Europe was over.

Graduated from boot camp in the summer, Mitchum was transferred to Fort MacArthur. He was made a drill instructor, imparting
the freshly received wisdom of his training to even newer recruits.
His qualifications, he said, were that mean face Pop Sherman had
tagged and the biggest mouth on the base. There was a lot of drilling
at MacArthur, where the presiding general thought the best way to
keep everybody out of mischief was to have them marching a hot,
dusty parade ground as often as possible. Mitchum found that some
of the officers didn't care if you drilled or not as long as you said you
did, and many days he let his guys stay in the barracks and sleep late.
One day he met a colonel from the Medical Office who told him his
talents were being wasted.

"I'm perfectly content, sir," said Mitchum.

That turned out to be too damn bad. They needed somebody like
him in the medical department. Mitchum told them he got queasy
at the sight of blood. But the orders were already in the works, and
he next found himself in the offices of the Medical Examiner,
according to Bob an old Kentucky abortionist in civilian life.

The doctor trained him to assist with physical examinations of
the recruits. One of Mitchum's specialties—as the years grew longer,
he would come to claim it as his single mission in the service—was
rectal exams; he became the chief of the "keister police," telling nine
hundred men to turn around, bend over, and spread their cheeks.
Using a spotlight attached to a metal headband, he made brief but
thorough searches for abnormalities, "piles, hemorrhoids, bananas,
dope . . . you name it." There was a science to it, this peering into
the void, and even something of an art. "I could diagnose all your

ills," he would say. "I could prognosticate the future." For years afterwards, he or his brother John would run into veterans of those intimate inspections, fellows gleefully recalling how they had "mooned" Bob back at Fort MacArthur.

And thusly did Mitchum spend some of the final days of the Second World War.

*

In July *The Story of G.I. Joe* was ready for release. Producer Lester Cowan devised a publicity campaign for the picture that began with screenings for influential members of the American military. General Eisenhower was among those who saw the film and was much impressed, calling it the greatest of all war movies, and he was willing to be quoted to that effect. Through his military connections, Cowan arranged for Robert Mitchum to receive a four- to six-week working furlough to promote *The Story of G.I. Joe*. The army liked the idea of a movie star who was an ordinary dogface, very democratic.

Bob walked out on a long line of bare-assed recruits and caught the next plane to New York.

The reviews for *G.I. Joe,* when they began appearing, were extraordinary. *TIME* magazine hailed "a movie without a single false note," an "enduring memorial" to Ernie Pyle. James Agee in *The Nation* compared the film to the great and beautiful war poems of Walt Whitman, calling it "a tragic and eternal work of art" and the first triumphant combination of fiction and documentary. And for all the raves, no single aspect of the film received more praise than the performance of Robert Mitchum (though the work of lovable Freddie Steele came in a close second).

The powers that be at RKO might have been slow, but they weren't stupid. As *G.I. Joe* broke, they woke up to the fact that they had under seven-year contract not a journeyman B Western star, as they had thought, but the most acclaimed young actor in Hollywood. There was talk of an Academy Award nomination for

Mitchum. RKO assigned its own publicity people as consultants to Bob's cross-country jaunt for Cowan and United Artists, setting up still more interviews and public appearances and reminding everyone along the way about which studio the man would be returning to when he got out of uniform.

They showed him off to the gawkers like a talking horse. At a premiere, fans crowded around for autographs until, as Mitchum remembered it, the "gendarmes" had to be called in to calm things down. Shifty-eyed girl reporters flirted with him, and doughy, cigar-chewing photographers with gravy on their lapels flashed their Speed-Graphics in his face. He went on local radio shows where one confused host told him how proud they all were of what he had done in the war and was it difficult playing yourself in a movie? "That guy's dead, lady," he explained. Mostly he said to the press what the studio wanted them to hear, but one time at the bar of the 21 Club in Manhattan he told a group of reporters how the army had employed him as a "poop chute inspector," and the attendant publicist slowly died inside.

The hoopla for the new star continued long after Private Bob had been returned to Fort MacArthur, continuing through the rest of the year, moving from the daily papers and Sunday editions to the monthly movie magazines trumpeting Mitchum's breakthrough. There were profiles, mentions in the gossip columns, captioned news photos showing him shaking hands with the postmaster general and other magnificos. Fan mail began to arrive at Gower Street in massive quantities, with weekly requests for autographed pictures that soon numbered into the thousands. Most were from females, and most of these were young. While the critics and generals applauded Mitchum for a moving and emotionally incisive performance, the response of this first wave of devoted fans was more primal. There was something about the actor's brooding, dirty, bearded appearance—he looked far scruffier in *G.I. Joe* than he had as a lowlife henchman in *Border Patrol*—that struck like greased lightning in the breasts of the era's teenage girls. Other teen idols were on the scene—Van Johnson, Robert Walker, Guy Madison—but their appeal was of the boy-next-door, let's-share-a-milkshake sort. Mitchum's was plainly more . . . mature. *Photoplay* magazine reporter Eleanor Harris, investigating this lustful reaction, got the lowdown from heavy-breathing bobby-soxers coming out of a showing of *G.I. Joe* at the Pantages Theatre in Hollywood.

"*He's got sex appeal in an evil sort of way,*" said one precocious jitterbugger.

Another undone nymphet opined similarly: "*He has the most immoral face I have ever seen!*"

In August atomic bombs were dropped on Hiroshima and Nagasaki. After that, what remained of the war was paperwork. On October 12 the U.S. Army released its claim on freshly promoted Private First Class Robert C. D. Mitchum. "I came out of Fort MacArthur," he recalled, "I had a suit and a bottle of Scotch in my locker, and I put on both of them. The next thing I knew I was in a Marine uniform and we were up to take twelve. . . ." Immediately upon his discharge, Mitchum was rushed to the location for a new film, *They Dream of Home,* already shooting at the marine base in San Diego.

As head of production at RKO, Charles Koerner had continued to chart a very profitable course for the studio (not to give the man undue credit: during the war years, entertainment-hungry audiences made it difficult for any picture maker to lose money; these circumstances would soon be reversed). Lately many of the studio's most successful releases (e.g., *Notorious, The Spiral Staircase, The Bells of St. Mary's*) were only nominally RKO creations, made through Koerner's partnership deals with outside independents such as Samuel Goldwyn, Leo McCarey, Frank Capra, and David O. Selznick. *They Dream of Home*—the title changed during production to *Till the End of Time,* exploiting a Buddy Kaye/Ted Mossman song adapted from Chopin's Polonaise in A-flat Major—was developed by Selznick's Vanguard Films division and Selznick's top man, Dore Schary; financed by RKO and shot on their facilities; and employed a mixture of DOS and RKO personnel. Top billing went to a pair of Selznick "discoveries," Dorothy McGuire from the New York stage, and Guy Madison from the U.S. Navy. The timely story line, from a novel by Niven Busch (*Duel in the Sun*) and scripted by Allen Rivkin, dealt with the readjustment difficulties of servicemen home from the war. Mitchum's was a supporting part in the story but a good one. RKO was eager to capitalize on the actor's new-found acclaim and added him to the cast within hours of learning of his imminent discharge.

A limousine was dispatched to take Bob to the U. S. Grant Hotel, where cast and crew were being comforted at a cost of twelve dollars per person, including bountiful meals (it said so right in the initialed agreement with the studio: "no limit to the amount of food any individual consumes"). There he met the director, Edward Dmytryk, one of RKO's creative stars. At thirty-seven, the Canadian-born Dmytryk had already spent more than two decades in the business, having risen from messenger boy to become Paramount's most valued film editor and finally a director (after a false start a few years before) in 1939. His early B films, mostly thrillers and horror pictures, showed great talent, and his sensational handling of the lurid *Hitler's Children*, released in 1943, gave RKO a box office smash. Elevated to A picture ranks, he made *Murder, My Sweet*, an adaptation of Raymond Chandler's *Farewell, My Lovely*, starring Dick Powell as private eye Philip Marlowe (the role Robert Mitchum would reincarnate thirty years later). It was Dmytryk's intensely imagined, phantasmagoric *Murder*, as much or more than any other film, that established the cinematic high style of '40s film noir. Dmytryk had also given RKO big profits with the cloying *Tender Comrade*, about women on the wartime home front, and he seemed a natural for *Till the End of Time*, one of the first films to deal with the travails of veterans in postwar America.

"I first got to know Bob down there at the location," Dmytryk, in his ninetieth year, recalled. "We shot at the military base in San Diego and we were staying near the racetrack in Del Mar. The whole crew was staying there and we spent a lot of time together. I saw right away that he was going to be very good. And he had the great-est photographic memory of any actor I ever worked with. If you changed lines, cut out lines, it didn't matter. He could adjust with-out hesitation. He was the most cooperative guy I've ever known. As

I got to know him, though, I found that he held something back. Always kept himself in firm control. I don't think he ever let go on the picture the way that he could when the cameras weren't turning. We used to play pool in the evening after dinner, and he would open up then. He did characters, accents. He would turn his cap backwards and do a German character, an Irishman, just perfect and very funny. Off camera he was a very free spirit."

Dmytryk, like others before him, was struck by the quality of Mitchum's mind. "It wasn't what I had been led to expect. I remember one night we'd been out driving, and we drove out to the pier and parked there, shooting the breeze. And we talked. Talked philosophy, talked about the world. It took me by surprise. I thought, 'Gee, this is a very intelligent guy.' Not just intelligent but articulate, learned. I saw there was a lot more to this guy than people thought there was."

When filming continued on the RKO lot, other members of the company got to admire Mitchum's "surprising" characteristics. Actress Jean Porter, playing the spunky girl-next-door with a crush on Guy Madison, was impressed and delighted when Bob whipped up a comic verse on the subject of the production at hand. "He had a typewriter in his dressing room," she recalled. "He would go in there and type things. And one day he wrote this poem he called 'Dream,' so clever and funny. I kept it all this time." Fifty-five years later the witty ode to the "docile disciples of Schary" sat in a frame in the Encino home of Edward and Jean Dmytryk (director and actress met during the production of *Till the End of Time* and never parted).

Johnny Sands, the young David Selznick contractee playing Jean Porter's high school swain, remembered Mitchum as a larger-than-life presence on the lot and the subject of much idle speculation. "The story was that he drank a fifth of vodka and smoked eight 'pakalolos'* every day," said Sands. "We'd watch Mitchum come out of his dressing room and walk right up and do the scene. He was absolutely as perfect as you could imagine. And we're all thinking, '*Man, he's gonna slur some words, huh?*' But he was just absolutely

*Hawaiian slang for marijuana cigarettes.

fantastic. Shoot the scene, go back to his dressing room, back to his vodka and pakalolo—his grass. Dorothy McGuire would look at him like she was looking at a superstar. All the movies she had starred in! He was not impressed with her. He just did his thing, man, and everybody get the fuck out of my face! Ha!"

*

Mitchum's performance in the film was outstanding. In casting him as the cowboy war hero Bill Tabeshaw, RKO had insightfully found a part that built upon the tough, stoic style of his breakthrough characterization in *G.I. Joe* while looking ahead to the wry outsider persona with which he was to become so strongly identified. A one-time rodeo rider from Stinking Creek, New Mexico, badly wounded in a Pacific battle—his head trepanned and a silver plate inserted—Tabeshaw floats in and out of his buddy Cliff Harper's life in Southern California, beset by restlessness and the recurring agonies of his head wound, making plans to buy a chicken ranch one day, blowing the grubstake on Tijuana B-girls and card games the next. With Dmytryk's discerning cooperation, Mitchum molded and personalized the part, rephrasing Tabeshaw's dialogue with some of his own favored hep talk and cynical humor and imbuing him with a cool, existentialist aura, creating an original and unpredictable character. Ostensibly in a supporting part, appearing only intermittently, Mitchum's presence on screen overwhelmed the more modestly gifted star, sunny Guy Madison, as the mopey Cliff Harper. What Mitchum did, said Edward Dmytryk, what all the great movie stars did, was to inject an element of the personal, even the autobiographical, into a performance. "The big stars—and I've worked with just about all of them—formed the characters they played at least in part from their own identity." It was what made "simplistic notions like the 'auteur theory' so silly," the director believed. In a collaborative enterprise like a Hollywood movie, degrees of authorship could be credited to a number of people, "and certainly to a strong actor like Mitchum, making use of his own thoughts and experiences. Oh, I think he knew that character very well. He had talked about his earlier days, how he had drifted around the country, run away from home. He identified with this character, sure."

Till the End of Time received lukewarm reviews on release, its timely subject matter not carrying much weight with critics, who found it slackly paced and clichéd, though Mitchum's appearance was generally singled out for praise. The verdict seems severe—the film is touching in its warm-spirited treatment of broken and uprooted people trying to cope and has a quiet lyricism in scenes evoking the simple pleasures of life in hometown America—barbecues in the backyard, skating rinks, swing music on the jukebox. Though he had made his name with the baroque *Murder, My Sweet,* Dmytryk directed here with an open, relaxed style, making effective use of real locations and much natural source music for the soundtrack. The director's real-life attraction to Jean Porter, playing the cute-as-a-button bobby-soxer, is evident in a pair of adoring sequences, Porter on the ice in a solo skating turn and doing a pull-out-the-stops jitterbug with Guy Madison.

The film's most memorable scene, leading into a brawling climax, would give Mitchum his best moments. It's a display of the character's deadpan decency and has a Capralike power. The scene, as well, serves to further establish a screen persona in the making: a man with a distant, disreputable surface masking reserves of heroic resolve. In a barroom, some sleazy crypto-fascists try to recruit Harper and Tabeshaw into their hate group.

"Of course, we don't know whether you men are eligible. You see, we have certain restrictions. . . ."

"No Catholics, Jews or Negroes."

A black soldier playing pinball nearby slinks away, embarrassed. Mitchum takes this in with seemingly sleepy-eyed bemusement. "You know," he says at last, "we had a friend named Maxie Klein. . . . Maxie was here, he'd probably spit right in your eye."

"Yeah?"

"Yeah. . . . But . . . Maxie's dead in Guadalcanal. So just for him *I'm* gonna spit in your eye."

And he does.

Whatever impression *Till the End of Time* may have made on release was all but erased a few months later with the arrival of Samuel Goldwyn's similar *The Best Years of Our Lives*, one of the most acclaimed and awarded films of the decade and an altogether more grandiose look at postwar readjustment.*

Much had changed for Robert Mitchum in the seven months he had been away in the service. He was now famous—not Gable or Cooper famous maybe, but close enough. "I'd played fags and winos and other weird parts until the war," said the actor, explaining these circumstances with typical self-aggrandizement, "and then suddenly there was this thing for ugly heroes, so I started going around in profile." He was the new young star in town, the first fresh face of the postwar era. The first big hunk of man since Errol Flynn, said the gossips, or since Sterling Hayden, or John Wayne, or whomever. Famous. Well . . . all it meant as far as Mitchum was concerned was that wherever he went now, he was better than likely to find people staring at him or somebody whispering or giggling behind his back like his fly was open or there was toilet paper trailing from his shoe.

"It was just anathema to him, the attention," said Julie Mitchum. "The fuss that people made when they saw him now. And the vulgarity of it all. I was coming to meet him one time and he had just arrived ahead of me up the street, and there was a crowd, a mob of people following him. They were screaming and grabbing at him. And one young girl held up her hand, screaming, 'Look! I've got his button!' She had torn a button right off his new jacket. And it was constantly like that for him now wherever he went."

The boy who had once dreamed of being invisible now found himself, even standing alone at the dark end of a barroom, feeling

---

*The quiet virtues of *Till the End of Time* were not without their impact. Screenwriter Allen Rivkin recalled for me: "There was a character in there, a prizefighter who lost his legs on Guadalcanal, and he came home and had to cope with it. I got a call one night from a soldier who had also lost both his legs. He just wanted to tell me that he had been planning to commit suicide and then he saw the picture, and on account of that he had changed his mind."

the gaze of unseen strangers on the back of his neck. Some were looks of curiosity. Some were of idolatry or lust. Others were poisonous, from belligerent guys with a load on—maybe their chicks had expressed a little too much interest in the big movie star. Though he had yet to so much as kiss a woman's forehead on screen, the studio had begun pushing him as a sex symbol. Press releases and photo opportunities downplayed the fact that he was long married and the father of two kids and promoted his growing appeal to hep teen females. The studio helped form a young bobby-soxer fan club called "The Mitchum Droolettes." Now there was a high-class image, he told the publicity department: salivating jailbait. He posed for pictures with some of the handpicked sweater girls, their braces glittering as they gaped at the new screen idol.

RKO produced an official biography composed of facts, half-truths, and some outright fantasies. In this document, Bob was a child vaudeville performer and had sailed to South America on a freighter, graduated from high school and "matriculated at Duke University, Durham, N.C., where he stayed for two years." While studio publicists seldom needed help in redecorating the truth, some of this embroidery had a familiar ring—wish fulfillment supplied by the subject himself.

"He has no affectations," it went on, "no foibles. He likes people, is a great kidder, hates pretense of any kind, wears no make-up on the screen; has no desire to own a ranch or work around a house and garden; never rides a horse except for pictures; is not fussy about his food. . . ."

*

The studio urged him to raise his public profile, attend more premieres and parties, do interviews with whatever correspondent or columnist wandered onto the lot. From the beginning, Mitchum resisted what he saw as attempts to turn him into another "Hollywood asshole," another "movie star fruitcake." He refused to cultivate the sort of good press relations enjoyed by many stars. Journalists complained to the studio that he was foulmouthed and rude. A movie magazine reporter with a questionaire asked the actor what valuables he would grab first in the event of a fire at home. Mitchum said, "My balls."

"If some reporter asked him a stupid question, he told them it was a stupid question," said Edward Dmytryk. "You weren't supposed to do that. You were supposed to put up a front, you know. Smile and tell them how great everything was. But he was a cynic. He couldn't make himself do that stuff. And he loved to pull the legs of these interviewers, to shock them. One old lady said to him, 'What is your favorite pastime, Mr. Mitchum?' I won't tell you what he answered, but it stopped her dead."

Colloquies between stars and reporters were generally formal affairs arranged by the studio and were looked at as an adjunct to their publicity department's own fantasy-spinning. Savvy careerists like Joan Crawford or Cary Grant approached them as public performances even when they took place in their own homes, as opportunities to present a predetermined image of doting mother or grinning poolside playboy. Many columnists and fan mag journalists used to these posed, nearly scripted encounters clearly found Mitchum's seemingly unguarded authenticity refreshing. Appreciative pieces spoke of his "free style," his "brilliant sense of independence and individuality," his "provocative and impudent conversation." Reporters visiting him at his house would find no servants, stylists, or handlers, only the star, barefoot in jeans and T-shirt, ready to say whatever crossed his mind. Of course, Mitchum as rugged antistar was a marketable image, too, and his behavior before the press might well have contained as much calculation as Crawford's Mother of the Year act. Nonetheless, there was an unprecedented iconoclasm to many of Mitchum's remarks in these earliest press pieces. Years before Brando and the age of the Angry Young Actor, Mitchum was going on record disdaining the Hollywood establishment, calling producers liars, and saying of his pictures, as he did to Ruth Waterbury in *Photoplay,* "The dialogue in most of them is so bad, you have to spit it out like dirt in your teeth."

In his private life he made no big star friendships, preferring to hang out with old pals like Tony Caruso and low-level industry workers he befriended—gaffers, stuntmen, extras. His few "name" cronies were on the far fringes of stardom, denizens of the night brought together by their taste for booze and other substances, brawling roisterers like Bruce Cabot and J. Carrol "Joe" Naish (the oily character actor, in real life a rabid and surprisingly successful womanizer) and fellow hipster John Ireland (Shelley Winters recalled watching the two young men hilariously smoking a reefer under a table at Lucey's, a hangout near RKO and Paramount, then Mitchum taking off with Ireland's steak and twenty of his dollars). Army buddies from the days at Fort MacArthur looked him up when they came through town and were given sleeping space on the living room floor, staying until someone in the family would ask them to move along. With the better part of two households depending on his weekly paycheck, there never seemed anything left for savings or extravagances, and for some time Mitchum's lifestyle remained modest in the extreme.

Henry Rackin, a production assistant whose father and uncle had worked at RKO, became friendly with Bob shortly after they both got out of the service in 1945. One day on the set of *Till the End of Time* he found Mitchum contemplating nearby Guy Madison, who was being made much of for his blond, sexy looks. "I'm going to change the title of this picture," Mitchum growled.

"To what?"

"*Beauty and the Beast.*"

Rackin went to visit him at the house on Palm Avenue. "It was right below the Sunset Strip, a little rundown bungalow with a big backyard in what was a seedy neighborhood at that time, and they didn't have a dime to their names. Dorothy, his wife, was walking around in an old cotton dress. He said they couldn't afford under-wear. So whatever money he was making, it was gone. I said, 'Hi, where's Bob?' and she told me he was in the backyard. And I went around back, and there he was with some tin cans with dirt in them, and he was dropping water out of an eyedropper. I said, 'What are you doing?' He said, 'I'm growing my seeds.' Marijuana." Contrary to the RKO publicity bio, Mitchum did enjoy a little gardening.

He went out drinking and barhopping most nights, and for a time Rackin accompanied him as the designated driver. "I would meet him at a bar. He had a whole list of favorite places. There was one he liked on Sunset and Gardner where he would usually start. And I would meet him there, and then we'd get in my car and go to various other spots. I was really a chauffeur for him. And I was the only one of his friends his wife could tolerate for a while. I was never a big drinker, and she thought there was a good chance I could get him back home. She would say, 'I don't care how late he's out, just so he comes back.'"

With a handful of drinking buddies gathered around at one watering hole or another, Mitchum would hold court, telling rowdy stories and keeping his pals in stitches. "He had a wicked sense of humor," said Rackin. "He would tell story after story, and he did many of them in character. He did a great impersonation of a gay guy, a real swish, and people would sit around roaring with laughter. And he was a great connoisseur of 'Rastas' stories, and he would tell them like he was imitating Stepin Fetchit. I know that's not the greatest picture in the world of black people, but I never heard him say anything derogatory about black people. You heard all these Polish stories, too, and I'm Polish and used to laugh like hell."

Some of Bob's buddies, particularly the stuntmen, were tough to an absurd degree and loved to prove it. One time they formed a circle on the barroom floor—all of them pie-eyed—trying to win a bet or something, and one guy standing there would punch the guy next to him, and that guy would hit the guy next to him, and around in a circle, and the last one standing won the bet. Jaws were broken, fingers were broken, blood everywhere. Good times.

By law the bars in LA had to close at twelve midnight in those days. Dedicated drinkers were just getting started by that hour, and to accommodate them a network of illegal after-hours joints sprang up at scattered addresses in Hollywood and downtown LA. Some were in basements and back rooms in the commecial districts, some were in private residences, like the mansion on Normandy above Wilshire where you had to say a password into a slit in the door, like at an old speakeasy. Some offered only setups, you brought your own bottle, but others peddled drinks, drugs, and whatever else your after-midnight heart desired. Mitchum knew them all. "One night," said Henry Rackin, "Bob says, 'I want to go to Brothers.' It was a place he had talked about. It was downtown, in a very bad neighborhood. He said, 'Let's go.' I said, 'Fine. Show me how to get there.' And we drove down there. It was a bad area, and you had to walk down a dark alley between two buildings. I was scared to death. And we came to a door and Bob talked to the guy at the door and they let us in. It was a terrible place, a toilet, hardly any light and it was dense with smoke, and the smell of marijuana made you woozy. There was a bar, people drinking, but a lot of them were smoking. People were sitting on the floor, along the walls. And Bob says, 'I have to go to the john, order us a couple of drinks.' And he was gone awhile, and when he came back he was screaming, 'I don't believe it, somebody stole my wallet!' So I was stuck with the bill."

On February 2, 1946, Charles Koerner, who had given RKO its most profitable years, died of leukemia, leaving the studio once more in search of a production chief and setting the stage for the bizarre final chapter in the company's history. Corporate president N. Peter Rathvon filled the post in the interim.

For his performance in *The Story of G.I. Joe,* Robert Mitchum was nominated for the Best Supporting Actor award by the Academy of Motion Picture Arts and Sciences. The Oscar went to James Dunn, heartbreaking as the doomed, happy-go-lucky father in *A Tree Grows in Brooklyn.*

"Hell, even I voted for Jimmy Dunn," said Mitchum. "The Academy," he liked to point out in the decades ahead, "never messed with me again."

Brother John Mitchum had gotten out of the service after nearly three years. He had not been sent into battle, but he had certainly done his share of fighting, in Florida, Hawaii, and elsewhere. A brawl with an officer had gotten him railroaded into the brig, and on a happier note, he'd won an assortment of boxing championships for his regiment. He returned to Los Angeles with a plan to study for a career in music under the GI Bill. When he had gone away, his brother was a struggling B movie bit player. Now Bob was a movie star. John had seen *G.I. Joe* in a crowded theater where he was stationed, and it filled him with pride. But back in Robert's orbit in LA, the difference in their status made for a certain added tension in the relationship. Bob's constant complaining about the way the studio took advantage of him wore on John's nerves. He was trying to make ends meet on a ninety-dollar monthly government stipend. One night, John told Mike Tomkies, Bob was waving around a check from RKO, squawking about how much tax had been withheld or something.

"Why don't you shut up?" John told him. "You're whining like a child. There are people coming back from the war with one leg, no legs . . . and here you are, bitching about losing a little money. . . ."

At that Robert hauled off and slugged him.

"We had both been drinking, of course," John said. "He hit me right in the head, and that started it. We fought so hard we did two thousand dollars' worth of damage to the den—and he'd just fixed it all up. . . . It could have got a lot worse, but Dorothy finally stepped in and stopped us."

Robert had not won an Oscar, but as they say, "It was great just to be nominated," and he—or his contract holders at any rate—profited from the honor as the Academy nod spurred other studios to make big-money offers for his services. MGM was one—paying twenty-five-thousand dollars per performance for two films shooting back to back that spring: a suspenser titled *Undercurrent* and a romantic melodrama with a wartime background variously referred to as *Sacred and Profane, A Woman of His Own, A Woman of My Own, Carl and Anna, Karl and Anna,* and, finally, *Desire Me.*

But first RKO rushed him into something of their own, *The Locket* (called *What Nancy Wanted* during production), starring Laraine Day and produced by Bert Granet.

"*Men worshipped . . . Cursed . . . Hated . . . Loved Her!*" moaned the ads.

Evil women were all the rage in 1946, and *The Locket*'s Nancy was the latest addition to a growing noir sisterhood, whose ranks included the femmes fatales of *Double Indemnity, Leave Her to Heaven, Scarlet Street, Woman in the Window,* and *The Strange Love of Martha Ivers.* Obsessed and psychologically twisted by the humiliations she'd suffered as a little girl, the bewitching adult Nancy is a daring kleptomaniac whose criminal behavior drives numerous men to madness and suicide. Mitchum was cast as one of the latter, a bohemian painter with a photogenic New York atelier who takes a swan dive through a skyscraper window after Nancy gets done with him. Olivia De Havilland wanted the lead, but producer Bert Granet's friendship with Laraine Day overruled box office considerations—it would turn out to be Day's best part and the most interesting performance of her career. In addition to Mitchum, the major male roles went to Brian Aherne as a psychiatrist and Gene Raymond as Nancy's would-be groom. To direct, the producer borrowed John Brahm from 20th Century-Fox. "At Fox," said Granet, "he had done a very good suspense picture about Jack the Ripper called *The Lodger.* He was a German—but not too German—and I thought he would be good to direct this and give it some of that same atmosphere he had in *The Lodger.* And we had Nick Musuraca, a marvelous cameraman."

The film is best remembered today, somewhat derisively, for its extensive use of the flashback. This narrative device had become popular, particularly in the densely layered film noirs (four of Mitchum's next five films, in various genres, would make extensive use of flashbacks). *The Locket* took things to extremes with, at one point, a flashback going into a flashback going into a flashback. "That complexity was really what enticed me to the material," said Granet. "It was like an enigma within an enigma within an enigma. It was an enticing script by Sheridan Gibney . . . maybe more so than the picture."

Mitchum did what the producer thought was a great job in the film and caused no problems. Granet remembered it as a happy time. One Sunday everyone in the cast, including Bob plus Mrs. Mitchum, went up to Brahm's small horse ranch in Malibu, and on another weekend they were all invited to dinner at the home of

Gene Raymond, where his wife, Jeanette MacDonald, entertained. But there was some tension on the set. Though Mitchum and Laraine Day had been friendly when they knew each other in Long Beach and at the Players Guild, during the shooting of *The Locket* he wanted nothing to do with her. Day claimed she'd been pleased to hear that her old Long Beach colleague was cast in the film and thought his performance marvelous, but when she approached him off camera he cut her dead. Years later Laraine would hear that Bob was nursing a grudge: that he believed she had snubbed him once, at Schwab's drugstore, when she had made it in movies but he was still a nobody. How funny! Day had thought he'd acted so strange because of the dope he was taking.

A stylish collection of suits, sports jackets, and tuxedo was created for Mitchum to wear in the film. They were clothes like nothing he had ever had in his own wardrobe and he decided to keep them. Someone from the studio demanded he send them back. Mitchum bristled at the humbling request. Other stars got to keep their wardrobe, why couldn't he? With some consternation, the studio's Jack Gross came back and told him they would do as they had done with Cary Grant and let him keep the wardrobe for the token payment of one dollar, for accounting purposes. Mitchum told him he wouldn't pay it. "I stole the clothes. Tell that to the accountant."

And on to MGM.

Undercurrent and *Desire Me* were oddly parallel projects. Both were planned as plush vehicles for Metro divas, Katharine Hepburn in the first and Greer Garson in the latter, each one playing an anxious married lady torn between two men. The male leads went to Robert Taylor in *Undercurrent* and newcomer Richard Hart in *Desire Me,* while Mitchum—though given costar billing—would play much smaller—though crucial—roles, characters more talked about than actually seen on-screen. Both projects offered Mitchum the kind of high-priced glamour and distinguished castmates his home studio could not readily provide, and they would give him exposure to the worldwide audiences in Metro's vast theater chain. To RKO, still figuring out what to do with their boy, a loan-out was not only profitable but served as a promotional campaign for Mitchum, with a rival studio picking up the tab.

Undercurrent derived from a magazine serial in *Woman's Home Companion,* the story of a plucky New England spinster who marries a charismatic millionaire gradually revealed to be a murderous paranoid with an obsessive hatred for his missing—possibly murdered—brother. The plot cobbled together elements from *Rebecca, Suspicion,* and *Gaslight,* with a few moments from *Woman of the Year* and *Philadelphia Story* thrown in for good measure. Directing the overheated but undercooked proceedings was Vincente Minnelli—it was the first of his string of neurotic melodramas—providing the film with a characteristic visual elegance and sheen but unable to provide much in the way of real suspense or interest.

In the role of the mad millionaire, Robert Taylor was resuming his career after several years in the navy. He looked middle-aged now, and his jet black, brilliantined hair and moustache seemed from another era, particularly in contrast to Mitchum's sleek, vigorous appearance as Michael, the mysterious rival sibling, decked out in a formfitting turtleneck sweater and leather aviator jacket. Still, the role was no plum for the younger Bob, physically present for not more than ten minutes of the nearly two-hour running time, excluded from the big climax (his *horse* gets to save Kate's life), and unconvincing as Hepburn's Brahms Fourth Symphony–loving aesthete soul mate at the final fade-out.

Mitchum's lack of on-screen chemistry with Katharine Hepburn extended beyond camera range. The actress had a pronounced superiority complex, loved to bait others, but did not take well to jokes at her expense. She seemed to turn a cold eye on the sleepy-lidded Mitchum from the start, and the chill only increased when he began entertaining the crew with an imitation of the actress at her most lockjaw affected. Such impudence. She told his stand-in he really must do something better with his life than work "for some cheap flash actor like Mr. Mitchum." When a take went poorly, she read her costar the riot act. "You know you cahn't act. If you hadn't been good-looking, you would never have gotten a picture. I'm *tired* of playing with people who have nothing to offer . . . *rahlly I am.*"

Mitchum gave the big shrug. He began referring to the movie as *"Underdrawers."*

If *Undercurrent* proved disappointing, Mitchum's other MGM assignment was a disaster. An assortment of writers worked on the script before and throughout the production of *Desire Me,* trying unsuccessfully to make something coherent, if not convincing, from the story. Set in a Brittany fishing village, it concerns a woman who wrongly believing her husband has been killed in the war is drawn into a romance with a mysterious stranger, who as it turns out had secretly betrayed her husband during a prison camp escape. Mitchum was cast as the scheming stranger, with Robert Montgomery as the missing husband. Then Montgomery dropped out, and producer Arthur Hornblow decided to make Mitchum the husband and give the role of the mysterious stranger to a little-known Broadway actor named Richard Hart, leaving Mitchum not only without the better part but now playing second fiddle to an unknown (perhaps Montgomery had noticed this as well). It was a confused, inauspicious start for the project, and things never did get better.

Mitchum, coming to work with a chip on his shoulder over the casting switch, chose to find the whole MGM ambience too damn refined for his tastes. They all wore their tradition-of-quality consciousness on their sleeves, and there was a rigid caste system in place. "L. B. Mayer would lick the floor clean at the approach of Greer Garson," Mitchum said. "I was always an outsider and I wasn't subjected to that caste system, so I'd speak to anyone. But there were definite demarcations in the hierarchy." He began to appreciate the "democratic" style at RKO, where the bosses were barely distinguishable from the grips.

There was nothing like an aura of elitism to bring out the vulgarian in Bob. He took to calling Miss Garson, Metro's stately queen of the lot, "Red," and claimed to have come to their kissing scene after a robust lunch full of onions and Roquefort cheese, making the great lady's eyes roll to the back of her head. He had no rapport with director George Cukor, who—perhaps having conferred with his friend Kate Hepburn—seemed to treat the young RKO loan-out condescendingly, as mere beefcake. Mitchum worked up an imitation of him, too, all puffy lips and lisping effeminacy.

"The two did not get along much, clash of personalities I suppose," Metro research librarian and Cukor friend Elliott Morgan said. "But the whole thing was a disaster, you know." Shooting on location at Victorine Ranch in Monterey, Garson was doing a scene on the rocky shoreline when she was hit by a sudden ten-foot wave that mashed her against the jagged stones and then washed her out to sea. The cameraman jumped in and saved her, but she suffered numerous scrapes and bruises. Taking stock after seeing how she had nearly sacrificed her life in the making of a stinker, Garson began demanding what proved to be impossible improvements in the amorphous script. There were long delays while the queen of the lot remained in her dressing room awaiting the rewrites and refusing to speak to Cukor. "Things have come to such a pass," wrote a visiting reporter, "that when the director wishes to speak to her, he tells his assistant; the assistant tells Miss Garson's maid; the maid delivers the message, then comes out again and tells the assistant director, who tells the director. Everybody is in a state." Mitchum's good graces mattered little to an MGM house director like Cukor, but Garson's growing displeasure was another matter. He assessed the situation, said, "Oh dear," and called in sick.

With Cukor out for the duration, the studio recruited Mervyn LeRoy to fill in. LeRoy tried to make sense of the various script revisions, worked for some weeks, and then disappeared, replaced by Victor Saville, Jack Conway, and anyone else with some free time on their hands. Shooting and reshooting continued into the summer, followed by months of editing and reediting. All the fiddling ultimately left the film with a free-floating, dispossessed sense of time and space, the narrative assembled as if at random out of flashbacks within flashbacks and multiple voice-overs. Cukor refused to have his name on it, LeRoy followed suit, and *Desire Me* would become the first Hollywood feature released without a director credit. As Mitchum said of the experience, "Nobody desired anybody."

Central casting had tossed up a stand-in for Bob Mitchum named Boyd "Tyrone" Cabeen. It was a lowly job—you stood on a hot set during lighting setups so the star could relax in his dressing room— but to watch Cabeen in action you might have thought he'd been cast for the lead in *Hamlet*. He had matinee idol good looks, an impudently charming personality, an assortment of little-exploited talents from sketch artist to fashion designer, and was a demonic, dedicated womanizer, boozer, and hell-raiser. He and Mitchum got along like gangbusters and soon became inseparable drinking buddies and mischief makers. "Mitchum would say anything and do anything—he didn't give a shit," said James Bacon, the Hollywood reporter and columnist. "And Tyrone was worse! He was crazy, this guy. You never knew what the two of them might do. Tyrone thought nothing of seeing some girl he didn't even know and going under her skirts and giving her head, in public. One time I was sitting with Bob at a place called The Coach and Horses over on Sunset, and we're watching Tyrone, he's got this broad he just met and he's screwing her at the bar. And she's loving it. And at one point there he stops long enough to pick up her drink off the bar and he dips his cock in it and stirs it around!"

Cabeen suffered along with Mitchum as the production of *Desire Me* became mired in delay and confusion. While he still labored on the film, director Cukor and assorted script doctors came up with new scenes and revised old ones, and shooting dragged on month after month. Added to this uninspiring work were days of retakes for *Undercurrent*. Mitchum would report to the MGM soundstages in Culver City at 9 A.M. and shoot with Minnelli and Hepburn until noon, then be flown directly up the coast to the *Desire Me* set in Monterey, returning in the evening. Sometimes he would be required to do a third session as well, working at night back at the studio. It was after one of these morning-to-midnight shifts that Bob and Tyrone perpetrated their legendary hairdryer-and-hairpiece heist.

Already drunk in the evening when they were at last dismissed— and with another 9 A.M. call for the next morning—the pair drove off to a barroom where additional alcoholic refreshments served to fan the flames of their resentment. A few hours before dawn, they drove back to the Culver City studio and were admitted and signed in by a half-awake guard. Mitchum and Cabeen staggered around the lot, ending up in the studio makeup department where they proceeded to ransack the place and remove anything that wasn't locked up, from towels and brushes to custom-molded head forms and Lucille Ball's wig. Mitchum grabbed a big Turbinator hair dryer, thinking it a good present for his tried-and-true wife, then returned with Cabeen for a couple more of them, thinking they might also make good presents for some girlfriends.

The next day the burglary and vandalism were reported. Studio investigators quickly determined that the two heavily intoxicated men witnesses had seen roaming the lot were in fact Robert Mitchum and his stand-in, Boyd Cabeen. MGM's private police chief, A. Q. Hodgett, had Cabeen hauled in while Bob, working on the set, was reached by phone. Both admitted to participation in what they described as a "gag." Hodgett, Cabeen, and some studio policemen then went to retrieve the stolen property from the two miscreants' residences. According to a report found by author George Eells, the recovered loot included: one bottle of spirit gum, one Sunbeam shaver, twenty-five sable brushes, three small towels, one eyelash curler, one plaster mask of Henry Hull, and one bundle of hair. As it is told, the studio police arrived at Mitchum's house just at the moment when the long-suffering Dorothy Mitchum was placing her wet head under the lovely professional hair dryer her husband had given to her that morning.

MGM raged at RKO for the behavior of their employee and threatened to have Mitchum prosecuted for grand theft. In the end, of course, with two of their own pictures set to star the accused, Metro decided to let bygones be bygones, merely billing RKO for damages incurred.

At Dorothy's persistent urging they began looking for a house to buy—Robert would have lived in the seedy, rented shack in West Hollywood until the owner threw them out for all he cared about where they called home. They settled on a four-bedroom place near

Universal Studios at 3372 Oak Glen Drive. The price tag was $12,500. Even with his contractual pay raises, Mitchum was still crying poor and so asked RKO to loan him $5,000 toward the purchase of the house. The family moved in that summer. It was a modest place, a world away from the movie star mansions of Beverly Hills. But it was theirs—once that RKO loan had been paid off—their first home. Dorothy was pleased. Bob said, "At least now the bums who visit won't have to sleep on the floor."

That year Mitchum had been drawn into the activities of a group of local actors and stage folk and surprisingly agreed to invest in and assume the presidency of—and most importantly, perform with—a new acting company to be called the Theatre Production Guild. The members had grand ambitions to build it into a western equivalent of New York's legendary Theatre Guild. Their first scheduled production, starring Mitchum, would be an original play called *The Gentle Approach* by John O'Dea, a slightly risqué comedy about a returning serviceman eager to resume his sex life and a wife who would prefer to take things more slowly. Harold Daniel directed the production, and the cast included Jacqueline DeWitt and Marcy McGuire. It was a showcase production, scheduled to be performed for a weekend apiece in Long Beach and Santa Barbara. It was a modest enterprise, not likely to make him any money; but Bob had a lingering affection for his nights on the boards, and it was also a chance to show audiences, including perhaps his Hollywood employers, that he could do a comic part as well as he did his taciturn tough guys. Mitchum was focused and disciplined throughout the few weeks of rehearsals and performance, showing a personal interest in all aspects of the enterprise.

Instead of the scheduled Santa Barbara performances, the production was moved to the resort island of Santa Catalina, a weekend getaway for Southern Californians. Dorothy and the kids came along to make a holiday of it. They chartered a small cruiser for the twenty-six-mile voyage. To publicize the production, fan magazine writer Jane Wilkie and a photographer were invited to accompany them. It was a rough crossing, the sea filled with whitecaps. Mitchum stood at the helm with the captain, while most of the

THE MAN WITH THE IMMORAL FACE

other passengers, including the photog, hung over the railings throwing up. Wilkie got her bearings sufficiently to sit near the cockpit and ask a few questions of the notoriously circumspect movie actor. "He could be garrulous once prodded into speech," wrote Wilkie, "spewing anecdotes that curled the hair. . . . But he was not prone to let anyone penetrate so much as a crack into his wondrous psyche."

"My close acquaintances," Mitchum told her, "—that's four people—keep asking me where I am, who I am, and I tell them I'm an open book. But they all say, oh no, that I'm an island, an island they can't find. . . . I'm not anyone else's property, am I? All life is spent in obeisance to the id."

"Who's your closest friend?" Wilkie asked against the buffeting wind.

"I don't have one."

"Come on. Someone in the family?"

"My family is baffled."

"Do you baffle yourself?"

"Hell, no. I have the key."

That night in Avalon, after they had put the kids to bed, Bob and Dorothy strolled barefoot to Santa Catalina's famous bandstand. The band played "To Each His Own" and the couple danced in the moonlight. *The Gentle Approach* made local history as the first play ever performed on the island. The fan magazine photographer shot the Mitchums posing before Catalina seascapes and in front of the Avalon Theater, and snapped Bob in the racy, curtain-closing moment when he hoisted DeWitt over his shoulder, held her around the thighs, and stalked offstage to conjugal bliss; but by the time these appeared, *The Gentle Approach* was ancient history, and no one else from Hollywood appears to have caught the play in its brief run or come away proclaiming Mitchum's talent as a farceur. It was his last appearance on a "legit" stage. The Theater Production Guild was never heard from again.

Pursued was the brainchild of Niven Busch, a journalist turned screenwriter and more recently a successful novelist (*Till the End of*

Time had been based on his book *They Dream of Home*). After years of hackwork in Hollywood, working on assignment, Busch was now dedicated to controlling his own film projects. He entered into a partnership with Milton Sperling, a Warner Bros. son-in-law who headed quasi-independent United States Pictures with the brothers' indulgence. A few years before, Busch had wandered around the Southwest gathering lore. It was a trip that had inspired the writing of his novel *Duel in the Sun* and now—*Pursued*. In El Paso, Texas, he read an old newspaper story about a blood-soaked feud between two families and a young boy who had survived to be brought up by the family that had destroyed his own. Busch thought, "Jesus, what was the fate of that little boy? He's going into a family that has killed his parents and his relatives . . . a wonderful classic springboard." Busch envisioned a Greek tragedy out West, familial curses and inescapable destiny. The screenplay contained more modern influences, too, interpolating newly popularized Freudian concepts like childhood trauma, repressed memory, primal fantasy. The finished script was so unusual, so richly, weirdly detailed, with its one-armed villain, whiffs of incest, hallucinations, and fragmented dream sequences, that the assigned director, Raoul Walsh, asked Busch to stay nearby during shooting and be ready to tell him what the hell was going on.

Pursued is the story of Jeb Rand, a boy saved from the horrifying site of his family's massacre by Medora Callum, who raises him as her own with her son, Adam, and daughter, Thorley. Grown up, psychically haunted, and, he comes to realize, physically hunted by his father's murderers led by the obsessed Judge Grant Callum (Medora's former brother-in-law), Jeb is doomed to follow a path strewn with tragedy and destruction, killing his adoptive brother and marrying the "sister" who is plotting to shoot him on their wedding night. Finally, on the verge of being lynched by his pursuers, Jeb's life is again saved by Medora, her long-ago adulterous affair with his father at last revealed as the cause of the blood feud.

The film's leading lady was a given, as Busch had written the part of Thorley for his wife, the incandescent Teresa Wright. To play Jeb Rand, Busch wanted a strong, new actor, someone the audience couldn't immediately identify as a conventional hero. From the New York stage, Montgomery Clift was brought out for a screen test. Posed in cowboy gear, Clift was thought to look ridiculous and quickly sent home (ironically, he later achieved stardom with another Western role in *Red River*). Newcomer Kirk Douglas was impressive in his test, but Jack Warner was repulsed by the cleft in his chin. Someone suggested Robert Mitchum—Warner considered *his* cleft acceptable. Busch was not too keen at first, but Mitchum looked great on film and the writer-producer soon became an ardent admirer of the actor's talent. The deal to borrow Mitchum was made with Selznick's Vanguard Pictures, whose periodic ownership of the actor's services was currently in play. The acclaimed Australian actress Judith Anderson—frightening Mrs. Danvers in *Rebecca*— was cast as Jeb's ambivalent "mother," and Mitchum's *When Strangers Marry* castmate Dean Jagger would play the relentless Grant Callum.

To give the film the dark, violently dramatic images the story demanded, the producers hired one of Hollywood's most talented and adventurous cinematographers, James Wong Howe. As for the director, the material would seem to have called for a past master of fatalism such as Fritz Lang or an up-and-coming specialist in violent neuroses like Anthony Mann. Instead the assignment went to Warners house director Raoul Walsh, a roguish old cowboy from Manhattan, maker of nearly a hundred movies since 1914 (including *What Price Glory? The Big Trail*, and *The Roaring Twenties*) and probably one of the least neurotic men in Hollywood. His most personal characteristics as a filmmaker were a lusty humor and an improvisatory naturalism. The humorless portentousness of *Pursued* hardly looked like his sort of thing on the face of it, but Raoul had done every possible type of film in his long career, and if the new trend was for dark, anxiety-filled movies, he could do those, too.

Walsh and Mitchum got along well (the director would later call him "one of the finest natural actors I ever met"). Mitchum enjoyed the old pro immensely. He looked like a pirate with his big, black eyepatch—orb lost years ago when a jackrabbit jumped through his windshield as he was driving to a desert location—and acted a bit like one, too. He had a glint in the remaining eye that ladies found irresistible, and there seemed to be a different big-bottomed blonde sitting on his lap for every day of the week. Walsh's approach to directing was so relaxed it bordered on the disinterested and sometimes crossed right over the border. He would often turn his back or wander off during a take, more concerned with coordinating his pouch of tobacco and his rolling papers than in watching the actors. "He would roll cigarettes with one hand on the blind side," Mitchum recalled. "And as he was walking away from the set the tobacco would fall out, and he would light it and—phew! Roll another one, light it—phew! Finally there would be a protracted silence, and he would say, 'Is it over? Okay, cut. What's next?'

"He never even watched," said Mitchum. "But he was marvelous, he had great confidence in everybody, so if you told him it was good, that was fine." Walsh lost his easygoing demeanor only when one of his team threatened to take this moviemaking business too seriously. Walsh considered Niven Busch "an eccentric" who "literally fell in love with his scripts." The writer, standing on the set to explain "what the hell was going on," gushed in such detail that the director could bear no more, crying, "Good God! Stop it, that's enough!" He also showed considerable irritation with James Wong Howe (though the two had worked well together in the past) and his complicated, time-consuming, lighting setups. "He knew what a great cameraman Jimmy was," said Niven Busch, "but he didn't give a shit about camera art."

Walsh would grumble, "The goddamn Chink is going to put us behind schedule."

Twenty-five-year-old Harry Carey, Jr., had appeared briefly in one B movie before signing on for the role of Prentice McComber, Thorley's doomed fiancé in *Pursued* (two appearances that did not keep John Ford from claiming to have introduced him to the movies in the credits of the later *Three Godfathers*). Carey's father was one of the original screen cowboys, and Junior, known to friends as

Dobe, had been around movie actors and stars all his life. But Dobe did not think he had ever seen anyone, on or off the screen, quite like Robert Mitchum. "It's over fifty years later," Carey said, "and I still haven't met another guy like that in my life. He was just an overwhelming personality. Big. Powerful looking. I mean, I knew Duke Wayne, and Mitchum at that time was a much more overpowering figure than Duke Wayne was, no question. And Mitchum—I don't know if they even had the word then—but Mitchum was *cool*. If they didn't have that expression he must have invented it, because he was just the coolest guy that ever lived. He had his own outlook on life and he didn't let anyone interfere with it. Totally opposite from me. I remember we'd be sitting in his dressing room doing nothing and there would be some commotion on the set like they were ready, and I was so eager I'd jump up to go on the soundstage. And Bob would say, 'Where you going?' I'd say, 'Well, they might need me.' And he'd say, 'Fuck 'em! They got little guys they send over to tell you that. That's their *job*, man!'

"Bob wasn't arrogant, don't get me wrong. There are plenty of people in this business who like you to kiss their feet, and Mitchum wasn't one of them. He was the least starlike movie star you could imagine. He didn't care anything about that, how things might look to other people. Bob had that background, wandering around on the road, and I think part of him always remained kind of a tramp. I used to drive him home from the Warners lot every day when we were making that picture. He'd had his license taken away, so he couldn't drive and needed a lift home. I had a 1937 Olds, a ten-year-old heap. Here's the star of this Warner Bros. movie, bumming a ride, climbs into an old jalopy. Didn't give it a thought. He'd tell me to let him out at a spot off Ventura Boulevard, and he'd walk the rest of the way. I can still see him there, by himself, hiking his way up into the hills."

At the studio, Carey—"I had the look of a fellow who had never even kissed a girl, let alone gone to bed with one"—observed with awe Mitchum's effect on the opposing gender. "He was big and powerful and handsome in a different way. Sex appeal and then some. And the women just sort of went crazy for him. Not that he was—how did they used to say—a pussy hound. He didn't chase it, just sort of a sideline. Never on the make. If it's there, take it; if not, the hell with it. But he had this aura—like he'd been to bed with hundreds of women. And I mean it made some women nervous to be around him."

According to Carey, Teresa Wright was foremost among those made nervous by Mitchum's erotic *aura*. "Bob scared her. She found him physically overpowering, and with that sort of bad boy sexuality, she just became out of sorts when he was near her. It was a strange thing to see. She was married to Niven Busch, the guy who wrote the thing, and she had been around in movies for years, but I guess she was very naive in some ways. And it wasn't put on; it was real. Teresa Wright, the little leading lady, she became terrified of him. She was scared to death, afraid he was going to do something to her, tear her down and rape her or something. And Bob was not that kind of guy."

The director and some of the other men found Teresa Wright's sexual anxiety quite amusing. Raoul Walsh loved a good practical joke—as the story went, he had once borrowed John Barrymore's corpse from a funeral parlor to give a drunken Errol Flynn a good scare. On this occasion he and Busch and Mitchum dreamed up a gag. It was the wedding night scene, Jeb carrying Thorley over the threshhold. The scene was rehearsed and ready to shoot when Walsh told Mitchum to take her to the bed and "make like you're jumping her bones. Hold her down and start trying to rape her."

The camera turned, and Mitchum carried the petite Teresa onto the set, but instead of lowering her to the ground, he tossed her onto the bed and crawled all over her. Wright screamed in terror.

"It was kind of cruel," said Carey, "because they scared the hell out of her before they let her know it was a gag."

The completed film was a strange, original, extraordinary work. Its grave yet delirious romanticism played like *Wuthering Heights* transplanted to a gunslingers' New Mexico (Raoul Walsh giving to this film the feverishness absent from William Wyler's prosaic version of the Brontë novel), while the fractured storytelling, violence, and shadow-haunted images strikingly introduced film noir to the Old West. James Wong Howe's photography, Fordian deep focus for the stark, high desert location footage, noirish underlighting, and low angles for the interiors, was—for a Western *certainly*—imposing and experimental (Howe's innovations included the first use of infrared film in a Hollywood production). Flanking Mitchum's central role, Judith Anderson was expectably powerful as the steely and tortured mother, and Teresa Wright, a testimonial to nepotism, was sublime—few actresses in film history could so enticingly express romantic yearning and vulnerability.

For Mitchum, *Pursued* was yet another proving ground. Though he had made four features since *G.I. Joe* thrust him into the big time, this was his first real lead in an A production. And it was a performance, and a role, requiring a dramatic leap beyond the behavioral naturalism of his previous characterizations. Jeb Rand, as written, was a ripely melodramatic part—the character is, after all, literally haunted by ghosts from his past—erupting with outbursts of passion, fear, and violence. Mitchum compellingly adapted the part to his own strengths, playing down the hysteria in the material—one could imagine a very different approach from Kirk Douglas—giving a kind of voluptuous passivity to Rand's enigmatic resignation in the face of a malignant, seemingly inexorable fate. The part was Mitchum's first romantic lead, and the actor was presented in a way guaranteed to set the bobby-soxers' hearts racing: an alluring object of desire, a figure of power and sensuality with his heavy-lidded, "immoral face," the glistening dark pompadoured hair, the massive physique towering over the low-angled camera, and an unusually flamboyant wardrobe (puffy-sleeved white shirts, extravagant Indian blanket coat). Mitchum's brooding, darkly sexual characterization in *Pursued* would anticipate the supposedly groundbreaking style brought to the screen by Marlon Brando and later still by Elvis Presley.

Pursued itself proved to be inarguably influential. Niven Busch's introduction of dark themes, classical allusions, and Freudianism to the horse opera plus the film's baroque style helped to launch the era of the so-called adult and neurotic Westerns, a range of distinctive films from *High Noon* and *The Gunfighter* to *Johnny Guitar, Forty Guns,* and *One-Eyed Jacks.**

Mitchum returned to RKO to take his first real lead in a major production at his home studio. It would become another great vehicle for the young star—and ultimately one of the two or three most important films of his career—though typically, even at this late date, he was not the first actor RKO considered for the part.

Daniel Mainwaring had been writing mystery novels since 1936. He wrote private eye stories set mostly in the California hinterlands (the rural, central region where he grew up) and published them under the pen name of Geoffrey Homes. They were among the best works of their kind, but they had never enjoyed more than moderate success. For years Mainwaring worked a day job as a publicist at Warner Bros., until in 1943 he broke into screenwriting, churning out scripts for Pine-Thomas (Bob Mitchum's low-budget employers, the Dollar Bills). Scripting even B-minus movies paid considerably more than he had ever seen from his crime fiction, and he would soon turn his back on book writing and stick to screenplays for the rest of his life. But Mainwaring had one last novel in him, not another series detective story but a one-shot—this time his hero wouldn't live to detect again.

It's the story of a private eye and his search for a missing girl and all that happens to him when he finds her. A sprawling story, it moves from the author's beloved California mountains to New York, Acapulco, and Nevada. The novel was called *Build My Gallows High,* and it was published by Morrow in 1946. William Dozier of RKO bought the book (for twenty thousand dollars) prior to publication and the author with it. After a George Gallup poll found that the title *Build My Gallows High* sounded too unpleasant to American ears, the studio changed it to something less provocative though no less poetic: *Out of the Past.*

Mainwaring went to work on a screenplay, condensing some

---

* *Pursued*'s influence was still being felt twenty years later in the Freudian flashbacks in Sergio Leone's spaghetti Westerns.

elements from the original, expanding others, creating an elaborate narrative structure with multiple flashbacks—there was simply no avoiding those flashbacks in postwar melodrama—and voice-overs, including a long section narrated by a young deaf-mute. Producer Warren Duff then hired the legendary James M. Cain, author of *The Postman Always Rings Twice,* to take a crack at it. Cain changed characters' names, removed every last shred of lovability from the femme fatale, added a few more murders, and came up with a simpler two-part structure with one long flashback sequence narrated by the hero. Warren Duff was hoping to have Jacques Tourneur direct the film—Tourneur had done *Experiment Perilous* for him the previous year. He showed the director both scripts, and Tourneur made several suggestions. Duff assigned a third writer, Frank Fenton, a veteran RKO scenarist and script doctor (and occasional novelist) with a string of "Falcon" and "Saint" mystery movies on his résumé. Fenton removed most of Cain's additions and excesses, streamlined Mainwaring's draft, revised and polished, and wrote new dialogue for nearly every scene. Mainwaring may have taken a final pass at the thing—in any case, under his Homes pen name he was the only one of the three contributors credited on-screen.

Here was what these assorted hands came up with:

In a small town in the mountains, Jeff Bailey leads a quiet life running a gas station and fishing on the river with his local sweetheart, Ann. A black-clad figure from his past—Joe Stefanos—drives into town one day and tells him that an old friend, wealthy criminal Whit Sterling, wants to see him again. Ruefully accepting the inevitable, Jeff agrees. He decides the time has come to let Ann know the truth about himself, and on the long drive to Whit's Lake Tahoe compound he tells her the tale. Once a New York private eye named Markham, not Bailey, Jeff took a job from Sterling—to search for the gambler's missing girlfriend, Kathie Moffett, who had shot him, stolen forty thousand dollars of his money, and disappeared. Jeff follows leads across the country and then to Mexico, where in an Acapulco cantina he finally crosses paths with the alluring young woman. Not letting on why he's there, the detective becomes romantically involved with her. Kathie eventually realizes that Jeff has been sent to bring her back, but by then he is fully smitten.

As they embrace on the tropical beach, Kathie begins to protest her innocence of Sterling's charges, but Jeff cuts her off: *"Baby, I don't care."*

After nearly being found together by Sterling and Stefanos, the couple flee to California, keeping a low profile until they are discovered by Jeff's treacherous ex-partner, Fisher, now employed by Whit. Tracking the pair to a backwoods cabin, he tries to blackmail them. Kathie shoots him dead, and before Jeff can react she is gone.

Finishing his sordid story, Jeff sends Ann home and goes in to see Whit. To his shock and disgust he finds Kathie there, returned to the fold. Sterling wants Jeff to make up for his betrayal and to avoid being turned in for Fisher's murder by helping him with another job: grabbing some incriminating documents from a blackmailing accountant named Eels. After exchanging a few bitter words with Kathie, Jeff goes off to San Francisco, meeting another Sterling confederate—comely Meta Carson—who aids him in the scheme to separate Eels from Whit's tax records. But Jeff deduces that he's being set up as a fall guy. Eels is killed, and Jeff is implicated, but he gets his hands on the tax ledger, hoping to barter his way out of trouble with Whit's help. Kathie is found to be calling the shots on the double-cross, but when she begins to plead his forgiveness and remind him how things had been in Mexico, Jeff finds himself weakening again. He hides out in the mountains, where Joe Stefanos is sent by Kathie to kill him. Instead, Jeff's deaf-mute friend, The Kid, hooks Joe with a fishing line and plunges him to his death on the rocks. Jeff returns to Whit for a final deal—a cash settlement and the Eels death pinned on Joe in return for the tax ledger. Sterling agrees, but when Jeff returns for his money he finds the racketeer dead, shot by Kathie for a second and final time. She tells Jeff they will go away together—"You're no good for anyone but me." Jeff seems to numbly accept his destiny, but while Kathie is getting ready to leave, he makes a phone call and the pair drive straight into a police roadblock. Realizing Jeff is responsible, Kathie shoots him and the car crashes, leaving them both dead. Some time later, a stricken Ann asks The Kid if Jeff had really intended to go away with the woman from his past. To spare her being haunted by what might have been, The Kid nods his head, knowing it is a lie.

By his own admission, Daniel Mainwaring had swiped elements of *Build My Gallows High* from *The Maltese Falcon,* the gold standard for detective thrillers (big and small echoes of the earlier book and film can be heard throughout *Out of the Past*), and so it was not surprising that the writer would suggest the screen's Sam Spade, Humphrey Bogart, to play Jeff Bailey. Producer Warren Duff, another Warner Bros. veteran and friendly with the actor, concurred. Mainwaring went to see Bogie on his boat at the marina in Newport and left a copy of the script. Then Warners nixed it, claiming the star was booked for the next year. There was talk of offering the part to Dick Powell, a profitable Philip Marlowe for RKO a couple of years before, and reuniting him with his *Murder, My Sweet* director, Eddie Dmytryk. But in the end, the meaty role was assigned to the studio's rising young tough guy actor. And about time. *Out of the Past* was his first starring vehicle at RKO since *West of the Pecos.*

With Mitchum in the lead, Duff and Executive Producer Robert Sparks opted to cast all the other principal parts with young and relatively fresh faces. As the smooth, deceptively even-tempered racketeer, Whit Sterling, Kirk Douglas, in his third film role, was the highest-paid member of the group, taking home $25,000 for two-and-a-half weeks' work (Mitchum, on salary, earned a mere $10,333.33 for his ten-and-a-third weeks with the production). It would be the motion picture debut for stage actor and director and former ballet dancer Paul Valentine, the husband of sumptuous stripper Lili St. Cyr, and at the time of his hiring still known as Val Valentinoff, cast to play Whit's equally smooth and oddly attentive henchman Joe Stefanos (a handsomer and more charming equivalent of *The Maltese Falcon*'s "gunsel," Wilmer). Dickie Moore, onetime child actor, still adolescent-looking in his early twenties, would enact the small but memorable role of the deaf-mute, The Kid. Just out of the veterans' hospital, still recovering from a rare, crippling

virus, Moore would spend four weeks with a tutor learning the rudi-
ments of sign language.

The part of Kathie Moffitt, the story's motivating force, its irresistable Circe, was assigned to the beautiful RKO starlet Jane Greer.
She was just twenty-two in 1946 when *Out of the Past* went into production. Only four years in Hollywood and Greer had already had
more than enough colorful and bizarre experiences for one lifetime.
While still in high school Jane—née Bettejane—had worked as a
vocalist at the Del Rio Club in Washington, D.C., and as a model,
posing for a recruitment poster wearing the newly restyled uniform
of the Women's Air Corps. Legendary industrialist–test pilot–movie
producer–owner of Trans World Airlines, compulsive-maniacal
skirt chaser Howard Hughes had seen the girl on the poster and sent
his team of talent scout–pimps to find her and bring her to California at once. Bettejane and her mother were put up in a
Hollywood apartment, all expenses paid, and waited there under
"house arrest" for four months until Greer, desperately bored,
began slipping out at night to have a little fun. On one of her secret
jaunts she met Rudy Vallee, the middle-aged actor-bandleader, former recording sensation of the Jazz Age. They began going out on
dates. Only then was she summoned to meet her mysterious bene-
factor, Mr. Hughes. It was the middle of the night, and Greer was
dragged out of bed for a rendezvous in a dirty old screening room.
Hughes told her he had people following her, knew everything she
had been doing with Vallee, and ordered her never to see him again.
Greer told him he had no right to tell her what to do, and Hughes
angrily dismissed her. Vallee continued his pursuit, and at last the
eighteen-year-old, would-be actress agreed to be his wife, to
Hughes's disgust.

When the marriage turned rocky, Hughes came back into Greer's
life, this time pouring on the charm. He wooed her like a high school
boy, taking her to the carnival, riding the merry-go-round with her,
and winning her some kewpie dolls at the midway games. They
began a love affair. But before long the high school suitor act faded
and Hughes's erratic behavior—for instance leaving her alone in a
restaurant for an hour while he disappeared to wash his clothes

compulsively in the men's room sink—proved too much for the teenager. She went back to Vallee, who was eccentric and a bit kinky—he had a fetish for dying Jane's hair jet black, painting her face milk white, and dressing her in black lingerie, black stockings, and black spike heels that made her teeter—but at least he was predictably weird. A year later, though, the marriage ended, and Greer then wed a considerably more stable and younger man named Edward Lasker, an entertainment attorney and aspiring producer.

RKO had signed her to an acting contract in 1945. With her dyed black hair she was invariably considered for heavies—bad girls— and stardom eluded her. Then producer Joan Harrison thought of her for the part of a glamorous New York adulterer in the noirish murder mystery *They Won't Believe Me*.

Harrison told her, "I want to test you. But I want to test you as Jane Greer, not as Gale Sondergaard" (the raven-haired Spider Woman from the Sherlock Holmes series). "I want to put a soap cap on your head. It lightens your hair, doesn't make it blonde, but lightens it, gives it life. Because your hair is dead." They made the hair change and tested her with star Robert Young. Harrison said, "The difference is astounding. Now you look like a human being, like a beautiful young woman. You've got the part."

Her appearance in *They Won't Believe Me*, Greer felt, turned RKO around in her favor. When the role of Kathie in *Out of the Past* came up, she was thrilled that they didn't want to shoot a test, simply told her she had the part. She was even more pleased when she read the script. "It was a great, great part," Greer said. "Anybody would die for a part like that. The way they build her up before you even see her. It was like that Alan Ladd thing, *Whispering Smith*. The whole first half is all 'Who is Whispering Smith?' and 'Boy, you never met anyone like Whispering Smith!' And by the time little Alan Ladd shows up, five feet four or something, he looked six feet nine. In my story it was 'She shot me, she took my money, but don't hurt her, I just want her back.' And then the next guy sees her falls instantly in love with her. This is some kind of woman. How can you go wrong? It was a part made in heaven."

*

On Saturday October 19, at seven-thirty in the morning, a sedan left
the RKO lot in Hollywood and headed for the town of Bridgeport,
California, 356 miles away in the eastern Sierra Mountains. Inside
the car was the assigned director of *Build My Gallows High,* Jacques
Tourneur, and his key technical personnel, cinematographer
Nicholas Musuraca, head grip Tom Clements, and assistant director
Harry Mancke. The crime drama was the second collaboration for
Tourneur and Musuraca, whose teamwork had created the
exquisitely evocative atmosphere of the first of Val Lewton's
groundbreaking horror films, *Cat People.* Jacques Tourneur was the
French-born son of Maurice Tourneur, an acclaimed Euro-
American director of pictorially rich silent films. Jacques had grown
up in Hollywood and returned as an adult, working his way through
the ranks from directing second units and short subjects to B features. The success of *Cat People* and its marvelous follow-ups, *I
Walked with a Zombie* and *Leopard Man,* elevated him to A picture
assignments at RKO. His first two of these, a war film, *Days of Glory,*
and a Gothic suspense story, *Experiment Perilous,* netted mixed
results, but on a loan-out to Walter Wanger at Universal, Tourneur
directed another unique and consummate work, *Canyon Passage,*
among other things one of the most beautiful color films ever made.
Tourneur was a director of style and delicacy, and though he could
dissolve into wispy anonymity with hopeless material, under the
best of circumstances his films possessed an ethereal mysteriousness
unlike the work of any other commercial filmmaker. That morning,
on the long drive to Bridgeport, Tourneur had no great enthusiasm
for the assignment at hand. He found the plot rather confusing, but
it was sexy and adult stuff by Hollywood standards and looked to
offer some good opportunities for a few pleasing visual grace notes,
s'il plait à Dieu and with the help of his comrade behind the camera.

Nick Musuraca, Italian by birth, began his life in the movies as
the chauffeur of early film pioneer J. Stuart Blackton. He became a
cinematographer in the 1920s and had been shooting for RKO from
the studio's inception. Noted for his moody underlighting (a recent

credit was *The Locket*), his name is frequently invoked as one of the inventors of the film noir style—indeed Musuraca was director of photography for the 1940 RKO release *Stranger on the Third Floor*, often cited as the very first film noir. His penchant for shadows actually had less to do with any feeling for noir's dark deeds and paranoid atmosphere than with his dedication to simplicity and realism over "technical window-dressing." For Musuraca, complicated lighting setups were compensation for a lack of perfection. "All too often," he said, "we're all of us likely to find ourselves throwing in an extra light here, and another there, simply to correct something which is a bit wrong because of the way one basic lamp is placed or adjusted. . . . If, on the other hand, that one original lamp is in its really correct place or adjustment, the others aren't needed. Any time I find myself using a more than ordinary number of light sources for a scene . . . I'll find I've slipped up somewhere, and the extra lights are really unnecessary. If you once get the 'feel' of lighting balance this way, you'll be surprised how you'll be able to simplify your lightings. Usually the results on the screen are better, too." In addition to providing a showcase for his skill with low and natural-source lighting, *Out of the Past* offered Musuraca a chance to display his now less well-remembered skill with outdoor photography. Like *Pursued*—that "black" Western—*Out of the Past* was an anomaly: a film noir full of spacious, sunlit exteriors.

In the small rural town of Bridgeport, the *Out of the Past* people took over most of the available accommodations, rooms and cabins at a couple of no-frills motor courts intended for visiting fishermen and hearty hikers. On the weekend, Tourneur and his crew toured the locations: the courthouse, a service station, the highway, and the forest and granite cliffs around Lower Twin Lake. On Monday a fleet of cars and buses from the studio arrived carrying cast, more crew, equipment, wardrobe, props, and stand-ins. Robert Mitchum, still in Hollywood, was scheduled to arrive later in the week. Meanwhile Tourneur began shooting the film's opening and closing scenes, the coming into town of Joe Stefanos (excitingly filmed with the camera mounted on the moving car), and the wistful coda after Jeff's death.

On Thursday morning Mitchum, along with a studio accountant and an assistant to Warren Duff, took off from the Los Angeles airport aboard a tiny four-seater airplane bound for Bridgeport. Three hours later they came in sight of the tiny airstrip south of town and began to descend. At the moment the wheels touched down, Mitchum, in the front seat beside the pilot, heard him emit a whispered but nonetheless disquieting oath:

"*Fuck!*"

The plane rushed along the tiny strip without slowing, heading straight for the trees beyond the runway. "At the last second," as Mitchum recalled it, "he jammed down and threw the throttle forward and took a right oblique."

The aircraft smashed through a fence, hopped a ditch, and knocked over an outhouse before it came to a complete stop.

The two men in the back were unconscious. The pilot said, "No brakes."

*

Cast and crew were having lunch when word arrived of the crash. There were no details at first, who was hurt and how badly. Some people drove over to the airstrip, others went off to phone the hospital. Paul Valentine and a few others were still in the restaurant when Mitchum arrived. He had crawled out of the crumpled plane, dusted himself off, and hitched a ride into town.

"He walked in on us," Valentine remembered. "Everybody looked up. And the first words out of his mouth were 'Anybody here got any *gage?*'" *

The company remained in the mountains for three weeks. With the tourist season over and winter coming early in the Sierras, life was bleak in Bridgeport. On the twenty-sixth of October it snowed while they were at the lake, sending them back to base early, and on the twenty-ninth they lost a whole day to a freezing windstorm. The

*Jazzman for marijuana.

Hollywood people had little to do when they weren't shooting. At the end of the day, many found their way to a roadhouse tavern a few miles outside of town. RKO sent up a projector and some spare prints, so in the evening people would gather around and watch Tom Conway as The Falcon and call out bored, inside jokes. "We all got a little stir-crazy very fast," said Paul Valentine. A studio publicist rounded up some of the local members of the Shoshone Indian tribe and convinced their genial Chief Owanahea to initiate Mitchum into the tribe. The chief and the actor posed for photos in feathered headdresses, giving each other the secret handshake. Some nights Mitchum would lie on his bed and write poetry, in the morning circulating the results to a select readership. One of those favored, Dickie Moore, was greatly impressed by Bob's gift for language, though the subject matter was sometimes less than worthy. "One pithy sonnet," Moore recalled, "in flawless rhyme and meter, was about a farting horse."

Virginia Huston, sweetly romantic as Ann, the "nice" love interest in the movie, was said to have developed a bit of a crush on the film's star. "It was her first film," Paul Valentine recalled, "and he was a big star, and she just followed him around like his pet poodle. But he brushed her off. He had other fish to fry."

One night a few people were sitting in Virginia Huston's cabin shooting the breeze. All of a sudden Mitchum, back from the bar, loaded, *bare-chested*, in a rage, stormed through the doorway, cursing in all directions.

He turned to the wooden door and put his fist through it. He moved over to the wall and put his fist through it. "I scooted out of there at that point," said Valentine. "The man was shouting, he didn't have a shirt on, he looked like he was ready to kill somebody. You didn't want to mess with him. Everybody got out as fast as they could."

Valentine ran into Huston later that night.

"Are you all right? What was up with that guy?"

"Oh, it was so *exciting*," she said. "And you know what he called me? *Little chickenshit!*"

"She was thrilled."

In a memo regarding expenses incurred on location, it was noted that payment had been made "for damages caused by Robert Mitchum to Slick's Cabins, Bridgeport, cost $135.00."

On November 7 cast and crew were back in Los Angeles and resumed filming on the RKO lot. Jane Greer, preparing for her first scenes, met with Tourneur to discuss the performance. She found the rotund director a calmly mild-mannered fellow, sweet and charming.

"*Zzjjane*, do you know what *ahm-pahs-eeve* mean?" he asked the actress.

"Impassive? Yes."

"No 'big eyes.' No expressive. In the beginning you act like a nice girl. But then, after you kill the man you meet in the little house, you become a bad girl. Yes? First half, good girl. Second half, bad girl."

"I get you," she said. That was his direction, Greer recalled. "But I did throw in a few big eyes anyway. I couldn't help myself."

Tourneur also discussed with her his plan for the character's wardrobe, something typical of his films' subtle, insidious visual design. "At first you wear light colors. After you kill the man, darker colors. In the end, black."

Greer: "And it would have worked had they not screwed up the production schedule and made us do some later scenes early and the clothes weren't all ready, so you wore whatever fit. Things went ahead so quickly on a picture like that that you didn't have the luxury to wait for anything."

Her first scene with Bob Mitchum was their clinch on the beach at Acapulco. The two had run into each other around the studio and at parties, but they were essentially strangers.

"Nobody thinks about that sort of thing, whether it's awkward or not to start two people off with a love scene. You're supposed to say hello and get started. But on top of that, I'm looking at Bob and I see he has something on his mouth and it looked funny. Finally I got courage enough to say, 'Excuse me, Bob, but they've done something with your makeup; I think they messed it up. Your lips, that brown lip liner, or whatever it is, is smeared."

Mitchum said, "What are you talking about?" He yelled for the makeup man.

"They bring a mirror," said Greer, "he takes a look into the mirror, and he says, 'Oh, honey, that's just *chawin' tabbaky*.'"

Bob wiped his mouth with the back of his hand and resumed kissing position.

Greer thought, "Well, this movie is going to be different!"

She found Mitchum's carefree style amusing and infectious. "He would arrive for work in the morning and say, 'What are the lyrics?' That's what he called his lines, his dialogue. He hadn't gotten around to looking at the script yet, he'd say. 'Somebody give me the lyrics.' And I thought that was the secret to doing the lines like he did them. You don't learn them in advance. 'I'll go in each morning and I'll learn them in makeup.' Oh, dear, was I wrong. I was stumbling over my first line. And he knew the script backward and forward. It was part of his act . . . 'What are my lyrics?'"

Director and star proved to be ideally matched. In Mitchum, Tourneur had found the most expressive embodiment of his own cinematic aesthetic of eloquent, subversive reticence and oneiric sensuality. Tourneur loved Mitchum's physical grace, the gliding, pantherlike movements, and his underplaying and powerful silences, his expressive quiescence thrilled the director whose films were among the *quietest* in the history of talking pictures. He savored Mitchum's ability to *listen* in a scene. "There are a large number of players who don't know how to listen," said Tourneur. "While one of their partners speaks to them, they simply think, I don't have anything to do during this; let's try not to let the scene get stolen from me. Mitchum can be silent and listen to a five-minute speech. You'll never lose sight of him and you'll understand that he takes in what is said to him, even if he doesn't do anything. That's how one judges good actors."

As Mitchum's opposite, the sort who tried "not to let the scene get stolen," Tourneur might possibly have been thinking of Kirk Douglas. With his explosive starring roles—*Champion, Ace in the Hole, Detective Story*—still a few years off, Douglas was becoming

typed for intelligent, urbane characters, supporting parts. As Whit
Sterling, certainly among the most well-spoken and civilized of
ruthless racketeers, Douglas gave a brilliantly controlled and charismatic performance, but he could not have been thrilled by another
second-fiddle part—especially second fiddle to Mitchum, who had
already taken from him the lead in *Pursued*. The two got along well
enough off the set, but the rivalry would flare as soon as the camera
began to turn. Since Tourneur was not about to accept any obvious
histrionics in his diminuendo world, Douglas was left to try and
out-*underact* Mitchum, an exercise in futility, he discovered. He
tried adding distracting bits of business during Mitchum's lines and
came up with a coin trick, running it quickly between the tops of his
fingers. Bob started staring at the fingers until Kirk started staring at
the fingers and dropped the coin on the rug. He put the coin away.
In another scene, Douglas brought a gold watch fob out of his coat
pocket and twirled it around like a propeller. This time everybody
stared.

"It was a hoot to watch them going at it," said Jane Greer. "They
were two such different types. Kirk was something of a method
actor. And Bob was Bob. You weren't going to catch him *acting*. But
they both tried to get the advantage. At one point they were actually
trying to upstage each other by who could sit the lowest. The one sitting the lowest had the best camera angle, I guess—I don't know
what they were thinking. Bob sat on the couch, so Kirk sat on the
table, then one sat on the footstool, and by the end I think they were
both on the floor."

Tourneur, no martinet, liked to give his performers a lot of freedom and waited out the one-upmanship antics with a weary grace.
"Quoi qu'il arrive, restez calme," he liked to say.

Actors were actors. One night he was screening the rushes of a
scene with Mitchum and Douglas talking to each other on either
side of the frame and was startled to see how Paul Valentine—
placed in the background and without a line of dialogue—had
craftily picked up a magazine and was flipping the pages with an
altogether distracting intensity, hijacking the scene.

"*Oh, Paul,*" he said to the actor, "now I have to keep an eye on you, too?"

Tourneur was happy to have two such sympathetic producers as Warren Duff and Robert Sparks, who allowed him to work with little interference though they were often present on the stages and available when any problems arose. Sparks, the executive producer, was, in Daniel Mainwaring's words, "a very nice guy, dignified and sweet." His position of authority, however, was sufficient cause for Mitchum's disdain. One day in his dressing room the star was being interviewed by columnist Sheilah Graham. They were interrupted by an acquaintance of Mitchum's, a slow-witted old lavatory attendant who needed to borrow five dollars. Mitchum gave him some money and then told him to get the hell out, he was busy.

"Oh my, who was that?" Sheilah asked.

"A very sad story," said Mitchum. "That's our producer, Robert Sparks, a terrible alcoholic."

He provided Graham with enough "sad" details to make for a juicy item in her column. Luckily a publicist introduced her to the real Robert Sparks before she left the studio.

For the most part it was a convivial set, a family-like atmosphere, according to more than one veteran of the production. Mitchum and his leading lady, Jane Greer, established a friendship during the filming that would remain warm for a half a century. Paul Valentine and Mitchum became pals, too, though their relationship would not outlast the filming. Valentine and his wife, blonde bombshell Lili St. Cyr, were invited to the house on Oak Glen Drive. "It wasn't much of a place. Nothing fancy in the least. Mitchum would sit in a cheap chair in the living room with his drink and his cigarettes, talking, while his two boys would jump all over him. They liked to run and throw themselves onto him, land on his shoulders or his leg, and he was so strong that he didn't even flinch. They would charge him, leap up, then hang onto him like little birds. He'd hold them up, play with them, toss them off, they'd come running back and jump onto him again, and he'd go on talking and sipping his drink, like he didn't even notice them flying through the air."

As for Mitchum and Kirk Douglas, they attained a certain affability with each other in public, but it was clear that their rivalry went on percolating just below the surface—they would never be friends. Douglas tended to paint Mitchum, with his outlandish stories told and retold, as a consummate bullshit artist, while for Mitchum, Kirk Douglas would forever after be the name he chose to invoke when ridiculing movie star arrogance and pomposity.

Filming would be completed by December, with a brief postproduction period to follow, Jacques Tourneur working closely with editor Samuel Beetley, a rare enough occurrence in an era when directors commonly went on to their next assignment and left the responsibilities of even a first cut to supervisors and technicians. With so much effort expended on perfecting the screenplay, the narrative itself needed few changes at this stage. One adjustment was the snipping of Kathie's shooting to death of Whit, filmed but cut in favor of having the audience discover Whit's dead body just as Jeff does. Among other stylistic touches Tourneur imposed on Beetley's editing was to insist upon never returning to the same camera angles when intercutting scenes, thus keeping the visuals from becoming stale and maintaining a sense of forward movement in the storytelling—aesthetic subtleties the average filmgoer was likely to perceive only subliminally if at all.

Out of the Past was not released until almost a year after the production ended. Mitchum would make his next film and see it open before the earlier one reached a single theater. Why the long delay for a film completed with dispatch and with good commercial prospects? According to Daniel Mainwaring, a change in administration at the studio left his movie in the lurch. Producer Warren Duff was fired, and, said Mainwaring, "[Dore] Shary didn't like *Out of the Past* because it had been bought before he came. He didn't like anything that was in progress at the studio when he got there. He tried to get rid of all of them. He just threw them out without any publicity."

Reviews of the film were positive, though far from ecstatic. The appreciations came with an air of condescension toward the confusing plot complications (Mitchum himself would always maintain that some crucial script pages had been "lost in mimeo") and perceived familiarity of the character archetypes. But Mitchum's notices were his best since *G.I. Joe*. James Agee at *TIME* had ambivalent feelings about the film and the characterization, though he would compose one of the more amusingly evocative and knowing comments on Mitchum in performance: ". . . his curious languor," wrote Agee, "suggests Bing Crosby supersaturated on barbiturates."

Out of the Past would achieve its classic reputation only belatedly, decades later with the rising critical and popular appreciation for a genre known by name to only a handful of French cinephiles at the time of the movie's release. What in 1947 seemed to all concerned "just another private eye movie" would become more properly seen as one of the masterworks of golden age Hollywood, an extraordinary confluence of art and craft in the name of entertainment: the brilliant cast of whispering performers; the lyrically cadenced, hardboiled dialogue; and narration comparable to Chandler at his best, endlessly quotable (Ann: *She can't be all bad. No one is.*/Jeff: *She comes the closest*); the haunted light patterns supplied by Nick Musuraca, setting a new standard for Hollywood chiaroscuro ("It was so dark on the set," said Jane Greer, "you didn't know who else was there half the time"); and Jacques Tourneur's hypnotic direction, eschewing the sharp edges and bombast of the Germanic nightmare style of noir for the opiated atmosphere of a waking dream. Like many of the greatest examples of film noir, *Out of the Past* was both richly representative of the genre and utterly original, pursuing its own eccentric impulses beneath the generic conventions, a violent, pessimistic mystery thriller that was as well a poetic exegesis of temptation and annihilation.

Even more than a great film, this was a great vehicle for the young actor, *the* great, defining role, the one that took all the ingredients that had shown in bits and pieces in other films and blended them into something coherent and lasting. In *Out of the Past* it all came together, the combination of psyche (cynical romantic, comic pessimist, fatalist) and image (trench-coated pulp knight, honorable tough guy, outsider) that transcended any individual film, that defining mix of art and nature, of personality, physicality, talent, and metaphysics that made the difference between a movie actor— even a great movie actor—and a star.

CHAPTER FIVE

The Snakes Are Loose

On January 1, 1947, forty-one-year-old Dore Schary became head of production at RKO. A failed playwright and actor from Newark, New Jersey, Schary had come to Hollywood in the early '30s and found work as a screenwriter. After negligible credits on films with titles like *Chinatown Squad* and *Girl From Scotland Yard,* he wrote the screen story for *Boys' Town,* the heartwarmer about the priest and his colony of young delinquents, and won an Academy Award. Louis B. Mayer pegged him as executive material and put him in charge of Metro's B films. He fell out with LB over interference and creative second-guessing, then took an offer from David O. Selznick—the ultimate meddler, but swearing he'd behave—to head his Vanguard Pictures division, in which capacity Schary produced several films in partnership with RKO, including *Till the End of Time.* He was known in Hollywood as an earnest and conscientious man, an active liberal Democrat, and a filmmaker with the ability to produce intelligent commercial entertainment. Schary had a Sunday schoolteacher's taste for stories with a message, movies that climaxed with a little civics lesson or humanitarian kicker. The first project he approved for production after taking the RKO post was a controversial screenplay by John Paxton titled *Cradle of Fear.* The story came from a hard-hitting novel by Richard Brooks, *The Brick Foxhole,* about the murder of a homosexual by a viciously bigoted soldier. Schary would boast that three other RKO executives had already rejected the transgressive script.

Paxton developed his adaptation with producer Adrian Scott and director Edward Dmytryk, his creative teammates from *Murder, My*

Sweet, the acclaimed film version of Raymond Chandler's *Farewell, My Lovely.* In *The Brick Foxhole,* which the three agreed was lacking in focus, Brooks's villain did not discriminate in his hatred. "He hated everyone and everything," said Paxton, "officers, fags, Jews; he hated period." The first third of the novel was excised and the screenplay began with the murder. Early on the three made the decision to change the victim from a homosexual to a Jew. "It was a simple, practical matter," said Dmytryk. "In those days we had the Code and you simply could not mention or even imply that a character was homosexual. There were people like Franklin Pangborn who played what we called sissies, and if you were a little sophisticated you might suspect something there, but that was as much as you could get away with. So we didn't even attempt it. The picture would never have been made. And how many people could you get interested, in those days, in something about the death of a homosexual? So we decided to make him a Jew, which made it a much more interesting picture, right then after the war. And anyway, it didn't make any difference—it was still a picture against prejudice."

Cradle of Fear, retitled *Crossfire* during its third week in production, was a hard-boiled murder mystery on the face of it. A man named Joseph Samuels is brutally slain in his apartment after being visited by some drunken soldiers. One of them, Mitchell, gone missing, is implicated in the crime; but Finley, the police detective investigating, begins to suspect his army buddy, the unpleasant and rabidly bigoted Montgomery. With the help of a reluctant Sergeant Keeley and another more naive soldier on leave, the detective lays a trap for the killer. Montgomery, who murdered Samuels merely out of a hatred for Jews, tries to escape and is shot down in the street.

Paxton set the compressed story almost entirely at night, in a series of nondescript, urban warrens. Isolated in the screenplay for the benefit of the production department, the list of settings read like a little poem of noir seediness:

Int. Cheap Rooming House
Ext. Police Station
Int. Hotel Washroom

Ext. Park Bench
Int. Hamburger Joint
Int. Moviehouse Balcony
Int. Bar
Int. Ginny's Bedroom
Ext. Street of Cheap Rooming Houses

It was a good, taut script, and there remained a potentially first-rate, sordid film noir for the making, even if they were forced to eliminate the controversial aspects of the story. But Dore Schary wanted it as Paxton wrote it, believed in the material, and saw it as the kind of bold, adult project that would put his new regime on the map.

The subject matter played into one of Schary's personal interests. "For years," he said, "I had worked in the fetid field of combating anti-Semitism and I knew something about the steamy current of hatred." During the war he had given lectures on the causes of racial and religious intolerance and had heard first-hand reports about the violent bigotry in the armed services. He believed that a film dramatically revealing of such behavior would serve a very worthy purpose. Few in the executive circle agreed. Peter Rathvon, president of RKO, and even an outsider like Jack Warner, who had heard of the story line, tried to get Schary to drop it. Everybody knew there were people like that, Warner told him—Jew-haters, racists—but that didn't mean you had to make a fucking picture about the schmucks. Schary considered his instincts correct, though, when Darryl Zanuck, boss at 20th Century-Fox, called him to announce that he had bought the screen rights to a new novel on the same subject, *Gentleman's Agreement,* and did not appreciate the competition. Schary told him he was sure there was enough anti-Semitism around for two movies at least.

Still, the new production head conceded it was a financially risky proposition. The studio had taken one of its so-called Want to See polls measuring public response to upcoming titles and stories and found that almost no one wanted to see such a picture. Edward Dmytryk made it easier on Schary, proposing what was a B picture schedule and budget: twenty days and $250,000. Dmytryk: "It was no hardship. I was pleased to do it at that pace. On a schedule like that, everyone is at a creative peak and you never get the chance to get paranoid. A long shoot and you begin to worry who has their knives out for you. You get worried, question what you're doing. You get tired, want to go home, for Chrissake. It's a terrible strain. But this picture was one of the most pleasant experiences I ever had."

Crossfire would have three stars: Robert Young (as Detective Finley, the story's conscience, in a salt-and-pepper toupee that lent him a distinct resemblance to director Dmytryk), Robert Mitchum as the cynical sergeant, and Robert Ryan as the murderous bigot—"the three Bobs" as they came to be called. Ryan was a favorite of Dmytryk's. The director laid claim to putting him in his first film, *Golden Gloves,* in 1940. Ryan had worked steadily since then, but in underwhelming leading man parts. In casting him as the despicable Montgomery, Dmytryk would unleash the actor's powerful capacity for conveying evil and launch him on the most memorable phase of his career, brilliantly playing neurotic antiheroes and ruthless villains. The other featured role went to Gloria Grahame, Mitchum's brother's sister-in-law, borrowed from MGM to play the sweet-and-sour platinum blonde bar girl Ginny.

Production began on February 21. Things had moved so rapidly that Mitchum had to be brought back from a vacation in Miami. He was reluctant to go, but Adrian Scott and Dore Schary pleaded, telling him how great the film was going to be and what a wonderful part they had waiting for him. He didn't get to read the script until the day before his first scene and then realized it was smaller than he had been led to believe and could easily have been done by another actor on the lot.

"Why did you lie to me?" he asked Scott.

"We needed your name on the marquee," the producer told him.

The filming was fast and furious. To maximize his chances of making a creditable film with a programmer shooting schedule, the director and his venerable cameraman J. Roy Hunt attempted to reverse the usual production ratio of 80 percent preparation—getting the camera and lights ready—and 20 percent actual shooting. "There were people working then," said Dmytryk, "like Charlie Lang when he was at Paramount, would take two days to light a single scene. Everything with its own key light, back light. Two days!" Dmytryk used some of the techniques he had learned churning out B horror and action pictures and experimented with new ideas for streamlined production. "How do you light quickly? You light the actors and the background, just throw a dash of light on each and that's it. Shadows work for you. You don't have to worry about the things you can't see on screen." The director staged a number of scenes in long, uninterrupted takes, dollying in for close shots instead of cutting, and generally restricted himself to the absolute minimum of "coverage" for each scene. There was barely a frame exposed that wasn't used in the final edit. "I only had 147 setups on that entire picture," said Dmytryk.

Saving more time and money, everything in the film was shot on standing sets—offices, bedrooms, and staircases that had been used before in a hundred B movies and looked it.

There was a feeling of common cause among many of the people making *Crossfire*, pleased to be part of a film attacking bigotry and, in the metaphoric big-picture political sense, skewering right-wing intolerance. (Screenwriter Paxton would note that "a character like Monty would qualify brilliantly for the leadership of the Belsen concentration camp. Fascism hates weakness in people. . . .") Dmytryk and Scott were left-wingers and at least briefly "card-carrying Communists"; Schary, Paxton, Bob Ryan, and Young all FDR liberals. Mitchum, like Groucho Marx, professed to be wary of any club that would have him as a member. And in light of subsequent ugly accusations hurled at him in years to come—charges of making anti-Semitic and variously "insensitive" statements—his very participation in the film would come to be viewed by some as ironic. Dmytryk, though—who *would* observe changes in the actor's attitudes in the 1960s—here found him to be sympathetic and in synch with the movie's humane theme. "Very much so. He hated bullies and spoke very much in favor of the working man. He had seen a lot of things done to people who were down and out by people with a little power to back them in his hobo days, and that stayed with him.

I once heard him talking to a reporter on the set. She asked him why he was doing this picture and he told her, *'Because I hate cops.'* What a thing to say. I don't know if she printed it or not, but what a thing to say to a reporter!"*

However much Mitchum may or may not have endorsed the film's noble mission, it did not affect his desire to make a little mischief. Everything was so grim and dimly lit on the set that Mitchum perhaps thought it his duty to lighten things up. He had a new toy, an air-powered BB gun, and occasionally stalked the sets and dressing rooms, firing off rounds at his coworkers. Steve Brodie, who played Floyd Bowers in the film, got shot in the leg. It gave him a huge bruise that he said lasted forever. Dmytryk's status didn't exempt him from becoming another target. "I was sitting on the set and it hit me right in the fanny. Shot by a BB gun. I looked around and caught Bob standing on the sidelines pretending not to be there." Brodie, a practical joker himself, would later get revenge, sneaking into Bob's dressing room and coating his clothing with a toxic powder that made a person do a kind of Saint Vitus' dance when it touched the skin.

There was another stalker on the *Crossfire* set, Gloria Grahame's creepy and abusive husband, actor Stanley "Stash" Clements, a diminutive figure with a snarling Brooklyn accent who got movie roles as jockeys and young toughs. As Grahame's career was taking off toward stardom and his sputtered nowhere, Clements took out his frustrations by beating her, threatening to shoot her with a shotgun, attempting to kill her mother with a knife, that sort of thing. After each incident Gloria would forgive him and they would have a long, violent, sexual reunion. Bob would hear from brother, John, how he would be called well after midnight to run over to their apartment when the situation got dangerous and disarm Stanley and knock him out. Bob thought Gloria sweet and talented but wacky, and he kept away from her private life. Grahame had lately been trying to dump Clements permanently but without much

*Discussions of *Crossfire* seldom recall—there is only a single mention in the dialogue—that the loathsome racist Montgomery was a Saint Louis policeman in civilian life. "Four years in the jungle on the East Side," he says to Finley, "I know the score."

success. The way he hung around the *Crossfire* set pestering and intimidating his wife, and her ambivalent feelings, were strangely similar to the situation Gloria's character was going through in the movie. Perhaps the parallels added something to her great performance as Ginny, the caustic, disappointed bar girl. It took just three days to complete and earned her an Oscar nomination.

Three weeks after filming began, just ten weeks after Dore Schary had first agreed to make it, *Crossfire* was in the can, a tough, uncompromising movie, bluntly revealing an ugly American underbelly. There had been nothing quite so raw made in Hollywood since the uninhibited pre-Code days of the early talkies. The economizing, the stripped-down mise-en-scène, the secondhand sets, the speed with which it was shot, far from compromising the project, all seemed to work in its favor. The dark, depopulated look of the film evoked a bleary, hungover, four-in-the-morning world. The compressed story line and no-nonsense staging produced a rare immediacy—it played as if in real time, as if it had all been filmed in one clammy all-night session.

Each one of the three Bobs performed memorably. Robert Young, always an undervalued movie actor, projected a probing intelligence and moral fortitude as the tough but humane police detective. As the designated messenger for the film's explicit political and moral stand against racial hatred, he did his best to underplay the explicitly message-laden portions of the dialogue. Mitchum's world-weary sergeant perfectly fit his persona—a smart, cynical, hard-boiled former newspaperman, sleepy but sharp-tongued, reluctant to get involved, wary of authority. Keeley is spokesman for the film's existential and poetic currents, seeing the nightmarish events in noirishly fatalistic terms as part of a general uncertainty and malignity that has infected them all.

"What's happened?" the hunted Montgomery asks in the dark back row of a theater balcony. "Has everything suddenly gone crazy? I don't just mean this; I mean everything. Or is it just me?"

"No," Keeley says, "it's not just you. The snakes are loose. Anybody can get them. I get them myself. But they're friends of mine."

Whatever his marquee value, the studio chose to give Mitchum second billing to Robert Young, a man at the end of his career as a movie lead. It didn't matter. Mitchum knew that in terms of impact, the picture belonged to the guy billed third, Robert Ryan: his Montgomery, seething, unctuous, animalistic—like a rat suddenly exposed beneath a rock—was a fantastic, daring piece of work. That was the way to do it when you played the bad guy, Mitchum thought: no compromise, take it all the way down the line.

The film was a spectacular success. Earning $1,270,000 in profits, it was RKO's biggest hit of the year and one of the most acclaimed films in the studio's history. Reviewers in near unanimity hailed it as a benchmark for Hollywood's supposedly growing maturity, raved over the filmmakers' skilled mingling of strong message and riveting entertainment. It was awarded a Grand Prix at the Cannes Film Festival, topped most publications' Ten Best lists for the year, and received five Academy Award nominations, for Best Picture, Director, Screenplay, and Supporting Actor and Actress (Ryan and Grahame). It won no Oscars, as it turned out, but this probably reflected external circumstances affecting the final vote. The Best Picture award went to that rival message picture with the similar theme, Darryl Zanuck's *Gentleman's Agreement*—it was the year of anti-anti-Semitism.

And it was the year of anti-anti-Americanism. The death of the invincible President Roosevelt had unleashed the dogs of reaction in the nation's capital, and the growing "Cold War" had done the rest. The anxiety felt by Americans in regard to world events, such as the encroachments of the Soviet Union and Mao's Red Army and the rising tide of anticolonial revolution in Africa and Asia, was to be ruthlessly exploited by big business interests, anti-Communist zealots, and right-wing politicians on the make to create a long-lasting, poisonous atmosphere of paranoia, suspicion, and hate. A Congressional House Un-American Activities Committee had been charged with rooting out subversive influences in U.S. society. In search of publicity for their efforts, the committee set their sights on the glamorous motion picture industry, and in the autumn of 1947 the assault on Hollywood began. At the studios there had always been an ebb and flow of political tensions between the ranks, occasionally flaring into bitter civil wars, as in the various fights to establish the screen guilds and unions. Overall the big studios had tended to operate as relatively forgiving, laissez-faire kingdoms where the talent of the employees ultimately counted for more than their particular crackpot ideology. On some level the moguls realized that it took all kinds to make hit movies, and in the peculiar assembly line artists' colony that was Hollywood there had always been room for right-wing crazies and limousine Leninists alike. Until now.

As the HUAC hearings began in Washington, ten of an initial nineteen so-called unfriendly witnesses were subpoenaed to give testimony. Of the ten, only two were not screenwriters—producer Adrian Scott and director Edward Dmytryk, the producer and director of a current hit film some of the committee members regarded with particular contempt. Said Joan LaCoeur, future wife of Adrian Scott, "Adrian . . . and Eddie Dmytryk were subpoenaed not because they were important in the Party or because they were big names but because of *Crossfire*. Two or three weeks before the subpoenas came out, federal agents came to the studio and demanded to see *Crossfire*. It was totally because of the content that they were subpoenaed."

A kind of unified approach had been agreed upon by the ten—a decision that was subsequently considered a disastrous mistake. They would stonewall the committee's prying and—they believed—unconstitutional questions about their political beliefs, and each would read a speech extolling their version of American patriotism and decrying the evils of the HUAC. They were not allowed to read the speeches; after a few sentences the gavel sounded. Some of the witnesses were obstreperous, hard to silence, and had to be dragged away. Dalton Trumbo shouted, "This is the beginning of the American concentration camp!" Scott and Dmytryk remained relatively composed, Dmytryk in particular grimly fatalistic as he saw his place in the world crumbling. When asked if he was now or had ever been a member of the Communist Party, Adrian Scott said, "I believe that I could not engage in any conspiracy with you to invade the First Amendment." Dmytryk also refused to answer the questions posed. In turn the committee did not permit him to read his statement about the attempt being made to censor a screen that had just begun to express its "responsibilities to the people of this nation and of this world." Even as Dmytryk was being silenced by a pounding gavel, citizens across the country were buying tickets to see *Crossfire.* The film seemed to hover over the proceedings as a kind of rebuke to the congressmen, some of whom no doubt thought the Robert Ryan character had gotten a raw deal. Screenwriter Samuel Ornitz, another of the ten, invoked the film in his prepared speech: "I wish to address this Committee as a Jew, because one of its leading members is the outstanding anti-Semite in the Congress and revels in this fact. I refer to John E. Rankin. . . . I am struck forcibly by the fact that this committee has subpoenaed the men who made *Crossfire,* a powerful attack on anti-Semitism. . . ."

You couldn't buy publicity like this, they were saying back at RKO, with their heads in their hands.

The ten—the "Hollywood Ten"—were cited for contempt and handed sentences of up to one year in prison. "I was the hottest director in Hollywood," said Dmytryk, "and I was going to jail."

On November 24, the same day the Ten were being cited, Dore Schary reluctantly joined a group of moguls and board chairmen from the various studios meeting at the Waldorf Hotel in New York City. Concluding that the movie industry could not afford to be seen as soft on Reds in the current volatile climate, the group issued a collective statement of intent, a virtual oral massage to the backsides of the committee members, to wit: "We will forthwith discharge or suspend without compensation those in our employ and we will not re-employ any of the ten until such time as he is acquitted or has purged himself of contempt and declares under oath that he is not a Communist. On the broader issue of alleged subversives and disloyal elements in Hollywood, our members are likewise prepared to take positive action."

It was the beginning of the witch-hunt years in Hollywood, an ongoing industrywide purge of suspected Reds. The film colony split into an assortment of warring factions, the superpatriots and fascists of the Motion Picture Alliance for the Preservation of American Ideals proferring their blacklists and loyalty oaths, the concerned liberals of the Committee for the First Amendment inef-fectually marching on Washington, and the leftists and progressives fearfully awaiting their subpoenas or forced to go underground or to squeal on their comrades and try living with that.

In later years, when asked about the blacklist in Hollywood, Robert Mitchum would speak only a few cryptic, hipper-than-thou words to the effect that he had seen it all coming, and what did you expect? He would recall with contempt how it had been "chic" for people in the movie business making huge salaries to call themselves Communists, how it had amused him to see someone like Eddie Dmytryk sitting on the set reading the *Daily Worker*, reveling in a fashionable concern for the common man. But Dmytryk had found Mitchum to be sympatico in those days, before it was dangerous, and the actor had been friends with leftists and soon-to-be blacklist victims such as Trumbo, director Joseph Losey, and writer Howard Koch. Mitchum, Losey, and Koch had even planned to collaborate on a theater project in 1947, a political play called *The Glass House*. "He was an interesting man. Smart. Spoke very knowledgeably of the political climate at that time," said Koch, the screenwriter of *Casablanca* and *Sergeant York*. "I think people tend to see him as another John Wayne figure; maybe he turned into that, I don't know, but I found that to be very far from the truth at that time. I liked him. I'm sorry we didn't get to work together."

It is surprising that Mitchum—a man with such associates and known to make mention of his days as a longshoreman (one of the more politically suspect forms of labor at the time) and of his authorship of a play, *Fellow Traveler*, not unsympathetic to Communist strike leader Harry Bridges—did not himself become a target for any of the self-apppointed investigators and Red-chasers, who cast their nets wide and recognized no statute of limitations on radicalism. "The play . . . remains unknown," he told writer Jerry Roberts. "The HUAC never had any interest in me." And that was that.

Anyway, Mitchum would soon have more than enough trouble on his hands just trying to be a good capitalist.

After the success of *Pursued* and *Crossfire* and with a growing positive reaction to his performance in *Out of the Past*—seen by industry and press people in private screenings, the film still held from
release until late autumn—Mitchum was shaping up to be perhaps
the major new screen personality of the era. RKO still seemed not to
know what to do about it. In recent years the big names had come
to RKO for specific projects and short-term deals. The studio
hadn't had to take charge of a truly homegrown star since Ginger
Rogers's peak of popularity in the early '40s. David Selznick, still
part owner of the actor's contract, was little help. He had yet to use
Mitchum in one of his personal productions (which were becoming
scarcer as the decade continued), preferring to rent him out to the
highest bidder. When the studio began negotiating with the Berg-
Allenberg agency for the services of Loretta Young, Bert Allenberg
made a play for Mitchum. Allenberg argued that Mitchum's current representative could not properly exploit a major star, keeping
him in the public eye via live appearances, radio programs, and
recordings, and thus ever increasing his value to the studio. Getting
Mitchum for Berg-Allenberg somehow became tied in to Loretta
Young's availability for the RKO project. The studio and the agency conspired to wrestle Mitchum's contract away from Paul
Wilkins—the man who had taken the actor from Long Beach theatrics and Lockheed assembly lines to movie stardom. The final deal
would give Wilkins an ongoing but reduced piece of Mitchum's
income for the remaining years of his stay with RKO. That done,
Phil Berg, in the serpentine manner known to Hollywood agents
worthy of their percentages, immediately strong-armed a new contract for their new client. RKO and minority shareholder David
Selznick would now be paying the actor three grand every week, less
twelve weeks of unpaid layoff per year.

At $120,000 per annum, Mitchum's base pay was considerably
less than the $468,000 Humphrey Bogart earned that year as the
highest-paid actor in the world, but for a man who continued to see
himself as essentially a drifter "between trains," the numbers seemed
unreal, beyond his grasp. He still lived in a shitty little house, often
bummed a ride home at night, and dressed like a ranch hand. He

still could not manage to hold on to much cash, and in those postwar years the income taxes on big earners were all but confiscatory. Anyone without the savvy to have capital gains or other tax shelters could find himself taking home ten cents on the dollar. "I always spend all I have—much or little," he told a friend. "It really doesn't matter to me." He was known as an easy mark for a quick loan. People would promise to pay it back the next day, but the next day he often couldn't remember who they were or what he had given them. Someone introduced him to a business manager by the name of Paul Behrmann. He was a slick character with an Errol Flynn moustache who favored flashy custom-made blazers and carried himself at all times in a manner that suggested he had the world by the testicles. Behrmann met Mitchum for lunch at Mike Romanoff's.

"Let's talk turkey, Bob," he said. Behrmann told him he was going to have to decide, when it all ended, did he want to go out like Greta Garbo, with a fortune tucked away, or did he want to get out like Buster Keaton, a bum over at Metro—he's a *gag writer* now— scrounging for peanuts from the people who used to work for *him*. Behrmann said the time had come for Bob to start investing his dough, and wisely. Mitchum spoke of his distaste for the RKO brass telling him what to do and confessed to his ambivalent feelings about acting, how he sometimes dreamed of chucking the whole thing. "Sure!" Behrmann said. "But for that you need 'Fuck you' money. *Like Garbo*."

A few liquid lunches later, Mitchum signed on with the dapper financial guru. His paychecks and bills would now be sent directly to Behrmann's office, while he and Dorothy would be given a small weekly stipend to cover household and incidental expenses. Behrmann told him that if he stuck with the program, in four, five years he could be a millionaire.

That summer another Mitchum entered the picture business. As he had followed in his brother's footsteps so many times in the past, now John Mitchum found himself working as a movie actor. An agent ran into him on Santa Monica Boulevard and told him he looked perfect for a role in a picture they were currently shooting over on Cahuenga. It was something called *The Prairie*, starring someone called Alan Baxter. The director, a German émigré named Frank Wisbar, looked him up and down and said, "Jah." A couple of scenes later, a stunt coordinator rehearsed him for a brawl with the star. He was to throw a left, then take a right from Baxter, then go into a clinch. John recalled in his memoir, "I hadn't been told that I was supposed to 'pull' my punches in accepted film-fighting style." His left pounded into Baxter's face just above the left eye, blood squirted across the set, and it took six stitches to close up the wound.

The film for which RKO had sought Loretta Young was called *Tall Dark Stranger*, the title eventually changed to *Rachel and the Stranger* to accentuate the presence of Ms. Young, then enjoying the biggest success of her long career as Katie in *The Farmer's Daughter* (she would win the Best Actress Oscar for it). Based on stories by Howard Fast and scripted by Waldo Salt, *Rachel and the Stranger* was a pastoral love story with dollops of comedy and adventure, set on the Pennsylvania frontier of the 1800s. Davey, a dour, widowed farmer, takes a spunky bondwoman as his wife to do chores and care for his young son. Ill-treated by her husband, Rachel is drawn to his friend Jim Fairways, a dashing and seductive backwoods hunter. Jealousy and an Indian attack spur Davey's romantic feelings, and he and Rachel decide to live happily ever after, while Jim returns to his life of adventure.

Obeying no discernible logic, RKO had once again chosen to cast its own hot property in a supporting part. Mitchum as Fairways would be billed third after Young and William Holden. Holden, the fair-haired boy-next-door in a number of prewar movies, had returned from several years in the armed service looking considerably more mature and ready for the tougher, more cynical parts that would define his career. But *Sunset Boulevard* was still in the future, and Holden's postwar comeback vehicles, *Blaze of Noon* and *Dear Ruth*, would hardly seem to put him in a superior position beside RKO's biggest male star. But what the hell, Mitchum decided. If they didn't know what to do with their investment, it wasn't his lookout.

With three thousand coming in every week, he went along without complaint, looking at the bright side—it was a change of pace for him, a good-natured role, and a chance to sing (vocalizing "Londonderry Air" in the tension-filled atmosphere of *Pursued* hardly counted as a musical showcase). Something new, and at the same time another variation on the established Mitchum persona, the Fairways character was described in the film as "a walking man with an itch in his heels"—rootless outsider, adventurer. He would have at least the opening sequence to himself, begun with the credits still fading, an unhurried walk in the forest, strumming a guitar and crooning in a pleasant if tenuous voice one of Roy Webb and Waldo Salt's ersatz folk tunes—"O-he, O-hi, O-ho." It was the first of six originals written for him to sing in the film. That was more songs than Crosby did in an average musical.

Norman Foster was directing. A callow actor in the talkie era, when he was known as Mr. Claudette Colbert due to his wife's greater success, he turned to directing in the '30s, mostly Mr. Moto and Charlie Chan pictures until an association with Orson Welles set him off in unexpected directions. He had only recently returned from making films in Mexico. Mitchum rolled his eyes when he heard that Foster—married now to actress Sally Blane—was Loretta Young's brother-in-law, but the director showed no inordinate signs of favoritism or indulgence and was amiable and amenable to all concerned.

Only four years older than Mitchum, Loretta Young had been a movie star for two decades. She had a steely capacity for self-preservation and, like Marlene Dietrich and a few other savvy veterans, cultivated a technician's knowledge of lights, lenses, and camera angles so as to better maintain her celluloid allure. Mitchum would watch with amusement as she calibrated her head movements just before the camera rolled, making the infinitesimal adjustments that would let the light fall on her face with enchanting perfection.

"I'm afraid I threw you a little into the shadow then," she said guilefully after a take.

"Honey, I don't give a damn," he told her, or said he did.

In August the *Rachel* company left Hollywood for a six-week stay in Oregon, filming exteriors in the woods of Fox Hollow and along the Mackenzie River near Eugene. The principal actors and Foster were assigned houses rented from the locals. Mitchum's had a scenic view of the chilled Mackenzie. Provoked by locals and sportsmen gushing over the river's bounty, he took up fishing in his off-hours. Grabbing a rod, a book, and a bagful of beers, he would amble off by himself for the entire day or until somebody came to retrieve him, a habit he would continue at future locations on many another film when an unspoiled waterway was at hand.

Though they would call themselves friends in the years ahead, and Mitchum would speak approvingly of Holden as a man and as an actor, the two stars seemed in the beginning to be far from compatible. Holden was prone to melancholy and bouts of debilitating self-doubt. He was a heavy drinker but a lonely one, more likely to hide away with a bottle than to hoist a few with some comrades. In Oregon, Mitchum's self-assurance and flamboyance only increased Holden's funk. Loretta Young, among others, observed his plunge into insecurity on the days when Bob was on the set.

"Why are you so nervous?" she said to him. "You have the lead role. He doesn't get the girl, you do."

"I don't know what you mean," said Holden.

"You know what I'm talking about. Bob Mitchum has gotten under your skin."

"You're crazy," said Holden, but his discomfort continued to show.

Loretta Young could be a pious and preachy character, Mitchum found. One morning following a dinner party she had thrown at her rented home, she cornered her costars and confronted them about their previous night's imbibing. After berating them for drinking nearly two bottles of whiskey, she declared that they were both going to be big stars for years to come and if they turned into drunks they would never get to enjoy it.

An obsequious Holden mumbled that she was probably right.

Mitchum momentarily raised an eyelid. "Are you finished, Mother Superior?"

A devout Catholic, Young frowned on unseemly behavior of all kinds and particularly disapproved the use of bad language in the workplace. It was generally understood that there was to be no swearing by anyone within miles of Loretta's delicate ears, a tall order considering that in the movie business even the child actors cursed like sailors. To enforce this edict, Loretta instituted her infamous "curse box," requiring an immediate donation (to be forwarded to one of her Catholic charities) by anyone on the set uttering a forbidden epithet. This provoked one of the most durable of Mitchum anecdotes. In the pithiest version of the story, an assistant explained to Bob how the curse box worked, with its sliding scale of penalties.

"It's fifty cents for 'hell,' a dollar for a 'damn,' a dollar-fifty for 'shit'—"

"What I want to know is," said Mitchum, in a voice that could be heard throughout Oregon, "what does Miss Young charge for a 'fuck'?"

To further publicize *Rachel and the Stranger,* and by way of fulfilling his agency's promise to spread his stardom to other fields, Mitchum was signed to a recording contract with Decca Records. At the company's Hollywood studio, he sang full-length and more carefully produced versions of the six songs written for the film. With "folk" still a decidedly obscure wing of the popular music scene in America, these were more easily seen as novelty recordings, partly sung, partly spoken, with only the spare backing of jazzman Dave Barbour picking at a guitar and Walter Gross playing an authentically Early American–sounding harpsichord. As he had in the movie, actor Gary Gray joined Mitchum on the comical "Just Like Me," lyrics revised here to refer to his "Uncle Bob." They are interesting, odd recordings. Mitchum's singing voice is musical but frail, barely able to hold up to the modest range of the tunes. The spoken parts came in plenty handy. No trace of Mitchum's iconic personality shows through; instead he sings "in character," and a retrospective listening finds certain moments like the weirdly cross-talking monologue section of "Foolish Pride" rather creepy, as if one were listening to crazy Preacher Powell from *Night of the Hunter* making *his* first record. Decca released "Rachel" and "O-he, Oh-hi, O-ho" as a double A-sided 78, to not much success, and the company made no further requests for the actor's time.

Mitchum himself would continue to believe in his possibilities as a singer. Music was important to him, as it was to his mother and brother and sister. He was a great appreciator of music, from Beethoven to Dizzy Gillespie, with an adventurous ear, an aficionado of swing and bop and later of country and calypso, an amateur musicographer with an ever-growing record collection to which he enjoyed listening, alone, for long hours without a break. Mitchum, in fact, identified far more with the life and style of the gypsy jazz musicians, drifting across the country from sleazy nightclub to nightclub, than he did with any of his Hollywood peers in their baronial splendor. Mitchum's whole private persona, the sleepy nihilism, the jive talk, the taste for weed, were all much more in the style of some hipster musician than of any previous species of Hollywood movie star.

He still blew a saxophone when the urge struck, noodling in his dressing room or at home, and he sang in public with little urging, at parties and public appearances, occasionally in tune and frequently with a swaggering enthusiasm that could turn an audience on. A female publicist who heard him at a party where much drinking had been going on thought he sounded like a young Bing Crosby and tried to arrange a deal for him with Columbia Records. Label president Paul Weston agreed to let him record a couple of duets with Jo Stafford. But Mitchum's then boss Howard Hughes got into the middle of the negotiations and the offer dissolved. Mitchum would not have his voice on another record release for ten years following his Decca debut.

There was anyway no lack of movie work. He happily agreed to a loan-out to producer Charles K. Feldman and Republic Pictures for a film version of John Steinbeck's *The Red Pony*. Steinbeck had been a literary hero of Mitchum's since he first read him as a teenager on the road, huddled behind the shelves in the library of some small town not his own. It wasn't just any Steinbeck adaptation either.

The script was by the author himself, and he was personally involved in preparing the film with director Lewis Milestone, who had previously transferred Steinbeck to the screen in 1940's *Of Mice and Men*. The production was conceived as prestigious all the way, with the participation of the famed novelist, the still reputable director, music by Aaron Copland, and film processing by Technicolor (it would be Mitchum's first color movie). With Orson Welles's *Macbeth* and Frank Borzage's *Moonrise,* the release of *The Red Pony* was part of oater-and-cliffhanger–prone Republic's brief, aberrant bid for "respectability."

Mitchum was to play Billy Buck, lone ranch hand on a small California spread owned by city-bred Fred Tiflin and his wife, the daughter of an aged pioneer. The story centered around Tom, the couple's young boy, his attachment to Billy and to the pony given him by his father. Costarring was Myrna Loy as the mother, with Shepperd Strudwick playing her husband, Peter Miles as Tom, and Louis Calhern in Buffalo Bill–style white hair and beard as Grandfather. The film begins as a sprightly, lyrical tale of childhood, with young Tommy fantasizing a ring of performing circus horses and his hero Billy as an Arthurian knight, and Milestone's flat, homespun staging looking like the simple color illustrations in a storybook. But the tale soon turns more neurotic and unpleasant, the Tiflins revealed to be on the verge of separation, Grandfather with his endless stories of taming the West a great bore, and when the red pony gets caught in a rainstorm, the maudlin account of his illness and death takes up a good quarter of the running time. Mitchum as the laconic hired hand gives a simple, self-contained, and convincing performance, though the story makes the character tiresome as he heedlessly steals the boy's affections from his caring father.

During filming, Mitchum offered his usual share of practical jokes and risqué stories for the amusement of the other players. Myrna Loy, though, proved to be something of a challenge, an utterly dignified creature whose poise and withering gaze had the ability to deflate his enthusiasm when many a good gag or raunchy witticism came to mind. He would study her as they sat together in the broiling sun on location. While the sweat poured down his back, Myrna remained cool and crisp in a high-buttoned dress without a pore out of place. "Why don't you undo a button?" he would ask, confounded. "Aren't you hot?" She would lift her slender nose haughtily. "Not particularly."

Still, she was not entirely imperturbable, and he evidently was not completely deflated. Loy recalled, "Robert Mitchum was a devil. He just about tortured me with his pranks during shooting—particularly when he had an audience. He seized one opportunity when Hedda Hopper came out to the ranch where we were shooting to interview me. As she angled for a story, Mitchum sat there on the porch watching. 'You know,' he suddenly interjected, 'at one point Myrna comes out into the corral and does a dance of the seven veils. . . ,' which he demonstrated in vivid detail, managing to fluster even a tough old bird like Hedda."

Writer Luke Short's *Gunman's Chance* was a property that had been kicking around at RKO for some years when director Robert Wise and editor and aspiring producer Theron Warth became interested in it. Wise had been at RKO since he was a kid, working his way up the ladder from porter to assistant cutter (his first assignment, to sync up the beeps on RKO's beeping tower logo) to editor (*Citizen Kane* and, more notoriously, *The Magnificent Ambersons*) and finally director—taking over a Val Lewton picture, *Curse of the Cat People,* in midproduction. Since then he had toiled in the B unit, but the quality of his work made it clear that Wise was meant for bigger things, so Dore Schary listened closely when the director and Warth pitched their Western. Schary had no interest in hoss oprys per se, but the two employees spoke to him of a mood piece, something realistic, darkly dramatic—something like *Out of the Past,* like *Crossfire.*

Schary assigned an "inexpensive" writer to the project, fifty-six-year-old veteran Lillie Hayward, whose long list of credits ranged from Boris Karloff horrors and Dorothy Lamour sarong sagas to *My Friend Flicka* and *The Biscuit Eater,* and two months later she turned in a finished script. "She did a damn good job," said Wise. "And we got ready to make the film. Then I got a call from Sid Rogell, an executive producer, and he told me I better come up to Dore Schary's office before they gave the picture to another director. A couple of fellows from my own agency had come in and wanted Schary to let one of their more expensive clients do the picture." The person they had in mind was Jacques Tourneur, and the agents talked up a repairing of the *Out of the Past* team; this would be a perfect project for Tourneur and Bob Mitchum. Schary told them, "No, this is Wise's picture, he and the producer dug up the material, we'll stay with them." But he liked the other half of their idea, and *Blood on the Moon* as it was now called (coincidentally, the title of a novel by Mitchum's boyhood literary hero Jim Tully) had found its star. Jim Garry was another of Mitchum's outsider roles, a solitary gunfighter-for-hire with a conscience, the script's mysterious stranger about to be made even more mysterious by the actor's enigmatic style. The rest of the cast fell into place—architect Norman Bel Geddes' refined young daughter Barbara, recently signed to a long-term contract; Robert Preston, playing *his* patented role of the corrupt best friend; Walter Brennan as a grizzled homesteader.

Robert Wise had a craftsman's soul. Without any need for personal expression in film beyond the telling of a good story, still his craftsmanship was thorough, even obsessive. Synthesizing techniques he had gleaned from his two creative mentors, Val Lewton and Orson Welles, Wise set out to make *Blood on the Moon* a studied, uniquely atmospheric Western. He familiarized himself with the styles of the period and the mundane details of cowboy life by poring over stacks of old photographs. Cinematographer Nicholas Musuraca—it would be something of an *Out of the Past* reunion after all—was chosen to give the film a downbeat, realistic look, to capture a dark, wintry outdoors and the dim, shadowy interiors of an era lit by flickering oil lamps. Having spent all that time looking at *Citizen Kane* rushes in his editing days, Wise knew the dramatic effect of sets with ceilings, and he had the *Blood on the Moon* interiors built with visible, realistically low-slung ceilings wherever possible, one more ominous, claustrophobic element in what would be the moodiest Western ever made. To costume the film, Wise hired

Joe DeYoung, a specialist in Western attire who had also worked on Howard Hawks's *Red River*. DeYoung came up with the authentic but idiosyncratic, sometimes bizarre outfits (bearskin and gaudy plaid coats, derby hats) that would give the film another of its distinctive qualities.

Mitchum, in beard, greasy hair, high-domed Stetson, and chaps, was going to look like anything but the conventional well-groomed, respectable Western hero. Wise: "The first scene we shot after Mitch got outfitted was in the barroom. Walter Brennan was sitting at a table with a couple of pals and Brennan was very interested in the Old West, it was a hobby of his. And I'll never forget when Bob came on the set, just standing there, with the costume and the whole attitude that he gave to it, and Brennan got a look at him and was terribly impressed. He pointed at Mitchum and said, 'That is the *goddamndest realest* cowboy I've ever seen!'"

Location shooting began outside Sedona, Arizona, where a studio construction crew built ranch houses, corrals, and other sets from scratch. The stunning red clay hills of Sedona gave Wise pause. "I took one look at that scenery and realized how beautiful it would be if we were shooting color," he said. "But I didn't regret using black-and-white. The stuff Musuraca shot was just marvelous." True enough: the cinematographer's shimmering blacks and whites in his cloud-covered Western landscapes look like Ansel Adams photos come to life, while the predominantly nocturnal town scenes and interiors are every bit as atmospheric and painterly as Musuraca's work in *Out of the Past* and his other noir extravaganzas. Bad weather plagued the company in Arizona. Preproduction delays plus a looming deadline before Mitchum went over to Selznick had put them on a tight schedule. Now snow and heavy cloud cover that not even Musuraca knew what to do with began to cost them whole days. It was Wise's first A-budget picture and he was determined not to blow it. "We tracked the weather like we were at NASA with a rocket launching. Every day I received three different weather service reports, one from a company in California, one from a government weather bureau, and one from some station in Winslow. Not one of them got it right." The only solution was to stay nimble. When the good weather shifted to another part of the valley, the company would quickly pack up and shoot something there. In the end they would have to return to California with some scenes—including the big cattle stampede—left unshot, filming these at a ranch in Calabasas.

"Bob was just fine to work with," Wise recalled. "He liked this part and he contributed a number of ideas. It was interesting to watch him working out the scenes. He never wanted to do *too much*. Just enough and then hold back a little, leave something a little unspecified. He was very bright, very facile, quick with language. But he liked to give the impression that he somehow wasn't articulate. I always thought he was a little embarrassed to be an actor. That this was sissy stuff. He should be a stevedore or a fireman or something. He never said this, but it was a feeling I had about him.

"Mitch and Bob Preston became pals and they spent a lot of time getting under the skin of the girls, Barbara and Phyllis Thaxter. Teasing, practical jokes . . . nothing sexual particularly, well, nothing inappropriate, but they gave them a hard time." (Bel Geddes already had enough irritation to deal with from her lack of previous riding experience, nursing a perpetually tender rear end.) Mitchum and Preston agreed to Wise's suggestion that they film their big fight scene without stunt doubles. "In keeping with the realistic style of this film I wanted to avoid one of those extremely staged-looking fistfights used in all the movies, where the stuntmen did this elaborate, acrobatic fighting and you saw the real actors only in closeups. I wanted this to look like a real fight, with that awkward, brutal look of a real fight, and when it was done for the winner to look as exhausted as the loser. And Mitch was excited about this. He knew exactly what I was going for. I think he probably knew more than I did about barroom fights like this one." For three days the actors crashed around the set, creating the film's most memorable sequence, an ugly, ferocious and realistic brawl, two figures clawing at each other in the near darkness, fists and faces smeared with glistening blood.

Blood on the Moon was, after *Pursued,* the Western genre's second and even more visually evocative move into the dark world of film noir. And Robert Mitchum was the one and only noir cowboy. It was a long way from heroes like Hopalong Cassidy or Jim "Nevada" Lacy to the brooding, brutal, unpredictable Jim Garry. In a performance that mixed a familiar, audience-friendly Hollywood archetype—the tough, laconic Westerner, the reluctant hero—with distancing characteristics of alienation and nihilism not yet codified by any modernist "school," Mitchum again proved to be an actor of stunning originality.

*

Paul Behrmann's system of handling all Bob Mitchum's financial affairs and giving Bob and Dorothy a small weekly stipend was awkward at times, a bit humbling, but it was working. It freed Mitchum of irksome everyday responsibilities like paying bills on time and balancing a checkbook, and now—via Paul—they were putting away some real money for a change. The savings account was approaching six figures. Bob told Dorothy they were going to put a good piece of it toward a big house in a better neighborhood. It wasn't safe for the kids where they presently lived. You couldn't go out the front door without fear of being hit by a car or truck, and the air was foul. Traffic in Los Angeles seemed to double with every passing year, and the main road just below the house was now a roaring effluvium he referred to as "Monoxide Alley." Big house with a good chunk of land around it, that was what he was going to get them, he said.

Paul Behrmann became a personal friend. And a generous one. He frequently took the Mitchums dining at good restaurants all over town, and often after that to a nightclub for a show and drinks, always picking up the tab. Paul made himself almost one of the family, an uncle or big brother dropping by the little house in the Valley for breakfast, sitting at the built-in table in the tiny kitchen in his natty blazers, reading the *Times* and *Variety* while the rest of the household scuffled about sleepily in pajamas and T-shirts; he'd sidle up to Bob with a bit of gossip about his other celebrity clients, and then it was time to dash off and make them all some more money.

Or maybe not. When the Mitchums returned to Los Angeles from Oregon, Dorothy couldn't reach Behrmann and went to the bank to get some cash. She found to her shock that all but fifty-eight dollars was gone from their accounts. Bob told her to let him handle it and went to see Behrmann. "My best friend and trusted manager," Mitchum would later say of the incident, "admitted the complete disappearance of my funds and refused an accounting." Saying he was "more hurt than angry," Mitchum declined to prosecute. In private, though, he brooded over the matter, contemplated revenge. One night with a buddy he got a little "hot" and planned in detail a torture murder of the man who'd betrayed him. *"How close I came to killing the son of a bitch,"* he would recall. Mitchum heated up but did nothing. In light of subsequent events, it's possible that the actor knew or learned more than he was telling about Behrmann and his activities, perhaps concluding that doing nothing was the safest way to proceed. In any case, Mitchum's seemingly passive acceptance of the theft left his family reeling in disbelief. Bob had behaved strangely in the past, to be sure. Even those who knew him best often said they never had a clue what the man might do next. But there was something about his reaction to this incident that seemed so weird to Mitchum's mother that she met with Paul Behrmann herself on the q.t. and came away with Behrmann's very different version of what had happened to the bank accounts. Behrmann had instilled in her, said Mitchum, "the belief that I . . . in reality was myself the thief." It was hard to know what to believe, but Julie Mitchum liked Behrmann and believed in him, and she had heard some shocking things from people in her circle that Bob's studio RKO was out to try and sever their star from his influential manager. In any case, Bob was clearly a confused character, and it was thought that he might benefit from some professional attention. "My mother and sister," said Mitchum, "doubting my sanity, implored the cooperation of my wife in suggesting a visit to a psychiatrist."

Mitchum agreed to their suggestion—"What could I do? It was

the family consensus"—and submitted himself to the leather couch in the Beverly Hills office of Dr. Frederick Hacker.

"Mr. Mitchum, do you know why you have come here?" asked the doctor, described by the patient as a dead ringer for Walter Slezak.

"Because my family thinks I'm crazy."

"Very interesting," said Dr. Hacker.

He saw the shrink a few more times. They "kicked things around" and Mitchum regaled the doc with stories of his life in Hollywood and the characters he knew there.

"Mr. Mitchum, you suffer from a state of over-amiability," Hacker concluded, "in which failure to please everyone creates a condition of self-reproach. You are addicted to nothing but the good will of people, and I suggest that you risk their displeasure by learning to say 'No' and following your own judgement."

Mitchum translated this into layman's terms when he got home: "He said I should tell you all to go shit in your hats."

Bob had not heard the last of Paul Behrmann. In February 1949, the agent and manager went on trial charged with grand theft. A Burbank housewife by the name of Wanda S. Schoemann had accused him of swindling her out of ten thousand dollars, supposedly to be invested in one of his clients, Anne Nichols, author of the play *Abie's Irish Rose*. Nichols denied any knowledge of the loan. Behrmann's lawyers subpoenaed several showbiz personages who were supposed to vouch for his honesty. Prosecutors countered this by subpoenaeing Robert and Dorothy Mitchum to give testimony against their former associate. Behrmann didn't take this move lightly, vowing vengeance.

"It's a subpoena, man," Mitchum said. "How does he think I'm gonna avoid that?"

Behrmann told Bob's assistant, Richard Ellis, the assistant claimed, that he knew Dorothy Mitchum had volunteered negative information. "He said that if Mrs. Mitchum didn't stop making trouble for him, he would do something violent. He said he would do away with her."

Mitchum testified. The whole mess with the missing money and the embarrassing business of Mitchum's twenty-dollar allowance was reported in the papers. It made the tough guy actor look like something of a chump. Behrmann was found guilty. The prosecutor publicly thanked Mr. Mitchum for strengthening their case and helping to send the con man to San Quentin. "We couldn't have done it without him," the papers quoted him. "And thank you," Mitchum grumbled, "and the horse you rode in on."

He began receiving threatening messages. Dorothy was terrified. She didn't know the half of it. But, hell, what she did know was enough.

It was all, Mrs. Mitchum decided, more than enough: the drinking, the smoking, the coming home at dawn or not coming home at all, the lowlifes and freaks her husband cultivated, the bimbos ever ready to drop to their knees for him, and finally the business manager who took all their money and then threatened them! This is what their life had become? Robbed of their savings and their lives threatened? If this was movie stardom, they could keep it. "Bob has gone Hollywood," Dorothy said to friends, and she wanted to go someplace else. One morning she told her husband she was taking the kids and getting away from the picture business. They would head back East and stay with her folks in Delaware. Ignoring any larger implications in her decision, Bob agreed it was a good idea for them all to get out of town, give the business with Behrmann and all that some time to cool down. He was on a layoff now, nothing to keep him in California.

They left town in April, crossed the country, got to Delaware, and moved in with the Spences of Camden. Dorothy's relatives and old friends came to visit. People she barely knew came to visit, too, rubberneckers wanting a peep at the famous movie actor in their midst. "Dot, can you ask Bob is Greer Garson just as sweet in person as she is in the pictures?" And "Wasn't it hard watching Bob kissing all them good looking actresses?" All Dorothy wanted was to forget that Hollywood even existed. The Maple Dell Country Club, the *prestige* club in those parts, threw a party in Bob's honor. He went over to have a look. Everyone was in their best bib and tucker, ready to drool over the local boy made good. Mitchum's old classmate Margaret Smith, now O'Connor, a member in good standing at Maple Dell, saw him arrive, saw him go. "He looked around, said, 'They didn't think I was good enough for this place when I lived here,' and he left. Haha! He didn't put on the dog or anything, you understand; he just told it like it was. I give him credit for that. Turned and walked out on his own party!"

Restless after weeks in the sticks, Mitchum took his wife to New York for some high life. She went shopping; he found other things to do. They had been in Manhattan for a few days when Bob picked up a call from David O. Selznick. The coowner of the actor's contract was in New York on business.

"Bob," Selznick said, "I just found out you were in town, too. You should have called me."

"Uh? Well . . . sorry about that," Mitchum said.

The actor and producer had met only briefly in the past. Mitchum, at the time he signed his first contract, had wondered why David wanted a piece of him. All Selznick's pictures seemed perfect for Joseph Cotten.

"I'm not your kind of actor," Mitchum told him.

"Oh yes, yes you are my kind of actor," Selznick said. But in the four years of their contractual association, D.O.S. had never done anything with Mitchum but loan him out—at great profit—to other producers and studios. Once, due to scheduling problems, he even got to collect top dollar for letting RKO have use of their own boy. He was currently negotiating his loan to something called Trinity Film Corp. for something called *If This Be My Harvest*. To Mitchum it sounded like a good title for a Joseph Cotten picture. But now at last Selznick had a production of his own with a part in it for Mitchum. It was an adaptation of Henrik Ibsen's *A Doll's House,* to costar David's inamorata Jennifer Jones, from a commissioned screenplay by a young Ingmar Bergman.

"You have to come over here and discuss this, Bob," said Selznick on the phone. "This is going to be quite a challenging role for you."

"Sure, all right. I can drop by a little later."

"I'm at the Hampshire House and I'll see you at three."

Bob decided to write Dorothy a little note telling her where he had gone, and he did this task in the hotel bar over a couple of drinks. Later, making his way to the street, he ran straight into an RKO acquaintance, screenwriter Herman Mankiewicz. There were two rounds of double scotches before Mitchum could tear himself away and resume his journey to the Hampshire House where, in the lobby, as he would tell it, he ran straight into another acquaintance, Barney Ross, the well-known boxer and morphine addict. Some drinks later, quite shitfaced and very late for his appointment, Mitchum found his way to the elevator and rode up thirty floors to David Selznick's suite. The producer had turned the place into Selznick International, East, with a receptionist and a lineup of publicists and writers waiting to see him. From an improvised meeting room David came hurrying out, greeted Mitchum heartily, and offered him a drink, which Mitchum claimed he tried to turn down but Selznick, running back to conclude his meeting, insisted. So Mitchum told Selznick's girl he would have a double scotch and water. Somehow, some undetermined number of drinks later, Mitchum found himself in Selznick's improvised office with Selznick sitting across from him and talking, talking—lecturing, really, the genius to the idiot boy, thought Bob. As Selznick raved on and the drunken Mitchum tried in vain to fathom what he was saying, the actor found himself overcome with an aching, uncomfortable sensation he could not quite locate. Selznick went on and on, a nagging drone in the background. *A fantastic step up for a person like you, Bob. . . . I don't know if you're familiar with Henrik . . . of course George Cukor would be marvelous . . . and Jennifer said . . . and then when I made* Gone With the Wind . . . Mitchum could not listen, pulling off his trenchcoat and twisting in his chair, finally, almost too late, realizing that what he was experiencing was a simple, overwhelming need to urinate. Unable to interrupt Selznick's self-absorbed chatter and reaching a point of unavoidable physical consequence, a moment away from sitting there in his seat and filling his pants with liquid, Mitchum remembered looking up at the chattering mogul one more time and then awkwardly tearing open his fly, twisting himself off the side of the chair, and pissing a hard, steady stream onto the Hampshire House carpet.

Selznick stopped talking.

Mitchum slowly raised himself up from the side of the chair, crushing the raincoat over his splattered trousers, thanked the speechless producer for his time, realized it was best to leave it at that, and staggered out.

He was due to begin work on a new picture at the end of May. Dorothy refused to return with him. They argued. Bob pleaded. Dorothy was adamant. She wanted . . . she didn't know what. For him to quit the movies? To divorce him? All she could really say for certain was that she was not ready to go back to Hollywood, not today, and not tomorrow.

Bob headed west, alone.

Even as Mitchum was traveling across the country, negotiations were being finalized for the secret sale of RKO to Howard R. Hughes, the beginning of what would come to be known as the most bizarre chapter in the history of the Hollywood studios. For a price of $8.8 million, Hughes would purchase 929,000 shares of RKO stock from Floyd Odlum. Odlum was a businessman, not a picture maker, and had never been seduced by the creative or hedonistic pleasures of the film industry. And lately business had been problematic. Profits had shrunk since the end of the war, costs had nearly doubled, in Great Britain and other countries they were now imposing stiff taxation on imported American features, the U.S. government was demanding that the studios divest themselves of their theater chains, unions were increasingly troublesome, congressional committees were labeling RKO a hotbed of Red subversion, and Floyd Odlum's arthritis was driving him crazy. It was time to take the money and run.

Hughes had been a colorful presence in Hollywood since the tail end of the silent era. A young millionaire bored with his inherited Texas tool company, he'd migrated to Los Angeles, where the quality of the women in the movie colony encouraged him to become a producer. In the late '20s and early '30s Hughes made a number of successful and critically acclaimed films—*The Front Page, The Racket, Scarface*—strong, attention-grabbing entertainments that made brilliant use of some of the great talents of the day, including Howard Hawks, Lewis Milestone, Paul Muni, and Ben Hecht. Hughes even ventured into directing with the World War I aviation epic *Hell's Angels,* feeble in its down-to-earth scenes but intensely exciting in the air. He then gave up moviemaking for nearly a decade, though he kept his hand in, so to speak, by dating an unending series of silver screen goddesses, including Katharine Hepburn, Ginger Rogers, and Bette Davis. As a test pilot during this period, his daring and record-breaking flights made him second only to Amelia Earhart as the country's most publicized aviator.

In 1940, he made a directorial comeback with a notoriously sexed-up Western called *The Outlaw.* Hughes's erotomanic approach to the staging and publicizing of *The Outlaw,* and his decade-long defense of the film against Production Code censors, defined his own outlaw status among the Hollywood hierarchy. In a business fearful of audience backlash and government interference, his urge to challenge the accepted proprieties was considered irritating and dangerous to the industry leaders who were doing quite well playing by the rules. The millionaire's reputed anti-Semitic feelings no doubt further isolated him from the brotherhood of the mostly Jewish moguls and major independent producers. But he remained a popular and glamorous figure to many others in the film community, especially the female stars he relentlessly wooed. When Hughes crashed his experimental XF-11 aircraft on Whittier Drive in Beverly Hills and lay near death in a hospital bed, the waiting room and hallway outside drew more big-name actresses than the Oscars.

In 1944, Hughes had attempted to create his own ministudio with writer-director Preston Sturges, but this had not worked out, and four years later he began quietly shopping for an established production company. For one thing he was in increasing need of someplace to employ his growing harem of starlets—formerly models, sales clerks, high school cheerleaders, nurses, carhops, baby-sitters, jitterbug contest winners—the young ladies with dark eyes and nice breasts he continually signed to personal contracts and kept stashed in bungalows and apartments all over Los Angeles, where they awaited their promised screen debuts.

Odlum let the new owner of RKO announce the sale to the press. Hughes gave the exclusive to Bill Feeder at the *Hollywood Reporter* before hiring Feeder as his personal publicist. Hughes had assured the old regime's Peter Rathvon and Dore Schary that things would stay essentially the same at RKO (though he'd already told Feeder, "I suspect Dore Schary's a Commie"). But soon after taking over he began making his distinctive presence felt, canceling the studio's high-minded projects and firing nonbabes like Barbara Bel Geddes. Schary called for a showdown. The elusive millionaire, who refused to set foot on the RKO lot, had his production head meet him at a borrowed place on the beach. A man who valued his dignity, Schary understood that his term at RKO was over as soon as he entered the unfurnished house and his boss greeted him from a side room where he was helping a woman hook up her bra.

Once Schary was out of the way, Hughes went to work retooling RKO to his own tastes and business needs. In short order, nearly half the studio personnel were pink-slipped, and work on new productions was brought to a standstill until Hughes had time to personally review scripts and personnel. Millions of dollars in pay-or-play contracts with stars and preproduction costs had to be written off. For much of that summer RKO felt like a ghost town, and even those who remained on the payroll came to work in a state of uncertainty. While Dore Schary had been a reluctant supplicant to the Hollywood Red-hunters, Hughes now appointed himself the movies' first Witch-finder General. In addition to his private staff of business advisers and procurers, he established a secret police force to investigate and spy on RKO employees and other potential subversives as well as commercial rivals and future girlfriends. The squadron, made up mostly of ex-cops, operated, according to one of its members, very much like the FBI.

*

Robert Mitchum returned to Los Angeles to find that he had a new boss and no work. The movie he had been scheduled to begin in mid-June was canceled, and nobody could say what he was going to be doing next. He went to the studio and looked at his mail and went over to Lucey's for lunch with anyone who still had a job. His personal assistant had mysteriously disappeared after the Behrmann trouble. He needed somebody to help him out with his correspondence and phone calls, remind him of his appointments, keep track of his scripts. There was a young woman he knew slightly, a friend of his sister Carol's from high school. "We met at his sister's party," Reva Frederick recalled. "He was just a very nice, polite guy. And I never expected to go work for him. It was just supposed to be for a short part-time thing at first. And before you know it, you're doing this and that and looking at scripts and it became a full-time job." Reva was smart, obviously efficient, was both no-nonsense and nonjudgmental. She could get things done, but she could blend into the scenery when that was called for. Bob was a man who could easily not bother to put on his second sock, let alone care where he was supposed to be in a week's time, so Reva quickly proved to be an invaluable asset. As Mitchum grew comfortable with her, he began to delegate to her all the parts of his life that bored or overwhelmed him. A good secretary, they said, was one who did things before the boss even knew they needed doing. In Reva's case she would have to deal with a boss who, about so many things, didn't want to know.

Reva became part of Mitchum's modest entourage, along with stand-in and play pal Tim Wallace. Offered up by the studio as a replacement for the troublesome Boyd Cabeen, by then virtually blacklisted for his rowdy behavior, Wallace was a dese-dem-dose Brooklynite, an easygoing bruiser, utterly without ambition. Uninhibited—vulgar said the easily shocked—he shared with Mitchum a predilection for scatology, with an enduring love of fart jokes. "Tim was an exact body double for Bob," an associate recalled, "except for the face, which looked like it had been hit by a frying pan." Wallace would be the gofer, the driver, the drinking and fishing buddy, the audience for the quips and stories when no one else was available, and the go-between in tricky encounters with the public. "He was actually very good at defusing situations," said Reva. "If someone wanted to pick a fight or took offense at something, before it could blow up, Tim could go over to the other person and try and talk him out of it. He'd tell him, 'Let me buy you a cup of coffee.' Or, 'Come have a cup with us. We're all friends here.' He went everywhere with Robert for many years, and they were close. Close friends? No, I don't think you could call it that. Robert didn't look at him like a close friend. He didn't really ever have one of those."

*

It was a long, hot summer in Los Angeles, with little for Mitchum to do other than wait for RKO and Hughes to sort out his future and ponder whether he would ever have his family back again . . . and drink and smoke. He played in a charity "all-star" softball game and got more applause than Frank Sinatra. The press called him the bobby-soxers' "new idol." Briefly he resurrected his dormant talent for writing specialty material. He became friendly with a tap dancer named Pat Rooney, half of a struggling comic, song-and-dance team called Rooney and Rickey, and he offered to write some new routines for them. He went out to see them perform at a club in Palm Springs and ended up on the stage singing a duet with Errol Flynn. The party moved on to Don the Beachcomber's, where Rooney recalled Mitchum eagerly reading him the new jokes and special lyrics he had written, impervious to the fact that Flynn had gotten into a brawl with three waiters and bodies were falling all around him.

Back in LA, Mitchum remembered his promise to Dorothy to move them all to a bigger house and better neighborhood. It was the best lure he could think of at the moment: to keep that promise, to find a nice new home for his wife and boys. In anticipation of putting his current place on the market, he began doing the repairs he had been putting off for months. Out in the sun working on the roof was good exercise and kept him out of trouble.

He had a friend, Robin "Danny" Ford, an itinerant bartender who was trying to make it as a real estate agent. Not everyone liked Ford as Bob did. Tim Wallace considered him "a rat." But Mitchum felt that if he started avoiding every trouble-prone character he knew, he wouldn't have any buddies at all. Anyway, he thought he might let Danny find a buyer for the house, get him a little commission, and maybe they could go drive around and look at some other properties for sale. Danny was good company.

He was hip.

"Lila Leeds," said columnist James Bacon, "was one of the most beautiful women who ever landed in Hollywood. She looked like Lana Turner. But cuter."

"I thought she was the prettiest damn thing I had ever seen," said Jack Elam, an accountant who became a most memorable character actor and worked with Lila on his first movie job. "By God, this girl was so pretty you just stood there with your fucking mouth hanging open."

She was born Lila Lee Wilkinson in Iola, Kansas, moved to Clovis, New Mexico, when she was twelve, and ran away from home a few years after that. At seventeen, the way she remembered it, working as a dancer in a Saint Louis jive joint, she met some guys from the Stan Kenton band. Lila and a girlfriend went up to their hotel room for a drink. Sprawled all over the beds and the floor, they were passing around hand-rolled cigarettes that burned with a sweet, strange aroma. One of Kenton's guys showed her how to smoke, to draw it into your lungs and let it out nice and slow. "I felt," said Lila, "as though I'd been released from my body and was floating in air. It was like there were two of me, one up on the clouds looking down at the me who was on the ground. It was a dizzy feeling, like being filled with air."

A couple of months later Lila got sick with some bug and asked her mom to come and get her. They went away from the cold weather and settled in Los Angeles. "I had no trouble landing a good job at one of those glamorized drive-ins where they almost dress the girl carhops—in shorts and V-necked sweaters. I was a big girl. I already had the measurements." The former child actor Jackie Coogan approached her on the street one day and told her she should be in the movies. So he got her a job as a hatcheck girl at Ciro's. The job wasn't as easy as it looked. In Hollywood they all had such big egos that no one could bear to take a hat check like a normal person. You were supposed to know everybody on sight and remember what hat they were wearing. Famous movie stars were one thing, but every roly-poly old producer wanted the same treatment. When it got busy on the floor she had to come around from behind her counter and help the cigarette girls selling smokes, dolls, toy pandas, and other gimcracks, and that job was worse. "A cigaret girl has no closed season on her," said Lila. "Every man who enters a nightclub takes it for granted he can make a suggestive remark, a pass, or a proposition."

Tired of wrestling with scores of guys each night, she married one of them, an older guy, Little Jack Little, a bandleader and racehorse owner. They eloped to Las Vegas and had some fun for a month. But the marriage didn't take. He had forgotten to get a divorce from some other wife.

Lila had to go to court to annul her vows. "You mean," said Judge Charles Haas, "you were so much in love that you didn't take the trouble to find out if this man was lying when he said he was divorced?"

Lila nodded.

"Then you learned about men from him, didn't you?" asked the judge.

Lila nodded. She was not quite nineteen.

With a hundred dollars in savings in her purse, she decided she'd had enough of hats, toy pandas, and black-and-blue marks on her fanny; and she invested in an acting course at the Bliss-Hayden School of the Theatre in Beverly Hills. Lila worked hard and won a good part in a school production of a farce called *Campus Honeymoon*. "There were talent scouts from every Hollywood studio in the audience on opening night," she remembered. "I knew my lines, and I changed sweaters five times in three acts. Next day I had three good offers."

Lila signed with MGM. Nine months from the day she hit town, she was standing on a soundstage at Metro. She worked with Red Skelton in *The Show Off*, and Robert Montgomery directed her in *Lady in the Lake*, from the Raymond Chandler novel about private eye Philip Marlowe. It was a small part, but it was thrilling to be in the movies, and people at the studio told her she was going to go places she was so pretty and talented. Somebody told her she was going to be the new Lana Turner. "I found out later it didn't mean a thing," Lila said. "Few people know for sure if a girl's been signed up because she can act or because some producer or star has a special interest in her. Either way she rates attention, and the wise guys deliver the attention." She went to classes for diction, singing, ballet, and fencing. It was just like going to school. She tested for parts every week. Then she got a little role in *Green Dolphin Street*, starring the old Lana Turner. It should have been her big break, but the television scare had hit the studios, she would say, and Metro was going through their postwar slump and decided not to renew her option. They didn't even give her billing when *Green Dolphin Street* came out. It left her shaken up, depressed. She would spend long nights at the bop clubs in Hollywood and on the Strip, chasing her blues away. Lila had always been jazz-happy, and she knew many of the local musicians. She smoked reefers with them in the dressing rooms and in the parking lots, even at the tables if the owners were cool. "I smoked socially . . . the way some people take a drink. Pot doesn't affect me much—just makes me sleepy and relaxed. I've heard of people who go crazy on pot. But, so far as I was concerned, it just relaxed me." Smoking the stuff was a great comfort after things fell apart at MGM. "It was a mental crutch. A way to forget my troubles."

A new agent came along and got her a contract at Warner Bros. But nothing great happened there. Bit parts and "Joe Doakes" two reelers. Lana Turner wasn't worrying. At Warners they ran a tight ship. When Lila didn't show up on the set one morning, they suspended her. "I had overslept after a marijuana party," she said.

Now it seemed like there was nothing to do but get into trouble. She started seeing her name in the papers for all the wrong reasons.

The police were called in to break up a catfight at the Mocambo nightclub between Lila and a platinum-haired model named Kitty Hamilton. The press called it "the battle of the blondes." Shortly thereafter she figured in a threeway scratch-your-eyes-out brawl with Miss Hamilton again plus actress Cara Williams, this time at Ciro's. One night she was discovered in a semicoma and rushed to Hollywood Emergency Hospital, treated for an overdose of sleeping pills. "I wasn't feeling well," she told a police officer. "I went to the medicine cabinet for some pills. Later I realized I'd taken the wrong bottle from the cabinet."

"FILM ACTRESS ON MEND AFTER DRUG ERROR," said the news item.

It was the summer of bad breaks. She had met a guy earlier in the year and was that way about him, but one day after an argument he walked out on her. A few weeks later she heard he was marrying another girl. "I was lower than an earthworm," Lila would recall. She told herself she was going to "make hey-hey while the sun shone—and after it went down, too." She drank too much and smoked too many reefers. She went away for a week to see her mother in San Antonio. Mom entered the bonds of matrimony for the fourth time, and Lila tried to be happy for her. She went back to LA and heard that Warner Bros. was going to give her another chance, a small part in *The House Across the Street*. She bucked up. There was even talk of a featured part after that. "According to the grapevine I was set for the biggest role of my career—and then something else happened."

"You have to see this chick," Mitchum's friend told him. "Bee-yoo-tee-ful, man."

Robin Ford had met her at a party in Santa Monica, at Pat Di Cicco's Ocean House, the old Marion Davies place. They talked over cocktails and it turned out she was looking to get out of her apartment in town, and Ford told her how as a rising young realtor he had insider listings and maybe he could find her something nice. She gave him her number, and then he started calling and asking her out for a date, but she wouldn't give him a tumble. One evening he and

Mitchum were at loose ends, and he decided to see if the kid would come out and play.

"I've got a friend who really wants to meet you, baby," he said. "You'll want to meet him, too. I'm telling you. A great actor and a real nice guy. Come out to dinner with us."

They picked her up at her apartment on Franklin Avenue in Mitchum's new green Buick and went to a restaurant in Hollywood. If Ford had thought this was a good way to make time with Lila he was misinformed, as the blonde beauty was digging Bob exclusively. So as soon as they were done eating, Robin made himself scarce. Bob never said a word or made a gesture, but you didn't remain friends with movie stars by crowding their action.

Lila liked Bob all right. Compared with all the sleazy Hollywood types she had encountered, all the creeps who couldn't wait to tell you how privileged you were to be in their presence, Bob Mitchum was a real doll. He downplayed his fame and fortune, didn't take anything seriously. And Bob played it straight, didn't try to hand her a line. Instead he told her right out, "I'm married and my wife's back East with the kids. We've had a disagreement, but I hope she comes back."

"I liked Bob," she said, "not because he was a big star but because he was a good guy. I knew a lot of stars, and there had been plenty of them who had wanted to know me who couldn't get to first base. It wasn't glamour or reputation that made Bob attractive. It was just that he was a regular fellow."

They left the restaurant and went to a couple of places for drinks. Somewhere in the chitchat they confessed to each other that they smoked pot, and Lila would recall that they made an open date to have a reefer party at her house sometime.

"Bob and I saw quite a bit of each other in the next few weeks," Lila said. They went to the beach. They went to bars. Smoked tea. Reporters would recall, after the fact, observing the pair together at assorted nightspots, but nothing was ever printed in deference to Mitchum's marital status. When it came to a man's private behavior, it was live and let live in those days, unless you crossed the line or got in trouble with the law.

Leeds found a new place to live in the last weeks of August. An actress she knew from someplace, Ann Staunton, gave her an unofficial sublease on a little cottage on the hillside high above Sunset. The rent was $150 a month. The tiny three-room house was furnished, but Lila didn't think it looked feminine or hep enough and she brought up a few of her own furnishings as well as clothes, cosmetics, her record player, and some records. A friend hooked her up with a pair of puppies, cute little boxers. She thought they would be good watchdogs up there in the hills at night.

She could never remember who had introduced her to Vicki Evans, a blonde dancer from Philadelphia come to LA to try and break into pictures. On August 27 she ran into Vicki, and the girl said she'd heard Lila had a new place and was there a chance she could room with her for a little while till she got settled? Lila said, "Sure, kiddo."

On August 29 she was with Vicki in a Vine Street café when they saw another of her pretty girlfriends, Betty Doss, in the company of a pockmarked man named Rudy. Later that evening Betty called and said she and Rudy wanted to come up for a visit. Lila refused to invite them. She had a bad feeling about the pockmarked guy. She had a feeling he was a cop from the Vice Squad. Lila believed that she received psychic premonitions from time to time, and always regretted that she did not act on them more often.

On August 31 Robert Mitchum and Robin Ford went house hunting again. He was going to spend all day at it. He needed to have a good prospect he could describe to his wife the next time they spoke. Dottie had called earlier in the week to let him talk to the kids. He told her he was looking for a new place for them. He was on his best behavior, said whatever he could think of, determined to make a good show for her. Didn't the kids have to come back soon and start school? he asked. But Dorothy wouldn't commit to anything. There was still a lot of fence-mending to be done, that was clear.

He and Robin Ford had driven all over the place, from towns in the Valley out to the ocean. It was early evening when they got back to Ford's place on North Havenhurst. Mitchum called his agent, Phil Berg, and discussed a script they had received. The Korda people in England wanted him to do the lead in a film of Joseph Conrad's *Outcast of the Islands*. It would mean working in London and on location in Southeast Asia. Mitchum told Berg he would be eager to read the script. Conrad had long been one of his favorite authors, and he had dreamed of visiting the Orient since he was a kid.

It was after seven when he and Ford drove up to Bob's house. Reva Frederick was waiting for him there. She reported the day's business. At his insistence she had canceled tomorrow's public relations appearance at City Hall. The studio had arranged for him to meet the mayor and speak to a group of young people about the dangers of juvenile delinquency. Tomorrow was National Youth Day. Bob had said to tell them he had laryngitis. Reva gave him a list of telephone messages. One was from Lila Leeds. He gave her a call. She told him about her new place and how she wanted him to see it. Lila could tell he had been drinking. Not much, but enough to make his voice fuzzy, she would remember. Bob said he would call her later, maybe drop by. Lila told him Vicki Evans was with her, and he said he would bring along Robin Ford. Lila said, "Come after ten o'clock."

Mitchum remembered telling her that he would but thinking that he would not, being very tired.

"Ford and I then went to the kitchen where we drank a fifth of Scotch while talking. My secretary reminded me to get something to eat and left for home."

*

At the house on Ridpath Drive, Lila told Vicki they were going to have a party. She phoned a pusher and asked him to bring up five sticks of marijuana. Later she had one of her funny premonitions and remembered asking herself how long it would take her to go into the bathroom and flush the tea down the toilet if a cop ever came to the door.

As the sun went down that evening, two figures moved out from the undergrowth and the shade trees around the house that clung to the hillside above Ridpath. They slipped around the tangled laurel and cactus and, like a team of professional peeping toms, moved into positions at the bedroom and living room windows. The windows were open, bright lights were on, and the two men could hear and see everything as clearly as if they had sneaked into a stage show. Or at least a burlesque house. The two blonde young ladies inside were getting ready for company. Lila Leeds wore a pair of white shorts and a bra top and an open corduroy tommy coat. The other one had on blue shorts and a loose top. Lila sat her friend down on a chair and stood behind her, putting up her hair. A lit stick of marijuana clung lightly to her cherry-red lips.

A couple of hours passed. It was getting close to twelve when the phone rang. Lila answered, speaking softly. Then she put down the phone and one of the men at the window heard her say, "It's the boys. They're at the bottom of the hill. They're lost. And they're loaded."

Bob Mitchum drove the big new Buick up Laurel Canyon. The lights of Sunset Boulevard faded behind the woods and the rocks. They rode along, slowing at each crossroad until they found the right one, taking a left and then winding round and continuing to climb as the streets narrowed and became almost vertical. Ford spotted the place. A small, frame bungalow, it was perched on a steep slope above an open two-car garage. The street was bathed in moonlight and silent but for the wafting sound of a Victrola playing Anita O'Day—"Hi Ho Trailus Boot Whip." An outside light went on, and Lila stood on the landing with her tommy coat hanging open and waited for them as they came up the rough stone staircase. Mitchum was a garish sight in a shiny brown-striped jacket and a red-and-black checked lumberjack shirt. Two frisky boxer puppies were at Lila's feet and jumped excitedly to greet the newcomers.

"Watch out, they're ferocious," Lila said, and they all laughed.

Mitchum moved inside, raising his hand to his brow. "Let's turn the lights down," he said, "they're hurting my eyes."

The lights were dimmed. The dogs ran around yipping noisily. They had been acting excited all night, Lila said. She put them in the enclosed porch in the back and shut the door. Mitchum said he thought there was someone at the front window. He went over to the window and looked out but saw nothing. He crossed the room and joined Robin Ford on the davenport. Bob took out a Philip Morris pack and threw it on the coffee table.

He said, "Let's get high."

Lila shook out the contents of the pack.

"You've got brown ones and white ones, too."

Lila lit a stick, then took it from her lips and passed it to Bob. Then she lit another one. Robin Ford fended for himself.

Vicki Evans leaned nearer. "Gee, what will it do to me," she joked. "And what happens if I get knocked out?"

Bob said, "Oh, daddy!"

But Vicki didn't take a stick, and Lila would later remember that Vicki hadn't smoked anything all evening.

The clock ticked past midnight. It was officially National Youth Day.

The two men skulking and spying at the windows moved swiftly to the back of the house, around a laundry line and garbage cans, and up to the porch. The screen door wasn't locked and they stepped inside, where the dogs were waiting for them. The boxers growled, but one of the men took some doggie treats out of his pocket. The puppies happily bit into them and were shoved outside.

When Lila heard something on the porch she got up to check, but Vicki moved past her, saying, "I'll take care of them."

When Vicki unlocked the kitchen door, the two men charged inside, the one in front grabbing the girl and using her as a shield.

Lila Leeds gasped.

Bob Mitchum, holding the stubby remnant of a joint, lurched from the couch and picked up a small table to throw at the intruders. In the same instant the men dropped Vicki Evans to the floor and aimed their revolvers at the actor's head.

"Police officers! Freeze!"

Mitchum froze. It took him several moments to comprehend that the flaring roach he still held between his fingers was burning a hole in his flesh.

CHAPTER SIX

Occupation:
Former Actor

Mitchum cursed softly and released the burning stub.

Robin Ford was sitting motionless, staring fixedly at the opposite wall, as if thinking he might go unnoticed. His only movement was to take the joint from his mouth and flick it under the couch. One of the policemen—Det. Sgt. Alva Barr—came up, retrieved it, then scooped up what Mitchum had dropped. He crumpled the tips and then placed them in the breast pocket of his jacket. Picking up the Philip Morris pack on the coffee table, he examined the contents.

He looked at Mitchum and said, "These are yours?"

Mitchum said, "No, they're not mine." But the words seemed to evaporate in the back of his throat.

Barr said, "Don't give me any business and we'll get along fine."

The other officer—Det. J. B. McKinnon—closed a pair of handcuffs on Robin Ford's wrists. Mitchum then offered up his own.

Barr stepped over to where Lila sat and took one partly burned cigarette out of her hand. It had red lipstick around the tip. He told her to empty her bathrobe pocket, and she took out something wrapped in a page of the *Herald Express*. The cop unwrapped it and found what appeared to be three more hand-rolled marijuana cigarettes and eight Benzedrine tablets.

He told them they were all under arrest and then picked up Lila's phone and called headquarters.

Vicki Evans said, "It's just like the movies."

*

In a matter of minutes the tiny bungalow was filled with lawmen, including Federal Narcotics Bureau investigator William Craig. Mitchum and Ford were frisked, photos were taken, evidence was secured. Policewoman Eleanor Whitney took the two ladies into the bathroom and searched them. Then the cops led the four accused miscreants downstairs and put them into the waiting police cars. The men were driven to the county jail, the women to the Lincoln Heights lockup. They were all booked on the same charge of narcotics possession, a felony with a penalty of up to six years in prison.

Reporters and photographers were already gathered outside both stations, alerted to the celebrity dope arrest. Ford and Mitchum entered past a gauntlet of flashbulbs and barked questions. One photographer snapped Bob with his features contorted; in the printed photo he was barely recognizable. The picture wrote its own caption: "A MAN IN THE GRIP OF DEMON DRUGS." Inside the station Mitchum and Ford were booked. Name, age, address, identifying marks. When the policeman asked Mitchum his occupation, he replied, wittily, "Former actor."

According to police, Mitchum had already made a lengthy and damning statement following his arrest by Detectives Barr and McKinnon. In the report, an oddly voluble and square-sounding Mitchum confessed, *"Yes, boys, I was smoking the marijuana cigaret when you came in. I guess it's all over now. I've been smoking marijuana for years. The last time I smoked was about a week ago. I knew I would get caught sooner or later. This is the bitter end of my career. I'm ruined."*

Amazingly, the arrest report on Lila Leeds contained a similar unprompted confession with a number of duplicated words and phrases, as if the two suspects had issued a joint statement. *"I have been smoking marijuana for two years. I don't smoke every day. I was smoking that small brown stick when you came in. . . . I'm glad it's over. I'm ruined."*

Police released Robin Ford's incriminating statement as well. *"Yes, I was smoking that cigaret. I haven't smoked marijuana for a long*

time. I really don't know who lit the cigaret for me. I was smoking it—
ain't that enough? This will ruin me."

Clearly a side effect of the dope—everyone spoke the same catch
phrases.

It was the middle of the night when a Howard Hughes flack got
word of the Mitchum arrest. He put a call through to his boss and
imparted the bad news. Hughes took it calmly—his anger was
reserved for Commies and intransigent females.

"Well, who do we pay to kill this thing?" Hughes asked.

In Hollywood everything from rape to hit-and-run homicides
could be—had been—hushed up if you knew the procedure.

But it was too late for that. The press already had the story. In a
few hours there would be headlines.

Howard said, "Let's get him out of jail, keep him from talking,
and for Pete sake will somebody call Jerry Giesler."

In the morning, as attorneys arrived to bail him out, Mitchum was
telling reporters a different story from the one the police had supplied. He denied confessing to anything. He had been out house
hunting and didn't even get a chance to join the party.

"I was *framed.*"

Anyone expecting to find a distraught, ruined man was in for a
surprise. Mitchum's demeanor was coolly sarcastic. "I'm sorry if my
new look doesn't appeal to you," he said, referring to his jailhouse
denim uniform. "It doesn't appeal to me either. I left the house last
night to get something to eat. I swung by Lila Leeds' place. I sat
down, then boom! What makes it worse is that I still haven't had any
dinner. As a matter of fact, I haven't even had my morning coffee."

Mitchum sat there with his bare chest sticking out of the denim
jacket, chatting and laughing with Ford, sitting next to him, as the
photographers snapped away. "Don't take my picture when my eyes
are shut," Mitchum said. "It makes me look like I've just been hit on
the head by a stick."

"Who's going to bail you out, Bob?" a reporter asked.

"Who knows! I've got two bosses—David O. Selznick and RKO.

Have you ever listened to Selznick or RKO when they're peeved? I think I'd just as soon stay in jail. Anyway, if Selznick calls I'll hang up on him."

Asked if he expected to be reconciled with his wife, Mitchum smiled wryly. "What, *now?*" he said. "I would like to hope so, but my wife is a very resolute woman."

Over at Lincoln Heights, Lila Leeds and Vicki Evans were also sparring with the press, and they, too, were seemingly undaunted by a night behind bars or the potential six-year prison sentence that loomed before them. Posing for the cameras, Vicki pulled up her skirt while covering her face. "How's this?" she said. Both girls dissolved in laughter. Lila complained about the poor job performance by her two boxers. "They must be police dogs in disguise," she cracked.

Someone arrived with a morning paper and the first account of the arrests. Lila read it aloud with enthusiasm, like it was a review of *Campus Honeymoon.*When she reached a mention of the blue bathrobe she'd been wearing, Leeds exclaimed, "Gad! They could at least have said I had my shorts on."

The four prisoners were released on a thousand dollars' bail each, pending a habeus corpus hearing on September 3.

Los Angeles woke up to the first wave of news stories.

Robert Mitchum Faces Marijuana Count with Lila Leeds, Two Others"
"Nabbed at Asserted 'Marijuana' Party"
"Bob Mitchum, 3 Others Jailed After Dope Raid"

The cops had spoon-fed the press Mitchum's alleged spoken confession. By the time he denied ever telling the police anything, the first reports were already in print. Rather than investigate the discrepency or question the LAPD's version of events, later editions would refer to Mitchum's "contradictory statements," continuing to validate the confession and perhaps to imply drug-addled confusion as well.

Later that morning the police held a press conference starring the arresting officers and a selection of federal narcotics investigators. In contrast to the unflappable Mitchum and Leeds, their demeanor was anything but cool.

"We're going to clean the dope and the narcotics users out of Hollywood!" screamed one of the narcs. "And we don't care *whom* we're going to have to arrest! This raid is only the beginning!"

"There is a lot of '*stuff*' being used in Hollywood. We have, besides Mitchum, a number of other important and prominent Hollywood screen personalities under surveillance. Not only actors and actresses, but others prominent in pictures."

Det. Sgt. Alva Barr revealed that Mitchum had been under police surveillance since the beginning of the year. "When sources reported to me that Mitchum was using marijuana I personally started investigating him. I followed him to various nightspots. I would tail him from home and follow him around all evening. We followed him to parties at several other movie stars' homes, then to late eating spots and then would wait until he went to bed. Last night we were investigating Lila Leeds when who should walk in but Mitchum."

The conference concluded on a note of intrigue and the promise of more excitement to come. "Many of the big shots—the stars and other top names—do not patronize small street or corner peddlers, for fear of a shakedown or other dangers. However, we have reason to believe there is an '*inside ring*' of perhaps no more than three persons, right inside the film industry, who are supplying a large number of narcotics users. Most prevalent use is of marijuana, but we know that other drugs are being used. Information is hard to get. But we get it.

"*Hollywood can let this serve as warning! We are out to get the 'inside ring'!*"

With Mitchum whisked into seclusion, the press sought comment from his employers. Columnists like Louella Parsons, with the clout to have their calls taken, found RKO execs—sitting on millions of dollars in unreleased Mitchum pictures—guardedly loyal. No one at the studio, they stated, believed Mitchum was an "addict." He had never given any signs of being doped and had turned in some very fine performances. David Selznick, typically voluble and opinionated even without any hard facts at his disposal, declared the boy was "sick" and should go into a sanitarium immediately to undergo treatment for his "shattered nerves."

Parsons, in a column printed the day after the arrest, mindful of the studio's investment, was conciliatory but stern and reflected a typical *Reefer Madness*–era knowledge of marijuana. "He could still be cured," she wrote, "providing he wanted to be. Barney Ross and other addicts have been successfully treated, and certainly this 31-year-old actor, who is at the peak of his fame, should realize it is up to him to get himself on his feet.

"Mitchum," she revealed, "was in a state of mental collapse following his release. He was ordered to bed and to sleep and not to talk."

Mitchum had left the jailhouse and disappeared. Reporters staked out the Oak Glen house, the RKO lot, and the Berg-Allenberg offices hoping to catch up with him, with no luck. Now it can be told: Howard Hughes asked his trusted publicist Perry Lieber to keep Mitchum under wraps, and Lieber took the actor to his own house. The publicity man's teenage son, Perry, Jr., came home to find Mitchum installed in the guest room. "He was just hanging out. Very friendly, a great guy. He didn't seem particularly nervous or upset or anything like that. He was just taking it one hour at a time. He ate dinner with the family. He played the piano, sang. He didn't act like he was worried about anything." Perry brought a couple of girlfriends over, impressing them greatly when he introduced his new housemate. "I got very popular with them," he recalled.

As Mitchum played the piano and flirted with the high school girls, the senior Lieber held a strategy meeting with attorney Jerry Giesler. Considered the most brilliant trial lawyer in California and renowned as the "attorney to the stars," Giesler's headline-making Hollywood cases included a Charlie Chaplin paternity suit and the first of the Errol Flynn rape trials. "Bob had nothing to do with getting Giesler," said Reva Frederick. "It was all Howard Hughes's doing." Lieber and Giesler went over what scant information they had so far and crafted an official RKO-Selznick joint statement.

"All the facts about the case are not yet known," it read. "We urgently request the press, the industry and the public to withhold its judgment until these facts are known.

"Both studios feel confident the American people will not permit Mr. Mitchum's prominence in the motion picture industry to deprive him of the rights and privileges of every American citizen to receive fair play."

Asserting his handling of the case, Giesler himself issued a similar statement, adding, "There are a number of unexplained facts and peculiar circumstances surrounding the raid in which Robert Mitchum was involved. His many friends have expressed their opinion that when all the facts are known that he will be cleared."

The only statement from Lila Leeds's camp was less optimistic. Her fair-weather agent, Louis Shurr, told reporters, "She had a promising career and was headed for success, if she had only behaved differently. It looks now as though she's blown her chances sky high."

The following day, September 2, with more details about the raid plus the police press conference, newspapers everywhere spread the story across the front pages, with banner headlines. The issue of the *Los Angeles Examiner* became a kind of Robert Mitchum Special Edition, with a front-page feature and no fewer than seven sidebar articles, including "'I'M RUINED,' SAYS MITCHUM AFTER MARIJUANA ARREST," "POLICE TELL HOW THEY PEEPED THROUGH WINDOW AND JAILED FOUR," "MITCHUM HOLDS HOBO INSTINCT: HAD VARIED JOBS BEFORE FILMS," and "MITCHUM 'SICK,' EXECUTIVES SAY." Articles reported that the actor's coworkers were stunned by the reports: "News of Mitchum's addiction to marijuana took the movie capital, and the nation, by complete surprise."

The papers reported an instant freeze in the Hollywood-area marijuana trade. "Insiders" told how the homemade cigarettes, "up to now relatively easily obtainable at a dollar apiece if one knew the contacts, couldn't be bought for any amount of money. The scare is on. Those that had it have ditched it, and those that use it are laying off."

Then, as if to calm these insiders' rattled nerves, it was announced that Capt. Lynn White, police narcotics detail chief, was out of town on a fishing trip and the narcotics division had decided to pause in their investigations until dope users, frightened by the Mitchum case, "were not so chary of their conduct."

"Perry Lieber had made the call to Dorothy," said Reva Frederick. "They had been separated and she was going to stay back East, as I understood it. Perry called, said, 'You must get out here right away.' They needed to show him back together with his family. And I think she realized that if his career went downhill her prospects went downhill. So she came. But I think she headed back with very little knowledge of what the hell sort of commotion was going on."

Dorothy Mitchum and the boys and a relative who had offered to help with the driving headed west from Delaware. The car barely stopped until they reached Las Vegas, Nevada, where it was arranged for Dorothy to rendezvous with RKO representatives. Alerted reporters were waiting for her, describing Mrs. M. as "nervous and distraught." They stayed for an afternoon and evening at the El Rancho Hotel, then departed in the middle of the night, crossing the desert to Los Angeles, reaching the Oak Glen house just after 10 A.M. The crowd that had been gathering since dawn closed in on the arriving sedan. Dorothy cried, "Please, I'm awfully tired," and herded the children to the front door. Bob stepped into the doorway, the family embraced, then disappeared inside.

Reva Frederick arrived and left an hour later with Jim and Chris. "They were very worried about the effect on the kids and thought it best to get them far away from there," Reva recalled. "It was such a madhouse. So I got them and took them to my mother's house. And she took them out to Palm Springs for a week."

At one in the afternoon the RKO reps began admitting photographers and reporters, four or six at a time, all that could fit into the living room of the modest home. Bob and Dorothy—the wife wearing a "ballerina gown" and looking as if she had been crying, Bob dressed up as if for church—sat on the sofa, clasping arms, rubbing their cheeks together and kissing.

Dorothy wished to speak only via a typewritten statement handed out by a man from the studio:

> Everybody ought to be able to see that Bob is a sick man. Otherwise he couldn't be mixed up in a situation like this.
>
> Our differences were the same kind all married couples get into. We have made them up. I love my husband and am back home to stay with him.
>
> I am indignant that not only Bob but our whole family should have to suffer simply because he is a motion picture star, because otherwise I don't think that all this fuss would be made.
>
> I'm sorry that I can't answer the newspaper people's questions today. I have driven all day and all night to my sick husband as fast as I could and have had no sleep at all, so I hope they will understand this and forgive me.
>
> I have only one favor to ask and that is that nobody bothers our children. They're very young and they love their father and they don't understand what it's all about.

"Anything you want to add?" Bob was asked.

"Just 30—at the end," he said.

"Is this a reconciliation—or were you ever separated?"

"Reconciliation is a hard word. Reunion is better."

"How do you feel about it?"

"I'm very happy about my wife's attitude."

"Was your marriage ever in jeopardy?"

"Every time I went to the studio," Mitchum said, smiling.

"And every time he didn't shave," said Dorothy.

"What are your immediate plans?"

"Lunch," he said.

It was during this period of anxiety and uncertainty that Robert's mother and sister, Julie (and soon after, his half-sister, Carol), began their involvement with a spiritual order that was to become a part of their lives forever after. Two actor friends of the family had come to offer support and, along the way, preach the benefits of their faith. They were Baha'is, members of the modern-era religion begun in Iran—dismissed as a mystical sect by some majority religions—that stressed principles of tolerance and universal brotherhood. "They invited Mother to a Baha'i 'Fireside,'" said Julie. "I wouldn't go. I wanted no part of *religion!* We found out that Mother had read all about the Baha'i long ago in a Charleston newspaper after a visit by the son of Baha Allah. And she came to realize that what she had read had stayed with her and that she had been a Baha'i in essence for decades. At first I was reluctant to open myself to what she had found. I was probably one of the nastiest agnostics that anyone could ever be. But I finally got the picture." Julie would speak to Robert about the faith, found him quite sympathetic—even an ad hoc adherent—to many of its philosophical and spiritual tenets, but Robert was sceptical—that was the nice way to describe it—regarding any organized religion, and not even in this time of crisis could he be persuaded to give up his status as a registered "independent."

Attorney Jerry Giesler declined the district attorney's invitation for Mitchum to appear before a grand jury, declaring he would need more time to investigate "a chain of odd coincidences, if coincidences they were." Attorneys for Leeds and the others followed suit. Proceeding without the participation of the accused, prosecutors offered grand jurors just two witnesses, Det. Sgt. Alva Barr and police chemist Jay Allen. Barr recounted his version of the bust, while Allen displayed the evidence. From three manila envelopes he removed nineteen cigarettes and six "roaches"—"underworld parlance for partly smoked marijuana cigarettes"—all containing "the flowering leaves of cannabis sativa." Allen displayed several of the joints, on which the name "Bob Mitchum" was now printed. "It was not a very good grade of marijuana," the chemist concluded smugly. "I would call it a medium mixture."

Everybody was a critic.

The proceedings lasted two hours. Following the lab man's testimony, the jurors were closeted with narcotics chief Captain White, freshly returned and rested from his fishing getaway. In an "off-the-record" session, White explained to them the extent of drug use in Los Angeles and what was being done "to rid the county of its terrors." Jurors then "pledged their support and assistance in continued investigation of the dope traffic" and minutes later returned indictments on two counts, charging Mitchum and the others with possession of marijuana and conspiracy to possess, violations of the State Narcotics Act. Conviction on the first count carried a penalty of from ninety days to six years in prison, depending on circumstances, with no probation. Conviction on the conspiracy count carried the same penalty but with the possibility of probation.

The following day, Mitchum and the three others surrendered themselves to the court of Superior Judge Thomas Ambrose. The LA *Daily News* reported: "Mitchum, his handsome face haggard with strain and worry, shouldered his way through a mob of applauding fans. Accompanied by the man and two women who were caught with him in an alleged Hollywood marijuana party, Mitchum drew from the throng of admirers, young and old alike, a warming vote of confidence.

"The eighth floor of the Hall of Justice was jammed. The two blonde women accused with Mitchum arrived first. And while actress Lila Leeds took the whole thing in her stride,"—looking ultra-glamorous in black high heels, royal blue suit, silver fox scarf and shimmering neon-red lip gloss—"equally blonde Vicki Evans quailed before the eyes of the multitude. Vicki seized her attorney, Grant Cooper, around the neck as flashlights blazed and eager people surged forward with pens extended for autographs. Mitchum, looking drawn and even thin from the terrific ordeal, willingly scribbled his signature for his beseeching fans, while his attorney, the famous Jerry Giesler, puffed a panatella and beamed approval of what he called the 'temper of the mass mind.'"

Arraignment was set for September 21.

On the twenty-first Mitchum and his three playmates returned to the courtroom. This time Lila and Vicki offered the judge a more demure vision of femininity. "Both blond women," wrote one investigative journalist, "have muted their chemically gold hair to lesser shades of brilliance." Evans dressed in black and Leeds in a tailored, cream-colored Roz Russell–style suit that tried hard—but failed miserably—to conceal her curvacious figure. The proceedings were cut-and-dried. Judge Ambrose ordered the quartet's return on the thirtieth, at which time he would hear their pleas of guilt or innocence.

Rumpled, balding, charismatic friend to the press Jerry Giesler had kept a relatively low profile in these first weeks. Columnists anxious to convey some of Giesler's legendarily colorful courtroom behavior were not rewarded until the September 30 appearance before the judge, when the attorney floridly demanded that all charges be dropped as unconstitutional due to the fact that the indictment "was not returned in clear English." The section charging Mitchum and the others with "possession and conspiracy to possess flowering tops and leaves of India hemp (*Cannabis Sativa*)," said Giesler, "might as well have been written in Japanese or hieroglyphics!" He quoted state law to the effect that all indictments must be drawn in pure and simple English so that defendants might clearly understand the accusation. Giesler said that "hemp" to his knowledge was used to make rope, and he comically stumbled over the pronunciation of the word *cannabis,* provoking laughter from the onlookers. He then left them in stitches by declaring that the only Latin he knew was Xavier Cugat.

Judge Ambrose overruled the demure. The defendants pled not guilty, and Ambrose designated Clement D. Nye as trial judge, trial date to be determined.

On October 2 Jerry Giesler was returning home to Beverly Hills when his car went out of control and climbed halfway up a palm tree. Several ribs broken, he spent the rest of the week in a hospital and was not expected to be on his feet for the better part of the month.

From Judge Nye came word that the trial would begin on November 21.

In the days and weeks following the arrests at the Ridpath party, the Mitchum case was kept alive by journalists, pundits, and moral watchdogs across the country. "MITCHUM'S SINS," "WHOSE RESPONSIBILITY?" "MITCHUM CASE TOUGH BLOW TO HOLLYWOOD," "FLAY STUDIOS FOR CONDONING MORAL LAXITY THAT LED TO DOPE SCANDAL," cried the headlines to these various screeds and editorial thumb suckers.

From the Saint Louis *Globe-Democrat*:

"Misunderstood" Hollywood has let the lid off the garbage can again. Now we have a young swoon actor, the idol of teen-agers, caught with two actresses and a real estate man indulging in a reefer-smoking fest known to the trade as "kicking the gong around." Moreoover, he makes no bones about admitting a long addiction to the narcotic weed and seems remorseful only because the exposure may write finis to his career. Not a word, mind you, about the thousands of impressionable young fans who think he is "simply out of this world."

Like the United States presidency, part of the cost of some occupations is forfeiture of the usual individual rights of privacy. Hollywood has long known this, yet it refuses to accept the responsibility. Will the admittedly numerous upright, hard-working members of the film profession begin to police their own ranks? Or will they wait until some monstrous stench over-whelms them all?

Harold Heffernon in the Indianapolis *Star*:

It has been common gossip for months that a dope scandal was hovering dangerously over the film colony. Luncheon crowds discussed it freely wherever film folks and newspaper cor-respondents gather.

What will Hollywood do now, officially, to clean its house and try to win back some of the public confidence it has destroyed in the disgraceful mess of the past few weeks?

Right now Hollywood has the biggest problem of all on its hands. The public never did—*never will*—laugh off a dope scandal involving a favorite screen performer.

Tough-guy syndicated columnist Robert Ruark had a more jaded perspective:

I don't quite savvy all this sudden bleating over the plight of Robert Mitchum, a droopy-eyed young movie actor who seems to have been caught by the cops with a couple of blondes. For one thing, it is not an unusual offense in Hollywood. Dragging the weed ranks roughly in the film colony with taking Benzedrine as a substitute for sleep and sobriety. Some medics think it less harmful to the user than the habitual dosage of sleeping potion, or goofballs, which by now are as static a Hollywood prop as the yellow convertible. . . .

I don't believe Mr. Mitchum's guilt or innocence should affect his career one way or the other. So many of Hollywood's idols of the young have persisted despite the company they kept, be it gangsters, dope-dealers, murderers, or other folks' wives, that a little thing like a drag on a muggle shouldn't bother a man who has charm for the kiddies.

Hedda Hopper, trying to distract the ad hominem attacks on her beloved movie industry, lashed out at others:

It is so axiomatic that any lurid story with a Hollywood background is sure-fire for black scareheads, that there's even a wild rumor behind the scenes here that the police decided to pull this caper with Mitchum in order to draw the heat off the department because of their inability to deliver any kind of a case on last week's gangster killing of one of Mickey Cohen's hoodlums.

Her readers, too, bore some of the blame for the present mess:

> The public makes them gods and goddesses. Yet the public can never understand when they turn out to be mere human beings. So, in this case of Bob Mitchum, let his trial be that of any individual citizen, as it would be for you or me or somebody we know who lives down the street. He—not Hollywood—is on trial.

Howard Hughes, RKO, and David Selznick had observed the developments in the Mitchum prosecution like ambivalent caregivers attending an infectious patient. To look after the boy and risk catching something or throw a sheet on him and dump him in an alleyway—that was the question. Any overt attempt to help the actor or influence the case became ammunition for the DA's office and the Hollywood- and Hughes-bashers who floated rumors that the moguls were "pulling political strings" to subvert the law and let Mitchum get away with it. Hughes and Selznick both issued official "hands-off" statements regarding the actor's defense.

The public response to the scandal was mixed. The studio received hundreds of letters decrying Mitchum, many from teachers, parents, and clerics bemoaning the actor's setting a terrible example for the kids. A far larger group, however, appeared to be titillated by the hunky actor's rowdy behavior. Trailers for *Rachel and the Stranger* reportedly elicited applause and hoots of approval from audiences, and when the film went into general release in October there were lines around the block. No matter what Loretta Young's and William Holden's agents were telling them, RKO understood that Mitchum was drawing those crowds. As far as the ticket-buying segment of the public was concerned, Bob's reefer rap was no more than they expected from the Hollywood "bad boy" and only served to make him more alluring on the big screen.

*

Early in November, with Jerry Giesler supposedly still on the mend from his auto accident, Mitchum, Ford, Leeds (Vicki Evans had now disappeared to somewhere "back East"), and attorneys Norman Tyre and Grant Cooper appeared before Judge Clemence Nye to request a continuance. The judge agreed to a new trial date of January 10.

Blood on the Moon opened in November and, like *Rachel and the Stranger*, was a solid performer at the box office. The returns increased David Selznick's belated professional interest in the star. He lobbied for Mitchum to play the role of criminal mastermind Harry Lime in *The Third Man*, but coproducer Alexander Korda and director Carol Reed preferred Orson Welles.

With the threat of Bob's imprisonment looming and the whole humiliating scandal never far from anyone's mind, the Mitchum family's Christmas of 1948 was far from joyous. As Dorothy had feared, the kids would not escape the consequences of so much lurid publicity. One afternoon Josh came home from school crying, taunted by classmates: "Is your old man out of jail yet?"

Robert was a big boy, and he at least could handle the occasional wisecracks he ran into in public. As he was coming out of a restaurant one evening, two cops sitting in a squad car called him over, big grins on their mugs. *"Hey, Bob, we're keeping Lawrence Tierney's cell warm for ya."* Mitchum gave them a friendly wave and thought, You want to suck *what?* More dangerous were the characters—car parkers, delivery boys—who winked or made the OK sign and offered to share a joint or put a little present in his pocket. He was sure that the city had police spies watching his every move. Now and then he'd see what he thought was a stakeout car or some flatfoot studying him over the top of a newspaper. What he didn't suspect at the time was that Howard Hughes also had men tailing and bugging him. He tried to leave home as seldom as possible.

On January 6, 1949, an advertisement appeared in the *Canyon Crier*, a community newspaper. The ad, taken out by Miss Nanette Bordeaux, actress and owner of the house at 8443 Ridpath Drive, announced the sale of the remaining furnishings and bric-a-brac used in the recent notorious reefer party. The ad read in part: "Charming sofa and arm chair. New slipcovers hide cigaret burns. Robert Mitchum sat here. $15."

*

Jerry Giesler, on his bed of pain, devised a bold, unexpected, and risky strategy. Having urged Mitchum to plead not guilty to the charges, the attorney had initially expected to battle for victory in the courtroom. His investigation had shown evidence of the frame-up Mitchum declared the morning after his arrest. The police stake-out had ignored the hours and days of earlier drug use in the Ridpath house only to start their raid within minutes of Mitchum's arrival. Giesler had been given off-the-record information from at least one journalist that there had been a tip-off about the arrest of a "big star" hours before it happened. A good case could be made from the telephone calls Mitchum received and other calls made by Leeds and Ford on August 31 that Robert had been deliberately lured to the house that night. Was Lila Leeds involved in the setup? Bob was convinced that it was his malevolent ex-business manager, Paul Behrmann, who had put the cops onto him, and Giesler found out that Behrmann had once been Lila's agent. Hollywood was a small, incestuous town, but that was curiously coincidental. Still, after several decades as an attorney, Giesler had great respect for coincidence. Leeds was a dizzy dame and a magnet for trouble, but would she have deliberately engineered the potential destruction of her own career prospects? Lila, for her part, also suspected a setup. Wasn't it odd how Vicki Evans had deliberately refrained from touching the stuff that night? How she had been the one to go back to the porch and unlock the door for the police? And Vicki— Florence they called her in court, whatever her name was—had now disappeared. And then there was Robin Ford, Mitchum's direct connection to Lila Leeds. Bob's double and pal Tim Wallace would remain forever convinced that *Ford* was the link to the cops, that he had an earlier charge hanging over him—dealing, Wallace figured—and had turned stool pigeon. Reva Frederick voted for Ford, too

("Sleazy . . . a user . . . if there was a buck or a deal to be made he was there"). There were other theories making the rounds. Julie Mitchum, gleaning inside info from her own network of showbiz pals, held to a more elaborate conspiracy theory. Fifty years later she hadn't changed her mind: "Bob had told me and had told them at the studio he wanted to break his contract. He was sick of them telling him what to do, sick of their trash scripts. He told me he was going away to the Bayou country and just write. That was all he wanted to do. The studio, of course, could not let someone walk away like that. So they set him up for the marijuana thing. It was the same with Bob's business manager. They didn't want Bob protected, so they had to get his personal manager out of the way. That guy ended up doing five years in the penitentiary. They said he had taken everybody's money and he hadn't taken a nickel from anyone. He was a lovely person and he adored Bob. Two radio announcers who testified against him whispered to me that he hadn't really taken anything from them."

It was like one of those Charlie Chan mysteries, Giesler thought. Everybody in the room was a suspect. The attorney didn't know what to make of Mitchum, an intelligent man, a great success in his field, idol of millions. He could be sitting on a yacht with liveried retainers feeding him lobster and champagne, but he preferred the company of lowlifes and police informers. Giesler had gotten to know many movie stars in his career and they never ceased to amuse him, although right now, with his ribcage broken and bandaged, it hurt to laugh.

His enthusiasm for a courtroom battle began to dissolve when he learned of some potential ammunition the prosecution team had been gathering, evidence of Mitchum's uninhibited lifestyle. The DA's office had a lot of dirt on the boy. Giesler realized he could very possibly win a not guilty verdict and yet prosecution evidence and witnesses might still damage Mitchum "beyond hope of rehabilitation." Reva Frederick remembered a conversation with Giesler. "He said to me, 'The reason I'm so good is that I always prepare the opposition's case first. I don't even think about what I'm going to do until I know what the other side is planning.'" RKO execs agreed that although the actor's current notoriety had not so far lessened his popularity—quite the opposite—a long trial filled with scandalous revelations making headlines every day would be likely finally to turn the public against him and destroy his movie stardom for good. Giesler and the studio also agreed—possibly without any input from Mitchum—that if the actor were to get off scot-free it might look like "special justice" for a celebrity and cause a renewed backlash against the movie industry.

Giesler's plan: "I proposed simply to ask the court to decide his innocence or guilt on the conspiracy-to-possess-marijuana count on the basis only of the transcript of the testimony before the grand jury."

In essence, Mitchum's attorney had decided to offer no defense and throw him on the mercy of the court.

Hughes did not want to lose Robert Mitchum's services if he could help it. He was a big Robert Mitchum fan. Since taking over RKO, Hughes had privately fixated on Mitchum as a kind of fantasy alter ego. He spent many a predawn hour in his personal screening room watching the actor's pictures, particularly *Out of the Past*, studying the clinches of Bob and ex-girlfriend Jane Greer with feverish interest. Hughes's position in life would seem to have placed him beyond envy or hero worship; but to the scrawny, hard-of-hearing, whiny-voiced, and paranoid Texan who felt compelled to offer money, fame, wedding rings, or threats to desired females, Mitchum's brawn, bourbon voice, imperturbable cool, and natural allure to women represented his ideal masculine image. (Hughes biographer Charles Higham posited the millionaire as an active bisexual; for what it's worth, both Mitchum and Hughes's second-favorite male star, Victor Mature, had certain physical characteristics in common with Howard's favorite female type—dark eyes, thick hair, and a big chest.)

Regardless of Hughes's personal enthusiasm, from a business point of view Mitchum was currently RKO's most valuable asset. The scandal publicity had made him more famous than ever. Aware of Jerry Giesler's intended trial tactic, Hughes and his new production head, Sid Rogell, now came up with a scheme they hoped—if their star was found guilty—might influence the judge to offer probation or—if it came to a jail term—allow them to have another Mitchum picture to exhibit while he was otherwise engaged. They determined to get a film into production immediately. With only a matter of days to prepare something, various remakes were considered, but Hughes finally settled on a pulp story by Richard Wormser ("The Road to Carmichael's") that had once been intended for George Raft. A script was already partially written, and *Out of the Past* scribe Dan Mainwaring was assigned to finish it in record time. It was a simple cops 'n' robbers chase set in rural Mexico. For the female lead the studio quickly negotiated to borrow Lizabeth Scott from Hal Wallis. Hughes personally picked a little-known outsider to direct, Don Siegel. A Warner Bros. staffer for fourteen years, doing montage and second-unit work before directing two features, Siegel had then been fired and found himself unemployed for months, reluctantly returning to second-unit jobs. Years ago he had turned down Howard Hughes's request that he direct retakes on the Faith Domergue debacle *Vendetta* (it had already exhausted the talents of Preston Sturges and Max Ophuls), declaring the thing was unfixable. Hughes had appreciated his honesty and now offered him the Mitchum project. It was an assignment with built-in aggravation, Siegel thought—no story, little script, a crazy schedule, and a star who might be headed for prison—but he was grateful to Hughes for a chance to restart his stalled career. Howard himself came up with the title for the picture—*The Big Steal*.

January 10. Mitchum, Leeds, and Ford filed into Judge Nye's courtroom, looking as grimly resigned as if they had already heard a guilty verdict. In a sense they had. They had all agreed to follow Jerry Giesler's plan of action—inaction better described it—which allowed for an almost certain criminal conviction. Vicki Evans did not appear for her court date. She had been tracked to New York City where her attorney informed the DA's office that she was without funds to return to Los Angeles but would report to them as soon as possible.

Det. Sgt. A. M. Barr, the man who had led the raid on Ridpath,

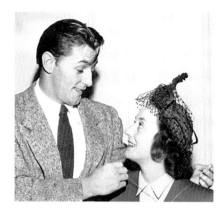

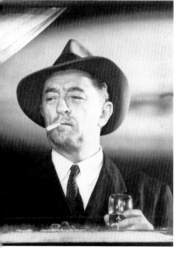

Robert Mitchum in *Farewell, My Lovely*
(1975).
Copyright © 1975, E. K. Corporation/Courtesy
Museum of Modern Art

William Boyd (as Hopalong Cassidy) and
Robert Mitchum (as a badman) in *Hoppy
Serves a Writ* (1943).
Courtesy Museum of Modern Art

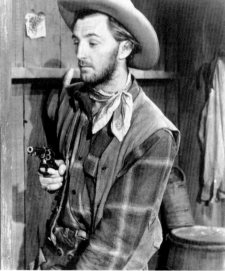

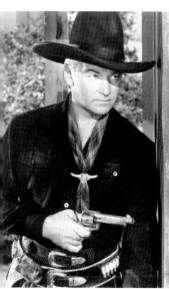

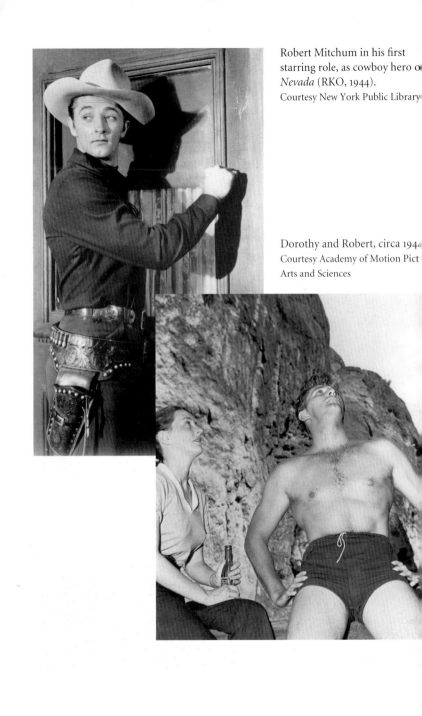

Robert Mitchum in his first
starring role, as cowboy hero of
Nevada (RKO, 1944).
Courtesy New York Public Library

Dorothy and Robert, circa 194
Courtesy Academy of Motion Pict
Arts and Sciences

olicity portrait, circa 1944.
urtesy New York Public Library.

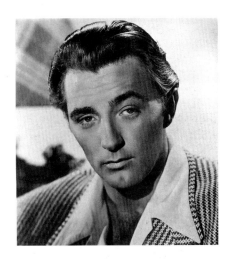

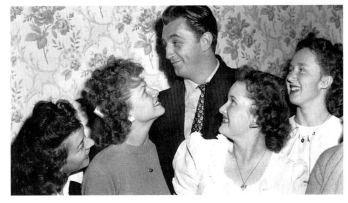

bert Mitchum and newly organized
1 club, the Mitchum Droolettes,
46.
urtesy AP/Wide World Photos

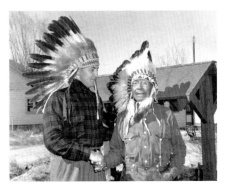

ducted into the Shoshone Tribe,
itchum gives Chief Owanahea the
cret handshake.
urtesy AP/Wide World Photos

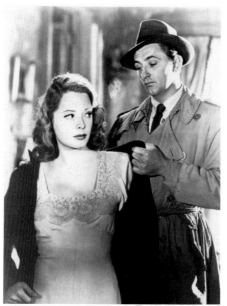

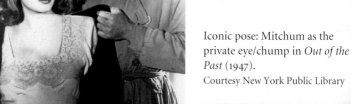

Jane Greer and Robert Mitchum in *Out of the Past* (1947).
Courtesy Museum of Modern Art

Iconic pose: Mitchum as the private eye/chump in *Out of the Past* (1947).
Courtesy New York Public Library

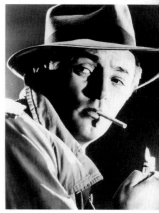

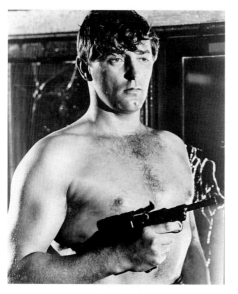

Mitchum in the frenetic climax to *His Kind of Woman* (RKO, 1951).
Courtesy Cinedoc

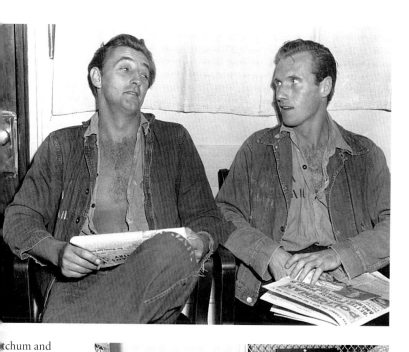

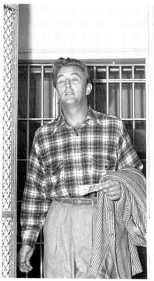
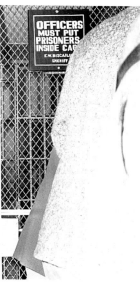

...tchum and
...bin Ford in
...ice custody,
...rdrobe by
...PD.

...urtesy AP/Wide
...rld Photos

..."ficers Must Put
...soners Inside
...ge": released on
..., September 1,
...8.

...rtesy AP/Wide
...ld Photos

Mitchum behind bars for marijuana possession. Note fine-grained cordovans.
Courtesy AP/Wide World Photos

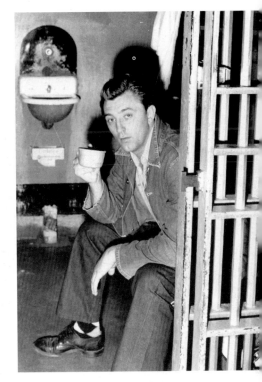

Courtroom hearing: Lila Leeds, attorney Grant Cooper, Vicki Evans, attorney Jerry Giesler, Robert Mitchum.
Courtesy AP/Wide World Photos

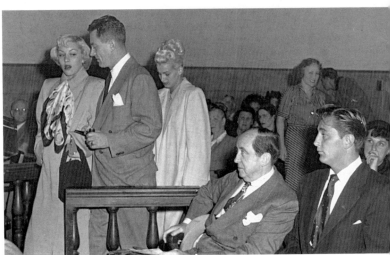

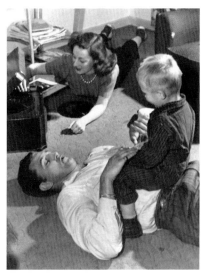

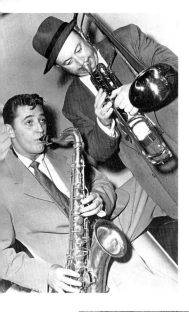

Mitchum learned to play the saxophone
during a brief term in high school.
Robert Mitchum and tiki girl, circa 1950.

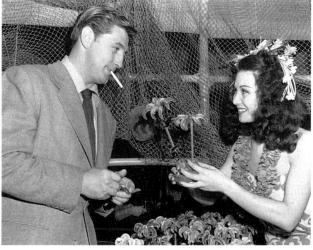

Advertisement for *Where Danger Lives* (1950) starring Robert Mitchum and Howard Hughes protégée Faith Domergue.
Courtesy Cinedoc

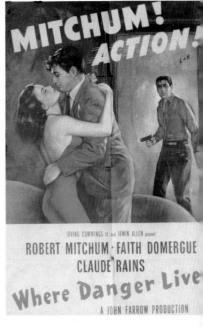

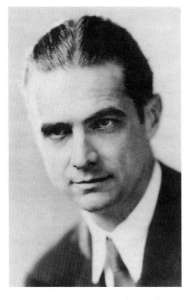

Mitchum's boss at RKO: Howard Hughes.
Courtesy Houston Public Library

Advertisement for *His Kind of Woman* (1951), directed by John Farrow (and Richard Fleischer). The quirky film noir was a pet project of RKO boss Howard Hughes and remained in and out of production for more than a year.

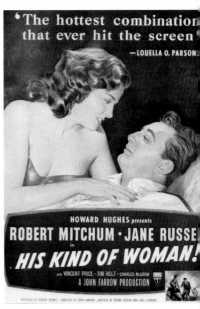

approached Mitchum in the courtroom and handed him a thick packet of letters, most of them already opened. They had been addressed to the actor care of the police station, Barr said tonelessly. It was fan mail wishing him good luck.

The trial began. The defense attorneys spoke. On the charge of conspiracy to possess marijuana, their clients would offer no defense and agreed to waive a jury trial and have their cases decided upon a reading of the testimony by the arresting officers given before the county grand jury. As Giesler had prearranged, the other charge, of possession, was held in abeyance.

Mitchum sat calmly for the sixty minutes it took Judge Nye to return with a guilty verdict for each of the three defendants. Nye set a court date of February 9 for probation hearing and sentencing.

In the hallway reporters rushed at the departing criminals. Asked about the unexpected "defense," Giesler said, "The evidence was in the transcript. Mitchum wouldn't perjure himself. He would have had to tell the truth." Giesler had "thrown in the towel," he said. When asked, Ford's attorney, Vernon Brumbaugh, echoed by Lila's Grant Cooper, said he believed probation was definitely possible in a case like this one.

Prosecutors held their own brief meeting with the press. Deputy DA Adolph Alexander was asked if he expected Mitchum and friends to do jail time. "Mitchum," he said, "will be treated no better or no worse than any other persons found guilty of narcotics charges." He then informed them that if Mitchum received probation it would be the first time in local history that a narcotics user got off that easy. "Of course," he said, "it's up to the judge whether he gets probation."

As Mitchum and Leeds exited the courtroom, they were served with a summons. The pair were being sued by one Nanette Bordeaux, "actress," for damages done to her house at 8443 Ridpath Drive. Miss Bordeaux alleged that the two, described as trespassers, had carelessly and negligently burned her furniture and walls with cigarettes and, further, had caused her property to be unfairly publicized as a "shack" and a "marijuana den," when in reality, said the suit, "it was an attractive hillside cottage."

Prepared at lightning speed, *The Big Steal* was ready to begin shoot-ing by the day of the trial. Then came the guilty verdict. Hal Wallis decided it was just too risky putting his valuable property together with a freshly convicted felon and abruptly withdrew Liz Scott from the picture. With the clock ticking, several other stars were contact-ed, all of them unavailable or reluctant to take the job. Hughes had deemed a shoot-'em-up quickie unworthy of his own carefully nur-tured discovery, star of *The Outlaw,* Jane Russell, whose recent appearance in Paramount's *The Paleface* had legitimized her career; but now he changed his mind. Hedda Hopper, in her January 19 column, announced the Russell-Mitchum teaming for *The Big Steal* and predicted "a box office bombshell." Then Hughes changed his mind again. It was possible that Hal Wallis knew something after all, Howard thought. If there was a backlash against Mitchum, he didn't want to taint a second valuable property.

Rogell and producer Jack Gross warned the dithering Hughes that Mitchum's sentencing was ticking closer. At last, with a combi-nation of practicality and perverseness, Hughes picked the girl for the part. She was one of the studio's own contract players, a woman whose talent and beauty he greatly admired but whose ingratitude had turned him against her. Since taking control at RKO he had been determined to wreck her career. She was the perfect actress for this risky project. What did she have to lose?

"After *Out of the Past* I felt I was finally getting somewhere," said Jane Greer. "I had gotten a chance to show what I could do, I thought the studio was behind me, I had a contract for years to come, I was set. Then came the news that Howard had bought the place. A few days after he took over, he sent for me."

It was years since they had last seen each other, and Greer had been happily married to businessman and producer Edward Lasker for most of that time. She greeted Hughes as an old but distant friend.

"I'm so excited for you, Howard," she said. "It's a wonderful stu-dio. I think you'll love it."

Hughes, acting not like a friend or employer but like a just-spurned lover, wished only to discuss her private life.

"You don't want to stay married," he told her. "You aren't happy."

"Yes I am, Howard, I'm very happy," Greer said.

"No. Deep down you're not satisfied."

"Yes . . . I am."

They argued some more along these lines, to no purpose. Then Hughes said, "I've decided that you will not be appearing in any more pictures, Bettejane. You will remain under contract to me and continue to be paid every week. But as long as I own the studio you will never work again. What do you think of that?"

"It means the end of me as a movie star."

"Yes, I guess it does."

"Well then," said Greer impassively, "I'll just have to stick with being a wife and having babies."

Hughes's tiny black eyes glared furiously. It looked like a scene from *Out of the Past*, with Hughes in the Kirk Douglas role, the powerful man undone by his unpredictable Circe. Jane Greer smiled, said good-bye, and went home.

"He kept his word. I hadn't worked in ages. Then Sid Rogell, who was running the studio, came by my house. He said, 'Whatever you do, don't let Howard know that I came here, you know how he is; but he is going to call you. He wants you to do a picture with Bob Mitchum.' I said, 'He wants me to do a picture with Bob?' Sid said, 'Yes, yes, he doesn't have anybody else. Wait for his call. And remember . . . don't say that I was here. *You never saw me!*'"

Moments later the phone rang.

"Bettejane!"

"Yes. Is that you, Howard?"

Sid Rogell, dignified Dore Schary's successor, crouched behind a big chair.

"How would you like to do this picture with Mitchum—*The Big Steal?*"

"I'd like to very much, Howard. I love Mitchum, and I want

him to know how much I'm pulling for him. I know how unhappy he is."

Hughes said, "You're going to have to go into Liz Scott's clothes, because we don't have time to wardrobe you."

"Well, that's all right, Howard. I'm about her size."

"You start on Tuesday."

"OK. I'll be there."

"Oh, there's something else."

"Yes, Howard?"

"You're knocked up."

"What?"

"The rabbit died."

Greer had gone to the doctor a few days before for a pregnancy test and was still waiting for the results. "Howard found out I was pregnant before I did. He broke the news to me. He had spies everywhere."

As part of his appeal for probation from the superior court, Mitchum was required to submit a written autobiographical statement that would include an account of his crime and, presumably, indications of remorse and rehabilitation. It was a revealing and detailed manuscript and, from the rich vocabulary and self-conscious locutions, clearly written by the man himself. Indeed, Mitchum seems to have approached it as something of a showcase for his neglected literary skills. While the typical plea from a felon read like a passage out of *The Postman Always Rings Twice*, Mitchum's appeared to be in thrall to a bad Victorian doorstopper.

"Publication of infantile verse and prose," wrote the actor, "which I composed to delight my mother was climaxed by featured interviews and photographs, which small spotlight on our material impoverishment inspired in me an introspection ever at odds with my desire for expression."

And later: "The rumor spread that . . . I was associating with people who indulged in the use of marijuana. This last gossip brought a swelling stream of acquaintances who appeared to accept me as one of their number, although their curious jargon was foreign to me, and their pressing invitations hinted at a social pat-tern of some mystery. Although progressing famously in my pro-fesssion, I was constantly obsessed with the phantom of failure, and in the next two years I several times answered entreaty by sharing a cigaret with one or more of these sycophants.

"The only effect that I ever noticed from smoking marijuana was a sort of mild sedative," he continued, "a release of tension. . . . It never made me boisterous or quarrelsome. If anything it calmed me down and reduced my activity." Mitchum asserted that he had first smoked the weed in Ohio in 1936 and then not again until 1947 and unequivocally declared, "My attitude with respect to the future use of marijuana is that I will not use marijuana at any time whatsoever."

Concluding the document with a self-pitying flourish, Mitchum told of his belief that he had already, before and after his conviction, been punished far more than the law itself had envisaged for a first offense. "Time in jail," he wrote, "would add nothing to the subjec-tive feeling I already have about what I have done."

Robin Ford's probation hearing was scheduled for January 27. On the night of February 26, Ford and a man described only as "a well-known musician" were driving away from a Sunset Strip nightclub when a pair of narcotics officers pulled them over. The cops claimed they discovered a stick of marijuana in Ford's hip pocket, and he was arrested. A reporter found him nervous and pale-faced, sitting alone in the narcotics squad headquarters at City Hall. Mitchum's pal said, "Guess I'm just a bad-luck charm for everybody."

*

On the last day of January, Robert Mitchum showed up at the office of attorney Leonard Wilson to answer the damage claim of actress Nanette Bordeaux. The LA *Mirror* was there to give the play-by-play:

> "If the kid's looking for a screen job, I hope this will get it for her. A publicity stunt? Could be?" shrugged the bobby soxers' pride. "What do you think?"

As casual as though he were shoving a movie villain over a cliff, Mitchum and his civil attorney Martin Gang appeared for filing of the deposition this morning. The gist of his statement was that (1) he had only been in Miss Bordeaux's house once and thus couldn't have damaged her furniture and (2) he not only couldn't have but didn't.

Having thus deposed, Mitchum made one of his characteristic slump-shouldered exits, to the tune of Gang's stern warning to the press—"Absolutely no pictures with cigarets!"

Lila Leeds was nearly twenty-one years old now and she knew she was never going to be the new Lana Turner. For a while after the arrest it had seemed almost fun to get the attention, to see her face in the paper, to have people on the street asking for an autograph, even if there was a shifty look or a raised eyebrow attached to the request. As the months passed, however, it became harder to see any good in it. She wished she was like Bob, with powerful people to look after her, to give the good word to the columnists, keep her name from being buried in the dirt. Lila knew she was washed up in Hollywood. After the guilty verdict she was depressed, scared of going to jail. "I cracked," Lila said. One night a few days before her sentencing, she met up with a friend from the clubs who promised to give her a new kick, help her forget her troubles. The friend took her to a place in Santa Monica. Five of them came to the party, plus the host, a skinny little man they called "the chef." They all sat in a circle on the floor while the skinny man laid out what looked like a random collection of trash, a cough medicine bottle, a glass straw, steel wire, a can of petroleum jelly, a hollowed-out orange, other odds and ends. Deftly he assembled a homemade smoker, lit it up, nursed the small blue flame. From an aspirin tin he scraped a black gummy substance onto the tip of the wire, rotated the wire between his fingers, and held the pea-sized black gum over the flame. The stuff looked like a tiny, crackling black marshmallow. The chef told her exactly what to do when he finished cooking the ball and slid it into the bottle.

"Now," the chef said.

Lila lay on her side so she could breathe deeper, emptied her lungs, then sucked on the glass straw with one long drag.

The Big Steal began shooting on the RKO lot with a cast that included—in addition to Jane Greer—William Bendix, Patric Knowles, John Qualen, and former silent star Ramon Navarro. Most of the interior sequences were completed, and a location trip to Mexico was optimistically scheduled for the weekend following Mitchum's sentencing.

On Wednesday, February 9, the crowd outside the courthouse began gathering at dawn. First the contingents of teenagers and other devoted fans, young girls mostly; then the representatives of the press, from crime reporters to gossip columnists and newsreel cameramen; finally the idle curious, passersby, and local workers randomly stopping to see the movie star come to receive justice. Mitchum arrived, dazzling in a light gray suit, white shirt, and silver tie, the crowd oohing and ahhing like it was a premiere at the Chinese Theatre. Dorothy did not accompany her husband. Lila Leeds came elegantly attired in her tailored, cream-colored suit and black heels, a small black purse in her left hand. Her mouth was painted a glistening candy-apple red. Her eyes were red, too, and she appeared unsteady. A spokesman told the press she had been ill and in bed for the last eight days.

Inside the packed eighth-floor courtroom of Judge Clement Nye, counsels Jerry Giesler and Grant Cooper completed the final legal fine-tuning before the punishments could be pronounced. Due to a more recent legal dispute, the sentencing of Robin Ford had been postponed, and the would-be realtor currently languished in a jail cell without bail (the new charges against him would ultimately be dismissed). Judge Nye asked if all concerned parties had read the reports prepared by the probation department. Mitchum's concluded that the individual was "psychologically ill-equipped for his sudden rise to fame."

The judge addressed the actor: "I realize that you are idolized by hundreds of thousands of people. However, you have overlooked the responsibilities that go with such prominence. You have failed to set an example of good citizenship.

"I am sorry for both of these defendants but respect for law and order must be taken into consideration. This case has attracted attention not only locally but throughout the world and I am treating it the same as I would any other case of a similar nature."

Judge Nye sentenced Mitchum and Leeds to a year in the county jail. He then suspended the sentence and placed the pair on probation for a period of two years, sixty days of that to be experienced in the confines of the county jail. The second count of possession was taken off the court calendar, which was understood to mean that it would be dismissed. A recess was called, and as the judge moved out of sight, the crowd moved in. Photographers trampled each other, desperate to shoot the convicts in the throes of anguish, fear, whatever. Fans and spectators jammed into the courtroom, shouted Mitchum's name, and cried out words of encouragement. A squadron of RKO reps bumped heads in a huddled meeting. Mitchum stood, showing no emotion, bending his head to Jerry Giesler's whispered wisdom, while Lila Leeds, standing a few feet to his right, mouth hanging slackly, quavered at the onslaught of exploding photo flashes. Asked if he had come prepared to go to jail Mitchum said that he had forgotten to bring a toothbrush. "I travel light, but this is too light." Then Deputy Sheriffs Walter Horta and Marjorie Kellogg took Mitchum and Leeds into custody, handcuffed them, and led them away from the frenzied audience. The quartet boarded an elevator bound for the jail cells on the top floors of the building. Women's quarters were on the thirteenth floor. Lila Leeds said, "Lucky thirteen."

Mitchum exchanged his suit for jail-issue denim blues, though he was allowed under jail rules to keep his own footgear, an expensive pair of brown Cordovans. And he exchanged his old identity for a new one: prisoner #91234. From the concessionaire he bought four quarts of milk and two cartons of cigarettes. No supplies from outside sources were permitted. The chief jailer explained some more rules. Other than his attorneys, he was allowed two visitors per week. All correspondence going in or out had to be scrutinized and censored. Breakfast was at 6:30, soup at 10:00 A.M., dinner at 3:00, lights out at 9:00. The prisoner was given a cup and spoon, which he was required to keep clean.

He was taken to his cell, a tiny cubicle with steel bunks, pairs of two-inch mattresses and wool blankets, a sink, a toilet. It slept two, but for now the actor had the place to himself. The cell door clanged shut. He sat on the bunk, lit a cigarette, and stared down at his cordovans. Sixty days. He thought about Jerry Giesler and his massive fees. They would have to sell the house to pay him off. For what? Any court-appointed pro bono correspondence school ambulance chaser could have gotten sixty days.

At dawn they woke him, gave him a mop and a bucket, and told him to clean up. He was finishing up when they let in some reporters and photographers. It was arranged by—somebody.

A reporter asked him how he'd slept. Fine, fine. He was beginning to like it there. No pictures through the bars, boys, that's all I ask. I don't want my kids to see that and get scared. He mopped some more. What did he talk about with the other prisoners? "Oh," Mitchum said, "we just discuss our lives of crime."

In the mess hall, slurping his soup, he had a conversation with the tank trusty. "Be careful," the man said. The word was that somebody wanted to set him up, rack him up in the joint. "They wanted to make me for the whole deuce," Mitchum would remember. "They didn't want to be wrong. I didn't know which side of the fuzz it was. . . . Man, they can do anything they want, you know—charge you with some minor infraction of the rules and you end up doin' two big ones in Quentin. No fuckin' way. I couldn't hack that."

RKO and Jerry Giesler arranged for their boy to be transferred out of the county jail to the sheriff's Wayside Honor Farm in a rural area forty miles north of Los Angeles. On February 16 he joined seven other prisoners boarding the sheriff's shiny new bus for the ride to Castaic. Someone had alerted the press, and a motorcade of reporters followed the vehicle as it pulled away from the Halls of Justice. Mitchum sat in the last row against a barred window with his hat pulled down over his eyes. On arrival his jail cell denims were taken away and replaced with honor farm overalls. The preening supervisors put him through a humiliating performance for the sake of the newspeople who had come all this way to see the actor's new digs. Everyone tramped over to the dairy barn, where a guard commanded Mitchum to milk a white cow named Daisy Mae. Squatting on a stool he fiddled with the udders, squirting streams of milk all over the place while the cameras snapped and snapped. Then it was on to the cement plant and more forced poses for the photographers. After all this bullshit, the supervisor told him he had missed out on lunch.

Days at the honor farm were long and wearying. You arose at 5:30, ate breakfast, began making cement blocks by 7:00, worked until 4:30 with a half-hour off for lunch. You had the evenings mostly to yourself. You could read books from the library, listen to the radio, play cards. It was a mindless grind. All Mitchum could say in its favor was that he hadn't slept so well in ages.

He wasn't, as it turned out, the only celebrity at Castaic. Big Bill Tilden, at that time the greatest and most famous tennis player in the world, was doing a year for contributing to the delinquency of a minor—he had stuck his hand in the fly of a sixteen-year-old male hitchhiker. (Jerry Giesler had refused to accept Tilden as a client.) Mitchum seldom saw the famed sports figure. Among the prisoners, child molesters were targets for physical abuse, and so Tilden was isolated and given work that kept him out of harm's way.

Visitors came up on the weekends. One of Hughes's secret policemen drove Dorothy to Castaic on two occasions. Reva Frederick visited once. "Howard Hughes said I had to take Robert candy—Hershey bars—to keep up his energy. He was very worried about that. So I brought those up. You went in. There was a table where you met the prisoner, and a bench on either side. Robert seemed fine. Relaxed. Listened to the news I had and then said goodbye. And we made the long drive back." Mitchum's friend Joe Losey appeared one weekend, toting a container of chili from Barney's Beanery in West Hollywood. Don Siegel, about to leave for Mexico to shoot some more of *The Big Steal* with the unincarcerated actors (using a double for Mitchum wherever possible), also came up, ostensibly to drop off the newly revised script. The manila envelope bulged suspiciously from the candy and things people at the studio had slipped into it along with the mimeoed pages, but the guards didn't give it a second glance; Siegel realized he could as easily have brought in a couple of guns or some heroin for all anyone seemed to care. Nevertheless, Mitchum emptied the package and quickly hid the contraband under his shirt.

"You are my favorite director," he said.

"Oh, it's really nothing," said Siegel. "Calm nerves, courage, and hatred for authority."

"We share many, many things."

Most visitors reported Bob as healthy and happy enough, considering the circumstances. He was at peace with the world, he said. If that was the case, then Associated Press correspondent James Bacon caught him on a very bad day. "I went to see him at the honor farm after he'd been there a little while," Bacon remembered. "Just to see him as a friend, really, not as a reporter. He was in a kind of a black mood, I guess. He said he had ruined everything, had screwed up all the breaks he had gotten, and why had he done this to his family, all this kind of thing. And he was crying. I mean real tears. I had never seen him like that, never did again. I told him the scandal had made him more famous, and I thought he was going to be bigger than he had ever been. I believed it, but what else was I going to say to the guy?"

Worrying about Mitchum's state of mind, Howard Hughes decided to go up to Castaic himself and give the boy a pep talk. Hughes had a liaison arranged with the sheriff to allow a special weekday visit and to let him meet with Mitchum in a private room without any guards listening or looking at them. He and Perry Leiber rode up to Castaic in Howard's old sedan. Hughes was wearing a particularly old and sloppy outfit, faded khakis, a stained shirt, his cracked old aviator jacket, and torn sneakers. They stopped at a roadside store along the way, Howard announcing he had a craving for ice cream. He went into the store and came out some minutes later telling Lieber he didn't have any money on him. Lieber couldn't understand what had taken him so long in that case. Hughes tried to explain himself. It was like a Laurel and Hardy routine. They were two hours late for their appointment at Castaic. The captain in charge, under orders from the sheriff, came out to greet the scruffy visitor and offered Hughes the use of his own office for the meeting with Mitchum. Seeing the multiethnic mix of prisoners working on the grounds, the phobic and racist Hughes requested that no prisoners be allowed anywhere near the office while he was still there.

Hughes and Mitchum sat on either side of the desk in the captain's office.

"Bob, I just came up here to reassure you that RKO is with you one hundred per cent. And I want to ask you if there is anything that I or the studio can do for you under the circumstances?"

Mitchum said, "I need fifty thousand dollars to pay off my legal fees and to buy a decent house for my family."

"I'll see to it." It would be a loan, at 5 percent interest.

Then Hughes handed over the gift he had brought for the actor, a brown paper sack filled with vitamins.

Meanwhile: After jumping bail and becoming the subject of a fugitive warrant, Vicki Evans returned to Los Angeles. On March 10 she went on trial. In a curious turn of events, the testimony of prosecution witness Det. Sgt. A. A. Barr seemed to paint Miss Evans in a sympathetic light. Barr testified that Vicki had not been smoking anything when they broke into the Ridpath house and then quoted her as valiantly trying to save her guilty pals. *"Can't I take the blame for this?"* Barr said she asked him. *"Bob and Lila have so much to lose."*

The jury found Evans not guilty.

On March 24, a week before his scheduled release (ten days shaved from his sentence for good behavior), Mitchum was expelled from the honor farm and sent back to the county jail. Chief Jailer Charles Fitzgerald assured reporters it was no reflection on Mitchum's behavior at the farm, but a steady stream of visiting agents, writers, and reporters from Hollywood had begun to interfere with the work schedule at the brickyard. Climbing off the bus in Los Angeles, Bob was bronzed from the sun, had grown a thick moustache, had lost ten pounds. Reporters caught him en route to his cell.

"I feel wonderful," he declared. "I worked hard, slept well and batted .800 on the softball team. We won seven out of eight games." Castaic, he said, was "like Palm Springs, without the riff-raff."

The final week went by without incident. After breakfast on Wednesday, March 30, Mitchum was released from custody. Reporters were waiting. "I've been happy in jail," he told them, tailoring his opinions for public consumption. "Nobody envied me. Nobody wanted anything from me. Nobody wanted my bars or the bowl of pudding they shoved at me through the slot. I did my work and they let me alone." He had developed a new taste for privacy. "I'm through with my so-called pals. I'll see only my wife, my two children, and a couple of close friends. Parties? I'd stand out like a monster at a party. I'm typed—a character—and I guess I'll have to bear that the rest of my life." He was going back to work as soon as possible, he told the group. "I've got to. I'm broke. . . . And now, if you'll excuse me, I'm heading for home."

The house on Oak Glen offered more of the same. The studio had sent a publicist to take charge. Dorothy couldn't believe it. Her reunion with her husband was to be a staged event for publicity purposes. She held her tongue, but it wasn't easy, watching the RKO man posing them, patting their hair like he was grooming a couple of poodles. Bob put a comforting arm around her, and she pressed her head to his chest and smiled thinly at the far wall as the strangers asked questions and scribbled in their little pads, took pictures, flooding the room with flashes of ugly white light. Yes, it was great to have Bob home again, and thank you for asking.

An article Mitchum supposedly penned himself, published in *Photoplay* magazine a few weeks after his release from jail, asked the question: "DO I GET ANOTHER CHANCE?" (subtitled: "Sixty days—time enough for a man to think").

In the last few months I've been surrounded by shadows. Deep, dark shadows through which little sunlight has filtered. Financially I am back where I started. But the bitter pills I have swallowed have made me a better man. I have attained a peace of mind which I did not think possible.

I think too many of us are apt to carelessly overlook little infringements of the law and the moral code. Some of us find ourselves taking one step too far . . . refusing to heed the little warning signals of our conscience until it is too late and disaster has overcome us.

Now I am facing life with a new sense of responsibility to the world, to myself, and above all to my wife and our two sons. No matter what is cooking for me in the future, I am dedicating my life to dispelling the cloud hanging over my family. . . .

A stirring plea for understanding and forgiveness from a reformed sinner, it shared the *Photoplay* page with an advertisement for a Lysol douche. "Be confident of your appealing feminine daintiness," read the ad, "truly *cleanse* the vaginal canal."

CHAPTER SEVEN

Phantom Years

Down in Tehuacan, Mexico, in the rift valley 150 kilometers southeast of Mexico City, director Don Siegel had been wrestling with a dilemma: how to make a movie starring a man who was not there. The screenplay had been revised and stripped down to accommodate the special circumstances, making *The Big Steal* even more of an exercise in abstraction. The whole thing had devolved into an endless car chase—no premise, no plot, just chasing. All day long on a highway in the sun-roasted valley he filmed the actors driving from right to left, left to right, occasionally directing them to look in the rearview or over one shoulder. Siegel had wanted to postpone the location shoot until Mitchum was available, but still more scheduling problems prevented that—William Bendix and Patric Knowles had commitments to other studios, the permits from the Mexican government were restricted to certain dates. Why they weren't shooting the whole megillah on the Gower Street lot and in Griffith Park Siegel didn't have a clue. *The Big Steal* had started out as a tough thriller, but as the project fell into disarray on location Siegel felt that no one could take it seriously, and he began to direct the actors to play everything for laughs, or at least tongue-in-cheek.

At last came word that the production's greatest problem, the absence of the leading player, was about to end. Mitchum, just a few days out of the jug, had landed in Mexico City and was on his way. Knowing how much had to be done and how little time he had, Siegel prepared to shoot Bob's first scene as soon as he arrived.

The hired car rolled into town just after noon. A boy from the hotel ran to get Siegel and brought him over to the entranceway where a big black sedan was standing, a couple of hotel staffers peering into the back windows. The driver from Mexico City was sitting on the curb smoking a cigarette.

"Where's Mitchum?" Siegel asked.

The driver blew smoke and pointed to the car. Siegel cracked the door and saw his star and another man—described facetiously as Mitchum's bodyguard. The other guy was passed out cold, but Mitchum seemed to be conversing with him anyway.

"Drunk?" Siegel asked the driver.

"A whole bottle of tequila. Maybe two."

With the help of perhaps three-quarters of the hotel staff, the two big men were extracted from the automobile and carried to their rooms. Bystanders watched the amazing parade, the mumbling Hollywood star crossing the lobby atop a human palanquin, another man being toted horizontally as if on a stretcher, and a third man, the gringo movie director who looked like a seedy version of Harry James, walking upright and cursing the other two.

Siegel was damned if he was going to lose the whole day to this nonsense. Up in the actor's room he ordered a pot of coffee and made Mitchum suck it down. Patric Knowles popped in, and Siegel showed him the problem. Knowles said they had to get him down to the hotel's steam room. It was a trick Errol Flynn had taught him.

"A half hour of steam and he'll be good as new."

Mitchum was already becoming a bit more cooperative, Siegel thought. He and Knowles got him up, one under each shoulder, took him downstairs to the hotel gym, and led him inside the steam room.

"Steam's the thing, Bobby," said the dapper Knowles.

Mitchum punched him in the head. Knowles cracked his skull against the sweaty, hot wall and then lost his footing on the damp floor. Mitchum pulled him halfway up and clobbered him some more.

Knowles screamed.

Mitchum proceeded to beat the tar out of him. The director, trying to stop him, leaped on Mitchum's back and was instantly thrown off. He did it again. "When I tried to grab him, he would spin his shoulder, which sent me spinning around the wet walls." It was all that goddamned exercise in prison, Siegel decided painfully. "Mitch was in the best shape of his life." Siegel crawled over to help the groggy, moaning Pat Knowles, and the pair struggled out of there.

"He was one tough hombre," said Siegel, "with a mean streak that we could not handle."

*

"Bob joined us in Mexico straight out of prison," said Jane Greer. "His hair had been chopped off. He had a great tan, he was in great shape from breaking rocks, and he looked wonderful. I didn't know how they were going to match him with the film they had shot before he went away."

Seeing Greer and Mitchum together as he lined the pair up for a shot, Don Siegel wondered how he was going to match either of them. Mitchum was certainly tanner and leaner. He had trimmed at least three inches from his gut. Greer, though, now well over four months pregnant, had developed a noticeable pouch. Christ, Siegel thought, *they've exchanged stomachs!*

"I didn't want anyone to know I was pregnant," said Greer. "But there was no place to hide down there. I wore one outfit, and it was ridiculous for anyone being pregnant—a slim skirt, a little bolero jacket, a tight sash around the waist. And every scene in that open car. I had to stay on a diet like crazy. Cottage cheese and fruit.

"The location was a little rugged, you know, a long drive up these winding roads, nothing around but the natives with their little huts. Then all day in the car getting shot at by Bill Bendix. And I was prone to morning sickness. I had a supply of these little pills I took so I could get through the morning and the rest of the day. I was driving out in the limousine with Bendix, and I sneaked a pill into my mouth. He wanted to know what it was. I said, 'It's for the *turistas*. Montezuma's Revenge.' He said, 'Oh really? Give me some of those.' And he liked them and starting taking them from me every day. He thought the pills protected him, and he drank all the local water, ate the ice. I had to send to my doctor for more pills. But I didn't want to tell anyone I was pregnant."

The South of the Border intestinal disorder known to strike visiting Americanos had spared the *Big Steal* company until one fateful day on a rural location. Siegel was rehearsing a scene with Mitchum and Greer and was ready to roll when Mitchum suddenly took off for the bushes. Siegel decided to do a close-up of Jane Greer instead, and cameraman Harry Wild lined it up. Then Greer ran away. Siegel looked around. "Jesus Christ. Shoot Pat Knowles through his window," he told Wild. Wild was nowhere to be seen.

"I showed no sign of diarrhea until early afternoon," Siegel recalled. "Then Montezuma struck." Two presumably nonunion grips held him over a small stone bridge above a stream "for what seemed like hours."

Considering Mitchum's recent troubles, Hughes and RKO had shown either great ignorance or a perverse sense of humor in sending the actor on to Mexico, particularly to a region known for the high quality of its cannabis crop. "In Mexico they knew all about what had happened to him," said Jane Greer. "He was treated like a hero. They worshipped him because of the marijuana. And they would come up, smiling, offering him some samples. Slip it into his pockets. Peasants would put some in the cuffs of his trousers— 'Here, please try our crop of marijuana, Señor Mitchum!' Oh my, he had a hard time keeping away from it because they just loved him down there."

Siegel's skills as a montage director at Warners served *The Big Steal* well. He was required to help Sam Beetley piece together a relatively seamless finished product out of footage that—due to the protracted shooting schedule—jumped from winter to spring landscapes within the same sequence and revealed his stars to have amazing weight gains and losses within the brief span of the film's story. In the end, the slapdash quality of the film seemed to work in its favor. Brisk, amiable, pointless, it resembled a seventy-one-minute live action Roadrunner cartoon. The *New Republic* reviewer said it best, calling *The Big Steal* "a ludicrous miscarriage of an adventure picture"—and he *liked* it. For Siegel, in retrospect, it was the real beginning of what would be a long and frequently distinguished career as a maker of fast, tough, action movies.

Dorothy had joined her husband in Mexico for the last week of filming. While they were away, the children were left in the care of a nanny. On April 28 a precocious five-year-old Christopher Mitchum and four other kids had a run-in with a store owner on Cahuenga Boulevard, not far from the Mitchum home. When the store owner chased them away, young Chris ran into an oncoming car. He was rushed to Hollywood Receiving Hospital and treated for cuts and bruises. When Bob and Dorothy got back and heard of the incident, they were newly motivated to move out of the small house and congested neighborhood.

They both wanted a place with plenty of breathing room, a place in the countryside with space for the kids to play and—Dorothy doubtless hoped—to isolate Bob from trouble and his odious cronies. Old friend Tony Caruso knew just the place. "I talked him into moving out by me in Malibu Canyon," said Caruso. It was an unspoiled and underpopulated area. People kept horses and rode them in the hills. You could be a forty-minute drive from the studios but feel as if you were in Oregon. "I said to him, 'Bob, they're bothering you everywhere you go in town. You move out there, nobody'll find you, you'll get some peace.' And we found him a property on Mandeville Canyon Road, just a half block away from me. And he bought it and we were neighbors for quite a while." As he had promised he would, Howard Hughes OKed a loan to the Mitchums for fifty thousand, to be paid back in installments beginning six months hence.

The Mandeville place was luxurious but down-home, a rich man's farmhouse. The interior spaces were huge by Mitchum family standards, and when they unpacked their meager furnishings from Oak Glen, the rooms seemed to tower over everything like the great halls of a castle. The master of the house settled into a relatively idyllic existence. He swam, sat by the pool, played with the kids for long hours, lay on the floor listening to records and reading Josh and Chris the funnies while they crawled across his stomach. He was all any parole board could hope for. Other stars eventually moved into the neighborhood. Richard Widmark. Gregory Peck. Tony found Don Defore a place across the street from Bob. An El Rancho Broke-O reunion. But the canyon remained off the beaten track, out of the limelight. "It was a quiet life," said Caruso. "No fancy party scene. People would get together for a drink. Bob would come over to my house; he'd invite Toni and me over to his. I don't remember ever seeing many people at his place in all those years."

Under the terms of his parole Mitchum was forbidden to associate with known criminals and undesirables, which officially cut him off from most of his old hangouts (though he did heedlessly play host to a couple of friends he had made in Castaic). To his wife's delight, they were forced to socialize with his more respectable acquaintances. Jane Greer and her husband, Edward Lasker, became good friends of the couple and often had them over to their soirees. At one of these, Greer seated Mitchum next to a recent Nobel Prize winner: "I thought William Faulkner and Bob Mitchum would be a good match so I put them together. Loretta Young was there with her husband, and they were very, very Catholic. Loretta's husband, whose name escapes me, heard that Faulkner was writing *The Left Hand of God* for Howard Hawks and he was grilling him. 'You're writing about a priest, a man of God? I don't think you're the right one to write this.' And Faulkner said, 'Oh? Well, they're paying me to write it.' And he was relieved to turn to Bob, whose colorful manner of speech really tickled him. I remember they were talking about studio contracts and Howard Hughes and Bob said, 'Well, you see, I'm a tall dog on a short leash. It's long enough to let me up the wall, but if I try to jump off the other side I'm hanged.' And Faulkner said to me later on, 'I really like the way that boy talks.'"

Hughes did put Mitchum on a leash while the actor was on parole. He assigned a man to keep an eye on him, Kemp Niver, a big, glowering ex-cop and Commie hater who looked a bit like a wolf drawn by Tex Avery. He had been operating a private detective agency in LA (Discreet About Others' Indiscretions was the agency's motto) until Hughes lured him away to head up his secret police force. Now he was playing Bob Mitchum's baby-sitter, supposed to go everywhere Mitchum went, leaving him alone only when they got back to the man's house in the evening.

"Yeah, I remember him," said Tony Caruso. "He was like a parole officer. He was assigned to try and keep Bob out of trouble. . . . *Hahaha. . . . Good luck!*"

Mitchum didn't much enjoy having the fuzz, even the ex-fuzz, constantly underfoot. "The crew at the studio hated him," said Reva Frederick. "They just didn't like the idea of a snoop. Some of them got a big bucket of paint and threw it all over Niver's convertible." Eventually Hughes's private dick agreed to loosen the strings a bit and allow Bob to go out and about without a chaperone as long as he would tell Niver in advance where he was planning to go and would check in periodically by phone. One night Bob and Dorothy came back to their car and found that someone had put a couple of joints on the front seat. Mitchum called Niver, and he rushed over and extracted the contraband. They never found out who planted the stuff, but there was a strong feeling that the actor was still under threat of another setup.

Niver was, in fact, only the most visible of Mitchum's watchdogs. The actor was under nearly round-the-clock observation during this period, Hughes's ever-growing corps of spies and electronic eavesdroppers tailing him, tapping his phone, bugging his office and trailer and probably his house as well. Mitchum's uncertain legal situation was the ostensible excuse, but Hughes was doing the same thing to dozens of actresses and politically suspect employees at the studio, as well as to a number of women he merely hoped one day to meet and date. He had become a Hollywood J. Edgar Hoover, a lascivious Dr. Mabuse, ever poring over surveillance photos and telephone transcripts, gathering info, intimacies, dirt. Ever since the Beverly Hills plane crash, said friends and associates, Hughes's behavior was becoming stranger and stranger.

In July Mitchum started work on a picture, *Holiday Affair*.

Something different now, a sweet comedy with a Christmastime setting. Producing and directing was Don Hartman, a longtime Paramount screenwriter who'd worked on some of the Hope-Crosby "Road" pictures. The story concerned a war widow with a young son and her conceivably amusing entanglement with a free-spirited drifter-through-life. A bit of *Bachelor Mother,* a touch of *Holiday,* and plenty of schmaltz. Although he would not be beaten, pull a gun, or ride into the sunset, the character of Steve Mason was still a recognizable Mitchum archetype, footloose, antiestablishment, an outsider.

Holiday Affair's costar was to be the sparkling young actress Janet Leigh. Under long-term contract with MGM, Leigh was being loaned to RKO on a three-picture deal, a situation that left her feeling anxious and a bit betrayed. Although she had not been in Hollywood long, Leigh already had an unpleasant history with RKO's odd owner. Her publicity buildup at Metro, the widely dispersed photos of the fresh-faced bubbling beauty, had caught Hughes's eye; and in his usual fashion he ordered his quasi pimps, "Get me that." Leigh's agent pressured her into going on a date with Hughes. As a potential romantic interest she found him resistible—as old as her father, presumptuous, and generally a weirdie. He conned her into taking a brief airplane ride, and then flew her to Las Vegas for a long, pre-arranged occasion. It was the sort of Hughes schtick that had made lots of actresses melt in their bucket seats, but not this time. Leigh felt only angry and frightened. Hughes persisted with his unwanted attentions, began following her to restaurants when she went on dates with other men or on evenings out with her parents, seating himself at the next table and staring at her. "He was stalking me!" Janet Leigh remembered. "It was nerve-racking. You can imagine how I felt when Bennie Thau called me into the office and said, 'Janet, I have wonderful news. RKO is going to borrow you for three pictures. You'll be working with Robert Mitchum and John Wayne. It's a tremendous opportunity for you.' And for the studio, because they were going to make a fortune on the loan-out. Which I didn't mind at all. I was happy if I could help them because they were sure helping me. But RKO! I said, 'You don't understand. This man has been trying to intimidate me. All these things have been happening. I don't know what he has in mind for me if I go over there.' And the man at MGM just said, 'Now, honey, we're sure there's nothing to worry about. This is a business situation, nothing more. There's no funny business. We're talking about a lot of money at stake here. So you go and do as we say.' And I must have still looked nervous because he added, 'Look, I'm a phone call away if anything goes wrong.' And that was all they wanted to hear about that."

Leigh would not escape serious aggravation and harassment from Hughes during her lengthy stay at RKO, but the making of *Holiday Affair,* at least, with the avuncular and easygoing Don Hartman in charge and Bob Mitchum for her love interest, she would recall as a happy and fun-filled experience.

"I was a fan of Bob's from seeing him in the movies, and I was excited to be working with him," said Leigh. "I was pretty naive and green then, and the fact that he had been to jail and that he had *actually smoked marijuana,* wow, this sounded really exciting and dangerous. And when I *did* see him for the first time it pretty much confirmed my impression of him. . . . I had driven onto the lot at RKO. I noticed some commotion from one of the bungalow dressing rooms, and then I saw coming out of the bungalow Mr. Mitchum, *playing a saxophone* and leading an entourage of six or seven people behind him. Like the pied piper! And they headed down the studio street, Bob playing the sax and his entourage marching and dancing behind him, the way they do at those New Orleans funerals, where they play 'When the Saints Go Marching In.' That was my first sight of Bob Mitchum. And it made a very vivid impression on me.

"When we did start to work together I found him to be just the most delicious person in the world. An extremely good actor, as everybody knows now, but he was so easy and cool, he never looked like he was acting. He was actually very intense and focused on what he was doing, but you were never aware of it. And working with him, he brought out that quality in you, which was great. I learned a lot from him. But he was such a tease. And I was so gullible and such an easy target!"

In a breakfast scene with child actor Gordon Gebert, Leigh stopped acting after the kid lost his concentration and started playing with his cornflakes. Don Hartman said, "Janet, don't you ever stop in a scene like that! You missed a great opportunity. When something like that happens, you improvise. You should have stayed in character as his mother, told him to listen or told him to stop playing with his cornflakes, as you would have done in life."

"He was absolutely right," said Leigh. "It was a great lesson. I never stopped a scene again. But, oh, then Mitch took advantage of it. I was in the kitchen and he's supposed to come up and turn me around and give me a little kiss and I'm supposed to be a little surprised. Instead he comes up, turns me around, and kisses me in a way that you would never do on a first date! And I knew he did it just to catch me off balance, and he did. I was so shocked I couldn't speak. And Don Hartman liked my reaction so much they kept it in the film.

"Both Bob and Wendell Corey were such devils with me. There was a scene at the Christmas dinner table, I'm sitting with my mother and my father and my son, and Bob and Wendell, my two suitors, one on each side of me. And they were so naughty, each time while I did the scene Bob and Wendell would reach under the table and put a hand up either leg. And I didn't know what to do. I thought, 'If I react to it and stop the scene going on with all the other actors, I'll just look like a complete ninny.' And I would tell myself, 'They aren't really going to go any farther with it,' but then I would think, 'With those two, God, maybe they will!' Oh, they just did it to unnerve me. It was so funny. And they never cracked a smile. They were both so cool.

"It was really a very happy set and we did good work. Bob and Wendell played off each other so well. I thought it was a charming, wonderful picture."

The gentle film had none of the sexual or violent content that generally provoked Howard Hughes's interest or meddling. Aside from private instructions to the hair and wardrobe people (he had them make Janet Leigh wear a shoulder-length fall and in one scene a sweater so tight it made her breasts stand out like traffic cones),

Hughes left *Holiday Affair* alone. The film was completed on the second day of September and was playing in theaters by Thanksgiving week. Other Mitchum starrers for Hughes would not have such an easy time of it.

Back in the Halls of Justice curious events were unfolding. Corruption and mob activities in Los Angeles had reached one of their periodic breaking points. It was widely understood that Mickey Cohen, king of the dope, prostitution, and gambling rackets, had a sizable percentage of LA city and county law enforcement in his pocket, and reform-minded elements in the DA's office were aching to take him down. Investigations into organized crime activities had been going on throughout the summer of 1949, with a grand jury sworn in and wading through a mounting dunghill of incriminations. Enter, stage left, Paul Behrmann, former actor's agent and business manager convicted on grand theft charges, at liberty on five thousand dollars' bond while awaiting an appeal decision and desperate to stay out of San Quentin. He contacted the office of District Attorney William E. Simpson with an offer of evidence concerning a big-time sex-and-extortion crime ring headed by one Mickey Cohen. Simpson rushed him before the grand jury and Behrmann spewed a lurid bouillabaisse whose ingredients included beautiful hookers, horny businessmen, candid photographs, tax-free payoffs, mob enforcers, an "assistant of Claude Marsan, French love teacher," and a woman known only as "Bootsie." He detailed a thriving racket involving reputable rich men being entrapped by party girls, then shaken down for large sums, Mickey Cohen collecting 60 percent of the take and the girls keeping the rest. He named names, including two that were familiar to scandal buffs: Lila Leeds and Vicki Evans (both women indignantly denied any such involvement in the racket). The DA invited or subpoenaed testimony from everyone Behrmann mentioned, including the victims.

Lila, linked by Behrmann to the shakedown of Ben Klekner, owner of a Hollywood correspondence school, was grilled at length about her relationship with the former agent. Her behind-closed-

doors recounting of the Ridpath reefer pad raid triggered an unexpected reaction from DA Simpson, who suddenly announced that
the Mitchum conviction might be "reinvestigated to determine
whether extortionists had engineered the case." Behrmann suddenly didn't feel like talking anymore. When Simpson attempted to
have him cited for contempt, he disappeared; the DA then peti-
tioned a bench warrant for his arrest. Behrmann surrendered days
later, claiming it was all a misunderstanding, but Judge Clement
Nye—the same man who had sent Robert Mitchum and Lila Leeds
away—remanded him to a jail cell pending a new bail hearing.

For more than a year the district attorney's office quietly looked
into the circumstances surrounding the Mitchum arrest. On
January 31, 1951, just days after the completion of the actor's parole
period, the Los Angeles Supreme Court quietly announced an
extraordinary legal reversal. *"After an exhaustive investigation of the
evidence and testimony presented at the trial,"* said Judge Nye, *"the
court orders that the verdict of guilty be set aside and that a plea of not
guilty be entered and that the information or complaint be dismissed."*

If anyone was expecting Mitchum's exoneration to generate the
headline-making frenzy of his arrest, they were to be very disappointed. As the actor liked to put it, the headline "MITCHUM
SUCKS," sold a lot of papers, but "MITCHUM DOESN'T SUCK AFTER
ALL" not a one. He himself said little of the "vindication," and his
lifelong and atypical circumspection regarding this strange devel-
opment can only lead to the suspicion that he was never fully
informed of the DA's findings or else was warned to keep his mouth
shut—certainly the retroactive dismissal of the case was an embarrassment for the county and its agencies of law enforcement. But
Mitchum's cryptic comments plus the accusations made prior to
the reinvestigation and dismissal encourage a connect-the-dots
conspiracy theory: that the events leading up to Ridpath Drive were
engineered by a vengeful ex-associate, mobster Mickey Cohen, and
some corrupt faction in the sheriff's department ready to do
Mickey's bidding.

Better luck next time, fellas. Mitchum put down the phone call
with the news about the overturned verdict and strolled back to the

soundstage, picking up where he had left off, in the middle of groping the bountiful Jane Russell.

Having championed Mitchum through the dark days of the scandal,
Howard Hughes decided he did not now want to share the man's
services with anyone and bought out David Selznick's half of the
actor's contract for four hundred thousand dollars. In the five years
to come, Mitchum would be the studio's busiest and uncontestably
its biggest star—though under Hughes's tenure this would prove to
be a somewhat dubious distinction.

Increasingly, Hughes would run RKO less as a place of business—and it was, after all, still one of only seven major motion picture studios in the country—than as a personal, rather perverse
hobby. Much of his workweek would be taken up in such nonprofit
activities as ferreting out leftists, elaborately seducing starlets, settling private grudges, and studying the screen tests of still more starlets. The actual movies being produced at RKO were more and more
reflections of Hughes's psychological fixations, political obsessions,
and sexual fantasies. His self-indulgent need to see certain things on
film exactly as he anticipated them, his demands for retakes and
retroactive recasting of films till they met with his satisfaction,
would mean continual production delays and cost overruns and the
destruction of RKO as a reliable source of product for exhibitors. A
personal, obstinate, and perfectionist style of moviemaking—with
its echoes of Griffith and von Stroheim—might have been seen as
admirable or heroic, even in Hollywood, except that the things
Hughes obsessed over were cleavage and fistfights and projects that
everyone else looked at as pulp trash.

Mitchum never forgot that Hughes had stuck by him after his narcotics arrest when he could so easily have thrown him to the dogs and
ended his career forever. Mitchum would bitch and moan about
many of the subsequent decisions Hughes made for him, and he came
to agree with those who thought the aviator was losing his marbles,
but he would never forget Howard's loyalty and would continue to
refer to him as a friend long after they had seen each other for the last
time. At RKO Bob's nickname for Hughes was "the Phantom" for his

mysterious and nocturnal comings and goings, and sometimes "the Thin Man." Aware of the rumors that Hughes had all the dressing rooms and offices bugged, Mitchum would amuse onlookers by talking to the wall or under a desk—"Did you hear what I said, Phantom, you deaf fucker? You want me to repeat it?"

Because so many of the RKO personnel were intimidated, mystified, or repulsed by Hughes, Mitchum's directors and costars would sometimes ask him to convey their complaints to the man. Mitchum would tell them it was no easier for him to see Hughes than it was for anybody else. His rare meetings with Howard were arranged like a scene straight out of an RKO film noir—a midnight call, an anonymous driver picking him up in a sedan with tinted windows, taking him off to some stripped-down hotel bungalow or to Hughes's dirty office or screening room. Occasionally he was transferred into another car, one idling on a street corner or in an alleyway outside a warehouse. Howard would be there sitting in the backseat, sometimes in a suit and tie, sometimes in dirty work clothes and smelling a little ripe, but acting as if everything was as normal as could be, greeting him warmly, asking about the family. They would sit in the backseat, Mitchum would light up a butt and maybe tell some ribald story, and Hughes would hold his head down and cock his left ear, then laugh with that high-pitched squeak that sounded like you'd stepped on a cat's tail. Not that he always got the jokes. Hughes struck Mitchum as completely humorless and very much a Texas square. Hughes, for his part, thought Mitchum the most cynical and carefree man he knew. "Bob," he told him, "you're like a pay toilet—you don't give a shit for nothing." That was a Hughes joke. One night Mitchum got into a car with him and they drove off down the coast to a waterside hangar where Howard brought the actor on board the legendary/notorious birchwood troop carrier he had built, the HK-1 *Hercules,* better known as "the Spruce Goose." "You'll enjoy this, Bob, having worked at Lockheed." Does this cat think I designed airplanes there? Mitchum wondered. He went through the spectacular craft with awe, sat down in the cockpit next to the Phantom, and didn't know what to say. Howard was a strange, amazing man.

In the last months of 1949, Mitchum made *Carriage Entrance,* eventually released as *My Forbidden Past,* a vehicle for Ava Gardner, one of Hughes's off and on lovers. Set in 1890s New Orleans, it was the sordid story of a sexually obsessed heiress with an "unholy ancestry" and a young doctor wrongly accused of murdering his wife. With the exception of Melvyn Douglas's fine work as Ava's cruel cousin, it was a film entirely without merit. Cold and wooden throughout, Mitchum seemed to deliberately withhold anything resembling a performance. Hughes fiddled with the editing for over a year, holding up release of the film until spring 1951.

Gardner impressed Mitchum with her tough-talking, heavy-drinking, hard-living style. Described by one biographer as "sluttish" and by columnist and pal James Bacon as a "nymphomaniac," she was, to be more polite, a sexual adventuress with a string of high-profile lovers currently in tow—including Hughes and Frank Sinatra—but Ava always had room for one more, and shortly after filming began the actress set her sights on her latest costar. In their first kissing scene she pulled the same gag he had pulled on Janet Leigh, only she wasn't kidding. He began taking her home at night. They began an intensely sexual affair. She was the most beautiful, exciting woman he had ever known. As an afterthought, Mitchum put a call through to Hughes, who had dated Gardner off and on through the years, concerned—a little late—that Hughes might find out Mitchum was screwing her and take offense. He made a joke of it, asking the Phantom whether *he* thought Mitchum should sleep with the dame. "You might as well," said Hughes. "Everyone'll think you're a fag if you don't."

Mitchum would tell friends that Ava got serious fast. She told him they should go away together; he should leave his family and keep house with her. He told her she'd have to ask Dorothy about that. And she claimed that she did. Ava said she phoned the house, said, "You've had him for ten years. Give somebody else a chance."

"What does Bob say?"

"He said to ask you."

"Okay, so you asked me. The answer is no."

Ava would get sentimental in old age, reflecting, "I think every

girl who ever worked with Bob Mitchum fell in love with him."
Mitchum, unsentimentally, would speak of Ava's fondness for performing an intimate act known as a "golden shower."

After a brief respite for the Christmas season, Mitchum was back
before the cameras in January 1950, shooting *Where Danger Lives*
with another Hughes-tested actress, Faith Domergue. Craftily
weaned away from her parents by the millionaire, the big-eyed, sultry brunette youngster had lived with Hughes from the time she was
fifteen, ostensibly being readied for silver screen stardom. After long
years of nurturing, Domergue took the lead in Howard's expensive,
avenging-Corsican disaster, *Vendetta,* still unreleased five years after
the production had wrapped. By default, Domergue would make
her official cinematic debut in a comparatively modest and altogether superior film, one of the darkest and most unrelenting examples of the film noir genre. Scripted by Howard Hughes pal and
suspense whiz Charles Bennett (*The 39 Steps, The Man Who Knew
Too Much*), *Where Danger Lives* is the story of the gorgeous and psychotic wife of a rich older man who implicates her young
doctor/lover in the murder of her husband. The doctor struggles
with the growing agony of a head injury as the pair flee to the
Mexican border and to the violent culmination of their fatal attraction. The tale contained favorite motifs of the conflicted misogy-
nist/girl crazy Hughes—the danger and duplicity of beautiful
females, the painful cost of lust and sexual obsession. For Mitchum
the role of Dr. Jeff Cameron was a kind of surreal amplification of
Out of the Past's Jeff Bailey, another corruptible man passively
accepting his own destruction, here the idea of losing one's mind to
an alluring woman made literal by the character's nearly fatal brain
concussion. The quality of a nightmare was expertly achieved by
director John Farrow's harsh staging and the bleak, shrouded
images caught by noir's king cameraman Nicholas Musuraca—
another Mitchum picture, as the actor said, "lit by matches."

Johnny Farrow was the only director Bob had ever met who
could outdrink him. The good-looking, blond, former Australian
seaman (he'd entered the United States by jumping ship from a

windjammer) and father of future Mitchum costar Mia, Farrow was known as a mean, ruthless son of a bitch by everyone who knew him, except for the coteries of Roman Catholic priests with whom he spent much time in pious and arcane discussions of Church doctrine and ecumenical history. Mitchum, like everyone else, had a difficult time equating the roistering philanderer he knew with the man who wrote devotional biographies of the saints and of Father Damien, "the leper priest."

"D'ya ever *dare* go to confession?" Mitchum asked him.

Farrow said he went every week to one of the oldest Spanish churches in California, downtown near Alvarado Street, told the priest everything, and received absolution. "The poor bastard doesn't speak a word of English."

"He was a professional Catholic, Farrow," said Reva Frederick. "Always surrounded by nuns and priests. But his private life was entirely different. He cast the extras—the women—almost entirely with women he wanted for his own amusement, girls he would make at his command." Mitchum enjoyed Farrow's company in a bar, but at work he could be unbearable, pinching every female's ass (he caddishly gave his wife, Maureen O'Sullivan, an unbilled cameo as an "understanding" girlfriend) and revealing a sadistic streak when it came to putting the actor through his paces. In a scene in a sleazy bordertown hotel, the injured, barely conscious Mitchum character (having just been beaten up by Domergue) is required to crawl out of his room and then slide and tumble down three flights of stairs. Farrow demanded they shoot it without a stuntman, with the camera on a descending crane following Mitchum's fall. The hastily constructed staircase set was open at the sides, and when Mitchum started tumbling he nearly slipped over, just avoiding a thirty-foot drop to the wooden plank floor. Sid Rogell happened to come onto the set as the take began and ran screaming at Farrow's throat.

"You goddamn idiot! Are you trying to kill him?" said Rogell.

Carpenters put in a railing, and Farrow restaged the shot to minimize the risk to the performer. Rogell wanted them to use a stuntman. Mitchum refused—he wasn't going to have Farrow calling him a fairy for the rest of the shoot. Down he tumbled. But when the director blithely called, "All right, let's try it again," Mitchum told him to go fuck himself.

Howard Hughes was so pleased with the nasty, brutal results of this creative collaboration, he put Mitchum and Farrow together again for an immediate follow-up, a project that began life as *Smiler with a Gun* but would come to be known to the ages as *His Kind of Woman*. For this one, instead of the problematic Faith Domergue, he would use another, more abundantly talented actress he had also nurtured since her teens: Jane Russell. In 1940, she had been nineteen years old, a chiropodist's assistant and aspiring model, with a prodigious 38-22-36 figure, a dedicated churchgoer living with her family when Hughes discovered her and cast her in *The Outlaw*. Publicity photos of Jane, massive bosom upheaving, had made her a household name years before her furiously hyped and controversial debut ever hit the theaters. She was the actress most closely identified with Hughes in the public's mind, though she was one of the few female performers of his acquaintance with whom he was never romantically linked (she preferred less scrawny and diffident men, and in 1943, she married Bob Waterfield, a well-known football player). Russell's acting in *The Outlaw* had been fairly terrible, but she had improved greatly since then; and in 1950, her down-to-earth charm, luscious physique, and big-limbed grace made her one of the real pleasures of the current cinema.

Mitchum and Russell: It was an inevitable pairing for RKO. The studio's biggest assets, the screen's two greatest chests, together for the first time. Hughes's excitement overflowed at the prospect, and he was imagining the sort of lurid publicity campaign and colossal erotic images he would commission even before the first frame of film was exposed.

Farrow began with the idea of making another grim film noir, but the script by Frank Fenton, the man who had supplied so much of the great, glistening dialogue for *Out of the Past*, turned out to be very different from the overwrought *Where Danger Lives* or even the darkly romantic *Out of the Past*; nor did it have much in common with an antic adventure picture like *The Big Steal*. It was quirky, going this way and that, light in parts, shot through with a cool, ironic wit and mischievousness while still being bluntly violent, lascivious, dark, with lots of room for the beatings and breast shots that Hughes and Farrow demanded. Fenton knew Mitchum well, and the script became reflective not only of the writer's sardonic point of view (the script's major subplot, for example, was a satire of certain absurd Hollywood types) but of the lead actor's own style and outlook—detached, amused, off-kilter. Fenton even wrote in bits and pieces of Mitchum's personal history and a few private jokes. It was a strange sort of a script, with the plot mostly at the very beginning and end and a long middle section where nothing much happened. To Farrow's credit, he never tried to resolve the script's tonal inconsistencies but ran with them all the way.

The slender plot line begins with a down-at-heels gambler, Dan Milner, fresh off the prison farm, hired for a mysterious high-paying job that sends him to a luxurious resort in Baja, Mexico. With no idea of his mission, waiting for his contact to show, Milner interacts with a number of colorful and some suspicious characters staying at the lodge, including playgirl Lenore Brent, narcissistic movie star Mark Cardigan, a mysterious German "writer," and a drunken pilot. Eventually Milner learns that he's been lured down there to become the patsy in an exiled mobster's scheme to sneak back into the United States by switching identities with him, a rootless loner no one will miss. Taken captive aboard the gangster's yacht, Milner turns the tables and the bad guys are captured or killed. Back in his hotel room, Dan and Lenore, broke but happy, decide to keep company. The End.

Supporting Mitchum and Russell in the cast were Vincent Price as the egotistical Hollywood actor, Tim Holt (the B Western star whose boots Mitchum was once assigned to fill) as an immigration agent, Jim Backus as a Wall Streeter on vacation, Tony Caruso and Charles McGraw as mob henchmen, and Howard Petrie in the role of the deported mobster Nick Ferraro. Cinematography was by studio regular—and Jane Russell's particular favorite—Harry J. Wild. Planning to shoot nearly everything indoors at the studio, Farrow had a massive main set built, the Morro's Lodge, where most of the action took place, a functioning, tropical rustic moderne resort complete with manmade beach sprawling across three soundstages ("You really thought you were there," Jane Russell recalled). Farrow and Wild would unveil the set in a showy single take with a smoothly gliding camera moving across the sand and through the lobby, slipping up behind the derriere of a silk-pajamaed cocktail waitress twitching briskly down the length of the bar ("*That* was John Farrow," said Mitchum of those moments of twitching. "*A signature shot!*"), moving among the tangoing couples on the dance floor, swerving away just in time to catch Mitchum in suit and tie striding in from the swimming pool, camera backtracking now as he seats himself at the bar and orders a drink ("Ginger ale, please"). Cut.

Filming went smoothly, although John Farrow's tough, even cruel behavior toward the crew and supporting and extra players continued to rub Mitchum—and now his costar, too—the wrong way. "He was nice to us, but he would be nasty to some of the other kids," said Russell. "Needling all the time. If you needled him back, that was okay, but if you didn't think you could do that . . . other people were kind of terrified." Farrow had a bottle of rare scotch in his trailer adjoining the set and sampled it daily. A raiding party from the crew went into the trailer one evening, emptied out half the bottle, and then, ritualistically, three or four took turns pissing into it. After that, evil grins met Farrow whenever he poured himself a belt of the prized whiskey.

Bob and Jane got along like old buddies. From her stand-in and friend Carmen Cabeen, the sometime wife of Boyd Cabeen, Russell was already well acquainted with some of Bob's more depraved antics and she had prepared herself for his "shocking" side, but that he was also so "intellectual, gentle, caring" came as a most pleasant surprise. She would rave about his astounding command of the English language—even as he would tell her she was the most inarticulate girl he knew. He would tease her about her God-fearing ways, but he understood she was no Loretta Young, wallowing in piety. He loved to tell the one about the pestering reporter who couldn't believe a girl with her "image" read the Bible and went to church each Sunday. ""Hey buddy," she told him, "Christians have big breasts, too." She was good-natured, generous, strong-minded when she had to be, a stand-up guy. Mitchum nicknamed her "Hard John." They became fast friends.

The *His Kind of Woman* mutual admiration society also included the erudite and amusing Vincent Price, thoroughly enjoying himself in a self-mocking performance as the film's vain, Shakespeare-spouting thespian. "Jane was a lovely, funny girl, with a great attitude," said Price, "and Bob was just hilarious." Many a time Price, a gourmet cook, hosted the other two for lunch, serving fabulous meals he had whipped together from scratch. Some days they would all remain on the perfectly pleasant Morro's Lodge set during the noon break, spread a blanket on the faux sand beach, and have a family picnic, Reva delivering baskets of chicken and potato salad, bottles of wine and beer. "We had a lot of fun on that picture," Vincent Price recalled. "At least in the beginning, before it got so . . . crazy."

In mid-May Farrow shot the last pages of the script and went home, the picture completed. Or so he thought.

With a growing logjam of unreleased studio features to preoccupy him, and busy with various business concerns and a hectic social life, Hughes would not even look at *His Kind of Woman* until several months after the production had closed down. Then the tinkering began. Hughes had Robert Stevenson direct some mundane pickup shots and retakes in the last week of October. Then, in December, Hughes summoned scenarist Earl Felton and director Richard Fleischer to his diurnal headquarters at Bungalow 19 of the Beverly Hills Hotel. Felton was a veteran hack writer of the Pat Hobby sort, a cynical wit, and a robust character despite a handicap that required him to get around on crutches. Fleischer was the talented young son of animation maestro Dave "Popeye" Fleischer and a B movie pro looking to move up in the ranks. His crackerjack noir thriller *The Narrow Margin,* written by Felton, was being talked about as the no-budget sleeper of the year, but Hughes had yet to schedule its release (at one point he had considered permanently

shelving the B version and remaking it with Mitchum and Russell).
The three discussed the climax of *His Kind of Woman* and all agreed
that the scene Farrow had directed—Mitchum and the bad guys in a
brief scuffle on the bridge of a yacht—could be expanded and made
more exciting. They sat together all afternoon improvising the additional action, Hughes wanting to work out each and every new slug,
kick, and gunshot, Fleischer and Felton screaming their comments
for the sake of the aviator's failed hearing.

Hughes suggested that the whole assignment could be done in
ten to fourteen days, but the story conferences alone continued for
the next six weeks, many hours at a time, with Hughes ever increasing the scope of the film's violent climax. The action would now take
place not only on the deck of the yacht but inside as well, in the
engine room, in the wheelhouse, there would be a torture scene, a
beating, a bursting steam pipe. Nothing had been built for the original production but the small prop bridge, so an entire yacht had to
be constructed over the water tank on the Pathé lot. Hughes thought
up an elaborate rescue attempt by Vincent Price's character and
some of the hotel guests and some Mexican policemen, a comedy
sequence with a sinking rowboat.

On January 10, 1951, shooting began again on *His Kind of
Woman*. As Hughes examined the daily footage, he would send long,
critical memos with maniacally detailed descriptions of the action
he wanted to see on film.

The comical sinking of the skiff beneath Price and his posse did
not meet Hughes's expectations as filmed, and bulldozers were
brought in to deepen the cement water tank so that the boat would
submerge another thirty inches.

Of all the newly invented material, Hughes had become most
excited by the scene in which an ex-Nazi plastic surgeon offers to
dispose of the Mitchum character with an injection of an experimental drug. Hughes declared that he would write the dialogue for
this scene himself, and to Fleischer's amazement Hughes not only
wrote it but sent along an acetate recording of himself speaking the
German doctor's lines in a high-pitched TexaBavarian accent.

Mitchum balked at the new "injection" sequence wherein he was to struggle against Ferraro's thugs and the doctor trying to shoot him up, the syringe pressing against his exposed vein. "No way Bob wanted to do that scene," said Tony Caruso. "He'd say, 'What's Hughes trying to do to me, man?' He'd just got over that drug rap and Hughes wants him on screen with a needle going in his arm! And they wanted to have a needle actually piercing his skin, you know? They were gonna have a real doctor do it, everything sterile, but Bob absolutely refused. They told him 'Look, this is what Hughes wants . . . let's try to do it.' Hughes wanted to see that thing going in the skin. And I can remember Bob telling them what he thought, refusing adamantly in no uncertain terms; he was not going to have a needle in his flesh. But Hughes was sending all these messages, 'Do this, do that. Have Caruso hit him harder. Hit him in the gut. I want to see his fist go in *deep*'—all that kind of crap."

Filming continued off and on for three months. One day Vincent Price threw a party on the set, an anniversary celebration—he had begun working on *His Kind of Woman* exactly one year ago. Fleischer took the miles of footage to an editor and put together the new climax. With all the material Hughes had asked for, the first cut of the climactic scenes alone ran an hour and twenty minutes.

Hughes eagerly viewed the edited reels at his private screening room in the Goldwyn Studios. Afterward he lavished praise on Fleischer and his colleagues. It was great, great stuff. But there was one problem, and it wasn't the fact that the movie now ran an impossible three hours. Hughes said, "I don't like the actor who plays Ferraro."

Fleischer said, "But he's in nearly everything I just shot."

"Yes, well," said Hughes, "we'll get another actor and redo everything."

Fleischer was then directed to begin a comprehensive search for a replacement Ferraro. After narrowing the candidates to three finalists, Hughes had Fleischer direct each of them in a test scene with Mitchum—the scene in which the star received his on-board beating. They settled on a man named Robert J. Wilke, and Fleischer went right to work reshooting the scenes. He was nearly finished when a man collared him outside his office. The man's name was

Raymond Burr. He was an actor. Howard Hughes had sent him over. He would be replacing Robert J. Wilke.

"Mr. Hughes said to tell you I will be playing Ferraro now."

As Fleischer recalled it in his autobiography, throughout the maddening months of their work together, Mitchum's behavior had been exemplary. But now at last, in this sixth or seventh go-round for these same bruising scenes, the actor began to show the strain. "Mitchum took to drink. . . . He began stashing vodka in water glasses at strategic places all over the set. Whenever there was a delay of some sort, there was always a glass at hand. I didn't catch on for quite a while. It often puzzled me how he could start a scene sober and finish it drunk."

Late in May the last shot was at hand. As sick of the proceedings as everyone else, Fleischer dreamed of nothing but wrapping it up and getting the hell away from there. The lighting for the setup wasn't ready until late in the afternoon, and Fleischer knew that in these hard-drinking final days it was not a good idea to ask anything of Mitchum past 5 P.M. But the desire to conclude the whole awful assignment was so tremendous, the director decided to chance it.

It was not a wise decision. A very drunken Bob Mitchum arrived on the set. Two stuntmen playing tough thugs were supposed to drag him into the salon of Ferraro's yacht and hold him before the German doctor. When Fleischer called, "Action!" Mitchum unexpectedly swung the two men ahead of him and sent them crashing onto the floor. Fleischer stopped the take. Thinking it was some kind of misunderstanding, he again explained what he needed, and Mitchum and the stunt guys started over. Again the pair were thrown to the floor. Even as he knew he was courting disaster, Fleischer felt compelled to go on. The third take was nothing but a brawl, the stuntmen now responding in kind to Mitchum's experiment in improvisation. Fleischer screamed, "Cut! Cut!" as the three men rolled around the set, knocking over the furniture and nearly giving a heart attack to the elderly actor who played the German doctor.

The stuntmen scrambled or were thrown to a neutral corner and Mitchum stood alone on the set, hunched down, panting savagely.

The crew stood around in stunned silence. This was Fleischer's first opportunity to work with a major movie star. It was not going as he had hoped. In a quiet, controlled voice the director told Mitchum he had made a fool of them both.

At this mild rebuke Mitchum exploded. Screaming obscenities and violent threats, he began throwing things, overturning the lamps, collapsing a heavy poker table, tossing chairs. He smashed the windows out, kicked down plywood walls and doors, toppling the entire set, then staggered off the stage, grabbing for every stray chair and sending it flying through space.

"I've had it with this fucking picture! I'm sick and tired of being taken advantage of. . . . Stinking directors, and fucking fag actors riding on my back! Fuck you! And fuck Howard Hughes, too!"

He raged his way across the hall, lurched into his dressing room trailer, and slammed the door shut.

Fleischer tried to keep from being sick. He quietly told his assistant to get the set fixed and then went home. After a sleepless night, the director returned to the studio next day full of anger and outrage. He stormed into Mitchum's trailer to demand a public apology. Mitchum saw him, moaned, *"Oh God,"* falling to the floor and crawling underneath his couch, disappearing completely. Mitchum couldn't face him, he said, and begged him just to go away.

Fleischer felt the wind go out of his rage. "You . . . son of a bitch."

"I must be," said Mitchum.

In spite of—or aided by—its spasmodic production history and cluttered auteurship, *His Kind of Woman* would turn out to be one of the most original and entertaining of Mitchum's RKO releases. Unlike Hughes's other fussed-over features, with their choppy editing and reduction to just-the-facts simplicity, *Woman*, two hours long in the final cut, was luxurious, digressive. John Farrow's careful staging was left intact, the film full of atmospheric long takes and sweeping tracking shots until Fleischer's takeover and the gritty climax on the boat, all percussive cutting and unusual handheld camera work. A worthy bookend to his work on *Out of the Past*, Frank Fenton's dialogue was tart and tough throughout, full of memorable, wised-up banter. Showing no indication of the genre-busting turns to come, the opening scenes were purest noir, a shadowed, violent, after-midnight landscape of all-night diners, rented rooms, snarling guard dogs, crooks, cardsharpers, a beating around every corner. The dialogue invoked Mitchum's personal identification with the alienated loser hero in his first moments on screen at an LA greasy spoon.

"Where you been?" asks Sam the counterman. "I ain't seen you since the last rain."

"Palm Springs."

"Hustling the millionaires?"

"I went down there to cure a cold. I wound up doing thirty days."

"For what?"

"For *nuthin'!*"

The expressions of Dan Milner's amiable, weary nihilism might have come direct from a Mitchum press interview of any vintage. "No, I'm not busy," says Milner, about to be hired for a mission to oblivion. "I was just getting ready to take my tie off, wondering if I should hang myself with it."

With Mitchum's third-reel arrival at the Baja resort, the film would shift gears and keep on shifting them, alternating unpredictably between tropical moonlight romance, comedy, murder mystery, and extreme violence (only Anthony Mann's brutal noirs contained anything to match the sadistic fury of Fleischer's and Hughes's belt buckle and hypodermic melee). The unhurried narrative easily made room for random, beatific vignettes: Jane Russell's squalidly glamorous introduction in a flyblown Nogales cantina, warbling an insouciant Sam Coslow ditty ("Five Little Miles from San Berdoo"); Vincent Price's farcical assault on the villain's yacht, with offhand tribute to Buster Keaton; and Mitchum standing over an ironing board ironing the wrinkles out of his cash ("When I'm broke I press my pants," he explains), a moment worthy of Buñuel.

As Hughes and everyone else had suspected, Russell and Mitchum made a wonderful team, a young man and woman who looked, in critic Manny Farber's phrase, as if they would do in real life what they did here for RKO. Magnificent physical specimens ideally paired, together on the screen they appeared at all times as if just back from or en route to the nearest boudoir. Hughes loved the film and excitedly made plans to exploit what his friend Louella Parsons was calling "the hottest combination that ever hit the screen!" On Wilshire Boulevard he hired a massive billboard and had the film's poster art—the stars in a languid horizontal embrace—loaded into a bright golden frame studded with gas jets ejaculating fire. The first night it was up and running, Hughes arrived at 3 A.M., stood on the street corner, and stared for some time at the blazing creation, Jane and Bob cuddling in the flaming sky. Then he got back into his car and ordered the whole thing torn down.

His Kind of Woman opened to mixed reviews—the *New York Times* called it one of the worst Hollywood pictures in years—and moderate earnings. The film would have registered a nice profit but for the nearly one million dollars Hughes had spent on five months of retakes, added scenes, and cast changes.

Just three months after shooting on *His Kind of Woman* concluded for the first time, Hughes reteamed his brawny stars for another exotic thriller: *Macao.* "There is no other place like it on earth," claimed the screen treatment. "Macao, in the China Seas across the bay from British Hong Kong. Where gambling is the heavy industry and smuggling and dope peddling come as naturally as eating. To this island of commercial sin comes NICK, a young grifter wanted back in the states—and NORA, a girl who never got the breaks. Both hard as nails, cynical, strangers. And on the same boat, posing as a salesman, comes a hardboiled New York cop, sent out to capture a fugitive-racketeer who is now the Frankie Costello of Macao. . . ."

On this premise, fashioning a shooting script, slaved writers Norman Katkov, Stanley Rubin, Edward Chodorov, Walter Newman, Bernard Schoenfeld, George Brickner, Frank Moss, and most likely anybody else at RKO with a working typewriter.

Early in the summer, second-unit man Dick Davol was dispatched to Hong Kong and Macao to shoot background footage. Davol found Asia in an annoying tizzy when he got there.

Cameramen were not welcome and everyone had their hand out. He cabled Hollywood to be prepared for his whopping big expense account:

> It was necessary to pay for every setup under cover. Here are a few of the people who were appeased:
>
> Macau Chief of Police
> Propaganda Minister
> Immigration Officers
> Custom Officers
> Macao Harbor Police
> Hong Kong Immigration Officers
> Hong Kong Policemen
> Communist Custom Patrol Boats
> Sampan Owners
> Chinese Junk Owners and Crews
> Communist Business Owners

Screenwriter-producer Jules Furthman, Howard Hughes's most valued creative collaborator, had urged his boss to bring Josef von Sternberg back from an involuntary retirement to direct John Wayne and Janet Leigh in *Jet Pilot*, an anti-Communist aviation romance. Sternberg was one of the handful of true artists of the cinema's first half century, but a surfeit of arrogance, artistic intransigence, and bad box office had sent him wandering in the wildnerness, without a feature film credit in nearly ten years. Always a connoisseur and exponent of movie eroticism, Hughes remembered fondly the humid results of Sternberg's work with such screen beauties as Evelyn Brent, Esther Ralston, and Marlene Dietrich. It was an arousing idea, to unleash the director's caressing camera on some of Hughes's own objects of desire—Janet Leigh and a collection of shiny jet-propelled aircraft.

Sternberg performed his task professionally if without much enthusiasm (Hughes was to keep *Jet Pilot* in postproduction for nearly a decade), and he was then sent across the lot to take the helm on *Macao,* which began principal shooting in August. This one at least sounded like a more sympathetic assignment, the title evoking memories of the maestro's brilliant earlier forays in the mysterious East, *Shanghai Express* and *The Shanghai Gesture.* Indeed, the opportunity to linger in another Oriental dreamscape of his own creation captured von Sternberg's attention at the start. He oversaw the design of a vivid backlot Macao of latticework fishing nets, artfully bobbing sampans, black cats, streets filled with gaudy chinoiserie signage, and cast a populous of exotic bit parts, Sikh traffic cops, blind beggars, beautiful Chinese "high-low" gamblers in slit skirts.

The project offered all sorts of intriguing possibilities, not the least of them in the matchup of director and star. By all rights Mitchum should have been ideal raw material for von Sternberg's molding. In *Morocco* in 1930, the director had drawn from Gary Cooper a sensational performance unlike any other in the actor's career, impudent, languid, *cool*—it was, in fact, a kind of proto-Mitchum performance. Now the director would be working with the real thing, so to speak. As to the script, the trivial intrigue of *Macao*'s plot was no pulpier than most of von Sternberg's earlier classics, and one could imagine, left to his own devices, his magically transforming the prosaic screenplay into something like another exotic reverie in the manner of *Morocco, Shanghai Express,* or *The Devil Is a Woman.*

The circumstances, alas, did not prove conducive to flights of oneiric self-expression. RKO in 1950 was not Paramount in 1930, and the director's despotic methods and arrogant manners were no longer looked upon as those of a world-renowned cultural icon but of a tiny, obnoxious has-been. Mitchum would recall him with little more than contempt: "He was very short and sort of arty, and he was from Weehawken, New Jersey, but he had a German accent—he was very German. I said, 'Where did you get that accent, Joe? You're from Weehawken, N.J.,' and he said if I wanted to know anything about anything, to come to him, he was the omniscient artist. He had a junk shop in Weehawken."

Jane Russell remembered, "According to Sternberg, we were not supposed to eat or drink on the set. No grip was allowed to have a

Coke in the corner. Nobody." Mitchum began bringing in bags of food and coffee, and handing them out to one and all. Sternberg was enraged, told Mitchum he was going to be fired. Mitchum said, "If anyone gets fired, it'll be you." Sternberg had a lecturn at which he would stand and where he would place his copy of the script. No one was to go near the lecturn, so Mitchum began having his lunch there, leaving half-eaten pickles and greasy wax paper all over the director's pages.

"Joe was really something," said Mitchum. "He told me, 'We both know this is a piece of shit and we're saddled with Jane Russell. You and I know she has as much talent as this cigarette case.' I replied, 'Mr. von Sternberg, Miss Russell survives, so she must have something. Lots of ladies have big tits.'"

Speaking of which:

Howard Hughes, monitoring the daily footage, took his usual great interest in Jane Russell's appearance on screen. Regarding a gold lamé dress worn in one sequence, Hughes wrote a long and vividly detailed memo. "The fit of the dress around her breasts is not good," Hughes complained, "and gives the impression, God forbid, that her breasts are padded or artificial. They just don't appear to be in natural contour . . . It would be extremely valuable if the dress incorporated some kind of a point at the nipple because I know this does not ever occur naturally in the case of Jane Russell. Her breasts always appear to be round, or flat, at that point so something artificial here would be extremely desirable if it could be incorporated without destroying the contour of the rest of her breasts. . . . I want the rest of her wardrobe, wherever possible, to be low-necked (and by that I mean as low as the law allows) so that the customers can get a look at the part of Russell which they pay to see. . . ."

With so much of Jane Russell filling the screen, there was hardly any breathing room for the film's second female lead, Gloria Grahame, performing the underwritten—she claimed "unwritten"—role of the villain's croupier mistress, a part originally earmarked for Jane Greer (Hughes still in the grip of his love/hate fixation with that alluring woman). Grahame thought Hughes was deliberately sabotaging her career, too. He would not even look at her brilliant work opposite Humphrey Bogart in *In a Lonely Place* (directed by her new and soon-to-be ex-husband, Nicholas Ray) and he refused to loan her to Paramount to costar in *A Place in the Sun* (the part that would bring Shelley Winters an Oscar nomination). Instead of that she was doing *Macao* and a part requiring only that she look sexy and blow on dice.

The atmosphere on the set continued to deteriorate, von Sternberg becoming victim to variations on the "Farrow treatment," his belongings tampered with, a reeking Limburger cheese smeared through the engine block of his car. Mitchum claimed to have taken him aside and warned him not to make "assholes" of the technicians and grips. "He'd be nice when I was there and when I was away, not so nice," he told Dick Lochte. "What was I gonna do, bat him around? He only came up to here."

Upon its completion, the film was put through a grueling preview process, shown to random audiences in return for their critical reaction. New production head Sam Bischoff (replacing Sid Rogell, who finally decided he had taken his last 3 A.M. call from Howard) gauged the audience responses and mixed in his own hard-nosed musings for a consensus opinion. *Macao* was too atmospheric, too weirdly sexy, too full of irrelevant details and artistic filigree. Apparently, instead of another *Jet Pilot,* the director had delivered something like a Josef von Sternberg picture. One preview card noted that a bare-chested Mitchum (waiting for his laundry) looked fat, and one card from a twelve-year-old girl said that he smoked too much. Bischoff decided that the picture was going to need a lot of work, though not necessarily from Josef von Sternberg. "Instead of fingers in that pie," wrote the director of what was to be his final American feature film, "half a dozen clowns immersed various parts of their anatomy in it."

A few days before Christmas, the Hollywood Women's Press Club announced Mitchum the winner of their annual Least Cooperative Actor or Sour Apple Award. Olivia DeHavilland, winner of Least Cooperative Actress, did not acknowledge the honor, but Mitchum wired the club at their annual luncheon: "Your gracious award becomes a treasured addition to a collection of inverse citations. These include several prominent mentions among the Worst Dressed Americans and a society columnist's 10 Most Desirable Males list happily published on the date I was made welcome at the county jail."

Present at the luncheon to receive a Solid Gold Apple Award as Most Cooperative Actress was Miss Loretta Young.

The production of *The Racket* in 1928, an adaptation of a hit Broadway play by Bartlett Cormack, was one of Howard Hughes's earliest ventures in the cinema and a groundbreaker in the nascent gangster genre. Like so many of the plays, novels, and films of the era written by wised-up big city reporters, *The Racket*—the story of a tough cop out to bring down a big crime boss—daringly and thrillingly exposed the corrupt underbelly of American society. Twenty-two years later, in the wake of the headline-making Estes Kefauver investigations into organized crime, Hughes decided the time was right for a remake of his early hit.

Hughes commissioned another ex-crime reporter and a hot screenwriter of the moment, Samuel Fuller, to write an updated version of the Prohibition-era text. The irrepressible Fuller turned in a typically provocative, anarchic script in which the good cop and the bad crime boss were two sides of the same coin—both of them uncontrollable psychos. Hughes and producer Edmund Grainger opted for something more conventional, and a shooting script was quickly flung together by William Wister Haines and W. R. Burnett (one of the inventors of the gangster genre and a past master of incorruptible-lawman stories). Mitchum would play the cop hero, one of his rare establishment roles, though Captain McQuigg's straight arrow is certainly an outsider in his bought and paid for metropolis. Mitchum's glum, stone-faced performance evidenced a distaste for the part. He was reteamed with his *Crossfire* costar Robert Ryan snarling his way through the role of the old-style racket boss Nick Scanlon.

The new film, directed by John Cromwell, another man whose once distinguished reputation had become faded, would turn out old-fashioned and a bit oafish but still hard-hitting in its blunt portrait of the pervasive corruption and criminal domination of a big American city. Hughes's update anticipated what would become the dominant thematic trend in the gangster genre in the next decade, the view of crime as another form of efficient big business with corporate rules of behavior and no room for hotheaded mob bosses determined to take things "personal." *The Racket* would also anticipate the fascist cop fantasies of the Dirty Harry '70s, with its non-judgmental display of matter-of-fact police brutality and necessary rule-bending. In the course of his investigation, McQuigg blithely sanctions the beating and jailing of an innocent bail bondsman, tears up a writ of habeus corpus, and calls for a suspect's arrest in this sarcastic exchange:

McQuigg: If he resists there's a city ordinance against expecto-
   rating on the public pavement.
Officer Johnson: That includes expectorating *broken teeth,* sir?
McQuigg: Oh yes, that's very unsanit ary.

Some of the right-of-center contributions by W. R. Burnett went even further in this vein—for example, having the cops kicking and wiping their feet on Scanlon's dead body—but these were not included for fear of censorship.

The Racket was shot quickly, in thirty-two days in April and May of 1951, and a seriously ailing John Cromwell left it at that. Hughes and Burnett then cooked up a few new scenes—a violent chase and gun battle—and a framing device with a crusading crime commissioner (Hughes belatedly remembering to tie into those Kevauver Committee headlines). These were directed early in June by Nicholas Ray, Mitchum doing this work just days after he finished wrecking the *His Kind of Woman* set.

Ray did such an efficient job that he was handed another ignoble task, directing retakes and new material for *Macao.* These took up most of July and a few days in August. In the time since von Sternberg had been removed from the studio, Sam Bischoff and his minions had made such a botch of dismantling and reediting the unsatisfactory director's cut that Mitchum claimed his character would come through a door and run into himself on the other side. The revised script pages were considered so hopeless and unplayable that Ray and Jane Russell drafted Mitchum to take a whack at it. "Jane and Nick came up to me with a big legal pad and several pencils and said, 'Write it!' So I got in the dressing room in the morning . . . they got a secretary to type it up . . . and we'd shoot it in the afternoon." Exactly how much he contributed to the released film is difficult to say—the Ray-directed scenes add up to about one-third of the release cut—but there seems some agreement that the amusing scene with Russell wielding an electric fan and spraying the room with pillow feathers ("What are we, delegates to a peace conferance!") is the work of screenwriter Mitchum.

Gloria Grahame, in the process of divorcing Nick Ray when she heard he was reshooting and reediting *Macao,* cracked, "If you can cut me out of the picture entirely I won't ask for any alimony." (In fact, she would have to appear in some of the new scenes, these directed by yet another overseer—Mel Ferrer.)

To Mitchum it was a season of déjà vu, returning to one unfinished project after another, traipsing from set to set, climbing into the costumes and parts he thought he had discarded months before. At any given time he had three pictures in various states of incompletion. Hughes had movies piling up all over the place, movies being rewritten, reedited, movies just lying on the floor somewhere, some of them two years or more out of production. It was a helluva way to run a railroad, Mitchum thought, but as long as his paychecks cleared, it was really none of his business. Doing the public a favor, keeping some of those things out of the theaters, he figured.

CHAPTER EIGHT

Our Horseshit Salesman

One Minute to Zero was Mitchum's first war picture since *G.I. Joe*, but genre and a noisy soundtrack were about all it had in common with Wellman's masterwork. A tale of the then-current Korean "conflict," it was action-packed, jingoistic propaganda, notable mainly for the unprecedented use of gory combat footage (e.g., charred corpses) and a grotesque and miserably self-justifying sequence (apparently based on fact) in which Mitchum's Colonel Janowski orders the murder by shelling of innocent refugees, including old people and small children, because there are Communist soldiers hiding among them. Slackly directed by veteran Tay Garnett, the film suffered as well from poor writing, terrible comedy relief, and a dull romance.

It didn't help that the production had fallen into disarray from the beginning. Exteriors were to be filmed in the rugged country surrounding Camp Carson army base ten miles outside Colorado Springs, Colorado. When the company arrived in late summer, the area was experiencing unseasonably bad weather. In September it snowed for days on end. Costar Claudette Colbert was struck down with pneumonia and a 104-degree fever, stayed under doctor's care for a week, and then flew home. Actor William Talman became afflicted with the same ailment, while director Garnett was hospitalized with influenza. Actor Charles McGraw stepped into a hole and broke his ankle, and crew members housed in Anderson tents at the base came under attack by rattlesnakes. After weeks of futile negotiations with Joan Crawford, Colbert was replaced with Ann Blyth, and the script had to be revised to accommodate the considerably younger actress. RKO sent writer Andrew Solt to the location, where he would hole up with Garnett every night, then type out new scenes hours before they were due to be filmed. All the delays necessitated the company remaining in Colorado for an additional month, by which time the weather had long turned seasonably bad, with snow and hailstorms, and leaves having to be wired to trees to match the shots taken in summer. John Mitchum, now billing himself as John Mallory, had nabbed a small part in the film as an artillery officer. He was supposed to stay with the company for less than a week, but the weather problems and various screwups conspired to keep him on the payroll for nearly two months.

With the filming proceeding in fits and starts, cast and crew were provided with a great deal of free time, which the majority devoted to drinking, card-playing, and skirt-chasing. Until he was asked to go elsewhere, Bob Mitchum could be found most nights at the Alamo Hotel's Red Fox Lounge, a local hangout. Colorado Springs was 5,800 feet above sea level, and Bob soon learned the mixed delights of high-altitude boozing, where one drink hit you like two. One night word had spread of his attendance at the Red Fox, and people from all over the area, mostly females—schoolteachers, mothers, women from the air base, girls below the drinking age— crowded into the lounge, surging around Mitchum, who was way beyond plastered. Breaking free from the clawing hands of auto- graph seekers, he climbed onto a couch, emptied his drink, then turned his posterior to the frenzied fan club and exploded a noi- some fart.

There was another nightspot in town, a black club called Duncan's, where hot jazz bands performed. A bunch of the guys from the movie arrived for the show, filling a big table near the stage. Charlie McGraw spotted some good-looking local girls in the audi- ence and invited them over, and John Mitchum was immediately taken with one of them, a sweet young woman named Nancy Munro. It turned out to be a momentous night for them—John fell in love, and he and Nancy became husband and wife some months down the road (after a complicated split from his current spouse, Gloria Grahame's sister, Joy).

On November 7 Bob and RKO stock player Charles McGraw—who proved to be a compatible sidekick, a kind of mini-Mitchum who reputedly drank two cases of beer and slept four hours per day—were standing at the bar of the Red Fox in conversation with a lieutenant colonel and an off-duty military policeman, both from Camp Carson, when in through the doorway from the Alamo lobby came a private named Bernard Reynolds. According to eyewitness reports of the incident, the lieutenant colonel looked over the private and ordered him to button up his jacket.

"Reynolds said something to the colonel," recalled Lee Haynes, the military cop who was standing beside them. "And that's when Mitchum grabbed him."

"I grabbed him by the lapels," said Mitchum. "He kept yelling and swinging his arms around and I grabbed him. I asked him to behave himself, but he shook his right arm loose and swung at me. I ducked the punch and we both fell to the floor."

Haynes said he thought that after Mitchum had shaken the soldier it was all over, and he turned away. "When I looked back, I saw Mitchum had Reynolds down on a couch and was banging his head against a table." Some bystanders tried to pull the men apart. "They had Mitchum standing up," said Haynes. "It was dark in there, but I saw Mitchum kick Reynolds in the head." Another witness, George Wright, a civilian worker from the base, told police that he saw Mitchum kick Private Reynolds in the face.

It turned out Reynolds was a sometime heavyweight prizefighter who had knocked out nineteen of twenty-eight opponents and was ranked tenth in the world at that time.

"I stopped in the joint for a hot buttered rum," Mitchum reflected, "and bang, I was right in the middle of it. I wasn't angry. It was just a saloon hassle. I just roughed the guy up a little but that's all."

Reynolds was taken to the camp hospital and treated for a possible skull fracture.

"An actor is always a target for the belligerent type of guy who thinks he is tough and movie he-men are softies," said Mitchum, in a studio press release run up the flagpole by RKO's Phil Gersdorf. "I never start a fight, but I assure you I can always finish one if there is no other way out. This one was unavoidable and I'm sorry it happened."

"MITCHUM KICKED SOLDIER, SAYS BRAWL WITNESS" and "COL. BOB MITCHUM IN BAR BRAWL; GI HOSPITALIZED" were a couple of the headlines that appeared across the country the following day. Back in Hollywood an RKO spokesman claimed that Mitchum was simply trying to protect fellow actor Charles McGraw. "Mitchum's rough and ready," said the spokesman, "but he's not the vicious type."

He would later cop to the kicking charge, sort of. "It wasn't the Marquess of Queensberry rules," he said. "I brushed my foot across his head to say, 'See, fucker, you see what I could do to you?'" (Or as he put it to another reporter, "*When you fuck with the ape, be ready to go the route.*")

Howard Hughes hated sharing his stars with other studios. Loan-outs generally meant huge profits (the vast difference between a star's loan-out price and his actual salary), and if done with care and the projects became award-winning hits, say, they could greatly increase the value of these human assets. But as the head of RKO, Hughes's eccentric methods showed little concern for profits and even less for prestige. It is impossible to say what direction Mitchum's career might have taken had Dore Schary and David Selznick remained in control of it, but there is evidence of some places it did not go, thanks to Hughes. He refused to respond to feelers from the Broadway producers of *A Streetcar Named Desire,* who wanted Mitchum to follow Marlon Brando in the role of Stanley Kowalski. The great Howard Hawks had hoped to work with Mitchum on one project or another for years, but the director's feud with Hughes kept it from happening. And Columbia head Harry Cohn begged Hughes to let them have Mitchum for the role of the top kick in *From Here to Eternity,* the part that ultimately went to Burt Lancaster. "Jesus, Bob," Howard told him in explanation, "you don't want to be going over there with those Jews. You don't want to be associated with those people. . . ."

A producer at RKO had once laughingly explained to Mitchum

his place in the Hollywood hierarchy. "Every studio has its horseshit salesman," he said. "And you're ours."

Mitchum tried never to think about the lost opportunities. Why fight City Hall. Paint his eyes on, change the leading lady, and shout, "Roll 'em." Did it matter which fucking picture you made? They were all just masturbation aids, something for the folks to think about when they got back home and took their pants off. "Have you ever seen a typical Mitchum fan?" he asked a reporter. "Glazed eyes . . . haven't shaved . . ." All his movies, he would explain, were a variation on a formula he called Pounded to Death by Gorillas. Fade in on broad-shouldered Bob as a huge gorilla looms up behind and hits him on the top of the head. Boom! He crumples. Boom, boom, he keeps falling down, but he keeps getting up again. Cut to a little girl skipping through fields of daisies. As the writers didn't have that part figured out yet, they cut back to Bob. Boom, boom, the gorilla still knocking him down. At last the ape collapses from exhaustion. The little girl comes in, says, "I know he's around here someplace, I just know it." Finally, she peels away the gorilla and there lies the hero. Cradling him in her arms, the girl looks straight into the camera and says, "I don't care what you think—*I like him*." Fade out. The End.

Restlessness still plagued him. He usually left town whenever a picture wrapped. Sometimes he would just climb into his car by himself and drive away with no destination in mind. Dorothy told a reporter, "Bob is really a bachelor at heart." But there were great times with the family as well, long afternoons in the pool, or playing croquet, or taking the boys on long treks deep into the wilderness. Times like he had dreamed of having with his old man when he was a kid.

Some of the crew guys at RKO—in appreciation of Bob's loyalty to them—had helped him to construct a compact mobile camper when such things were not yet commercially manufactured. To the open bed of a Ford truck they attached a removable corrugated steel cabin containing a refrigerator, butane stove, sink, water tank, a single bed hung from chains on the ceiling, and a convertible double bed on the floor. With Tim Wallace and the boys on board, he took the camper on an inaugural journey, pursuing salmon in the rivers of Idaho, catching two massive beauties that left a choking stink in the cabin when the refrigerator broke down. They drove to Colorado in time for the *One Minute to Zero* premieres in Denver and Colorado Springs, meeting up with Dorothy for the festivities. She and the boys then departed for Delaware and a lengthy stay with her family. Bob and Tim loaded the truck with alcohol and chili beans and set off to do some spearfishing in the Arkansas backcountry. It turned out that John Mitchum was down in Little Rock finishing up the required ninety-day residence for a "quickie" divorce, a plan that was foiled when he failed to bring a corroborating witness to court. He was standing on Main Street, forlorn, when the camper—now dubbed the "Oochee-Papa-Poontang Wagon" for reasons unspecified but easily guessed at—rolled into town. He grabbed hold of Tim and rushed him to the courtroom, where Wallace gladly improvised lurid tales of John and Joy Mitchum's incompatibility, and the divorce was granted.

Howard Hughes had succeeded in turning RKO into a ghost of the once thriving studio, a growing joke and embarrassment in the Hollywood community. With fewer and fewer pictures scheduled and "finished" films piling up or endlessly revised at the boss's unfathomable whim, there was little product to sell and the studio began losing money at an ever-advancing rate. The need to have something to distribute, no matter how unpromising, meant an increasing dependence on fly-by-night outside sources, expanding the definition of an RKO picture to include Italian art movies (ruthlessly reedited and dubbed) and a ten-year-old Swedish documentary about Siam.

Relief seemed on the way when Hughes signed a fifty-million-dollar, five-year deal to finance and distribute sixty films produced by the independent team of Jerry Wald and Norman Krasna, a pair of highly regarded pros who boasted that Hughes was giving them "full autonomy." Instead Hughes gave them the same interference and disappearing act he gave to everyone else. In the three years they remained at RKO, Wald and Krasna were able to make just four completed features. The last of these and the best—perhaps the very last RKO film to be widely considered a classic—was *The Lusty Men*.

Jerry Wald had seen a magazine article by Claude Stanush about modern-day rodeo cowboys. He hired the writer and put him together with a migrant New York novelist named David Dortort to develop a screen treatment on the subject. They came up with a heavily detailed, sort of semidocumentary account of the tough, rowdy, often sad lives of the rodeo tramps, moving from town to town across the West, risking their lives for a chance at some elusive prize money. After Robert Parrish dropped out of the project early on, Wald turned to an RKO contract director with whom he had been eager to work: Nicholas Ray.

The intense, innovative director—formerly Raymond Nicholas Kienzle, Jr., of Galesville, Wisconsin—was a product of the experimental and revolutionary stage companies of the '30s in New York—the Theatre of Action, the Federal Theater—and a disciple of Elia Kazan. His directing career in Hollywood had gotten off to a flying start with the remarkable RKO release *They Live by Night* in 1948, and he had remained under contract to the studio ever since (loaned out to Humphrey Bogart on two occasions). Ray's first seven pictures varied wildly between brilliant and personal works (*In a Lonely Place, On Dangerous Ground*) and craftsmanlike jobs of utter anonymity (*Flying Leathernecks*). Howard Hughes had taken a liking to him, going so far as to overlook Ray's left-wing associations (even forgiving him after he refused to direct *I Married a Communist*, a Hughes litmus test), but saw only the craftsman, indiscriminately assigning him to those thankless retake jobs on *Macao* and *The Racket* and the outrageous Vestal Virgin Bathhouse sequence added to *Androcles and the Lion*. It was the pattern of Ray's entire career, great original film art mixed in with meaningless hack work, right up until bad luck and self-destruction afforded him a premature "retirement."

Happily signed on for Wald's project, seeing it as an extension of his work in the Southwest in the '30s with folklorists John and Alan Lomax, Ray began soaking up the background from Stanush's files and looking over the locations and dates of the next regional rodeo circuit. There was still no script, just incidents, data, a rough outline of a story. To come up with a filmable text, they sought out a reliable hired gun named Horace McCoy. McCoy was a journeyman screenwriter with the sort of background a journeyman screenwriter often had in those days—World War I flier awarded the Croix de Guerre, Dallas sports and crime reporter, one of the original hard-boiled pulp writers for *Black Mask* magazine, and author of the acclaimed novels *Kiss Tomorrow Goodbye* and *They Shoot Horses, Don't They?* He had also been a rodeo aficionado since boyhood and had his own store of anecdotes and lore to bring to the project. McCoy went to work at once, putting flesh on a skeleton of a plot about a washed-up former rodeo champ who agrees to manage the career of an ambitious newcomer, and how the new champ comes to resent and humiliate the mentor and drives him back into the arena, with tragic results. Typical of McCoy's best work in Hollywood, it blended strong, flavorful writing with backlot clichés.

Everyone agreed that Robert Mitchum was the man for the part of the broken-down cowboy—everyone except Hughes, who had to be convinced by the actor himself. Nick and Bob had known each other from the time of *They Live by Night,* when Mitchum had been ready to play the Indian bank robber Chickamaw in that film (the part eventually played by Howard DaSilva), even making a test with his hair dyed black; but the higher-ups had vetoed it—not a proper role for a star. Now the director talked to him about *Cowpoke,* as it was then known, craftily connecting the washed-up, drifting character of Jeff McCloud to things he knew of Mitchum's personal history and inner life. Mitchum thought Ray sounded like a screw-loose prophet when he got going on a subject, but Ray had pushed the right buttons—Mitchum's fondness for losers and outsiders, his memories of Depression wandering and homelessness—and the actor came away eager to take on the role.

Arthur Kennedy was picked for the part of McCloud's ambitious partner, the new rodeo champ whose arrogance leads to tragedy. Kennedy had doubts that the role was for him and questioned whether there was enough story to make a picture, but Ray convinced him during a long, liquid lunch at a restaurant across the street from the studio. The supporting role of Booker, a grizzled rodeo veteran gone punchy, went to a character actor recommended by Howard Hawks, Arthur Hunnicutt, then at the start of a noble career as the cinema's seediest-looking scene stealer.

Something like two-thirds of the script had been written when it was learned that Susan Hayward, a very big name and yet another actress Howard Hughes lusted after, was joining the cast. This presented a bit of a problem as there was barely a part for her to play. The role of Arthur Kennedy's wife would have to be rewritten and expanded to fit a major star. And on the double: Hayward, borrowed at great expense from 20th Century-Fox, was available only for a specific block of time that began almost immediately. The actress came over to RKO for a meeting with Ray and Mitchum. Ray talked about the characters and their dreams and feelings in his tangled, inarticulate way.

After a while, Hayward put down her knitting and said, "Listen, I'm from Brooklyn. What's the *story?*"

As Mitchum recalled it, Nick turned to him at this point. "Tell her, Bob." So Mitchum started improvising, trying to catch her interest.

"She said, 'That's all right. Is that on paper?' And Nick said, 'Of course!' and he dragged out toilet paper and all sorts of things. So he convinced her, I guess, that we had a script."

Horace McCoy revised his pages to accommodate a role worthy of Miss Hayward's stature. Louise Merritt became the third side of a triangle, the strong-willed wife who agrees to follow her husband's dangerous season on the rodeo circuit in pursuit of her own dream, the money to buy a home. The script remained unfinished, though, when McCoy dropped out just before filming was to begin. He had a book deadline looming and more movie offers (he would cowrite the *other* rodeo movie of 1952 as well, *Bronco Buster,* directed by Budd Boetticher), and a frantic Jerry Wald had begun pestering him with suggestions. Mitchum's absurdist recollection of the writer's departure went like this: "Horace came in one day—he had undergone some strange metamorphosis and was sort of jiggling up and down—and he had a paper, and he said, '*Now, she's standing at the exercise bar and stretching out like this . . . and the miner's lamp is still burning in his hat, he's got a lunch box. . . .*' He read us this scene and we didn't know what the hell. . . . Nick said, 'What's that?' and Horace said, 'Only the greatest damn scene ever written!' and he turned around and walked out." McCoy would not be back until months later, returning on a whim to compose the rodeo announcers' authentic-sounding introductions and comments heard over the loudspeakers.

David Dortort was reassigned to the project, and another writer, Alfred Hayes, worked on several scenes from ideas Mitchum and Ray came up with during the filming. Jerry Wald contributed a few moments here and there, and yet another writer, *One Minute to Zero*'s rewrite man Andrew Solt, served as a stopgap for one scene without even knowing what the picture was about. Many of the sequences shot on location at actual rodeos would be very close to pure improvisation. As in that better-known make-it-up-as-we-go-along movie, *Casablanca,* the ending—Mitchum's death—was uncertain through most of the production. As Ray remembered it, "We started shooting with twenty-six pages of script and we wrote every night. So there wasn't much besides instinct and the reactions of my actors to what we had done the day before to what we were going to do the next day."

Filming got underway just after Christmas, beginning, in continuity, with McCloud's poignant return to his childhood home and his first meeting with Louise and Jeff Merritt. Despite all the pressures surrounding the production—particularly Susan Hayward's looming departure date—Ray worked slowly. And mysteriously. He felt his way around each scene like a blind man and often took to his director's chair for long periods of staring at the set or at an actor and pondering his next move. Bob nicknamed him "the Mystic." Ray liked to have the actors take part in his search for the psychological or poetic values in a scene, in part a tactic to keep them concentrated, stirred up, make them active collaborators, not just line readers. For Mitchum, who had made forty-five films now without even speaking to some of the directors involved, Ray's detailed, dramatic approach to the job took some getting used to. "When I act, I come in and say, 'What page is it and where are the marks?' But Nick is a fellow who likes to discuss the scenes with the actors . . . what my background was, what the background of the rodeo bulls and horses was. . . ." Mitchum cracked that he was out of the frame a lot of times because Ray kept his camera on the actor who had listened the most when he was "talking about Stanislavsky and those people."

Despite the mocking recollections, Mitchum and the director got along very well. Ray, for all his Russian theater "mysticism," was no aloof Sternbergian aesthete but eager for creative collaborators and all too human, another macho fuckup—boozer, ladies' man, degenerate gambler. Mitchum found himself drawn more deeply into the creative process in the making of *The Lusty Men* than he had ever been before. Ray came to feel, as a few other directors would throughout the actor's career, that Mitchum's legendary indifference was a protective mask against disappointment or humiliation; and if you could prove to him that the job was worth the risk, he would work as hard as anybody. Ray found that Mitchum had several characteristics in common with that other notable tough guy actor, Humphrey Bogart. Both were genuine sight readers, and both were good for up to six takes only and then would stray or dry up. If there was still a problem or a technical mistake with the sixth take, Ray would go to something else and come back to it later. As for Mitchum's fondness for drink, another trait he shared with Bogie, Ray had been told that he was "the second biggest lush in town" and warned to beware of shooting past sunset. But, happily, in the entire production they would lose only one morning to Bob's being "too red-eyed" for the camera.

Nick Ray did his best to bond with Susan Hayward as well—he zeroed in on a mutual enjoyment of Thomas Wolfe—and certainly drew from her an excellent performance, but she remained typically tempestuous and cranky—Mitchum called *her* "the Old Gray Mare"—and on one occasion held up production when she refused to play a scene as written. With her contract running out, an emissary was sent running from the stage to the writers department to grab the first writer he saw. "I went down on the set where sat, pouting, Susan Hayward," said Andrew Solt to Ray's biographer Bernard Eisenschitz. "This woman had the foulest mouth that I've ever heard in my life. She sat there and said, 'No, I'm not going to say these lines, they insult me.' And there sat Mr. Mitchum, who couldn't care less, and Nick blowing his top." Taken aside, Solt was informed about Hayward's imminent departure. Solt wanted to read over the script. "You can't read the script!" he was told. "You must start now!" Demanding to hear at least the briefest precis of the story, Solt then managed to come up with some dialogue which, if nothing else, Miss Hayward found not insulting.

The actress's final scenes were completed in a flurry of activity, then she hurried off to Fox to shoot *The Snows of Kilimanjaro* and an exhausted Nick Ray went into the hospital. Robert Parrish, the director originally set for the film, took over for a week and shot three scenes. Ray came back and completed the remaining studio sequences before heading off with cast and crew on a two-week location jaunt (all of Hayward's scenes were filmed on the soundstage and at a couple of rustic spots in Los Angeles). The man who had directed Mitchum's first starring vehicles, the man who had gotten him his first dressing room, Ed Killy, had fallen in the ranks by this time and worked as Ray's assistant during the location shooting. At Tucson, San Angelo, Pendleton, and other rodeo venues, they filmed the events as they happened and then shot improvised scenes with the actors, some of them made up on the spot. It was in the footage shot on location (not the unfortunate soundstage "outdoors" of some scenes) where Ray's handpicked cinematographer, the legendary Lee Garmes ("a renegade," the director called him) really showed his stuff, in windblown images that evoked for some the photographs of Walker Evans or the Dust Bowl scenes in John Ford's *The Grapes of Wrath*. "The whole quality of it was something," said Nick Ray. "I think the kind of loiny sexiness of the hills, of the foothills, was treated as no other cameraman I've ever seen do it, in black-and-white, particularly."

As the company moved from rodeo to rodeo, and despite the number of bones they saw breaking before their eyes as cowboys tumbled through the air and crumbled in the dirt, Mitchum and

Kennedy fell under the spell of the testosterone-charged atmosphere, and each took a turn—violating the terms of their studio insurance coverage—riding a wild horse and a Brahma bull. Mitchum would recall his bumpy ride: "I get on . . . and they all say, 'It's OK, he's just a retired old bronc,' and this thing is turned loose . . . and I can't get off him. They'd go in and try and pick me off and my horse would turn around and kick the pickup horse. . . . I'm bleeding from my hair by this time. . . ." Even Ray felt compelled to show he had what it took, hopping aboard a bucking bronco at the San Francisco Cow Palace. "I guess," he said, "we all have a little of that wildness in us."

They returned to Hollywood, filming a few more bits and pieces, and then Ray began putting the whole thing together. At Jerry Wald's insistence, an alternative version of the ending had been shot, with Mitchum surviving and going off into the sunset with an ex-girlfriend. David Dortort believed that Jerry Wald never understood what the picture was about and cared only that audiences liked happy endings. In the end Ray prevailed, and Jeff McCloud expired as planned. Mitchum claimed he had Reva sneak into the editing room and throw Wald's version in the incinerator.

The actor was sufficiently intrigued about how it had all turned out that he did something he hadn't done in a long time. "Have you got any film cut together that I can see?" he asked the director.

"Sure," Ray said, "I've got about seven reels for you."

He set up the screening for that evening. Mitchum sat by himself in the dark watching the two-thirds of the picture, and afterward, said Ray, "came out of the projection room walking about ten feet high." A celebration was in order, and they went across the street to Lucey's. Ray crawled for home some hours later, recalling that when he had last seen his star, Mitchum and some new pals—a pair of drunken FBI agents—were lurching about in the restaurant's kitchen, Mitchum firing an FBI handgun at Lucey's dirty dishes while the kitchen staff ran for cover.

A key work in the postwar era's advancing demythification of the Hollywood West, *The Lusty Men* (a Hughes-approved title; *The*

Losers would have been more appropriate) depicted the pain and despair underlying the rodeo's festive surface. Anything but conventional, romantic, heroic figures, the film's cowboys are crippled, scarred, middle-aged, and mostly dim-witted men living a sleazy, nomadic existence in a world of cold-water trailers and domestic strife, men sustained by a few dangerous moments of "buzz" when they're in the saddle, and the dream of prize money that will be squandered come morning. Evidencing the formula-driven thinking of assembly-line scenarists, the story itself and many of the dramatic ingredients were hardly groundbreaking—a rehash of *Test Pilot, The Crowd Roars, Manpower,* and all those two-men-and-a-woman-plus-a-dangerous-profession pictures—but Horace McCoy's incisive and poetic writing of individual scenes (the author of *They Shoot Horses* clearly had a feel for life's failures) and Nicholas Ray's nuanced, artful direction gave *The Lusty Men* moments of lyricism and psychological resonance that set it apart from those earlier tales of risk-taking roustabouts. Though he would be best known for his films' neurotic energy bordering on hysteria, Ray here obtained some of his most powerful effects from emotional restraint and simple staging, most memorably in Mitchum's last scene. The offhand style and quiet underplaying only increased the scene's emotional force: the broken cowboy sighing his last ironic aphorism ("Guys like me last forever"); and even more devastating (Ray repeating a bit from *They Live by Night* but to much greater effect here), the almost imperceptible cutaway to the young tomboy, Rusty, standing in the background and silently mouthing "I love you . . ." to the dying ex-champion.

Typical of Ray's work, the performances were all strong and three-dimensional, from the leads to the smallest bit parts, including, most memorably among the supporting players, a sad/funny turn by Arthur Hunnicutt and vivacious work by Eleanor Todd as a hilariously sexy lover of the rodeo, branding men with her teeth and guzzling from a phallically extended bottle of champagne. Only Arthur Kennedy, an excellent actor but looking more like a crafty traveling salesman than a potential rodeo champ, was manifestly miscast. Susan Hayward, too, was something less than authentic-seeming as a former Southwest tamale-joint barmaid, though her powerful and discerning performance more than compensated for her lack of a rustic personality. As to Mitchum (beefier than he had ever appeared on screen), he was both believable and superb, carefully tempering his charisma and sex appeal with a distant sadness that perfectly illuminated the character of Jeff McCloud as a man caught between past glory and a future of lonely failure, a man who has come to accept that life is a matter of "chicken today, feathers tomorrow." He was as authentic-seeming a Westerner as Gary Cooper but unromanticized in a way Coop would never have allowed—Jeff blithely living off a friend's hard-won winnings, coveting the same friend's wife, then throwing his life away in a moment of wounded pride. Another portrait in his gallery of existential loners, outsiders, and drifters, McCloud was Mitchum's subtlest and most enigmatic characterization to date.

Mitchum and Ray: a marvelous pairing that should have continued. The director tried to land Mitchum for the Sterling Hayden role in *Johnny Guitar* over at Republic but got nowhere. They never worked together again.

The Lusty Men received mostly excellent reviews, Mitchum heaped with praise, something he had not seen much of in the last few years. But as Jerry Wald feared, audiences didn't know what to make of a drab modern Western with a tragic ending. Nicholas Ray was to say of the film's characters, "They had all lived up to what they were supposed to live up to." And so, in their way, did the public, staying far from anywhere the film played.

*

On March 3, 1952, Dorothy Mitchum gave birth to a third child. The seven-pound, ten-ounce baby girl was named Petrine after Bob's much loved and recently deceased grandmother (it was a long way from frigid Norway to sunny SoCal; Petrine would eventually be trimmed to a perkier-sounding Trina). RKO dispatched photographers to record the baby's arrival at Mandeville, flashing their bulbs as Daddy dandled the infant on his knee. It was good to let the press know Bob did something other than get into bar fights when he wasn't working.

The rest of the Mitchum brood, James and Christopher, were now ten and eight years old respectively. They were healthy, good-looking kids. Jim's appearance was a perfect amalgam of his mother and father, though as he grew older and took on his father's physique, people would speak of the two as dead ringers. Many thought Christopher looked like his mother, a resemblance that was accentuated by the feminine softness of his features and a gentle disposition. In adolescence the boys seemed to divide between them Robert's twofold nature. Jim was the tough kid, an outdoorsman, liked to have fun, was drawn to acting, and acting up. Christopher was the quiet one: thoughtful and bookish, a good student, he dreamed—as his father had done—of becoming a writer.

As a parent Mitchum would be both doting and distant. When the boys were young, especially, through the first decade of his success and with his own childhood deprivations still fresh in his memory, he was generous and attentive, eager to see them enjoy the luxuries and pleasures money could buy and experience the joys of a loving father that he had never known. When they were old enough, Mitchum took them on long hunting and fishing trips, camping and roaming in the wilds of California and throughout the West, wonderful memories for all of them. At home, the boys might not see their father for days at a time—weeks or months even when he was on location or in prison—but Robert did all he could to keep weekends for home and family, and Sundays were inviolate. Photos and home movies show glimpses of the endless California summers spent by the big swimming pool, or playing ball, or riding in go-carts, faces full of grins and high spirits. In time, as the boys grew older and used to their privileges, their father's earlier impulses would fade. The past was done and Robert had new lives to lead. In the years ahead, the changing exigencies of moviemaking took Mitchum farther and farther away and for longer periods of time—ten, eleven months a year at his busiest. Dorothy would diligently try to maintain the family unit however she could, packing them all up and shipping out to follow the wandering movie star—to Greece,

Australia, England, the Caribbean. But these visits, and Mitchum's own sojourns back at the homestead, were only interludes of domesticity for someone who would pull off the rare trick of maintaining the vestments of both family man and wayward bachelor for most of the rest of his life.

Jean Simmons had come to America to marry Stewart Granger. The young Englishwoman, acclaimed star of *Great Expectations, Black Narcissus,* and Olivier's *Hamlet,* was not long in the throes of wedded bliss when out of the blue came news that her contract with the J. Arthur Rank Organization in London had been purchased outright by that rapacious admirer of full-breasted brunettes, Howard Hughes. Despite the presence of the strapping "Jimmy" Granger, Hughes quickly and shamelessly imposed himself on newlywed Simmons's private life. "I realized," said her then-husband, "that Howard Hughes, instead of wanting this lovely actress to make films for RKO, just wanted to screw her." At first intrigued by Hughes's mysterious methods and contemptuously amused by his lasciviousness, Simmons soon came to despise and fear the eccentric Texan. In addition to his unwanted personal advances, he seemed intent on destroying her prospects as a film star. The situation became so ugly and inescapable that, according to Granger, the couple actually considered luring Hughes to their cliffside home and murdering him. In the end they took a more conventional means of redress and sued the man. The two sides came to a bitter standoff—Simmons agreed to appear in three more RKO productions, but all three would have to be completed before a specified, imminent date.

A furious Hughes put his minions to work preparing quickie vehicles for the woman who had spurned him. Two of these, filmed back-to-back in May and June 1952, would costar Robert Mitchum. The first was released in 1954 under the Hughes-chosen title of *She Couldn't Say No* (like so many of Howard's titles, it sounded like it came in a plain brown wrapper). The story was of a wealthy woman (Simmons) returning to the small Arkansas town where the residents had generously taken care of her when she was a sickly infant, and the havoc that ensues when she tries to pay them back.

Mitchum was cast as the woman's bemused love interest, a lazy physician. Handed the script and a starting date, Mitchum promptly disappeared. He found the offered role embarrassingly bad and refused to have anything to do with it. It was only days before shooting was to begin that RKO tracked him down in Dallas, Texas, and wheedled his reluctant return. *She Couldn't Say No* was intended to be a kind of Capraesque comedy of philanthropy à la *Mr. Deeds Goes to Town* and *Lady for a Day*, a goal it missed by some distance due to a weak, mirthless screenplay and the fact that it was directed not by Frank Capra in his prime but by Lloyd Bacon in his dotage.

The second of the Simmons-Mitchum projects was of considerably greater interest. *Angel Face* (given the generic title of *Murder Story* during its fleeting production history) was a black-and-white film noir, one of the last of its kind, as it would turn out, and the very last of Howard Hughes's touching tributes to homicidal females.

With only a brief window of eighteen days in which to squeeze out another feature with his despised star, Hughes knew he would need a fast and efficient director for the job, a disciplinarian who would crack the whip at the first sign of recalcitrance. Hughes decided the man for the job was Otto Preminger, a Viennese Jew and a sophisticated and liberal man in private life but reputed to be a pure Junker sadist on the set. An occasional film actor, he had portrayed Nazis on the screen more than once and quite convincingly. Darryl Zanuck, Preminger's boss, agreed to loan the director to Hughes, and a screenplay was sent over at once. By Chester Erskine, it was based on the actual murder trial of a couple accused of killing the woman's parents. Preminger read it and thought it a piece of *scheisse*. So Hughes drove over to Otto's house at three in the morning and took him for a ride. They drove around the deserted streets of Los Angeles in the battered Chevy as Hughes told of his travails with Jean Simmons and begged him to take the job.

"You hire any writer you want to, any number of writers to rewrite the script, as long as they are not Commies," said Hughes. "Nobody will interfere with you and that includes me. Come to my studio tomorrow and you will be like *Hitler*." In his whining, outraged voice, Hughes said, "I'm going to get even with that little bitch."

Accepting the assignment, Preminger turned to his agent brother Ingo for a writer, and Ingo told him he would send over "a genius" named Oscar Millard, screenwriter of *Come to the Stable* and *No Highway in the Sky*. Millard went to work. "Relations with Otto steadily deteriorated," he recalled. Then Preminger—feeling there was no such thing as too much genius—hired another scribe, Frank Nugent, to finish the thing off. A sordid noir drama with an Electra complex subtext, *Angel Face* was about the beautiful, emotionally disturbed Diane Tremayne, unhealthily devoted to her father, a complacent, faded English novelist under the thumb of his wealthy, shrewish American wife. Summoned to save Diane's stepmother after a suspicious accident, ambulance driver Frank Jessup falls under the sexual spell of the scheming young woman. He accepts a chauffeur's position at the Tremayne manor, continuing his affair with Diane in secret. Jessup comes to realize that Diane is planning to murder her stepmother, though he is morally incapable of doing anything to prevent it. She rigs a car to plunge over a cliff with Mrs. Tremayne behind the wheel, but Diane's father unexpectedly goes along for the fatal ride. The bereft daughter and Frank are both arrested for murder. A clever attorney has them married to attract sympathy and then convinces a jury of their innocence. Diane seeks salvation in her love for Frank, but the chauffeur rejects her, tells her he's going away forever. Offering to drive him to the bus station, Diane recreates her parents' fatal trajectory and sends the car backward over the cliff, killing them both.

Preminger himself came up with the idea for the automotive murders. "That was taken from my personal experience," he recalled. He'd pulled up past the lines at an intersection, reversed, forgot to shift back, hit the gas. "You see, I'm not a very good driver."

Herbert Marshall, Mona Freeman, Barbara O'Neil, Leon Ames, and Jim Backus were added to the cast. Fast-moving cinematographer Harry Stradling was borrowed from Samuel Goldwyn. The Lewis estate in Beverly Hills was rented for the role of the Tremayne estate. Filming began on June 16.

The feud between the RKO mogul and Jean Simmons had grown

ever more virulent. Inflamed by Hughes's fetishist dictates concerning her hairstyle, Simmons had abruptly taken a pair of shears and hacked off her rich dark locks till what remained was a variation on the hairdo worn by Stooge Moe Howard. Wigs had to be quickly prepared to disguise the damage.

Speculation as to just what sort of treatment Hughes had instructed Preminger to give Miss Simmons was fueled by the director's gratuitously brutal behavior toward the actress. "He absolutely, totally destroyed me," Simmons would remember. Shooting a scene at the studio, they reached a moment early in the script that required Mitchum to slap Simmons on the face. Mitchum effectively faked the blow, barely grazing the actress's cheek. Preminger, standing just behind him, screamed, "No, no!" The camera was tight on her face, too close for such fakery, said the director. "Slap her for real!" Mitchum tried again. Preminger didn't care for it. "Again!" Simmons braced herself, her cheek already flaring. The camera rolled; Mitchum slapped her. "No good! Do it again!"

Jean Simmons's eyes began to water from the impact. Mitchum thought she was crying. "Oh Christ," he muttered.

"Vunce more!" Preminger barked.

Mitchum slapped her again.

"Vunce more!"

Mitchum spun around. "Once more?" he said and either slapped Preminger across the face, with just the force the director had been asking for, or very nearly did the same.

Preminger scurried away. He demanded that Mitchum be replaced. He was told to go back and finish the picture before Jean Simmons decided to cut her nose off. Thinking this was not how they would have treated Hitler, Preminger readjusted his pride and returned to the set.

"Well, do you think we can be friends?" the director asked the actor.

"Otto," Mitchum said with fiendish affability, "we're all here for you."

Like Preminger's other noir features (*Laura, Fallen Angel, Where the*

Sidewalk Ends), *Angel Face* was cynical, perverse, and glamorously sleazy. However much or little the director had to do with it, the lead actors were extraordinarily good: Mitchum's amoral, disengaged Frank Jessup was the most spookily apathetic of the star's fatalistic noir losers, while Jean Simmons's simmering, Siamese-catlike performance as Diane Tremayne was among the greatest of her career, though she would probably gag at the thought of it. Perfectly reflecting the circumstances of its production, the entire film quivered with an air of frustration and resentment—there is nary a shred of sympathy evoked for anything on screen, living or dead. The glacial final image—following Mitchum's and Simmons's berserk death scene—of a taxicab pulling up and idling before the ghostly mansion, is a moment of haunting emptiness like nothing else in the American cinema.*

Barely a decade old, film noir, the genre that didn't know its own name, had already reached a decadent phase. Like the Western, noir had become ritualistic, scavenging its own clichés. Seen with a harsh eye, *Angel Face* appeared rewoven, put together from remnants of assorted earlier black melodramas. The aberrant female, the male patsy, the whiffs of incest and sexual obsession, the ironic deaths— all familiar motifs by now, though they had been shocking and fresh just a few years before. The film's trial sequence was a wholesale purloin from James M. Cain's *The Postman Always Rings Twice*, with Leon Ames virtually recreating his role from the MGM version of the tale. Other elements were more than vaguely reminiscent of *Sunset Boulevard* and *Where Danger Lives*.

The golden-age cycle of film noir that had begun in the early '40s with *The Maltese Falcon* and *Double Indemnity* was drawing to a close. Shadowy black-and-white crime dramas, filmed on artificial backlot streets and soundstages, would be fewer and farther between, replaced by genre works considered more up-to-date, more appropriate to wide screen and color. Femmes fatales and trench-coated crime solvers would now, for the most part, be rele-

---

*Angel Face was a particular favorite of Parisian cinephiles in the 1950s. Jean Luc Godard came to rank it one of his ten all-time favorite American films.

gated to the B movie ranks and to the ignominy of television. For Mitchum, anyway, whose close identification with film noir was almost unmatched by any other actor, *Angel Face* was the finish, if not the capstone, to an extraordinary ten years in cinema's shadowland. His last moment on screen was a fitting nihilistic exit for noir's great corruptible chump/hero: seated on the passenger side of an open-topped sports car beside his final fatal woman, pouring a glass of champagne as the vehicle screams into reverse and shoots them through space and to their just desserts.

The African adventure story, yet another generic staple of big-studio-era filmmaking, had experienced a recent rise in prestige after the critical acclaim and popular success of *King Solomon's Mines,* starring Stewart Granger, and *The African Queen* with Bogart and Hepburn, both films shot in color and on dangerous "Dark Continent" locations. Otto Lang, an Austro-Serbo-Croat alpine sportsman and Darryl F. Zanuck's skiing instructor at Sun Valley, Idaho, had followed Zanuck back to Hollywood and became a movie producer at 20th Century-Fox—quite a good one at that, his credits including *Call Northside 777* and *Five Fingers.* Lang was eager to make a film of a book he had read, *White Witch Doctor* by Louise Stinetorf, a fictionalized memoir of the relationship between a saintly old missionary woman and her young novice working with the tribes of Central Africa. Zanuck agreed to purchase the film rights. Lang was delighted, sure that the touching and unusual story would make a memorable motion picture. With enthusiasm he arrived at the first preproduction conference with DFZ, where Zanuck told him the following: "We do not want a picture based on the 'exploits of a woman missionary' struggling for courage in the African jungle. We want a picture about two interesting people, a woman missionary and a white hunter, a story full of physical excitement, physical violence, and *sex*. We do not want a picture about a woman struggling with . . . locusts and other depressing things."

And thus did Lang's moving drama of the hardships of two selfless, celibate Christian ladies become a lusty tale of adventure, a vehicle for sexy Susan Hayward and Bwana Bob Mitchum.

Lang, Roy Baker (an up-and-coming young English director who had just completed *Don't Bother to Knock* at Fox), and a small camera crew took off for the Belgian Congo on a search for suitable locations. Venturing deep within the Congolese jungle, the team faced great hardships, constant heat, rot, insects, and disease. Baker, a "pale-skinned . . . ultrasensitive Englishman" (per Otto Lang), collapsed with fever and had to be shipped home. Lang forged on, returning to Hollywood with lots of exposed film and the realization that no stars could be taken to the pestilent hellhole he had just visited, so *White Witch Doctor* would have to be made on the lot or at Griffith Park. Loaned to Fox in reciprocation for RKO's use of Susan Hayward, Mitchum was teamed with his *Lusty Men* costar for a second and final time. Hard-nosed director Henry Hathaway was assigned to the Technicolor production, guiding the performers around all the potted foliage, process screens, and pot-bellied extras in leopard-skin loincloths. Otto Lang's spectacular location footage would be interspersed with the glaringly phony soundstage exteriors. The film's exciting action highlights included Susan Hayward's molesting of a rubber tarantula and Robert Mitchum's epic brawl with a man in a gorilla suit.

Otto Lang: "The character of this white hunter was a man with a shady reputation, and a sultry guy, and we thought Mitchum would be perfect for the part. I know he had up and down periods where he was under the influence, but he had periods where he was completely sober and normal and no one was better than he was. We had nothing but the best experience. He was on time, always ready to go. Do whatever had to be coped with. He and Susan Hayward got along, but there was no particular charisma between them, or any attraction. She was going through a difficult divorce at the time and was not really approachable as a person. In other words, she kept her distance. And Henry Hathaway was a very strong director. Very forceful. And the stars respected that, Mitchum respected that. No one made any difficulties."

Notwithstanding Henry Hathaway's ugly tendency to direct screaming tirades at his crew, it was an easygoing shoot, and Mitchum—not unaware that the picture was as foolish as anything he'd ever done—settled into a big Fox trailer and tried to enjoy his first job in four years away from RKO's cramped quarters. Between scenes, Mitchum would converse with the production's technical adviser, Dr. Conway Wharton, a medical researcher who had spent twenty years in Africa. "He wanted me to trace the ethnological history of the little-known Bakuba tribe in the Congo Basin," Dr. Wharton recalled. For several sequences involving jungle drumming, a percussionist named Eddie Lynn was brought in to establish some authentic-sounding rhythms; and Lynn was working out on the skins one day when Mitchum came over and joined him in a hot, polyrhythmic jam session. "Man alive," said Lynn, "he was real solid!"

One afternoon, killing time on the set while waiting for the gorilla suit to come back from the steam cleaner, Mitch put his feet up, tipped back his pith helmet, and favored the press with a philosophical discourse on a favored topic. "I believe," Mitchum pronounced, with the conviction of Lincoln freeing the slaves, "the average woman should never wear a girdle! I believe a well-proportioned woman is an object of great beauty. I feel that the lines that nature gave us are the ones we should show. . . . I always have had an intense dislike for anything that detracts from the feminine qualities of a woman, and I look upon a girdle as such a device. I don't see why you should not be able to recognize a person from the back as well as the front."

The weird, hard-to-believe saga of RKO under Howard Hughes was moving ever closer to its inevitable, annihilating conclusion. In September 1952, Hughes unexpectedly sold his controlling interest in the studio to a quintet of businessmen, a syndicate headed by Ralph Stolkin of Chicago. Within weeks of the syndicate taking charge, a New York newspaper exposed the members' various ties to racketeering and organized crime. The revelations shocked Hollywood's scandal-fearing poobahs and infuriated the already shaken RKO stockholders. The confusion brought activity at the Gower Street property to a standstill. For several months in 1952–53, as studio chroniclers Richard Jewell and Vernon Harbin described it, "RKO had no president, no chairman, no production head, and was controlled by men who couldn't run it and wouldn't allow others to take charge." The new owners tried to dump their shares, but no one wanted to go near such an albatross. Finally, to the rescue came . . . Howard Hughes, who in February agreed to take control of the studio once again, keeping the syndicate's $1.25 million down payment for his pains. Hughes was ready to go on as before, but this was not going to be easy now, with so many suddenly alerted to RKO's strange state of affairs. With the company drowning in red ink and ridicule, stockholders began looking into Hughes's management style, incredible squandering of company funds, and sleazy self-indulgence—the vanity productions, the endlessly shelved features, his virtual white-slave racket, filling the payroll with imported starlets, most never even to glimpse a working movie camera. Hughes was pelted with lawsuits, many of them containing lurid accusations regarding his private life. People joked that RKO now employed more lawyers than actors. Thumbing his nose, Hughes announced the studio's first new production in seven months, a "spectacular" adventure called *Second Chance,* to be filmed in color and in the exciting new "3-D" photographic process, and starring Robert Mitchum.

*

Dorothy had once said that her husband was a bachelor at heart, but that didn't mean she liked it. With a new baby in addition to two adolescent boys to be minded, she found Bob's honorary bachelorhood increasingly hard to stomach. Early in March 1953, Hollywood gossips reported that the actor had been kicked out of his home and was living in a rented apartment in Beverly Hills. A series of indiscretions or one lease-breaking outrage—the exact cause of the rift was never revealed, but Dorothy's anger was sufficient to make her change the locks and the phone number at 1639 Mandeville.

Mitchum explained it to the press like this: "I guess I was pretty irresponsible and brought too many people into the house and

Dorothy felt I was a complete nuisance." He hoped the "trial separation" would be brief. He was "very much in love" with his wife, he said. "I want to live with Dorothy and my three kids. I am going to do everything in my power to win her back. Sunday is our thirteenth wedding anniversary, and I'm going to ask her to have a date with me."

On Sunday a sheepish Mitchum showed up at the Mandeville doorstep, bearing gifts—a Spanish lace mantilla and a silk skirt and blouse from Italy. He took her to Ciro's. Bob said he was sorry and wanted to come home. He would be going to Mexico soon for two weeks to shoot the new picture and wanted her to come with him. Kind of a little honeymoon. No kids. Just the two of them—and a Hollywood film crew.

Bob played it hangdog back at the doorstep at the end of the evening. "Can I take you out again?"

"You may call," she told him.

Second Chance was about an American palooka fighting tank town matches somewhere south of the border, and how he becomes involved with a dame on the run from a gangland enforcer. To get permission to shoot in Mexico, RKO had to send the script to Mexico City for approval. The propaganda minister sent it back with a letter telling RKO it had been an honor to read the truly fine tale of the American palooka and demanding that the script be changed to eliminate a number of scenes and references insulting to all Mexican people and their Spanish-speaking neighbors. These offending passages included the hero's depreciative classification of Latin American women as "tamales," another line stating that "there is no hot water South of Laredo," and a dialogue sequence about the battle of the sexes, all of which were found offensive, including the line "Latin American men beat their women once a week regularly and if they did not the women would miss the beatings." Although they regretted compromising the integrity of a piece of fine art like the *Second Chance* screenplay, RKO agreed to the changes and deletions, and the filming permit was granted.

A few weeks before shooting was to begin, Mitchum got a copy of the script. He sat down and tried to read it, but every few pages, he said, he found himself going back to the front to look at the names credited with writing the thing. He was sure they must all be the producer's grandchildren. The hero was some kind of chickenshit fighter who had killed a guy in the ring and was very sensitive about it. In the movies the fighters were always sensitive, and people were always trying to pay them to take a fall and they were never interested in that kind of thing. He had known a lot of boxers in his time, Mitchum reflected, and he had never known one like that. Sometimes a fall was the best thing for everybody concerned. You got tired, you stuck your chin out, took ten, and settled down for a little rest. Why not get paid for it? He went to a story conference with director Rudolph Maté, producer Edmund Grainger, and their associates. Grainger, said Mitchum, liked to analyze the structure and meaning of the screenplay and was fond of big words like *regenerated* and *catalyst* when explaining why one character did this and another did something else and how it all tied together with a pink ribbon. The others would listen, said Bob, wait until it sounded like the guy had come to the end of a sentence, and then nod with enthusiasm.

"Give us your thoughts on the script, Bob?" someone said and Mitchum started flipping through the pages, offering his own insights."Here's a new twist, the heavy smiles all the time. . . . Now this is a real moll . . . she can't have babies or nothin' . . ."

"Yes, but," said the producer, "she's regenerated in the catalyst!"

Sydney Boehm, an ex-crime reporter, was called in to do a rewrite.

If the script was stricly B-unit stuff, the studio's big "comeback" picture would at least be given the veneer of a superior production, with color (a first for Mitchum at RKO), exotic location shooting, and most exciting of all . . . 3-D. The invention with which Hollywood hoped to counterattack television, 3-D was a stereoscopic process supposedly offering audiences an illusion of lifelike depth, though it was quickly perceived as a gimmick best utilized for special-effects sequences and for throwing things at the camera.

Howard Hughes, who had already experimented with three-dimensional effects in the way he had costumed Jane Russell, Janet Leigh, and Jean Simmons, was immediately intrigued by the process.

Cast opposite Mitchum as the "moll" was thirty-two-year-old Linda Darnell. A frequent Hughes bedmate for many years (he had once offered to "buy" her from her husband, cinematographer Pev Marley), she had come to RKO after more than a dozen years at Fox. Hughes had great respect for her talented curves and believed they would make a fitting subject for his studio's first use of the 3-D camera (though Darnell, feeling overweight, would end up refusing to wear the revealing dresses of Hughes's imagining and spent most of the film in a conservative dark suit). The villain of the piece, a ferocious mob hit man, would be played by Jack Palance, the fascinating and often disturbingly intense Elia Kazan discovery who had been in Hollywood for three years, alternating between eccentric leading man parts and great scene-stealing heavies. He would give Mitchum one of his rare opportunities to do cinematic battle with a bad guy his own size and strength.

On April 11 the *Second Chance* company flew to Mexico City and from there continued by car and bus to the scenic colonial town of Taxco. So many scenes had been dropped or rearranged for filming on their return to Los Angeles that what they did shoot amounted to a week's worth of the stars running back and forth across the cobblestone streets and coming in and out of an assortment of doorways. Maté attempted only one elaborate sequence, Bob's big boxing match, filmed at the Plaza de Toros in Cuernavaca, with locals filling the seats and cheering the all-day match between Mitchum and a young former boxer named Abel Fernandez. Hour after hour the pair bobbed and weaved under the killing Mexican sun, while Maté and his crew strove to maintain the precision focus required for 3-D filming. Inevitably, as the wearying fake fight continued, some of the blows the two exchanged landed with unintended impact. "I got knocked out three times," Mitchum recalled. "Cut!" Rudy Maté would shout. "Bob, it is in the script, you are supposed to win the match!" The star's agony would be mostly in vain because problems with the extras staring into the lens and the erratic lighting conditions meant that the fight would have to be at least partly restaged back in Hollywood.

Dorothy had agreed to accompany Robert on the trip, and he had tried to stay out of trouble for the entire week. But sometimes trouble found you. The RKO publicists had arranged for Mitchum and Palance to attend a charity dinner for Boys Town in Mexico City on the Saturday before their departure. Mitchum was brought up on the podium to hand over a (studio-supplied) check for five thousand dollars. An American college boy got into an altercation with the actor en route to the toilets and ended up sprawled across a table. There were shouts and curses, and it looked like the boy's friends wanted to stage a second assault. As photographers jockeyed for a good angle, the RKO publicists decided it was time to get the celebrities out of there.

Bob and Dorothy, Jack Palance, and the rest of the *Second Chance* group were taken to a popular nightclub on the Reforma, where they were joined by a party of Mexican film people, including Emilio "El Indio" Fernandez, the well-known actor-director (a seminal figure in the Mexican cinema but perhaps best remembered for his portrayal of the evil warlord Mapache in Peckinpah's *The Wild Bunch*). They had barely gotten to their table when a drunken stranger—as it turned out, a member of the military elite—came over to meet the Hollywood *estrellas*.

Jack Palance recalled the night: "I'd had a couple of drinks at a party and because of the altitude I was feeling pretty awful. Mexico City is eight thousand feet above sea level. Mitchum and I had already escaped one near brawl, so we went to a club somewhere and as we came in a big Mexican general got up and embraced Bob. He tried to do the same with me but I wasn't feeling like it, so I pushed him away. And he fell, right there on the floor. Well, you know what a general is in Mexico? God—right? The next thing you know he'd drawn a gun on me. . . ."

Emilio Fernandez rushed in to halt the conflict, a dubious choice for peacemaker as he was notorious for his hot temper and was rumored to have shot a number of people, including a movie critic who had offended him with a bad review. Sure enough, things heated up again, with Fernandez shouting, "Fucking Mexicans!" and pulling out a pistol. "I'm getting the ladies out of here," said Mitchum and rushed for the exit. One of the general's men fired what sounded like a machine gun. Palance picked up a table and hurled it at him.

"Suddenly," said Jack, "there was this big drama going on."

People dropped under tables in screaming confusion while shots zinged back and forth across the room. As El Indio continued firing, giving him cover, Palance made his way out through the kitchen and escaped. By then Mitchum and company were safely inside their limousine and heading across town.

The "general," it turned out, was the big cheese in federal security and had a nasty reputation for unwarranted arrests, torturing suspects, that sort of thing. Jack Palance was put under wraps until someone could locate the offended officer and RKO could write out a large check for another charitable donation. Palance told reporter Roderick Mann, "Of course, when I got back to the States, I found old Mitchum had taken all the credit for my rescue."

•••

With everyone safely returned to Los Angeles, filming continued on the studio lot. The climactic scenes, conceived for maximum stereoscopic thrills, took place on a cable car suspended between two mountain peaks in the story's imaginary Andean locale. When the car stalls at the midway point, Mitchum is elected to swing from a rope to the nearest ledge and scramble for help. He returns with a rescue team and confronts killer Palance. The pair slug it out as the last threads of cable snap from the dangling car.

Palance was an idiosyncratic method actor known to lose himself in his characters, a risky pattern for one who enacted so much on-screen mayhem. "He would go back behind the set and work himself up to a real state," said Reva Frederick. "Huffing and puffing. It was odd." A stuntman warned Mitchum that Jack was planning to give him a hard time in the cable car fistfight and to keep his guard up. The two rehearsed their moves, but once they began battling their way in and out and on top of the set it was difficult to stick to the script. Palance gave him a hard one in the head. Mitchum's ears were ringing and he lost his footing for a moment, then, sure the punch had been intentional, moved back in with a fury, slugging the other actor in the gut. Palance let out a growl and vomited across Mitchum's shoulder.

Second Chance opened to good business and moderately positive reviews. Critics were distracted by the ocular assault of the 3-D effects, not by the story, which seemed even more threadbare on the screen than it had on paper. For RKO's vaunted big picture of the year, the film was sloppy and cheap. The location trip to Mexico had provided little more than some raw-looking, second- unit-type footage. The rest was a cramped, operetta-style soundstage South America, the cable car climax a cheesy mix of obvious toy miniatures and back projection. Even the music sounded subpar, like the generic library cues used by Poverty Row studios for their three-day Westerns. But "the great unwashed," as Mitchum referred to his loyal fans, seemed to enjoy it. What the hell. The film was as effortlessly watchable and as easily forgotten as a gaily colored dream. Mitchum performed his empathetic tough guy characterization with a refined minimalism. Given nothing to do, he did it to perfection.

Due to RKO's ever-increasing deficits and its stockholders' constant scrutiny, Howard Hughes no longer had the luxury of turning down high-priced offers for his biggest star's services. Mitchum was thus loaned to 20th Century-Fox to costar with that studio's latest and greatest asset, and an old acquaintance of Bob's, Jim Dougherty's former teenage girlfriend, Norma Jean Baker. After seven years of wiggling at the periphery of the movie business, Marilyn Monroe had at last achieved fame if not fortune, and with her appearances in *Niagara, How to Marry a Millionaire,* and *Gentlemen Prefer Blondes* had become the most exciting and talked-about movie star of the day. (Nevertheless, Mitchum's representatives waged a successful battle for their client to be given top billing in all studio advertising and publicity.) *River of No Return* was to be a superspectacular aimed—like *Second Chance* but with considerably better prospects—at separating TV-addicted audiences from their living rooms. It would be produced not with the sideshow gimmickry of 3-D but in Fox's own revolutionary technical process, anamorphic wide-screen Cinemascope, with multitrack stereo sound, color, awesome locations in the Canadian Rockies, marauding Indians, white-water rapids, and Marilyn Monroe squeezed into revealing dancehall-floozie mufti and skintight blue jeans.

Actually, *River of No Return* was a cheap B Western that had just growed like Topsy. Fox originally planned to shoot it in a couple of weeks on the wild Snake River in Idaho. Paul Helmick, scheduled to be the assistant director and unit manager on that picture, had scouted the locations. "It was going to be a small thing," Helmick recalled. "About twenty-five people, cast and crew sleeping in tents and eating at the campfire. All of a sudden Zanuck decided it was going to be a big picture with Marilyn and Mitchum, and Otto Preminger was going to direct. I thought that meant I was off the picture because I had done one with Otto before and that did *not* work out. So I thought the minute he was assigned I was out, which was fine with me because I did not care much for Otto. But I was very much in. So now we had to rethink where the picture could be made, now it was a matter of finding locations where you could have a good hotel, food and lodging for a hundred, hundred-and-twenty-five people, an airport not too far away, good communications, and so on."

New ultrascenic locales were chosen at Jasper and Banff Springs near Lake Louise in western Canada and comfortable accommodations secured at the stately old Banff Springs Hotel. There was still snow on the mountains and some of the roads had been clear for only a matter of weeks when members of the company began arriving in June, making preparations for the complicated and dangerous river rafting sequences that were the film's primary raison d'etre. A special train brought the cast and Preminger the eighty miles west from Calgary to Banff, a publicized event that brought out curious ogling Canadians all along the route.

A sweet but often intransigent personality even among sympathetic collaborators, Marilyn did not react well to Preminger's patented screaming-Prussian act. "Otto," said Paul Helmick, "was a complete pain in the ass. Vicious, impatient, very crude to people, especially to women." Filming had barely begun when Monroe and the director stopped speaking to each other. "Not a word. It was the biggest mismatch I'd ever seen," said Paul Helmick. "They absolutely detested each other." The telephone lines to Los Angeles sizzled, with each camp complaining about the other's bad behavior, and Fox telling them both to shut up. The *Angel Face* contretemps forgotten, Preminger turned to Mitchum for help; and Bob would become the single tenuous line of communication between Monroe and the director.

A major source of unpleasantness, and not just to Preminger, was the presence of Monroe's drama coach—really her surrogate mother—Natasha Lytess. "Horrible woman," said Reva Frederick. "And smelly. If only someone had taken her out and given her a bath." Otto dismissed Lytess as an annoying phony from the get-go—"She was passing herself off as a Russian, for reasons of her own, but she was in fact German"—but Marilyn had an absolute Trilby-like devotion to the woman and her professional advice. Lytess would sit at the sidelines during filming, conferring with the actress before a take, overriding the director's instructions, signaling Marilyn to demand another take or to refuse to do another one, depending on whether the coach was satisfied with the first. Her most damning influence on Monroe's performance was an insistence on every syllable of every line being enunciated distinctly, advice the actress followed to an absurd degree. Marilyn, said Preminger, "rehearsed her lines with such grave ar-tic-yew-lay-shun that her violent lip movements made it impossible to photograph her." To Mitchum, holding her in his arms for a shot, she looked like she was doing an imitation of a fish. He slapped her on the ass—which he found was also undulating uncontrollably—and snapped, "Stop the nonsense! Let's play it like human beings." He managed, said Preminger, "to startle her and she dropped, at least for the moment, her Lytess mannerisms."

At other times, when Marilyn was not in need of her aid, Natasha would wander among the rest of the cast offering unsolicited advice in gloomy Garbo-like tones, as when she told the boy playing Mitchum's son, Tommy Rettig, that child actors lost their talent at just about his age. Rettig immediately began having trouble with his lines and sobbing before a take. Preminger had Lytess barred from the set. Then Monroe refused to come out of her dressing room. Darryl Zanuck wired Preminger that Marilyn was "money in the bank," and he would have to do whatever it took to keep her working. Again Preminger must have thought, this was not how they would have treated Hitler.

Monroe's peccadilloes seemed never to bother Mitchum. He thought she was an essentially sweet and funny but often sad and confused person. Eternally vulnerable, uncertain of her talent, she was prey to exploitation and a victim of her own bad judgment. Perhaps a key to their relationship—and he would have no easy time convincing anyone about this—was that Mitchum found Monroe sexually unappetizing and never tried to bed her. While others cared to see only her voluptuousness and easy availability, Mitchum saw a frightened and possibly disturbed child-woman, not his cup of tea. Perhaps, too, his lack of ardor had something to do with what he claimed was the secret source of Monroe's neurotic temperament and chronic lateness: her vagina. Due to the peculiar nature of her female plumbing, Mitchum discovered, Marilyn would experience an unusually strong, debilitating menstruation and an excruciatingly painful premenstrual period that could sometimes last for nearly the entire month. Mitchum claimed that many a time, as people on the set stood around cursing her selfishness, Marilyn lay in her dressing room immobilized with cramps, embarrassed and suffering.

While in Canada—and until her boyfriend Joe DiMaggio arrived, hot on the heels of a rumor that Monroe and Mitchum were having an affair—Bob assumed a kind of older brother role for Marilyn—if a teasing and mischievous older brother. Mitchum was amused by her attempts at intellectual self-improvement, mockingly claiming she was forever studying books on psychology or human sexuality, looking up from the pages now and then with wide-eyed innocence to ask him, "What does the author mean by . . . *anal eroticism?*" One day she yearningly remarked that she hadn't seen her man Joe in some time, and Mitchum's boisterous stand-in Tim Wallace supposedly suggested they take up the slack with "a round robin."

"What's that?" Marilyn asked.

"You know, *you* and *me* and *Mitch,*" Wallace said, leering.

"Ooohh," said Marilyn. "That would kill me!"

"Well, nobody's died from it yet!" Wallace snickered.

"*Oh,* I bet they *have,*" Marilyn told him. "But in the papers they just say . . . the girl died from natural causes. . . ."

"I wouldn't say she was dumb," said Reva Frederick. "She was just a very young woman in her mind and had a lot of growing up to do. She was a nice girl, always said hello to everybody, asked how they were, caring. But it was all a bit overwhelming for her. She was very simple and sweet. I remember once we were in her dressing room and she was dying to show us a present she'd gotten from Joe DiMaggio. It was a gorgeous, very expensive black mink coat. And she grabbed it and put it on and everybody said, 'Marilyn, don't put that on, you've got body makeup on, you'll stain the whole coat!' And she said, 'Oh, it's all right. I've got orange sheets, too!' But she was a nice girl."

As Mitchum, Monroe, and Preminger filmed and fought, the second unit was putting together the action and stunt sequences on the same locations. There were setbacks. The Indians on the warpath in the film were to be played by a contingent of authentic tribesmen from the area, but they kept falling off their horses and were eventually replaced by cowboys from Saskatchewan, who could ride but not bareback, and they too spent much of their time tasting dirt. The work on the wild Bow River was exceedingly dangerous, made even more so apparently by the caliber of the local assistance. Roy Jenson, working as a stunt double on the picture, recalled, "One time the stunt coordinator, Fred Zindar—he and Norm Bishop were taking the raft down the rapids with the camera mounted on the nose— nearly washed down the river to Hudson's Bay because the guy in the rescue boat was out of gas. These guys were major idiots. I remember the first time we came down the river, and one of them was supposed to throw me this rock tied to the end of a rope. I would then take it, tie it off, and pull the raft in to shore. I wasn't even looking up, and he throws it and hits me in the head with the rock."

Big Roy Jenson, an aspiring movie actor, was playing football for the Calgary Stampeders that summer when he talked his way into a job as Robert Mitchum's stunt double. Coming from the area, Jenson had found it easy to convince Otto Preminger that he was an expert at running the Bow, but this was in fact his first attempt at such a thing. Jenson, veteran stuntwoman Helen Thurston doubling for Monroe, and Harry Monty, a midget (and formerly one of the Wizard of Oz Munchkins) doubling for Tommy Rettig, would have many moments of sheer terror before their job was done. "Some of that stuff still comes back to haunt me today," said Jenson forty-five years later. "We were up at the top of the river one time, and we had to go over these Mickey Mouse falls. They didn't look like anything. Six- or eight-foot drop, not shattering, a flow drop. But unknown to us there was a big rock, and when we went over on that damned raft it hooked on the rock and started to tip over. The only thing that saved us was I used to work in lumber camps and I had spikes on my shoes. I was on the back panel, and I remember Harry the midget going by in his corduroy pants and I reached out for him, and the adrenaline was going so strong through my entire body that I pulled out the entire crotch of his pants. I got to the other end and swept it off. But we all thought we had had it. The closest people were a couple of hundred yards away. The midget was in total shock, but Helen was cool, she was an old-time stunt gal. I was too busy trying to save our lives, my life, to get scared. I got scared later on, back in the motel room I shared with the midget, remembering what had happened."

Mitchum would often appropriate the incident, telling people he and Marilyn had been on the overturning raft, but in fact the stars were permitted to work only on a raft that had been secured to the riverbank. Not that they had it risk-free: Monroe painfully twisted her leg scrambling on the rocks and was reduced to walking with crutches by the time she left Canada.

Due to the odd liquor laws in Alberta, Mitchum and many of the others in the *River* company spent most of their free time within the confines of the Banff Springs Hotel, one of the only places in the area where you could get cocktails or hard stuff, outside of the government-run liquor store. "Bob would be at the bar, telling stories, or in his hotel suite, sitting up on the armoire with twenty people below him, sitting on the armoire with a bottle of gin, telling stories for days, and he was a marvelous entertainer," Roy Jenson recalled. "Really great. And I was young and naive and everything and trying to keep up, but no way. I was so far out of my league. Mitchum was incredible. The guy could drink two or three quarts of gin and not even show it. One night I went out with Bob and Murvyn Vye, he was the heavy in the picture. And we were drinkiing for hours. I'm just ripped out of my mind. I finally go away and I get a steam bath and a massage and a nap and have some dinner and I come back, and they were still there, talking and drinking! Christ!"

Later in the summer another team of filmmakers arrived in Alberta to shoot a Universal International production about the Canadian Mounties, *Saskatchewan*. Raoul Walsh was directing and the star was Alan Ladd, playing a part that had originally been offered to Mitchum. A number of the *Saskatchewan* people moved into the Banff Springs Hotel. Ladd was a recluse, seldom seen. One of the other visitors from Hollywood was apparently not so stand-offish. The woman in question, Paul Helmick recalled, "had the hots for Mitchum. She wanted to get into bed with him, made it clear. And he made it clear that he didn't want to by peeing all over her. They went up to her room. I saw him right afterward; he came back to the dining room or wherever we were, and that was what he told me he did. Pissed all over her."

River of No Return was completed in Los Angeles, where Mitchum and Monroe would do their white-water rafting indoors on a hydraulic platform in front of a giant process screen, while men stood to the sides and splashed them with buckets of water and shot steel-headed arrows into the solid oak logs at their feet. Having reached the end of his contract with Fox, Preminger left for Europe with the Indians still on the warpath, and a number of brief scenes and retakes were directed by Jean Negulescu. The simpleminded but exciting and colorful film was hugely popular, Mitchum's most successful picture to date, though it would be hard to deny that the larger share of the audience came to gaze upon second-billed Marilyn Monroe, the most talked-about woman in the world. Marilyn, anyway, was his fan. "Mitch," she told a reporter, "is one of the most interesting, fascinating men I have ever known."

RKO, wriggling in its death throes, exercised the final contractual option for another year of Robert's services. His salary was now five thousand dollars a week. But he was not happy. The money was at most a third of what he might be making on the open market; and RKO, now clearly incapable of competing with the rival studios, was threatening to diminish his future prospects as well with every lousy project they threw at him.

He turned down his next assignment, *Susan Slept Here,* set to costar young Debbie Reynolds, saying he was not prepared to attempt a part requiring singing and dancing (the eventual film, made with Dick Powell, would have little of either). Mitchum had been a cooperative employee all these years—barring a few broken chairs and windows and some bad publicity brought on along the way—and had done pretty much any piece of shit they had offered; nevertheless, the studio refused to back down. Playing hard ball, they sent notice to Mitchum's agent that he was required to begin work on *Susan* on the morning of November 13 or be put on suspension without pay.

Fuck 'em. He took the suspension.

Now with some free time, he pondered life after RKO. All too aware that owners kept the big money, he and a collection of drinking buddies—Paul Helmick from *River of No Return,* a Texan named George McGee (the brother-in-law of New Orleans hotelier Frank Monteleone), Paul Lally, and David C. Moore—announced the formation of a television production company they were calling Westwood Productions. Incorporation papers were filed in

Sacramento on November 23, and a press release detailed their plans to rent studio space and begin production of their first series program in the spring. Helmick: "Mitchum and I used to do quite a bit of drinking. So we were sitting around one day and he says, 'We ought to get into the television business.' I said, 'Well . . . that's right.' He said, 'Let's do a series or something. Maybe more than one series.' I said, "OK.' And TV McGee—we called him that because he wanted to be a partner—put some money behind this company we formed. And Mitchum said, 'Come up with an idea.' And I said, 'I've got one.' I said, 'You take the *Saturday Evening Post*?' He said, 'Yeah, I think so.' And he called to his wife, Dorothy, to get him a copy of the *Post*. I said, 'Look at the back page.' And the back page was a maid—what was her name? A cartoon. *Hazel*. I said, 'There's our show.' He said, 'That would be a good show; you're right.' But the guy who did the cartoon wouldn't give us bunch of guys the rights to it. He didn't want any part of Robert Mitchum and this crew doing his beloved Hazel. So we discussed this among ourselves and somebody said, 'Screw it, he's got no rights if we do the same thing about some other maid. What's another good name for a maid?' So I said, 'We'll call her Amy.' Bob said, 'Great.' We formed a company, we went looking for a studio and found some cheap space with standing sets. But Mitchum kept procrastinating. Then he got a picture to do out of town. And then he came back and said, 'Let's do it,' but I was going off to Egypt for a year to do *Land of the Pharaohs* with Hawks. So that was kind of the end of that."

A few moments after midnight on December 2, Off. J. N. Ryan saw a dark Jaguar roar across Wilshire Boulevard on San Vicente at approximately seventy-five miles per hour, which was approximately forty miles above the speed limit. He kicked his motorcycle into life and gave pursuit, with red light flashing and siren on. The Jag did not slow down but took evasive action, turning off the boulevard and onto the dark side streets. The chase continued on to Brentwood where, at Avondale Avenue and Hanover Street, the speeding automobile pulled to a sudden stop. The door opened and

Robert Mitchum stepped from the car, holding his keys out to the uncertain motorcycle cop.

"What . . . what are they for?" Ryan said.

"Maybe my driver's license is in the trunk," Mitchum said, cryptically.

The cop stood there confused. Then Mitchum abruptly produced the license from his wallet and handed it over. "What have I done?" he asked.

"You were driving fast."

"How fast?"

"Over seventy."

The officer started writing out a citation.

Mitchum lit up a cigarette, took a few puffs. He said, "Do you have any witnesses, man?"

Ryan said, "Just you and I, I guess."

"In that case I'm leaving," Mitchum said, got back into the car, waved, said, "By-by," and roared away.

By the time the officer had revved up his motorcycle, the Jag and the movie star had already vanished into the night. He returned to the West Los Angeles Police Station, where desk officer David Sellars was just then answering a call from an irate Mitchum, who was threatening to file a complaint for theft against one of their officers for stealing his driver's license. Sellars turned the call over to Officer Ryan.

"I asked him why he fled the scene like that," said Ryan. "He replied, 'I wasn't sure you were a cop, Dad . . . thought you were a bandit, and so I just took off and went home.'"

An arrest warrant was issued for speeding, resisting an officer, and evading arrest, the latter two high misdemeanor charges carrying maximum penalties of five years in prison. Still missing in action, Mitchum called the police station in the afternoon and ranted, "What are you guys trying to do? Make a big production out of this? A hundred people a day do the same thing!"

On December 8 in West Los Angeles Municipal Court, Judge Leo Freund agreed to drop the more serious charges in exchange for guilty pleas to Delaying an Officer in the Discharge of Duty and

Speeding in Excess of 70 Miles an Hour, for which the fines were $150 and $50 respectively.

"Don't you think you were kind of stupid?" the judge asked.

Mitchum said yes, he had been stupid.

The judge nodded sagely. "Your realization is the best punishment for you."

Robert could not have agreed more.

Late in December, after nearly two months without a paycheck and with Christmas expenditures now to be accounted for, Mitchum began to feel the pinch and rendered himself unto RKO once more, saying he was ready to go to work immediately. The studio played it spiteful, taking advantage of a contractual clause allowing them an additional six weeks to prepare a project for the actor's return without paying him a dime (a bitter victory, since RKO needed Mitchum as much as he needed the five grand a week). From now on, all communications between the star and the studio brass would be made through his agency. Personal allegiances dissolved after Mitchum tried several times to meet or talk to Howard Hughes but could never track him down. Hughes, caught up in legal battles and a difficult attempt to buy out the studio's stockholders, had become more and more removed from daily production matters. The studio arranged to loan Mitchum to Fox for another Cinemascope epic, *Untamed,* to be shot in South Africa in June and July. The studio went ahead filming action scenes, second-unit stuff, with a Mitchum double. But the leading lady—Susan Hayward again—was going to be delayed on another picture—*The Conquerer,* with John Wayne as Genghis Khan—making it impossible to finish *Untamed* before the end of Bob's RKO contract, so Mitchum refused to do it. Fox threatened to sue for their huge second-unit expenditures (the Mitchum double would remain in the finished film, though he would end up passing himself off as Tyrone Power instead).

Mitchum picked up the phone one morning in March and somebody offered him a free ten-day visit to the French Riviera. Because

of the caller's thick accent, Bob couldn't make out what he was saying and thought he'd won a radio contest, but it turned out it was a
representative of the Cannes Film Festival.

On their first-ever trip to Europe, Bob and Dorothy were flown
to Paris, where they spent two days mostly posing for local photographers and ordering room service, and then on to the
Mediterranean as special guests of the film fest, a glamorous and
sleazy annual gathering of international cineastes where, at that
time, appearances by major Hollywood stars were still far from
commonplace. Mitchum was the belle of the ball, eliciting screaming pandemonium from press and gawking civilians wherever he
went. It was not the balmy Riviera sojourn he had envisioned. The
whole town was a mob scene, and the Cannes organizers expected
him to pay for his freight in a dawn-to-dawn round of public appearances. He was a "shuddering wreck," he claimed. "Every one pushes
you around. You come down at eight o'clock and . . . they've got
you visiting some old broken-down maharajah who has a villa overlooking seven thousand other villas overlooking the sea. The only
time the photographers and journalists—you don't know whether
they work for a Hollywood peep show or *Pravda*—will leave you
alone is when someone yells, 'Free lunch!'"

The adventure reached an appropriately photogenic climax when
Mitchum and his wife attended a publicity event at nearby Lerins
Island. Dressed like a Saint-Tropez playboy in tan slacks and a florid
horizontally striped sport shirt, Mitchum was standing at the edge
of a cliff above the sea posing for half a hundred snapping cameras
when a lovely and well-endowed red-haired woman in a pink trans-
parent scarf top and tiny grass skirt slipped over to stand next to
him. It was already a Cannes tradition, the presence of starlets and
would-be starlets looking for publicity, and Mitchum good-
naturedly posed with the girl. "What could I do?" he would say later.
Suddenly, the girl—Simone Silva was her name—whisked off the
pink veil and, as Dorothy Mitchum stood a few feet away in angry
disbelief, pressed her massive bare breasts over every part of Robert
they could reach. There was a crush of humanity as the photogs
went into a feeding frenzy, and three fell off the rocks and into the

sea, one suffering a fractured elbow. Saying he had been not quite sure what was going on, Mitchum put his hands over the girl, to cover her nakedness, he would say, though some of the photographs mistakenly made it look like he was "copping a feel." Within the week the pictures—the more sedate shots the law allowed—had appeared in newspapers and magazines around the world. Bob, said the news reports accompanying the torrid photos, was in the doghouse with his wife on account of the incident. There were also quotes from Miss Silva, an aspiring British actress, who explained, "As long as sex is box office and I keep my figure, I'm out to be the sexiest thing on two legs. So I took off the scarf."

In May RKO delivered Mitchum to John Wayne's Batjac Company at Warner Bros., where he was to take the lead in *Track of the Cat* under the direction of that old star maker Wild Bill Wellman. The cast, in addition to Mitch, included Teresa Wright, Tab Hunter, Diana Lynn, Hedda Hopper's son William, and Carl "Alfalfa" Switzer, playing a mystical hundred-year-old Indian.

Based on a novel by Walter Van Tilburg Clark, whose *The Ox-Bow Incident* had provided the text for an earlier and highly acclaimed Wellman movie (a Mitchum favorite; he claimed to watch it every year), *Track* was a grim tale of the brooding, feuding Bridges family, mountain ranchers haunted literally and symbolically by a murderous panther. The much talented novelist and film writer A. I. Bezzerides (*On Dangerous Ground, Kiss Me Deadly*) was put to work on the script.

Bezzerides: "Wellman gave me the book to read and I loved it. I told him, 'Let me write the script and then we'll talk and we'll see what we have to do.' So I wrote it. He loved it. I had a big drunk scene in there. Wellman and Wayne and all of them were big drinkers, bottles all over the place. And Wellman came in after reading the scene and said, 'You're one of us!' He thought that to write it as I did, I had to drink like they did. And boy, did they drink. I said, 'Bill, I wrote a scene. I don't drink.' Well, that was the last I heard from him for a while. . . . So then I finished the first draft of the script. And John Wayne called me in—it was his production company—and said how wonderful it was, and if he was younger he'd have liked to play the part. I said, 'It's just first draft. It needs cutting.' He said, 'I understand.' But Wellman didn't want it changed. I said, 'Bill, it needs cutting. It'll take a couple weeks.' He said, 'No, I like it. Any changes, I'll do them.' I said, 'Don't you understand? It's overwritten. The scenes have to be worked on.' Wellman said, 'No, it's perfect.' He had so fallen in love with the script that he wouldn't touch a word of it. And he didn't. And oh my God, that's going too far. I'm not untouchable. But he wouldn't listen."

Wellman had long nursed an aesthetic fancy, an idea of making a black-and-white movie in color—that is, shooting it with color film but designing it with a palette of nothing but blacks and whites. A film of Clark's spare, winter-set story of the hunt for a killer black cat seemed the perfect opportunity to attempt this visual experiment. Every element in the production obeyed the severe color scheme, from the clothing and the furniture to the white oleomargarine on the kitchen table, the only exceptions being one yellow shirt and the blood-red mackinaw worn by Mitchum. Wellman's brilliant cinematographer, Bill Clothier, shared his enthusiasm for the experiment and even more so when they looked at the results. "Never have I seen such beauty, a naked kind of beauty," Wellman recalled. "Bill and I saw the first print back from the lab. We sat there together, drooling." Said Clothier, "For the first time, you really noticed people's features. When I made a close-up of Diana Lynn, you saw the blue eyes and her hair was such and such a color and she had a flush in her cheeks."

Jack Warner, financing the picture, was less enthused at first. "I'm spending five hundred thousand dollars more for color and there's no color in this damn thing!" Wellman sent a message: "If he doesn't like it he can go shit in his hat."

The outdoor scenes demanded deep snow, and Wellman and his assistant director Andrew V. McLaglen went on what became a frantic last-minute hunt for an appropriate location. "Bill and I went all over," said McLaglen, "up in Truckee and Big Bear and you name it, and we couldn't find any snow. We finally found what we needed at

Mount Rainier and we got the crew and actors up there to do the scenes. We stayed at the base of the mountain, drove up to the base and stayed at the cabins they had there. There was a lot of snow and we were prepared for it. But it was rugged. Very rugged. And on July Fourth, on Mount Rainier, we had a blizzard."

Snow roared down, accompanied by whipping winds. They squeezed into the small, primitive cabins and huddled around waiting. And when the weather calmed, they were left with locations newly covered in twenty- and thirty-foot snowdrifts. Everything moved at a snail's pace, the crew aching, the equipment freezing. Mitchum would forever remember *Track of the Cat* for the worst, most difficult conditions he ever experienced in making a film—bitterly cold, physically exhausting, all day sinking or falling over into the bottomless drifts.

Equally chilling was Mitchum's characterization. Growling brother Curt Bridges, a "cheap dirtymouth bully," was the most unsympathetic lead role Mitchum had ever attempted. A. I. Bezzerides, watching from the sidelines—still hoping for a chance at that rewrite—was impressed with the star's uncompromising approach. "Bob Mitchum was fantastic. He carried scenes that needed to be polished, and his performance made some of it work. I got to know him very well and I thought he was a wonderful guy. But cynical . . . *God* is he cynical."

In the end, audiences did not warm up to anything in *Track of the Cat*. With its talky interior sequences and shallow pretentiousness (the "painter" supposedly stood for all the evil in the world), much of it came across like summer stock O'Neill. Wellman's subtle approach to the panther attacks, emphasizing the idea of the cat as an abstraction, put a further strain on the moviegoers' shriveling interest. The director realized in retrospect that he should at least have shown the cat tearing Mitchum to pieces.

"The audience's imagination failed to imagine," said Wellman, "and my arthritis became my black panther; and the son of a bitch has been prowling through my system ever since."

But one could not call *Track of the Cat* a failure, for it contained elements that were unforgettable: Wellman's drained, bloodless color scheme was eerily, uniquely atmospheric, while the hard-won exterior photography, in CinemaScope, of shadowed trees and tiny figures on vast expanses of snow, included some of the most amazing and starkly beautiful images ever shot.

As the clock ticked on Mitchum's RKO contract, the studio tried to negotiate an extension that would accommodate Fox's production of *Untamed*. He was not interested. Bitterly, the studio tried to squeeze a humiliating last performance out of him, casting him as the Indian brave Colorados, a supporting part in a Ronald Reagan Western, *Cattle Queen of Montana*. Mitchum replied that he would rather go fishing and then did.

On August 15, 1954, his ten years as RKO's favorite horseshit salesman—that sobriquet a studio exec had mockingly awarded him—were over.

And now, freedom. Or something.

Mitchum's departure from the studio, where he was virtually the last remaining major asset, only quickened the spiral into oblivion. Twenty-eight months later there would be no RKO. The company that had created *Top Hat, Citizen Kane, The Informer,* and *Out of the Past* ended in a fire sale, its final spawn—a couple of Westerns, a George Gobel comedy, and the like—scattered to other studios for distribution like orphans to foster homes. The lot itself would be bought by the enemy, a pair of television producers (and one-time RKO contract players), Desi Arnaz and (Bob's old ship in the night) Lucille Ball.

Mitchum would not encounter Howard Hughes again for many years. They kept in touch, sort of. Every month or so until the billionaire's strange demise, there would come a call out of the blue, one of Howard's Mormon minions on the phone, merely wanting to make certain that they had the correct number should Mr. Hughes ever need to reach his friend Robert Mitchum. By the late '60s, Hughes had entered the reclusive, druggy, and increasingly deranged last phase of his life. Mitchum had gone to Las Vegas, at the request of Perry Lieber, to the reopening of the Desert Inn, one of the string of casino resorts Hughes had begun buying in the

Nevada gaming capital. During the festivities, someone slipped up to Mitchum and whispered in his ear that Mr. Hughes would very much like to meet with him upstairs. He was taken by private elevator to the top floor of the casino, led to the ornate doorway of a corner suite, and told to go inside. Mitchum stood in the empty, gold-embossed living room until one of the bedroom doors opened and Howard Hughes—older, frail of body, but with much the same dark-eyed intensity as in the old days—stepped into the room.

"Good to see you, Howard," Mitchum said.

The Phantom smiled grimly. He said, "Bob, forgive me. I have to go make a phone call, if you don't mind waiting."

Howard Hughes turned and went back into the other room, closing the door behind him.

Mitchum waited. A couple of minutes maybe. He moved closer to the door behind which Hughes had disappeared. He couldn't hear anything. After another few minutes he gave the door a knock, then opened it a crack. It was silent as a tomb in there. He opened the door and looked inside. It was an empty, undisturbed bedroom. There was another connecting door. It was locked. He went back into the living room and waited, found the toilet and took a leak, then went back downstairs to the party. He never saw his old boss again.

Part three

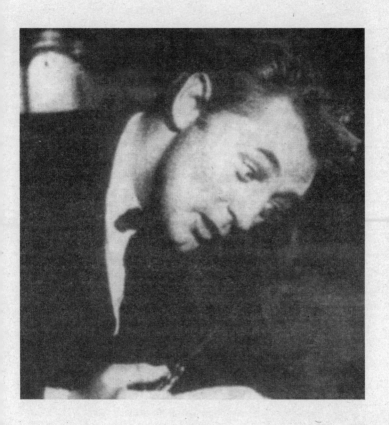

CHAPTER NINE

The Story of Right Hand/Left Hand

Departing RKO for good in August 1954, Robert Mitchum was among the very last of the important postwar stars of his generation to escape the shackles of the long-term stock contract. Such relationships had become a remnant of the past. The Hollywood studio system as it had existed for decades was unraveling. The rapid rise of television, the government enforcement of antimonopoly statutes that wrested away the studios' control of exhibition, the decline of the original tyrant-moguls, and other factors had combined to undermine the studios' near-feudal control of the American film industry. Increasingly their power would have to be shared among independent producers, talent agencies, and ambitious stars demanding control of their creative and financial destinies. Actors such as James Stewart, Cary Grant, and William Holden now made deals guaranteeing them a sizable share of a film's profits, while others—Burt Lancaster, John Wayne, Kirk Douglas—were establishing their own production companies, developing their own projects, coming to the studios only for financing and distribution.

As a sign of his intention to join this elite group, Mitchum rented an office suite at 9200 Sunset Boulevard. When opened for business, it had a staff of two (Reva Frederick and former RKO publicist Gloria Pogue), a well-stocked bar, and a big desk where the boss could sit and make like David Selznick. He had already lined up his first two jobs months in advance of his actual emancipation from RKO, both in projects distinctly un-Hughes-like on the face of it, one to be based on a blockbuster novel, best-seller of the year, while the other offered a daringly unconventional part and a distinguished creative collaborator. The two might make critics and audiences sit up and rethink their notions of a Robert Mitchum movie.

While still at RKO he had gotten a call from Charles Laughton.

"Bob," said Laughton, "we have a story here we are hoping to turn into a little film, and I would very much like to talk to you about the leading role. The character is a bit different. He's a terrible, evil . . . *shit* of a man.

"Present," said Mitchum.

Charles Laughton, the man Laurence Olivier described as the acting profession's only genius, was in the midst of a professional revitalization as the director of a series of theatrical triumphs—the powerful all-star readings of *Don Juan in Hell* and *John Brown's Body* and the imaginatively conceived Broadway production of *The Caine Mutiny Court Martial*. Just four years earlier, Laughton had been drifting, appearing in increasingly undemanding roles and ignoble fare (suffice it to say, *Abbott and Costello Meet Captain Kidd*). Then a young William Morris agent named Paul Gregory saw Laughton on a live television show reading from the Bible, found it a stunning experience, and came to the actor with an idea for a series of similar dramatic readings in a theatrical setting. The national tour of this one-man show was a considerable critical and commercial success, and Gregory and Laughton continued their alliance—now a formal partnership—with more elaborate and equally successful productions. Late in life, Laughton was revealed to be a great, original directorial talent, compared with the young Orson Welles for his dazzling creativity.

After their success on Broadway, the team of producer Gregory and director Laughton were eager to return to Hollywood and make a motion picture that would be as unique and memorable as their acclaimed works for the theater. An agent friend in New York sent Gregory the prepublication galleys of a novel called *The Night of the Hunter* by West Virginia native Davis Grubb. Gregory felt at once that the material could be turned into just the sort of startling and unexpected film he and Laughton were hoping to make. He rushed the galleys over to his partner, and Charles instantly agreed with his assessment. "You've got your finger right on my pulse," Laughton said. "I would love to direct this."

The strange, brilliant novel was an American Gothic, written as if by some collaboration of William Faulkner and H. P. Lovecraft, mixing a rustic tale of terror with gallows humor and experimental prose. In the Depression-ravaged South, a psychopathic evangelist named Harry Powell, a charismatic black-clad preacher with the words *Love* and *Hate* tattooed on his knuckles, wanders the back roads doing a peculiar version of the Lord's work, killing stripteasers, whores, lonely widows, and other wantons. Grubb wrote: "Sometimes he wondered if God really understood. Not that the Lord minded about their killings. Why, His Book was full of killings. But there were things God did hate—perfume-smelling things—lacy things—things with curly hair—whore things. Preacher would think of these and his hands at night would go crawling down under the blankets till the fingers named Love closed around the bone hasp of the knife and his soul rose up in flaming glorious fury."

In prison for car theft, the preacher meets Ben Harper, a condemned man who, broken by the hard times, had robbed and killed to feed his family. Harper is executed while his ten-thousand-dollar swag remains missing, and Powell goes off to acquire it. He cozies up to the widow Harper and her children, Pearl and John, marries the widow, kills her, then turns on the children, who are the keepers of the secret of the hidden loot. John and Pearl barely manage to escape, fleeing upriver where they are taken in by the eccentric old Miz Cooper, mother hen to a houseful of stray children and outcasts. Preacher Powell pursues them, and by nightfall he lays terrifying siege to Miz Cooper's house. But goodness prevails. Miz Cooper traps Powell in her barn and turns him over to the police. In the jailhouse for murder, Powell is seized by an angry mob and lynched.

Having purchased the rights to the novel, Gregory and Laughton pondered the proper casting. "Right away I thought of Mitchum," said Paul Gregory. "He was a man who could project great charm, and yet there was a sense of evil lurking there under the surface. Charles asked me if I saw anyone for the role of the preacher and I said, 'There's one American actor I think could do a good job with this, Robert Mitchum.' And Laughton said, 'Jesus Christ! That's right. He'd be wonderful. I can see him, yes. . . .' And we decided to waste no time. Charles knew him slightly and he came to my office and called him at home."

"Present," Mitchum said.

Laughton asked him if he might have time to take a look at the novel.

"I'm just twiddling my thumbs here. Sure, send it over, I'll take a look."

Mitchum read it that very afternoon, sprawled in a lounge chair beside the pool. He loved it—Davis Grubb's corrosive take on the world, the fiendish humor, the portrait of a rural, near-medieval South that rang true to his own Depression-era wanderings there, the whole subversive attack on religious hypocrites and nut cases and psalm-singing yahoos. Said Julie Mitchum, "Bob told me he was going to do that one to show people not to follow some character because he's got a Bible in his hands, or because he's got his collar on backwards, to alert people to these kinds of characters. And he was always very sympathetic to the exploitation of children, always very sympathetic to the innocence of children. He thought this would get that out there." But were they really going to be able to make a picture about a wife-murdering, child-stalking maniac of a preacher, doing his evil deeds in God's name? Well, if they were, Mitchum decided, he wanted to be in on it.

He went over to Laughton's house the following Saturday afternoon to discuss the project. Laughton called Paul Gregory immediately afterward. "He was on the ceiling with excitement about Mitchum. He said that Mitchum had been wonderfully enthused, had so many ideas to offer." Mitchum quoted from the book by memory and at one point got up before his adoring host and began crashing about the living room, acting out the love/hate sermon, the story of "right hand/left hand," knuckles upraised. "Of course," said Gregory, "they had had quite a few drinks."

Mitchum visited Laughton frequently in the months ahead, coming for lunch or dinner. According to Laughton's wife, Elsa

Lanchester, the two were a natural team: "They were kindred spirits, both what you call rebels, with no respect for formal religion or Hollywood society." Lanchester, always prone to a snit when her husband was fawning over another man, thought Mitchum a bit of a poseur, trying overly hard to convince the couple he was no dumb cowboy. "Charles knew enough to let a person have his head if he wanted to appear to have an intellectual approach. I don't know, maybe Bob Mitchum is very bright, but I never heard such a lot of words—big, long words, one after the other. Perhaps he felt insecure with Charles and he was only trying to impress him. . . . Charles was patient with him because Mitchum was going to be one of his children."

An agreement was made to begin filming in August, giving Gregory and Laughton time to finance the picture and prepare a screenplay and allowing Mitchum to conclude his term at RKO. Gregory took the project to the studios. Warner Bros. turned him down. Columbia was interested in the material and Laughton as a director, said Gregory, "but Harry Cohn just absolutely wouldn't go with Mitchum. He wouldn't even discuss it with Mitchum."

A deal was finally made with United Artists, the "nonstudio" studio, offering a meagre $595,000 for the whole production.

At some point in the months before filming began, Laurence Olivier entered the picture, suddenly eager to play Preacher Powell under Laughton's direction. The idea was not unexciting, and Laughton didn't know what to do. "Larry" discussed it with Laughton's partner. Gregory felt they had the right person with Mitchum, but he ran it up the flagpole at the studio. He found that United Artists "would not be interested in putting up any money for *The Night of the Hunter* with Larry Olivier."

To write the screenplay, there was brief consideration of setting Davis Grubb to the task. "He was an odd man, to say the least," Gregory remembered. "Number one, he said he could only write on a train. And he refused to travel other than on a train or a bicycle. You could hardly get him into a car. And he was . . . troubled. Very troubled. He never spoke much. Only thing I remember, he asked, 'Do you know Tennessee?' I said, 'Tennessee? Well, I know a few things, through a friend of mine.' He said, 'Oh, tell me about it!' He said he was curious about Tennessee, liked to read about it. Hmm. Other than that, I can't remember him ever saying a thing, only that he liked the movie. He thought it was true to the book. Of course it was."

So Grubb went home—by rail and pedal, presumably—to Philadelphia, but Laughton stayed in touch. He had learned that Grubb was an amateur sketch artist who liked to draw scenes and caricatures of the people he created in his fiction. Seeing the value in such visualizations by the hand of the author himself, Laughton had him send them to Hollywood and phoned him up begging for new ones throughout the production, sometimes specifying that Grubb draw in the exact expression on a character's face that he'd had in mind while writing a particular scene. The writer produced over a hundred of these pen-and-ink drawings for the film. "I declare, perhaps immodestly," Grubb said, "that I was not only the author of the novel from which the screenplay was adapted but was the actual scene designer as well."

Gregory and Laughton settled on another literary figure to write the screenplay: James Agee, the acclaimed critic and novelist who, pertinently, had written the classic study of Depression-ravaged Appalachia, *Let Us Now Praise Famous Men*, and had one notable screenwriting credit for *The African Queen*. Unknown to Laughton and Gregory at the time they hired him, *The African Queen* had been largely rewritten by John Huston and Peter Viertel, and Agee was currently well into the last phase of his alcoholic self-destruction. "That was our first big flub," said Paul Gregory. "He was drunk all the time. And he couldn't get along with Charles. It was just terrible." At first Agee worked at Laughton's house, going out by the pool each day with a typewriter and a bottle of Jack Daniels. When Laughton couldn't take any more of the puking and passing out, they moved Agee to Gregory's place at the beach. Then to a hotel. Gregory: "He was a wonderful writer. But the poor man was tormented by something. I don't know what. At times he would cry for hours. I went and sat with him at his hotel one night, and he just sobbed and sobbed. I thought he might commit suicide. I had never seen such behavior."

Agee refused to show anyone a page of script until he was done, then turned over something the size of a New York phone book (Grubb's novel was slender) and full of unfilmable descriptions, stream of consciousness, and indications for frequent cutaways to old newsreels. Time and thirty grand unpleasantly wasted! Laughton ended up writing most of the screenplay himself, though he wouldn't take a credit. Agee was dead before the picture was released.

Laughton imagined *Hunter* having a deliberately archaic look, something like the early silent films he had seen as a youth. At New York's Museum of Modern Art he screened a number of D.W. Griffith's works and became reacquainted with the singular artistry of Lilian Gish. They took tea together in Manhattan, and he offered her the part of Miz Cooper (his wife, Elsa Lanchester, having already turned it down—she didn't want to be near him in a "hypersensitive" situation). He told Gish, "When Griffith was making those films, audiences sat bolt upright on the edge of their seats. Now they sit slumped over, feeding themselves popcorn. I want to make them sit upright again." For the role of the doomed widow, Laughton and Gregory had one actress in mind from the beginning: Bette Grable. She hemmed and hawed, unsure of her availability, uncertain of the strange project. Laughton and Gregory remained hopeful of signing her until a few weeks before filming was to begin. Reluctantly, they considered a list of other actresses, including Teresa Wright, before abuptly offering the part to Shelley Winters, the zaftig blonde from Brooklyn, and a student in Laughton's advanced acting class. Mitchum objected. "She looks and sounds as much like a wasted West Virginia girl as I do," he said. "The only bit she'll do convincingly is to float in the water with her throat cut."

Mitchum favored shooting the picture on authentic Appalachian locations, but this was vetoed as too expensive. Besides, Laughton had something other than authenticity in mind. Filming would be done on stages at Pathé and Republic studios and at the Rowland V. Lee ranch in the San Fernando Valley. Laughton protégés Terry and Dennis Sanders were sent to film second-unit material along the Ohio River.

To photograph the movie, Laughton hired a cinematographer he had gotten to know in Paris on the set of *The Man on the Eiffel Tower* (and became reacquainted with in Hollywood shooting—yes— *Abbott and Costello Meet Captain Kidd*), Stanley Cortez. Nicknamed "the Baron," the elegant brother of silent star Ricardo Cortez was an extremely creative technician, best known for his amazing work on Welles's *The Magnificent Ambersons,* who nonetheless found himself most of the time shooting B picture junk. Cortez met with Laughton every Sunday for six weeks before shooting began, showing him how the camera worked, piece by piece, lens by lens. In turn, Laughton found prints of Griffith's silents for Cortez to study.

Though he had been making movies as an actor and sometime producer for nearly thirty years, Laughton approached his directorial debut as if it were to be his first moment on a film set. He considered no element of the enterprise unworthy of his attention, for all that it was not a luxurious production, and the strained budget and tight shooting schedule left him little time for rehearsals or for much advance work on the production design. Mitchum was not legally available to them—still with RKO—until three days before filming began. Laughton had to depend on inspiration, luck, and teamwork.

"I have to go back to D. W. Griffith to find a set so infused with purpose and harmony," wrote Lilian Gish. Said Stanley Cortez, "Every day the marvelous team that made that picture would meet and discuss the next day's work. It was designed from day to day . . . so that the details seemed fresh, fresher than if we had done the whole thing in advance." As soon as filming concluded in the evening, Laughton, Cortez, set designer Hilly Brown, and assistant director Milt Carter regrouped at the Frascatti Inn on La Cienega to consider the possibilities for the upcoming sequences. Some scenes came together only hours, even minutes before they were to be shot. Laughton encouraged contributions from everyone involved. Mitchum delighted him with clever suggestions and bits of business that were instantly incorporated—like the idea of speaking his lines inside the prison cell while hanging upside down from his bunk. A creative synergism developed among the artists and technicians that allowed scenes to blossom and achieve sudden, unexpected new levels of expressiveness, as when a last-minute adjustment of a few lights before shooting Preacher's murder of his wife turned the A-frame bedroom set into the outline of a church with shimmering spire. Freed of any allegiance to realism or the favored stylistics of the day, Laughton's technical team was encouraged to employ visual tricks that had fallen out of favor in the naturalistic Hollywood of the '50s. They made flamboyant use of shadows and silhouettes. Some sets were built in perspective for artificial, dreamlike vistas. Instead of a time-consuming, expensive crane shot of a boy outside a basement window, Cortez offered to zero in with a mechanical iris, a device that had rarely been used since the coming of sound—the look was pure Griffith.

Laughton could barely contain himself. "He was such an inspiring figure," said Cortez. "You were ready to do all you could to give him what he wanted. You didn't care about the hours spent. You were not working for the paycheck, you were working to help Laughton, to help him achieve all that he wanted." To reveal the dead Shelley Winters seated in her car underwater, Laughton desired a bright, ethereal image, her hair floating like seaweed, and a slow, unbroken camera movement rising to the water's surface. Cortez went all over town trying to find a water tank that his lights could penetrate sufficiently, settling on the one owned by Republic Pictures. A platform suspended by a crane held eight blinding Titan sun arcs. Wind machines had to be carefully employed to blow the hair and weeds without making waves. The camera operator and an assistant worked underwater in scuba gear. The amazingly lifelike dead Shelley Winters was a wax dummy.

As for Mitchum, he, too, gave Laughton everything he wanted—and more. In the spirit of Laughton's eccentric and expressionist approach, he abandoned his usual low-keyed behaviorial style in favor of intense theatricality, eye-rolling flamboyance. The director confided to Lilian Gish that he had to hold Bob back lest he go so far with his inspired malevolence that he ruin his career, making women and children run when they saw him. ("I think," said Mitchum, "I was still fairly despicable.") Laughton felt such confidence in his star that he even allowed Mitchum to take over direction of the film on a couple of occasions, scenes involving little Sally Jane Bruce and Billy Chapin, though in truth Laughton was only too eager to have someone else work with the children. He was not simpatico with the young actors and thought the boy a perfect little monster. "Charles was not able to get through to them," said Paul Gregory, "and thought that maybe Mitchum could talk to them and make them a little more relaxed." Mitchum theorized that child actors instinctively sought direction from the adult actors they worked with and that it was natural and less confusing for them if an actor actually did give the directions. "Mitchum got along great with the kids and they got some damn good footage," said Paul Gregory. "Charles told me how very tender he was with them."

Neither Mitchum nor Laughton seemed to be particularly tender with Shelley Winters. "Shelley was such a good actress," said Reva Frederick, "but sometimes she would have little screaming jeebies over something and Robert used to not be tolerant of that kind of attitude. And *Charles* . . . the way he dealt with her . . . Once she was making a scene over a piece of wardrobe that didn't fit or something, or she thought it didn't fit, and Charles just walked over to her and slapped her across the face. He said, 'Stop it!' And we were all like, 'God, did I just see what I saw?' And Shelley just blinked and snapped to and went back to the work."

Robert's devotion to Laughton and the project had begun to fade by the final week of the thirty-six-day shoot. Gregory: "Laughton had a keen thing for Mitchum, and Mitchum said all this shit about how he loved Charles, but he was on drugs, drunk, and what have you, and there were times when Charles couldn't get him in front of the camera. He put us through a lot of hell on that. The picture went two hundred thousand dollars over budget." To Gregory, Mitchum at times seemed uncomfortably like the character he was playing. "He was a charmer. An evil son of a bitch with a lot of charm. Mitch sort of scared me, to tell you the truth. I was always on guard. He was often in a state, and you never knew what he would do next. He would be drunk or in a fight with this flunky he kept around, and kicking him all over the place. I came from the world of the theater and I had never seen anyone quite like this."

One day they were shooting an exterior scene at the Lee ranch in the Valley. Shelley Winters arrived late, coming from rehearsals for a television appearance. Mitchum arrived staggering. Laughton said nothing but phoned his producer for help. "What the hell, Paul," he said, "we can't shoot. Mitchum is so high . . . it's just not possible." The thing was—Mitchum *insisted* on working.

Gregory, ever mindful of the production's strained budget and all that he and Laughton had riding on this initial effort, hopped into his car and sped to the location. He would recall having words only with Mitchum, though Shelley Winters recollected also receiving a tongue-lashing from the producer. "He was running around the set screaming about how much it would cost if the stars delayed like this all through the picture," she wrote. "Gregory's screaming unnerved me. . . . I was hoping somebody would shut him up. Good acting cannot be performed in an ambiance of chaos and pressure."

Gregory confronted Mitchum. "He was all puffy-eyed. Could barely see. I said, 'Mitch, sweetheart, you're in no condition to go on camera.'"

Mitchum said, "What the fuck you mean I'm in no condition?"

Gregory said, "You're in no condition. You're all puffy-eyed!"

Mitchum raised his eyebrows—though drooping eyelids did not follow. He seemed to ponder for a moment, considering this red cape of authority that had just been shaken in his face. Then, said Gregory, "he opened his fly and whipped his dick out."

The door to Gregory's Cadillac convertible was wide open, and Mitchum moved over behind it to urinate. "I stepped back to give him some room. I thought he was trying to hide behind the door for modesty's sake." But no. "I looked back and see that he is pissing on the front seat of the car where I had been sitting. It went on and on, filling up the seat with piss. I stood there. I couldn't believe it, that's all. And then he put his cock back in his pants and turned around with a look on his face like that was just the *dearest* thing he had ever done in his life! He staggered away, and I stood there looking at the seat of my car. Finally I closed the door and went over by the crew and got one of the prop boys. I said, 'I wonder if you could get me a sponge or something. I just had my car seat baptized by Mr. Mitchum.'"

Nearly five decades later, thinking back on that day of infamy—nothing like it in the theater!—Paul Gregory would start to laugh. "He was . . . a funny guy, *I'll admit it*. Funny in many ways. Oh, I wanted to kill him. . . ."

Gregory and Laughton went to view the finished film for the first time, by themselves, in a tiny screening room at the Beverly Hills Hotel. The producer was amazed by the artistry and creativity displayed. Mitchum was remarkable, Gish wonderful . . . but . . . what to think . . . seeing it all cut together now he hadn't expected the film to be quite so odd, so . . . out of the mainstream. He thought perhaps Cortez had been an overwhelming influence, too far out, offering Charles too many possibilities. The lights had gone up and the two sat there. "You had to be careful what you said to Charles. He didn't believe you if you said it was wonderful, and he would have killed you if you said you thought it was awful. But Charles and I had had a relationship for about six years by then. I was not one to bullshit him. I looked him right in the eye and I said, 'Charlie, they're not going to know how to sell this picture.' And he said, 'Oh, my god, why, old boy?' I said, 'It's . . . they're going to call it an art film, a picture for the art houses. And I think we're going to be in trouble. It has nothing to do with the fact that you did a fantastic job, but I think it's going to be a tough sale.' Well, he hadn't dreamed of such a possibility. But I turned out to be right. The fact that *The Night of the Hunter* was not a commercial success devastated him. He went into a slide, a depression that lasted for about seven months and ended with our breaking up our partnership. We had contracts for him to direct *The Naked and the Dead,* and he was just out of sorts, couldn't do it. And I had to go on and do something with it; I couldn't just sit there. Terrible how it turned out. He never directed another film, of course. . . . He was a terrific guy. I loved old Charlie. . . ."

It was one of those rare Hollywood films—like *Citizen Kane, King*

Kong, The General, and few others—that seemed to come out of nowhere, following no tradition or precedent, a work of astonishing originality. Laughton had reconceived Davis Grubb's dark, often savage novel, with its switchblade killings and carved-up hookers and other niceties, turning it into something equally strange but airier, like a fractured fairy story or folk tale, beginning with the opening moments—the disembodied Miz Cooper reading Scripture as she floats among the stars—and on to the enchanted river journey with its scuffling bunny rabbits looking on and the final Grimm battle of the surrogate mother and father. It was the story as it might have been drawn directly from a loopy child's imagination—direct, say, from the mind of strange, wild-eyed Pearl. The film's odd, multilayered sensibility invoked the lost world of Griffith, the Manichaean-Victorian melodrama of *Way Down East* and *Broken Blossoms,* even as its insidious black comedy and strange satire anticipated the "put-on" and "sick" humor of the '60s, of films like *Lolita* and *Dr. Strangelove* and *Psycho.* Mitchum's performance—a bone thrown to all those critics incapable of appreciating his usual subtly nuanced naturalistic acting—was a grandly unbuttoned, theatrical piece of work unlike anything he had ever attempted or would ever attempt again. Whether greasily charming his backwoods admirers, preaching the tale of "left hand/right hand," singing various renditions of "Leaning on the Everlasting Arms," contemplating the murder of a burlesque queen, making his psychotic hog caller's cry of "*Children!*" or taking a pratfall like some diabolical Keystone Kop, Mitchum's wonderfully sinister, appalling, ridiculous Preacher Harry Powell was the powerful, crucial fulcrum in the film's risky imbalancing act. There would be many who would call it his best performance, and sometimes Mitchum would agree with them.

Despite the audiences' indifference and the tepid enthusiasm of reviewers at the time, the film would go on to achieve classic status, eventually, decades later, showing up in critics' polls of the greatest movies of all time. Francois Truffaut, in the pages of *Cahiers du Cinema,* wrote of *The Night of the Hunter,* "It makes us fall in love again with an experimental cinema that truly experiments, and a cinema of discovery that, in fact, *discovers.*"

Charles Laughton was done with film directing, but he would remain a Mitchum enthusiast for his remaining years, speaking of him warmly to a reporter just months before his death in 1962: "He is a literate, gracious, kind man with wonderful manners and he speaks beautifully—when he wants to . . . Bob is one of the best actors in the world . . . a great talent. He'd make the best Macbeth of any actor living."

Stanley Kramer was Hollywood's most distinguished independent producer, with a string of box office and/or critical hits that included *Champion, Home of the Brave, The Men, The Wild One,* and *High Noon.* At a time of Red scares, blacklists, and avenging superpatriots, when Hollywood seemed to be covering its head and running in fear from subjects concerned with American social problems and matters of conscience, Kramer made them his specialty. A high-minded liberal humanist, Kramer's productions were predominantly dramatic explorations of timely and controversial topics such as race, the handicapped, delinquent youth. Even his Gary Cooper–starring horse opera, *High Noon,* was a blatant if metaphoric attack on McCarthyism. Kramer ignored the truism that Western Union, not Hollywood, was the place that delivered messages, but his pictures were tough, dynamic dramas, and he always kept an eye on the box office. An excellent overseer with a keen instinct for fresh talent (Kirk Douglas, Marlon Brando, Carl Foreman), Kramer nonetheless longed to move into the auteur's chair. And now the time had come. For his directorial debut he chose to make a film out of Morton Thompson's popular novel about doctors and the nurses and patients who loved them, *Not as a Stranger.*

While Kramer had made his reputation with small, high-fiber, low-budget films using new or little-known performers, he decided to launch his directing career with a two-million-dollar all-star— Robert Mitchum, Olivia DeHavilland, Frank Sinatra, recent Oscar winner Broderick Crawford—extravaganza derived from 1954's thickest and most melodramatic best-seller—948 pages of C sections, stitches, and sex. Not that it was a project without a socially relevant subtext. The Thompson novel had provoked readers with its scathing exposé of the medical industry, and Kramer declared that his film was likewise going to pull no punches in depicting the private lives of the "men in white."

Hard to fathom now, with the novel so long unread and forgotten, but *Not as a Stranger* would top the best-seller lists for two years running, and the prospect of its adaptation to film was cause for much excitement and speculation across America. Like the debate over who would play Rhett Butler in *Gone With the Wind,* readers and media folk pondered the proper actor for the role of Dr. Lucas Marsh, the "brilliant physician who must learn to be a human being." It became apparent after the casting choice was made that there was at least one person whom readers did *not* want for the role, and that person was Robert Mitchum. Columnists reported hearing from "thousands" of readers deploring the casting and printed some of the more outraged letters. "What in the name of heaven have they done to that sensitive part that a burly, crude lead such as Mitchum would even be considered?" went one irate missive. And another: "I found Lucas Marsh a quietly intriguing and intelligent man; he is the kind of man I married. Lew Ayres or Cornel Wilde could do the part justice. How shocked and distressed I was when I read they had chosen Robert Mitchum of all people to play this nice fellow!" On the face of it, the novel's driven, neurotic Dr. Marsh did seem better suited for—well, if Cornel Wilde was not available, someone along the lines of a Brando or Montgomery Clift, and not the king of apathy and cool; but Stanley Kramer saw Mitchum's powerful, unemotional presence in his vision of Dr. Marsh and he stuck to his choice despite the outcry.

Kramer put his trusted and estimable team of Edward and Edna Anhalt to work on a script (author Morton Thompson, briefly consulted, died, an apparent suicide, while the movie was in production) and they began transforming the nearly one thousand pages in the book to a manageable if still unusually long 173-page script. The Anhalts updated the story from the 1920s and lopped off hundreds of pages about Lucas's Dickensian childhood. In advance of filming, and in pursuit of a detailed realism for the medical scenes, Kramer hired a team of technical advisers—doctors, surgeons, and

registered nurses—to watch over the production and the performers
and keep all hospital procedures scrupulously authentic. In further
pursuit of this goal he arranged with several area hospitals to allow
himself, Ed Anhalt, Mitchum, and several others to observe a variety
of actual operations and to follow some doctors on their daily rounds.

Mitchum, Sinatra, and Crawford attended a hospital theater
autopsy similar to one staged for the first scene in the film. Seated
among a small group of hovering medical students, they watched as
a pathologist ripped the sheet off a corpse, inserted a scalpel, and
opened the body from throat to pubis. Broderick Crawford immediately got up and headed for the exit.

"Where you going?" Sinatra asked.

Crawford said, "*Malibu!*"

At the Veteran's Hospital in Los Angeles, Mitchum, DeHavilland,
Kramer, and Anhalt, all in full surgical costume, stoically observed a
number of operations—an appendectomy, a gastrectomy, the
removal of a tumor from the spinal cord. "Everybody was surprised
and, if you ask me, disgusted that none of us got sick," said
Mitchum. As one surgeon stood poised to make his first incision, he
told Bob and Olivia, "If you faint, I'd appreciate it if you faint backward." This line and a number of incidents the group observed went
straight into the screenplay. Kramer and Mitchum watched an operation on a man with a gangrenous intestine. When the patient was
wheeled into the operating room, the surgeon told him, "These two
people here"—Mitchum and Kramer—"are observing your operation for a movie they are making."

"Oh?" said the man on the operating table. "What's the movie?"

"*Not as a Stranger,*" said the surgeon, through his surgical mask.

"Oh, I read that. Who's playing Dr. Lucas?"

"Robert Mitchum."

"Robert Mitchum? You got to be kidding. . . ."

Paying no heed to such critics, Mitchum stayed the course
Kramer had prescribed. Technical adviser Dr. Morton Maxwell
worked closely with the actor, answering his many questions and
teaching him the mechanics of the profession, giving him instru-

ments to practice with at night—on Dorothy or the kids, presumably. Morton said he was "astonished at the speed with which Bob Mitchum learned to percuss a chest wall, tie sutures, and handle surgical clamps. . . . Bob learned in hours what it required medical students weeks to master."

But Mitchum and his colleagues were not quite ready to take the Hippocratic Oath, as they proved soon after the hospital training period ended and filming of *Not as a Stranger* began. Kramer had unwittingly loaded the picture with a number of Hollywood's most ferocious drinkers. "Mitchum, Sinatra, Brod Crawford, Lee Marvin—every one a teetotaller!" said Ed Anhalt, gleefully recalling the well-lubricated cast. "Myron McCormick? Broadway actor played the anesthesiologist in the picture? He'd fall asleep during a take, wake up screaming, and fall off the set! I'm very fond of Stanley, but he was a good boy, didn't drink, and . . . Stanley had no idea what he was getting into with this mob. "

"It wasn't a cast so much as a brewery," said Robert Mitchum. The tippling would begin early, and by late afternoon the sets at the California Studios would become a full-blown bacchanal. Fights, with fists and food, erupted at a moment's notice. One day the gang toppled a trailer. On another occasion they broke through the side of a dressing room. Telephones were ripped from the walls. It reminded Stanley Kramer of that picture he had produced about the motorcycle gang taking over the town, only that time the gang was working from a script and he could count on a happy ending.

One day Broderick Crawford went berserk. The scrawny but fearless Frank Sinatra enjoyed needling the huge, powerful Crawford, likening the actor to the retarded character, Lenny, in *Of Mice and Men*. "He could be mean, Sinatra," said Anhalt. "Why he was so mean to Brod, I don't know. And you didn't want to make Brod lose his temper if you had any sense." Crawford—Mitchum called him "the Crawdad"—took all the needling he could stand one day and attacked Sinatra, holding him down, tearing off his hairpiece, and . . . *eating* it. Someone screamed, "My God, Crawford's eaten Sinatra's wig!"

"Mitchum tried to pull them apart," said Anhalt. "He liked Brod, and he liked Sinatra, too. And like the Good Samaritan he ended up getting socked for his troubles. And Sinatra took off, disappeared, having instigated the whole thing. So Mitchum's fighting with Brod, and Brod throws him through the window onto the balcony outside. Mitchum was big and strong, but Brod was even bigger."

The Academy Award–winning Crawford began choking on the fake hair he had ingested. Someone ran in with technical adviser Dr. Maxwell, and they attempted to make Crawford vomit the hair clump up. Anhalt said, "I don't know whether they were trying to save him or save the hairpiece, because it was the only one they had. Anyway, it was mangled and they couldn't use it, so filming had to be postponed for I don't know how long, until Sinatra could be fitted for a new toup."

At the end of one exhausting day—blissfully without incident—Kramer dismissed the cast with a polite request: "Tomorrow morning we shoot one of the most difficult scenes in the picture and I want you all clear-eyed and no hangovers. *Please* . . . everybody promise me you'll go straight home now and get a good night's sleep." They promised. Kramer stayed late working with the film editor, then wearily got into his car and headed for home. He stopped at a red light on a seedy corner not far from the La Brea studio and saw a violent commotion outside a bar. He blinked a few times before he realized what he was looking at. It was three, no, four members of his cast, one of them lying sprawled on the asphalt, two in a ferocious fistfight. The light turned green and so did Kramer, cursing to himself and laughing mirthlessly; he drove on and didn't look back.

The refined Olivia De Havilland, hair dyed blonde and having to speak all her lines with a "yumpin yiminee" Swedish accent, was subject to practical jokes, roughhousing, and "fanny pinching" (per Kramer) on the set, yet remained a figure of calm amid all the chaos. Anhalt: "She would never react to any of it. But I would feel bad and say to her, 'You know, they don't mean half the things they do or say.' She said to me, 'I know that. They don't bother me. I've been around drunks.' I said, 'I don't know how you do it.'"

The other woman in the cast, Gloria Grahame, making her third film appearance with Mitchum, had entered the "toilet paper under the upper lip" phase of her career. "She put tissue under her lips because someone told her a thrust upper lip was sexy!" said Stanley Kramer. "See what I had to cope with?" After many hours of shooting, the toilet paper would begin to wad up with saliva, making her dialogue incomprehensible. When Mitchum tried to kiss her in the film's big passionate love scene, he found flecks of wet tissue coming out of her mouth. And she smelled funny. "She's a nut!" he told people.

Mitchum and Sinatra became instant friends. Mitchum greatly admired Sinatra's musical artistry going in, and Sinatra found Bob's don't-give-a-shit manner perfectly compatible. Sinatra was a short fuse with a crazy Napoleon complex, but he was certainly fun— there was always something happening when Frank was around. Mitchum earned the entertainer's undying admiration by passing on his recipe for a can't-fail hangover cure. "It's like mother's milk," Mitchum said. A gratified Sinatra took to calling him "Mother" from then on. For years he would send him a greeting card on Mothers' Day.

Mitchum and Eddie Anhalt became good buddies, too. "Everybody called him Mitch. I only called him Bob, for some reason. We went out just about every night when we were making that picture. Used to go to this place on Sunset Boulevard a lot. I drank martinis. He drank vodka. Sometimes he brought along a sidekick, kind of like Sinatra's Jilly. Big guy, looked like the Hunchback of Notre Dame." Tim Wallace, perhaps? "Don't remember his name. He wasn't illiterate, but he was close. But Bob was a smart guy. And he could write. Wrote some awfully good poetry. He wanted to be a writer at one point, but he probably got a look at some writers, somebody like you or me, and thought, 'I don't want to turn out like that,' so he became an actor."

One night—it was the night of November 5, midway through filming *Not as a Stranger*—Anhalt and Mitchum were sitting at the bar in the Villa Capri. They were expecting to be joined by Sinatra and some others from the picture. Mitchum tapped the screenwriter, telling him, "Hey, look, there's DiMaggio. He looks terrible."

Anhalt looked, agreed. Joe DiMaggio was standing a little farther down the bar and appeared morose. Mitchum said, "Do you know him?" Anhalt said no. Mitchum said, "Let's ask him if he wants a drink." Anhalt said, "Yeah, he might appreciate that." They waved Joe over. Just about then Frank Sinatra and Lee Marvin showed up. Everybody had a drink. Sinatra knew DiMaggio well and got the ex-ballplayer to admit what was bothering him. Of course, everybody knew that DiMaggio's marriage to Marilyn Monroe had gone south. DiMaggio said that Marilyn had disappeared; she was hiding from him. He needed to talk to her, and he'd been frantically trying to track her down for days. Everyone commiserated. A lot of drinks later, DiMaggio went off to the men's room and Sinatra said, "You know, we ought to do something for him. He really is in terrible shape. We got to help him get to Marilyn."

"But she's hiding out," somebody said.

Frank said, "I know where she is. We'll go over there and we'll tell her that she's got to talk to him."

"This didn't make a lot of sense at first," said Eddie Anhalt. "But the more we drank, the more it began to seem reasonable. And we got to the point where someone said, 'What if she won't open the door?' And Lee Marvin says, 'Well, we'll break it down.' And DiMaggio says, 'Break a door down? Who's gonna do that?' And Mitchum says, 'Well, Brod Crawford could do it; he's strong enough. He's like a mountain.' So then the cry went up, 'Where's Brod? Let's get Brod!' And I said, 'He hangs out at the Formosa.' So we decide to go over to the Formosa and see if he'll come with us to visit Marilyn Monroe. So everybody's drunk and we all pour out to the parking lot and drive off in this parade of cars. Those were the days when we all had XK 120s. Mitchum had an XK 120. I had an XK 120. Sinatra had a car with a driver, which was smart. And DiMaggio came along, but he was very quiet and sad and probably very drunk by that time.

"We went over to the Formosa and I went inside with Mitchum. And there was Brod, and we came up to him and we said, 'Brod, you can knock down a door, can't you?' He said, 'I can do anything!'

And I said, 'We want you to knock down Marilyn Monroe's door.' It all seemed perfectly reasonable by now. So we all went back to our cars and drove off to this address Sinatra told us. Now it was funny how Sinatra knew all this, and later I found out he was balling Marilyn himself, but we didn't think of that at the time. And we got out. Everybody's staggering around on the sidewalk trying to stay upright, and we head into the building, Sinatra and his guys, DiMaggio, Mitchum, Lee Marvin, Brod, everybody who was there. And I said, 'What apartment is she in?' And Frank said, with great authority, 'She's in 3A.' And we all went upstairs, as many as could manage it. And Brod and some other guys leaned on the door and broke it open and went tumbling inside this apartment. And inside was a little old lady who looked nothing like Marilyn Monroe, and she started screaming. So everybody says, 'Oh shit! Let's get outta here!' They're knocking each other over to get back out through the doorway. And everybody staggered back out on the street and got back into their cars and drove away. Somebody called the police, of course, and they reported it in the papers, what happened, and this woman said she had seen all these movie stars come breaking into her apartment, and I think maybe everyone thought she made it up, that she had had an attack of dementia."

It was what came to be known in the annals of showbiz gossip as the "Wrong Door Raid," after a story appeared nearly a year later in the pages of *Confidential* magazine—at a time when Robert Mitchum was in the process of suing that same periodical. Two years later the report of the raid became a focal point for a California State Senate investigation into the scandal magazine industry, and Frank Sinatra was subpoenaed. Accused by some of perjury, Sinatra gave obfuscatory and understandably irate testimony and managed to take the investigators down a dead-end street leading nowhere. Details of the legendary evening, and the actual stellar cast of characters involved, remained a mystery for nearly fifty years.

"I guess nobody will mind me telling about it at this point," said Eddie Anhalt. "Everybody is dead now except for me."

For all its iconoclasm and presumed authenticity, *Not as a Stranger* proved to be little more than a bloated, lurid Dr. Kildare episode without the MGM gloss of that old movie series (visually the film looked more like one of the black-and-white TV doctor shows its success would spawn). A majority of reviewers found Robert Mitchum's Dr. Lucas lacking. His characterization was variously described as "monotonous," expressionless," and an exercise in "stunned lethargy." The *Harvard Lampoon* cited him for the year's "Most Cretinous Performance."

Audiences, lured by the opportunity to see cretinous, stunned lethargy for themselves, made *Not as a Stranger* the fifth-highest-grossing film of the year and Mitchum's biggest box office success to date.

Even after what he called "ten weeks of hell," Stanley Kramer remained Bob's steadfast—if guarded—admirer. Mitchum, Kramer said, "thinks it's weakness to care about something or someone, so he pretends that he doesn't." He gave to the actor a lavishly Morocco-bound copy of the script as a keepsake and wrote: "To Bob, who possesses within himself the unfortunate power to be whatever he wishes!" Kramer would later offer him the lead opposite Sidney Poitier in his escaped prisoners drama about an angry black man and a racist white man discovering their common humanity, *The Defiant Ones*. Mitchum, Hollywood's self-avowed voice of experience on the subject of incarceration down South, turned it down, citing a phony premise—no white and black would ever have been chained up together in that part of the country, Mitchum said. A mangled version of his reponse would be told through the years—that Bob Mitchum refused to be in *The Defiant Ones* because he didn't want to work with a Negro.*

John Wayne's production company, Batjac, in association with

---

* Kramer's difficulty in landing a star for *The Defiant Ones* was the basis for a joke that made the rounds of the Hollywood party circuit, supposedly revealing of certain actors' proclivities, their respective egotism, bigotry, or pretentiousness: Kirk Douglas agreed to make the film but only if they cut out the role of the other prisoner; Mitchum agreed but only if the other prisoner was white; and Marlon Brando would make the film but only if he could play the part of the black man.

Warner Bros., signed Mitchum to star in *Blood Alley*, a $2 million pulp adventure story about an American soldier of fortune in Red China helping a boatload of refugees escape to Hong Kong. The salary was $150,000 plus a very healthy 16 percent of Batjac's profits. It would be much the same team that had done *Track of the Cat,* Wayne and partner Robert Fellows producing, William Wellman directing, Andy McLaglen his assistant director, photography by Bill Clothier. Mitchum's starting date was January 20.

Having made two pictures back-to-back with barely a day off, he had rented a house in Palm Springs for four weeks and on December 15 headed off for some uninterrupted rest and recreation in the desert resort.

One week into the new year, Wellman and crew arrived to do second-unit filming at locations around San Rafael and Belvedere Island on the north coast of San Francisco Bay, mostly hoping to get a lot of footage of the film's main prop, a vintage ferryboat, as it plowed around in the fog. Wellman had an idea: "Wouldn't it be great if we could get Bob up here for this and shoot him at the wheel of the boat instead of a double? We could move in closer . . . it would be a helluva lot better. Let's call Mitchum's manager and see if he'll do it. We can't put him on salary, it's not in the budget, but tell 'em we'd like him to do us a favor and come on up. Hell, we'll give him a limousine and he can go into San Francisco every night and have a good time."

Reva Frederick took the request and passed it on to Mitchum in Palm Springs. It meant cutting off his R and R by ten days, but Mitchum agreed and a day later climbed into his Jaguar and drove up the coast to the Bermuda Palms Motel in San Rafael. Things did not get off to a great start. On arrival, Mitchum was unhappy with his room and, to make his point, pounded a fist through the adding machine of the company's one-armed accountant. Given new accommodations, Mitchum was then housed directly over the room occupied by William Wellman. Mitchum had some guests that night, and to Wellman trying to sleep downstairs it sounded like they were playing football with the furniture. "Bob and somebody were up there having a scuffle," said Andrew McLaglen. "It was a friendly scuffle that turned into kind of a real scuffle, but it was mostly just kidding around. The next morning, Bill was a little grouchy about it, said Mitchum had kept him awake all night. And Bob didn't seem any the worse for wear—Bob's an amazing guy because whatever he does the night before, the next day he's as good as gold."

They shot on the ferryboat all that morning. At noon a couple of boys from the Coast Guard came by and introduced themselves. They were sent to invite Mitchum to their nearby ship for lunch. Wellman had no objection and Mitchum didn't mind. He went off to be guest of honor on the Coast Guard vessel and returned in the afternoon, climbing back on board the old ferry. "I wouldn't say that Bob was drunk, but he'd had a couple," said McLaglen. "The production manager, Nate Edwards, and the transportation man, George Coleman, were having a little conference, just going over the logistics for what they needed to do that afternoon. Bob ambled over to them and just sort of stood there listening. They saw him listening and they stepped away from him. With that, Mitchum came forward and grabbed hold of Coleman, sort of yanked him around—and that got turned into a lot of horseshit in the papers about Bob shoving George into the water, but it never happened, I was standing right next to them. And Bob said, 'Don't walk away from me like that! I'm a partner in this picture.' Which he was—he was getting a percentage. He said, 'I can listen to whatever I want to listen to.' And he shouted at Nate Edwards, 'Nate, I've known you a long time. Where do you get off acting like that?' Somehow . . . Bob doesn't get steamed up easy, but for some reason he got steamed up over this."

When neither man reacted, Mitchum turned in Bill Wellman's direction, as if determined to find an opponent. Wellman hadn't said a word to him, but he went toward him anyway.

Mitchum said, "Well . . . I certainly couldn't hit an arthritic old man like you."

"He didn't mean anything by it," said McLaglen. "He was just running off at the mouth. Bill was, what, fifty-nine then, but he was a feisty little guy. He didn't mean anything against Bill at all. But he said some things that he shouldn't have said and . . . one thing led to another. Bill, I think, had Nate Edwards get Duke's partner, Bob Fellows, on the phone; and Fellows said, 'How's it going?' and Bill must have said, 'Tell you what, I'm not too happy with Mitchum.' He was angry at him for what he said for a lot of reasons. He was angry, thinking, I made this guy a star. . . . But I do not think what happened was all Wellman's doing at all. I think Fellows had something in mind, and he picked up on an opportunity. If you really want to know what I think, I think Bob Fellows all of a sudden said, 'Boy, here's a chance to get Duke to do this part, and we'll save the percentage and we'll have a John Wayne picture.' And Fellows said, 'Let me talk to Jack Warner about this. We'll get him fired.' And that's exactly what they did."

John Wayne, the man drafted to be the star of *Blood Alley*, did not want to be the star of *Blood Alley*. He was at that moment in New York on his honeymoon. When he got word of the flare-up in San Rafael, he called McLaglen and told him, "Andy, whatever you do, make sure that Bob doesn't get fired!" But it was already too late. Jack Warner had signed off on Fellows's request. Mitchum was history. Fellows penned a circumspect press release—"Robert Mitchum has been fired after delaying production and refusing to apologize for creating disagreements among the production staff. . . ." Delaying production? Mitchum had come to work ten days ahead of schedule—and for free! The press release brought reporters rushing up to San Rafael for the story—major movie stars did not get canned every day. The Fellows/Wellman camp heated up the story, as if fearing their abrupt action might be considered frivolous. Someone heard someone say Mitchum was "on dope . . . always walking about six inches off the ground. He punched a guy, one of the drivers, knocked him into the bay, damn near killed him."

Mitchum held a very impromptu press conference in his motel room, sitting in bed in blue-and-white-striped boxer shorts and clasping a bottle of red wine. He told the gathering of journalists that the trouble had all started when he'd tried to help some of his fellow workers who had been deprived of much needed supplies, such as shaving cream and razor blades. "It was all," he said, "a result of my championing of the little guy. I always have and I always will establish myself as a human arbitrator, but don't get the idea that I'm a *hero*. It's just that lots of little people have spoken up for me. I want them treated right." Mitchum then said that he was "very, very tired" and wearily raised the bottle to his lips.

In the morning came the headlines: "MITCHUM FIRED FOR PUSHING AID INTO FRISCO BAY" . . . "BOB MITCHUM FIRED FOR DUNKING FILM MANAGER" . . . "MITCHUM LOSES STAR ROLE IN FILM FOR HORSEPLAY" . . . "PRODUCERS HUNT SEDATE SUB FOR GAY BOB MITCHUM." The papers had printed whatever the hell they felt like, describing in detail "Bad boy Mitchum's dunking of a 250-pound co-worker in the icy waters of San Francisco Bay" and the man's near drowning, and the fierce scolding Wellman had given Mitchum in front of the crew and costar Lauren Bacall, who wasn't even in California at the time.

"The next morning Bob came around," said Andy McLaglen. "And I'll always remember, Bob came in all shaved, blue suit and white shirt and tie, looked like a million bucks. I was very impressed with him. And he came over to me, said, 'G'bye, Andrew,' gave everybody a little salute, and then went over to Bill and said, 'Goodbye, Bill. Be seeing you.' And with that, with his head up, you know, he turned and went on his way."

Pilar Wayne, a fiery Peruvian and the Duke's new bride, would hold a lasting grudge against Mitchum for causing the premature termination of her honeymoon. It would be some time before her husband could persuade her to forget about it and invite Bob and Dorothy to one of their parties. That time had finally come, and as the Mitchums arrived at the Waynes' Encino home for what was a gala event, Pilar dutifully came out to greet them, letting bygones be bygones. According to the Duke's daughter Aissa, the first thing Mitchum did when he came through the doorway was peer down her mother's low-cut gown and mutter, *"Boy, do you need a new bra."*

All her stored up anti-Mitchum fury returning in a flash, Pilar cried, "Leave here! *This instant!*" and chased them out of the house.

An astonished John Wayne joined his wife at the front door just in time to see the couple scurrying to their car. "When my mother told him why the Mitchums had gone," Aissa recalled, "my father was careful not to crack the thinnest smile."

A few days after the *Blood Alley* firing, having had his sudden availability so well publicized in the press, Mitchum was offered the lead in *Man with the Gun,* the premiere producing effort of Samuel Goldwyn, Jr., and the directorial debut of Orson Welles's former longtime right-hand man, Richard Wilson (this would be the third of four Mitchum features in a row helmed by first-timers). The others in the cast included Jan Sterling, Karen Sharpe, and Henry Hull. Following in the bootsteps of *The Gunfighter* and *High Noon, Man with the Gun* was another heavy-handed, psychologically oriented oater about glum, tortured Westerners who never get to leave their backlot towns. Mitchum's long-faced peacemaker, Clint Tollinger, spends much screen time trying to get information about his abandoned daughter from his ex-wife, now a madame at the local whorehouse. It was a long ride from *Hoppy Serves a Writ.* When Tollinger finds out that the girl is dead, he goes berserk and nearly burns down the town he's been hired to protect, one of the movie's two memorable sequences (the other: classic bad guy Leo Gordon's amazingly mean-spirited shooting of a little boy's puppy).

With Mitchum's trouble-making image freshly on everyone's mind, there was a sense of anticlimax to his display of nothing but efficient and amiable professionalism. Karen Sharpe, a young and lovely actress playing the film's spunky ingenue role, recalled, "Jan Sterling and I would get together in the dressing room and talk about him and wonder what sort of colorful things he was going to do. But he was so *tame* on our movie. And we'd say, 'Oh, he's nothing like his image!' He was such a sweetheart. And he was so wonderful to me. I was just starting out, and he took such good care to make sure I had the right angle and gave me time for my lines. So generous." Said director Wilson, "Mitch never gave anyone a bad moment. He was never late for work, and he stuck right to his knitting. He worked very hard to bring the picture through on schedule." Mitchum was almost too cooperative. For the saloon fire sequence, where his character was to be seen coming out with one of the villains slung over his shoulder, Mitchum refused to let them use a stunt double. Reluctantly Wilson went along, then crossed signals kept Mitchum inside the burning building too long, and by the time he came running out—carrying a stuntman—his shirt and pants were scorched and smoking, and the stuntman wasn't feeling too good either.

Leo Gordon: "He was a first-class actor, Mitchum. First-class movie actor. We were watching him shooting a scene and somebody said, 'He doesn't do anything. He's not reacting.' I said, 'You don't understand what he does. The camera can pick up things that the eye can't. Wait till you see it on the screen.' And sure as hell there it was. I thought he was a helluva guy, just as easygoing as can be. We would sit around on the set bullshitting in those canvas-back chairs, and Mitchum loved to regale us with stories of his amorous adventures. I remember there was one he told about being down in New Orleans sometime before and how it was hotter than hell in his hotel room . . . and—he's telling this—he's lying naked on his bed and the phone rings. So he picks it up and hears a voice say, '*Mistah Meetchum? I'm so-and-so, Miss New Aw-lins for nineteen-whatever, and I'm the mayuh's official welcomin' committee, sugah, and would y'all mind if I came up and said hello?*' And Mitchum says, '*Hell no, I wouldn't mind.*' and so then she comes up to the room, the door's unlocked . . . well, anyway, it went on from there and . . . I don't suppose I better go into the details on this one, but he was quite a damn good storyteller."

Mitchum and some of the cast members went on a publicity junket to New York City when *Man with the Gun* was about to open. "I went—and my mother was even with us because I was so young," said Karen Sharpe. "It was my first trip to New York and Bob was excited for me. We were on the plane and he'd say, 'Come here, I want to show you the Statue of Liberty,' and I saw the Statue of Liberty for the first time. It was like he didn't want me to miss a thing. And we got off the plane, I think it was about seven in the morning, some ungodly hour, and there were lots of reporters there to meet us. And just to give them a good picture and—he was so sweet—just to make sure I got my picture in all the papers, giving me a boost, he took me up in his arms and carried me right off the plane! Oh, but when that picture got printed, my boyfriend of the time, Al Martino, got jealous; he thought there was an affair going on, and that really upset the relationship, but that's showbiz! And Bob was just a wonderful host on that trip for the two or three days we were there. We had to go from one radio show or one newspaper interview to another, very busy, but he showed me around, really watched out for me. And so generous—he took me to Toots Shor's, this great old hangout in Manhattan, and I remember how he told them that whenever I came in there, I was to be his guest. 'When you're in New York,' he said, 'you come here, whether or not I'm here or I'm dead and gone, it's on me.' That was how sweet he was. I must have been pretty naive back then, but I really couldn't understand how he had gotten such a bad reputation. The one and only time when I thought, Hm, maybe it's true the things they say, was when I had to do an early morning newspaper interview with Bob at his hotel. I went up there—I was staying at the Warwick; he was at the Sherry Netherland—and the reporters were there already, and, yeah, it looked like Bob had had a very big night. He was sitting in his underwear, in his shorts, giving an interview. And he was pretty hungover. And Tim was there, his bodyguard and stand-in, and Reva, and they were always together and I wasn't sure what the relationship was; I was kind of naive about all that stuff. But Bob was sitting in his underwear and giving an interview. He may have been slightly blasé—well, I never saw him very passionate about anything, don't think he was very impressed with himself or anybody else—but he didn't miss a beat, was up and awake and did his thing, very dependable no matter how awful he must have been feeling."

As part of his publicity duties, Mitchum made an appearance on network television—his first ever—guest hosting CBS's *Stage Show* variety program. Another, more intriguing TV gig was planned—Toots Shor's acquaintance Jackie Gleason talked him into appearing on that week's episode of *The Honeymooners*—but Mitchum left town and it didn't happen.

*

On March 8 he made official the formation of DRM Productions
(from his and Dorothy's initials) for the purpose of creating or
coproducing Robert Mitchum movies. It was good for taxes when
you did it this way, and, very important, it was a lot harder to get
fired when you were your own boss. And more: He really did want
to start creating his own stuff. He had even begun coming to the
office on Sunset and working on a couple of projected screen stories
(in addition to writing new lyrics and patter for his sister Julie's latest cabaret act). Nothing esoteric—he wasn't about to get nutty and
make art movies with his own income at stake—but he thought they
could be good commercial pictures with things in them the public
hadn't seen a million times already and maybe contain a few personal elements as well. One idea, about moonshiners and fast cars in
the Deep South, he had been tinkering with for years, but it still
needed work.

On the heels of DRM's announcement, Mitchum signed a long-
term, five-picture deal with United Artists, the financing and distribution organization for which he had just made three films in the
last eight months.

Confidential Magazine: the most scandalous scandal magazine in the
history of the world, Tom Wolfe called it. Created by New York
publisher Robert Harrison, the William Randolph Hearst of sleaze,
the man who had given to America *Titter, Wink, Flirt,* and *Beauty
Parade, Confidential* was the prototype for a new generation of
movie magazines not dependent on studio support and eschewing
regurgitated publicity-department fodder in favor of hot gossip, pillow talk, lurid disclosures of celebrities' hidden pasts and secret sexual preferences, and, on a slow news week, pure and simple slander.
In May folks picking up the new issue of *Confidential* found an article by a certain Charles Jordan, Hollywood investigative reporter.
The title of the story was "Robert Mitchum, the Nude Who Came to
Dinner," and the jaunty, cryptic deck read like this: "The menu said
steak. There was no mention of a stew. And one guest was not only

fried—but peeled . . . It's a pretty crazy story even for a guy who did time in a Hollywood clinic on charges of flying too high with Marijuana Airlines!"

All was explained on the pages that followed, an intimately detailed account of a party supposedly cohosted by Charles Laughton and producer Paul Gregory at Gregory's home on Ocean Front Walk in Santa Monica. Arriving late with an anonymous female friend and three sheets to the wind, wrote Jordan, actor Robert Mitchum proceeded to take off all his clothes, then lurched his way to the dinner table where, as Laughton and others averted their eyes, he doused his nude body with ketchup. "This is a masquerade party, isn't it?" said the brawny star. "Well, *I'm a hamburger!*"

Mitchum called up Jerry Giesler. Publisher Bob Harrison, editor Howard Rushmore, the managing editor, and two associate editors were slapped with a lawsuit asking one million dollars in general, exemplary, and additional damages. No one had thought to do such a thing before. It was a risky proposition for Mitchum of all people to sue an underhanded rag for such a trivial story, especially when the magazine could so easily fill an entire special double issue with more authentic and more damaging tales of his misadventures. Possibly he was bowing to family pressures. It was believed that when his son Jim had recently been eased out of a snooty private school he was attending, it was because the principal was repelled by the Mitchum reputation. (Jane Greer and Dore Schary promptly removed their own children from the school in protest.) Dorothy told a reporter, "The backwash of these sensational stories about Bob is hurting our children. Jim idolizes his dad, and the other kids keep ribbing him. He's always getting into fights sticking up for Bob." But the press couldn't really take all the credit for Mitchum's rep. That was what you called blaming the messenger. Mitchum said it was "a case of fighting for your good name. People are inclined to believe what they read in magazines." But it was the lawsuit that spread the story, garnering him a new wave of newspaper headlines, his most peculiar yet—including "MITCHUM DENIES ROLE OF NUDEBURGER; SUES"—and millions who had never even heard of

Confidential now woke up to read—and perhaps believe—an account of the magazine story Mitchum was denying.

Overnight he was hailed by his fellow movie stars as a hero, a crusader. A blow for liberty had been struck at last! Published since December 1952, *Confidential* had entered the movie capital like a festering contagion. What made it seem so threatening to so many celebrities was that the scandal rag burrowed deep within the substratum, relying on a newly tapped network of paid industry insiders to provide information, luring them—local reporters, wardrobe ladies, butlers, bartenders—to violate the Hollywood *omerta,* the code of silence that had previously protected so much bad behavior. The magazine used private detectives, people settling grudges, people telling tales out of school, people informing, naming names—it was like the HUAC witch-hunt days all over again, except that instead of Commies *Confidential* was rooting out adulterers, drunks, and scumbags.

"You know what that Mitchum *Confidential* story was?" said James Bacon, syndicated columnist and friend of the offended party. "That was based on a story Mitchum told me, and he probably told a lot of other people. He said he was with Charles Laughton and this other guy, and of course the two of them are both fags, and they're eating dinner and, I don't know, they can't take their eyes off Mitchum, I guess. So Mitchum said he opened his pants, took his cock out, laid it on the plate, and poured ketchup over it. And he says to them, '*Which one of you guys wants to eat this first?*' Now that's the story he was telling. And I guess what happened is a reporter in Hollywood, one of them writing for *Confidential* on the quiet, anonymously, wrote this story up but it was too raunchy for the magazine and the magazine changed it around to 'I'm a hamburger' or whatever it was, so they could publish it. And the funny thing is, Mitchum became convinced for a while that I had written the story. We'd run into each other and he'd give me a funny look and say, 'Hey, Jim, still writing for *Confidential*?'"

Giesler wanted no settlement or apology, only a courtroom trial and a million bucks. Believing that a jury was more than likely to side with a handsome movie actor over a sleazy scandal rag, and further believing that once they settled with or lost a lawsuit to one of their celebrity subjects they would be inundated with more of the same and be run out of business, Harrison and his crew decided to try and defeat Mitchum . . . the *Confidential* way.

Bob's brother, John, remarried, was back in Los Angeles and working regularly these days as a journeyman actor in the movies. Not long after news of the lawsuit hit the papers, he was making a picture called *Man in the Vault* with William Campbell. One evening they were shooting some scenes in Art Linkletter's bowling alley in West Hollywood and an off-duty deputy from the sheriff's department was providing security. The deputy struck up a conversation with John Mitchum and invited the actor to come over to his place for a drink when they were done shooting. Mitchum dropped by as he said he would. The cop had impressively luxurious digs and a new Cadillac in the driveway. The drinks flowed, and the deputy started talking to him about Robert, feeling him out, making cracks. "That brother of yours probably acts like a real big shot, huh? Everybody's got to kiss his ass, I bet. . . ."

Long story short, it turned out the deputy knew some people willing to pay real big bucks if John was able to get them some evidence proving his brother wasn't such an upstanding citizen. John told him he would think about it. Next morning he went to Jerry Giesler's office and repeated all he had heard. "Those *Confidential* bastards!" Giesler cried. He came up with an idea: John should pretend to accept the offer and try to find out what they were plotting. And so did Brother John become an undercover agent in Jerry Giesler's counterintel plot to beat the *Confidential* boys at their own game. John began meeting with the deputy, stringing him along with fake glimpses of Robert's dirty laundry and promises of something big to come. It went on like that for a while, with nobody getting much in the way of evidence against anybody.

One day the sheriff's deputy waylaid John on the street and told him his people were through waiting. He made John get into the gold Cadillac, drove him across town, and took him into a ground-floor apartment in a luxury apartment building in Beverly Hills, the offices, it would turn out, of Hollywood Research Inc., command central for *Confidential*'s fact-gathering and surveillance agents. The place was filled with big, tough-looking guys, and some of them looked like they were packing heat. There were desks around the apartment topped with phones and recording and listening devices and files and photographs. John was taken over to the head tough guy and recognized him—it was Fred Otash, a notorious ex-LA cop turned private eye, Hollywood fixer, problem solver, leg breaker, a big mean Lebanese, looked like Joe McCarthy with muscles.

"Where the fuck's that story you're supposed to deliver?" Otash screamed.

John wrote of the moment, "I looked over at Otash's silent, glowering gunmen with the bulgy jackets. It was confession time. 'I tried. God knows I tried.' My voice was trembling and I started to cry. 'But he's my brother and I just couldn't bring myself to do it.'"

Otash screwed his face into a meaty mass of disgust. "Get out . . . you sniveling bastard!"

Mitchum got out.

Apprised of the situation, Giesler told John his life was probably in danger and thanked him for his time.

John took his family and got out of town for a while.

Confidential's lawyers fought the Mitchum suit for over a year. In the end they successfully argued that the publication had technically never done business in the State of California and the case was dismissed. By then, however, other celebrities had followed Robert's lead, and many of these subsequent lawsuits were successful in court, greasing the way for *Confidential*'s emasculation in1957 and the end of a brief but colorful era in the history of journalism.

Of the five men Mitchum had tried to sue, one died of cirrhosis of the liver a few months later, one was shot in the Dominican Republic and went into hiding and an early retirement, and one— editor Howard Rushmore—was in the backseat of a taxi on Manhattan's East Side when he pulled out a revolver and murdered his wife and then stuck the barrel in his own mouth and put his thumb around the trigger.

But that, as they say, is another story.

CHAPTER TEN

Foreign Intrigue

In June 1955, the Norwegian tramp *Fern River* carried the Mitchums across the southern Atlantic from New York. For a week they moved slowly over an empty ocean, doing nothing. There was nothing to do. Sit in the sun, read—half his luggage was books—eat in the tiny dining room. It had taken a day out of New York for the six other passengers—retirees and college professors—to get used to the movie star on board. Now he was just Bob, stretched out on the deck, telling stories at the captain's table at dinner. One morning he woke up, looked through the porthole, and saw Africa on the horizon. They moved up along the coast of Morocco that morning and entered the port of Casablanca. The Norwegians advised them to stay on the boat as there had been much unrest in the country of late and many foreigners attacked on the streets. Bob said, "Hell, they were probably just having a little fun with 'em." He and Dorothy and two other passengers hired a taxi to take them around. They left the car at the entrance to the walled medina and walked through the old gated entrance, settling down for a drink at a café on the square. Gawkers began to whisper to each other, gathering for a look at the famous visitor. In no time, Mitchum recalled, the square had filled with "ragheads," maybe three hundred people pushing, edging forward, surrounding them on the narrow street. People whistling, shouting in Arabic. Somebody, said Mitchum, "remembered that it was to crowds like this that revolutionaries come to start a riot." He got his party up and moving as the crowd followed, many of them chanting his name, eyes full of fire. The others hurried to the car, unsettled, with hundreds of Moroccans in cotton frocks closing in behind them. "Get in the car, Bob!" someone shouted. But Mitchum paused, basking like a Roman emperor, until someone grabbed the back of his shirt and pulled him into the car and the driver hit the gas.

And on to Europe.

Sheldon Reynolds was American television's expatriate boy wonder, only twenty-six in 1951 when he began producing, directing, and writing a weekly series called *Foreign Intrigue,* a cloak-and-dagger drama distinguished by its authentic European backgrounds. Reynolds staggered Hollywood TV producers with the amount of production value he could squeeze into a low-budget show—each episode seemed to be shot in a half-dozen countries. This he accomplished through a variety of clever improvisatory strategems, shooting exterior sequences for an entire season at each location, then returning to his bases in Paris and Stockholm to write scripts and shoot interior scenes that would match up with what he had shot on the streets of Rome and Berlin and so on. The show was a hit, running for five seasons and 156 episodes. Then Reynolds came to Hollywood, wanting to "expand his horizons" and set up his first feature film. He shared the same agent with Robert Mitchum, and so they were brought together for a meeting on the set of *Not as a Stranger.* Mitchum liked Reynolds, knew his TV show, liked his nontraditional ideas about shooting a picture, and liked the idea of hanging around in the glamorous capitals of Europe. Mitchum said, "Let's do something." The problem was Reynolds didn't have a script—he didn't have a story even. The agent said he would be committing Mitchum to a summer picture within the next two weeks. Reynolds said that if he'd wait two weeks, he would have a script. He sat down and batted out a complete screenplay in the next eleven days. Mitchum liked it, United Artists liked it, and the picture was on.

Bob decided to spend the entire summer in Europe, half work and half vacation. He arranged passage on a freighter bound from New York to Genoa—it was a boyhood fantasy, crossing the ocean on a rusty old tramp.

Foreign Intrigue was not the title Sheldon Reynolds had intended for his feature debut. It was not a spin-off from the series, he insisted. But the script, about an American public relations man wandering the boulevards and back alleys of Europe investigating the death of his employer, had enough in common with the TV show to make UA feel they could profit from the association. Otherwise the studio left the producer-director to his own proven devices. It was a ten-week schedule with locations in three countries and a start date in early July.

Filming began on the Riviera, in Nice and Monte Carlo. Mitchum hated the expensive wardrobe that had been prepared for him—"There was a Swedish version of a Made in Paris suit with an Edwardian cut," he said. "I looked like Johnny off the pickle boat"— and elected to wear his own clothes in the picture. These included a trench coat (a staple garment of the *Foreign Intrigue* TV hero, making the movie look all the more a continuation) given to him as a going away present by Reva Frederick. Too-tight clothing aside, Mitchum relished the production's European style—the tiny crew, the minimal technical gear, the ability to move from one setup and one location to the next in a matter of minutes. Reynolds had eliminated all the flab and fuss of big Hollywood filmmaking. There were no story conferences, no production design sketches to be approved, no big sets to be built. The efficient operation Reynolds had put in place for his television show meant they had access to lights, recording equipment, film stock, and personnel wherever they went, allowing them to travel from country to country carrying little more than their personal luggage. They just got up in the morning at one luxurious hotel or another, had a big breakfast, and started shooting something. Mitchum didn't know if the finished product would look like a movie or a newsreel, but it was certainly pleasant putting the thing together.

The unit moved along the Mediterranean, then up to Paris, Versailles, on to Stockholm and the islands of the Swedish archipelago. The Mitchum boys were shipped over at the end of their school term (Trina left at home with a nurse). Dorothy schlepped them to the obligatory monuments and museums along the route, but more time was devoted to finding them Coca-Colas and properly prepared hamburgers. From Sweden they took a brief trip to Oslo, Norway, and arranged to meet some of Bob's Norwegian relatives. They were lovely people and in no way fawning—Bob had a feeling they hadn't gotten a chance to see any of those newfangled talking pictures yet.

He listened to stories of his mother and grandparents. A cousin and some others would stay in touch, writing him letters through the years.

"Mitchum was marvelous to work with," said Sheldon Reynolds, "extremely knowledgeable, understood the kind of filmmaking we were doing, could adjust and improvise to any situation. An incredibly fast study and with an amazing ear for language. We had a scene where he is supposed to be making a phone call and speaking four or five lines of French. Not one word made sense to him—he learned it phonetically—but he did it instantly, and his accent was excellent. And as an actor, if there was a hole in a scene, in the story line, he could find a way to fill it, to play through it and make it logical, because he understood story and everything that was going on. And he was extremely generous with the other actors. If he was not on camera and a bit player was saying some lines—normally, you had a script girl or the director reading the off-camera lines while the star went somewhere to rest, but Mitchum was always there to feed the cues to everyone. They all enjoyed working with him.

"He was a marvelous man, and we became very good friends. I found that his Hollywood image was a facade. He was very smart and learned, and if you wanted to discuss literature and poetry with him you had to hold your own because he knew what he was talking about. He was always eager for new experiences, not parochial at all. We went to dinner together every night, in Paris and elsewhere, and he was eager to try new things, taste new foods, frogs' legs, anything.

"He loved wine and he particularly loved cheese, cheese of all kinds he was eager to try. And while we were shooting, his thirty-eighth birthday came up. I told everybody on the set not to say a word, not to say 'Happy Birthday.' So we went through the whole day shooting and nobody said a thing to acknowledge it. And he was in his dressing room, taking off his makeup and cleaning up, and then I came in and told him I wanted to show him tomorrow's set. And we went out and everyone was there to yell 'Happy Birthday,' and we had the whole place covered with barrels of wine and giant wheels of cheese, about thirty-six different kinds of cheese. And that was the only time I ever saw him get emotional."

For the rest of his stay in Europe Mitchum would provoke the wrath of hotel keepers and gagging chambermaids, not to mention family members, as he gorged on great slabs of Roquefort and Gorgonzola and Brie and left unwrapped, unrefrigerated portions behind under the beds and in dresser drawers. "I remember, he talked a lot about cheese," said Harry Schein, the Swedish theater director and husband of Ingrid Thulin. "He was crazy for cheese, that man."

Ingrid Thulin (billed phonetically as Tulean in the credits), a successful young actress on the Stockholm stage (and with legendary performances for Ingmar Bergman and Luchino Visconti still in the future), was making her film debut as *Foreign Intrigue*'s leading lady. "I was so nervous to meet this famous Hollywood star, and he looked so big—he seemed like a giant, such shoulders! And I met him and I saw that he was reading Simone de Beauvoir! And I thought, Well, I have never seen a *man* reading Simone de Beauvoir, this feminist writer, not even in Paris. And he talked to me about the book and had me read it—and I am really thankful to him for that! So I was so surprised, this 'tough guy' was a real intellectual.

"He was very funny. In Paris, the French journalists would come around and someone asked, 'Can you say something in French?' And he said, '*Cognac!*' And one time he was urinating in the street, an alley, and someone yelled to read the sign over his head—it said, in French, Do Not Piss in the Doorway—and he was very angry. 'What kind of town is this!' he said. 'Take that sign down!' And then another day, we were up at the place where they had the Eternal Flame. And he heard that some Dane had been able to put it out by urinating on it. And he said, 'Oh, I can do that,' and he made a bet with someone and pissed and he managed to do it!"

Just once, on the Swedish archipelago, were the tables turned, Mitchum getting a chance to be shocked, when the director called a lunch break and—it being a hot day for Sweden, about 45 degrees Fahrenheit, according to Bob—the cast and crew, wardrobe lady, everybody stripped off their clothes and ran naked into the nearby sea. "Well, summer lasts about two days up there," he said. "Doesn't pay to invest in a bathing suit."

"He was such fun," said Ingrid Thulin. "He would tease me a lot. You know, my English wasn't at all good. I had only school English for three years. And Bob would correct me and tell me how to make it sound better. And we had a scene, we were walking and it's very foggy, and I was to say to him, 'Oh, I really like the fog.' But he told me I wasn't pronouncing it right. So he rehearsed me, and when we shot the scene I said it the way he told me: 'Oh, I really like *to fuck*'!"

He enjoyed the four-month jaunt, far from agents, trade papers, producers, and scandal magazines—at least any that he could read. "Whatever you do," Mitchum said, "the Europeans couldn't care less. No one bothers you. They leave you alone. They believe in individual liberty." His last night in Paris he did it up right, closing down a jazz club and bringing the American combo with him to a party he had heard about, where old pal Vic Mature was on hand to greet him—"Bobby, *sweetheart!*"—hopped over from London on the midnight plane in the middle of shooting *Safari* with Janet Leigh, hadn't even changed out of his great white hunter costume, mamboing around the joint in his pith helmet and khaki jacket with a bottle of Remy in one hand.

*

Foreign Intrigue: It was one of those movies that was no doubt more fun to make than to watch. A detective story at heart, the plot followed the hero's uncovering of a blackmail scheme involving a cabal of World War II quislings, with much footage devoted to Mitchum in his belted trench coat ambling iconically, though often listlessly, across elegant hallways and down dark alleyways. Though lacking in dynamism, the film was an aesthetic pleasure with its Riviera vistas, regal interiors, and sensuous Eastman color photography. *Foreign Intrigue* bombed in America but became a sizable hit in Europe, oddly, where the title and its association with the television series meant nothing.

Earl Felton, the man who had scripted the revised ending to *His Kind of Woman,* had been without the full use of his legs since childhood, a victim of polio and complications, getting around on crutches and leg braces; but he'd never allowed that to keep him from a life of amiable debauchery. He and Mitchum often palled around, closing taverns, getting into mischief. They made quite a duo wandering into a joint together, the big movie star and the man on the crutches, but Mitch never acted as if they were anything but evenly matched as they swapped lies and argued over who was going to get to bed some passing skirt.

Earl knew that Bob saw himself—not inaccurately—as an adventurer, a man who went looking for the fun and danger in the world, regardless of the consequences. "I've always liked the taste of the expression *soldier of fortune,*" Mitchum once said. Felton told him he wanted to write a script about a soldier-of-fortune character that would fit him to a T. He fiddled around and one day came through with a treatment about a movie company in Mexico during the 1916 revolution and the American adventurer who was Pancho Villa's right-hand man. Everyone who read it loved it. Felton got producer Robert Jacks and United Artists interested, Mitchum signed on at once, and Felton's friend and frequent collaborator Richard Fleischer read the treatment and agreed to direct. Felton and Mitchum took a trip to Mexico and looked at some locations, closed some cantinas, and worked on the material. Mitchum went to Europe. Felton sent him the script he'd written, and Mitchum cabled a response: "What happened to that other story?" Felton cabled back: "The idea which looked so good over Mexican beer hadn't come out when bathed in black typewriter ink, and this current plot had reared its exciting head instead." When Fleischer read it, he asked, "What happened to that other story?" There was no more movie company, no more Pancho Villa, no jokes, and no clever Pirandellian self-reflection. It didn't even read like a finished script, just a lot of shooting with an American gunrunner doing little more than ducking bullets. Fleischer said he was bowing out, but UA told him he'd be sued if he quit and undermined their investment in the project. Fleischer succumbed but told Earl to pack his typewriter; he was coming along to Mexico to rewrite the thing. Felton would be working on scenes throughout the production, sometimes sitting on the set and turning in pages of script even as the camera was being set up to shoot them.

The project had a title now: *Bandido!* In addition to Mitchum it would feature Zachary Scott as a rival gunrunner, German actress Ursula Thiess (who had recently wed Robert Taylor) as Scott's wife, with Mexican-born Gilbert "Amigo" Roland as a Villaesque bandit leader and, like the trailers used to say, a cast of thousands.

The filming schedule covered over a hundred sites in central and coastal Mexico, from Cuernavaca to Acapulco. Many of the sites chosen were the actual battlegrounds and byways of the revolt of forty years before, the town of Tepotzlan and the Dominican Cathedral built by Cortes, the Palo Balero Falls, Yaltapec, where Zapata was killed. For still more authenticity, the extras in the film, local villagers, would include numerous elders who had been witness to the revolution and participated in bloody events like those depicted on the screen.

Since Mitchum had a share in the film's potential profits—DRM was coproducing—Fleischer expected he would be on good behavior for this one. And he was, or something close to it. But Fleischer hadn't counted on Mitchum's bringing down a couple of surrogate troublemakers to take up the slack. The star arrived with an entourage consisting of Reva, Tim Wallace, and Layne "Shotgun" Britton, makeup man, another refugee from RKO. One night after Mitchum had gone back to his hotel, Wallace got into a brawl at a party. Whether Bob's stand-in was an instigator or an innocent bystander, Dick Fleischer couldn't say. "What was clear, once the dust settled, was that a pretty senorita had been at the receiving end of a haymaker and lay unconscious on the floor." It turned out she was the mistress of a high-ranking Mexican policeman, and the Mexicans were saying that the girl had been kayoed, not by Robert's look-alike stand-in, but by Mitchum himself; and that Bob was about to be arrested or shot or both. Nobody disbelieved it. The town was full of *pistoleros* and shotgun-toting police. One afternoon several *Bandido!* people saw a cop and a bus driver get into an argument on the street, and the cop shot him without a second thought.

"Jesus Christ," Mitchum said, "we went through this shit the last time I made a picture here!"

Fleischer was living in a small posada in the mountains (Robert had preferred a hotel amid the downtown tequila joints). That night Mitchum moved his stuff over to the posada and took a seat in the lobby. He said he was certain he was going to be attacked and told Fleischer to sit with him and keep him company. He kept him there practically till morning.

"What you need is a bodyguard," Fleischer said, blinking back sleep.

"I've got a bodyguard. He got me into this mess."

In the morning the injured mistress vindicated Mitchum but put the finger on Tim. It was arranged for a private plane to touch down at a rural airfield and fly the stand-in to Mexico City and out of the country.

Next it was Shotgun Britton's turn to stir things up. "People stood, stared, and gaped when he passed by," Jane Russell wrote of the man. He was a flamboyant, one-of-a-kind, sometimes hard-to-take character who dressed in garish outfits of purple and orange and spoke an indecipherable drawling hipster double-talk. He was also an unreconstructed Texan whose treatment of the local Mexicans was something worse than condescending. Now came reliable word that some of the insulted locals had decided to assassinate him. "Old Shot had grab-assed a young Mexican maid in Cuernavaca," said Reva Frederick. "The Mexican crew took great exception to this and he had to go. At one point the negative of the picture was taken. They wouldn't give it back till things were settled."

The *Bandido!* emergency airlift flew again, and Shotgun was whisked away at dawn.

It was an enormously physical production. Scenes called for huge battles involving hundreds of people, machine guns and cannons firing, horse falls and other stunts, explosions everywhere as armies of *Revolucionistas* and *Regulares* battled in the streets. A first aid station had a line halfway through Tepotzlan with bleeding, bruised, broken-boned extras and stuntmen. The principals got their share of purple hearts, too. Zachary Scott dislocated a leg in a leap. Ursula Thiess suffered serious bruises and a state of shock when the railroad car they were working in took a sudden lurch and sent her flying from one end to the other. Mitchum had the skin shredded off one of his legs when he fell through a rooftop. Richard Fleischer's dynamic staging and mobile camera craning and tracking throughout—plus Mitchum's disposition—required the star to do most of his own stunt work. He rode horseback for miles on the roughest terrain, leaped off a moving train, came face-to-face with a shark while swimming underwater in a lagoon, and dodged real bullets from a supposed sharpshooter when the planted squibs they had expected to use failed to explode. The one occasion when he demanded a double was for an unathletic but spine-splitting ride in a springless 1915 Model-T Ford on a rocky, unpaved road. Tim Wallace would take the ride for him, cursing all the way.

The moviemakers did nothing to make things easy on themselves. For a chase scene they went to a densely overgrown mangrove swamp miles to the east of Acapulco that could be reached only by canoe. It was a nightmare of heat, steam, and muck, large insects and rodents running around, conditions made no more pleasant by the fact that a goodly portion of the American crew had come down with the turistas and were vomiting and shitting even as the camera was turning. One of the few remaining blissfully undiscomfited was Earl Felton, sitting on the shoreline watching the filming, sipping a cold drink. At the end of a take Mitchum came out of the swamp dripping with slime and spitting refuse and looked at the screenwriter with fury.

"What kind of fucking sadist would write a chase scene in a dirty goddamn swamp!" he squalled.

Felton took another refreshing sip of his drink. "Don't you remember, this was one of your swell ideas," he said.

Mitchum glared at him. But come to think of it, he remembered the swamp had come from him. "I shut my mouth," he said later, "and prepared to duck under the murky waters again and see what new garbage or ravenous animal I would meet."

The picture finished shooting with a week of interiors done at the Churabusco Studios in Mexico City. On the night before they were all to fly back to Los Angeles, Felton and Mitchum got into Bob's chauffeured car and were on their way to a restaurant in the *zona rosa* when a dark sedan sped in front of them and four large Mexicans jumped out, flashing police badges. They rousted the driver and had him open the trunk, then extracted a heavy brown paper bag that turned out to be filled with marijuana.

The driver said it wasn't his. Bob said it wasn't his. Mitchum told Felton, "This is a setup."

"Oh shit," Felton said.

Earl spoke a little Spanish and asked the Mexicans to take them back to their hotel where it could perhaps all be straightened out. The cops thought taking them to the prison was a better idea. Felton pleaded. The cops took the evidence, everyone got back into their vehicles, and they drove to the hotel, took Mitchum up to his room, and kept him there under guard.

An assortment of people—Mexicans from the studio and the hotel, members of the crew—were huddled in the lobby. A little later a squadron of burly police officials arrived and went up in the elevator. They conferred with Mitchum. Mitchum talked to John Burch, the film's production manager, in charge of the per diems and other money matters. Ten thousand dollars was packed into a small suitcase and the police squadron went away.

Fleischer wrote, "Nobody was late for the plane the next morning."

Bandido! is a signature Robert Mitchum movie—for all its spectacle, pulp drama, and exotica, one of his most personal works. This was Mitchum as he saw himself, the adventurer's adventurer, bringing his gaudiest daydreams to life and allowing audiences, if they so desired, to share in the fun. Felton had cut Mitchum's part to order. The American gunrunner Wilson is a fearless, hard-drinking, wife-stealing contrarian and outsider, crossing the border into war-torn Mexico as everyone else is lined up to escape the other way; an opportunistic idealist, not above making a peso off of both sides of the revolution but ultimately a sentimental fighter for the little guy, taking a stand with the cop-hating peasants. The early scenes in particular are prime Mitchum in all his insouciant glory, hailing a taxi to the battlefield, standing on his hotel balcony in his wrinkled white suit and wide-brimmed hat, a glass of whisky in one hand and a grenade in the other, happily blowing up government troops in the street below.

The direction of the much underrated Richard Fleischer (with the great aid of Ernest Laszlo's cinematography) perfectly complemented Mitchum's swaggering style. Fleischer's muscular mise-en-scène, here seen at its best in raucous action scenes, with a fluid free-roaming camera that turned whole whitewashed towns into the film's exploding sets, was one of the great justifications for the cinemascope lens and the gigantic new screens of the day. The version seen for decades on television, with faded color and cramped pan-and-scan compositions, is a travesty of the exhilarating original and its extraordinarily vivid wide-screen images.

Mitchum and Earl Felton vowed to do another project together someday, but the writer was just as notorious a procrastinator as the actor, and their assorted plans never came to anything. Earl's physical problems got worse through the years. His handicap was very demeaning to him and very painful, but he hated to be pitied. He began to withdraw from life. Reva Frederick remembered how Mitchum would go over to see him when he was under the weather, stopping at his favorite restaurants to get him soup and sandwiches. Felton would come to the Mitchum house from time to time and Robert would go into the kitchen himself and fix something special that Earl liked. But no one had all the time it took to fight the man's growing despair. One Sunday in 1972, bored and lonely, the caustic and clever Earl Felton took a gun and blew his brains out.

The movies had entered an international phase in the mid-'50s. Where in the past all roads led to Hollywood, now many of the graduates of the old studio system were wandering the world, making pictures everywhere but on those hermetically sealed LA soundstages. The blacklist victims had been among the first to go, turning up in the European film centers of London and Paris and Rome. Then came the footloose and independent spirits like Orson Welles and John Huston, now more likely to be shooting in Morocco or the Chad than in Culver City. Then off went a contingent of the over-the-hill and the out of work, faded names whose Hollywood résumés were still able to command respect at Cinecittà and Hammer. Even Gary Cooper had arranged to work outside the States for a year, in Mexico and the South Seas, taking advantage of an expatriate's tax loophole. The American studios themselves endorsed this rising exodus, sending productions to all points from Fiji to Capetown, taking advantage of their blocked funds in foreign countries, taking advantage of cheap labor costs overseas, and hoping to lure TV addicts with ever more spectacularly scenic and exotic visuals.

For Robert Mitchum, imbued with an impulsive restlessness and wanderlust and an unquenchable thirst for adventure, it was a fine time to be a movie star. Now, and for much of the twenty years to come, he would spend a great part of his life wandering in strange and distant lands, a tramp again, though a very well paid and glamorous one to be sure.

His next job was to take him to London and to the islands of the Caribbean. *Fire Down Below* (the double-entendre title sounded like one by Howard Hughes) was a British-based production but financed by Columbia Pictures in Hollywood and put together by American expatriates. The London-based producers were Irving Allen and Albert Broccoli; the director, Robert Parrish; and the screenplay by Paris's favorite Brooklynite, novelist Irwin Shaw. It was the tale of two American roustabouts in tropic waters, owners of a small tramp cargo boat, who get mixed up with an alluring woman on the run. The two partners have an inevitable falling out over the female, reuniting briefly when one must save the life of the other after a disaster aboard an old freighter; but the bad blood remains, and they go their separate ways.

It was a film with three strong lead characters. Mitchum was cast as the more nihilistic partner who steals the girl, the "nice" roustabout role to be played by Jack Lemmon. The producers tried to get Ava Gardner for the part of the bruised-by-life adventuress but without success. Irwin Shaw suggested Rita Hayworth to his friend Bob Parrish. The director tracked her down at the George V in Paris. She was miserable, in the midst of half-a-dozen personal crises—failed marriages, deadbeat ex-husbands all over the globe, her youthful beauty gone, her endless alliance with Columbia and the despised Harry Cohn coming to a bumpy end. It took some doing to get her to connect, but Parrish talked up the Shaw script and made three months in the Caribbean sound like a wonderful chance to escape from the world and all her problems.

Late in May Mitchum took a flight from New York to Trinidad. The arrival had been heavily publicized and the tiny airport was packed with local press, movie fans, and gawkers. As he walked across the tarmac in 90-degree heat and withering humidity, reporters peppered him with what seemed increasingly ridiculous and trivial questions, and his responses were mostly abrasive. When someone asked what he was carrying with him, Mitchum cracked that he had "two kilos of marijuana" in his bag, and "a quart of Jewish blood, taken by transfusion, in my veins . . . so I can stay even with those guys."—meaning agents and producers, one of those "Jew jokes" and ethnic references that would come out of Mitchum's mouth not infrequently through the years. Just Bob being outrageous, friends would say in explanation.

In the limousine riding into town, the local chauffeur told him about Trinidad. "You will love dis island, sir. *Not one virgin older den t'irteen!*"

As any travel agent could have told them, though apparently the producers of *Fire Down Below* did not ask, May, June, and July were off-season months in the Caribbean, when there was always a strong possibility of overcast skies and tropical rains. Sure enough, after a couple of weeks' work, the production was shut down by overcast skies and tropical rains. It rained and rained, while cast and crew sat on hotel verandas and watched it come down. It looked like a scene out of Rita Hayworth's last picture, *Miss Sadie Thompson,* the better part of which took place at an island hotel in a downpour. Some wag suggested they do a remake.

While they waited for better weather, the visitors occupied themselves as they might. Jack Lemmon, his first marriage in the process of dissolving, was restless and lonely. Mitchum thought Jack needed calming and claimed to have introduced him to a beautiful, charming island woman Mitchum had recently met. Lemmon took her out and liked her very much. The actors were invited to a dinner at the governor's mansion, the fancy dress event of the summer, and Lemmon intended to bring the lovely islander. Mitchum decided it was time to tell him that the girl was a very widely known prostitute.

"She screwed the entire U.S. Navy!" said Mitchum.

"That's their problem," said Lemmon. "She's my girl, now."

Mitchum himself, after his wife had come for a visit and departed, was making a close study of the local flora and fauna. Like that other intrepid seeker of new and unusual thrills, William Burroughs, who about this same period was combing the Amazon in pursuit of the legendary telepathic drug *yage,* Mitchum spent some of his free time chasing down a rumored backcountry substance reputed to be the one true aphrodisiac. The love potion was derived from the bark of a certain rare tree, and Mitch and an English pal from the crew eventually obtained a sackful of the stuff from some ancient herbalist. They followed his directions, cooking the bark in a pot until a small bit of sap was obtained. Then both of them chickened out—what if the stuff was toxic and we keeled over dead? they asked each other nervously. Or what if it made your dick hard and it never went down again? Deciding like any good scientists that they should experiment first on guinea pigs, Mitchum solicited a pair of paid volunteers for the job. "Two young native kids," according to Jack Lemmon, "a boy and a girl who looked about fifteen years old."

Mitchum and his partner sat on the couch in his hotel room and waited for results after the experimental couple ingested the sap, but the boy and girl turned out to be only as horny as any ordinary pair of fifteen-year-olds. Disappointed, Mitchum tossed the rest of the bark off the balcony. Twenty bucks down the drain!

Ears always attuned to appreciate all styles of music, Mitchum was thrilled by the indigenous sounds of calypso and the other sinuous Afro-Carib rhythms by artists like the Mighty Sparrow that he heard in the bars and dance clubs of Port-of-Spain and on the records screeching tinnily from the windows of every island home. He bought drinks for local music legends and jotted down the lyrics of their songs, some of them quite amusingly risqué. Ever the quick study and perfect mimic, he was soon hopping up on stage and belting out the raunchiest versions of "Mama, Looka Boo Boo" and "Matilda" with perfect Trinidadian inflection. He shipped home every local record he could find to add to his already massive collection.

The company moved on to the island of Tobago, known as "Robinson Crusoe's island," for it was thought to have been the setting of Defoe's novel. A small freighter was chartered and everyone lived on board for a couple of weeks, the only link with the outside world being a twice daily speedboat run from the tiny town of Scarborough. With nothing else to do, the players might have been expected to concentrate on the work. But a malaise set in—they became spiritually becalmed. Producer Cubby Broccoli came back to the ship after being away overnight and found no activity whatsoever. Parrish took him over to where Mitchum was lying on the deck, passed out and unwakable. The high point of each day was producer Broccoli's lunchtime arrival with the mail. The isolated, bored group then spent an hour or two sprawled about the vessel reading their forwarded letters, advertisements, and out-of-date copies of Variety and the Times of London. Rita Hayworth's mail, rerouted from Europe, New York, and Los Angeles, arrived all at once in a huge canvas sack and sat untouched. One day Lemmon and Parrish came upon Hayworth sitting by the railing, tearing up the unread mail piece by piece and tossing it into the sea.

"Rita, what the hell are you doing?" they screamed. "Aren't you going to open any of it? There may be checks inside!"

Hayworth shrugged, smiling ruefully. "There's bound to be more trouble than money."

One day Broccoli arrived with a visitor. It was one of Harry Cohn's minions, come to keep an eye on Columbia's investment. Mitchum immediately began calling him "Spy," as in, "Hello, Spy," "Out of my way, Spy." The man was well known to Hayworth from her years at the studio, and she treated him like the plague and fell into an even deeper despondency.

She was another Marilyn, Mitchum thought, another Love Goddess who could never find happiness—and not much love either. "He described her as a rather lost little girl," said Kathie Parrish, the wife of the director. "She wasn't the sharpest knife in the drawer, and everyone took her for something. But Mitch and Jack and my husband loved her, and they were very sweet with her.

"She got married again not long after that and she wanted us all, Mitchum and Lemmon and Bob, to come to meet the man, Jim Hill; and it was an awful evening, terribly stiff. Jim had these terribly square parents from Colorado or someplace. They were very religious and they were nondrinkers. And Mitchum, the moment anything got stuffy, he got dirty. And when he heard that Jim's mother frowned on drinking, he said to her, 'What's the matter, does it make you fart?' Followed by dead silence. Oh, it was just an awful evening."

*

Irwin Shaw's original screenplay had been constructed with a framing device. The rusting old freighter is about to blow up, and a man—the Jack Lemmon character—is trapped in the engine room. As the trapped man waits to be rescued, his story is told in flashback. For the finale, the story returns to the burning boat and the

Mitchum character's last-minute rescue of his former pal. The producers cut this structure to make the narrative linear and supposedly did a number of other things of which director Parrish disapproved. Whether or not there was a better film hiding behind the producer's reedit, what went into release was not much—pretty to watch but empty and disconnected at the center. It was like a grim, sordid version of a "Road picture," with Mitchum and Lemmon's Hope and Crosby battling for the hand of Rita Hayworth's melancholy, frowzy Dottie Lamour.

Mitchum's agent had signed him to a two-picture deal with 20th Century-Fox. Although he believed his days of being forced to do this or that movie were over, the agreement with Fox turned out to have a couple of overlooked knots in it that effectively removed his power of veto. In London to shoot the interiors for *Fire Down Below,* he learned that he was about to start filming *Heaven Knows, Mr. Allison,* with John Huston directing. Mitchum said the first thing he knew about it was when Huston's cinematographer, Oswald Morris, came by to measure him for a marine's uniform. The assignment was to turn out so splendidly and, on a personal level, so satisfyingly, that Mitchum would later claim that all he needed to know about the picture was that John Huston and Deborah Kerr were involved and he was there. But in fact the actor had a sizable if short-lived snit when he learned that Huston had first tried hard to get Marlon Brando for the role and that *Heaven*'s three-month shoot, beginning a few weeks hence, would be done entirely in . . . Tobago. Nearly four months he had been down there, the sand was still coming out of his ears, and now he was getting on an airplane and going right back.

Huston thought the novel—about a U.S. Marine and a nun cast away on a Pacific island during World War II—too salacious, with the characters entertaining illicit thoughts on every page (which may have been just what led producer Eugene Frenke to buy the screen rights in the first place). So Huston got together with veteran screenwriter John Lee Mahin (*Red Dust, Treasure Island*) in Ensenada, Mexico (the director was an American tax exile) and knocked out what he considered a palatable adaptation of the material. Producer Frenke objected to Huston's and Mahin's more celibate script and less lascivious nun—*"She's gotta have an itchy cunt!"* he screamed at them—but headman Buddy Adler gave their version the nod. With the adventurous, exotic setting and only the two mismatched characters on screen for nearly the entire picture, *Heaven Knows, Mr. Allison* was clearly seen as a variation on Huston's greatest box office hit, *The African Queen,* and Fox was hoping lightning would strike twice.

An advance team arrived on Tobago in August, renting all the rooms in four of the eight existing hotels, commandeering nearly every taxi and truck, and building a faux village and church. Returning to the island in September, Robert Mitchum was a little slow getting back up to speed. The first morning the English crew (*Heaven,* like *Fire Down Below,* was a "British quota" picture, utilizing Fox's blocked pounds sterling) were ready to shoot the opening moments of the film, showing Mitchum floating in to shore on a raft. But Bob was working on a bottle of vodka in his tent and refused to be removed from it. An assistant director was sent to reason with him and came back many minutes later, reeling drunk. At last Huston had to humble himself and make a personal appeal, after which Mitchum—showing no outward sign of having consumed a bottle of hooch by 9 A.M.—accompanied the director down to the beach. Huston could be a son of a bitch, with a mean streak nearly the size of his considerable charm, and he never let a slight go unanswered. Mitchum got on the raft and lay there, bobbing up and down in the water under the fierce tropical sun, waiting to shoot the scene. Sending out one excuse after another, Huston managed to keep Mitchum bobbing and broiling for nearly two hours.

It could have been the start of a very unpleasant three months—Mitchum wasn't the sort to let a goddamn director get the better of him for long. But as in one of those old Eddie Lowe, Victor McLaglen battling buddy movies, Mitchum and Huston sized each other up nose to nose, decided they were evenly matched, and agreed to be friends.

Huston was the artist as buccaneer, sailing through life in search of adventure and booty, stopping now and then along the way to make some of the world's greatest motion pictures. "Sure," said one friend and admirer. "He couldn't help it! John was a guy who had an appetite for the best of everything. Of course he would make the best movies, too!" Huston, like Mitchum, suffered from wanderlust and a restless nature. Huston, like Mitchum, could drink mere mortals under the table, or certainly tried to at every opportunity. And as an inveterate tale teller, Huston's accounts of his swashbuckling early years—including a stint in the Mexican cavalry—were, Bob had to admit, even more colorful and preposterous than his own. The director's range of experience and understanding of life's darkest secrets impressed Mitchum and gave him confidence in the work they were to do. Whatever the situation, Mitchum said, "you knew John had been there."

Mitchum found that as a director Huston had a distinct sense of rhythm he could impose on a scene and a painter's eye for detail, but he allowed for the randomness of real life to enter the frame as well, keeping the scenes fresh, unstudied. When dealing with actors, Huston believed that once the proper person had assumed a given role, that performer brought with him the nuance and personality the role was meant to have. He therefore said very little to the actors before shooting a scene, although, unlike the other tough guy directors Mitchum had worked with, Huston had the intellectual capacity and education to verbalize whatever subtleties and values he sought should the need arise. Mitchum claimed that the most direction Huston ever gave him was to say, at the end of one take, "I think, kid . . . *even more.*" As he did so often, Mitchum used his observational skills and talent for mimickry and accents to bring the simple U.S. Marine character to idiosyncratic life. "Robert based his Mr. Allison character entirely on Tim Wallace," said Reva Frederick. "He decided that was the perfect model for that part, with the Brooklyn accent and everything, and the whole performance was a perfect imitation of Tim."

Huston would sing his star's praises forever after: "A delight to work with, and he gave a beautiful performance. He is one of the finest actors I've ever had anything to do with. His air of casualness, or rather, his lack of pomposity is put down as a lack of seriousness, but when I say he's a fine actor, I mean an actor of the caliber of Olivier, Burton, and Brando. In other words, the very best in the field." If Mitchum walked through many pictures with his eyes half open, said Huston, it was because "that's all that's called for, but he is in fact capable of playing King Lear."

After making a poor show of his first scene, Mitchum quickly set about regaining Huston's and the crew's confidence by giving his all to the next day's action, which called for him to crawl across the razorlike coral reef and through the underbrush beyond the shoreline. By the time he'd finished crawling and the director called, "Cut," he had scraped his flesh open in a dozen places. Huston and assistants ran down to look at the streams of blood.

"Jesus Christ, Bob!" said Huston.

Mitchum shrugged. "You work, you suffer."

He didn't know the half of it. There were still palm trees to be scaled, gullies and swamps to fall into, giant tortoises to ride. The three-hundred-pound turtle towed him for what seemed like miles. He was supposed to be catching the creature for food but, said Mitchum, "it was a wonder the damn thing didn't eat me. As it was, he almost dashed me against the coral reef." He caught his foot on a tree root and nearly twisted it in a full circle. "The bastard Huston's going to kill me," he moaned en route to a doctor. And then there were the mosquitoes that infected Mitchum and several others in the company with dengue, a painful, infectious tropical disease producing high temperature, body rash, and swelling of the joints.

The comelier half of the virtually two-person cast had no easier a time of it. It was like they said about Ginger Rogers—she did everything Fred Astaire did, and backward. For the scene in which the nun runs away and passes out in a mangrove swamp, Kerr had to spend days half submerged in horrible slime and wads of sticky alligator shit. "Deborah had to lie down in this mess," said Huston, "and she did it without a word of complaint. It was only years later that I discovered . . . she had dreams of this swamp for weeks afterward."

Kerr, too, would get a dose of dengue and spent several days in the local hospital. But her most unrelieved agony was undoubtedly her wardrobe, the heavy nun's habit that had to be worn from dawn to dusk in the scorching tropical temperatures. "Talk about mad dogs and Englishmen," she gasped, scratching and sweating in the itchy costume. Mitchum claimed that two members of the crew were employed entirely for the purpose of holding Deborah's skirts up between takes and "cooling her ass with a fan."

Kerr and Mitchum were a magical team. The actress likened their work together to a perfect doubles pair at tennis. Getting to know him in those first days on Tobago, as they sat on the "soft pink sand," Kerr recalled finding herself "listening to an extremely sensitive, a poetic, extraordinarily interesting man . . . a perceptive, amusing person with a great gift for telling a story, and possessed of a completely unexpected vast fund of knowledge . . . Bob was at all times patient, concerned, and completely professional, always in good humor, and always ready to make a joke when things became trying." Laura Nightingale, a wardrobe girl on the film, described Mitchum's great sensitivity toward his costar to journalist Lloyd Shearer: Sensing that her feet were hurting from the sharp rocks she'd been standing on, "He just kneeled down, unlaced her white sneakers, removed them and massaged her feet. It was lovely and compassionate the way he did it. . . . Then he put her sneakers back on and said kind of brusquely to hide his tenderness, 'Gotta keep you alive for the next scene.' Then he walked away. Deborah was so touched she cried."

Deborah became Bob's great platonic love. He would speak of her ever after as his all-time favorite actress and the "only leading lady I didn't go to bed with"—an exaggeration in any case, but meant somehow as a compliment. When they met he had been expecting a prim Englishwoman like the rather frosty ladies she often played on screen, but Kerr turned out to be one of the boys. She was a rare delight, warm, wise, earthy. One time she was rowing a raft in open water during the tortoise-chasing scene, Huston constantly shouting, "Faster! Row faster!" The wooden oars split in half in her hands, and Kerr, in her damp nun's habit, screamed in fury,

"Is that *fucking* fast enough?" Mitchum, floating nearby, swallowed a gallon of saltwater laughing.

Kerr and Mitchum collaborated on the most amusing moments of the whole shoot during a visit by an inspector from the Catholic Legion of Decency, the self-appointed censorship board. Invited by Fox to verify that the film's depiction of Miss Kerr's nun character was entirely respectable, the Legion sent a suitably severe man of the cloth down to Tobago to observe the filming. He soon began making complaints and demanding changes, perceiving something smutty in the most innocent line and gesture. One day he arrived on the set as Huston was preparing a scene between Mitchum and Kerr. Huston greeted the priest and then called for "Action." Director and crew were deadpan as Bob and Deborah spoke their lines, then moved closer together, Mitchum sliding his hand under nun Kerr's breasts while she cupped his buttocks and they began to kiss with open-mouthed abandon. The Legion of Decency man's eyes widened; he grasped at his heart and screamed, "What is going on there?!"

"No talking, Father," said Huston. "Dammit, now you've gone and ruined a perfectly good take."

The only other speaking parts in the film belonged to the Japanese soldiers, heard conversing among themselves in one scene. Waiting till the last minute to find Japanese-speaking bit players, the casting scout wound up on a frantic island-hopping search, finally securing the services of eight émigrés living in a Japanese farm colony in Brazil. To play the nonspeaking Japanese forces, the film drafted fifty Chinese from the restaurants and and hand laundries of Trinidad. The film's American invaders were a hundred actual marines.

For the filming of the bombing raid, everyone had come down to the beach to watch the fireworks. There were supposed to be a couple of dozen explosions scattered across the sand over the span of a couple of minutes. But the powder man's setup short-circuited and the explosions went off prematurely and all at once, nearly blowing the beach off the island. There were remarkably few injuries considering the destruction, but one special-effects man was temporarily blinded.

You might be called on to take your lumps for Huston even when the cameras weren't turning. The director had hired a local driver and baby-sitter for his visiting kids, a young islander named Irwin. He was a handsome, muscular giant and an amateur boxer, and the more Huston saw of him, the more he began to envision him as the next heavyweight champion, with Huston himself the lad's manager and chief beneficiary. He goaded a reluctant Mitchum into going a few rounds with the new champ, and a little boxing ring was rigged up. Mitchum stepped in and looked up and up at his towering opponent. The bell sounded and, said Mitchum, "I just stuck my left hand out and he fell down."

A more noteworthy battle took place at the veranda bar of the Blue Haven Hotel where Bob and Dorothy were having some refreshments one evening. Three American marines from the ersatz invading force arrived with, it seemed, the express purpose of getting into a brawl with the mighty Mitchum. Whether they had originally intended for the whole trio to attack one actor at the same time or whether this became an emergency tactic once Mitchum's interest was engaged is not known. A first soldier reportedly tapped Mitchum on the shoulder and told him he could knock him off his feet with one punch, and what did he think of that? Mitchum told him to take a shot, which the boy did. Then, deciding to avail himself of another try without first asking permission, the marine found himself on the floor, seeing stars of a different variety. The other patrons at the bar watched in wonderment as the American movie actor began punching the daylights out of his countrymen, one tumbling down the staircase, another slugged in the head and dropping to the floor, out cold, and a third man dragged over to the railing of the veranda from which Mitchum had planned to toss him twenty feet to the wading pool below when he felt blows rain down on his head and neck from a high-heeled shoe.

"Hey . . . you're supposed to be on my side!" he said.

"You were starting to enjoy it," Dorothy told him.

The film was a beauty. It was a movie that was stripped to the bare essentials, but not a thing was lacking. It was funny, tender, exciting, visually enchanting, the empty blue sky and sea a soothing treat for the eye; Kerr was superb, and Mitchum, playing dumb as the good-hearted marine whose only knowledge of life is "the Corps," gave a deceptively simple performance that was in fact a fully created characterization of inestimable grace and charm.

Huston and Mitchum: They had grown to be close friends during the filming, or as close as two larger-than-life rogues who both preferred the role of top dog in the pound could ever hope to be. There were long bull sessions together, in the evenings and late at night or in the long days when this or that crucial member of the company was laid up in bed moaning with fever. They drank, played poker, and, of course, traded stories, usually with a retinue of idolators lounging around them for an audience. They talked about making movies and adventures in foreign lands. Mitchum was delighted to learn a salient fact about one of his small handful of favorite films, *The Treasure of the Sierra Madre,* shot in Mexico—John told him they were all smoking grass down there, high as clouds for most of the picture. Huston spoke of films he planned to do someday. There was a sense, not quite spoken but both of them felt it, that they could go on together, a creative partnership making great movies one after the other, the way Huston had done with Bogart in years past. They spoke of Huston's dream project, a grand-scale film of Kipling's adventure story, "The Man Who Would Be King." He had once thought of it for Bogart and Gable, but Bogie was old now and sick.

"We could have some real fun making that one, Bob. We'd shoot it all in Bhutan, in the Himalayas."

"How do you figure we could do that, John? They don't permit foreigners, and there's no road in or out."

Huston's eyes went wide, like a little boy's on Christmas morning.

"Parachute, kid . . . parachute."

CHAPTER ELEVEN

Gorilla Pictures

"The three toughest guys in the movie business," said Budd Boetticher, the great American film director, bullfighter, horseman, "were Jack Palance, Bob Ryan, and Mitchum. And Mitchum was the toughest. And very soft and tender, like a lot of really tough guys. We met when I first got started directing and he was just starting out, and we were dear friends. We never got to see enough of each other, but the times we were together we had a lot of fun. Once when I was working at Universal he came and took me over to meet what he said was 'the dumbest girl in the world.' And it was Marilyn Monroe. And we went over when she was making a picture called *Don't Bother to Knock* and he said, 'This girl is really off the wall.' And of course she wasn't really. She could be very smart about some things. But Bob said what he thought, and he was funny as hell. We would always talk about doing a picture together. I wrote *Two Mules for Sister Sara* for Bob. It was going to be Bob and Silvia Pinal, and it would have been a helluva picture. They took it and messed it up, and with my friend Clint in it. But me and Bob were always hoping to work together, right up to the end.

"Back in the 'fifties, I got an invitation for the inauguration of the new governor in [a state in northern] Mexico. I was to go down to lead the parade before the afternoon bullfight on Sunday with Carlos Aruzza, taking down one of my fancy Spanish horses. Then there would be the inauguration and a big dinner party. I was told I could bring a guest and so I took Bob and Dorothy, who I loved dearly. The bullfight went off well, the opening parade was great, and we went to the dinner party. Now along the way Bob was inter-

ested to hear about the outgoing governor because he had the reputation for being the worst politician in the history of Mexico—and
boy, if you know Mexico, that's really being crooked. He was smuggling hookers and dope and gold and everything else. But he had
had his six years and he was out. Well, after the bullfight we're all at
the big dinner, and Bob and Dorothy are seated right next to the ex-
governor. And everybody was drinking and having a good time. But
I guess Bob never knew who he was sitting next to because all of a
sudden I hear Bob's voice and he's saying to ex-Governor———
'Well, it sounds like they got you into office just in time. I understand that that son of a bitch who was here the last six years was the
biggest damn crook in the country, he had a whore racket, and he's
running a dope ring.' And the ex-governor is looking at him as he's
saying this and he's not happy with it; it's in front of everybody, all
these distinguished guests. And I tried to get Bob's eye and I
couldn't and finally I just muttered to him, 'Bob, that's the former
governor you're talking to.' And Bob just blinked, didn't miss a beat,
and he said, 'And you know, Governor . . . , my pappy always told
me, when you grow up, son, whatever you do you try to be the
biggest and best in the whole damn world, whatever it is. And I
always thought that *I* was the biggest and best no good son of a bitch
in the whole damn world, but . . . here I am *talking to him. And it's a
real honor.*' And the man didn't know how to take it, but he decided
it was all in fun and he started laughing; and he says, 'This guy's got
balls!' Which of course he did."

"Bob was by nature a very lonely person," said his sister Julie. "He
had a sensitivity that was difficult for him to reveal to outsiders. He
never let many people see that side of him." Mitchum kept no child-
hoood pals, no bosom buddies. "I don't think he ever really wanted
or needed anyone like that," said Reva Frederick, "someone you
talked to every week or month, someone you shared your problems
with. There were people he was delighted to run into, to take a call
from and catch up on the news with, like Victor Buono and Sinatra
and people like that, they got along great, but then he went on his
way. Perhaps it would have been a problem for him, opening him-

self up, letting someone understand you, know your problems, your feelings, the way you would do with a real friend. Robert, I think, had a great deal of sensitivity and a lot of fears that he would not want to share with anyone. But I have no idea. I really have no idea if that's what it was. Tim Wallace was the closest person that Robert ever had as a real friend. But Tim was older than Robert, and Robert was so superior to Tim in so many ways, intelligence, talent, money, he was over Tim, it was in no way a friendship of equals. Tim was just there, company. If Robert wanted to drive up to Montana he could always grab Tim and Tim would say, 'Sure!' He was always delighted to go anywhere, do anything. He would tell jokes, do whatever you needed, including get out in the middle of a freeway and change a tire. He was an ideal companion who never asked anything of you and always did what you wanted. That was Robert's one friend. The rest were guys he could talk to at lunch or have a few drinks with. That was all he wanted. He didn't need anyone getting closer to him than that."

A loner, but a gregarious one, Mitchum had people he called pals, male and female, all over the world and in all variety of high and low places. "He was extremely adaptable," said Reva. "You could toss him down anywhere and he could find someone to talk to. And I mean anyone. He could have a conversation with people from every conceivable walk of life." Through the years he had passing acquaintanceship or intermittent friendships with generals, makeup men, politicians, ex-convicts, surgeons, stunt guys, Nobel Prize–winning scientists, salesmen, cowboys, barflies, stewardesses, government leaders, strippers, even a few policemen (he told people that the cops always had the best dope). He liked the company and conversation of writers and had proudly bent an elbow with John Steinbeck and with A. B. "Bud" Guthrie, author of *The Big Sky*. For many years he kept in touch with novelist James Atlee Phillips, the man who wrote *Thunder Road,* and he had a long-standing acquaintance with Barnaby Conrad, the author of *Matador* and the owner of a hip watering hole by the same name. Conrad first met Mitchum at his San Francisco nightspot, the actor taking up the Matador's weighty guest book and scribbling, "*Compadre . . . When all the broken crock-*

*ery of desperate communion is swept from under our understanding
heels we may find on that clear expanse of floor the true and irrevoca-
ble target of infinite thrust."* Forty years later Conrad was still trying
to figure out what it meant.

In Los Angeles, his actor and performer pals tended to be from
the fringes of the showbiz hierarchy, colorful or eccentric characters or good storytellers or good listeners. There was Richard
"Lord" Buckley, the avant-hip nightclub comic and monologist—
as in "The Nazz," his swinging history of Jesus Christ—with whom
Mitchum shared a love of esoteric language and black dialects (it
was because they both had part American Indian ancestry, they
decided, and thus were both "honorary niggers"). There was actor
Billy Murphy, who'd been in *G.I. Joe* and *The Sands of Iwo Jima,* a
strange cat who dressed all in black like a Western bad guy and had
a favorite saying ("You bet your life, mister—and you may *have
to*") and a personality that struck fear in the hearts of directors and
casting agents. There was Morty Guterman, an agent with the
Feldman Company and Robert's favorite companion for deep-sea
fishing trips to Baja, and Peter Simon, a paraplegic who had worked
with Marlon Brando on *The Men* and whom Robert became friendly with through Dorothy's work with Los Angeles charities. There
was actor Robert "the Wing Commander" Rothwell and movie
extra/construction worker George Fargo, aka "Gray Cloud"
because of the cloud of smoke that seemed always to be swirling
around him. (Mitchum's world was at times like one of those
Howard Hawks movies where everybody had a nickname. There
was "the Hog" and "Seed Sacker," and the man himself was known
to the gang as "the Goose," as in the one that laid golden eggs and
from his peculiar chest-out-thrust walk.) "The way Sinatra had his
Rat Pack, Bob had a lot of guys he could pull together when he
wanted to go off somewhere," said actor Roy Jenson. "He'd say,
'We're going to New Orleans,' or down to Mexico. And he'd go off
for days or weeks, someplace like Mazatlan, he loved it there, taking
four buddies with him, to drink with him. And there had to be four
guys because it was like duty, nobody could keep up with him the
whole time."

Sheldon Reynolds remembered a Mitchum gathering in the late '50s. It began, for him, one night in Paris: "It was about three o'clock in the morning, I was not entirely awake, and the phone rang. It was Mitchum. I said, 'Hi.' He said, 'Let's get together.' I said, 'Wonderful. Why don't you come to Paris?' He said, 'Well, that's a long way. Why don't you come to California?' I said, 'Well . . . let's compromise, we'll meet in New York.' And he said, 'OK,' and hung up the phone. I went back to sleep and in the morning I said to the woman I was going with, 'Was I dreaming or did I get a call last night from Robert Mitchum?' She said, 'Yes, I think you did.' So I called his number in California and I spoke to Dorothy. I said, 'Could I talk to Bob? He called me last night but I'm not sure what we said.' And she said, 'I don't know either, but he got in the car and said he was driving to New York.' I said, 'Well, do you expect that you'll hear from him soon?' And she said, 'I think I will hear from him. He left without his wallet and he has no money.'

"Well, that was typical is all I can say. And we did meet in New York some days later. He had driven across country by himself. He would meet people and he could sleep anywhere and just took things as they came. I remember him telling me about driving into a gasoline station somewhere in the South. The man filled up the tank, and as Mitchum was paying, the man looked at him and said, 'Ain't you that actor fella?' And Mitchum said, 'Yeah.' And the man said, 'Well, how about that.' And he said, 'Have you had dinner?' And Mitchum said, 'No.' And the gas station man said, 'You want to come home; we'll give you something to eat.' And off he went, taken care of for that night. I asked him how was the food and he said, 'I think it was squirrel stew. Tasted like squirrel. Seasoned with buckshot.'

"In New York I stayed in the Hampshire House and he stayed in the Sherry Netherland, as I recall. And we picked up Trevor Howard, he joined the group. Trevor just showed up, I don't know from where. There was a lot of drinking. And Trevor said we must go to this great little jazz bar, very tiny place he had discovered. Trevor insisted nobody went there, it was an out-of-the-way place. So we got into a taxi and the little place was just above Broadway and

Forty-second Street. It was packed. The musicians were playing behind the bar, and they stepped down to come meet Mitchum. Everyone recognized him, and the place just kept getting more and more crowded. And things got out of hand, and the police came and they took us away in a police car. And Trevor, with this crowd around and getting pushed into the police car, said, 'I don't understand it; this place has gone all commercial!'

"And we had some days of this and then the two wives, Dorothy and Helen, Trevor's wife, arrived in town. And everyone was to meet at 21. It had been a very long night, the night before. And everyone met up at 21, but Trevor didn't show up. He hadn't come back to his hotel and Helen became worried. 'Where is he? Has something happened to him?' she said. 'Don't either of you know where Trevor is?' And we knew where we had last seen him, with some girl, but we didn't tell her that. So Mitchum and I went off to try and find Trevor where we'd last seen him. But all we could remember from the night before was that it was a building on Fifth Avenue, nothing more, and Fifth ran for a hundred blocks. We didn't know what to do. Then Bob remembered it was a building with a large doormat out front. So we drove along Fifth Avenue and at every building where there was a doormat, we stopped. And Mitchum would call to the doorman and say, 'Was I here last night?' And finally one doorman said yes, and Mitchum said, 'And where did I go when I was here?' And we went upstairs to somebody's apartment, some girl, and Trevor was up there sleeping and we got him back to his wife.

"At the end of the week, everyone dispersed. But Mitchum wanted to stay on the road. And I wanted to see my sister, who lived in Washington, so we drove there in his car. And we stayed with my sister and her husband. I offered him the spare bed, but he said he would sleep on the floor. He really could adapt to any circumstances. I don't recollect he had any plans after that. He had the ability to, as we say, *drift*. One day in Washington we said good-bye, and he got back into the car and drove off. I have no idea where he was headed and, I think, neither did he."

Not long after he returned from the Caribbean, Mitchum ran into Johnny Mercer in Beverly Hills and told him about all the great music he had heard in Trinidad and Tobago and perhaps even sang him a tune or two. Mercer sent him over to Capitol Records in Hollywood. Capitol had been talking to Robert about an album for some time, but no one had ever come up with a game plan. The calypso thing appealed to everybody. Harry Belafonte had recently made a huge splash with his recordings of authentic and quasi-authentic Caribbean songs, including the chart-topping hit "Banana Boat (Day-O)," and sexy, so-called exotica records, from high-octave Andean warbling to Balinese bachelor pad instrumentals, were all the rage. Now Robert Mitchum was going to be calypso's great white hope. He went into the studio for a couple of weeks in March 1957 with a crew of cocktail jazz and rock 'n' roll pros and some backup singers and made like Lord Melody on a dozen jump-up tunes, including "Coconut Water," "Matilda" (with an innovative calypso-rock arrangement), "I Learn a Merengue, Baby," and "Mama, Looka Boo Boo." The resulting album, *Calypso—is like so . . .*, was an enticing romp, equal parts Belafonte, Martin Denny, and karaoke bar. It was the first time—until his series of accented film roles in the '60s and '70s—that Mitchum got to show off his talent for foreign accents, belting out the Carib ditties with scrupulously authentic intonations. As Caucasian calypso albums went, it was a masterpiece; and the cover photo—Mitch and a fistful of Jamaican rum in a Technicolor beach bar, complete with vaguely dusky maiden—was alone worth the selling price. But music lovers didn't buy many copies, and the man went back to his day job.

In the summer, Mitchum was in Hawaii to film exteriors for *The Enemy Below,* the first of two films he made with the former boy crooner turned producer-director, Dick Powell. A drama of World War II set entirely at sea, it detailed a battle of wits between the commander of a U.S. destroyer and his enemy counterpart aboard a German submarine. Mitchum's Captain Murrell was his first establishment hero since his last war movie, *One Minute to Zero;* and the part did not inspire much enthusiasm from the actor—it was what they called a "solid" performance. *The Enemy Below* was part of the late-'50s trend toward antiwar films, specifically the liberal humanist subset that included *The Young Lions* and *The Bridge on the River Kwai*—films that in the cool of peacetime attempted to put a human face on the old enemy. When Mitchum had started in war pictures, it was all about slaughtering "krauts" and "Japs." Now the movies wanted you to understand them. A graduate of live television dramas, Wendell Mayes, wrote the script from a story by Comdr. D. A. Rayner. Powell and Mayes had originally intended the film to have a tragic, haunting end as Mitchum is trying to save Curt Jurgens's U-boat captain. "The moment Mitchum gets hold of him and starts pulling him aboard," said Mayes, "the ship blows up, and at that point you pull back to watch this tremendous explosion, and you keep pulling back until there's nothing left for the audience to see but the great vast empty sea. . . . There's much more feeling if they should die, one finally trying to help the other after trying to kill him. But the studio said, 'No, you like both of them. You can't kill them. It'll disappoint the audience.' So we had the ending with them standing smoking a cigarette on the back end of the destroyer."

There were the usual injuries and near disasters. Mitchum took a fall twenty feet down one of the ship's open metal stairways and landed on the deck on his back. The doctor told him, "Your back's sort of . . . broken." He returned to work in a brace. On another day, shooting aboard the destroyer escort *Whitehurst* at sea off the coast of Oahu, Mitchum as the pretend captain signaled the firing of loaded depth charges. The charges misfired or the men at the ash can racks misheard the order, and instead of two charges, nearly a dozen were exploded, making the entire ship convulse, sending everyone on deck tumbling, short-circuiting the engine room, knocking out one engine, and causing a leak.

David Hedison: "*The Enemy Below* was my first film under contract to 20th Century-Fox in 1957. Robert Mitchum had always been one of my favorite actors; and when I first met him on the set, I can remember being a bit awkward, but he very quickly put me at ease. It was Doug McClure's first film as well, and we were both very proud and happy to be appearing with Mitchum in our very first film—I mean, how lucky can you get? During the course of filming I had a line where I had to bark out a command: 'Right full rudder!' I thought I had delivered the line quite well, but Mitchum kept insisting I had said *ruther* not *rudder*. I told him he was wrong, but he wouldn't let it go, even after seeing it on film. More than thirty years later I bumped into him and his lovely wife, Dorothy, at a restaurant. 'Well hello,' I beamed. 'How have you been?' 'Just fine, Al,' he said, 'but I'm telling you, you said *ruther!*' "

The second of the Powell productions was *The Hunters*, based on a superb, cold-blooded novel by James Salter, the story of a warrior breed of jet fighter pilots in the Korean conflict.

"While we used the title," said writer Wendell Mayes, "what I wrote was from start to finish an original screenplay. There wasn't anything else to do, because the novel could not be adapted. It was too internal. They do make mistakes in Hollywood in buying material."

Powell lured Mitchum with a partial script. "It seemed fine to me. I got to fly a fighter plane and spend a lot of time in the Officers' Club in Japan. 'And you can go to Japan early and scout it out for a couple of weeks,' he said. That sounded good, so I said yes. Then he sent me page thirty-one. And I found out my plane crashed and I spent the rest of the film carrying some fellow on my back. 'You ought to cast that part by the pound,' I said. 'What's Sinatra doing?' But of course they saddled me with some hulk who got heavier by the minute." And no trip to Japan. "We did the whole thing on the Fox ranch."

He had originally planned to do a different Korean war drama, *Battle Hymn*, the story of Col. Dean E. Hess, a minister who became a fighter pilot and killed numerous Asians. Universal offered Mitch the part until the righteous colonel threw a fit. "I cannot possibly allow a man who has been jailed for taking drugs to play me on the screen!" said Hess. Mitchum couldn't find the piece of paper that said he had been exonerated and so let it pass. Hess happily agreed to have himself portrayed instead by Rock

Hudson, whose skeletons, unlike Mitchum's, were still hermetically closeted.

"You got problems?" asked Robert Mitchum in a flavorful article he
penned for the *Hollywood Reporter*. "Well, climb on the pad and tell
old Dad. I don't have any. Or, I didn't have until producing a picture
messed me up. As the man said, 'It all started with a cloud in the sky
no bigger than a man's fist.' Home crouched on the couch one
night, it occurred to me that we might get a motion picture out of
moonshiners and government tax men trying to outwit each other
in the southeastern area of these United States.

"Sure, actors have problems, but I've found production problems come lower than a hungover snake. . . ."

In fact, Mitchum had been fiddling with the idea of a "moonshine adventure" for years, letting it simmer and take shape in his
mind. It was now to become the subject of his first personal production: *Thunder Road*. Although he had influenced the final form of
many of his films through the years, writing dialogue, pinch-hit
directing, contributing to them in myriad small and large ways—
and he'd been the coproducer and uncredited cowriter on *Bandido!*—
it had taken him four years since his escape from RKO to take this next
important step toward complete creative independence.

He met a smart, affable writer working for Batjac, John Wayne's
production company. James Atlee Phillips was a Texas newspaperman turned mystery novelist (*The Case of the Shivering Chorus Girls,
Suitable for Framing*) and a tyro scenarist, a footloose character with
a fertile imagination. He and Mitchum hit it off, and they began discussing the actor's idea for a movie about the southern moonshine
business. Mitchum had worked up a story line concerning an ex-soldier returned to his Smoky Mountain home, running illegal liquor
across the state, trying to outwit and outrace the authorities; and
another writer, Walter Wise, had done a draft, but it needed a lot of
work. Mitchum wanted more details, an inside feel for the milieu.
He and Jim Phillips decided they would go to Washington, D.C., on
a research trip. Jim had a brother, David Atlee Phillips, a rising star
in the CIA. The men from Hollywood came to see him at his office,

which Mitchum claimed was located behind a false front, the facade of a brewery. Brother David made some phone calls, smoothing the way for them to meet with officials at the Treasury Department.*

Schmoozing officers of the department's Alcohol and Tobacco Tax Division, explaining his desire to make a film documenting their glorious battle against the moonshine menace in the American South, Mitchum came away with a promise of full cooperation for his project. For days he and Phillips pawed through Alcohol and Tobacco's criminal files and case histories, then carried on their research at the Library of Congress, learning about the ancestry of southern mountain families and spending some time listening to the library's collection of regional folk music and rare "hillbilly" recordings.

One day Mitchum turned up in Asheville, North Carolina, a scenic crossroads and summer retreat in the Blue Ridge Mountains. It was the birthplace of a writer whose work Mitchum had always admired, Thomas Wolfe (Wolfe on Asheville: ". . . the cool sweet magic of starred mountain night, the huge attentiveness of dark, the slope, the trees . . ."), and the town was no stranger to the moonshine trade. Mitchum checked in at the old Battery Park Hotel and, with an introduction and authorization from Washington in his pocket, he telephoned the treasury's man in Asheville, John Corbin, and asked if they could get together.

"Are you some kinda joker?" said Corbin. "Robert Mitchum the movie man?"

A meeting was arranged, and Corbin brought along Al Dowtin, a respected local legend and overachiever, former sports hero, former

---

*David Atlee Phillips was later connected with the Bay of Pigs invasion and numerous other attention-getting CIA operations in North and Central America. Conspiracy buffs have claimed for him a part in the assassination of President Kennedy. In the early '60s, his brother James began writing a series of paperback spy novels under an alias: Philip Atlee. The books were notable for their imaginative detail regarding clandestine operations. Mitchum remained good friends with Jim for many years and spoke with David from time to time, and they may have been the source for some of Mitchum's later "inside stories" of "spooks" and government plots and international conspiracies. James Atlee Phillips's son, Shawn, a folk rock singer, performed on Donovan's recording of "Sunshine Superman." What else do you want to know?

FBI agent, and champion golfer, now the head of the local ABC (Alcohol Beverage Control) Board.

"I was chief of the law enforcement for the Asheville ABC," said Dowtin. "The liquor stores had just been voted in in North Carolina, and so liquor sales had just become legal in Asheville at the ABC store; but prior to that the only liquor we had coming in to Asheville, which is a town of fifty-six thousand people, well, it was *illegal.* So mountain liquor—white liquor, corn liquor—was the basic alcohol used by most people. And they did a good business, I would say. There was stills all over them mountains in western North Carolina. About eleven hundred stills. And when I was working with Alcohol Tax we arrested over ten thousand people. You're asking me how did we find the stills? Well, we would get information. There's always some good people in a neighborhood who don't like to see people sellin' liquor."

Dowtin sat down with Bob Mitchum and they talked moonshine. "He was just about as down-to-earth a fella as you ever saw. And we talked, and he wanted to know if we could furnish him all the information he wanted on the moonshiners' tricks and how they operated and all that business. He asked a lot of questions. And o' course we wanted to help him anyway we could. So we filled him in on everything he wanted to know, told him some adventures. I had some car chases, shot down the tires on a car. Once or twice someone shot at us from up the hill. Most of the time, though, I told him, it was like this; we treated folks right, that was my belief. We'd arrest them, and rather than put handcuffs on 'em, we'd tell 'em, 'Come to the office on Monday and turn yourself in.' I tell you, we treated people right. . . . See, where you get in trouble in life is treatin' people wrong."

Mitchum returned to Hollywood and set about putting together a cast and crew for his moonshine movie. His choice to direct the picture was decidedly unconventional yet emblematic. Sixty-two-year-old Arthur Ripley was an eccentric and mysterious figure in American film circles. To those who had worked with him in the course of his peripatetic forty years in the business, his behavior and appearance had engendered as much comment as his undoubt-ed talent. He was a gloomy presence in his early days and prone to fits of truculent shouting as if, said one observer, "unseen demons were fighting his ideas." He seldom changed clothes or bathed; and while making a film for Walter Wanger in the '30s, Ripley looked so frighteningly unkempt that intermediaries hid him under blankets when the fastidious producer visited the sets. In the beginning a film editor (he chopped von Stroheim's *Foolish Wives* from twenty-four reels to fourteen on a train from Los Angeles to New York), then a Mack Sennett gag writer, he partnered with a young Frank Capra in creating a series of features for silent clown Harry Langdon. Ripley, it was said, gave Langdon his "dark" side. Joshua Logan, who codirected a film with him in 1938, declared, "Ripley was a true movie man. . . . He knew everything there was to know. An inspired man, almost a clairvoyant, it took careful knowing to appreciate him." In 1942, Ripley directed *Prisoner of Japan,* from a story by Edgar Ulmer, completing it in five days; the picture cost $19,000 and made $350,000. His mood-drenched romance of Nazi refugees in the Caribbean, *Voice in the Wind,* took eight days to shoot and the *New York Times* said it contained "more art per lin-ear foot than most Oscar winners." Ripley made one more feature in the mid-'40s, the great, bizarre film noir *The Chase,* starring Peter Lorre and Steve Cochran, from a novel by Cornell Woolrich. And then . . . mostly unemployment and obscurity. At the time Mitchum went looking for him, it had been over ten years since Ripley had directed anything.

"Anybody else would have tried to get some established director or some hot new talent that everyone was enthusiastic about," said Reva Frederick. "It was typical of Robert to come up with Ripley. He got these ideas from the back of his head, you didn't know where. He said he had seen one of the man's movies years ago, he couldn't remember it exactly, but he thought that was the sort of guy he wanted." Mitchum was intrigued by the filmmaker's outsider rep—he compared him to Nick Ray as another artist "people just didn't believe in"—and by his legendary economy. "He was a very gifted man and a drinking fellow," said Mitchum, "a tall, sonorous, big-nose character from Brooklyn, teaching at UCLA when we nailed him." Said Reva, "We found Arthur Ripley. Oh boy. He was one hundred and ninety years old or looked it. He liked to drink, and when he drank he didn't know where he was, where he lived, or how to get back home. Robert liked him."

His next idea was even more inspired, but by no means economical. Mitchum wanted to costar in the film with Elvis Presley. The young musical sensation had appeared in just one film so far, *Love Me Tender,* stealing the picture right out from under the nominal star (and Mitchum's friend), Richard Egan. In *Thunder Road,* Mitchum wanted Presley to play his character's upstart young brother.

He showed up at Elvis's hotel suite one day, with a screenplay in one hand and a fifth of scotch in the other. Members of Presley's omnipresent posse escorted him inside to meet the twenty-two-year-old King. Elvis was a confessed fan of Mitchum's and confided that the actor's high, upswept hairstyle in one picture had been the inspiration for his own much-talked-about pompadour. Mitchum chuckled, poured himself a drink. They chewed the fat, Bob trotting out some old standards, the escape from the chain gang, snapping hound dogs, and such. Elvis told his friend Russ Tamblyn that Mitchum's exciting stories had left him "all shook up."

At last, feeling the two of them had established a pretty good rapport, Mitchum got down to business. "Here's the fuckin' script," he said. "Let's get together and do it."

According to Presley's pal Lamar Fike, a witness to the meeting, Elvis told Mitchum they would have to discuss it with his manager.

Mitchum said, "Fuck, I'm talking to you. I don't need to talk to your manager. Let's do the picture."

"Well, I can't," Elvis said. "Not unless the Colonel says I can."

Colonel Parker didn't care about sentimental shit like Mitchum's influential hairdo. The price for Presley was most of *Thunder Road*'s estimated budget, and that was more or less the end of that. Presley did accept an invitation to come over to the Mandeville house one weekend. Young Chris Mitchum, used to seeing famous faces drop by and pretty blasé about it, was stunned by the visit. Gregory Peck,

Jane Russell, these people were just . . . neighbors. Here was a star! Presley ate roast beef at the dinner table, then played the piano and sang and did a couple of duets with his host. Bob's stock climbed several points in his children's eyes.

Mitchum's oldest son, sixteen-year-old Jim, had sprouted up to his father's size and was getting bigger, and people often joked that they looked like twins. Bob decided to give him a taste of the family business and cast him to play Luke's young brother, offering him a minimum salary of $280 a week. "I'm a producer first and a father second," Mitchum said. Other roles went to Gene Barry (the federal lawman), Jacques Aubuchon (the gangster villain), Mitch Ryan and Peter Breck (young punks), and to singer and Las Vegas lounge sensation Keely Smith, making her acting debut as Luke's chanteuse girlfriend. "Robert had come into the office one day some time before," said Reva, "and he said, 'I have heard the greatest record of all time!' He was just crazy about that record, Louis Prima and this girl he said had a great voice, Keely Smith. So fade out, and now we're casting *Thunder Road* and Robert says, 'Let's see if we can talk to Keely Smith about the part.' He wanted her and that was that. He had a theory that anyone who could sing, who could deliver a lyric, could act. This didn't turn out to be correct, but she was a very nice lady."

Mitchum cowrote two songs for the film, "The Whippoorwill" and a title theme, "The Ballad of Thunder Road." With the latter he had no luck fitting the lyrics to a piece of music that worked until his mother tried the words against an old Norwegian dancing tune she knew, sort of a polka. Eureka. Mitchum recorded a version of "The Ballad" for Capitol, which in September rose to number sixty-two on the pop-rock charts.

The legion from Hollywood descended on Asheville in the autumn of 1957. Mitchum took over the Governor's Suite at the local hotel, and *Thunder Road* people filled every other room in the place and a motel and a few boardinghouses as well. Locations were scouted and chosen all over town and on the roads and mountains outside of Asheville and over in nearby Transylvania County. Extras and all bit parts were cast from among the local population, including high school students, businessmen, and local celebrity Farmer Russ, a popular radio disc jockey who would play the laughing lout in the nightclub sequence. Al Dowtin took Mitchum next door from the ABC to Hoyle's Office Supply Store, a former car dealership that had its own parking garage, and they made an arrangement with owner Red Hoyle to use the garage and part of his outdoor parking lot and to build an office set in the back. "He came in and he said, 'We'd like to film a movin' picture in your parking area,' Red Hoyle remembered, "and I said fine, OK. And they made it into a body shop back there and filmed things and jumping out of the window and so on." The Hoyle building became *Thunder Road*'s improvised studio for a number of interiors and exterior scenes. The store remained open and people would come in to buy their pencils and stationery while Mitchum and the others walked in and out making the picture. "He was a fine fellow, Robert Mitchum," said Red Hoyle. "He treated me fine. They were there for some weeks and he brought a lot of people to the store 'cause he would come on in when he took a break, and walk around, sit down on the office furniture and say hello to people, so forth and so on. And people came around, two, three hundred women there all the time. Those ladies would come up and see him shoot scenes. I thought they were coming to see me, but they really came to see him."

The film company settled into Asheville, Mitchum telling them all to mingle, make themselves part of the scenery. It was the locals who had trouble acting natural as they gathered in crowds for hours at a time watching the filming or froze in place, slack-jawed, watching Mitchum and Keely Smith cruising down the main street in an open convertible. At night the movie stars were often to be found at the nearby nightspot, The Sky Club, located inside an actual castle built by an eccentric rich man. "They were all up there all the time," said Mickey Hoyle, Red's son. "That was a private club, the only place you could get drinks by the glass. Everywhere else you had to brown bag it. They shot part of the movie in there, too."

When word spread that Mitchum was living in Asheville, he was paid a visit by a committee of Indian tribesmen from Lane, South Carolina. Relatives, it turned out, from Mitchum's paternal grandmother's side of the family. Mitchum embraced them warmly and staked them all to a night's entertainment. "They were among the most frightening people I'd ever met," he said. "They were pure blooded Blackfoot, wild-looking men who, if you gave 'em too many drinks, would tear down the motel."

Very soon it became apparent that Arthur Ripley would not be making *Thunder Road* in anything like four days. The working atmosphere was extremely relaxed, the script vestigial. Bossman Mitchum ran a loose ship, to say the least, and the shooting schedule became a meaningless affectation. Gene Barry, playing Treasury agent Troy Barrett, arrived at the location for an expected three-week stay. "But I got there and—it was a nice little town, Asheville—I found they were making it up as they went along. Arthur Ripley was an elderly man, very intelligent, very articulate, knew camera angles, all the technical aspect. But he was very slow. And Jim Phillips, a nice guy, clean-cut looking young man, was constantly writing new scenes, taking advantage of whatever local color they found, and some of the people there were very colorful. And my three weeks were up and Jim Phillips would say to me, 'Don't go, I've written a great scene for you.' And my three weeks came and went and they kept me for another six weeks. And my wife would call and say, 'When are you coming home?' And I said, 'Don't complain, they're enlarging my role!'"

"Hell, yes, Jim got behind in the writing," said Al Dowtin. "Jim, he liked to drink a little beer, and I guess most all of us do a little bit, occasionally. And he had a hard time keeping ahead of what they were going to shoot and coming up with a script. He did all his writing in his hotel room. But anyway, he was a real nice guy. And I don't think Mitchum minded waiting for the pages, he was having such a good time."

Actor Jerry Hardin, playing one of the moonshine drivers, had been at a summer stock theater in Virginia when Mitchum passed through town and hired him for *Thunder Road*, his first film. "Mitchum," he said, "was the most laid-back man that I had ever seen. The business of acting was very casual with him. The thing that was of primary importance was his relationship with the company.

He loved to party and practical jokes were de rigeur. One night he got ahold of about six dozen baby chicks and put them into one guy's room—I think he was the stunt driver. And then everybody waited for the man to stumble home after having a good deal of liquor. And the man came and the chicks were everywhere and so were their droppings, and the guy was floundering and flopping about—this story lived on the set for weeks afterward.

"Mitchum represented to me the most extraordinary physical specimen. He partied all night sometimes, and he would come to the set, they put a little bit of makeup under his eyes, and he would work the whole day. You never could see it on the film. Absolutely astonishing. His conquests were a legend, all kinds of wild tales flying around. Women were coming from all over to pay attention to Mitchum, and Mitchum was, how shall I say, paying attention to them—until his wife showed up. There was talk about him making love with nearly every woman in North Carolina. I don't know how much of that was accurate, but he was clearly popular."

"Oh my, yes," said one Asheville resident, confirming this conclusion. "He was quite a ladies' man."

"There was one morning, after a very full weekend," a member of the company recalled, "and Mitchum was on the set, very abashed, and he was telling how he had partied so hard that the whole weekend had become a blank. His wife had just gotten into town, he said, but he had somehow lost track of her; and dawn came and he was confused, his head hurt, and he saw that he was in bed with some woman. And Mitchum thought, 'Oh shit! Where am I? My wife's in town; I can't get caught doing this again!' So he got out of bed very quietly, he could barely open his eyes, and he put his clothes on and climbed out of the window and ran away out of there and down an alley without looking back. He wandered around and made his way to the set and passed out. When he woke up and the crew were getting ready, he noticed that he didn't have his wristwatch. . . . He had forgotten his wristwatch in the woman's bedroom, and it was an expensive watch, a gift from his wife, had his name inscribed, a little message and everything. And he said, 'Oh, Jesus, I don't even know where I was, and I left my goddamn watch there. My goose is cooked.' And he was agonizing about this all morning, trying to remember where he was last night and who the woman was. And about midmorning his wife came to the set. And she said, 'Bob, I noticed you forgot your watch on the bedstand this morning; I brought it over.' He was so drunk he didn't even know he was in bed with his own wife and had snuck out of his own room. I don't know if the story is correct, but it has a definite ring of truth to it from what was going on there, and *he's* the one told me the story."

As if to forestall the same charges of nepotism he often leveled at the Hollywood establishment, Mitchum made sure not to play favorites with his sixteen-year-old son. "He's had no formal training," said the father, "so I raised hell with him on the set whenever he goofed or got self-conscious in front of the cameras. I was much rougher on him than on any actors I've ever worked with." With the rest of the *Thunder Road* company, Mitchum was both a benevolent and a creative producer. For many segments of the film he was codirector as well. Ripley at times restricted himself to the technical and visual details of filming while Mitchum would casually take over with the actors. Mitchum was particularly good at coaching all the film's non-professional bit players.

Along with everything else the cast and crew were soaking up, Mitch encouraged them to ingest the film's background and subject matter, to get involved. "Mitchum went to considerable lengths to expose us to the inner workings of the whiskey-running business," said Jerry Hardin. "He had guys talking to us who had driven the cars, and there were Drug and Alcohol people around telling their stories. A good deal of effort was put into wising us up to what was going on, so we knew what everything looked like and felt like. It was very important to Mitchum as we made this film that everyone felt like they were part of the atmosphere."

"I said to Bob, 'I'd like to know more about what these agents do,'" Gene Barry recalled. "And so he arranged it for me to go with some of the real guys on a raid into the hills. And this group of tough-looking guys came up to the hotel, said, 'OK, we're here.' And first they gave me a pair of boots to wear. Then they shoved a gun in

my hand. I said, 'What's this for?' They said, 'You may have to protect yourself where we're going.' And we drove around the back
roads up above Hendersonville, and then we went into the woods on
foot. And then we came charging into this still someone had built
there in the woods. But the moonshiners had been tipped off and
got away with their goods. Somebody told them we were coming. It
was very clannish around there. Or maybe Mitchum tipped them,
you never know!"

There *were* those who wondered just exactly which side Mitchum
was on in the struggle between white lightning and the law. At some
point during the shooting, two Alcohol Tax people Mitchum had
spoken to in Washington came down to see how things were going.
They came to the set and observed the shooting of several scenes,
and it began to occur to them that their friend Bob was not playing
a Treasury agent after all but was portraying a criminal whiskey
driver. "Here's what happened, and I don't know how you ought to
handle it," said a man on the scene who would prefer to go
unnamed. "They came down and saw what the picture was about.
And they saw how Bob was outsmarting the Alcohol Tax agent and
making the agents look kind of like the whiskey runner was a little
bit smarter person. Well, I mean this was purely fictional, but they
didn't quite like that. And they didn't know what to do, so they sort
of pulled out of cooperating, just backed away from the whole thing
and went back to Washington."

The cars that were used in the film had been obtained at no little
effort. Production manager John E. Burch was sent combing the
hills for the sixteen-year-old Mercurys and other hopped-up moon-
shiner transporters. "Here was old Dan with a pocket full of
Hollywood green," said Mitchum on the matter. "Everytime we
found what we needed, we also found one of the local mountain
boys had just bought it." Eventually, though, a souped-up fleet was
put together for the would-be bootleggers. "Everything we drove
was an authentic whiskey-running car they had gotten from
sources," said Jerry Hardin. "There was nothing faked. We were
running around town with these hot engines everywhere. Mitchum

was fascinated by the cars. And he was very proud of what the car he was driving could do, how it could outrun the police. Mitchum was really into it, like he'd become one of these whiskey runners. He was in the center of this world and really enjoying it."

While all the actors in the chase scenes were required to do some high-speed runs through the town and up and down the wooded highway, the difficult and dangerous stuff was left to an amazing stunt driver named Carey Loftin (the man with the baby chicks in his room). A Hollywood legend, Loftin had been driving—and crashing—high-speed vehicles in the movies for decades (and would continue to do so for another forty years). Loftin's dexterity at the wheel was extraordinary. It was believed that his vision was literally superhuman—he could see through fog, for example. "What would be a blur to you or me," said his widow, "was crystal clear to Carey. So it was like everything moved slower for him and gave him more time to adjust to it. His reactions were so fast that he could catch a flying bug between two fingers just putting his hand up—just two fingers."

Loftin arrived in Asheville direct from doubling Marlon Brando on a motorcycle in *The Young Lions*. His hair was still bleached blond for that picture, and Mitchum made a great show of taking him down to the local women's beauty parlor and having it darkened while townspeople looked in through the window.

A flamboyant, fun-loving character, Loftin enjoyed dazzling people with his legendary gifts. For *Thunder Road*'s big stunt—Luke Doolin driving to his death, the car rolling over repeatedly and crashing into an electric station—Carey went up to the cameraman and asked him for his "mark."

"What?"

"Where do you want the car to come to a stop?"

The car was supposed to flip over out of control and spin till it got to the jerry-rigged electric station. The cameraman wasn't thinking in such precise terms, but he shrugged and pointed to a spot on the ground. Carey took a last puff on a cigarette and tossed it on the spot. He got in the car, drove down the road and turned around, waited for the signal, then moved. The car screeched, skidded, flipped over again and again, and shuddered to a stop. Loftin climbed out, everyone applauded; they moved over to the front of the upside-down car and saw Carey's cigarette butt lying dead center below the front fender.

"Carey and Bob had a good time down there," said Mrs. Loftin. "He said they got stoned on some real moonshine liquor from the mountains, the kind in a jug, and you slung it over your shoulder and passed it back and forth. And they were seeing who could out-drink who, and they were very bleary-eyed at the end of it."

Yes, said Al Dowtin, "Bob was kind of interested in knowing about the white liquor. See, there was kind of a mystique to it. Whenever a still would start running, the first liquor that came out would be about a hundred and fifty proof. Then as the mash would run, it got lower. But all the liquor we confiscated always came out about a hundred percent. And about eighty-six is the average for tax-paid liquor. So the illegal stuff was always a bit stronger. Bob liked hearing about that, and I'm sure he probably drank a little of it when he was here. Somebody got some white liquor for him."

Was it possible to sample any of the moonshine that had been confiscated, an anonymous source was asked?

"No, no . . . don't say anything about that. No."

"Bob was just the most regular down-to-earth guy," said Al Dowtin. "And he always had time, even when he was working, to stop and say hello and kid with people. And I remember one time, I came over to where they were shooting with a good golfing friend of mine, Dr. Brutin. He was in charge of the medical department over there; he was sort of a character. And that day Bob had sent one of his drivers over to bring back a big tub of ice and cases of beer and some drinks. And everybody had their drinks and their ice. And Bob was drinking; he drank everything. And Dr. Brutin says to him, 'Bob, I don't know about all this drinking,' he says. 'At your age that stuff may not be good for you anymore.'

"And Bob said, 'Now lookee here, Doc,' he said to him. *'I know more old drunks than I do old doctors.'*"

With its B picture dramatics, certain zombielike performances, and flat, even primitive visuals (not discounting Ripley's random moments of surrealism and poetic images, like the final brief cutaway glimpse of nocturnal road, with distant car beams like lightning bugs at the very tip of the screen), it would be difficult to place *Thunder Road* among Mitchum's greatest works of film art. Its real distinction is more personal: the movie simply contains more of Robert Mitchum, more of his actual creative participation and more of his heart, soul, and mind than any other. From the sympathetic subject matter—the creation and distribution of high-octane alcohol—to the alienated, outside-the-law hero who feels without a home even in his mother's kitchen, the glimpses of a close yet dysfunctional family, the film's almost religious belief in rugged individualism, the obsession with the Deep South, the fetish for high-speed cars, liquor, lonely open roads, and an all-night life, the pessimistic, fatalistic perspective that harkened back to his ten years in the noir trenches—here, more than in any other single film, was Mitchum's ultimate cinematic statement, his personal vision of life transposed into lurid, downbeat entertainment. A cult film long before such terms for cherished yet disreputable works of art had gained popular acceptance, *Thunder Road* would foster a rabid underground following, a cross-cultural group of enthusiasts that included southern teenagers, vintage car buffs, film scholars, and an otherwise unclassifiable demographic that desired to watch over and over the cool way Mitchum, while tearing down Thunder Road, flicks a cigarette through the window of a pursuing bad guy's car. Pop culture critics would be inspired to flights of rhapsody about the film and its delirious allure, most notably Richard Thompson in an ode published in a 1969 issue of *December Magazine*. "*Thunder Road*," he wrote, "is a private myth irradiating the secret corners of a lost existence with the savor of true existentialism. . . . *Thunder Road* disciples envy those who saw it exactly right: at a drive-in, sitting in their customized Fords and Chevs, just after leaving the high school dance and just before juking on down to Shakey's Pizza Parlor." The film's afterlife in the South—where it was called the

"*Gone With the Wind* of the drive-in"—was a true cultural phenomenon. People would speak of seeing it—like a spotting of the
Loch Ness monster—playing to packed audiences in theaters in
places like Knoxville and Pikeville, twenty and more years after its
original release.

*

On January 10, 1958, Bob and his son Jim made an appearance on
Frank Sinatra's short-lived and poorly received ("One of the biggest
disappointments of the season," said *TV Guide*) weekly television
series on ABC. Sinatra, said the New York *World-Telegram*, "didn't
just walk through his show, he shambled, shrugged, and could not
have cared less." Clearly, then, what the show cried out for was the
caring presence of Robert Mitchum. He and Sinatra did a half
singing, half crosstalk number, a hipster's variation on an old
Gallagher & Shean vaudeville bit.

> FS: Oh, Mr. Mitchum!
> RM: Yeah, Dad?
> FS: I have heard that you've made records, more or less.
> RM: More or less would be more right, and unless you'd like to
> fight, that sarcastic tone I'd thank you to suppress.
> FS: Sarcastic? Me? Ha ha, perish the thought!

Jim Mitchum, after a taste of movie acting in *Thunder Road,*
announced that he was now planning to make a career of it. He
began trying out for parts and landed a role in an Albert Zugsmith
production starring Steve Cochran, *The Beat Generation.* It was the
sort of credit that had an asterisk attached to it—Zugsmith liked to
fill his teen drive-in pictures with a lot of starry surnames, and the
children of Edward G. Robinson, Charles Chaplin, and John
Barrymore were a lot cheaper than their famous parents would ever
have been. Jim certainly had more natural ability than some, but his
uncanny resemblance to his father minus the charisma would not
make things easy for him. Whether indicating reticence, disinterest,

or something else, Pappa Bob's public statements regarding his son's would-be career were never a public relations agent's dream. Aside from the very big break he handed the boy in letting him appear in *Thunder Road*, Robert seldom enthused over Jim's prospective stardom. Instead his tendency was toward blunt honesty, telling a reporter, "Jim is an overprivileged kid from Brentwood and likes whatever the equivalent of Schwabs is for his set." Mitchum added, "It's difficult for him; he's a grown man but has been deprived of the experience of maturity."

In the summer Robert and Dorothy went to Greece. *The Angry Hills* was a novel by Leon Uris about an American correspondent, a reluctant hero joining the Greek resistance fighters after the surprise German invasion in 1941. Buying it for the screen, producer Raymond Stross and associates had originally sought Alan Ladd for the hero role, Mitchum claimed. "But when they drove out to his desert home to see him he'd just crawled out of his swimming pool and he was all shrunken up like a dishwasher's hand. They decided he wouldn't do for the big war correspondent. Some idiot said, 'Ask Mitchum to play it. That bum will do anything if he's got five minutes free.' Well, I had five minutes free." (Back in the desert, according to Alan Ladd's biographer, the diminutive actor would read Bob's comments and have a severe attack of shingles.) Mitchum was once again playing the revolutionary and the outsider, and once more taking a three-month jaunt far from home.

It was a British production with Hollywood's Robert Aldrich—then in self-imposed European exile—hired to direct. Aldrich found the idea of the story alluring—"an American coming of political age and assuming commitment and responsibility during the early days of the last war." The screenplay by the novel's author, however, Aldrich thought completely unfilmable. But the commitments were irretrievably made. On July 1 the cameras had to turn. The director sent for one of his most valued past collaborators, A. I. Bezzerides (*Track of the Cat*), with whom he had made *Kiss Me, Deadly* several years before.

"The producer and Uris had worked for a year on a script and it had to be thrown out," Bezzerides said. "It was no good. The whole thing had to be rewritten, and the producer didn't like that much.... I was writing this thing while they were shooting."

Bezzerides renewed his acquaintance with Bob Mitchum. "He could never pronounce my name, so he'd say, 'Hey, Bazza ... Bizza ... Beezareet. ... Hey, man, what are you doin' here?' I asked him, 'Why are you doing this piece of shit?' We were on location in Athens. He said, 'Well ... I've never been to Greece.'

Director Aldrich's misgivings about the film only grew as the shooting began. The script was not coming together. The half Greek, half British crew did not get along. Few of the Greeks spoke English, so that instructions had to be relayed back and forth through translators, and there was a great deal of confusion. And then there was Mitchum. Aldrich was a powerful masculine personality who could bring out the best in many of the screen's toughest hombres, men like Jack Palance, Lee Marvin, Burt Lancaster, and he and Mitchum should have clicked—but did not. Aldrich had known Mitchum since assistant directing *The Story of G.I. Joe* (indeed, Aldrich sometimes claimed to have been Mitchum's "discoverer," the man who actually recommended him to Wellman for the picture), but they had never developed a friendship. Now, in Greece, as the cameras turned, the director came up against what he called an "inability to find any personal or creative or even emotional routes to discover whatever it is that must be discovered to make Robert Mitchum function as an actor."

Theodore Bikel, playing the movie's extremely seedy, wheeler-dealer, fifth columnist Tassos, observed the conflict between director and star. "Mitchum was very professional; he did everything really, really well. He also could turn ornery if you made him do something he didn't like. Let loose a whole string of invectives. But Aldrich was not intimidated. He was not the kind of director who gave in to anyone. He had a short fuse and he would yell. And so in the end Mitchum did what Aldrich wanted, but he didn't necessarily like it."

A columnist got Mitchum on the phone for a comment on the work in progress. "I play a mute war correspondent who gets to freeload on the Greek peasants," he said. "He has trouble with the goats. There are goats all over. . . . I don't know if he's a hero or a villain. I'll be clearer on that when the writer gets back."

They had been shooting for about a week. Everyone was staying at a lovely hotel on the beach just outside Athens. The picture was falling apart. After dinner one night Aldrich went down to Mitchum's cabana overlooking the water and told him they should talk.

Aldrich said, "We're making a lousy movie. I'm trying the best I can, and I sense you are, but it's not working and I don't know what to do."

Mitchum said, "Don't you understand what we're making? We're making a gorilla picture."

Aldrich stared at him. "What is a gorilla picture, Bob?"

"A gorilla picture is when you get two hundred fifty thousand dollars for doing all the wrong things for ten reels and in the last shot you get the girl and fade into the sunset. That's a gorilla picture. I don't care how well you make it, it's still going to be a gorilla picture. Now if you understand that, you'll be very happy. If you don't, you'll be very unhappy."

Aldrich said, "I don't understand that. So I'm going to be very unhappy. . . . I don't want to make a gorilla picture."

While Aldrich suffered, Mitchum enjoyed his Greek vacation. "We had a lot of fun on that location," said Theo Bikel. "There was a lot of music, there was a lot of good wine—well, perhaps not good wine, but a *lot* of it. The nights on the town could be excruciatingly late. Things don't start in Greece until midnight. There were quite a few nights when we would be in the nightclubs until four or five in the morning, and there would be a seven o'clock call on the set. Luckily my part in the film was such that I could go on camera looking like shit."

Mitchum had arrived in Greece without much enthusiasm for the local females. "They all look like they're wearing moustaches to me," he said. With time, though, he would come to have a more sympathetic point of view. "Women swelled around the movie set," said Bikel. "These were more liberated Greek women, fascinated with the stardom of Mitchum. One of them latched onto him. I would see her in the trailer a few times.

"He was very funny. One night in Athens we were at a nightclub and there was a female impersonator performing. Mitchum was quite taken by what he saw. He said, 'Boy, she is something! I've got to have her.' I said to him, 'Bob, you can't!' He said, 'What do you mean? Why not?' I said, 'Because, the person you're looking at . . . it's not a she, it's . . . it's a *he* . . . it's an *it*.' And he said, 'I don't care about the *plumbing*. She's gorgeous!'"

Another member of the cast, Stanley Baker, a legendary carouser in British film circles, had been eagerly anticipating his first drinking match with the man who—in regard to alcohol consumption—he took to be his American counterpart. The match ended with Baker unconscious and carried back to his hotel, while Mitchum carried on for another four or five hours until dawn and then headed off to breakfast and work.

"I had a very bemused view of all this," said Theo Bikel. "I tagged along, as the house intellectual. I liked Mitchum. He was pleasant, fun to be with. Sometimes we sang together, in the restaurants, sitting around in the evening. I would take out the guitar and do folk music, and then he would take a turn with it and do a blues number. Later, as the night wore on . . . Mitchum was not a particularly pleasant drunk. Some people when they drink get mellow. He didn't. He got robust and belligerent. And you got the feeling that you better steer clear of him when he was that way. He had a general orneriness. He was a bit of a redneck. His whole background came out of the sort of poor white trash environment where there was mistrust for anyone and anything that wasn't of their ilk. I got that feeling. And his tendency was to needle; and if you're sitting with him and you're a Jew, as I am, you needle the Jew. But he was very nice most of the time, and I don't want to neglect that. It's important to say that he was a very pleasant human being who had a dark side to him."

After more than two months in Greece, the company moved to London, shooting interior scenes at MGM's Elstree Studio.

Mitchum was lodged in a suite at the Hotel Savoy and settled into a comfortable routine, returned to the city by five in the afternoon to host a daily "happy hour" in his rooms. Ken Annakin, a talented English writer and director (he'd entered the movie business during the war, after retiring from the RAF with a case of amnesia; his later credits included *Those Magnificent Men in Their Flying Machines*), had a script he wanted to shoot, *The Gold Lovers,* and very much hoped to interest Mitchum in starring in it. "A great adventure story of a plane crashing in Ethiopia," said Annakin. "Hidden gold in the desert, a story of greed, adventure, a love story. Three people with their eye on the gold, even in the most dangerous circumstances. I'd gotten the script to him—I think I had given it to his representative. And I was going up to talk to him about it when he was staying in the Savoy. And I saw that it was going to be difficult to have a talk about the film under these circumstances. The suite was filled with people. Everybody in London seemed to come there, especially the ladies. Lots of actresses from around London, and some of them were quite well known. There was drinking and a little of the other stuff—white stuff—passing around. The ladies were all over the room, and there was Mitchum overseeing it all. I can remember him sitting in a great armchair by the window with the Thames behind him and looking like he was the Sultan of Borneo holding court.

"I tried talking with him but he was terribly busy with all of these social activities, and finally the only time I could attract his attention and be alone with him was when he went to the toilet. And so we went into the toilet and we start to discuss what I had come to talk to him about, and we talked *before* he was using it and gradually it got to where he *was* using it. But once I had his undivided attention there, he was right on the ball, he knew everything about the screenplay and what was involved. He was sharp, even if he was having a few drinks and a little of the other stuff. And I realized that underneath this freewheeling character was a very keen professional. And indeed he thought it was a wonderful story and thought we could make a great film. But he said he had to do this one and then the next one. And we had other meetings and talked about making it, but it just became one of those that slipped through the cracks. And eventually it became just a memory to me. But I would meet up with Mitchum years later at various functions, until his dying day, and he would always say, 'Ken, that's the picture we should have made. It would have been great.' One of those 'regret' stories."

At Elstree, Robert Aldrich continued to struggle with *The Angry Hills*. His star had continued to be a disappointment. "I have seen Mr. Mitchum be too excellent too often to doubt for one minute that he is an extremely accomplished and gifted artist," Aldrich said. "And since the performance that I was able to extract from Mitchum was neither sensitive nor accomplished nor in any regard gifted, it is impossible to escape the conclusion that my failure to connect with him is a liability that I alone, and not the actor, must assume."

The director put together what he hoped was at least a moderately coherent and exciting adventure story, clocking in at just under two hours. Producer Stross thanked him, showed him to the exit, and cut out thirty minutes. "He understood that Metro was buying film by the yard then, and Mitchum was reasonably hot. So they thought as long as it was an hour and a half with Mitchum and some Greek scenery it would work. Obviously, it didn't."

The Wonderful Country was a magnificent novel by artist and writer Tom Lea. It was the story of Martin Brady, a *pistolero*, an assassin for a Mexican governor, caught between two worlds, Mexico and his homeland across the Rio Grande, a man whose sojourn in a Texas border town leads him to question his past life of violence and irresponsibility. It would be the source for one of Mitchum's greatest and most underrated films (with *The Purple Plain,* one of director Robert Parrish's two masterworks), a contemplative, melancholic, and lyrical Western, beautifully shot, with a richly romantic central performance, certainly the most poetic and tender of Mitchum's assorted portrayals of alienated adventurers.

Author Tom Lea had befriended then film editor Robert Parrish during the shooting of another Lea novel, *The Brave Bulls.* "He was a good friend, and I knew him all the time I was writing *Wonderful Country,*" he recalled. "And Parrish said I would love to make that as a movie, so we shook hands on it and we were gonna be kind of partners. We thought the perfect guy for the part would be Henry Fonda, but he wasn't interested at all. And then we went to see Gregory Peck, and he had just married a very nice French girl and he wasn't interested. And Bob had done a picture with Mitchum before, and Mitchum said he was interested. And Mitchum had a very sharp lawyer, and finally he took the whole thing over. And it might interest you to know that the only pay I ever got for the use of my novel was what I made acting a bit part in the movie. And I decided to make that my last experience with Hollywood. The hell with this! I thought. But I got to like Mitchum. And Bob Parrish was a fine man. I always thought he didn't get to rise to the front ranks in Hollywood because he was just too nice a gent."

Lea wrote a screenplay that made the mistake of being reasonably like the novel he was adapting. United Artists wanted more scenes for leading lady Julie London. So Bob Parrish got another author friend of his, Robert Ardrey, to write a revised script. With DRM producing the picture, Mitchum took an active part in the casting, hiring old friends like Anthony Caruso, Charles McGraw, and "Bad Chuck" Roberson as his stunt double and stunt coordinator (Roberson would double just about every rider in the picture). Caruso: "Bob's company was doing that one and he just threw me the script and said, 'What part do you want? Pick one.' So I read it and said, 'I think I'd like to do that Mexican rancher.' And Bob said, 'You got it.'" Among the story's unusual elements was the presence of an all-black cavalry regiment, and for the part of the regiment's sergeant Mitchum suggested they hire the legendary black baseball player Leroy "Satchel" Paige. The fifty-something Paige was currently signed with the Miami Marlins but was at that moment doing time in a Florida jail. A judge agreed to release him to the production.

The entire film would be made in Mexico—Mitchum's fourth time working in that country—in and around the mining town of Durango. Durango had been attracting Hollywood Westerns for only a couple of years at this point. It was a real cowboy town, no frills, tough, could be dangerous, and people still rode horses because they had to. The roads were cobblestone or dirt trails and there was one hotel, the Mexico Courts, which leaned more than the Tower of Pisa and where the smell of backed-up toilets permeated the west wing. "It was a town, in those days," said Anthony Caruso, "full of bars and hookers and that's about it."

Mitchum arrived early, working with Parrish on various preproduction matters, then spent a couple of days in the courtyard of the motel, sipping tequila and greeting the members of the company as they straggled in from the States. Charles McGraw arrived, leaving his usual trail of anarchy behind him. Boarding the flight to Mexico City he'd managed to pick a fight with a sickly man breathing from an oxygen tank—a "Denver lunger" in McGraw's sympathetic description. The actor arrived in Durango unconscious. Julie London came with her boyfriend (eventually, husband) "Route 66" songwriter Bobby Troupe. London got the prized corner suite with the large windows that gave relief from the choking stink when the toilets got too unbearable. "Satchel Paige got to Durango with a very beautiful young girl in tow, a teenager," said Kathie Parrish. "People thought maybe it was his daughter."

"Who do we have here, Leroy?" said Mitchum.

"This is my child's baby-sitter," said Paige.

Mitchum paused a beat. "But your child's not here."

Paige said, "How about that!"

"He was a character, Satchel Paige," said Mrs. Parrish. "He was cooler than Mitchum!"

Tom Lea came down from El Paso, bringing along a vintage sombrero his father had gotten from a Mexican during the revolution. "I used to carry that thing around for some reason," said Lea. "Mitchum liked its history and decided to wear it in the film. But he always felt kind of funny in that big Mexican hat, and he was always trying to crease it and bring the wings forward so it looked more like a cowboy hat."

Lea was put back to work on the screenplay. Mitchum liked to confer with the writer about the man he was playing. "I would talk to Mitchum about the character, and he would ask questions. I told him that this was a man who had gone after his father's killer and now he was trying to be like his father, and he was very interested in that. But he fell right into the part, and he was working on his Spanish-Mexican accent and he did quite a job. And I think he liked to try and identify with the character a bit. He had that black stallion he rode in the picture, and Mitchum would say, 'That horse won't let nobody ride him but me.' And any kid stable hand could ride that horse he had. But I think he might have believed it when he said it."

Lea found himself unexpectedly working in front of the camera, too. "Bob Parrish wanted to get me some money out of the thing, and he said the only way he could do it was to put me in the picture. And I said all right. So I played the part of the town barber who gives Mitchum a bath and a shave. And a Mexican barber showed me what to do, how to hold the scissors. For the bathtub scene, the guy playing the doctor"—Charles McGraw—"wanted us to play a gag on Mitchum. I was supposed to throw a bucket of lukewarm water over him in the tub. And instead we got a bucket of water that was almost ice. Bob wasn't wearing anything and I poured this ice water right on his balls. He screamed and the rest of us nearly died laughing. And he thought it was funny, too, after he got over the shock of it. Then it took many tries to get that scene right afterward because every time we'd start it again we'd all start breaking up thinking on Bob's reaction.

"The most amazing thing about Bob Mitchum was, he'd be up all night, doing God knows what, and at 5 A.M. the bus would load up to go to the location and he'd be on the bus, fresh as a ten-year-old girl."

The nightlife in Durango certainly took its toll on *some* bodies. Mitchum and Chuck Roberson were knocking back the tequilas in a cantina one weekend when a fiery argument broke out between two Mexicans. Mitchum tried to catch the gist of the contretemps with his limited Spanish and offered Roberson a halting translation. It seemed that one man had gotten another man's sister pregnant, one man wanted the other man to marry the sister, and one man told the other man to go and stick his head up his sister's ass.

The tall hombre drew a pistol and shot the short man in the face and then ran out the door, but the short man with the bullet in his face ran after him. Mitchum and Roberson were remarking on the wonder of this when the short man staggered back into the bar.

Roberson wrote: "There was a small hole in his forehead and a trickle of blood ran down between his eyes and to the end of his nose. He was glaring right at Mitch with the wild eyes of a wounded animal. Mitchum gasped at him and then the man's eyes rolled back and he crashed to the floor.

"I thought for a minute Mitch might have a heart attack. He yelled something in Spanish to the bartender, checked the man's pulse, dropped the hand, and stood back horrified.

"He's dead. . . . Stone, cold dead."

Roberson couldn't believe somebody could run so fast with a bullet through his skull, and the hombre wasn't even a stuntman.

"Let's get the hell out of here," said Mitchum.

Roberson recommended they wait around for the police. Everyone knew who they were, and it wouldn't look right just to take off into the night. Mitchum looked in a state of shock, according to Bad Chuck, and couldn't take his eyes off the body. They gave their account to the police when they arrived, and then, said Roberson, "We high-tailed it back to the hotel and pretty much stuck around there from then on."

Another day, another adventure: Mitchum and Roberson obtained a bottle of homemade pulque from a peasant they met while riding along the river. After consuming the beerlike beverage made from cactus (Mitchum on pulque: *"Drain the sap out of the cactus, let it be for a minute. Viscous. Limpid. Full of gnats. Ferments in the warmth of the stomach. Smells like baby vomit"*), both experienced a horrifying hangover that kept even Mitchum in bed all day and an angry Parrish demanded everyone go on the wagon for the duration. Then food poisoning from a dinner of baked fish put the star—and numerous others—out of commission for three days, and Mitchum went back to drinking tequila with every meal and recommended it to everyone else, "for medicinal purposes."

"It was a beautiful picture," said Kathie Parrish. "Mitchum was terribly good. But he let someone who worked for him take over the picture at the editing stage. She wanted to oversee the cutting of it and she just took it away, wouldn't let Bob in the cutting room. And it wasn't ruined but there were all the little things he would have done differently, the pacing, the style, made sharper. And there was nothing Bob could do about it. Mitchum understood what was happening; but you know, with Mitchum, when it came down to the wire of having a conflict, he would back away. And he wouldn't fight for the picture. Bob—my husband—did an imitation of Mitchum that was just a gesture: putting his hands up. In other words, 'What can I do?'

"But he was an absolutely marvelous character. And Bob and Mitch were great together; they were terribly funny and had exactly the same sense of humor. And we stayed friends. And Mitchum came over to the house once after the picture, and he was trying to tell Bob that he liked the picture, that it had been a good experience and it was a good picture. And it was just so difficult for him. He could not say that he was grateful or that he loved you. It embarrassed him to show emotion, affection, even with Dottie. He could come on to girls and all that, but real emotion was difficult. He'd take a drink instead."

Tom Lea came out to visit Bob Parrish sometime after the movie had come and gone. "He decided to call up Mitchum and tell him I was in town, and Mitchum said, 'Well, bring him out.' And so we went to Bob's house out in the canyon. I remember it had a screened porch and he had some big macaws he kept there and he was very fond of them. He had taught them to shout obscenities. And Mitchum said, 'Well, we all got to celebrate.' And he went into a closet and brought out a bottle of very old bourbon. It had a big green seal on it and it was from the year 1917. I don't know where he got that, but it was damn good bourbon, and we had a damn good time drinking it."

In April 1959, the Mitchums paid a little under $140,000 for a 280-acre property called Belmont Farms at Trappe, Maryland, on Chesapeake Bay. For some time they had mused about getting away from Hollywood. Even after nearly twenty years in Los Angeles, Dorothy still tended to think of herself as an Easterner, an outsider in Tinseltown, and Bob—an outsider everywhere—had a visceral contempt for what he called "Beverly Hills values." Both thought the kids ought to get a chance to see what life was like in the real world (well, Chris and Trina; aspiring movie star Jim had decided that unreal Southern California was good enough for him). Making eight pictures in a row in nearly as many countries, Mitchum had proved that you no longer had to live in Burbank to be in the film business.

"They were burned out on Los Angeles," said Reva Frederick. "It's a sprawling city, but it's really a village. And I think Dorothy in particular may have longed to go back East—back home."

They had scoured the East for an appropriate place, starting in Delaware and working their way down. They had gotten as far as Maryland and were flapping around a town called Easton, Mitchum recalled."I asked this real estater what the natives did in these parts. He said, 'We don't do nothing but go crabbing and drink.' I knew he was telling the truth because right after he said that he fell on his ear. Man, was he stoned. I said, 'This is it! We'll dig in right here.'"

It was seventy miles from the Baltimore airport, in Talbot County, a remote and lovely area of old colonial farms, a few of them gone somewhat to seed since Independence Day. The main house was a three story, 110-year-old mansion, set back far from the road. The rear fronted the Choptank River with a mile of unbroken shoreline. To the nearest town, Easton, it was twelve miles by road, five minutes by boat, and from the house you could see approaching visitors on either side. "I could escape by land or sea," Mitchum said dreamily.

There were barns, stables. Most of the farmland was tilled by contract, by tenant farmers who planted and harvested barley, corn, oats, wheat, and rye ("all the fixin's for making whisky," said Bob) and kept chickens, horses, hogs, and white-faced Herefords. It was a working farm, not a weekend resort. Not that Mitchum himself planned on doing much in the way of work when he was there. He was an actor, not a gentleman farmer. When he looked around the sprawling place, he saw privacy, seclusion, his own waterfront, room to breathe and fresh air to go with it. He wanted to loaf, go fishing, maybe get back to writing. "If anyone were to come there to visit with me, fine—just going there would be the sign of true friendship," he said. It was as far away from Hollywood as you could get and still be in the same country.

They put the Mandeville place on the market and packed their bags. After more than two decades as a resident, he was kissing California good-bye. Came on a freight train, leaving a millionaire of global renown. Was he going to miss the Hollywood life? the columnists asked. "What Hollywood life?" Mitchum said. "I never traveled with the mob. I've only been to one movie star's home, Kirk Douglas's, and that was for all of ten minutes. All actors are freaks and I guess I'm a freak's freak. If I walked into a restaurant here people held their breath—they just waited for me to walk up and sock someone." In Maryland, he said, he was going to be just another citizen, trying to get through the day.

CHAPTER TWELVE

The Smirnoff Method

Within days of the Mitchum family's arrival at their new tidewater residence in the spring of 1959, Robert had gone to his next job. *Home from the Hill*, based on the novel by William Humphrey and a script by Irving and Harriet Ravetch, was MGM's latest foray into the then popular and surprisingly fertile Sleazy Southern Gentry genre. Ingredients common to this category were big old plantation houses, randy and/or cranky patriarchs and their neurotic sons and nymphomaniac daughters, nasty skeletons in the family closets (anything from drunken driving arrests to hereditary insanity), and lots of overripe, bourbon-and-magnolia-scented acting (examples of the genre include *The Long Hot Summer, The Sound and the Fury, Written on the Wind,* and *Cat on a Hot Tin Roof*).

For two hundred thousand dollars plus a percentage of the gross, Mitchum agreed to play "Captain" Wade Hunnicutt, the ferocious-ly masculine and debauched head of a wealthy East Texas family, husband to an embittered, sexually withdrawn wife (Eleanor Parker in the film), father to a sensitive "mamma's boy" (George Hamilton) and—officially unacknowledged—to a manly bastard (George Peppard). The role had originally been earmarked for Clark Gable who became unavailable, but it is unlikely that Gable, two decades older and gentler with his screen image, would have been capable of anything like the violent, intimidating physical presence of Mitchum or the cruel arrogance of the actor's uncompromising characterization. At the same time, it was revealing of a new stage of Mitchum's career that the studio now considered him for this kind of mature role. The film's director was Vincente Minnelli—at a career peak, the Oscar for *Gigi* still warm in his hand as filming began—who had first worked with Mitchum in *Undercurrent* when the actor had played Robert Taylor's fresh-faced younger brother. Now Mitch was forty-one and portraying a paterfamilias with a pair of grown sons. Were his days as a screen adventurer and love object fading into the past? reporters asked. All right with him if they were, Mitchum answered. Gray up my hair and let me play granpas, maybe they'll stop plaguing me with work. He confessed he had only taken the part because of a promise of lots of time off and a location jaunt to an area of Mississippi where he'd heard there was excellent bream fishing.

For a month they filmed in Oxford, William Faulkner's hometown. Mitchum found himself, so he said, once again hoodwinked, working long days without a break, the fishing tackle lying idle on the floor of his hotel room. The shooting went smoothly, Mitchum and the director working together with inspired synchronicity and a surprising enthusiasm for one another's seemingly very different styles—Mitchum the king of just-do-it, outwardly antifussy moviemaking, Minnelli a delicate, aesthetic personality and a rapturous stylist who could spend all day getting a leaf in a gutter to lie just so before committing it to film. Mitchum told Vincente he had many acquaintances like Hunnicutt and was basing his interpretation of the character on some of these men. Perhaps in the philandering and violently macho captain he may have seen aspects of an even closer acquaintance from which to draw his inspiration.

Mitchum had been around long enough now, his reputation on- and offscreen looming large before him, that the cast's two newcomers, the two Georges, tended for a while to stare and tremble when working with such a living legend.

"They were impressed because I was very impressive," said Mitchum. "I was like someone an old cameraman used to describe when I was over at RKO. He was an Argentine-Italian and I think illiterate. He'd probably started out as Bessie Love's gardener or something. To him, a woman artist was anyone who made over a thousand dollars a week. If she got less, she had to be a whore. Why else would she hang out with foulmouthed guys and juicers? I was an artist to Peppard and Hamilton in the same way."

"I don't know why Bob puts on his act," said Minnelli. "Few actors I've worked with bring so much of themselves to a picture, and none do it with such total lack of affectation as Mitchum does."

Speaking of affectation, both the young actors in the film were giving excellent performances, but Peppard's came with a lot of baggage. He was fresh from the New York theater and Strasberg's Actor's Studio, full of thespian theorums and wary if not outright contemptuous of the ways of Hollywood.

"Have you studied the Stanislavsky Method?" he asked Mitchum.

"No," said Mitchum, "but I've studied the Smirnoff Method."

Peppard and Minnelli did not see eye to eye. The actor did not like to do certain of his more difficult scenes until he could really *feel* them. Minnelli (ignoring his own directorial fussiness) told Peppard that was fine for Greenwich Village but in the movies you started to "feel" the scene when you got off the bus at the location. The hot-tempered Peppard decided that instead of compromising he was going to tell Minnelli and MGM to shove it, and shared his decision with someone he imagined would understand, that rebellious spirit Bob Mitchum. To his surprise, the older man advised caution. Mitchum said, "It'll be a very expensive hike. I'm sure the studio can sue you. I'm certain it will be your last job. Even though you think Minnelli is wrong, do it his way."

After three weeks in Mississippi, they moved back to the Metro lot in Culver City for a month, then off on a second location trip to the town of Paris, Texas ("Minnelli shoots all his pictures in Paris," Mitchum cracked), the actual setting of William Humphrey's novel. Most of the two-week visit was spent filming a wild boar hunt, *Home from the Hill*'s great visual showpiece, which Minnelli put together with all the cinematic flourish of his greatest musical sequences. They filmed in an area near Paris that Gigi would not have found *sympathetique,* a wooded, sulfurous swamp filled with copperhead snakes and quicksand.

The final stage of the hunt, with the battle between the wild boar and the hunting dogs, was shot back on the MGM lot. A big boar was imported from Louisiana but was found dead on arrival. Instead a big pig was used, and tusks were glued to its face. To make it stagger and fall over, they shot it up with tranquilizers.

After the last six weeks at the studio, the lengthy film (with a final running time of two hours and thirty-two minutes) was completed early in August, by which time Mitchum was already in Ireland on another job. With *Some Came Running, Home from the Hill* was the finest of Minnelli's operatic/neurotic wide-screen melodramas, a lurid, flamboyantly emotional and yet deeply incisive exploration of family life at its most destructive. Mitchum's powerful performance as the fierce, ultimately poignant Captain Hunnicutt gave more credence to those, like Laughton and Huston, who envisioned the actor triumphing as one or another of Shakespeare's tragic heroes. Critics applauded Mitchum's work, but they were more excited by the strong, youthful, and promising newcomer George Peppard. What could you expect, Mitchum would say. He had been around a long time since the press had first fussed over him in *G.I. Joe.* Yesterday's news and then some. It was like that old joke you heard actors telling around the lunch table, the rise and fall trajectory of a Hollywood star:

"Who is Robert Mitchum?"
"Get me Robert Mitchum."
"Get me a Robert Mitchum type."
"Who is Robert Mitchum?"

He began a new three-picture commitment to United Artists with a film produced jointly by Raymond Stross and DRM, *The Night Fighters* (aka *A Terrible Beauty*), an action drama of Irish Republican Army terrorists attacking British interests during World War II. As Dermot O'Neill, Mitchum would play yet another revolutionary and his most reluctant hero to date, a dim and drunken boy-o who joins the IRA on a whim, finds it not much to his liking, and in the end turns informer. Though Hollywood usually took the freedom fighters' side in films about "the troubles," this was a British production and so a more *objective* take on the subject, with

IRA members here including ruthless opportunists associating with Nazis and the protagonist a good man at heart who sees the light and betrays his revolutionary friends. At the least it was unusual and intriguing subject matter for a film, and its appeal to Mitchum—revolution, exotic setting, outsider hero, drinking scenes—was apparent.

Mitchum hired his *One Minute to Zero* director, Tay Garnett, whose career had fallen on hard times. He had not gotten a feature assignment in five years and was reduced to directing half-hour television programs. Thinking that perhaps his low fortunes were due to bad habits, he had given up drinking and become a member of Alcoholics Anonymous. Garnett thought *The Night Fighters* script lousy and believed it would invite invidious comparisons with Ford's classic *The Informer,* but he was in no position to promote negative thinking and hoped it could all be made right once they got to Dublin.

It wasn't. The film is best remembered, if at all, for Mitchum's impeccable Irish accent. "There is still an elemental force in the story," he said. "But it's like looking for a diamond that's been covered in sewage. You know it's there, but man, does it smell."

An incident in a Dublin bar after a day of filming at the Ardmore Studio got more attention than the movie ever would. A short, flyweight Irishman came up to Mitchum and poked him in the ribs with a pencil.

"Hey, movie star," he said, "give me your autograph. It's for me wife."

Mitchum said, "Look at the leprechaun," and told him to wait until he had finished his drink. "But, he didn't want to wait and told me so."

Mitchum took the man's paper and pencil and wrote, "FUCK YOU," signed it "KIRK DOUGLAS," and handed it back.

The man returned, having read the inscription, pulled Mitchum around, and threw a fist at his right eye. Mitchum looked down and said, "If that's the best you can do, little lady, you better come back with your girlfriends."

Richard Harris, Bob's drinking buddy and fellow actor in *The*

Night Fighters, said, "He hit Mitchum full in the face when he wasn't looking. Mitch could have killed him, but he just shrugged it off like he does in film fights. He was wonderful."

The man returned with a few more autograph hunters. Mitchum head-butted one of them and sent him reeling. Then two of the others attacked, inspiring Richard Harris and a couple of Abbey Theatre Players to come to Bob's aid. A huge "donnybrook" ensued, and the police were summoned to break it up. A colorful consensus account of the brawl animated the world's newspapers the next day, most of them delighted by the possibility that bruiser Mitchum had finally met his match—"MITCHUM REFUSES FIGHT WITH MUCH SMALLER MAN," "MITCHUM FLIPS FOR IRISHMAN," and "BLACK-EYED MITCHUM IS MEEK," said the headlines, one account describing how the movie star was "tossed for a loop by a short, limping Irishman," while another claimed the brawny Yank had been given a "ju-jitsu flip" and knocked out cold by a midget.

Warner Bros. and Fred Zinnemann were producing a film of Australian Jon Cleary's highly regarded novel *The Sundowners.* It was the picaresque story of the footloose Carmody family, Paddy, Ida and son Sean, and their wandering adventures in the rural Outback, the title derived from the family's nomadic existence— home was wherever they happened to be at sundown. In 1959, after a series of distinguished box office and critical successes (*High Noon, From Here to Eternity, Oklahoma, The Nun's Story*), Zinnemann was at his zenith, the standard-bearer for mature, adult, big-budget film-making. His movies were the sort the tastemakers considered good entertainment and good for you, too, and his projects and associates were invariable award nominees and frequent winners. For *The Sundowners,* Zinnemann cast Deborah Kerr as the loving, long-suffering wife (he had directed her to an Oscar in *From Here to Eternity*) and Robert Mitchum as the beer-swilling, sheep-shearing, irresponsible Paddy. (Zinnemann had long hoped to work with him and had originally cast him opposite Kerr in *Eternity,* but Howard Hughes had refused a loan-out). Kerr's involvement convinced Mitchum to sign on, though it would mean flying to Australia with barely a day off after his Irish sojourn. Others hired for the film were Peter Ustinov as a comical remittance man, Glynis Johns as a saucy hotel keeper, Michael Anderson, Jr., as Sean, Dina Merrill as a station owner's wife, and a few native sons like Chips Rafferty taking supporting roles. The Carmody's racehorse was to be played by a well-known retired turf champion, Silver Shadow, and pulling the family cart would be a thirty-year-old named Sam, once awarded the title Most Handsome Milk Horse in a Sydney beauty contest.

Jack Warner had attempted to get Zinnemann to shoot the picture in Arizona; there ought to be a couple of kangaroos in the Phoenix Zoo, he told him. Zinnemann was adamant, saying that without the uncountable atmospheric details of the genuine locations *The Sundowners* would look like nothing more than "a half-assed Western." Glancing again at the returns on Zinnemann's *The Nun's Story,* Warner agreed.

Mitchum arrived at Kingsford Smith Airport at three in the morning on September 28, straggled wearily from the plane he had been on for what seemed like weeks, only to see a mob of Aussie reporters charging him, he claimed, screaming, "How do you like our beer?"

Housed at the Hotel Australia in Sydney for a few days to rest and soak up the local speech patterns, Mitchum sparred with some of the nation's impudent newspapermen, who trotted out a long list of the actor's transgressions for amiable discussion. Sucking at a vodka and tomato juice, chain-smoking Mexican cigarettes, Mitchum claimed it was all a case of mistaken identity. "I'm no tough guy. . . . All the public knows is some silver, chromium-plated jerk. How could they really know what I'm like?" And as for that marijuana beef, Mitchum explained once again that his conviction had been removed from the record. "Well, all this was news to me," wrote one Down Under Winchell next day. "No mention of this *expunging* the conviction never [sic] got to Australia. But try as I might, I couldn't budge Bob Mitchum from his story. So that was the sum total: he isn't a jailbird, he isn't a drunk, he isn't a brawler. And he was too big for me to argue with. So I left."

With a cast made up largely of English and American actors,

Zinnemann prayed they would all be able to approximate an Oz accent that would at least not sound ridiculous. Mitchum astounded him. "His Australian accent was perfect; he had the uncanny knack of making any accent sound as though he had been born with it." Zinnemann found Bob amusing and delightful company, was much taken with his "colorful" way of expressing himself. "If, for instance, he had to go to the toilet, he would say, 'I've got to drain my lizard,'" Zinnemann said. "He is one of the wittiest and most respectful men I have ever met."

Deborah Kerr, arriving with boyfriend Peter Viertel, the movie writer and novelist, renewed her respectful love affair with Mitchum. "It was an honor to feed her lines," Mitchum said, "even in this godforsaken country."

They began filming in the area around the small town of Cooma. Mitchum moved into a hired house. He had a cook, a chauffeur, and an English secretary/manservant. He fished in the local "alpine" stream and caught a single trout. The weather was bitterly cold, and fires burned in every room of the house. It poured rain and production shut down. From the start, Mitchum seemed to react badly to the aggressively starstruck Australian public. "He didn't get along with the Aussies very well," said Fred Zinnemann. "He felt victimized and outraged by the blunt possessiveness of the local fans and autograph-hunters."

In Cooma he was followed everywhere he went. An audience gathered to watch him eat a steak in a local restaurant, standing stock-still for each course as if they were watching a play. The gawkers, a foul mood, and the rotten weather sent Mitchum into hiding in his villa at the edge of town. He was reportedly "bored stiff," but seldom ventured outside. "He's like a caged tiger waiting for production to start," said his shuddering personal assistant, Brian Own-Smith of London. "He's a regular Lonely Garbo," wrote one newshawk. Cooma's citizenry kept their eyes open, but spottings of the American movie star were rare and were much talked about when they occurred. There were tales told that he had insulted a woman in a hotel and that he had "jobbed" a man in a barber's shop. "He's a real sleepy lizard when he's sitting in the sun," a postman was quoted. "Then I watched him cross the street. He's the breathing image of Paddy Carmody, I tell you!" An eleven year old had a run-in on the road and reporters rushed to gather her story. "He gave me his autograph," said Bobundra's Jill Singleton. "Gee, he's a beaut bloke."

One Sydney reporter on the scene managed to wrangle his way inside the Mitchum manse and found the actor fixing an onion-laced beef stew. "Robert's a real homebody," said Own-Smith. "He's a marvelous cook, the dishes he makes are delicious! He went into Cooma twice, but many people followed him. Of course Robert likes meeting people and signing autographs but he doesn't like it when they crush all around him. Some people try to be too smart. They push an old piece of torn paper under his nose and say, 'Sign this, you!' and not even 'please.' That's when Robert jumps up and grabs them around the neck and says, 'Where are your manners, buster?'" In the kitchen Mitchum stood over a bubbling concoction while a maid scrubbed vegetables, the chauffeur searched for black pepper, and the valet drank vodka beside the broom cupboard.

"These rumors that my first housekeeper left because I was walking around undressed are wrong. I let her go because she never smiled. . . . I told her, 'Wash your hands, little lady, we don't need you around here any more. . . .' When the hell does it stop raining? . . . Sure, I get about two hundred thousand bucks for this picture, but I don't see any of it. Every cent of it goes into a Swiss company. It's held in trust for my kids. . . . 'Jobbed' a man in a barber shop? Do I look like a guy who's been near a barber shop? . . . I don't meet any people. I'm here for work. Pubs—I don't go into them. Not much. I like mixing my own drinks at home. I like my own cooking. . . . If you like, you can just call me Mother."

When Paul De Coque, the young Cooma man Warners had hired to drive Mitchum around, learned that a close relative had fallen ill in Sydney, Mitchum gave him several hundred dollars and told him to take the company station wagon. "If you need anything at all, don't hesitate to let me know," Mitchum said.

He spent a pleasant day with *The Sundowners'* author, Jon Cleary.

The Sydney *Sun* reported it with the headline "BOB'S NOT A SLOB." Cleary was quoted for the record: "Robert Mitchum is anything but a droopy-eyed slob once you get to know him. He is extremely well read and writes beautiful poetry."

On November 12, Dorothy Mitchum arrived in Sydney from California for a ten-day location visit, and reporters swarmed her flight, too.

"This Mrs. Mitchum's quite a doll," said the man from the *Daily Telegraph*. "Tall and slim and built to all the right specifications. 'I'm traveling reasonably light,' she announced when she arrived and wearily deposited a mink coat and a gigantic stack of parcels on top of her luggage. 'Usually I have to lug a whole strange assortment of things along for Robert. Records and sunglasses and what have you, because he's always giving things away.' We know, Mrs. M., we know. When we shot down to see him in Cooma he gave us quite a hangover!"

At the end of the month Dorothy had returned home, and *The Sundowners* company headed for Port Augusta in the south. From here they would be commuting most days to the sheep station at Iron Knob, a forty-minute drive from the port. Arriving at tiny Whyalla Airport where reporters and fans clamored in the 104-degree heat, Mitchum, looking like a "shaggy caveman" to one observer and hiding his "sleepy peepers" behind outsized sunglasses, brushed aside the crowds and motored off to the luxury cruiser *Corsair III* he had chartered at a cost of a hundred pounds a week. Dina Merrill recalled, "We saw little of him after work. Everyone else—except for Deborah, who found a little house, but she had most of her meals with us—was staying at this little hotel. We took over the whole place except for a couple of itinerant salesmen passing through from time to time. There were only four of us had their own bathroom, and I was very fortunate I was one of them! And they were the smallest rooms you ever saw in your life. Mitchum, though, spent all his time on his boat out in the harbor. He wanted to get away from all the people who were bothering him. But young ladies were known to swim out there to the boat. It was rather amusing—the women trying to climb on the boat and Mitchum trying to keep them away."

Adhering to the code of the sea, perhaps, Mitchum eventually let a few of these aquatic intruders come on board. Some local "sheilas" happily confessed to attending a "wow of a party" on the shaggy man's cruiser.

Each morning the company boarded vehicles to take them to the sheep station at Iron Knob, a long, bumpy ride across the hot, barren, fly-infested countryside. "You can't imagine how hot it was, how dry and dusty," said Mitchum. "I was clean only twice during the entire shooting."

"The dust flew along the whole road," said Dina Merrill. "It was terrible. I shared a driver and car with Peter Ustinov, who made it at least bearable. He liked to drive and so we used to put the driver in the backseat and the two of us would sit up front, and Peter would sing a different opera every day, not only singing the parts but doing the instruments. He had us laughing so hard we couldn't get out of the car when we got there."

At Iron Knob Mitchum encountered something even more intimidating than the local autograph seekers. "Those sheep in Australia stand as high as a pony, and I didn't know where the hair left off and the meat started," he said. He was always very tenderly disposed toward animals, and the prospect of shearing the plumply beautiful four-hundred-pound merinos—and doing it at top speed, taking the entire fleece off in one piece—filled him with dread. "He was terrified of cutting off a nipple, or a vein running close to the surface under the sheep's left jaw," Fred Zinnemann recalled. "This would make the sheep bleed to death. Mitchum was unable to do the job without first having several bottles of beer."

The actor was more in his element during the film's big brawl between the two rival gangs of sheepshearers. Now at last he found common ground with the Aussies who, on a merciless 108-degree afternoon, took to the action with ecstatic enthusiasm, slugging, jumping, breaking ribs, continuing long after Zinnemann and several assistants had repeatedly screamed, "Cut!" Mitchum, said the director, "had great fun."

*

On December 17 Mitchum, Kerr, Ustinov, and others from the production boarded a Pan Am Boeing 707 headed for the States and a Christmas break before a final few weeks of interior filming in London. Reporters and others once again dogging his trail, Mitchum remained grumpy and incommunicative, saying only that he had seen little of the country he was leaving, had done nothing else but work, and was completely "cheesed off." Harumphing his way to the aircraft, Mitchum was intercepted by a small girl and appeared to visibly soften at her request for an autograph.

"I have a little seven-year-old daughter, too," Mitchum said, and scribbled on the Aussie girl's pad: "In a country which with casual aplomb regards the anachronism of the kangaroo and the platypus—the being homo sapien is a disgusting oddity—Merry Christmas, Bob Mitchum."

He then picked up his bag and boarded the plane.

Mitchum's performance in *The Sundowners* met with universal acclaim. Perhaps the unusual backdrop and a contrived accent helped the critics to see beyond the widely perceived notion of Mitchum as an actor who simply "played himself." As Paddy Carmody, a living, breathing creation without a hint of artifice or theatricality, Mitchum gave perhaps the greatest demonstration of his supreme command of a naturalistic acting technique that was as rare as it was—generally—underappreciated. (Of course, this is not to deny that the charming but irresponsible and selfish vagabond Carmody had possibly more than a little in common with the man who portrayed him.)

It was a unique and wonderful movie, had a warm humanity, a jaunty sweetness, an enticing, lyrical aimlessness. The simple yet poetic imagery, the rowdy humor, the sense of the sublime in the everyday brought to mind the work of John Ford but minus Ford's sentimental or melodramatic excesses. *The Sundowners,* even Mitchum had to admit, was no gorilla picture. The film received numerous award citations and nominations at year's end, with

Mitchum named as Best Actor by the venerable National Board of Review in New York. *The Sundowners* got five Oscar nominations, including Best Picture and Best Actress for Deborah Kerr, but Mitchum, to many people's surprise, was not recognized by the Academy. The film was a good earner at its initial engagements in New York, Los Angeles, and other major cities, but its returns faded in the rest of the country. Zinnemann believed that a misconceived and misleading publicity campaign accentuating the sexuality of Deborah Kerr ("the impression given that she . . . could hardly wait for the sun to go down so she could lay her hands on Bob") harmed the film's potential success.

Although contractually entitled to top billing for *The Sundowners,* Mitchum ceded the position to Deborah Kerr at her request. "I told them by all means . . . and that they could design a twenty-four sheet of me bowing to her, I couldn't care less."

His curiously unpleasant relations with Australia continued long after his final departure. The country served him with a substantial income tax bill for his *Sundowners* earnings. He refused to pay, claiming he had never been working for an Australian employer, but the Oz tax collectors harassed him for several years to come.

Mitchum remained in London to make *The Grass Is Greener* for producer-director Stanley Donen. It was an ersatz Noel Coward drawing room comedy about a high-born English couple and the restless wife's tentative fling with a rich Texas tourist. The all-star production had Mitchum working once again with Deborah Kerr and Jean Simmons (his third go-round with each) and for the first time with Cary Grant, who took over when Rex Harrison withdrew after the death of his wife, Kay Kendall.

Mitchum and Grant fell into a mild, undeclared rivalry. Grant fretted that Mitchum's casual style was making him look over-rehearsed, and whispered to wardrobe that Bob's understarched shirts were perhaps a tad sloppy even for a Texan. Mitchum complained that his role seemed to be entirely a matter of saying, "Really?" and, "Oh?" in between Grant's monologues. He liked Cary well enough, found him expectedly charming, though rather odd and a solid square. "No sense of humor," he told Chris Peachment and Geoff Andrew. "His humor is sort of old music-hall jokes. 'What's that noise down there? They're holding an Elephant's Ball? Well, I wish they'd let go of it, I'm trying to get some sleep!' I guess that was when he was coming off his LSD treatment."

The finished film was a polished bore. Hollywood's Stanley Donen, in his expatriate phase, had directed with such artistocratic preciocity he might have been expecting a knighthood for his labors. Neither of the male stars was well served by the material. Grant's purring, ironic suavity always worked best when he played quasi-hustlers or schlemiels, not smug noblemen; and Mitchum, enacting a ballsier variation of what screwball comedy aficionados would know as the "Ralph Bellamy role," was constitutionally ill-equipped to do this sort of brittle, one-raised-eyebrow frolic. For Mitchum's sardonic wit and fatalistic insouciance to resonate he needed a dangerous setting, a life-or-death situation, not a plush London vacation. Sparkling Jean Simmons, with little to do in a ditzy best-friend role, stole the picture from all of them.

*

Even worse was an all-American comedy, The Last Time I Saw Archie, ostensibly based on the army experiences of veteran Hollywood scribe William Bowers and his adventures with an amiable con man of a private named Archie Hall. It was a first attempt at humor for the ordinarily glum producer-director-actor Jack "Just the Facts" Webb, the frog-faced star of television's Dragnet, here playing the wry, long-suffering Bowers to Mitchum's impudent Archie. Television was the operative word: The whole thing resembled an extended episode of a sitcom, from the cheap gray sets, functional photography, and presence of supporting players like Louis Nye, Don Knotts, and Joe Flynn, to the characters and jokes out of a lesser episode of Sgt. Bilko. It lacked only the canned titters and guffaws of a laugh track—and brother, it needed them. No attempt was made to make the supposed World War II setting look anything other than 1960s contemporary, and the cast of jowly, middle-aged actors were all twenty years too old for their parts. The film was relentlessly modest, even by sitcom standards, with little or nothing happening for most of the running time. The script posited Archie as a world-class operator who fascinates and infuriates everyone he meets, but the character Mitchum actually brings to half-life on screen is bland and indescribably lethargic. The real Archie Hall, William Bowers's army buddy, sued the filmmakers for invasion of privacy, but the dullness of Mitchum's incarnation made defamation of character a more appropriate charge. Mitchum relished referring to this mediocrity as his favorite film of all time, based on a simple equation: four weeks' work times a hundred thousand dollars a week.

During the Belmont Farms years, when work took him back to Los Angeles for weeks and months, Mitchum made his headquarters at the Beverly Hills Hotel, the "pink palace" above Sunset Boulevard. The hotel pampered its celebrated guests with customized service, and Mitchum's personal guest file included a stipulated eye-opener and hangover cure that was destined never to be added to the regular menu—bourbon and orange juice blended with honey and eggs.

As a guest, Mitchum did not always return their graciousness with model behavior. His suite became a rowdy bachelor pad at times. Longtime bellman Jack Keith recalled one four-day-long Mitchum bacchanale as most likely the wildest in the hotel's history. "It had everything—booze, broads, and guys. It went on in two suites, Mitchum's and this other fellow's, which were together. All I can remember is everybody walked around in various stages of undress."

*

Gregory Peck and British director J. Lee Thompson were making *The Guns of Navarone* in Europe when the star handed the director a copy of John D. MacDonald's novel *The Executioners*. Peck was going to make it the first feature for his new production company, with Universal picking up the tab. "We were working so well together," said Thompson, "and he was very happy with *Navarone*. He said, 'Read this. I'd like us to make this one next.'" John D. MacDonald, one of the last of the writers to come out of the hard-boiled pulp magazines, had written a tough, merciless suspense story, and screenwriter James R. Webb's adaptation would be even tougher: the story of a lawyer whose life becomes a nightmare when a sadistic ex-con he helped send to prison returns seeking revenge. No simple hooligan, Max Cady cleverly perverts the law to protect himself even as he stalks and terrorizes the attorney and his young family. Hitchcock's *Psycho* had recently set a new standard for movie suspense, and Peck thought that a film of *The Executioners* could deliver the same kind of terrifying thrills with a much more realistic story.

"I liked the book very much," said Thompson. "Greg had a script being prepared, we signed the contracts, and I came to make my first picture in Hollywood. Originally there was a certain budget, and it was assumed that Greg would be the only star in this, his own production. We considered some other actors. Rod Steiger was one, and Telly Savalas was another. We actually tested Savalas, and he gave a very good test for the part. But these were character actors, or at least secondary actors compared to Greg. At some point in discussing it together, we began to talk about having the villain played by an actor of equal importance, make it a much stronger matchup from the audience's point of view, and then Mitchum immediately came to mind. There were some problems—he was not available in the beginning and it meant changing the budget—but once we had seen Mitchum in the role we knew he was superbly right for it, and Greg did what had to be done to get him."

Mitchum came to a meeting with Thompson and Peck at Peck's office on the Universal lot. He had no interest in doing it, he said. He had been working too much. He was going back to his farm in Maryland and taking a long rest. Peck and Thompson got him talking about the script, about the character of Max Cady. Yes, Mitchum admitted, he had liked the story, the way it showed how the law really operated, how the cops held all the cards, bent the rules to serve their ends, and how one man gave it back to them.

That was something you didn't see too often. "Who else could do this, Bob?" Peck and Thompson asked. "What about Jack Palance?" That'd be over the top before the opening fade-in, Mitchum said. "The whole thing with Cady, fellas, is that snakelike charm. *Me*, officer? I never laid a hand on the girl, you *must* be mistaken."

"We discussed the part thoroughly," said J. Lee Thompson, "and when we heard Mitchum's thoughts we were more convinced than ever that he would be terrific for the role. And I think by the end of the meeting he now realized that himself. But he still couldn't make up his mind and wouldn't agree to it."

Mitchum flew back to Maryland. In the morning there was a delivery: a bouquet of flowers, a case of bourbon, and a note— "Please do the film!" A little later in the day he called Los Angeles. "OK. I've drunk your bourbon. I'm drunk. I'll do it."

They were calling the picture *Cape Fear*.

The MacDonald book takes place in the Carolinas. Director Thompson traveled around scouting locations mentioned in the book but didn't like any of them, then found a town in Georgia he thought would be perfect. "Fucking Savannah!" Mitchum said, when he learned where the film would be made. "They railroaded me in that town, man. They may still have a warrant out for me. . . ."

"Oh, he spoke at length about what he thought of Savannah," J. Lee Thompson recalled. "How much he disliked the people there. He had a definite grudge. And he had it the entire time we filmed. We got down there and he had a great big chip on his shoulder about the whole place, had contempt for everyone there. And he loved that he had come as a big movie star, where everyone was asking for his autograph, and before they had thrown him in jail."

"We were all put up at the DeSoto Hotel," said Assistant Director Ray Gosnell. "And word got around that Mitchum had had some problems in Savannah in the past, but I think he settled down and enjoyed himself. It was a very, very friendly place. And the day we arrived there was a convention of southern hairdressers, all these females from beauty salons all over the area, and they were very friendly and made quite a welcoming committee for Mitchum and some of the members of the crew. I don't think some of them ever got to their own rooms at all that night."

"You know, Mitchum would give the impression he didn't take the job seriously," said Thompson. "He would go out and have a good time all night and come to work and act like he hadn't learned his lines. You know, sort of saying, 'What is this thing; where are we?'—looking at the script like it was for the first time. But then he would work perfectly. Highly professional. He just goes in and does it. And he was superb."

The contrast between the characters of Cady and lawyer Sam Bowden was mirrored somewhat by the personalities of the two stars. Peck was a straight arrow, took the job of acting seriously, was thorough, analytical. Mitchum liked to make a show of being off the cuff, mocked seriousness. As if to emphasize that parallel, Mitchum did some taunting of his more regimented costar. "Peck," said Ray Gosnell, "always requested there be no distractions off camera. No one standing around in his eye line when he was doing a scene. So if there were grips or people standing around where he could see them, we always needed to clear them all out of the way. Mitchum always thought that was a joke. One time we had cleared the sight-line area for Peck to do the scene and Mitchum arrived to put on wardrobe for a scene and he went right over to where Peck could see him and started stripping, taking off all his clothes. I think it was just a gag; he was trying to see if he could shake him up."

What might have made the teasing more difficult to take was the realization that Mitchum was stealing the picture. "From the first time Peck gave me the book to read, he said that he would be playing the lawyer, and he said that Cady was probably the better part," said Thompson. "And when Mitchum signed on, Greg had a feeling he might run away with it. And as we came to shoot the film, his fear was being realized—Mitchum's characterization was so strong. But this was Peck's film company and he had hired Mitchum, and I know that Peck was very fond of Mitchum as a person and admired his performance all through the film. He never let it get him upset or felt any jealousy or anything like that, always full of praise for

Mitchum. And you know he gave a magnificent performance against a character that was far more colorful."

Weather conditions and various dissatisfactions brought the *Cape Fear* company back to Los Angeles sooner than expected. Interiors were shot at Universal, the last-act scenes aboard the boat and in the water filmed in the studio lake and on the coast around Ventura. Now they were shooting the film's most violent and emotionally charged scenes, and the nature of these became reflected in the atmosphere on the sets and particularly in the man playing Max Cady.

Mitchum said to J. Lee Thompson, "You know, I *live* a character. And this character drinks and rapes."

"That gave me pause, you know. And he did fulfill some of that. And when we had the violent scenes, he did work himself up. When he was playing one of those scenes he looked at you like he was going to kill you. You had to watch him because he really played the part. You had to be careful to control him—not the acting, but he might go over the top physically. There was a scene with Barrie Chase, where he's being very rough with her. And I had to stop filming at one or two points to let things cool down. But I was certainly glad to get it all on camera. Barrie Chase was frightened of him; I know that because she told me so. She admired him, as everyone did. But, you know, he made people frightened."

The climactic battle in the water between Peck and Mitchum took days to film, shooting at night on Universal's back lot lake. "It was freezing cold," Ray Gosnell remembered. "We put these warmers in the water, but you know there's no way of keeping a lake warm. And the actors had to wrestle in there for the better part of a week, at night."

"Mitchum enjoyed those scenes, I think," said Thompson. "He liked getting in the water and having that fight with Greg. I'm not too sure about Greg liking it, because he was on the receiving end. He had to be forced underwater, and Mitchum kept him under there for quite a long time. We devised a code so that Peck could come up if it was getting too much for him. But sometimes Mitchum overstepped the line. I mean, he was meant to be drowning Greg, and he really took it to the limit. We had to send a man in to get Greg up. It was a bit of a worry. But Peck took it marvelously; he never complained. I expected there to be some outburst from Peck, but he was a real sport about the whole thing. And it looked marvelous on film."

Cape Fear's most violent sequence, the last scene to be shot, involved Max Cady's brutalizing and sexual assault on Bowden's wife, Peggy, well played by Polly Bergen, whose usual elegance and poise made her violation and reduction to hysteria in these moments all the more frightening. Thompson, Bergen, and Mitchum all sensed the electric possibilities in the scene. Everything had been building to this, Cady's ultimate, horrible explosion of sadistic fury, meant to bring the audience to a peak of dread and anguish before the climactic release of the final battle and the—not triumph, but bare survival of good over evil. Mitchum roamed the set, bare-chested, sweating, building himself into a rage. There was no joking with the crew, tossing away a cigarette, and "Roll 'em" this time. "He was like a fireball," said Thompson. "You felt any moment he would explode, an eruption. We got ready for it, and we talked over the action. But there was no rehearsal. I thought we should just do it. We just talked it over a bit what they should do and added things, invented on the spur of the moment. And I improvised the business with the eggs. To crack the egg on the chest, the symbolism of it. Mitchum liked that very much."

The camera turned. Mitchum's fury was released.

"He just . . . lost it," said Polly Bergen.

"It went much further then we were ever able to use," said Thompson. "He smeared the eggs over her chest and down over her breasts and so forth."

Mitchum's flailing arm hit a cabinet, ripping his hand open. Dripping blood from his fingers, he grabbed Bergen by the shoulders and thrust her against the cabin door. The door was fixed to spring open, but as the actress remembered it the catch had come down and Mitchum simply broke it open, using her back as a battering ram. "His hand was covered in blood, my back was covered in blood," she said. He slammed her into the other room and continued the assault. The director called, "Cut!" Called it twice more, then people rushed onto the set to break it up. "We just kept going," said Bergen, "caught up in the scene. They came over and physically stopped us."

Mitchum realized what he had done, Bergen said, and took her in his arms, rocking her gently, saying, "I'm so sorry, I'm so sorry. . . ."

Then, according to Mitchum's less warm and fuzzy recollection of the moment, she told him, "Don't apologize . . . I dig it!"

Hollywood was in a transitional phase in the early '60s, the prim standards of the previous thirty years fading away, but the moral watchdogs were not yet ready for anything as dark and transgressive as the *Cape Fear* put together by Thompson, producer Peck, Mitchum, screenwriter James Webb, composer Bernard Herrmann (a brilliant Hitchcockian score, seething with menace), and the rest. The censors demanded that all use of the word *rape* be removed. They insisted that Mitchum's lascivious leering at young Lori Martin be cut to the bone. The assault on Polly Bergen and Mitchum's original use for an egg had to be similarly reduced to little more than an ugly implication and not the ejaculative horror they had shot. "They made us cut so much," said Thompson. "If we had made it a few years later we could have gotten it through, I think, but not then. Censors wouldn't stand for it. Would have been much stronger otherwise. Still, pretty good picture, I think."

Critics—some of them—thought it sadistic, repellent, "close to pornography," though few could deny it was spectacularly effective entertainment, a relentlessly gripping thrill ride, or that Mitchum's raping, murdering, dog-poisoning Max Cady, performed with absolute conviction and a quality of self-righteousness (Mitchum would reveal that, until things got out of hand at the end, the way *he* read the script was that *Peck* was the bad guy), a portrait of redneck monstrousness with his imperious strut and his fat cigars and natty Panama hat and his face of smiling hatred, was a stunning and utterly unforgettable creation.

"It's Bob's picture," said Gregory Peck, a gentleman. "Best performance he ever gave."

In the mid-'50s, Darryl F. Zanuck, the youngest of the original gold-en age moguls, had abdicated his throne at 20th Century-Fox and run out on his family, going abroad to produce his own films under the DFZ banner and to salve a midlife crisis with a series of Parisian mistresses. The DFZ productions that followed would be a mixture of dull exotica (*Island in the Sun, Roots of Heaven, The Sun Also Rises*) and debacle (*Crack in the Mirror, The Big Gamble*), and Zanuck was at a creative nadir and considered something of a has-been when he decided to make a film of Cornelius Ryan's nonfiction account of the June 1944 Allied invasion of France called *The Longest Day*. Zanuck quickly began to envision it as a sweeping, spectacular production, the war film to end all war films, and not incidentally a certain vindication and return to glory—at the least a last hurrah—for the tarnished Hollywood tycoon. Zanuck and his team put together an amazing collection of vintage and recreated military matériel and won the cooperation of American and French military commands for the use of equipment and working troops numbering in the thousands. For the film's most elaborate sequences, Zanuck commanded an operation very nearly as large as the actual D day invasion itself.

Spending freely, calling in favors, and making full use of any per-formers under contract to Fox, Zanuck tried to fill even the smallest of the more than sixty parts in the film with a name actor, everyone from Henry Fonda, Jean Louis Barrault, and Richard Burton (who flew to Paris for forty-eight hours during a weekend off from shoot-ing *Cleopatra* in Rome), to teen idols Tommy Sands, Paul Anka, and Fabian. In truth, though, the long cast list contained only two major stars at the time of the filming in 1961, John Wayne and Robert Mitchum, and Mitchum could arguably lay claim to having the film's leading or at least most substantial role. As Gen. Norman Cota, Allied commander of the Twenty-ninth Infantry Division at the bloody Omaha Beach assault where 7,400 American troops were lost, Mitchum would be seen in the tension-filled sequences prior to the invasion and then in the thick of the most spectacular and rugged fighting on the beach. And Mitchum would have the last, perfectly understated line in the epic picture, spoken to his driver after a final glance at the horrible carnage of victory: "OK, run me up the hill, son." Mitchum's powerfully assured and believable performance made General Cota the embodiment of the film's vision of heroic democratic invaders—humane, fearless, modest, and indomitable.

In November, when Mitchum arrived in France to shoot his outdoor scenes, Zanuck's D day had been under way for several months. He had now virtually taken over the Ile de Rey, two hundred miles south of Normandy in the Bay of Biscay. The filming had become the focus of great excitement throughout the country and had involved at some point almost every figure in French culture and politics up to and including Charles de Gaulle, who released to Zanuck the use of one thousand commandos brought back from the Algerian War and had threatened to imprison a group of oyster bed owners who had complained that some of Zanuck's forces were destroying their crop of crustaceans. The White House, Congress, and the Pentagon were also de facto advisers to the film, debating the degree of military cooperation, ultimately contributing two hundred fifty troops and millions of dollars' worth of hardware. Zanuck's principal director for the beach invasion scenes was Andrew Marton, best known as a second-unit man, a specialist in outdoors and action footage. Zanuck had also hired Ken Annakin for the scenes involving British troops and then, pleased with the work he was seeing, gave him other things to shoot, including the French-language scenes involving Zanuck's latest girlfriend, Irina Demick.

The low-lying Ile de Rey was often flooded, and the hotel where much of the *Longest Day* people were housed was provided with wooden planks on the floor so guests could go in and out without getting their feet soaked. This was as nothing compared with the conditions on the actual beach-side location (filling in for Normandy's Omaha) where at times the water hit like a crashing express train and the air was filled with stinging, needle-sharp sea spray.

On the day Mitchum began filming the arrival at Omaha, it was miserably cold and rainy, the seas rough. Mitchum and thirty others—actors, soldiers, and stuntmen—waded into the icy water to board a landing craft, which then motored back to the position in deep water where the sequence would begin. Unfortunately, things did not work out so expeditiously with the other landing vessels. There were delays getting the troops aboard, and one craft could not be operated properly and another one had to be brought up in its place. Meanwhile, Mitchum and the others swayed biliously in the rough seas, straining to figure out what was going on back on the beach. Some people got seasick and threw up everywhere. One man, a soldier, Mitchum claimed, kept accidentally firing his rifle and at one point discharged a blank cartridge directly into the star's backside. Mitchum grew furious as the delay went on. What was the problem? It looked like some of the soldiers didn't want to get their feet wet. And over on the beach, Mitchum said, he saw two generals watching the show only until they got a little chilly "and asked for a good fire to keep warm."

At last they were all in position and the filming began. Because of the difficult conditions, the use of military personnel and equipment, the long hours that would be required to load the boats and turn them around again or to replant the explosive charges laid out along the beach, it was crucial to get a good take or something close on the first try. This proved even less easy than was feared. At the signal for action, the beach became a scene of pure chaos. Just the moment before Mitchum leaped out of the landing craft, an explosion went off in the sand. The charge had been planted too near the water—or the tide had shifted—and when it went off it sent a giant plume of sea into the air and then down over everything in the filming area, soaking the camera recording the scene. Realizing that they were about to lose Mitchum's entire landing, Andrew Marton jumped up, tore his shirt from his pants, and wiped the splashed lens dry while the scene went on uninterrupted (Marton claimed he had moved so quickly they lost only four frames of film). The commander of each landing craft had a separate camera crew trained on his group, and forseeing the confusion that would occur, Marton had attached to each main camera the name of each main actor.

"That's your location," he told them, "and whatever you do, whenever you give your orders, you stop there. That's your own camera and you play your scene to it." The gimmick worked perfectly until Eddie Albert lost track of his sign and began stumbling around in confusion. Marton again refused to stop shooting, and ultimately much of the footage of the confused Albert remained in the finished film. "It looked perfectly natural!" said the director.

Both Mitchum and Albert were highly praised by Marton as he recollected to Joanne D'Antonio the trying circumstances of what was indeed a very long day: "Mitchum and Eddie Albert had to be in very cold water; they stood by and were absolutely marvelous. They knew they were doing something which was as close to reality as you could get without getting slashed to pieces."

Later, apparently still angry over the delay in shooting the invasion, Mitchum reportedly made some intemperate remarks to United Press correspondent Robert Ahier, recounting his uncomfortable hours in the landing craft and blaming it all on the cowardice of the participating American soldiers. "The sea was rough," said Mitchum, "and these troops were afraid to board the landing craft to go to sea." He also cast aspersions on the observing brigadier and major generals and their desire for a "good fire to get warm." Newspapers ran the UPI write-up with headlines like this: "GI ACTORS 'AFRAID OF SEA,' MITCHUM SAYS." In Washington, where some members of Congress and officers at the Pentagon had already expressed reservations about the advisability of offering military cooperation to Hollywood hucksters, the shit hit the fan. Zanuck, in a panic, released a statement discrediting the entire story, followed by Mitchum's own official rebuttal: "The statements attributed to me in my interview with the United Press are false and a complete distortion of what I did say. . . . I have the highest respect and admiration for the soldiers who participated with me in the landing scenes on the Ile de Rey. To quote me as saying that they were afraid to board the landing craft borders on the ridiculous." A new round of headlines followed. Typically: "MITCHUM DENIES HE LABELED GIs SCARED."

With the difficult battle scenes shot (many of them creatively and magnificently) and out of the way, and Zanuck having spent his budget and now dipping into his personal funds, the interiors were completed with dispatch at the Boulogne Studios in Paris, the American stars flown into town on a clockwork schedule, put through their paces as quickly as possible, then flown home again.

Ken Annakin: "I went out to visit Andrew Marton when he was in the midst of shooting on Omaha Beach. And Mitchum was there and we chummed it up, slapping of backs, that sort of thing. And I watched what Andy was shooting, wonderful stuff, never been done better. I learned quite a bit from him because, having seen what he was doing, when it came to my stuff I knew I had to at least equal him. By the time we got to the interior stuff I had been on the picture for nearly four months, doing the British scenes and finishing up all the French scenes. And there was never any question of Marton doing any studio stuff—he was a great expert on locations. So I was doing the interiors. We had two marvelous French camera crews. And each American star came back, including Mitchum. We isolated his stuff, and when he became free he came for three or four days in the studio. He came on knowing his lines; it was a job, and he was an ideal person to work with."

Zanuck considered *The Longest Day* his greatest single effort in the movie business and a personal triumph. Compelled by his obsessive attachment to the production, Zanuck expressed an unprecedented desire to assume the director's reins, at least symbolically and for a few moments only. He told Annakin that, although he was very busy upstairs, he thought he would "love to come down to the floor and say, 'Action,' and, 'Cut,'" if Annakin didn't mind stepping aside. "Why the fucking hell should I do that?" said the Englishman to his wife. She convinced him there was no harm in it, and after all they were having a very nice stay in Paris thanks to Mr. Zanuck. And so Annakin would work with Mitchum on scenes and then—on three occasions—wait for Zanuck to come down to the set and say, "Action," and, "Cut," after which, very pleased with himself, the producer would return to his upstairs office. Mitchum, who said he had worked with directors who had done even less, expressed no objection to the former mogul's little play act.

Against the odds, and with little enthusiasm from the studio he had created, Zanuck's "folly" would become his last triumphant success. *The Longest Day* was a tremendous accomplishment, an entertaining yet relatively uncompromised—no love interest, no subplot, no single hero to root for—war movie, a vast production with a sweep and scale greater than any previous Hollywood epic and yet as compellingly realistic—shot in cold tones of black and gray—as any newsreel, or at least any newsreel that included the presence of Fabian and Tommy Sands. It was hailed by most critics as one of the best war films of all time, saluted by veterans as a fitting tribute to the greatest military operation in history, and it was a worldwide hit.

Though his was a brief role in an episodic "all-star" production, Mitchum could share in Zanuck's glory. His prominence, bravura performance, and definitive portrayal of an archetypal American action hero (the intrepid yet unpretentious military man) offered a kind of unofficial confirmation of his rank (just below top-billed John Wayne) among those actors representing American masculinity on the screen, circa 1962.

He had been in the movies for twenty years now. A lot of bad pictures, quite a few good ones, and a handful of gems and masterpieces. He was forty-four years old. A little blearier, a recurring beer gut that had to be worked off from time to time, but overall a fine physical specimen, the passing years giving his ferretlike "garage mechanic's mug" a few more character lines and an added soulful weariness that did more good than harm. And as for the state of his acting, with recent efforts like *The Sundowners, Home from the Hill,* and *Cape Fear* among the incontrovertible evidence, Mitchum's great ability as a movie actor—his range, depth, and power—clearly overwhelmed all but a very few other stars on the scene. Mitchum was in a uniquely flexible place in the Hollywood hierarchy of the day: he was a veteran star with the stature to play the classic American genre roles like the cowboy and the soldier and give them an iconic power no young newcomer could match, and yet he was an adaptable and modern presence as well, a professional risk taker and not inextricably tied to a backward-looking style or genre like Wayne and other older stars. The movies were changing, the old taboos dying off. Hollywood was on the brink of a new era in film realism: more violent, more sexual, more unconventional; and Mitchum was, almost uniquely among his contemporaries, perfectly positioned to thrive in the iconoclastic climate to come. With the full maturation of his talent and the authority of middle age now upon him, and with the arriving zeitgeist embracing the sense of cool and the antiheroic attitude that had long been the actor's emblematic persona (embracing, even, the use of marijuana), the '60s—if such backward prognostications can be given any value—should have been Mitchum's decade much the way the '40s seemed to belong to Bogart. It would only have taken some interesting scripts, another series of challenging parts like the ones that had so frequently enlivened his career in the past few years, some continued alliances with talented directors like Zinnemann and Huston, a little good luck, and the ability to give a damn.

Part four

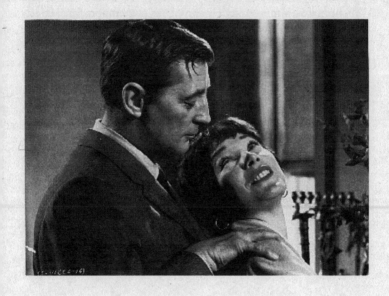

CHAPTER THIRTEEN

Poet with an Ax

Mitchum recalled the first years of his Maryland residence as a "lost, nostalgic, splendid isolation." He did not miss Hollywood; and the town, he said, did not miss him. "I was never very social in California and I'm not social in Maryland. But Maryland is a place in which it's easier not to be social. . . . In Maryland I can be as unsocial as I want . . ."

It was a place to do nothing. Belmont Farms so inspired Mitchum's native indolence that he found himself incapable of meeting even his modest goals of catching some fish or "writing a little." Returned from months away on a picture somewhere, he would quickly melt into the scenery, sleep when he could, eat, drink, watch the squirrels and the raccoons, wait for another beautiful sunset. "I wouldn't even crank up the boat and go fishing," he said, "just goof, sit there and stare. . . ." A place in town delivered the papers and magazines but he never read them, only the comic strips ("The only part that changes"). Never answered the telephone. He was up at six-thirty, sprawled on the king-size bed by nine in the evening. Sometimes he waited for the eleven o'clock news on the television, sometimes just drifted off. Dottie supervised what farming they did, the soybeans and corn, a few animals, and she managed the business dealings with the tenant farmers. Mitchum was pleased to know the place was self-sufficient, unless, he said, you counted the liquor bills.

His one active interest in those years was a growing involvement with quarter horses, the swift, muscular southwestern breed used in ranching and, to more glorious effect, in rodeos and special quarter-mile races. The cowboy from Connecticut who "didn't know a horse

from a mule" and could hardly get mounted in his Hopalong
Cassidy days had developed into a first-rate rider, winning compliments from expert horsemen like Budd Boetticher, and horses and
their breeding had become a subject of great fascination for him. He
had made a lengthy study of the history of Thoroughbreds and
could talk for hours about various breeds and breeding techniques,
could discuss the genetic formula of every champion, and trace the
pedigree of numerous top racehorses back practically to the conquistadores. At Belmont Farms he was able to take his hobby from
the theoretical to the practical, purchasing a racing quarter horse
stallion and a brood mare, eventually keeping a stable of more than
a dozen racing and working quarter horses and becoming part of the
network—a separate subculture, in fact—of wealthy western and
southern Thoroughbred quarter horse breeders. Now and again
Mitchum would load up a stallion and trailer him across country—
"I'm off," he'd explain happily, "to get my horse laid."

In Maryland he would occasionally come out of his refuge,
accepting a dinner invitation from one of the neighboring gentleman
farmers or venturing into town for a special event, to pin a medal on
a local beauty contest winner or some such. Visitors were rare, a relative now and then and that "true friend" or two who were willing to
make the complicated journey, flying into Baltimore, renting a car,
driving into the backwoods. One who came was Charles Laughton,
not long before he died, staying nearby in Washington, D.C., to
make what would be his final film, *Advise and Consent,* for Otto
Preminger. He was playing a Dixie senator in the movie and complained to Mitchum of his difficulty in getting the Deep South accent
right. "It's as if they had hired *you* to play a Cockney, Bob," he said.
Mitchum abruptly responded with perfect East End locutions.

"Remarkable," said Laughton.

One day a fellow came down the half-mile entrance drive and up
to the front door looking for the man of the house. Mitchum came
out, ready to throw the stranger off the property.

"You don't recognize me, do you, Bobby?" the man said.

It was Manuel Barque. They hadn't seen each other in thirty
years.

"I don't fucking believe it," Mitchum said. "You son of a bitch!"

Manuel laughed and told him to watch his language. Bob's old delinquent pal was an ordained Methodist minister these days.

The idle life at Belmont Farms never lasted more than a few months at a time. Eventually the call would come from good old Reva with a new job lined up for him. Sometimes she would airmail a script for his approval; on other occasions, if he was sufficiently restless, a brief rundown on the phone and a starting date would be all that he asked. And then he was off, leaving Dorothy behind to wonder what sort of mischief he might get into this time. Now, in Maryland, she was more cut off from his other life than ever. She couldn't keep him on the farm permanently. But did she even want to? The little flings were going to happen no matter where they called home. At least there was the satisfaction of knowing that was all they would ever be . . . little flings. The other women had never meant anything more than a cheap thrill, an inebriated evening's entertainment forgotten by the next morning. He had found his one soul mate, in sickness and in health; she could take comfort in that, anyway.

It was the prospect of working with Shirley MacLaine as his costar that finally got Mitchum to agree to do *Two for the Seesaw.* He had seen her in Billy Wilder's *The Apartment* and been struck by her offbeat beauty and sly, dramatic style. Perhaps with her, he thought, they could make something interesting happen on-screen, though he doubted it. He was convinced that they had found the wrong man for this picture.

William Gibson's play had been a sizable hit on Broadway, a two-character, bittersweet romance about a pair of mismatched lovers, a stuffy, midwestern lawyer running from a broken marriage and a spirited ditz living in Greenwich Village. The original production had starred Anne Bancroft as bohemian Gittel Mosca and Henry Fonda as Jerry Ryan, the depressed attorney. Walter Mirisch, whose company had produced *The Apartment,* no doubt had that Best Picture winner much on his mind when he put Gibson's play into production. Indeed, with its overcast black-and-white New York backgrounds, apartment-house setting, funny/sad romance, and, of course, Miss MacLaine there to play another lovelorn New Yorker, it was—short of Jack Lemmon's and Wilder's participation—as close as Mirisch could get to making *The Apartment, Part II.*

It's not clear why he became fixated on Mitchum for the role of Jerry Ryan, a character who would have much more comfortably fit any number of more conventionally middle-class and repressed-looking stars, including Gregory Peck, William Holden, Glenn Ford, and Fonda, several of whom Mitchum recommended to Mirisch after turning down the picture, twice. Hiring Mitchum for the part was—as would be the case with the later *Ryan's Daughter*—casting against type. But it was also miscasting.

In lieu of Wilder, Mirisch hired the man who was perhaps the second-hottest director in town after his spectacular success with *West Side Story*, Bob's *Blood on the Moon* director, Robert Wise. "It was one of the few times I went on a picture where the cast was already set," Wise recalled. "The two stars were signed and I had nothing to do with it. And no, I don't think Mitchum was ever quite right for the part at all. He was more believable and better in rougher, outdoor kinds of stuff. But as I say, when I came on, the casting was set."

The stars met for the first time in the producer's office at the old Goldwyn Studios in Hollywood. Mitchum arrived, barely acknowledging anyone's presence, lit a Gitane, and blew smoke at the ceiling.

MacLaine tingled.

She was seventeen years younger than Mitchum. She had been thirteen when *Out of the Past* played in the theaters in Virginia, and Robert Mitchum had become her girlhood idol. Most movie stars had once been movie fans like everybody else, and it was one of the strange phenomena of the business, this coming together as equals and working with people you had once known only as thirty-foot gods and goddesses on the big silver screen. It could feel like entering a dream.

"Don't let me take up too much space," Mitchum said, shaking her hand and then lumbering into a chair. "I'm basically a Bulgarian wrestler. I'm not right for this part."

"You're wonderful," MacLaine gushed impulsively. "I've admired you for so long. . . . I think you'll be great."

The cast and a few key technical people went to New York City for ten days of exteriors. "We opened it up a bit from the play," said Robert Wise, "just enough to give a sense of New York. And then everything else we shot on the stage back in California."

Soon after filming began it became clear that Mitchum and MacLaine were most compatible, were getting along splendidly. In public, on the set, they were a pair of cutups, entertaining each other and the crew to the point of exasperation for director Wise. "They got to ribbing and telling jokes and making us all laugh, so that the biggest problem we had was getting the two of them to settle down and get into the scene and rehearse. Finally I had to call the crew and everybody back twenty minutes early from lunch break and I talked to them. I said, 'Listen, guys, we've got to stop being such a good audience for these two. We simply have to stop encouraging them or we'll never get this picture done.'"

In truth, there was something beyond compatibility going on. MacLaine's girlhood crush had been reignited and was now combined with some deeper, more mature response to the enigmatic man she deemed in so many ways her exact opposite: a drifter through life, a dedicated underachiever. As they played their roles of Gittel and Jerry falling for each other, it was becoming a case of reality mimicking the movies.

Mitchum began driving her home from the studio. He would talk, tell stories, recite poetry. MacLaine listened, spellbound, reveling in the sensitivity she found lurking beneath the "Neanderthal" surface. Mitchum pulled out all the stops. He quoted Shakespeare, peeled pomegranates for her with one hand, told her he was a caged lion . . . "a poet with an ax."

Shirley swooned.

When she took a week off from filming and went to Hawaii to cool down and think things over, she returned to find Mitchum acting bereft. "When I didn't see you, I felt deprived," he told her.

The friendship deepened.

It was a banality of the business, the midproduction affair between male and female costars. Acting together, particularly in a love story, was such an intimate, vulnerable experience for some performers that brief backstage romances were almost inevitable, and with so much money riding on the hoped-for "chemistry" between a film's leads, such affairs were often encouraged by producers or directors, sometimes nearly insisted upon. MacLaine, though married (to Japan-based producer Steve Parker), was a free-spirited character and had experienced her share of flings and on-location alliances with previous leading men. Mitchum, though, from the start, seemed to hold the prospect of a longer-lived fascination. "I found him to be a complex mystery," she would write, "multifaceted, ironically witty, shy to the point of detachment. . . . I felt I'd be missing the adventure of a lifetime if I just did my job and walked away from what I intuitively knew was a deep and stormy fragility."

"Mitchum and Shirley liked each other very much, that was obvious," said Robert Wise. "They kidded each other and it was pretty spicy kidding, pretty ribald. I had to have a closed set for a while; I was kind of embarrassed over what they were saying to each other. I can't cite you chapter and verse of what it was, but it was pretty dicey [e.g., Wise, rehearsing the actors in a scene: Bob, can I see the end bit again?/Mitchum: You mean just the pink part?]. . . . Maybe they *were* having an affair. I don't know. I couldn't tell. But I had a difficult time getting them settled down to do a scene."

Jerome Siegel, Wise's assistant director, had a better view of what was developing between *Seesaw*'s stars, dealing with them away from the set and first thing in the morning each day of the production. "It wasn't an obvious thing by any means," said Siegel. "They were very subtle about it. You never saw anything where you could be sure there was a romance going on. But it didn't surprise me when I did hear about it.

"They were both very happy, fun, relaxed together. They kept the set relaxed, no tension. They were both very down-to-earth people—well, not down-to-earth, they were pretty unusual characters actually, but they acted like regular people, not big stars. Mitchum in particular was very warm, just one of the boys, a great guy. He liked to have his secretary bring in a bunch of stuff for lunch, and he'd invite the guys to sit around and shoot the breeze and eat lunch with him. No entourage, no yes-men. And surprisingly, the drinks were all Cokes and tea, no hard liquor at all."

Malachy McCourt, the Irish roustabout, raconteur, and actor, met Mitchum at breakfast time, not lunch, and had a different experience regarding the star's liquid intake. Playing a bit part in a party scene, McCourt mentioned to Mitchum that they had a mutual friend in Richard Harris. "Of course, once I said I was a friend of Harris's he just assumed that I was of the drinking fraternity . . . and he was quite correct in that assumption."

Mitchum invited McCourt to his dressing room one morning and brought forth products from the homeland, bottles of Guinness and Irish whiskey. "We had a long talk as we sampled these refreshments, and I found him to be a highly intelligent man, very well read. Had a good sense of irony, didn't take himself seriously. He had this tough facade but there was a softness within it all. Our conversation touched on many things and he spoke very eloquently of Ireland, he had a feeling for Irish mysticism, for the Celtic twilight. I found him to be a very bright man who had become a bit lost in his stardom, a man who thought he ought to be doing something else besides standing before the camera for a living."

The pair were eventually joined by Frank Sinatra, in the vicinity shooting *The Manchurian Candidate*. "He was just popping in to say hello, that sort of thing. They were very chummy, a very easy relationship there. And Mitchum sat him down and poured him two large beakers, one with Guinness and one with the Irish whiskey. Sinatra gulped with dismay, drinking at that time in the morning, but he bravely downed a very good portion of both, and then made his farewell. He was still a very thin man, Sinatra, and I'm sure it was hitting him harder than it hit Mitchum or myself. But at that hour of the morning it was a bit much even for me, to be quite honest!"

The assistants came calling—Mitchum wanted on the set.

"Fuck off," he told them.

"But Mr. Mitchum, Mr. Wise is ready for you. . . ."

"Fuck off!"

Glasses were filled, Mitchum gathered McCourt round. "'Sing "The Bold Fenian Man" for me!' saith this grand actor, and together we sang."

Whatever the qualities were that had made *Two for the Seesaw* a hit on Broadway, they did not appear to have been replicated in the film adaptation. And as Mirisch's *Son of The Apartment,* it lacked the wit and bite, the romanticism and ineffable weltschmerz of Wilder's masterpiece, or anything close to it. Mitchum had delivered a perfectly good and often touching portrayal of the depressed, square Middle American who cannot in the end cope with the unconventional. But as he had suspected he would, Mitchum brought to this homely role certain inappropriate physical and stylistic qualities, not to mention distracting biographical baggage, that were bound to make the customers uncomfortable. From the critics he received some of his worst and most contemptuous notices since the RKO days, as if the part of Jerry Ryan had been taken on not by a seasoned and acclaimed dramatic actor but by one of the cast from the Bowery Boys series.

"Intellectual snobs," Mitchum called them, and went home with the leading lady.

While their other in-production romances had faded away with the wrap party, Mitchum's and MacLaine's affair, much as she had anticipated, grew only stronger after the filming concluded, their pleasure in each other's company an irresistible force. They began seeing each other regularly, for days and weeks at a time. With his spouse in Maryland and hers in Japan, they had the rest of the world to themselves. MacLaine became Mitchum's partner in wanderlust and they journeyed off to favorite cities and far-off places. Paris. London. New York. New Orleans. They were happy, wealthy hoboes, bumming around the world, MacLaine following Mitchum's lead, having "no sense of time or purpose." In Manhattan they went to jazz clubs, hung out with Dave Brubeck and other Mitchum acquaintances, Robert discoursing on musical esoterica, playing hipster professor to MacLaine's doting student. In Louisiana they scored absinthe and buckets of oysters and gorged till they were seeing stars. They moved into an old barge on a secluded estuary in bayou country. Mitchum could make himself at home anywhere. Soon they were holding court with the locals, filling their cups, and trading tall tales.

Mitchum delighted in her lithe twenty-eight-year-old dancer's body and a face he told her was "treacherously beautiful . . . like some enchanted goblin's." She was bright, funny, spirited. Her days as the Sinatra Rat Pack's mascot had made her a sturdy drinking buddy and as unshockable as a Brooklyn stevedore, but she could be earnest and sensitive and had a burgeoning, ambitious intellectual curiosity.

Mitchum, to MacLaine, was a mysterious and fascinating creature, with his hidden depths and contradictions, variously cynical, poetic, coarse, romantic. She loved his stories and his rich, recondite, and often surreal verbiage, though many a time she didn't have a clue what he was talking about.

He was hard to understand in many ways. Once, in a farmhouse they rented outside Paris, he watched her taking a bath and tears began welling in his eyes; he told her he was crying because she looked so beautiful. The same man, she knew, was quite capable of outbursts of rage and violence. On one occasion he went after a driver who had cut him off on the road, ramming into him again and again for miles, grinning, eyes afire. MacLaine looked at him beside her and could only chillingly see the killer he had brought to life in *The Night of the Hunter*.

The two of them were together when President Kennedy was shot, and they sat side by side in front of the television, day and night, watching the news unfold. It didn't matter what you did with your life, Mitchum whispered after hours of silence, staring at Kennedy's coffin, there were always bastards out there waiting to grind you down.

When family or professional obligations took them in different directions, they might not see each other for months but remained in touch with long, intimate phone calls. His words would often haunt her, MacLaine remembered. They would visit each other's sets, and insiders' tongues wagged, though the affair would not be hinted at in the columns until much later. "I remember I was playing golf early one morning with Max Perkins, who was director of publicity for Warner Brothers," said showbiz reporter James Bacon. "And Max got a call from the head security guard at the studio, said Mitchum was in his dressing room with Shirley MacLaine and he was drunker than hell and making all kinds of noise, and everything else was going on in there. This is about seven, eight o'clock in the morning and they'd been there all night. So Perkins called Jack Warner and asked him what they should do. And Jack Warner said, 'Hell, if she keeps him in his dressing room we at least know where to find him. Tell the guard to make sure they have enough *ice*.'"

Mitchum and MacLaine would work together again, briefly, in *What a Way to Go!* the grandiose Comden-Green satire in which Shirley was to play a sweet small-town girl who weds and buries a series of millionaires, each husband played, briefly, by a major male star—Paul Newman, Dean Martin, Dick Van Dyke, Gene Kelly, and Mitchum, who took on the role of Rod Anderson, a jet-set industrialist.

The director was J. Lee Thompson. "We were setting up *What a Way*, and Shirley and I were in New York to meet with Darryl Zanuck. We were there about a week and Bob Mitchum arrived, and we would all go out to dinner together every night. So I knew the situation. They weren't broadcasting the fact. Well, they were both married. Shirley would never refer to Robert as anything other than a good friend. But they were having great fun together and were great fun to be around. And I think they were probably very much in love with each other.

"Frank Sinatra was supposed to be in the film. Each of the stars was getting a certain salary, and it was quite a lot for two weeks' work, but Sinatra suddenly wanted about three times that amount and the producers decided they wouldn't pay it. And so we moved on. I would have liked Gregory Peck to do it, but he turned it down or was doing something else. And I suggested Bob, and Shirley was consulted, and of course she liked that idea."

Mitchum's segment in *What a Way to Go!* had an odd, coinci-dentally metaphoric resonance for those in the know. His celebrity tycoon character is seen to lead a glamorous, globe-trotting exis-tence with sexy Shirley MacLaine in tow, while secretly longing to return to his overalls, jug of corn liquor, and favorite moo cow back on the rustic farm of his dreams (which, after he mistakenly tries to milk a bull's testicles, is the scene of his sudden, violent death).

For three years Mitchum lived in a floating captain's paradise, drift-ing shiftlessly from spouse to sweetheart and back again. He returned to the farm periodically, and Dorothy and the kids still joined him on location trips, coming to Hawaii while he filmed *Rampage* (a restfully enjoyable final entry in the dying Great White Hunter genre, with Jungle Bob tracking a mythical leopard-tiger. It was, said the star, "a lot of dancing girls, banjo playing, and bull") and keeping house in England during the shooting of *Man in the Middle*. Dorothy knew all about Shirley. She could count on old "friends" from Hollywood to keep her up to date on her husband's transgressions. It was another passing fling, she must have thought, but *Two for the Seesaw* came and went and MacLaine did not go with it. The gossip continued. Things appeared very tense as Mrs. Mitchum had to to confront the idea that her husband might final-ly have found someone else. There were reports of public feuding, of Dorothy arriving at the *Rampage* producer's party with some male friends and then departing in a fury the instant Robert arrived. Tongues waggled about a New Year's party at Romanoff's, Dorothy attending teary-eyed, and no sign of her husband. Hollywood hands wondered if they were finally seeing the disintegration of one of the town's longest-lived and supposedly indestructible marriages. Dorothy no doubt wondered the same thing.

She might have taken solace from the fact that Shirley MacLaine had no clearer idea of where it was all heading. Getting Bob to con-sider the future was like trying to catch a handful of air. For all their intimate time together, he remained in many ways as elusive and ultimately unknowable a character as when she had first determined to make him "a project." Peel away one layer, MacLaine found, and there was another enigmatic surface underneath. Sometimes it just seemed as if there was no *there* there. She believed that he had not a single strongly held personal opinion, was "emotionally committed" to nothing. "He had no desires," she wrote, "not in relation to food, an evening out, or an evening in. His attitude toward lovemaking was the same. He never took the initiative. He enjoyed it certainly, he was sweet and tender, but I never really knew what he wanted. Anything was OK."

His refusal to articulate his feelings on subjects about which MacLaine was contrastingly voluble made for increasingly explosive encounters. Once, in a hotel room in New York, she became so angry that she dragged him to his feet and out the door and shoved him onto the floor in the hallway. She paused before slamming the door shut, waiting for his response.

Mitchum, in the hall, on the floor, said only, "I'll tell him when he comes in."

At times MacLaine's frustration with Mitchum would grow so great that she would daydream—shocking herself—of committing some very violent act on him, something terrible, whatever it might take to stir the man from the world of indifference in which he seemed to be living. She would decide to be done with him and then find herself drifting back. They would make plans to meet somewhere in the world and Mitchum wouldn't show, no explanation. That was the end! No more. And then he would track her down somewhere, they would find the old harmony, and the affair would bloom again. Friends told MacLaine that she was drawn to difficult men, and she began to wonder if the key to the relationship wasn't somehow all tied up with conflicts in her past and with another difficult, distant man she had tried to love. In grappling with Robert, two decades older, MacLaine wondered, was she trying to resolve issues she had had with her father? Mitchum's opinion on this theory would remain unrecorded.

I'll tell him when he comes in.

One evening MacLaine showed up at John Mitchum's door—

according to John in his memoir—with a half-gallon of vodka in one hand and her high-heeled shoes in the other.

"Read this," she said, thrusting an unfolded letter before him.

John perused the letter. It was from Robert. In high-flown prose he described to her a painful, native loneliness he dared not ask her to share.

What did it mean? she wanted to know.

Assuming that honesty and utter frankness were the best policies, John told her it was "the kiss-off."

Sad to say, he had heard about similar letters forty, fifty times before. John told author George Eells that his brother went "into this deep, expansive, profound reasoning why he can't see them anymore, because he doesn't really want to get involved.... When it comes down to the decision, Dorothy always wins hands down. Talk about a con artist."

As John recalled it, MacLaine heard his blunt explanation, roared, "*That son of a bitch!*" and flung one of her high heels in the direction of the television set, which as it happened, in the way of a good Mitchum brothers story, was just then midway through a broadcast of *One Minute to Zero*, starring brother Bob.

"Robert had ... a tremendous fondness and love for Shirley," said Reva Frederick. "Under certain circumstances it would have ... what should I say ... could have culminated in something permanent. And he was very unhappy that something could not be done about a particular situation. He adored her. But he was not free to go further."

"Why couldn't he get free?"

"There was a hold on him. Maybe it was within his own mind. But he couldn't do it."

"Obviously you mean something to do with his marriage. Was this a general feeling he had, or are you saying there was some specific reason he felt he could not leave Dorothy?"

"Yes. Yes. A specific reason. I don't want to get that personal. I wouldn't want to hurt anyone. Too many people still alive."

"Is this reason he stayed married ... this *hold* he felt ... is it something ... is it a key to understanding Robert's character?"

"Oh, no. No. Oh, no, you'll never understand that. I don't know that anyone ever did."

From the moment he first read Arthur Miller's screenplay of *The Misfits*, John Huston wanted Robert Mitchum for the lead opposite Miller's wife, Marilyn Monroe. The character of the existential "last cowboy" was a perfect part for Bob, Huston thought, and the director looked forward to continuing the creative and personal alliance forged in those balmy tropical days and nights on Tobago. He tracked Mitchum to Dublin and sent him the script. Mitchum thought the thing made no sense at all but read with interest the scenes of the hero wrestling with wild horses on the desert flatlands of Nevada. Huston had nearly killed him the last time, Mitchum thought, and this looked like it would be his second opportunity. He alerted his secretary that if the director called, "Tell him I died." The part went to Clark Gable—who did die shortly after completing the film. Many said it was in large part due to the physical demands of *The Misfits* as well as the endless aggravations of working with Monroe. Mitchum would later regret his decision. Perhaps the great Gable—with whom he had spent many a pleasant evening over an open bottle—would still be around. And Marilyn—she was soon gone, too. Sad, scrambled child. Perhaps he could have helped out there as well, keeping an eye on her, bringing her back to earth with another slap on the ass. He liked to think he was one of the ones, the last few, she really trusted.

It was some time before he saw Huston again, crossing his path in a hotel bar in London. John gave him the reproving fish eye.

"I'm pretty disappointed in you, Bob," he said. "Turning me down like that."

Mitchum said, "What are you doing with that creature, John?"

Huston had a little pet monkey with him at the bar. The monkey's red-striped penis was extended and the director was plucking at it as he stood there, a drink in his other hand.

Huston smiled. "Well, kid, I think he likes it. . . ."

All was forgiven, the friendship continued. Huston soon offered him a small role—a guest starring appearance—in his delightful, gimmick-ridden mystery thriller, *The List of Adrian Messenger* (the leads going to George C. Scott as the detective and Kirk Douglas as the villainous master of disguise). The film was full of cameos by an assortment of famous name "suspects"—Burt Lancaster, Frank Sinatra, Tony Curtis—supposedly hiding under pounds of makeup, their identity to be revealed as each man ripped off his wig and rubber face in a jaunty epilogue. Mitchum was, in fact, the only one of the guest stars to actually play a real part—a scheming Englishman in a wheelchair who gets dumped into the river, making good use of the East End accent with which he had impressed Charles Laughton back in Maryland. "He was marvelous," said Huston.

Not long afterward, Mitchum considered another and more intriguing collaboration with the man. He read a play Huston had written in his youth, *Frankie and Johnny*, a flowery, hard-boiled dramatization of the lurid folk tale of love and murder—originally written for marionettes, no less. Mitchum wanted to make a film of it (with humans, not puppets), not starring but directing and producing. It would be set in '20s Chicago, with a lot of period blues and South Side jazz on the soundtrack and a few original songs by Johnny Mercer. He wanted Nelson Algren, author of *The Man With the Golden Arm,* to write a screenplay. The idea, of course, came to nothing.

The urge to direct a picture came upon him every now and then. Watching all the incompetents and dullards he found himself working with was its own sort of inspiration. Better me than let that guy waste someone's money again, he would say. "Most directors would be more gainfully employed sitting at Schwab's drugstore reading the *Hollywood Reporter* over somebody else's shoulder." But then he would imagine actually having to arrive on the set before anybody else, or sitting in a room for months with a *cutter* . . . or having to look at *dailies.* It gave him the creeps just thinking about it.

Max Youngstein, associated with Mitchum as a producer and executive at United Artists in the '50s, became more closely allied with the actor when he married Mitchum's good right hand, Reva Frederick. Working under the aegis of Mitchum's production

company (newly renamed Talbot Productions after the home county in Maryland), Youngstein became interested in a property, a
novel by Howard Fast called *The Winston Affair*. It was a story set in
India during World War II, concerning the trial of a psychotic
American lieutenant accused of murdering a British soldier. He
thought it would make a compelling and exotic courtroom drama
on film and that the character of the ambivalent American defense
attorney would be a nice change of pace for his star. Mitchum
agreed to do it, but by then they found that the rights had already
been optioned to Marlon Brando's Pennybaker Productions. As it
turned out, Brando himself was not interested in the project, which
came to be titled *Man in the Middle*, but his company had to make
something to maintain their legitimacy for tax purposes. Producer
and Brando's business partner Walter Seltzer explained,
"Pennybaker had to validate itself, and Marlon didn't want to work.
We had optioned Howard Fast's book, and Max Youngstein came to
me and said, 'You beat me to it. Can we throw in together?'"

Youngstein and Seltzer flew to London to meet with Mitchum,
then finishing his chores on *Adrian Messenger*. Seltzer: "And that
first meeting was the one time for me when Mitchum lived up to his
reputation as something of the playboy of the Western world and
beyond. It was at the Savoy Hotel in London. He was drunk. So
drunk he walked out of his shower and out of his hotel room and
wandered down the hallway and into the elevator, naked.
Completely starkers. I think he said he was trying to get a cup of coffee. It kind of startled me—as well as everybody else who was a resident at the Savoy Hotel. A waiter and a valet took him and ushered
him back to his room."

After working with Brando for several years, Seltzer was no
stranger to eccentric behavior, though Mitchum's nature walk did
give him pause. "But as it turned out, once we got started he proved
to be a professional in every respect. He was on time, knew his lines,
and didn't make any trouble. There was only one occasion when he
held up production and that was to take a call from Shirley
MacLaine in New York. They had a romance going on. He just
broke away in the middle of shooting a scene to talk to her for a half

hour and didn't care about anything else. But he couldn't enjoy the conversation much because I came and stood at his elbow, looking at my watch the whole time. Otherwise, he was a great professional and very helpful to the film as a whole. Bob was very good with France Nuyen, who was a little unsure of herself, and he did a lot to help her performance and boost her confidence. He was not quite as much help with Trevor Howard, who could be . . . odd."

Mitchum had been all for hiring his old buddy Trevor. The two—who first met in Mexico in the '50s while one was shooting *Bandido!* and the other was finishing *Run for the Sun* with Richard Widmark and Jane Greer—had had their share of adventures through the years, and Mitchum was, besides, a great admirer of the man's acting talent. However, Howard had been all but blackballed of late due to his drinking.

"He had a bum reputation then," said Walter Seltzer. "But he wanted this job very badly; and Guy Hamilton, the director, and I went out to visit him. He was with his wife, a lovely actress named Helen Cherry. And he was demonstrating to us that he was clean and sober. He very dramatically showed us that he was having tea while the rest of us were swilling drinks. And he did convince us he would be OK, and of course he was a fine, fine actor, and perfect for this role of a military doctor."

The problem with putting Mitchum and Howard together on a picture was that Bob could drink for days on end and still work, but Trevor could have two belts and lose all control. On Howard's second day on the film, he and Mitchum had done some private conferring before they were called to the stage. The Englishman was helped up to a platform on the courtroom set that had been rigged so a camera could shoot from a very low angle below his feet. It was soon discovered that Howard was very clearly wearing one brown sock and one white sock, and when this was pointed out to him, along with the fact that they could not shoot a British major in such attire, he went into a drunken fit, screaming, threatening all who approached, absolutely refusing to change his socks.

"I got a frenzied call to come to the set," said producer Seltzer. "Trevor was up there on this platform, really stoned, acting like he was under siege because they wanted to change his socks. And there was Mitchum, watching it all, very amused."

Guy Hamilton, who had not yet made his remarkable '60s spy movies, *Goldfinger* and *Funeral in Berlin*, had directed big Hollywood personages once before, filming *The Devil's Disciple* with Kirk Douglas and Burt Lancaster. "My pleasure and joy in working with Bob Mitchum," Hamilton recalled, "was in direct contrast to my previous experience with Hollywood stars. I still think of him as one of my favorite people, both as an actor and as a human being. I found him to be extremely professional for the ten, twelve weeks we were together. Always knew his lines, always helpful, never complained about anything. That was his approach to everything. Why make waves? As an actor Bob understood the importance of listening, which is very, very rare for American stars—they're the world's worst listeners. Bob listened very carefully. And if all else failed in a scene, you knew you could always fall back on Mitchum's reaction shots, which could say more than the dialogue. Also, Bob was an amazing sight reader. It was like a magic trick. I used to arrive in the morning with pages of script I'd rewritten overnight. I'd say, 'Bob, I'm sorry about this, but the dialogue is all changed.' I was expecting all sorts of troubles. And he would look at it and say, 'OK, that's fine. Great.' And he knew it all. And he knew everybody else's part. Tremendously helpful. The continuity girl didn't have to work because if anybody dried up on a line, Bob could read it to them from memory. He was a very generous actor and was enormously helpful with the less experienced members of the cast.

"I was very impressed with Bob as a person. He was huge when he stuck his gut out and walked around with that extraordinary sort of puffed-up pigeon chest of his. But he was a very gentle soul. A very liberal human being and quite modest. He liked to pretend that he was an idiot. And he was very happy pretending to the world that he was a moron, because it made life simpler. He could be left in peace and quiet. But he was a very bright human being. And, oh yes, he played a mean saxophone. We had a dummy band on the set—a recording played the actual music—and the instruments were left around. And Bob had wandered off into a corner with the abandoned saxophone, and I discovered him there, blowing away . . . a real mean, jazzy saxophone. Just wonderful."

With the filming of interiors at Elstree Studios efficiently concluded, it was belatedly decided to send Mitchum, Hamilton, and a small crew to India for a week, a kind of glorified second-unit shooting miscellaneous atmosphere and background shots in the streets and buildings of New Delhi. "We were not there very long, but it was a tough location," said Walter Seltzer. "I don't think anyone was prepared for the amount of dirt and squalor we encountered. Most everybody got sick—I didn't and Mitchum did not—alcohol might very well have helped there—but the rest of the crew reacted very badly to some of the bugs that one picks up. We had a number of dinners we were invited to, one at the British ambassador's house, and some other special evenings with the local dignitaries. And Bob went and behaved just fine, a fine representative of America. Bob was a consummate performer, and he knew when he could turn it off and when he had to behave."

On one of these "special" evenings, Mitchum claimed, he became the fixation of a maharajah's daughter, and the two reconvened in his hotel suite that night for a lengthy discussion of Hindu erotic art and other pertinent matters. Mitchum's driver, meanwhile, introduced him to the delectably powerful subcontinental strains of grass and hashish.

Mitchum sat between Hamilton and Seltzer on the long return flight to London. "It was an endless, very boring trip," said Guy Hamilton. "Sixteen hours? I can't remember. Touching down every five or six hours to refuel. But I was feeling relaxed, finally. The picture is over, the last shots are in the can. And there's a very helpful stewardess always asking, 'Can I fill your glass?' And I'm drinking away happily. But Bob's not having anything, which is slightly odd. And occasionally he would get up, go to the loo, come back again, go again. And I see that Bob is acting high; he's really flying. I think, how's that? He hasn't been drinking. Then I see, when he bends down, he's got one of those tiny little British Airways zip bags, flight bags, holding it between his knees.

"I said, 'What have you got in there?'

"He gives me a beatific grin and shows me, and it's absolutely stuffed with marijuana, raw, not rolled, right off the farm."

"What the hell is that?" Walter Seltzer asked.

"You know, man," Mitchum said.

Seltzer said, "No, I don't."

"It's hemp!"

Seltzer said, "Jesus, Bob, what are you doing? This is a public flight, not a chartered flight! Where the hell did you get it?"

Mitchum chuckled. "You're a naive son of a bitch. One of the drivers in New Delhi supplied the entire crew."

"And then," said Seltzer, "he peeled off some and rolled it. I said, 'Bob, you're not going to try to take that into London, are you?' He said, 'What do you mean, I'm not? Of course I am.'"

Guy Hamilton: "We started coming into Heathrow and Bob closed up his bag. And we land and head off for Customs. And I was thinking as we got off—oh, God, I still need him to do some post-synching and this and that; what will we do? And he's already got one strike against him for this sort of thing. And I was remembering some other actor who was picked up and how they threw the book at him. And I start falling behind, walking at a distance, feeling very nervous and rather sick. And Bob reaches the Customs man, who recognizes him, says, 'Hello, Mr. Mitchum! Anything to declare?' And Bob waves his little British Airways bag and the Customs man says, 'Right, carry on. Good luck!' And Bob walked straight through without a pause. I nearly collapsed. I went and retrieved my luggage and by then Bob was away and gone. . . ."

"I had to kind of admire it," said Walter Seltzer. "He wasn't scared of anything."

Returning to the States, Mitchum told a reporter that he'd been on his best behavior while abroad, trying to fight the misconceptions people had about him. "After making all those gangster pictures," he said, "there's a general impression I'm up to no good."

The Man in the Middle was not well received by the critics, most of them decrying its slow pace and Mitchum's sluggish performance. Fox dumped the film with little to no support, and it soon disappeared, barely earning back the star's salary.

The colorful story of *Mister Moses*, derived from a novel by Max Catto (*Fire Down Below* had been his as well), followed the adventures of an American con man and diamond smuggler in the wilds of East Africa, passing himself off as a savior to a dispossessed tribe, posing as an unlikely Moses leading them in an exodus to a new homeland. It was to be the first Western film shot in Kenya since the country's recent independence from Britain, though the story line of a white scoundrel leading an adoring African tribe was hardly an endorsement of the new self-rule.

Producing the film was Frank Ross, the man who had once interviewed an unknown Robert Mitchum to play Demetrius in an aborted production of *The Robe* back in the actor's $350-a-week days. Mitchum was now offered four hundred thousand dollars for his participation in *Mister Moses*, much of his role to be played atop the back of an elephant. One more time the actor's choice of project evidenced his preference for and identification with a reluctant adventurer, a man whose goodness is masked by a surface of cynical self-interest, a personable con man, outsider, friend to the disenfranchised. Carroll Baker, the sensuous blonde who had come to fame in 1956 as the thumb-sucking nymphet in *Baby Doll*, took the role of a missionary lady who fights and then falls for Robert's flimflam man. Others in the international cast included the black American actor Raymond St. Jacques, Briton Ian Bannen, and Canada's Alexander Knox, plus five hundred Masai tribesmen recruited for the bargain rate of a few shillings a day. Ronald Neame would direct. Once a premiere cinematographer, he had directed several excellent, intelligent British features—*Man With a Million, Tunes of Glory, The Horse's Mouth*—and was still several years away from the Hollywood superproductions like *The Poseidon Adventure* that would occupy him later.

"We met for the first time in Nairobi," said Neame. "I'd flown in from London and Bob from California, and we'd arrived within a couple of hours of each other. I phoned him, said, 'Let's meet and say hello. How about the bar at eight o'clock, and we'll have a couple of drinks to celebrate the start of the picture?' And we met and I found him to be, then and always, the most relaxed company imaginable. We had our drinks, and neither of us remembered that Nairobi is ten thousand feet above sea level, the alcohol hits you at least twice as hard, and instead of having dinner we both got so inebriated that the next thing I remember is being in bed. And that was my first very friendly and amusing meeting with him. And from the first day of production onward for twelve weeks or so he was the most congenial company and one of the best actors I have ever known."

Much of the shooting would be done near Lake Naivasha, three hours from Nairobi. Here an entire village of mud and dung huts was constructed to house the Masai and for use as a principal set. Each tribesman was allowed to bring along one wife apiece, with the exception of the chieftain, who was permitted a quartet. "The chief became my assistant director," said Ronald Neame. "He was the man who all the villagers followed, so he was my liaison with the Masai—who I have to tell you were really very charming, very nice people. Everyone thought of them as savages, but in their own way they were highly civilized. The chief spoke only Masai, that was translated into Swahili and from Swahili to English, and back again when I had to tell him something. It did get to be a bit much, but it worked. He was great. I wished I could have had him in Hollywood. The only problem was that they coated themselves with this mudlike ochre substance that had a terrible odor. Once you got used to it it wasn't so unpleasant, but when some of us would get back to our respective wives at night . . . mine would say, 'Well, you really do smell of Masai this evening.'"

The closest accommodations considered appropriate for the stars and crew were an hour and a half drive from the location in an old colonial hunting lodge at Lemura. Mitchum and Baker were installed in the lodge's two "luxury" bungalows, in actuality a pair of wooden huts with porches, separated from the main building by a hundred yards of overhanging vegetation, snakes, and ravenous insects. Everyone was advised to stay on the property at night as there were said to be contingents of Mau Mau terrorists still wandering about, robbing and murdering Europeans. Only days before the *Moses* people arrived, an Englishman who had been bicycling home in the evening was waylaid and hacked to death.

A hall in the main building of the lodge became a makeshift screening room. "The film we shot all went back to England for processing," said Neame. "Whatever we shot after lunch one day and before lunch the next. It was sent out in time for the five o'clock plane for Nairobi. Processed in England the following morning, printed by the next morning, and sent back to Nairobi. We had a terrible projector and a bedsheet for a screen to view the rushes on, and everything looked awful. It was better not to look at them at all. Bob never had any interest in seeing them. He was very casual about what we did after he had done his job. He was very secure as an actor and knew what he had given me. I'll tell you something about Mitchum. On the first day of shooting, a scene between Bob and Carroll Baker, the producer, Frank Ross, was standing discreetly a bit behind the camera. We finished the shot and I said, 'Let's print that. Move on.' And he came up to me and said, 'Ronnie, he didn't do anything. He just walked through it. This is awful. Why don't we get him to do more?' I said, 'Frank, wait and see what it looks like when you see it on the screen.' It was a wonderful thing about this man as an actor. He appeared to do nothing. Underacted. But some—I don't know what—some *magic* made it very powerful on the screen."

Each morning at dawn, Mitchum's driver, a local man named Sampson, would take him to work, a bracing wake-up ride over what was more trail than road. Sampson knew only one mode of driving—dangerous. He would take them along the dirt highway like a bat out of hell, all but running over anyone walking or riding on the same thoroughfare. More than once he barely avoided a head-on crash with a wild beast and Mitchum would go flying from his seat as they nearly toppled over, careening off the road and onto the grass, and would look up from the floor in time to see a giraffe prancing by on the road where they had been a moment before. Robert complained, but to no effect, even though Sampson professed great fear of losing his job. After a few days of these death-defying rides, Mitchum insisted on driving himself to the location, while Sampson moved into the backseat and napped or enjoyed the view.

An even more uncomfortable ride was the one Mitchum had to take aboard a supposedly trained pachyderm named Emily, imported from South Africa. Shades of Marilyn Monroe, the elephant actress proved to be difficult, often refusing to come to the set or to perform once she got there. The trainer had warned them repeatedly that Emily should not be separated from her girlfriend, Susie, but Susie had been considered an unnecessary expense. Now, seeing the error of their ways, they had the other elephant shipped in, and Emily became instantly cooperative. "The trainer was quite right," said Ronald Neame. "The elephant was a lesbian. Once we brought her girlfriend to the set, she would do anything we asked."

For Mitchum it was like a return to his first awkward days riding horses in Kernville but even more chafing and straining on the thigh muscles. Perched ten feet from the ground, legs widely splayed, he would roll and sway for up to six hours a day in the heat and dust. "Christ," he complained, "I might as well be with Ringling Brothers. At least there'd be a tent over my head, and I'd get to fuck the lady midgets."

Unlike Emily the elephant, the other female star of *Mister Moses* was no lesbian. Carroll Baker had come away from a problematic marriage to film and theater director Jack Garfein, and now, thousands of miles from home, in what she called the "primitive . . . titillating" atmosphere of the African wilds, she found herself falling under the spell of an erotically appealing leading man. Described by Baker as a "gorgeous hunk" who "paraded his manliness twenty four hours a day," Mitchum seems to have unwittingly reduced the actress to a state of almost painful concupiscence.

Placed within whispering distance of Mitchum in their isolated bungalows beyond the hotel, Baker found herself spying on him through her shuttered windows. "Barefooted and barechested," she recalled, "he would strut on his front porch . . . sheening with sweat. I was driven to distraction." He would pace the porch like a "tiger in heat," then lie half-naked in the hammock there, "hypnotically swaying toward me and away from me as a perpetual prurient invitation."

Baker's infatuation grew with each passing day and night, but the object of her affections seemed completely oblivious. Indeed, he would seldom have even a kind word for his costar. Mooning over Mitchum, Baker took cold showers, downed an herbal tea prescribed as a tranquilizer by a Masai witch doctor, and slid tribal "discouragement" charms into her undies. "I wanted so much to be faithful to Jack and our marriage vows," Baker wrote in her memoirs, "but where was I to find the strength?"

On one particularly torrid evening a couple of weeks into filming, her ardor at the boiling point, Baker finally made up her mind to throw caution to the wind and make her feelings known to the irresistible actor. In the midst of plotting her seductive next move, she heard a knock on the bungalow door. Thinking it could be no one else at that time of night but her coveted next-door neighbor, Baker recalled "shaking in anticipation" as she flung open the door and saw a grinning Shirley MacLaine standing there.

Hi!" Shirley squealed. "I just surprised Bob. He had no idea I was coming!"

"Oh . . . ," said Carroll. ". . . wonderful . . ."

MacLaine invited her to come on over to "their" bungalow for cocktails. Not wanting to be impolite—though she had certainly envisioned different circumstances for her visit to Mitchum's bachelor pad—Baker went, and found MacLaine wriggling on Bob's lap and the two of them smooching it up. So much for what John Mitchum had called the "kiss-off." The frolicking pair were already well into a large pitcher of bone-dry martinis. Baker drowned her disappointment, then stumbled back to her bungalow and passed out.

For the next few days, Mitchum and MacLaine were together happily as in the past, with no discussion of more recent acrimony and ultimatums. They frolicked with the Masai, "commiserated" with the whites still whining about Uhuru and Mau Mau, and drank. "Shirley was great fun, and the whole of the unit loved her," said Neame. "She loves any sort of adventure and she was really enjoying being there with Bob and everyone and getting to know our tribe. Several of the women had their babies on the set, and it was considered by the Masai to be good luck if the child is brought into the world by a white woman, so Shirley was present with the midwife for the delivery of two or three babies."

It was plain to MacLaine that as much as she still cared for Mitchum, the fire had cooled. His philosophy of life—his nihilism, his belief that shit just happened, his commitment to a lack of commitment—could never be her own. The sense of frustration he had provoked in her, though, she took as an object lesson. "I was drawn to him," she would write, "not only because he was nearly twenty years older and a father image, but because through him I could learn how essential it was for me to inform others of what I wanted, needed and was committed to in life."

She took off on a solo safari to the north and eventually went onward to India for some spiritual study. It was over, but MacLaine never quite forgot. "I don't think they saw each other or talked in later years," said director J. Lee Thompson, "though Shirley still cared about him, yes. I was doing a picture with Bob many years later and she called me, wanted to know—how is Bob? Is he OK? It was very sweet."

A journalist friend of the lodge's English proprietor had filed a story on the *Moses* group, strongly implying—before Miss MacLaine's arrival—that Mitchum and Baker were in the midst of a romance. This set in place a wave of gossip and countergossip back in Hollywood—which eventually brought both Baker's and MacLaine's husbands flying to East Africa to keep an eye on their women. Dorothy, though, told columnist Earl Wilson she wasn't going anywhere—"I've been through this a good many times before," she said.

When the troublemaking journalist showed up at the lodge again, Baker piled a tray full of food and dumped it on his head. The outraged proprietor then told Frank Ross they could all get the hell out. But it so happened that Baker, Mitchum, and a few of the other actors were going to Nairobi that evening for a state dinner with the country's new president, Jomo Kenyatta. Carroll told him of their imminent eviction from the lodge, and Kenyatta assured the beautiful blonde that his chief of security would "silence the landlord forthwith!"

The charismatic African leader was particularly delighted with Mitchum, who sat beside him during the elaborate dinner and regaled him with raunchy stories of Hollywood. (Mitchum would later boast to Tim Wallace how well he had hit it off with Kenya's "head nigger.")

*

Catching word of all the expected new arrivals, and having gotten pretty fed up with three hours of driving each day, Mitchum decided to forego the comforts of the sportsman's lodge and moved himself into a dressing room caravan out at the edges of the Masai village. And so, for the remainder of the production, he lived in the wild, keeping an eye out for beasts and becoming an honorary member of the adjacent tribe. He spent late nights around the fire in the camp, sampling the cow's blood milkshake the men imbibed for strength and passing around some of his own deadly brews. He took part in dances and ceremonies and learned the art of spear-throwing. "I loved it," he would say. "Those natives are honest folk— never steal anything except one another's women, but that's okay under their code. They hunt with their spears, can hit a dime at fifty paces, and the men do no work at all. They've got the right idea. Sleep, eat, make love, kill a few lions and when you start to get bored, move on to the next county. The only thing I didn't dig was all the blood you're supposed to drink."

He found the Masai women a fascinating, even alluring lot, shaved heads, greased in fat, earlobes stretched, sprinkled with cow urine, and all. He attended a ritual dance by the females of the tribe and called them "the most electrically feminine women—I mean you could feel it—I'd ever come across." As a token of their affection, several tribesmen offered him the loan of their wives. But

Mitchum, through with married women for the time being, graciously declined.

The downside to all that natural living was a nasty case of dysentery, chills, and severe diarrhea. His plumbing refused to settle down for several weeks. The doctor told him it would have been smarter if he had sought aid after the first symptom had appeared.

The first symptom was lethargy. Mitchum said, "How the hell was *I* going to recognize *that?*"

The good relationship between the film company and the Masai ended on a sour note after the manufactured village was burned down for the camera—as had been planned from the beginning. "The burning went well, we got it all on film," said Ronald Neame. "And then we broke for lunch. Suddenly in the middle of lunch there was a terrible explosion from the burned down village. We all rushed to see what had happened. A big oxygen tube that was used for lighting flares and things had been left on the ground. It had overheated and exploded. One of the Masai had gone back in among the rubble—presumably he had forgotten something, and he was there at just that wrong moment—and the explosion killed him. When the other tribesmen learned what had happened, it became very nasty for a time. They came after us, surrounded us, and pointed quite a few spears in our direction—which, by the way, were all made in Birmingham, England—and I can assure you it was no joke. When they threw those spears, they could kill a lion. And they were particularly angry with one of my assistant directors who they held responsible for the explosion because he had gone into the village first. And I was scared that they would kill him outright, right there in front of us. Finally they were convinced that it had been a careless accident, and that the man had brought it onto himself. The chief had a meeting with his committee and decided that five head of cattle should be given to the dead man's wife. Mitchum? Yes, he was there at the lunch table when the explosion went off. He took it calmly. Went on eating, probably."

Mister Moses would turn out to be a bright and gorgeously scenic adventure movie and one of the few films to make good use of Mitchum's talent for blithe comedy, here in a charming and funny performance as a lovable hustler who permits himself to be "out-hustled." The film's final image of Bob, Carroll, and elephant, Mitchum's latest variant family of sundowners, traipsing off to their next unknown adventure without a tribe or a home to call their own, was resonantly emblematic.

After *Moses,* Mitchum felt more than ever before a reluctance to go back before the cameras. He was forty-six, and already the word *retirement* fell easily from his lips. He remained in Maryland for some months, "goofing off." He was devoting more time and money to his horses. His racer Belmont Scare looked like a champion in the making. But even in this gentlemanly rich man's sport, his notorious past dogged him, biting him on the ass. Intending to run Belmont Scare in a quarter horse stake race at Sunland Park in New Mexico, Mitchum was found to have falsified a Racing Commission license application. On the form he had denied ever having been arrested or convicted on a criminal charge. His horse was denied a license, and Mitchum was barred from entering all New Mexico racetracks.

Jim Mitchum was still looking for stardom. He worked steadily, but a breakthrough role eluded him. He was impressive in Carl Foreman's antiwar movie *The Victors,* but it was a nasty part in a nasty film—it did not become his *G.I. Joe.*

His brother, Chris, had grown to young manhood on the farm. He was widely regarded as a very nice kid. Chris was intelligent, sweet-tempered, sensitive. He still hoped to be a writer and was a good student at the various universities he attended. He seemed to understand his father's temperament better than most and accept it, but the yearning for some more emotional connection with the man had to be there all the same. Chris had met a girl at high school in 1962. They went together for a couple of years, and then he and Cindy decided to get married. His mother thought he was being young and foolish, tried to talk him out of it. He couldn't remember his father having an opinion on the matter. Cindy came from a warm family. "Her father used to kiss her good night, and she'd kiss him good night. My family just isn't that way," Chris told a reporter. "I think Cindy felt, because she didn't walk in and get hugged and kissed, that she was unwanted. Which isn't the case. It's just a matter of our family structure being different."

Robert did not make the wedding, maybe didn't know it had occurred. "I don't even think he was in town at the time," Chris said. "He was off on a picture somewhere." There was always the telephone, the reporter offered—all he had to do was pick it up and break the news. "That's getting into sentimentality," Chris said. "He's not that way. He doesn't express it. I think my mother called and told him. He said, 'I hope it works out.'

"I think that being raised the way he was, having had such a tough childhood, Dad had to become the type of person who finds it actually embarrassing to express himself emotionally. I understand him as a person. I don't resent him or hate him or feel he's cheated me out of anything. . . . I respect and admire him. . . . Of course I love him. Very much so. Only sometimes I don't necessarily like him."

In the summer of 1965, Reva called with an offer. "Howard Hawks wants you to do a cowboy picture with John Wayne."

Mitchum said, "Tell Howard to call me."

He called.

"You want to tell me a little bit of the story," Mitchum said.

"No story, Bob. Just you and Duke."

Well, what the hell. Anything to get out of the house.

A year shy of seventy in 1965, Howard Hawks was coming to the end of an extraordinary career as a motion picture director. In the course of nearly fifty years of making movies, he had been responsible for a great many milestones of popular entertainment, including *Scarface, Twentieth Century, Bringing Up Baby, His Girl Friday, The Big Sleep, Red River,* and *Gentlemen Prefer Blondes.* Though for most of his working life he had no public profile à la DeMille or

Hitchcock, Hawks had long been held in the highest esteem within the mogul camps of Hollywood, a man known for decades as a hit maker and a star maker. He was drily funny, icy of manner, an American aristocrat; also self-absorbed, arrogant, and, according to his biographer, a credit hog and a deadbeat not above stiffing the local grocer. Beginning in France in the '50s and then—by the mid-'60s—in cultural and academic circles in Britain and the United States, Hawks had been "discovered" as the great unknown master of the cinema, with critics and movie mavens championing his weighty skill as a storyteller and explicating his peculiarly personal obsessions with masculine cameraderie, stoicism, sexual humiliation, and basso-voiced starlets.

Hawks had planned to make a film out of Harry Brown's novel *The Stars in Their Courses*, a violent and tragic tale described as a "Western *Iliad*," and put his frequent collaborator Leigh Brackett to work on a screenplay while he completed another film, *Red Line 7000*. A race-car melodrama for the drive-in set, full of vapid young faces, bad acting, and awful, ersatz à-go-go music, *Red Line* was Hawks's attempt to prove he was one sexagenarian who was still "with it," and at this he failed dismally. With the unreleased picture almost certain to crash and burn—and his previous film, the underrated *Man's Favorite Sport*, considered another disaster—Hawks scurried to reteam with his frequent collaborator and the movies' only sure thing, John Wayne (rebounding heroically after losing half a lung to cancer). Now having second thoughts about his dark, six-gun *Iliad*—the thing was just too damn sad; everybody died in it—he jettisoned Brackett's just-completed screenplay, which she considered the best work she had ever done, keeping only the title, *El Dorado*, and a couple of early scenes, in favor of something less tragic, less risky, and more fun, something not unlike his last Wayne Western, *Rio Bravo*. So much not unlike it that screenwriter Brackett referred to the revised story line as *Rio Bravo Rides Again*. As in the previous film, the plot would now center around a town and a jail-house under siege, with its cast of characters including a drunken lawman to be rehabilitated (it was Dean Martin in *Bravo*), an arrogant youth, a sassy female (or two this time), an old coot, and so on.

Brackett balked at the quasi- plagiarism—even though she was cribbing from herself, having written *Rio Bravo* as well—but could not stand up to the intimidation tactics of Howard and the Duke, who stood over her and growled, "If it worked once, it'll work again!"

*

El Dorado's central relationship was that of two old comrades, one an aging hired gun (Duke's role), the other a derelict sheriff. Hawks needed an actor who was vaguely contemporary with the fifty-five-year-old Wayne and had sufficient stature not to be (in Hawks's phrase) "blown off the screen" by the larger-than-life actor. Such personages were in short supply. Mitchum, indeed, seemed an all but inevitable choice. Mitchum's stoic masculinity, underplaying, and deadpan humor were right up Hawks's alley. Hawks had, in fact, placed the actor on his casting wish lists for many past productions.

But that was then.

"I was associate producer on *El Dorado,* and Hawks and I were very close by this time," said Paul Helmick. "I had been good friends with Mitchum, but we hadn't seen much of each other in a while. We were casting the picture, and Hawks was trying to think of somebody to play the Dean Martin part. I said, 'The guy for that part is Bob Mitchum.' Hawks said to forget it. We mentioned everybody in Hollywood, none of them as good as Mitchum. So I suggested him again. Hawks said he was good, but he was trouble. He'd heard too much about his drinking. I said, 'Howard, let me tell you something. Mitchum has done these pictures with these directors who don't know what the hell they're doing. And Mitchum loses interest, he goes off the deep end, parties all night, does whatever.' I said, 'Howard, with you, you know your business. When you want to do any experimenting, the actors are glad to do it; they trust you know where you're taking them. I don't think you'll have a problem in the world.' And Hawks said, 'Mitchum is real good. Let's try and get him. But I'm telling you I don't want any drinking.'"

Filming got started on the streets of Old Tucson (the same location used for *Rio Bravo*—of course) on October 11, 1965. Oddly, Hawks planned to shoot relatively few scenes using the bright blue Arizona skies and scenic landscapes but set most of the film's action on the Tucson streets at nighttime. They would be shooting "night for night," and the cast and crew were advised to get ready for an unusual schedule—work beginning at five or six in the evening and lasting until dawn some nights. Vintage Hollywood cameraman Harold Rossen was brought out of retirement with a mandate to light up the town in imitation of Frederick Remington's evocative nocturnal paintings.

Though the new version of *El Dorado* was mostly complete on paper and Leigh Brackett was in Tucson finishing it up, the relationship between what they filmed on a given day—or night—and anything written in the script was often tenuous. Hawks had a relaxed and semi-improvisatory approach to the work. "You have to run the thing," he said. "You have to tell them what to do . . . but they do it their own way and in doing so lead you into many, many things." He liked to sidle up to scenes, handing actors a revised line or two, giving them the freedom to get comfortable with their parts and make something unexpected happen. And sometimes, when nothing happened, that was all right, too. It was just a movie. Mitchum got a kick out of Hawks's studied casualness. He did an amusing imitation of him that involved standing silently at length, staring portentously, holding his chin as he pondered, then telling everybody they could go home for the day.

"Hawks was not like some of these directors, watching the clock, yelling and screaming," said Robert Donner, who played Milt, one of El Dorado's sleazier bad guys. "He took things at his own pace, had his own way of doing things. And Howard thought nothing of closing down the show and taking everybody down across the border into Mexico to eat at some restaurant he liked.*

---

*"We're all excited, thinking this must be some *incredible* restaurant the way Hawks has been talking it up. And we get to this *gas station* outside Nogales—a café run by the people who run the gas station. But, dammit, the food was just as great as he said it was!"

"The idea with Howard was to make a good picture but have a good time doing it. He didn't drive himself crazy with the little details. That's how you got that business with Mitchum holding the crutch under the wrong leg in some scenes—crutch keeps switching left to right in different scenes. So they stuck a piece of dialogue in there—'Don't you know which leg you got shot in?' or something. That was a result of the fact that Hawks saw the mistake and said, 'Hell, the audience won't give a damn. We're not gonna go back and reshoot for that.'"

Mitchum liked Hawks's way of working—it was what he ended up doing on his own on many films anyway, trying to get something halfway real out of dreadful scripts; but now it was done in a spirit of calm and of communal creativity, not desperation. Since nobody, including Hawks, had a real strong idea where it was all going from day to day—the script was "written in sand" as one cast member put it—there were some false starts. Mitchum had begun playing his soused sheriff—J. P. Harrah, "a tin star with a drunk pinned on it"—for realism, making him pathetic and terrifying. Hawks said, "Well, that's the way Dean Martin did it. What else have you got?" And so Mitchum went in another direction, to a broad comic style, mugging and doing pratfalls that had cast and crew in stitches. It was so well received that Mitchum set a new tone for the proceedings (Hawks liked to say he was happy to turn any picture into a comedy if he could). The film went into areas of pure farce at times (according to Hawks, James Caan, as the annoyingly callow youth Mississippi, never knew his part had turned into a comic one or he'd have "tried to be funny"; Caan said he *did* figure it out, and you can tell because he starts smiling after every line).

"You know, it got where I could read what Hawks was thinking," said Paul Helmick. "And when it came time to turn the camera on Mitchum the first day, he added so much to the scene that when it was over Hawks turned to me and I looked back at him, and he was so happy, like the cat that [sic] swallowed the canary. Because he knew damn well now that he had done the right thing in hiring Mitchum."

"It was the first time I'd worked with Mitchum," Hawks said. "I enjoyed it. The first time I work with a good actor I have fun finding things for them to do. You remember that scene in the bath tub? Well, it was Mitchum's idea that when the girl walked past, *he'd* pull the hat over *his* eyes. I laughed as hard as anybody. You can hear the crew laughing on the soundtrack because nobody knew he was going to do it. Those things are just marvelous."

Hawks said, "Any time you get somebody who's as good as Wayne and Mitchum, you're going to make better scenes than there are in the script. Because they're damn good, those two people are together."

Some weeks into the filming the director cornered Mitchum and told him, "You know, you're the biggest fraud I've ever met in my life."

Mitchum cocked a grin. "How come?"

Hawks said, "You pretend you don't care a damn thing . . . and you're the hardest-working so-and-so I've ever known."

Mitchum said, "Don't tell anybody."

"Hawks and Mitchum worked together just great, as I thought they would," said Paul Helmick. "Bob did a wonderful job on that picture. And I don't think he took a drop the whole picture. Now I'm not saying he didn't enjoy himself. I remember, a couple of days after we got started in Tucson, before an afternoon call, I was sitting at the table with Wayne and Hawks, we were eating our lunch. Mitchum walked in with one of the best-looking girls I ever saw in my life. I think she was some girl from the local college, a teenager. And he came over to us at the table and said, very straight-faced, 'Fellas, I'd like to introduce what's-her-name here. She'll be with us for the entire picture. She is my new drama coach.' And then he escorted her away. And Wayne made some crack, and Hawks laughed. And I said, 'This picture is going to be fun.'"

"Mitch was really a nifty guy," said Robert Donner. "Working with him, he was always, you know, saying, 'I could not fucking care less,' but he was always the one who was letter perfect, knew exactly what was needed, what was going on.

"Mitch and Duke got along great, worked real well together, but they were different types of people. Duke was wonderful, and he loved the people that he worked with all the time. But Wayne was always ready to tell you what to do, grab you by the shoulders and put you where he wanted you, tell you how to say a line." One night, Mitchum recalled, Wayne was sitting outside his trailer putting his wig on. He said, "Goddamn it, Mitch, when are gonna let me direct you in a picture?" Mitchum said, "Duke, that's all you do anyway."

"Wayne could get a hard-on against somebody," said Donner. "Duke didn't care for John Gabriel, who was one of the nicest guys that ever walked. (Gabriel: "I walked between Wayne and the camera, and he sort of manhandled me to show me you don't do that to John Wayne. But later he apologized and complimented my acting. Which was nice of him.") And he didn't like Ed Asner, always called him 'that New York actor.' What the hell he had against Ed I don't know. And Duke loved to argue about politics. He would sit sipping tequila with the still photographer, Phil Stern, and it was hours of 'goddamn liberals' this and Stern telling him 'goddamn conservatives' that.

"Mitchum was a lot more easygoing. You could play around with Mitch and didn't have to worry you had overstepped your bounds. He was very generous with the other actors. I remember him whispering something to Adam Rourke—they didn't know I could hear them—and making sure Adam got to shine in the scene. . . . And when the work was done, he was a lot of fun. He and old Arthur Hunnicutt were a riot together, sitting around remembering stories from the old days. Arthur had been quite a drinker in his day, and he still drank on days when he wasn't working. His idea of a martini was half gin and half vermouth, and he had it poured into what they called a bucket glass."

For nearly two months, shooting "night for night," the *El Dorado* company worked the graveyard shift. Work began around five, and dinner would be served at about ten, then filming would be resumed—some nights until they "ran out of dark." The actors and crew would try to sleep during the day, but it was difficult to adjust to the odd hours. Robert Donner: "You had breakfast at . . . I don't know when the hell we'd have breakfasts. You got so screwed up with the hours, you didn't know what time it was after a while. You just knew when the sun went down you were supposed to start working." During the night, many actors would slip off under a wagon or onto an unlit porch on the Old Tucson street and try and catch a nap, though it was hardly restful knowing that Hawks might be looking for you at any moment. "Mr. Hawks was spontaneous, always changing things," said John Gabriel, playing the varmint Pedro. "So you just had to hang around because you never knew when he would need you for a scene."

Donner: "I remember lying there on the street behind the wardrobe. It was getting to me, staying up all night every night. I sat up all of a sudden and screamed, 'I can't take this anymore!' And Jim Davis, stretched out near me, lifted his hat back and said, 'Aw, stop it, if you were home you'd be on unemployment anyway. Go back to sleep.' So I went back to sleep."

On a normal work night the actors might be dismissed at about 2 A.M. While some slid into bed at that point, others went looking for whatever entertainment might be had in Tucson Old or New at two o'clock in the morning. There were poker and blackjack games in the rooms. And for those who were up to interpersonal relations, there were a pair of local girls, possibly cousins, known affectionately as Filthy Phyllis and Rotten Ruth, who loved movie actors very much. The bar at the Ramada Inn, where most of the company stayed, could usually be kept open under special dispensation. One week there was a contingent of rowdy Lufthansa pilots in town for training. Seizing half the bar for a private Oktoberfest, they delighted in cutting off the ties and other articles of clothing from anyone walking near, pinning them to the bar, and generally acting like drunken morons. One night a bunch of the *El Dorado* guys were heading for a card game when Mitchum veered off, saying, "I'm going to the bar and check out the heinies." He was going to mess it up with the Lufthansa guys. Everybody rolled their eyes and went the other way. It was some time later when Mitchum showed up at the card game in Ed Asner's room, and he wasn't alone. Casual as can be, like nothing was out of the ordinary, Mitchum had a German tucked under his arm. Seeing a Lufthansa pilot in a head-

lock, people in the room shouted, "Hey, Bob, let that guy go!"
Mitchum said, "Oh, he's all right. We came to play some cards.'"

Bob Donner recalled, "With the German in the headlock he
comes over and sits down at the table. Keeps the German's head
tucked under his arm—the guy's on his knees now—and starts playing a hand. And Mitch'd lift the cards and he'd let the guy see and
he'd say, 'What do you think, heinie? Should we hit?'

"A little later things got pretty rowdy and there was a beating on
the wall. And Ed Asner says, 'Jesus, guys, keep it down, for god's
sake! Hawks is sleeping in the next room!' And it quieted down for a
while, and then Bob or somebody would start something and the
noise would start. All of a sudden we hear BAM! BAM! BAM! from
outside. And everybody runs to the door. And there's Hawks in his
long john pajamas with a six-shooter, firing away. And he
says, 'Goddamn it! If I see anybody not in their bed in five minutes
they're on the goddamn plane out of here!' And it was like rats in the
night, everybody scurrying!"

The company departed Tucson for Los Angeles on November 22
and continued shooting on the Paramount lot until the end of
January 1966, wrapping up some three weeks and a half million dollars over the original estimate. In April, in Palm Springs, Hawks
screened a preview for friends and family. His son told him, "A sheriff shouldn't sing," and so the director cut a jailhouse musical number with Mitchum singing and Arthur Hunnicutt playing
harmonica. The film opened in Tokyo and Osaka, Japan, at the end
of the year but was held back until the summer of '67 for its
American release. It was a smash everywhere it played; and in Paris,
where Hawks had become a brand name like Hitchcock, the lines
ran around the block all day and all night.

Then (as now) it was an enormously entertaining film. A sloppy
film, to be sure—meandering, misshapen, with bit and supporting
players giving line readings not worthy of a high school play, and the
lines themselves often not much better, wardrobe that had the neat-
ly pressed look of a dude ranch masquerade, continuity errors like
that notorious shifting crutch, and other failings. And yet it suceed-

ed in a way that many more ambitious and more disciplined movies never could. As Hawks had promised, in lieu of a plot it offered Wayne and Mitchum "riding again," a study more than a story—of friendship and redemption, danger and good times. For some admirers of *El Dorado,* its concentration on its heroes' infirmities and physical deterioration—paralyzing bullet wounds, alcoholism, both stars on crutches at the fade-out—and the inclusion of an Edgar Allan Poe poem with its references to failing strength and the Valley of the Shadow—revealed this as Hawks's elegy on aging and death. For many more, though, its value was of the less profound but likely more pleasurable sort, as a funny, violent, engaging, rather antiquated movie that played across the screen like a favorite old tune heard on the radio one more time.

It was arguably the last great Western for everyone involved.

"You ask if I have one favorite memory of working with Mitchum, and I do," said Robert Donner. "It was late one night in Old Tucson. There were hours when none of us had anything to do but wait, and if you were looking for Mitchum you could usually find him off by himself in the dark street. You could find him by the glow of his cigarette. He smoked those Gauloises, French tobacco, smelled like shit. And you'd go walking in the dark on the street there, and you could see the little glow. And from the dark he called out to me. He always called me 'Mother Donner.' And I sat down there and we talked. I was new in the business, and I didn't know my head from a hot rock and he knew it. And Mitchum talked and tried to tell me a few things, and finally he said to me, 'Just know that this business can afford you some wonderful opportunities. Don't miss them, boy. Don't waste it. You'll see great things. . . .' He said, 'The movie business has been like a *magic carpet* for me. I've been to places, seen things . . . *wonderful* things.' And I could not even begin to imagine what kind of things Robert Mitchum had seen, you know. So we just sat there in the night, and he went back to smoking that shitty French cigarette. I don't know. I guess it's not much, but that little conversation stayed with me. You remember funny things like that when you look back. . . ."

CHAPTER FOURTEEN

Baby, I Don't Care

"Some people in the Defense Department kept nudgin' me—
'Why don't you go find out?' Next thing I knew I was fallin' off an
airplane at Ton So Nhut . . . and it's 117 degrees."

The conflict in Vietnam was raging, no end in sight. At home,
public opposition to American involvement in the war was becoming more heated, soon to explode. Morale had begun its steady
downward crawl among the fighting troops. Hoping to raise the soldiers' spirits, as well as provoke some much-needed positive press,
the USO—in addition to sending out vaudeville shows of the Bob
Hope sort—had been organizing more low-key "handshake tours,"
asking Hollywood celebrities to go to Vietnam at government
expense and spend a little time meeting and talking to some of the
boys in the camps and hospitals. Those who went included Robert
Stack, Henry Fonda, Jimmy Stewart, Lana Turner, John Wayne,
Hugh O'Brian, and Martha Raye (who became a fearless virtual fixture in the war zone). Mitchum had never shown much interest in
the war till now (he had barely spoken a word in public about World
War II, for that matter). But maybe, he said, it was time he had a
look at what they were doing over there with all that tax money.
Protect his interests. It also sounded like a hell of an adventure.

Flown out on a government aircraft, Mitchum spent his first days
in Saigon, wined and dined in tropical colonial splendor, meeting
and greeting the military elite (General Westmoreland awarded him
an autographed glossy), hearing the company line on the war. He
was taken to military hospitals and toured the wards filled with
injured Americans, young guys with missing arms and legs and faces

half blown off. The visits had their intended effect—it wasn't easy to remain neutral or indifferent about the war when you saw what the enemy—whatever their cause—was doing to these hometown boys. He was taken out to villages and shown good works projects, Americans putting in sewage systems, building schoolhouses. He was impressed, and pissed off. Why didn't they show any of this noble shit on the news back home?

The greater part of Mitchum's two-week visit was to be spent in the field, roaming by helicopter and light aircraft from one U.S. encampment to another, fanning across the jungles north of the capital city. Dressed in the khaki safari suit favored by TV correspondents and Hollywood bwanas, Mitchum, accompanied by an army public relations man or other assigned "minder," would drop from the skies onto tiny landing fields the size of a parking space, where he would be welcomed by the top brass and shown around. The usual itinerary included a quick tour of the base and an hour or so of shaking hands and making small talk, encouraging words for the troops—then back to the Huey and the next camp on the list. He posed for pictures, signed autographs for anyone who wanted one, and collected phone numbers and messages from kids who knew their moms would be thrilled to hear Robert Mitchum telling them their boys were OK.

Special Forces veteran Daniel Carpenter, stationed at a Green Beret encampment "so far out in the bush that everyone seemed to have forgotten about it," would recall that the coded announcement of a VIP visit was greeted as an oncoming headache by the camp commander until the VIP was revealed to be Robert Mitchum.

"No shit," said the North Carolinian captain. "You ever see *Thunder Road?*"

Mitchum arrived by helicopter with a diffident navy lieutenant, got the usual grand tour, shook some hands. The navy man wanted to wrap things up and get back in the helicopter, but Mitchum said, "Relax, man. Anybody got a drink around here?" They trudged over to the local clubhouse, a contraption made of ammunition boxes and *Playboy* centerfolds. Mitchum asked what they charged for a drink, then asked how much it would be to buy the whole bar. The captain didn't know. Mitchum told him to figure it out. Then, Carpenter wrote, Mitchum "took a fat roll of bills from his pocket. It cost him a couple of hundred to buy the bar. The troopers drank free, on his tab, for months."

Mitchum played some craps, lost most of his roll, and took off.

Herb Speckman, another Vietnam War veteran in the field during Mitchum's tour, recalled his first sighting of the roving movie star:

"The gentleman landed at Dong Ha air strip and they wanted to take him up to Quangtri Province, where there was no runway. We didn't get many entertainers that far out, maybe two in all that time bothered to drop by. And Mr. Mitchum was going by jeep, about a ten-mile drive. They were worried about the man and decided to assign one of the most talented of our pilots—which of course would be myself—to escort the little convoy. Mitchum got off the airplane and got into a jeep. I was told to take care of him, flying overhead in an L19, stay close, make sure they didn't get attacked, that they got there all right. I watched them all load up, and then I got in my airplane, fired up, and followed them. And I stayed quite close, and then I came up from behind to get a better look. I made one pass and tore the antenna off the jeep that he was in. Scared the shit out of him. He was extremely irate. It was probably a twelve-foot whip antenna, and the wing of the airplane took it right off, which didn't bother me. I got a little closer than I intended. I didn't intend to kill anybody, just to give them a little fright. And I had a good three feet to spare before I would have actually hit Mitchum's head. But, you know, if you never had a big engine suddenly come at you from behind, just missing your head by a few feet, it can give you a little scare."

"Yeah, I remember when Mitchum came up there to Quangtri," said Norman Peterson, a pilot and air liaison officer at Mitchum's destination in the jungle. "He was the only one besides Martha Raye. Came in by jeep, which was a little dangerous coming through there. We called it Indian country. Friend of mine buzzed him, knocked his antenna off. He was angry. Said, 'Wait till I get ahold of the SOB that buzzed us!' See, if the enemy had attacked him on the road, he had no communication. But nobody attacked Mitchum. I don't know who'd want to.

"Yeah, Mitchum came in," said Peterson. He was wearing a bright pink shirt. It wasn't becoming. He went over to the officers' club, an old tin-roofed French building with ten bar stools, and he drank up my bottle of Johnny Black Label I was saving for me and another guy and the other guy got killed. Mitchum came in sober, got drunk, and they had to carry him out of there. Mostly what we had was cheap stuff, but Mitchum must have smelled my Black Label. Black Label was hard to find at that time. I had to bring it up there from Thailand. And I was sitting at the table with the rest of them, and the army said, 'Pete, you got a bottle of Black Label.' I said, 'Yeah.' 'Well, present it to Mitchum.' The way they said it, I didn't have much choice. And Mitchum uncorked the thing and he didn't even give me a drink of it. I told him, 'Give me a drink.' I put my glass out. Nothing happened."

Herb Speckman landed the tiny L19 and came to the camp to see what was happening. "It was the standard routine; the big man stands around, we all spit, shake his hand, he says, 'Hoo-haa.' He didn't sing or dance for us or anything. There was an Australian one time did a little magic act and brought in a couple of girl dancers. That was more appreciated, to tell you the truth, rather than the movie stars coming, saying, 'Here I am, boys, touch me.' I went over, shook his hand. He said, 'Oh, so you're the guy . . . That was damn close, mister.'' I said, 'Yeah, a little closer than I like, but it didn't scare me.' He kind of saw the humor in it by now. We shot the shit for two minutes. What else were we supposed to do, kiss the hem of his cloak? He drank a lot—but that's OK, most of us did—and went away."

"He just sort of slobbed into the jeep and he left," said Peterson. "I think the only reason he came up from Quantri is somebody told him there was a bottle of Black Label scotch there. And he found it."

These celebrity tours were not intended to be particularly dangerous—a killed or captured movie star would *not* be good publicity for the war—but Mitchum would come to claim numerous hair-raising adventures and close encounters with the enemy during

his Vietnam sojourn. There was the time, he said, when his helicopter transport got lost, wandered across enemy lines for a while,
finally found an American base, and touched down just as the place
was bracing for a major attack.

"Robert Mitchum? What are you doing here?" asked the CO, as
Mitchum recollected it for journalist Jerry Roberts.

"Anything to get out of the house," said Mitchum. "I take off,
eleven minutes later they got hit—six survivors. . . . That was the
beginning of the end of the Assau Valley Massacre."

"He got back from Vietnam with ninety million tiny scraps of
paper," said Reva Frederick. "Just about every boy he met over there
gave him a message to take back. Pieces of paper with phone numbers, names. And Robert sat down for days and called every number.
Just little brief conversations with wives and mothers and fathers. 'I
just saw your son and he wanted me to call and say hello. He's doing
fine, looks good. He's doing a good job over there.' Called every
one."

Mitchum signed up for a second tour, and in February 1967, spent
two more weeks roaming among the troop encampments and military hospitals. On his way home, he spoke at a news conference in
Bangkok, Thailand, offering a spirited and at times baldly propa-
gandistic defense of the Pentagon's enterprise. The United States, he
told reporters, was *not* engaged in a war in Vietnam. It was strictly a
self-defense action. "We are trying to build schools, roads, and hospitals. But the enemy is shooting, and the Allies must shoot back to
defend themselves." The Vietcong were enemies of humanity,
Mitchum explained. Referring to the antiwar efforts at home and
abroad, he said enigmatically, "Because of a very emotional involvement in Vietnam, the American image leaves something to be
desired. We have the largest standing army in the world. But there is
no need to display our power. Power rests in the unity of the
people."

Mitchum's two USO tours were ample evidence of his patriotism
and bravery, but he nevertheless seemed to feel a need to embellish

the visits with a greater strategic importance and an unlikely personal glory. He told reporters that he had certainly *not* gone to 'Nam on any *handshaking tours* but on what he referred to as "undefined missions sanctioned by the government." Through the years, and depending on the occasion and the hour of the evening, he would claim to have participated in as many as 152 missions, undefined or otherwise, many of them hush-hush dealings with CIA "spooks" and the like. Reva Frederick recalled, "I would hear him telling these stories to interviewers who were very gullible and were happy to get a good story, and nobody ever checked anything. I'd think, Holy shit, where is this stuff coming from! I'd just laugh and so would he, afterward."

Returning from Saigon, in his safari suit, lugging a souvenir crossbow, Mitchum stopped over in Honolulu. He looked like shit, people told him. He told them he hadn't slept in nearly three weeks. He put in a call to Dorothy.

"I expect tears of rejoicing that I'd been spared and that I'm back in one piece. And then she says, 'You know, I've sold the place.' And I say, 'What place?' And she, 'Our place. Belmont Farms. . . . I sold the farm—cows, farmhand, and all.'"

Dorothy had gotten to hate their Maryland paradise. Mitchum could stroll in, feed the horses and watch television, then slip off in the night to London or Mexico. There were snowstorms in the winter, heat, humidity, and bugs in the summer. Every time a wasp bit her, he said, Dorothy would look at him accusingly. "Sell the joint, if that's how you feel," Mitchum had told her more than once. "We can live at the Waldorf-Astoria for what it costs here."

Still in Honolulu, Mitchum called Reva in Hollywood. "You're in the middle of moving," she said, "so I've prepared a list of pictures you may care to do. It'll solve your problem of finding a roof over your head."

He picked *The Way West*, three months in the Northwest. It was from his friend "Bud" Guthrie's novel, the Oregon Trail jazz. The book had gone through a blender and came out like *Peyton Place Takes a Wagon Train*, and the backers were sure it would be a smash.

Directing the film would be Bob's friend from *Track of the Cat* and the *Blood Alley* debacle, Andrew V. McLaglen. Trained by Wellman, Budd Boetticher, and John Ford, McLaglen had gone on to a successful career in television and features, becoming one of the very last Hollywood filmmakers to specialize in the Western.

"I went to have lunch with Mitchum and Harold Hecht, the producer," McLaglen remembered. "Kirk Douglas was signed to the part of the senator. And we flat-out said to Bob, 'Which part do you want? The husband or the scout? Take either part, whichever you want.' And all during lunch he wouldn't say, just 'I don't care; I don't care.' And he never would say. So what the hell, we gave him the part we thought he was best for, the scout. And he shrugged, and I'm awfully glad it worked out the way it did, because Widmark was perfect for the other part and Mitchum was perfect for the scout."

Fine, Mitchum said. Love to play a trail scout. Smaller part, more time off. Good fishing in Oregon.

It was an enormous and complicated production, and for McLaglen and his crew as much a feat of engineering as of cinematic craft. Rivers had to be forded, wagons had to be raised and lowered from the tops of cliffs by antiquated means. It was no picnic for the cast either. "Physically, that was as tough as it could possibly be," said Jack Elam, Weatherby in the film. "Working on the cliffs and in the sand and all that shit. On top of a mountain, the top of a ski run that was bone dry in the summer. Everybody had to take a ski lift to the top. All the equipment went up by ski lift. You're up there, hundreds of feet up, nothing but rocks to fall on. Goddamn scary. And no facilities, just bare rocks. If you had to go to the bathroom, it was a matter of a half hour down and a half hour up, and we're up there all day. And then long days in the river, cold water, a lot of risks of drowning. Lowering wagons down the cliff, and we all had to take part in it. Some people landed in the hospital. So the whole picture was one tough son of a gun. But Andy—McLaglen— he was wonderful through the whole thing. Stayed calm through thick and thin."

"Andy really knew how to handle physical things," said Terry

Morse, assistant director on *The Way West.* "Well, he was about six foot seven himself, so nothing really intimidated him. A great, great guy. And for all the difficulties, he kept it right on schedule. We had a month in Eugene and two months in Bend. No interiors, studio stuff, to speak of at all."

Though they had both appeared in *The List of Adrian Messenger,* this was the first time Mitchum and Kirk Douglas had worked together since *Out of the Past.* Douglas's great success since then had, it seemed, done nothing to mellow his drive or competitiveness. "Kirk was arrogant and rude to everybody," said Terry Morse. "That's the kind of guy he was, and nobody really liked Kirk. He wanted everything his way. He was not a pleasant person to be around."

"My introduction to Kirk Douglas on that picture," said Harry Carey, Jr., "was while I was sitting in a chair, reading a paper. And Douglas comes over and jerks it out of my hand, says, 'That's my paper!' That's how he introduced himself. Later, we got to where we could just about say good morning to each other. But he was really full of it. A real pain in the neck. He tried to take over the thing at some point. Widmark got furious at it, very agitated. He screamed, 'You're not directing this goddamn movie!' Really raised hell with Douglas. But Bob just laughed at it."

"It was very dumb of him to try and provoke a confrontation with me," Mitchum told Dick Lochte. "So many guys wear their balls in their pockets. Tightening their guts, shouting 'Look at me, I'm a wrestling champion.' As far as Douglas is concerned, all I have to do is whack him one between the horns and it'd be all over. And he knows it."

"Well, somebody like Kirk Douglas and somebody like Mitchum, they were poles apart in personality," said Andrew McLaglen. "Bob was an easygoing guy, and Kirk was more volatile. But there was never a feud. I felt within myself that Kirk probably wasn't one of Bob's favorite guys, but you'd never know it. Bob wasn't the kind of guy that goes spouting off with that kind of stuff."

Mitchum was so laid-back during much of the filming that—while shooting scenes along the banks of the river—he would

actually pick up his fishing pole and cast a line into the water—
between takes.

"Sometimes," said Morse, "he would get so concentrating on the fishing that he would walk away from the set, start moving along downstream. All of a sudden we'd be ready for him and he'd just disappeared. We had to assign a production assistant to keep an eye on him when he started wandering off down the river. He loved to fish. He was a great guy. You know, his brother, John, came along for that one, had a small part. They got along great, and Bob took care of his younger brother."

"You never saw Bob at night," Jack Elam said. "The rest of us usually got together, most of us staying at the same motel, and we had cookouts and dinners, and John would be there every night playing his guitar. But Bob stayed by himself most of the time.

"We worked so hard on *The Way West,* it was a shame it got such mixed reviews and kind of died somewhere on the vine. At the time we were shooting it, we really thought we were making a damn good picture."

"The funniest thing I remember from that one," said Dobe Carey, "was one morning in the woods outside Eugene. It was about seven o'clock in the morning and Bob stumbles over to the set. It's a real cold morning and he's got an army fatigue jacket pulled up around his ears. His hair's a mess. He's got on dark glasses, and he's not even sure where he is yet. And this guy runs up in his face, yelling, 'Bob, I want you to meet the only lady sheriff in the state of Oregon!' And he pushes forth this fat little lady in her sheriff's uniform. And Bob takes a long pause to look at this woman, and he says, 'Glad to know you, Sheriff. Tell me something, do you know anyplace around here where a guy can go to get laid?' And oh God, they were both shocked. The woman couldn't believe her ears. And they both ran off. But, you know, it wasn't a good idea to bother Bob that early in the morning."

Despite some well-staged action, epic images, and beautiful photography, *The Way West* was not a success, hamstrung by the soap operatic plot and melodramatic overkill. As for the film's remark-

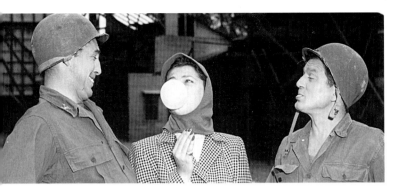

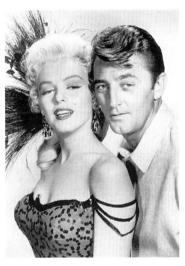

ert Mitchum's longtime assistant and
idante, Reva Frederick, teaching Robert
Charles McGraw how to blow a bubble
ng the production of *One Minute to Zero*
2).
tesy AP/Wide World Photos

Marilyn Monroe and Robert
Mitchum in Otto Preminger's *River
of No Return*, Twentieth Century-
Fox, 1954.
Courtesy AP/Wide World Photos

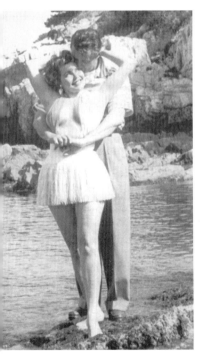

Mitchum on the French Riviera
with starlet Simone Silva: all an
unfortunate misunderstanding.
Courtesy AP/Wide World Photos

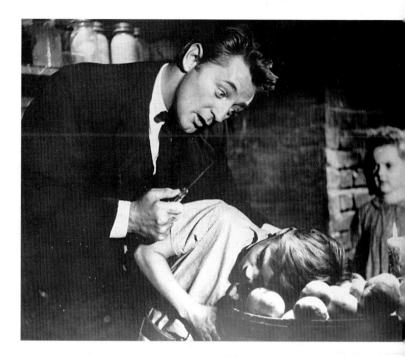

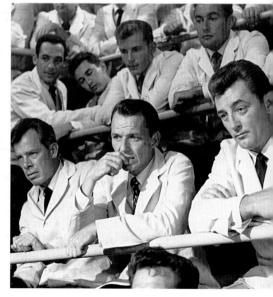

Preacher Powell and
the children: Robert
Mitchum, Billy Chapin,
and Sally Jane Bruce in
The Night of the Hunter
(1955), directed by
Charles Laughton.
Courtesy New York Public
Library

Observing an
operation, future
physicians Lee Marvin,
Frank Sinatra, and
Robert Mitchum, in
Not as a Stranger (1955),
directed by Stanley
Kramer.
Courtesy AP/Wide World
Photos

e great William A. Wellman,
ector of *The Story of G.I. Joe*, *Track
he Cat* and a would-be Mitchum
rer, *Blood Alley*. Here seen in San
ael, California, at the time of
chum's firing.
rtesy of William Wellman Jr.

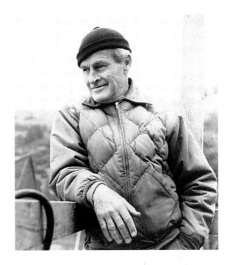

chum Confidential:
. *Herald Express* headline.

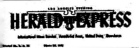

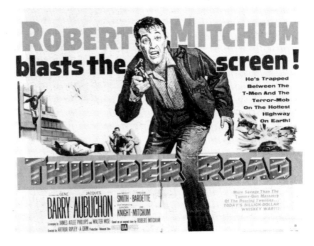

vertisement for
under Road (1958).
rtesy New York
lic Library

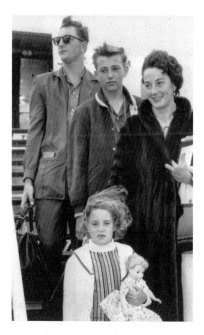

Robert Mitchum's wife, Dorothy, and their three children, Jim, 17, Chris, 14, and Petrine, 6, arrive at London Airport en route to Athens, Greece, to join Robert, filming *The Angry Hills*, June, 1958.
Courtesy AP/Wide World Photos

Deborah Kerr and Robert Mitchum in *The Sundowners* (1960).
Courtesy AP/Wide World Photos

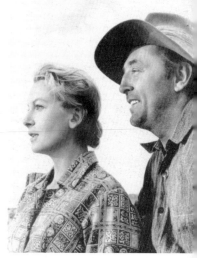

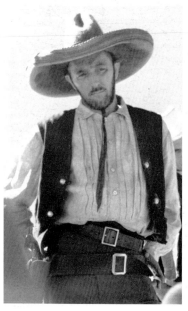

Mitchum as gunfighter Martin Brady in *The Wonderful Country*, from the novel by Tom Lea (United Artists, 1959).
Courtesy of author's collection

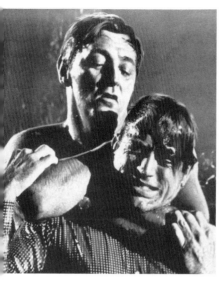

Robert Mitchum and his producer, Gregory Peck: the violent climax to *Cape Fear* (1962).
Courtesy AP/Wide World Photos

"Fun to be a movie star." Robert Mitchum and friends circa 1963.
Courtesy AP/Wide World Photos

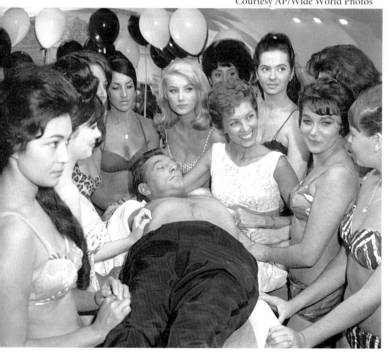

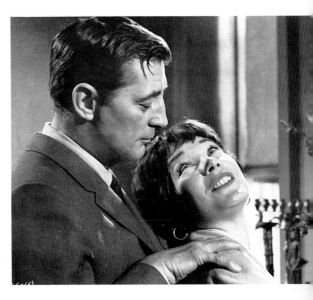

Robert Mitchum and
Shirley MacLaine in *Two
for the Seesaw* (United
Artists, 1962).
Courtesy New York Public
Library

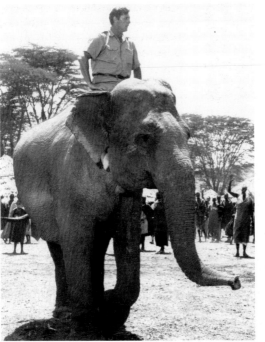

Robert Mitchum astride
lesbian elephant, filming
Mister Moses (1965) in
Kenya.
Courtesy AP/Wide World
Photos

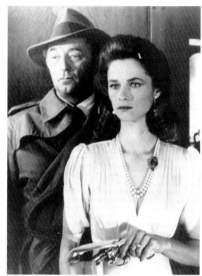

Robert Mitchum as Philip Marlowe, with Charlotte Rampling in *Farewell, My Lovely* (1975), from the novel by Raymond Chandler.
Courtesy AP/Wide World Photos

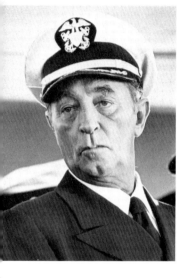

Robert Mitchum as Victor "Pug" Henry in the television miniseries, *The Winds of War* (1983).
Courtesy AP/Wide World Photos

Robert and brother, John Mitchum, Los Angeles, 1989.
Courtesy Andrew Fenady Productions

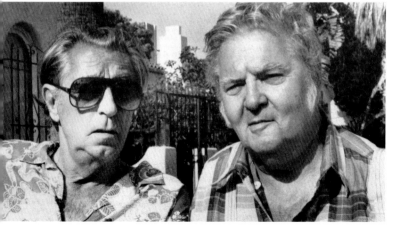

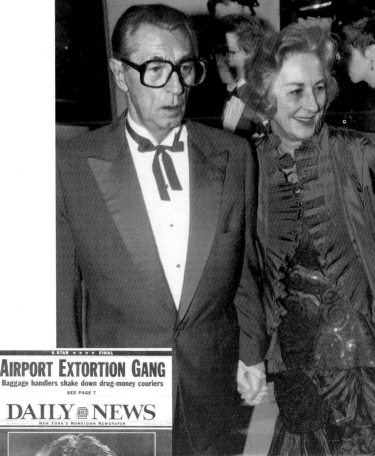

Robert and Dorothy Mitchum attending a premiere, 1995. Childhood sweethearts, together for more than sixty years.
Courtesy AP/Wide World Photos

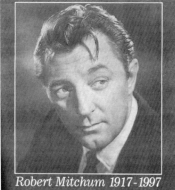

The end: the front page of New York's *Daily News*, July 2, 1997.
Copyright © *New York Daily News*, L.P. reprinted with permission

able star trio, for all of Douglas's dynamic histrionics and fine work by Richard Widmark, the consensus was that Mitchum (wearing buckskins and a shaggy wig he said made him look like "Gravel Gertie") walked away with the picture in a typically underplayed yet strong and moving performance as the old trail scout gradually losing his vision. Though he seems to have assumed it by happenstance, Mitchum's role was a custom fit, one more lonely, stoic outsider turning his back on civilization by the fade-out.

Driving himself up to Oregon, he had heard an obscure country and western record on an obscure country and western radio station somewhere beyond Bakersfield. The song was called "Little Old Wine Drinker Me," and it spoke to him. Later in the year he hooked up with Fred Foster, president and creative head at Monument Records, and traveled to Nashville, Tennessee (with some supplementary work in Hollywood), to record an album of easygoing pop and country pop tunes, some new, some old, including "Wine Drinker," "Sunny," "Wheels (Keep A-Rollin')," and two of Mitchum's own compositions, "Ballad of Thunder Road" and "Whippoorwill."

With jaunty, bleary, and on- and off-key vocal stylings like some hybrid of Dean Martin and Keith Richards, the record conveyed the ambience of something improvised at a truckstop roadhouse around four in the morning. The album, called *That Man Robert Mitchum . . . Sings,* was released with a striking cover photograph (and no type), a close-up of Bob in a pink shirt and a tousled, modified Beatle hairdo, and on the back were exuberant liner notes by Johnny Mercer. "I don't suppose Bob Mitchum is the greatest singer in the world," Mercer began, with candor, "but he is one of the greatest guys in the world. . . . The same carefree attractiveness that you find in his acting, you will find in this Monument album. . . . What some would call a 'maverick,' and that's how he is about how he sings . . . just as he always has been about his career and what people thought of him. His beat is impeccable, only a shade behind Bobby Darin, and if a note is too high for him, what the hell—he can act his way through it. I think the quality of his singing will surprise you. . . . If I sound like a 'fag,' sue me."

Released as a single in May 1967, Mitchum's "Little Old Wine Drinker Me" broke the pop charts and for several weeks was the number one country and western record in various markets across the country. Dino would later record the tune and have a major success with it, but Mitchum's 45 remained the preferred choice of jukeboxes throughout the Southwest for many years to come. Despite the record's good showing, Mitchum made no follow-up to *That Man.*

Back in Los Angeles after seven years, wanting to make an appropriately impressive return to their old stomping ground, Dorothy had taken a lease on a spectacular manor house on Rockingham in Brentwood that had been the home of Cole Porter for twenty-three years. "Comfortable, dreary, and expensive," Mitchum called it. Trina, now a stunning-looking teenager, was enrolled at the tony Westlake School for Girls. His beloved quarter horses were scattered, stabled at an assortment of California locales—"a couple of 'em in rooms at the Beverly Hills Hotel," he said. Eventually they would be brought together again at a small ranch—seventy-six acres—he purchased in rural Atascadero, a couple of hundred miles from town.

After the Mitchums' years of relative isolation in Maryland, there was a comforting feeling of coming home, being accepted back into the fold by the town's extended showbiz family. Bob could even be persuaded to put on a jacket and tie and attend an occasional party and public gathering. They met up with old acquaintances they hadn't seen in ages. Of course, some of these had been avoided with good cause. At a reception given by Henry Fonda for his daughter, Jane, and her husband, Roger Vadim, Mitchum and Wild Bill Wellman found themselves in the same room for the first time since the ugliness at San Rafael. "I went there with my father because my mother was ill that night," said Wellman's son William. "There was a ton of people at the party. At some point in the evening Mitchum arrived and worked his way to the end of the crowded hallway and came into my father's view. They'd had that feud on since the time he had fired Bob on *Blood Alley.* Dad was much older then and pretty tame, but he'd had a few beers and he was still capable of getting out of hand. Mitchum didn't see us. He was standing there smoking a cigarette and holding a drink. My father spotted him and started practically running at him. And I thought, *My God, he's going to hit Mitchum!* And I'm rushing through the crowd trying to catch him and protect my father. And when Mitchum saw him coming at him, he spilled his drink he was so startled, you know, about to get hit by this old man. And Dad grabbed him around the shoulders and hugged him, and Mitchum hugged him back, and the next thing they're grinning and sitting down and talking for the longest time."

Though they had known each other forever, it was during this period, after their pleasant months together on *El Dorado*, that Mitchum and John Wayne became—for a time—pals, roistering around town together—though never, of course, within sight of Mrs. Wayne (*that Blood Alley*–era feud remained alive). Mitchum was ever amused at the way Duke played his role in life to the hilt, wearing four-inch lifts to make his six-foot-four-inch frame still more impressive—gave him that funny walk, Mitchum said—having his car roof raised so he could comfortably keep his Stetson in place while driving. Once Mitchum came to Wayne's production office and listened to him screaming at his staff, knocking chairs over in a seemingly volcanic fury. Then, slamming his office door shut, he grinned from ear to ear and pulled out a jug. "You gotta keep 'em *Wayne-conscious*," he said. Despite his posture as a scold of young libertines, Wayne enjoyed getting smashed and, according to Mitchum, wasn't as square as he might appear. When a young actor and pot-smoking buddy asked, out of curiosity, whether John Wayne would ever get high when they were together, Mitchum told him, "Duke will do anything. He'll do it all."

"They were pretty funny together," said Paul Helmick. "I remember one time there was a big party to welcome Barbra Streisand to Hollywood. It was held outdoors at Ray Stark's house. I was invited because I was going to be the production manager on the picture *Funny Girl*. It was the elite of Hollywood there. And who shows up stumbling around in the garden but Mitchum and Wayne. Just the two of them, no women or nothing, crashing this party. I said, 'What the hell are you two doing here? This is a formal thing; they don't want a bunch of cowboys here!' They said, 'We want to meet Barbra!' And Wayne said, 'How'd you ever get mixed up with a nice outfit like this?' And I told him, 'I only do cowboy pictures if I can't get on a good musical. . . .'"

One of the Mitchums' new neighbors on Rockingham was the fabulous shock-haired comedienne, Phyllis Diller. "They were darling people," Diller recalled. "And he . . . *uh!* The voice, God, just the voice, the body, the attitude, what a guy! Exuded that maleness. And such a character. He would sit and regale us with stories. And he was so proud that he had been jailed thirty-seven times—it was his badge of honor!

"He was a world-class drinker, God, yes, we had that in common! *Ha!* He did as he pleased at all times. One evening after I had restored this lovely, beautiful old home of mine, I gave a big 'all-star' party. Very grand. A hundred and fifty sit-down dinner. And at every place setting was a large goblet of water with a large goldfish swimming in it. I thought it was amusing, and if they wanted they could take their fish home in a little compartment, a party favor. Mitchum sat down, picked up the glass, and drank it, fish and all! They were often guests in my home because I was crazy about both, absolutely nuts about them. And Robert was nuts about my chili. Well, and properly so! It's a hundred-year-old recipe, and it's the world's greatest chili. And when I had a buffet, there would be all sorts of lovely things, lobster and shrimp and huge roasts, and Robert would just fill up a bowl with chili and lick it clean.

"Dorothy was a darling person. Straight on. A good mother, a fine friend, no BS, just a nice person. You could feel very comfortable with her. A friend. No game playing. And she had her work cut out with that husband of hers. She'd tell me what a bother it was he was so untrue. But he would declare temporary insanity, and she would always forgive him. I tried to talk her into a divorce. I did! *A-haa!* We were away on a trip, a mutual friend, Lady Sassoon, her annual ball in the Bahamas. Both in the same guest house. And we were talking about him. You know, we were away from home, what are we going to talk about—men! Look, he would get out of her sight, he'd be surrounded by these beautiful young sluts—I mean starlets—that can't wait to jump into bed, they're throwing it in his face, and he couldn't resist. 'Temporary insanity,' he called it. I think the word is *horny*. And she was angry at him. And I told her there was only one thing to do, *divorce him!* I had had just enough to drink to tell the truth, to be brutally honest with her. She would have *none* of it. It was a lifelong affair, she said. They loved each other. It went back to the beginning; they'd been in love since they were kids. . . . Thank God I didn't marry *my* high school sweetheart . . . an ugly little rat! But I'm getting off the subject. . . ."

After twelve months—"when the rent came due," said Bob—they decided to leave the manor house on Rockingham. He had never cared for the place; it felt like old Cole Porter was turning over in his grave every time you belched or brought a muddy boot indoors.

They planned to rent something in town until an appropriate house could be purchased. That was all going to be Dottie's bailiwick. Mitchum told Reva to get him the hell out of town quick. He signed for two pictures shooting back-to-back in Europe.

Anzio was a Dino DeLaurentiis production with funding from Columbia Pictures, shot entirely in Italy with Italian technicians and Hollywood cast and director. Mitchum would be working with Edward Dmytryk for the first time in twenty-one years. After serving nearly a year in prison for contempt of Congress, blacklisted and broke, Dmytryk had made the difficult decision to cooperate with the witch hunters, the only one of the Hollywood Ten to "name names," after which he returned to work, picking up the pieces of his career, though a certain stigma would haunt him for all the years to come. It would be said of Dmytryk that—after this subjugation— he never again showed the creative power that had been so evident in his films of the '40s, but this is to ignore a number of creditable and unusual postblacklist works (such as *The Sniper, The Young Lions,* and *Warlock*). In any case, *Anzio* would not turn out to be one of them.

"DeLaurentiis was a deal maker more than a picture maker," said Dmytryk. "When the deal is made he thought the picture was made, all his worries were over. Things I was promised, the weapons, boats, the soldiers, never materialized. We had soldiers with rifles— the rifles were bending. I said, 'Jesus Christ, come here!' I looked at it; it was made of rubber, like a child's toy. All the guns were rubber, they were wiggling in the wind. I went to DeLaurentiis with the rubber gun. He said the guy with the good guns tried to cheat him. I said, 'I can't use these.' He said, 'Go ahead.' I said, 'I can't.' The whole picture I was back and forth all the time, demanding a ticket home."

The choice of subject matter reflected the spirit of the times, cynical, antiestablishment, antiwar, the era of *The Dirty Dozen* and *Kelly's Heroes*. No D day, the battle of Anzio had been one of America's worst military blunders, stemming from Gen. Mark Clark's reluctance to advance on an unprotected Rome, giving the Germans time to mount an attack on the U.S. beachhead—result, thirty thousand casualties. Mitchum had probably not even read the script (in which he was to play a sceptical war correspondent, a kind of hipster Ernie Pyle) before taking off for Rome that summer, but on arrival—fresh from his second inspiring visit to the grunts in Vietnam—he declared it to be "violently anti-American," a virtual "crucifixion" of General Clark. Dmytryk defended the facts. The script, he said, was historically accurate; the problem was that in all other ways it stank. Writers were flown in. Changes were made to appease Mitchum. Changes were made to appease Dmytryk. The script was rewritten just before they filmed, sometimes while they filmed; sometimes they went ahead and filmed without anything written down at all. The same old same old. Conceive, plan, prepare, rehearse, then—improvisation, anarchy.

"I hadn't seen Bob in a while," said the director. "We hadn't worked together since those days at RKO. A lot had happened since then. We'd gone our separate ways. He was still the same relaxed guy, good actor. There were changes, sure. He was a drunk now. But listen, I like to say that I directed all the great drunks of Hollywood. And most—maybe not most, but many of the great stars were drunks—Bogart, Gable, others I can name. And they were the best. And Mitchum would say, 'Don't use me after six o'clock.' But no matter how much he drank at night, or drugged, or whatever he was doing, in the morning he was there, perfect.

"There was a strange incident, when Bob first got to Italy and DeLaurentiis wanted to have a meeting. So we had a meeting. And when Bob wasn't working he was drinking and whatever. And Bob, when he began talking, it would become a monologue really. It was beautiful language, nice words, but sentences that went nowhere, absolutely incomprehensible. DeLaurentiis would ask a question and Mitchum would talk and it would be all nonsense. He didn't slur or stammer, but it made no sense at all. I've seen it before, schizophrenics do the same thing. And there was nothing to do. DeLaurentiis looked confused, but English wasn't his native tongue. So I just nodded and picked up the conversation like there was nothing wrong until Mitchum was asked another question. I don't know what DeLaurentiis ultimately made of it. Some day, I tell you . . . I'm going to write a book about all the movie star drunks I have known."

There were other changes in Mitchum, as Dmytryk perceived him, since those times on the stages at RKO long ago, in the halcyon days before Congressional investigations and wiretapped dressing rooms. "I remembered Mitchum as someone who was always talking up for the little guy, defending minorities, working people. And the Mitchum I saw in Rome had changed completely. He now had all these very right-wing views. Full of these strange conspiracy theories. He was right in the middle of all this kind of fringe political thinking; he had articles with him he could show you and everything. . . . He thought the government was secretly run by outsiders, that Lyndon Johnson had been involved in Kennedy's assassination, he was some kind of puppet leader. . . . Well, worse than that, worse than that. I don't want to . . . I can't begin to go into it, actually. But I must say, thank God, he realized this was something the two of us could not talk about, and it never went into any long discussion or argument."

Perhaps sensing condescension in the director's dismissal of these conversational gambits, Mitchum let it be known that he thought Dmytryk an "old fool." He would goof on him to the other actors. "Dmytryk had his barbells shipped here from Los Angeles, can you imagine?" he would say. One time Mitchum had to run up a steep hill and back for several takes. He found out it was a long shot, a double could have done it just as well. "Oh, Eddie's going to pay for this one," he told onlookers.

Anzio had roles for some other names from the RKO days. Robert Ryan, another *Crossfire* vet, played a general, and so did Bob's *Lusty Men* costar, Arthur Kennedy. But these were old men now, playing old men's roles. Mitchum felt more at home among the younger and more active members of the cast. Reni Santoni, who had just given a brilliant and hilarious debut performance in the film *Enter Laughing*, had been loaned to DeLaurentiis by Columbia to play a GI and comic relief sidekick for Mitchum's hard-boiled lead. "They figured I played a young actor in *Enter Laughing*, so make this one a guy who likes movies. And we'll call him Movie! That shows you the level of creativity going on in this thing. Every scene, I was supposed to do an imitation of another movie star. I did it a little bit, but Dmytryk—'Fast Eddie' we called him—had the good sense to let me take my own approach to it.

"It was a disaster area. The Italian way of filmmaking was baffling. Nothing got done. And I remember Dmytryk saying, 'I've had better production value on pictures that cost ten thousand dollars!' There was no script. There was some idea, which might have been cool, about men making war because they like to, because they need to. Somewhere that was in there. But what it turned into was seven dwarves lost in the woods. In this war movie, seven guys win the war.

"Mitchum . . . yeah. 'The Goose.' When I first saw him they were shooting out in Naples at this huge congressional hall, opening scene of the picture. We were introduced and he was curt. 'How are ya. So what . . .' I thought, Hm . . . OK. Kind of disappointing. I was very much a fan of his. I found out later he had just had a big disagreement with Dmytryk over something.

"When I was a kid growing up in the Bronx—I'm from a New York Puerto Rican background—they had an expression 'Moto eyes.' I guess it was tracked back to Mr. Moto—you smoke some grass, your eyes get an Asian look. And when I was a kid I remember my mother talking about Robert Mitchum, the pot smoker, and his Mr. Moto eyes. He was a consumer of marijuana, of all horrors! Fade-out, fade-in, I'm in my early twenties in a hotel room in Italy with Robert Mitchum and smoking some superior, superior grass! We eventually got to be friendly after that first gruff encounter, and he soon recognized me—it was the late '60s—as a guy 'of the time'; in other words, he figured, 'I can get loaded with this guy.' And we did, quite often. And it was the beginning of a beautiful friendship."

In Bari the drug dealer came calling with a huge attaché case for interested cast members. Drop it down on the bed, click, click, swing it open. Pills in one corner, hashish over there, hash oil, grass, kif from Morocco. All the world's bounty. Whatever your heart desired. "The Goose loved to get high. The first night Mitchum sent for me he says, 'Uh, I have some stuff that you might find . . . interesting.' And he had gotten some spectacular Afghanistan hashish. He would share his dope; I will say that. He was very, very generous. And he was a connoisseur, like a wine expert with this stuff. And he'd be interested in your opinion. 'Tell me what you think of this shit.'

"He was a great storyteller and a great mimic. Did voices, could imitate anyone. I did some routines, too, and he really appreciated my humor. I could do a dynamite black imitation. I could do some niggas would have him falling down laughing. He loved that stuff. He had a doper's perspective. Humor, rock music. What was he? Almost fifty. But he was hip. We're sitting in the hotel room in Italy one day. We were smoking some excellent grass. A friend had sent it from the States stuffed in a doll. And a friend of mine had just come from London and had one of the first copies of *Sgt. Pepper*—the Beatles. It hadn't even hit the States yet, not even released yet. And here we are high, listening to *Sgt. Pepper*, this incredible hip thing at the time; nobody had heard anything like this before. And at one point I'm so thrilled by something I hear I want to turn and share it with this old duffer, in my youthful arrogance, explain what it's all about to the old-timer. And I started to explain, and he very politely, with a little hand gesture, just kind of said, 'I'm already there, man.' He was incredibly cool. And there we are, I'm sitting with Robert Mitchum smoking dope and listening to *Sgt. Pepper* for the first time and we're wearing our World War II clothes, combat boots and dog tags! It was like I had left reality and gotten into some very unreal realm."

Mitchum took some of his castmates on night patrol. He dazzled them with his powers, left them in the dust—they were half his age! Just to watch him making his rounds through the Roman night was astonishing entertainment for the young actors. Watch the women, mooning and purring in the streets and lobbies and bars. Oh, Mr. Mitchum, and where are you staying? Oh, that's near my room, perhaps I can come visit. Running into a half-lushed Ava Gardner at Dave's Dive. They all go over and sit with Ava in this dark joint, while she and Robert canoodle in the booth. Holy shit, Reni Santoni remembered thinking, is this for real? "And for all that life, that movie god life he had, he never took it seriously. Always had that ironic perspective. Could not care less. Look who he picked for his entourage, an entourage of one: *Tim Wallace.* Tim was the coarsest creature on earth. Farting was Tim's chief amusement. He was riding in the elevator, three or four other people in there going down, Europeans. Suddenly the elevator is filled with the unmistakable stink of one of Mr. Wallace's gas specials. Lofted through the hotel. Mitchum turns to him and whispers, 'You . . . dog.' Tim looks around at the other people and says, 'What's the big deal? Dey don't none of 'em speak English.' He was quite, quite coarse. He'd see a girl sitting somewhere with her legs apart and come running to report: '*Jeeze, you can almost see her whole minge!*' This charming creature is who Mitchum brings to Rome!

"It was a joke to him, being a movie star. We were going into a restaurant in the city, about three or four guys, and just before we go through the door, he stops. Puts his shoulders back, adjusts that little tilt to his head. He said, 'Hold on, guys, I have to get my attitude ready. It's taken me twenty-five years to get this shit down. . . . OK. *I'm ready.*' And then he goes through the door as *Robert Mitchum, movie star!* Everybody bows down. 'Ah, *Signor* Mitchum, ah *signor!*

Ahh!' He was very aware of how absurd it all was, and he had a great sense of humor about it!"

A shabby, would-be *Longest Day* with a woeful lack of spectacle or firepower, *Anzio* was the least distinguished movie to which Mitchum had offered his services since his days as a B movie bit player. The film had one distinction: The theme song played over the opening credits, sung by Jack Jones, a cocktail cha-cha thing with lyrics (impossibly credited to the great Doc Pomus) about "gentle dreamers" finding "war is necessary hell," was the worst in the history of the cinema.

*

From Rome Mitchum went to Madrid to begin filming *Villa Rides*. Since Sergio Leone had struck gold there, it was the new home of the American West. Europeans had started making imitation Hollywood Westerns with great success, so now, of course, Hollywood had to come to Spain to make imitation spaghetti Westerns. *Villa Rides*, a version of the life of the Mexican revolutionary, was a project for Yul Brynner; and Sam Peckinpah, then drifting in Hollywood, had been hired to write the screenplay and—more tentatively—to direct the picture. Peckinpah turned out a typically intense and violent piece of work, a deeply ambivalent portrait of Pancho Villa as half-noble, half-monster. Yul Brynner read it, said it made Villa look like a bad guy, and Peckinpah left the project. So, no Peckinpah-directed life of Villa, and Mitchum would not get to work with a man who might well have proved to be a most simpatico collaborator. Buzz Kulik, a television director now making features, was hired. "The Peckinpah script? Three-quarters of it was in Spanish!" said Kulik. "I think he was married to a Spanish woman he was trying to impress. We threw most of it out, had to start almost all over again. Hired Robert Towne. He came to Spain, and he would be working on tomorrow's dialogue the night before."

Peckinpah had originally been told his screenplay would have to include "a white face" in addition to all those darker, revolutionary ones. He came up with an American mercenary character, "a man without direction or ambition, who seldom thinks about the future." For this part the producers thought of, yes, Robert Mitchum.

Towne summed up the proceedings as he saw them: "A million dollars tied up in salaries between the two guys, and they figure it will take maybe two million to make the movie, so they say, 'What the hell, we might as well go ahead and get something for an extra million. We'll come out of it somehow.' What happens is you pay a lot of people a lot of money to make a movie that nobody particularly wants to make."

They filmed in the hills and valleys outside Madrid and in the tiny village of El Casar de Talamanca, filling in for the Mexican town of Chupadero. The cast was comfortably housed at the Castellana Hilton. Brynner, wearing hair for the first time in years, thought Kulik an underwhelming talent. Kulik thought the same of Brynner. "He knew he wasn't that great an actor, so he was on the defense all the time. Plus, he had a bad back, so we were forced to do lots of cutaways when shooting him. He goes to mount a horse, you cut away, you cut back, and we've lifted him up on the horse.

"Working with Mitchum, though, was a dream. He had this facade he put out—'I don't know anything; I don't know what we're shooting.' But underneath, he was a man with great discipline. He knew everything. He was a genius! You talk about nuclear physics; he knew about that. Talk about the price of cattle; he could tell you. Nothing he didn't know. Extraordinary."

El Dorado was set to have its Spanish premiere during Mitchum's time in Madrid. In conjunction with the opening, a one-week tribute to the star was arranged. This was something new. A Robert Mitchum Film Festival. It lasted a week, opening with *G.I. Joe,* followed by screenings of *Night of the Hunter, Heaven Knows, Mr. Allison, The Enemy Below, The Sundowners, Two for the Seesaw,* and climaxing with the *El Dorado* debut. The festival givers wanted Mitchum to attend all the screenings. He told them he had been successful in avoiding seeing most of those pictures up to now and did not intend to spoil his record.

On the locations, Mitchum was graciously permitted to do his dozing and bullshitting inside Yul Brynner's one-of-a-kind, superdeluxe air-conditioned trailer, which Yul took with him wherever in the world he was filming. Mitchum and Brynner got along fine (it was third-billed Charles Bronson that Mitchum couldn't stand). "Yul had great respect for Bob, and affection," said the actor's son, Rock, hanging out with his father that autumn in Spain. "Found him a wonderful, thoughtful man, very humble, and yet with great pride in his work because he felt that he had always delivered the honest goods." Until the calming arrival of his wife and daughter, Mitchum and the two Brynners and a floating band of international revelers had an antic time among the bright lights of Madrid. "Bob enjoyed the Spanish red wine, and many other things he got his hands on," said Buzz Kulik. "I don't think he was ever a really bad boy with it, but he had his fun. There were always hangers-on trying to tempt him with something. People shoving women at him. Women—well, they didn't need to be shoved. I remember at one point he had two girls with him; I think they were twins. As I heard it, he was having them both at the same time."

Rock Brynner: "*Identical* twins. English girls, living in Madrid. One hung on each arm. Everyone called them 'the Bookends.'"

He kept his other amusements within reach, too. Veteran character actor Marc Lawrence, working in Europe since the blacklist days, remembered calling on Mitchum during this Iberian sojourn. "I smoked *shit* with him at the Hilton in Madrid! Yeah. We were all in Spain, and Phil Yordan wanted me to go over and talk him into doing some picture. I go over to the hotel and he doesn't listen to a word. 'Fuck the business talk, man,' he says. 'Let's smoke some weed.' Got me all fucked up. I told Yordan, 'Hey, I tried.' He said, 'What happened?' I said, 'I don't remember!'"

"Bob was such a passive guy for the most part, and had that comic, laconic outlook on life," said Rock Brynner. "One of the locations for *Villa Rides* was done just beside this huge open conduit for the city's sewage. And Bob viewed it and made this observation. He said, 'I wake up in the morning in my hotel, . . . take a dump, . . . come to work, and right in the middle of a scene I watch my dump go by. I find this very comforting."

Villa Rides was noisy, colorful, violent, watchable, forgettable. Mitchum had done it all—and done it better—a dozen years before, in *Bandido!* Sam Peckinpah, meanwhile, once dismissed, went on to make his own American-mercenaries-in-the-Mexican-Revolution movie: *The Wild Bunch.* He claimed to have reused many things he wrote originally for the *Villa* script. The character of Pike Bishop in *The Wild Bunch* would have been not just exciting and perfect casting for Mitchum but a great and defining end-of-the-decade role. Peckinpah's producers sent the script to him, but Robert opted for *Five Card Stud* instead—they were both Westerns, weren't they?— and the part in the epochal *Wild Bunch* went to Bob's old friend Bill Holden.

Five Card Stud was a production of Hal B. Wallis, the man who had supervised *Little Caesar* and *Casablanca,* still plugging away after a near half century in the business. It was an unofficial remake of one of the producer's old pictures, a 1950 film noir called *Dark City,* readjusted to the 1890s frontier. A card cheat is lynched by his fellow poker players and then each man in turn is brutally murdered by a mysterious avenger. The hero part went to Dean Martin. Mitchum accepted a colorful but subsidiary role as Rev. Jonathan Rudd, a gunslinging preacher "elected by God and Mr. Colt." The director was another Hollywood veteran, Henry *White Witch Doctor* Hathaway.

Filming got started in the spring of 1968. Hal Wallis didn't know from these half-assed, runaway, shot-in-Spain, faux spaghetti Westerns. He made *American* Westerns, and he made them where you were supposed to make them—in Durango, Mexico.

The summit meeting (as Sinatra liked to call these things) of Mitchum and Martin, Hollywood's two deities of indifference, produced no sparks, on or off the screen. Martin acted his part as if he had memorized the lines phonetically. He retired early, stayed in his room when he wasn't working. Observers say it was a quiet, uneventful shoot, with the exception of a collapsing camera platform that nearly hammered Mitchum into the earth. Calmly, like Buster Keaton in *Steamboat Bill,* he stepped aside just far enough and in time for the thousands of pounds of metal and lumber to miss his head by inches.

Roddy McDowall, another *Five Card Stud* player, had been talking on the phone to his friend Liz Taylor. Her new picture, *Secret Ceremony,* shooting in England, needed a big name for a small part; and he suggested Mitchum. Robert was taking some R and R in Mazatlan, on the Pacific Coast, when a phone call from London reached him. It was *Ceremony's* director, Joseph Losey, another old pal from the distant days at RKO. Losey talked him into this sort of guest star job, two weeks maximum, for $150,000. Could Bob handle an English accent all right? Like a jaded garage mechanic explaining a range of services, Mitchum listed the various regional British dialects he could offer. Losey said he wanted something that wouldn't overshadow the ersatz accents of his two other American stars, Taylor and Mia Farrow. He told Mitchum to see if he could come up with an "indifferent" English accent. Mitchum said he didn't think it would be a problem.

After being blacklisted in Hollywood, Losey had resettled in England, where he slowly established a reputation as a stylish and highbrowed *auteur. Secret Ceremony* was the latest of his series of opaque, architectonic films following a pattern set by his breakthrough hit, *The Servant,* and it was the second of his projects as the "house director" for the Burtons, Liz and/or Dick, then at their jetsetting, conspicuously consuming, bad-movie-making height. The film dealt with a wealthy, insane young woman's enigmatic, disturbing relationship with a prostitute surrogate-mother figure and a stalking, incestuous stepfather. There were echoes of *Night of the Hunter* in Mitchum's eventual characterization (as there had been, of course, in his *Five Card* part)—Albert, the leering, loathesome English professor, a kind of goateed, tweedy Preacher Powell for the

Swinging '60s. The film was modernist esoterica light years away from his usual genre stuff but Mitchum typically adapted without a hair looking out of place.

Mitchum moved into the Dorchester, where the Burtons were already enthroned on most of one floor (their puppies, due to quarantine, were kept on a yacht on the Thames). Mitchum enjoyed Liz Taylor's boisterous company, and their scenes together brought out the best of her performance in the mannered film. And he was entirely taken with the wispily beautiful, twenty-one-year-old Mia Farrow, dreamy flower-child daughter of his late drinking buddy and nemesis John Farrow and—though not for long—wife of his pal Frank Sinatra (whose hounding phone calls and cables were a source of aggravation during filming).

But Mitchum seemed to have nothing but disdain for the job at hand and something like outright hostility for his one-time friend Joseph Losey. "From the moment he arrived he was on the defensive," the director revealed in an interview, "and he was very unpleasant. So it was extremely hard for me to work with him. . . . In some curious way I must have made some mistake with him; I don't know what it was. But there was nothing ever that he did with any pleasure." Losey had been an associate of Charles Laughton's and had greatly admired the remarkable collaboration between Laughton and Mitchum on *The Night of the Hunter*. But Losey's attempt to spark a discussion of the subject with the actor was bluntly rejected. Mitchum was only sarcastic about Laughton, as he was about everything else. Losey thought Mitchum's attitude was perhaps a defense mechanism, a cover "for intense embarrassment . . . intense sense of failure." Losey was frustrated and haunted by Mitchum's inexplicable rejection—they had been friends, had a real rapport once. Mitchum had been engaged by life, spirited. Now, twenty-five years later, there was only a contempt for everything. "He was an extremely secret man. And he was writing poetry, which I found very beautiful, very sensitive. But he's an adamant, crazy, damned man, and there was no way of having any contact with him." But for all that, the ugly feelings, the end of communication between them—and in some silly, selfish way making it feel all the worse—Losey didn't know anyone who could have done a better job, with Mitchum's exactly right quality of "sensual contemplation." No British actor he knew of. Maybe Mastroianni could have done it, if he'd had the English, Losey mused pointlessly.

One morning Robert showed up on the doorstep of London residents Bob and Kathie Parrish. He had simply walked out on rehearsals at the art nouveau mansion in Kensington, drifted along the streets, and tracked down his old *Wonderful Country* friends. "We let him in, it was early in the morning," said Mrs. Parrish. "He asked for some tequila. In memory of our days in Mexico. He loved the kind with the worm in the bottle! And Mitchum drank some tequila and told us he had snuck out on Losey and Liz Taylor and Mia. They didn't even know he left. He said they were over there arguing over their motivation for the next scene. They needed to know what was the character's grandmother's maiden name. In other words, he was decrying that kind of acting. He drank some more tequila and then decided he better get going; they'd be looking for him. He said, 'I'll go back and hit my mark.'"

They moved to Holland for a week of shooting at the seaside town of Noordwijk, scenes of Albert the stalker following the two women to a weekend getaway. Richard Burton came along. He recited poetry, got bombed, needled his wife—all very *Virginia Woolf*. Burton and Mitchum: one might have expected something to blossom there. The Welshman, too, had lost a parent in childhood, had tossed around with relatives, grown up in poverty, a roughneck youth but extremely intelligent, erudite. A secret scribbler. Public roisterer. Burton had once said, "One drinks because life is big and it blinds you. It's grabbing at you from all directions all the time and you have to tone it down. Poetry and drink are the greatest things on earth." But neither man seemed to have the energy or inclination to pursue a friendship. Burton, rather treacherously, as Losey's disappointment with Mitchum grew, even quietly offered to do Robert's role should the director get rid of the other actor.

There was an incident in the dining room of the Hotel Huis ter Duin one evening, Mitchum giving Mia Farrow an "all-consuming" kiss, according to a news report, and Mia so distracted that her dangling cigarette burned the suit of another diner. The man got to his feet and yelled at Mia, Mitchum took his plate of salad and threw it at the man, the man reached over for his own salad and tossed it, mostly splattering Mia, and waiters rushed in as Mitchum gathered up a fistful of sliced tomatoes and flung them into the air. Someone should have turned a camera on—the morose *Secret Ceremony* could have used a good food fight.

Mitchum's contract stipulated such a brief availability, and Losey was so happy to be rid of him, that several of the actor's scenes were dropped and some revised for Liz Taylor to do instead, including, Mitchum claimed, the film's risqué two-in-a-tub sequence, which he said was originally intended for him to do with Farrow. "They turned it into a lesbian scene," he said. "And I'm just no good as a lesbian."

There was one aftereffect of Mitchum's brief participation in the film. The contracts had been drawn awaiting Mia Farrow's return to Hollywood to play the lead opposite John Wayne in *True Grit*. It was to be directed by Henry Hathaway. "Hathaway? Oh no. He's a screaming, bullying son of a bitch," Mitchum told her. "Screams all day long. You'll be miserable." Wispy Mia promptly cabled Hal Wallis to say she wouldn't work with Hathaway, to hire Roman Polanski instead. Wallis refused. She cabled back pulling out of the project. She would later say it was the biggest mistake of her career, and Mitchum would later pen an affectionate tribute to Hathaway for one of Roddy McDowall's celebrity portrait books, ranking the director among those whose "seamless armor shielded a depth of feeling and sensitive appreciation."

Whatever. Maybe he was thinking of some other guy.

*

They found a house in Bel Air, a modest—by Bel Air standards—ivy-covered four-bedroom place with a pool at 268 Saint Pierre Road. Mitchum was awarded the large den as his personal space. Here he put his stereo and a portion of his vast record collection, some books, a couple of photographs that amused him (an out-of-focus candid of him and Sinatra in a dressing room, Mitchum's white thigh near the lens, distorted, looking like it was springing from his crotch; "I've seen some big cocks, but this is ridiculous . . . Love, Francis Albert"). Unlike many stars—he claimed good old Kirk Douglas's den was the unofficial Kirk Douglas Museum—he neither displayed nor kept any memorabilia to advertise his career. "What am I going to do," he would say, "hang up a poster from *Hoppy Serves a Writ? Anzio?* The cleaning lady would laugh at me." His den was to be the pot-smoking headquarters—exclusively, by edict. The curtains and cushions in every room in the house weren't going to smell of that stuff in this place. He hid a marijuana plant in the garden and cultivated it with the love and devotion of a mother toward an infant, and it grew to be strong—six feet tall!—and bear much fruit. When it was in full bloom he took Polaroids of it and kept them around and in his wallet, like baby pictures.

It was now being said that Mitchum, having carried his anti-establishment, outsider persona into the Age of Aquarius, had become "in," a favorite with the teenage crowd. A survey of the nation's campuses reported that Mitchum was becoming a cult icon, the screen's new godfather of cool. He couldn't understand it, Mitchum said. They must have missed his last ten pictures before they took the vote. Anyway, it had to be a short-lived ascendency. It seemed to Mitchum there were pretenders to that throne all over the place now. The underplaying, the deadpan macho schtick, the cynical hipster outsider stance were all the rage in 1968. Steve McQueen, Lee Marvin, Clint Eastwood, Bronson. Were they trying to crowd his act? Forget it, fellas. Just my luck I'll be here till they set fire to my coffin. Anyway, if that was the competition . . . Steve McQueen? A McQueen performance, he believed, just naturally lent itself to monotony. Didn't bring much brains to the party, that boy. Marvin was the fourth med student from the right, back in *Not as a Stranger* days, and now he was a star, thanks to *Cat Ballou,* a part Bob had turned down. Fun guy, Lee, he thought—and they call *me* a mean drunk. Eastwood Mitchum remembered from the '50s, the shy, good-looking young man used to work construction jobs with George Fargo; Gray Cloud used to bring Clint along to the tavern so he could meet a real live movie star. And Bronson? Oh . . . forget about it. None of 'em was as popular as old Duke Wayne, and he weighed more than his horse these days and was working on one lung.

Speaking of young actors, Jim Mitchum was still trying to become a star. He was somewhere in Hollywood, but his father claimed not to hear from him for months at a time. The boy never came to him for his professional advice, he said, so he shared it with reporters instead: "I guess James is one of the 'now' generation. They're sure they can do it, *now*. I said, 'James . . . You've got to learn the trade first. Apply yourself.'"

And now there was another performer in the family. Chris Mitchum was at loose ends after graduating from the University of Arizona. His dream of becoming a professional writer remained just a dream. He and wife, Cindy, had two kids by this time, a daughter, Carrie, and a newborn son, Christopher Robert Mitchum. It had not been easy taking care of his family, but Chris did not like to go to his father for money. A point of pride, he said. Once, near Christmas, he had had to ask him for a hundred dollars and paid it back as soon as he could, to his father's evident surprise. He looked for work in various professions, with varying results. Employers discriminated, he said. They heard you were the son of the big movie star, and they couldn't believe you needed a paycheck. "My kids were starving and I was two months back on the house payments, and they wouldn't give me a job because they thought I was loaded. . . . It almost forces you to become an actor because you can't get a job doing anything else."

Which sounded, after all, just like Papa Bob's own rationale for remaining an actor.

Christopher made his screen debut with his father in *Young Billy Young*, his old man's latest Western. He played the sheriff's son in a flashback sequence. He fit in perfectly with a supporting cast that also included Dean Martin's daughter Deana, John Carradine's son David, and Robert Walker, Jr.

From a novel called *Who Rides with Wyatt*, about a purported friendship between Sheriff Earp of the title and boy outlaw Billy Clanton, the script by Burt Kennedy had originally been done for John Wayne. When the Duke decided against it, Kennedy wound up making it with producer Max Youngstein and Mitchum, who received a two-hundred-thousand-dollar salary plus 27 percent of the gross. Released in the time of *The Wild Bunch, Butch Cassidy and the Sundance Kid,* and *Once Upon a Time in the West, Young Billy Young* was a decidedly more traditional, modest enterprise (comely leading lady Angie Dickinson's nude scene excepted). It was Mitchum's least ambitious horse opera since the Zane Grey programmers at RKO. They shot it under the blue skies of Tucson, exteriors and all interiors, too, on a soundstage that subsequently burned down. Mitchum would sing the film's theme song over the opening credits (the strange, nearly all-percussion score for the movie supplied by jazz musician Shelly Manne).

"Bob was a great guy, did the job, no problems at all," said Burt Kennedy. "He was from the old school, like Duke, Henry Fonda. No problems, no questions, just get the job done. He liked to make wisecracks, put himself down. Mentioned *El Dorado* one time, said, 'On that one I played John Wayne's leading lady.' He was a bright guy, liked to pretend that he wasn't most of the time. But it was a joke. I remember one time we went to dinner, invited to the house of a friend of his. Turned out the guy was dean of architecture at Arizona University, and Bob sat all night talking about ancient architecture with the guy."

Reporter Tim Tyler found Mitchum's "get the job done" attitude to be undercut by frustration and barely contained loathing for the work—at times uncontained. In Tucson, observing the shooting of an uncomplicated scene among the crowd gawking at the "flat miserable" star in action, Tyler wrote, "As soon as the director yells 'cut' Mitchum explodes. Literally explodes. He sprays a string of four-letter words all over the astonished tourists who have come to watch their hero work. He dances and minces all over the Western street in a wild, furious and very accurate imitation of a fairy. Then, as the tourists stare dumbfounded at one another, he shuffles off in his

chaps to the location cafeteria, muttering, 'Every time the same goddamn role, the same goddamn role.'"

With barely a pause, Kennedy and Mitchum reunited for a second
Western, *The Good Guys and the Bad Guys,* shot in the mountains
around Chama, New Mexico, near the Colorado border. This one
was mixed with satire and farce, in the vein of Kennedy's earlier
comedy Western, *Support Your Local Sheriff.* As in *El Dorado,* the
film explored the idea of an aging cowboy hero, Robert Mitchum
here playing a lawman put out to pasture, teaming up with another
involuntary retiree, a train robber played by George Kennedy—an
exuberant, picture-stealing performance, particularly in contrast to
Mitchum's glum, even dull work in the film.

Maybe, at fifty-one, he was living the part. This so-called generation gap that they were writing think pieces about was beginning to
deprive Mitchum of some of his hip *edge.* Everybody was a rebel
these days, an outsider. Kids were all using drugs, marijuana was
practically passé. Some of the young actors he was working with on
the latest pictures were into the more advanced mind-altering
capacities of LSD. And on that other great controversial topic of the
day, Vietnam, Mitchum was now firmly entrenched on the counter-
countercultural side. At a party George Kennedy threw at a Mexican
restaurant, Mitchum went into a kind of kill-'em-all rant involving
mass bombings and how to destroy the North Vietnamese supply of
fresh water. "We'd all had a few," said John Davis Chandler, one of
The Good Guys' bad guys. "And he was just getting outrageous,
more and more out of line with this prowar thing. And I'd had a few
and I said something like, 'Well, I think we should get the fuck out.'
Something like that. 'If we can't win it, get out.' And he just turned
to me, furious. 'What the hell do you know? *I've been there.'* And I
thought, OK, you been there for a couple of weeks; you're the
expert. But I knew damn well he hadn't been in a uniform or had to
do any fighting. But what the hell; it was all drink talk. Like I said,
we'd all had a few by then."

Burt Kennedy was talented and good-natured, and the film was
efficiently made, but Mitchum was heard grumbling and grousing

throughout. "How in hell did I get into this picture anyway? I kept reading in the papers that I was going to do it, but when they sent me the script I just tossed it on the heap with the rest of them. But somehow, one Monday morning, here I was. How in hell do these things happen to a man?"

A complicated setup on a moving train caused difficulties. Everyone stood around, waiting for the engine to work. Mitchum said, "Why don't we quit and try something else? Like another movie. . . ."

With the exception of a brief role in a decidedly untraditional film many years later, *Young Billy Young* and *The Good Guys and the Bad Guys* were to be Mitchum's final Westerns. It was the genre in which he had done his first work in the movies and his first work as a star and the genre in which he had worked often enough to become identified as one of its A picture icons, with Cooper and Wayne. Nearly one-third of the eighty-five features he had appeared in by the close of the '60s had been Westerns. Most of these had been "the same goddamn role" no doubt, but a few had been much more than that; and some of those cowboy pictures were among the best, certainly the most unusual, the genre had ever produced. Ironically, even though a number of the most popular and talked-about films in the last year of the decade would be "hoss oprys," even as the form was being reinvented and given new life in Europe, the Western's days were numbered. In Hollywood the studios disdained the opportunity to make run-of-the-mill, old-fashioned cowboy movies like *Young Billy Young*—not enough profit potential, not enough pizzazz. The new Western prototypes were the easy rider and the midnight cowboy, a driftin' drug dealer and a Texas/Times Square male prostitute. In a few years the genre that had been a mainstay of American movies for most of the century would become a thing of the past.

Didn't bother Mitchum one way or the other. He was taking himself out of it now. Fed up, bored to tears. His back was broken; his ass was sore. The joke books these producers sent him were worse than ever. Let somebody else make faces at the gawk box. He had four or five million in the bank, fellas, or maybe it was six, and the time had come to saddle up and ride off into the sunset with the other old farts.

CHAPTER FIFTEEN

. . . I Used to Be Handsome

Retirement was the thing. He sat in meditation in his den that winter and into the new year, or made the two-hundred-mile drive to the ranch at Atascadero and let his mind look ahead as he drove, plotting what he would do—and all that he would not do—in the glorious, indolent future that lay before him. He thought about buying a ranch in New Mexico, a place he'd checked out near Santa Fe, build his quarter horse stock there, and maybe a winter place in the Bahamas. He wanted to get a boat, become a yachtsman like Duke Wayne, maybe a nice eighty-foot yacht, and cruise in warm waters, big game fishing.

The scripts and the phone calls continued to come into his production office. He was thinking of closing the place down. What did he need it for? Reva wouldn't be happy about that. Have to cut back her duties. Concentrate on answering the fan mail or something. One of the scripts she had tried to get him to read came in from MGM by way of London. Robert Bolt original, to be directed by David Lean.

"Send it back."

"But . . . it's David Lean! *Doctor Zhivago. Lawrence of Arabia. Bridge on the River Kwai.* They want you for the lead."

He looked it over. *Ryan's Daughter.* Very pretty. Lyrical even. He remembered hearing about how long Lean took to make each one of his pictures. Nine years or somethin'. And you had to do the whole thing on a camel.

"Reva, honey, NFI." No further interest.

Then, some weeks later, Bolt got him on the phone. They talked,

Bolt flattering, charmingly obsequious. Mitchum said Lean took a long time, didn't he? Bolt told him, ah yes, normally, but this was no *Doctor Zhivago*. This was an intimate little romantic drama and they would be in and out in two shakes. And besides, they were going to finagle the schedule so Mitchum could take off weeks at a time now and again. And so on. Kept talking it up. He couldn't get rid of the guy.

"Well, it's a nice offer but . . . just can't. . . . I have made other arrangements. I'm planning to kill myself."

"Planning what? Sorry, bad connection."

"I'm planning suicide."

There was a long pause on the other end. Maybe he'd hung up. Mitchum considered putting the phone down. Then Bolt said, "Yes, I quite understand. . . . But, well, if you would just do this wretched little film of ours first and then do yourself in, we'd be very happy to stand the expenses of your burial."

It had begun as an adaptation of *Madame Bovary* for Bolt's wife, Sarah Miles. Perhaps, he hoped, his *Lawrence* and *Zhivago* collaborator, Lean, would be interested in directing it. Lean said no, but something sparked when he read the script. What about an original, based on the Flaubert, same premise but new characters, settings? Lean had become world famous and enormously wealthy on account of his series of "thinking man's spectaculars"; but he had a prickly sensitivity to criticism and he had been stung by the talk that these big-hit superproductions were not as good as the good old lean Lean pictures like *Brief Encounter*, those simple, tasteful, and touching dramas with a human-sized canvas. Bolt's Bovary put things in motion for what Lean began calling a "little gem" of a story about romantic young Rosy Ryan, her marriage to a dull schoolteacher, Charles O'Shaughnessy, and her torrid love affair with a dashing, wounded, English military officer, the whole set in the Irish hinterlands at the time of the "troubles." The role of the husband, an inspiring romantic as Rosy's teacher but a dud as her sex partner, was offered to Paul Scofield, a superbly right casting choice, and he turned it down. Lean's producer wanted a little-known

Anthony Hopkins to take the part. MGM and Lean wanted a big movie star, a heavyweight to evenly stand up beside Marlon Brando, the actor who had been offered the part of the military man. His choice of Mitchum for the retiring schoolmaster and inept lover was considered odd in the extreme, but Lean had come up with a theory that a "dull" character had to be played by an actor with an opposite personality or the audience would go to sleep. Still, his people argued, Mitchum was *too opposite*. Producer Anthony Havelock-Allan told the director that no audience was going to believe Mitchum would allow somebody to screw his wife and not do anything about it: "He's not that kind of man. . . . He's a tough guy, a reactor, and a violent one at that." Lean stuck to his theory, and Mitchum was persuaded to come out of retirement for a payment of $870,000. Meanwhile, Brando was practicing walking around with an arm tied up so as to resemble the wounded, one-armed character in the script. He didn't like the look of it. Bolt said they would change it to a missing leg. Brando presumably hopped around and didn't like the look of that either. They were ready to change it to a sore foot. But Brando dropped out and was replaced by another American, young Christopher Jones, who David Lean had heard was shaping up to be the new James Dean. The rest of the cast was filled with top character players from the British cinema, Trevor Howard, John Mills, Leo McKern.

Locations were found at the far reaches of the Dingle Peninsula in County Kerry on the western end of Ireland. It was a landscape of rocky cliffs and long, sandy beaches and a pounding, merciless Atlantic. There a complete interior and exterior village set was built, forty-three different structures, most of solid stone. The new village was given the name Kirrary. Life in Dingle and environs was happily disrupted as the locals took lucrative advantage of the arriving film company's need for lodging, food, and alcohol (the latter available from some thirty pubs in the immediate vicinity; you could even buy a drink in the shoe store, according to actor Leo McKern).

Bags packed for Ireland, Mitchum took a few questions from the press, the usual surreal little playlet . . .

Reporter: What's the Lean film about?

Mitchum: (taking a sip of his double Ramos Fizz) I don't know what it's about.

Reporter: What part do you play?

Mitchum: A husband. A yoke carrier. If it had been made long ago—who was the actor who played the perfect husband, the one who was always married to Joan Fontaine?—well, that's who would have played it.

Reporter: What's the character?

Mitchum: (eyes widening) I just told you! A Jewish woman during the troubles. A husband who shows up whenever the call sheet calls him.

*

In February 1969, Mitchum flew to Germany, taking possession of a new white Targa at the Porsche factory in Stuttgart, then drove and ferried his way to Ireland. Arriving in Dingle, presenting a red rose to Sarah Miles (and reminding her that they had originally been meant to work together on *Mister Moses*), Mitchum was assigned to the tiny, whitewashed Hotel Milltown (the name, oddly, of a prescription narcotic in the states). The entire Hotel Milltown, all eleven rooms, was his. At one end of the hall was a bathtub and at the other, the toilet. The telephone at the front desk remained in service during his residency, and there would be the occasional call from people hoping to reserve a room. In the dark days of boredom to come, Mitchum was known to answer the phone himself and chat, take reservations, sometimes concluding by telling the caller, "By the way, you do know we're under new management? Yes, it's a nudist joint now."

Filming began with a sequence involving Trevor Howard and John Mills in a tiny fishing boat. The seas were wild that day, and the locals warned Lean not to send the actors out there. He ignored them, the boat was overturned, and Mills was knocked unconscious and nearly drowned. "He was very game," Lean said appreciatively. On another occasion it was Leo McKern's turn to be almost lost at sea. McKern had a signal to make if he was in danger. He made the signal. Lean refused to let the wet-suited divers run into the shot until he had what he needed. McKern was finally dragged out, but his glass eye was lost to Davy Jones.

At his first sight of Mitchum, bulging in his costume and standing beside one of the more diminutive English actors, Lean reacted like he was looking at King Kong. Surely no one had told him Bob was so bloody large! And the period suit and derby hat that had been prepared for him to wear made him look like Charlie Chaplin, or a giant ape version of Chaplin anyway. Lean felt unsure of his approach to Mitchum and not quite happy with the performance he was getting. Mitchum's casual attitude and sarcastic jokes left him unsettled. Mitchum would do his usual playing around up to the last moment before a take and then effortlessly go into character. Mitchum acted like the whole enterprise was no more important than one of his silly Westerns. At the end of one dramatic, emotional scene, Lean called, "Cut," and Mitchum said blandly, "How was that? Too Jewish?"

When, finally, Lean hit upon a scene that met with his satisfaction, and feeling he had at last found the key to getting what he wanted from Robert, he began shooting the previous scenes over again. Mitchum joked that they were going to spend the ten-million-dollar budget on rehearsals. He was also offended. He told Sarah Miles that if Lean hadn't liked his fucking performance the first time he should have been a fucking man and said so.

After ten days of shooting, they were seven days behind schedule.

The relationship between the star and the hawk-faced, neurotically obsessive English director would ebb and flow, mostly ebb. The imperious Lean was used to having his actors bow and scrape before him, but Mitchum mostly just laughed or gave him the middle finger. For weeks at a time they would barely speak to each other, communicating tart messages via Mrs. Bolt, who did her best to encourage a truce. At other times, Mitchum took a merely bemused or mocking stance toward Lean, who struck him as rather humorless and comically starchy, uptight.

The wedding night lovemaking scene between Rosie and

Charles—her underwhelming, disillusioning, first experience of sex with a man—turned into an unending goof for Mitchum and an embarrassing nightmare for David Lean. The director awkwardly coached the action with the most careful terminology while Mitchum sprawled informally in the bed in his nightshirt, groping Sarah Miles in her nightshirt and behaving like a jaded porn star.

"You lift up the . . . the nighties," said Lean. "And then you . . . you have intercourse . . . and then you . . . you . . ."

"Shoot my wad?" said Mitchum.

"Uh . . . yes . . . you climax . . . abruptly . . . and then withdraw."

"What style of this intercourse should we have, David?" Mitchum asked.

"What . . . style?"

"How about she climbs up on top and straddles me?"

"Good God, the girl's supposed to be a virgin!"

They went for a take. Mitchum wrestled with the long, heavy nightie. "What a task it turned out to be," Sarah Miles wrote in her autobiography. "On and on, he hauls away at great lengths of material. 'Cheat both nighties up a little,' said David impatiently. Mitchum pulled mine up. 'All the way up to your cunt?' he whispered in my ear. . . ." Mitchum mimed the act then fell away with an erection.

He said, "Careful, honey, or you'll crease my nightie."

Fastidious Lean called for another take. Mitchum's hands encircled Sarah's "lower cheeks" as she wrestled with an unavoidable sense of excitement. "He was a mixer all right." Miles found herself very drawn to Mitchum and spent much time in his "caravan," causing considerable gossip. There was a widespread belief that the two stars were "doing it," Miles herself admitted, though she heartily denied the act had ever occurred and found such speculation terribly tacky.

Miles and Bolt threw a big party at the manor house they were renting at the other side of Dingle Bay. Word had spread and security was nil, so there were a number of gate-crashers. Two of these, a man and a woman, surly and drunken trash from Dublin, encircled Mitchum as he sat downing a beaker of whiskey and demanded he get up to settle a bet—was the woman's strapping husband taller than the big film star? Mitchum reluctantly obliged. The man, pleased to be an inch taller, began feigning blows at the actor's face. Sarah Miles came over to break it up and was shoved aside by the man's horrid wife. The man swung; Mitchum swung back. The man lunged forward and raked his thumbnail across Mitchum's eye as if to slice it in half.

Mitchum screamed and reeled back, covering the bleeding orb. The Dublin couple hightailed it. One hand covering his injured eye, Mitchum lurched outside and stumbled to his Porsche, coming out with a gleaming hunting knife upraised. Roaring, "I'll get you motherfuckers!" he rushed back into the house. Mitchum crashed from one splendid Georgian room to the next, one hand clutching the dagger, the other covering his bloodied eye, as startled, shrieking party guests jumped out of his way. It looked like a scene out of a Hammer horror movie with Christopher Lee.

The shooting schedule had to be changed, and Mitchum could not do close-up work for weeks. Lean seemed not even to notice. What were a few weeks to him? He worked at the pace of a pyramid builder. It didn't hurry things any that the weather was atrocious for filming, pouring rain one hour, sunny the next, and back again, so overcast for days at a time that the cameraman got no reading at all on the light meter. When summer arrived, they had been shooting for nearly six months and there was no end in sight. Mitchum continued to feud with Lean. Once the director left him standing in wet sand for over an hour and then went off to do another shot without telling him. The next time Lean wanted a shot of him, Mitchum waited till the camera was turning, then exposed himself and began pissing.

Bored, cut off from all but those minimal comforts offered by Dingle, Mitchum felt obliged to be self-sufficient. He cooked many of his own meals and gradually became chef to a good portion of the company. He obtained a rare bundle of huge lobsters one weekend—lobster thermidor was one of his specialties—but before he could have his way with them, Sarah Miles—having seen their cute little crustacean faces—took them and threw them back in the sea. Mitchum vowed revenge, and later, she said, had it by announcing to reporters—accurately—that Sarah was a secret urine therapy adept—drank her own pee. He planted marijuana "trees" in the back garden at the hotel, which yielded a huge crop ("In my hands I hold the hopes of the Dingle Botanical Society"). Generously encouraging all and sundry to try a toke, he gave much of the inhibited British crew and cast their first experience with the devil weed. On one occasion Sarah Miles was startled to see Mitchum and her own mother sitting together sharing a joint. On another a Dingle policeman showed up at the Milltown to inquire about the unusual vegetation in the garden. Mitchum whipped out a sizable spliff, lit it, and goaded the cop into trying it. Soon other members of the constabulary were said to have stopped by as well for a sampling of the contraband.

With pubs galore and comrades like Trevor Howard in the vicinity, Mitchum was also known to open a bottle or two. He gave every watering hole his custom at some point. There was Paddy Bawn's, there was Tom Long's, there was Ashe's, his home away from the Milltown. Turned out the place was run by Gregory Peck's cousin, small world that it was. And—shades of *Thunder Road*—Mitchum sniffed out the local moonshine trade as well, sampling a regional, triple-distilled, untaxed liquid magic known as poteen.

Mitchum and others from the film would spend their lunch break at a bar, coming back to Kirrary blotto. Many scenes in the finished film had to be artfully put together so as not to reveal when the actors had obviously had a few. Regarding Mitchum's night-shirted walk along the beach after finding out that Rose is unfaithful, Tony Lawson, the assistant editor, told Kevin Brownlow, "In the rushes you could tell he was absolutely paralytic. I remember when we were cutting we had to look for the bits where he looked like he wasn't about to topple over." Mitchum himself liked to come with visiting girls and pals to the twice-weekly showing of rushes in the local cinema—barging in uninvited, Lean made note—and give a noisy and hilarious narration about which figures on screen had been totally shit-faced at the time of shooting.

Trapped in Dingle for month after month, Mitchum required conjugal visitations. First, of course, came those of his wife, who visited the location for weeks at a time. As soon as she had been safely set aboard a flight back to Los Angeles, Mitchum would begin shuttling in the relief catchers. "Mitch's dolly birds would fly in from all over the place," wrote Sarah Miles. "What I couldn't fathom was whether they came of their own volition . . . or Mitchum got them to come over and footed their bills. Were they simply dope carriers? The quality of most wasn't particularly appetizing, some of them being no more than scrubbers." The Hotel Milltown became jocularly known around Kirrary as The Dingle Brothel.

Mitchum had his fun, but then it would wear out again. And the filming just went on. "There's no reason for it," he growled. "I could have made three pictures in that time just as good as *Ryan's Daughter* will probably be. There's no reason to have to sit around like this. It's all inefficiency. . . . I sit home all day and eat potatoes. They did let me go to California for a visit. I went over the North Pole and spent a full sixteen hours in Los Angeles and they rushed me back, and then they didn't use me for three weeks."

It seemed that it would never end. But one day in November, finally, it did. He had been on the production for ten months, longer than his entire hitch in the U.S. Army. Mitchum wearily headed home. And they're *still back there,* he told people in horror, Lean and his merry cameramen chasing a parasol down a beach in Ireland somewhere in the pouring rain, David shouting, "Oh, *bugger!*"

Howard Hawks wanted him for another Western with John Wayne. They were calling it *Rio Lobo,* but it might as well have been *Rio Bravo, Part III* or *El Dorado Strikes Back.* Wayne said to Hawks, "Do I get to play the drunk this time?" Mitchum told the director he was done working. Wayne said, "Mitchum's been saying he was retiring since the first day I met him." Hawks persisted. Mitchum let it be known his price was a million dollars. Hawks decided to make do with a less expensive Mitchum, Chris. Mitchum visited his son, Duke, and the rest in Tucson while they were shooting *Lobo.* He watched Chris do a scene. Hawks told him the kid might be a star in the making. Mitchum told his son, "I figure to live, say, twenty years more. I might spend everything I've got. What would you think of that?"

"Go ahead," Chris said. "It's your money. Brother Jim and I will make our own."

Although he was a millionaire four or five times over, Mitchum seldom thought of himself as a man of great wealth, and he hated it when others thought of him that way. He never even touched the big paychecks; everything went through managers and accountants, straight to corporate bank accounts. The only cash he generally put his hands on came from his beloved per diems, the daily stipend for expenses he received during a film's production. He signed the checks when the relatives asked, but it was often accompanied with an air of disdain, even contempt. "Bob wasn't known to be the most generous man in the world. Some in the family wanted money from him *forever*," said a ten-year friend and business associate. "And Bob always resented it. When it was about money he could be the biggest prick. Bob always resented people wanting him for things." When organized charities came soliciting his services or an appropriately large donation, Mitchum's frequent response, via Reva, was "Absolutely, as soon as our accountant can take a look at your books."

His sister Julie believed Robert's generosity was simply not known to a lot of people because he wanted it that way. "He did all kinds of goodies for all kinds of people. But he didn't do it for the credit. He never wanted to leave any fingerprints."

"I think he was very aware that many people who came in touch or wanted to get close to him were trying to get something out of him," said Reni Santoni. "And so he was always a little sceptical. If you wanted to spend time with him, and I count myself among them, you had to have no other reason than to have laughs and be together with this very interesting guy. You did not go to Mitchum and say, 'Gee, I've got this good script I want you to see; you think you might—' No, you never hustled him or that was the end. And I would never think of asking him for anything; I would never want to muddy the waters like that. But if you respected that, then you saw that he gave openly and generously."

In addition to supplementing the incomes of his children when requested and offering the occasional boost to his brother and sisters and members of their families (brother John would write of Bob's paying for John's daughter's medical bills on one occasion and other generosities through the years), Mitchum paid for pleasant upkeep for his mother and stepfather for most of their lives. His family's involvement with the Baha'i organization was also supported by Mitchum, according to a family friend: "Their whole group, if they wanted to take a missionary trip or something, they would schlep the mother and Bob would pay for all of them." While his wife did much work for high-profile charities like the SHARE organization that involved celebrity participation and publicized events, Mitchum preferred to remain the barroom philanthropist, helping out old pals and the sorts of characters who didn't rate much in the way of Hollywood benefit dinners. His friend George Fargo, for example, a professional extra, was frequently in need; and Mitchum would often drive to the supermarket, buy eighty or a hundred bucks' worth of groceries, and drop it off at Fargo's with a bag of weed from his tree, giving the man sustenance for weeks at a time. Mitchum received many letters from prisoners through the years, some with desperate tales of having been abused by the justice system, railroaded into prison and such, and many times he would make at least the gesture of sending a check or recommending a lawyer and sometimes more. "Prisoners would write him or even call him," said Toni Cosentino, his manager and a friend for many years. "They figured, he'd been in the joint, he was a tough guy, not a namby-pamby movie star. He was constantly sending stuff to prison. People in prison just sort of had his heart, I don't know why. We all say, sure, that guy didn't really do it, but he gave everybody the benefit of the doubt. And just because other people said it was irrefutable evidence, he wouldn't take that as gospel."

"He called once, he was in town and he had some friends coming in," Reni Santoni recalled. "And his usual 'source' was not to be found, so he called me and I checked and this one guy I knew was around. So I told Mitchum, and we agreed on a time. He did kind of slip in the fact that he hoped there weren't going to be a bunch of people at this guy's place. So I called up this guy and told him who it was coming over to make a purchase and we wanted it low key. He said, 'That's cool.' So Mitchum picks me up in his little Porsche; we zip over to this guy's apartment in Hollywood. We go to this guy's apartment and there's two guys sitting there on the couch. And I think, 'Oh, shit.' Mitchum's very cool, he doesn't let on he's uptight or anything. He nods to the guys. One stares right at him and he can't contain himself. He gets up from the couch, runs over, he says, 'Hey, man, I had to stay to meet you!' And Mitchum starts looking at the floor, he's kind of embarrassed, he's not looking to sign any autogaphs. And the guy says, 'Man, you sent us that stuff, that gym equipment, those exercise bikes,' and he mentions some penal institution in northern California. 'Man, we didn't have shit in that place. When that stuff showed up it was like Christmas! I've got to thank you for myself and eighty other individuals. Shit, man, I always knew I'd meet you one day and thank you; I didn't know it would be here—while you were scoring!' And he pumped his hand, and Mitchum's all embarrassed. We did our business and got out of there. But that's the kind of cool things he did, just because he thought: those guys didn't have anything."

On March 16, 1970, Robert and Dorothy celebrated their thirtieth wedding anniversary.

"He asked me what he should get her for an anniversary present," said James Bacon. "I said, 'A Purple Heart!'"

People marveled at Dorothy's aplomb, her self-control. It could not have been easy being married to "a masturbation image," as Robert said she had called him. How often—at parties, social events, visiting on locations—must she have been been made to feel like an inconvenience, an intrusion, while the women—men, too—waited for Robert's undivided attention. Some didn't even bother to wait. Once at some party in London, Rex Harrison's soused wife, Rachel Roberts, had crawled on hands and knees across the floor to Mitchum—as Dorothy stood there beside him, no doubt aghast—and tried to pull his fly open with her teeth.

What kept them together? There were the standard-issue suggestions: love, habit, security. There were the cynical speculations: "The worst job in Hollywood is to be an ex-Mrs. Movie Star," said one showbiz veteran who knew both of them. "All of a sudden you're nobody. Even your own kids won't answer your calls!" Another: "Wife and family, that was Bob's safety net. When another woman tried to hold on to him he'd just say, 'I'd love to see you more frequently, but my wife wouldn't approve.' Or, 'You better ask Dorothy.'"

"She was his constant, his honing signal," said Reni Santoni, a frequent visitor to the Bel Air household. "Whatever crazy shit he got into anywhere in the world, he knew there was always one place he could still go where he would be welcome and where he didn't have to play the movie star. They were like Nick and Nora Charles together for a while. She was a handsome woman, very low key, sharp wit. And she wasn't any shrinking violet. She wasn't the kind to slip in from the kitchen and say, 'Can I get you gentlemen something?' She'd sit there with the guys as long as she wanted to. And she was always quite generous and very cool."

"Dottie sometimes says she hoped I would evolve," Mitchum reflected, "whatever that means. No way. People who've known me a long time tell her I was a bum when she married me, I'm a bum now, and I'll be a bum when I go."

For most of that year he drifted.

He would get in the Porsche and drive. He would roll into towns, try a few old phone numbers, stir up a drinking buddy or a friendly female, drive on. When he wanted to "get lost," he told people, he would put up at some nowhere motel for a time, take out his teeth, go unrecognized. "It gives me," he would say, "the temporary illusion that I'm real."

He went to Mexico for a while. Tourists spotted him on the beach at Mazatlan. You could see him lying on a lounge chair in the sun, sipping from a bottle of tequila, with a comely Mexican chick rubbing coconut oil on his chest and shooing away the riffraff. An American on vacation down there got close enough to ask him what he was doing. Mitchum opened one eye and said he was getting in shape for his next picture, *The Life of Sabu.*

He visited his mother and sister near Scottsdale, Arizona. Mother now lived with sister Julie and her jewelry executive husband, Elliott Sater. Bob's stepfather, the Major, was in his nineties by this time, completely deaf and ailing, consigned to a nearby rest home. He could still kick up his heels on a good day, still had a twinkle in his eye, and Julie and Mother were with him as often as possible.

The quarter horses took up some time, pleasantly spent. Mitchum kept between thirty and thirty-five animals on his seventy-six-acre ranch. He had raised at least one real champion: Don Guerro. Mitchum and trainer Earl Holmes and jockey Ronnie Banks ran the horse in the California derbies in the early '70s and won the Bay Meadows and Gold State stake races. Don Guerro was considered an "anxious colt," with a rare quirk, bursting from the starting gate like a streak of lightning but so fast and hard he caused the ground to break, tripping himself. The horse either won by a mile or he fell flat on his face at the gate. Pundits called him "the Stumbling Señor." After being written off by the handicappers, a four-year-old Don Guerro had a spectacular, unexpected win at the third running of the prestigious Champion of Champions race at Los Alamitos. With this glorious comeback, he was retired to stud. Mitchum could ask no more for himself.

People kept trying to get him back to work. The scripts came in. Reva would read them, make her recommendations. He would tell her to send them back. One day he got a call from Orson Welles. Orson said he wanted to direct him in a movie, and they had to get together at once. Robert thought this one at least was good for a lunch. Orson wanted to go to some French restaurant that cost about a hundred bucks a plate, plus wine. Orson didn't have enough in the bank for hot dogs at Pink's, so Mitchum was buying, so Mitchum told him they would go to the Polo Lounge. The waiter asked them if they were having any cocktails. Orson said he had stopped drinking all hard liquor. Mitchum ordered a large scotch, and Welles said he would have one, too, then drank up both at a swallow. He told the waiter, "Bring two more of those . . . and Mr. Mitchum would like another as well." Welles told him about the movie project, a spy story set in a French whorehouse, and he slipped Shakespeare and Hearst into it somewhere. It couldn't miss.

In the early morning of September 1, three eighteen-year-old girls came into the West Los Angeles Police Station. One girl had visible injury to her left eye in the form of a reddening of the eyeball and a slight laceration. A second girl had a visible injury on her right cheek, a fresh bruise and swelling. The girls told the police that they had been in their car, stopped at Sunset after midnight, when a white Porsche came up beside them and through the open window they saw a man they recognized as the actor Robert Mitchum. Mitchum, they said, asked if they were interested in going with him to "smoke some shit." The girls followed him in their car, up Benedict Canyon and into the hills, pulling up to a ranch house on a dead-end street. The three girls said there were other people inside the house, a couple and a single man at the other end of the main room, all of them smoking what smelled like pot. As the girls sat together nervously on the couch, they said, Mitchum offered them a lit marijuana cigarette, but one of the three "chickened out" and ran from the house and back to the car. Mitchum became angry, they said, yelled, "Don't fuck me," then struck one of the other girls on the leg and then in the eye. The two fled the house, they said, with Mitchum in pursuit, catching up with them and striking one girl on the cheek with the palm of his hand and then kicking the same girl as she tried to get into the automobile. They got the car going and drove off, leaving their host in the driveway staring after them.

At the West LA Police Station, Officers Capitain and Pedneau took one of the girls back to the Benedict house. Capitain knocked at the front door, got no answer, announced himself, and entered the house. The police report stated, "Officer Capitain located the Suspect (Mitchum) in bedroom with female/Caucasian and informed Suspect (Mitchum) that an individual fitting his description had been named in a crime report charging battery. Officer Capitain then obtained information from Suspect

(Mitchum) as to his name, address, etc. Suspect (Mitchum) made no statements concerning the incident."

No charges were filed. One of the movie magazines ran a near verbatim copy of the police report, including the names and addresses of the young women, with the headline, "3 TEENAGE GIRLS TELL POLICE: 'ROBERT MITCHUM HIT US . . . TRIED TO TURN US ON TO DRUGS.'" No reporters investigated the story. It was the autumn of 1970, and the press about Mitchum all concerned MGM's fifteen-million-dollar Irish romance, the studio's biggest picture in ages.

Ryan's Daughter would be released during the Christmas season of 1970. It was David Lean's first film since the phenomenal *Zhivago*, and the media were happily buying into the notion of *Ryan's Daughter* as a major cultural event about to be unveiled. Mitchum was brought to New York for various festivities and press gatherings anent the world premiere at the Ziegfeld Theater in Manhattan. He went wherever he was asked, talked to reporters, appeared on television programs, including the long-running *Joe Franklin Show*. "He came on the air wearing these large, thick sunglasses," Franklin remembered. "He looked like Stevie Wonder. I said, 'Bob, why don't you take the sunglasses off. That's good for Ray Charles, but let the viewers see those gorgeous eyes of yours.' He said, 'Not at these prices.'"

MGM held numerous press screenings and trotted Mitchum in when the film ended for a brief star-gazing and Q and A session with critics and entertainment reporters. One screening was arranged specially for student journalists. Carolyn Sofia, a twenty-year-old college student writing for her campus newspaper, *The Chronicle*, was among the twenty or so in attendance. She wrote up the event in the paper and recalled it again thirty years later: "I remember him coming into the big screening room after the movie. The theater was filled with nothing but young people, everybody with long hair, bell-bottoms. And he comes in in a dark business suit, wearing shades. He was a very big presence in the room. The way I remember it is like he was standing under a spotlight, but there was no spotlight.

He looked exactly like a movie star was supposed to look like. I didn't know much about him. Had no idea about any of his past history with the law or anything. And he was supposed to answer a few questions, I guess; and he took out what looked like a lunch bag, a brown paper bag. Inside was a brick of marijuana." Mitchum handed it off to a longhaired kid in the front row. "I was in the back, and not everyone realized what was going on at first, then everyone started to laugh and there was a sense of anticipation. He had them pass it around. Everyone was so polite they only took a very little and passed it, and I was the last person and ended up with the bag and a nice portion. No one asked for it back, so I took it and put it in my backpack and took it back to school with me. I had never used it before. That was the first time I had seen marijuana. But my pothead friends said it was great stuff. I was very popular for a couple of weeks."

Mitchum attended the film's gala opening night festivities, the Ziegfeld screening and the postpremiere party at the Museum of Modern Art, where the actor clownishly got up with the hired band and sang "Bill Bailey, Won't You Please Come Home." Cornered by one inquiring reporter as he came out of the theater, Mitchum announced that the film was too long and that it had given him cramps in his ass. Later in the evening, after studio publicists had restrained themselves from attacking him bodily, Mitchum was encouraged to explain that what he had meant by that was that the film was excellent and that David Lean was a great artist.

Though the picture got off to a good start, it was soon clear that *Ryan's Daughter* would not have the stature—or the "legs"—of *Lawrence of Arabia* or *Zhivago*. A portion of the critical fraternity seemed to take Lean's imperfect—overblown, wretchedly humorless—production as a personal affront, savaging him in print—and in person, in New York, during a little get-to-know-us session in which he was asked to his face how he could have made this "piece of bullshit." An irate female critic is said to have inquired, "Are you trying to tell us Robert Mitchum is a lousy lay?"

Lean was mortified. He did not make another film for fourteen years.

The film could not be considered a dud by any means—the determined MGM publicity machine and David Lean's vast reputation would simply not allow it. But the sense of a letdown was undeniable. It was as if the director had tried to make *Brief Encounter* on the budget of *Doctor Zhivago,* the result a case of cinematic elephantiasis. As for Mitchum, he had performed his wispy role with delicacy, his usually cynical and debauched gaze become a thing of sad helplessness in the person of the weak schoolmaster, Charles. Even as he physically towered over the rest of the cast, Mitchum's skill as an actor and presumably a great deal of willpower very nearly transmogrified his chesty brawn to a frailer form more appropriate to the timid soul on screen. As in *Two for the Seesaw,* he proved that he could play a dull, moping character effectively enough, but the question remained: Why would anyone want him to do that? Critical reaction was mixed, though on the average Mitchum was treated more sympathetically than Lean. If many found his part miscast, they were still impressed by his nobly self-effacing effort.

Though Mitchum received no mention among the honors and awards heaped on the film throughout the next year, his participation in it had certainly done much for his prestige. The association with Lean and the massive publicity push for *Ryan's Daughter* brought his name to the forefront after years of half-of-a-double-bill flops (much as Marlon Brando would soon be resurrected in *The Godfather* following a similar long string of bombs). Mitchum was once again "hot." For a time he seemed to be at the top of the wish list for every big action picture and masculine drama to be made. He was offered the leads in *Dirty Harry* and *The French Connection.* He turned them down. Aside from the usual lament about the need to retire and schedules without enough days off, his stated reasons for what he chose or rejected were often more or less esoteric. The drug-busting cop hero of *The French Connection*—an Oscar winner for Gene Hackman—apparently offended his sensibilities, as did *Dirty Harry*—Clint Eastwood's boost into superstardom. Mitchum thought that the latter script, like its director, Don *(The Big Steal)* Siegel, reeked of "drug store" tastes.

More difficult to understand was the rejection of another offer, to play Gen. George Patton in the film that would ultimately star George C. Scott. The producer, Frank McCarthy, thought Mitchum perfect casting for the lead. He sent him the script and got a thumbs-down. Some weeks after that McCarthy asked Mitchum to come to the studio for a meeting. Mitchum claimed to be busy, so McCarthy asked Reva Frederick to come by. "I went into his office at Twentieth, and he told me he wanted to show me something. He had a huge thing on the floor covered with a sheet. He said, 'I want you to see this!' and he uncovered it, and there was a very large painting, a portrait of Mitchum made up as General Patton, with these pearl-handled pistols. It was really quite something. And McCarthy said, 'This is how I visualized Patton. We want Bob for this role.' And he went on and on about what they were going to do. I said, 'Let me tell him about this. That's all I can do. I never answer for him.' He told me to take the new version of the script and ask him please to read it. 'I'll await your call.'

I went back and told Robert what had happened. He laughed. He said, 'What the hell is that all about? He got a painting made? Why would anybody do that?' I said, 'Because he sees you as Patton, and he wanted to show everyone what he saw. He sees no one else but you!' And Robert said, "Oh . . . OK.' Well, he was amused by that and he agreed to look at the script again. And he reread the script and he said, 'No. I just don't want to do it.' That was it. He said that he didn't see himself as that character in those situations. He said, 'It isn't me; I don't want to do it." In later years Mitchum would admit that the character of the controversial general fascinated him, and he had read everything that had been published about the man. So what was the problem? He said he knew what would happen: They'd all get to Almeria, they'd want to fuck it up, water the man down, and he'd let them do it because . . . that was what he did. Someone like George C. Scott would be willing to fight for the character, make the picture into something worthwhile, he said—a strange confession of professional defeatism.

Sarah Miles was nominated for the Best Actress Oscar and MGM brought her to Los Angeles for the ceremony. Her schedule was tight, but after the award show dress rehearsal she went to visit the Mitchums in Bel Air. She had a swim. Dorothy served tea. He looked buttoned up in his wealthy neighborhood, Miles thought, not the roaring, wild man they had known in Ireland. Dorothy said she would drive Sarah back to her hotel. Miles discerned an odd vibe from the woman but couldn't put her finger on it. Perhaps Mrs. Mitchum, too, had heard those unfounded rumors that Sarah and Robert had been shagging away back in Dingle. At the hotel entrance Dorothy gave her a kiss and told her to come visit again.

"I do believe you mean it," Miles said.

Dorothy smiled at her. "Robert will never leave me," she said.

Going Home was the story of a man who kills his wife. Harry Graham kills her in a drunken rage, witnessed by his young son, Jimmy. Years later he tries to rebuild a relationship with the boy, now nineteen, but Jimmy burns inside and secretly dreams of some act of vengeance. He rapes his father's kindhearted girlfriend, and Graham nearly kills him for it. In the final face-off, the son demands from Graham an explanation, a rationale for the brutal act he committed all those years ago, but there is none: It was a gratuitous, pointless tragedy that cannot be undone. They can only go on from there or give up trying. The boy asks, "What happens now?" The pensive father tells him, "You get to be twenty."

Retirement had proved bothersome after all. And costly. He told Reva he might possibly entertain an offer, if it did not involve any heavy lifting. "Two sets of guys come into the office," said Mitchum, "and the first set has this nice script about jazz musicians and they're going to shoot in San Francisco. I like that. A few days later I tell one set of guys, 'See you in San Francisco.' They look puzzled and say, 'No. Wildwood, New Jersey.' My secretary looks at me and says, 'Yep. You got them mixed.' I had signed for *Going Home*."

The director remembered it differently. "Mitchum liked this script," said Herbert Leonard, making his first feature after years of producing such television shows as *Route 66*. "I had worked very hard on it with the writer, Lawrence Marcus. I believed in it and I believed in the fucking picture that we made. Mitchum read it and he said, 'I want to do this picture.' He never copped to me what it was in the script that attracted him. So how can I know? The relationship between a father and a son, I suppose. Or maybe he always wanted to kill his wife! Who knows? But he was not being cynical this time or uninvolved. He was there. He wanted this one."

Leonard told Mitchum he was offering the role of the son to an acclaimed young actor. "Mitchum said, 'You're out of your fucking mind.' He said he looked like a fag. Not masculine enough to play his son. I said, 'Are you kidding? This guy's not only a good actor, but he's a tough little guy.' He says, 'Oh, bullshit! I'm not having him play my son, get somebody else.' I said, 'We'll go down to the YMCA and you two can put on the boxing gloves and you'll see if he can handle himself.' He refused. And that's how Jan-Michael Vincent got a break. I didn't want him."

Shooting began in Wildwood—with the star complaining about gawking, unruly rubberneckers trailing their every move (at one point a woman passed out from the excitement)—and then moved on to McKeesport, Pennsylvania. Leonard came to Mitchum's motel room every morning at seven-thirty and talked out the scenes to be shot. "He was stoned every day. Eight o'clock in the morning, forget it, he's already finished a half a bottle of vodka, and eight-fifteen he's got the vodka and a big pipe of marijuana. But he came to work knowing his stuff. Never came in without knowing what he was supposed to do. Don't ask me how he prepared or when he prepared! I don't fucking know! He was stoned the whole fucking time. It was an amazing capacity. I was bewildered by his ability to do it day after day and not suffer. He was doing everything he could do. He was sleeping with one of the actresses. I had someone in the cast stoned all the time, sleeping around with everybody, sleeping with Mitchum. And one time we had to do a porno movie thing to use in a scene. We shot that at this motel in an empty room and we got some local girls and he decided he had to be in on that, to be codirector.

"But he worked on this movie. And I kept at him. Sometimes it took fifty-two takes. He wouldn't get inside himself. This is not a knock on his ability. He was great. An incredibly great actor. But he wanted to just do a throwaway, and I wouldn't let him. We didn't print shit. Do it again! Fifty-two takes on that scene with the girl after she gets raped. I wanted the best fucking performance from him, and I didn't let anything just go by. We understood each other; we were both street kids, spoke the same language. And he support-ed me all the fucking way until just before the end. Other people complained; they'd complain to him about me being too rough. He'd say, 'Fuck you. Do what the man says.' He was wonderful. Until we got to the biggest scene in the picture. Then it came apart. That's when he did it. He waited until the climax of the fucking movie, and then he went crazy."

It was the final, brutal confrontation between the father and the son, Vincent's demand for a meaning to his mother's death and the Mitchum character's helpless and mournful statement of fact: "I was drunk and I killed her."

They were shooting at night outside the building, a kind of road-house/whorehouse in the movie. "It was the key moment in the film," said Herbert Leonard. "He's almost killed his son, and now he's got to almost cry as he faces the truth. And the kid has to face the truth. And now Mitchum comes around and we're going to shoot it and he says he wants to change the script. He had loved the script, talked about the ending, how much he liked it. Now we're coming to shoot it, and he doesn't want to do it. He has some all new ideas, a different climax to the movie. What his ideas were, it doesn't matter; they're not worth remembering they were so terrible. They were out of a different movie. They would have destroyed this movie. And after we had agreed twenty-nine thousand times that we liked the script. If there was an idea there, a suggestion that would have taken it to another level, something deeper, believe me, I would have bought it from him in a minute. But this was nonsense. And it wasn't about the script, I knew that. It had to do with his *self-destructive drunkenness*. He had tremendous self-destructive impulses in his life. He almost didn't want to see it be good.

"I said, 'Bob, we're not doing it like that. We're doing it the way it is in the script, the way we discussed it.' He said, 'I'm telling you how we're doing it.' And he told me his ideas again. I was holding the script, trying to listen to him, and I felt the script melting in my hands, a hallucination. I could feel it dripping. He said, 'No way. I won't do this other shit.' I said, 'No fucking way are we doing a scene like that. Now if you want to sit down and relax and talk about it, if you want to do it another day, whatever the fuck you want. But don't talk about some scene out of another movie.' He said, 'We're not doing it like that.' I said, 'I'm not changing nothing.' So then he says, 'I guess maybe we need to have a little fight, you and me.' He was a considerably bigger person. But I was in good shape; I was very athletic. And he's kind of stoned. He puts his hands up, and I say, 'OK, let's go!' And he starts swinging at me. He boxed me around. And I just ducked and moved around. I couldn't believe it. I was almost laughing. And after about three minutes, he wore himself out and sits down on the street. I said, 'OK? Now let's get on with it.' He said, 'No fucking way I'm doing it!' I said, 'Do me a favor, get your ass out of here, go home!' I told him we'd replace him. Replace him! We were one week from finishing the picture! So Mitchum gets up and goes away. We're in Pennsylvania. I call the studio. I told Jim Aubrey what happened. He said, 'You've got to stick to your guns. He can't fucking decide he's gonna do another script.'

"The next night we're back again. Does the same shit. Starts swinging his fists at me. I said, 'I thought you were flying home?' I taunted the shit out of him. He turns and disappears. I'm going crazy myself with this thing. It's a battle of wits; he's taking punches at me. And I've got no film, no ending!

"I'm having breakfast the next morning. He's having breakfast way over in the corner, with his manager, Reva. And I hear him screaming. I can't hear it all, just enough. What a fucking bastard I am. He'll kick the shit out of me. This kind of thing.

"The third night. The third night I'm waiting at the set for him. He comes out. He has a malted milk. No booze. Nothing. And we shoot the whole fucking three days' worth that night. He's a doll, acts like nothing ever happened. I act like nothing ever happened. It went perfectly. Maybe he realized the script was the way to go.

Maybe he decided he wasn't going to be allowed to fuck it up. I tried to think of his motivation. Maybe this was something too close to his life. Maybe it touched something distasteful to him. Something about it that made him so distraught that he just wanted to piss on the whole thing. . . .

"All I know is he was great. Three days' work in a night. He was amazing."

James Aubrey, head of MGM, "the Smiling Cobra," as he was known, took time from his busy schedule—selling off MGM's history in a tag sale (Judy Garland's ruby slippers, Norma Shearer's underwear, and the like) and butchering new films by Sam Peckinpah, Blake Edwards, and others—to shred fifteen minutes out of *Going Home* and schedule a seven-day run in four cities before removing it from circulation. Leonard took out an ad declaring that Aubrey had "Unilaterally raped the picture." Despite its flaws and abridgements, the film was a poignant and incisive character study. Mitchum's Harry Graham, a pitiful, destructive, and regretful loser, is played with such piercing honesty that he is at times almost physically painful to see—with every gesture, every tentative, unhappy line of dialogue, Mitchum stunningly conveyed a life diminished and overwhelmed by shame and regret.

Pauline Kael in *The New Yorker*, indifferent to the film itself, found cause to take stock of its star, a man she had long admired. Once, at a Manhattan gathering, a snide master of ceremonies had introduced the esteemed critic, praising her suppposed stand against the rising tide of lowbrow pop culturists, the silly sorts of film buffs at places like Britain's *Movie* magazine, who tended to worship "the likes of Robert Mitchum" no less. Kael got up and perversely delivered an impromptu glowing encomium to the disdained movie star. Now, in her review, Kael wrote, "Robert Mitchum has that assurance in such huge amounts that he seems almost a lawless actor. He does it all out of himself. He doesn't use the tricks and stratagems of clever, trained actors. Mitchum is *sui generis*. . . . His strength seems to come precisely from his avoidance of conventional acting. . . ."

*

Aubrey's handling of *Going Home* had a direct, negative impact on Mitchum's welfare. The actor had taken a lower salary in return for a hefty percentage of the gross, and with the picture buried there wasn't going to be any percentage. The only way to stay even with Aubrey was never to work for him again, Mitchum said, and then went right back to work for him. It was a high-adventure tale set in Mexico called *The Wrath of God.* The role of Father Oliver Van Horne sounded like it had been constructed from bits and pieces of previous Mitchum parts—he was a south-of-the-border mercenary *and* a homicidal man of the cloth. The story concerned a band of seedy adventurers, led by the renegade, machine-gun-toting priest, hired to assassinate a Latin American despot. Others in the cast included Ken Hutcheson, Victor Buono, Frank Langella as the chief bad guy, and Rita Hayworth as his mother. It was Mitchum, hearing that his former leading lady was having financial and professional problems, who urged director-screenwriter Ralph Nelson (*Lilies of the Field, Charlie, Duel at Diablo*) to give the part to the the aging Love Goddess.

This would be Mitchum's sixth time filming on Mexican locations, not counting the backlot-created Mexico of *Out of the Past* and *His Kind of Woman* (or the Mexico via Madrid of *Villa Rides*). They shot in Taxco, Cuernavaca, Guanajuato, and in the capital city. "Mitchum," said the film's producer, William S. Gilmore, Jr., "was the ultimate professional. He did the job, caused no problems. In all my years of making pictures, he was probably as professional as any actor I have ever worked with. He was very well liked by the crew and the rest of the cast. I can't say enough positive things about him. Mitchum worked hard and he played hard, and the only negative impact he had on the film was that some of the cast members tried to keep up with him, with disasterous results. We had serious problems with several members of the cast. Rita Hayworth was just off the deep end . . . and Victor Buono was a schizo. Mitchum and Frank Langella, John Colicos (only there for a few days), and a couple of others were the stable ones in the cast. Some of the others—it was a zoo. This was my first experience with drug use on a film. I mean I had worked for many years with drunken actors—you get some coffee in them and sober them up and stick them back in there. But this was a whole new ball game."

Ralph Nelson had an inkling that Hayworth was not operating at full strength when he came to visit her at the small house she was renting, and she sat with him in total darkness the entire time, laughing crazily, telling odd stories about people trying to kill her. It was the time to cut and run, but Nelson thought she was just having a bad day. She wasn't costing much, it was a nice addition to the cast list—Rita Hayworth, for gosh sake. In Mexico, her behavior proved appalling and pathetic. Her death some years later from Alzheimer's disease suggests she was already in the grip of mental illness, but she certainly didn't alleviate any incipient problems by boozing heavily day and night. Hayworth had screaming fits, refused to set foot on some of the sets, refused to ride in an elevator or be driven at more than twenty miles per hour, verbally attacked a number of women connected with the production, and could not remember her lines—couldn't remember more than one word at a time and couldn't read from "idiot cards" either. A disaster. Nelson ended up shooting some of her dialogue from behind her head so that you could not see her lips and dubbing later, shooting her in close-up in a mock set when she was slightly clearer-headed, or simply cutting her out altogether. William Gilmore: "Looking back it seems tragic, but at the time . . . I felt so sorry for Ralph Nelson having to deal with this woman. She could not remember her own name." Mitchum, like everyone else, was shocked by Hayworth's extreme deterioration. "He had gotten her the job, but no one held him responsible," said Gilmore. "He had no more idea than the rest of us that she was so far gone."

Victor Buono, a Mitchum pal, was a corpulent actor often cast as comically malevolent, epicene villains in this period. "A strange duck," the film's producer recalled. "Very strange. Would run around accusing people of opening his mail. I have no idea if he was involved in the drug aspect. But there was a lot of grass, hash cookies, going around. And they were drinking a lot of mescal, rough stuff."

The film's near undoing was an unfortunate accident suffered by a young English actor, Ken Hutcheson, playing a rambunctious Irish soldier of fortune. One night about six weeks into the filming, a week before Christmas, Hutcheson was in his hotel room when he cut his arm on some broken glass, flesh slashed wide from elbow to wrist. Dorothy Mitchum, in the suite directly above, heard Hutcheson's outcry and rushed down the steps to find the gruesome sight, the actor on the floor, his open arm, blood pouring everywhere. She quickly made a tourniquet to stop the bleeding, saving his life. He was rushed to the local hospital. "From that moment on," said producer Gilmore, "we lost control of the film. This actor was in everything. No one knew how long he would be in the hospital. We had about two days' work we could shoot without him. We could have replaced him and reshot but that meant six weeks of scenes thrown out. But we considered it. . . . We were shut down. It was an insurance claim. The insurance company was now producing the movie—they were responsible for everything above the ten-thousand-dollar deductible."

The insurer made the decision, based on medical reports and cost estimates, that they would wait for Hutcheson to return to work. The technical crew from Hollywood had to be kept on salary and per diem and spent the next month twiddling their thumbs in Acapulco and Puerto Vallarta. "Everybody sat by the pools, sipping margaritas, on full salary," said Gilmore. "A good deal for the crew. Ultimately Hutcheson's wound healed enough where he could return, but he couldn't do anything strenuous, couldn't really ride a horse effectively, arm had to be kept covered."

Hayworth, then Hutcheson, then an imposed vacation. Director Nelson came back to work, but his focus and enthusiasm were lost. Now all anyone wanted to do was wrap things up and go home. The finished picture tells the story—early scenes filled with the spirit of adventure, robust, funny, violently exciting, Mitchum, Hutcheson, and Buono a delightful trio of impudent rogues roaming the colorful Mexican locations. Then—confusion, continuity gaps, dislocation. Mitchum in his long, black soutane, toting Bible and tommy gun, stepping over firing squad victims he has just blessed or dangling from a cross in the film's absurd climax, seemed to be having a good time through it all, relishing his second most outlandish "man of God" characterization. Once again he proved to be a film's only real pleasure.

The Friends of Eddie Coyle was the first published novel by George V. Higgins, an assistant U.S. district attorney for Massachusetts. It was a story of Boston lowlifes and criminals, told mostly in dialogue through interconnecting vignettes. The dialogue was so idiosyncratic and sustained at such length that some—including Robert Mitchum—believed it was derived from transcripts of actual wiretapped conversations. In any case, the novel conveyed an unusually intimate and detailed view of everyday life in the criminal underworld, qualities that producer-writer Paul Monash and director Peter Yates hoped to repeat in adapting the material to film. Considering how perfectly he became the centerpiece in a large ensemble cast, Mitchum's participation seemed to be almost an afterthought. He was at first offered the small role of the bartender–hit man–police informer (ultimately played by Peter Boyle), a part that fit his request for no more than three weeks' work, but he wound up taking the title role—Eddie, an aging, small-time crook, three-time loser, a man so desperate to stay out of prison that he begins bartering for his freedom and selling out his associates. No master criminal, Coyle's treacherous schemes are a flop—the police double-cross him and the mob has him killed.

Monash's script tried to retain the distinctively cadenced dialogue and nuanced characterizations of the novel, and Yates directed in the fluid, coldly objective style of his breakthrough British film, *Robbery.* "We decided this would be almost documentary in style," said the film's cinematographer, Victor Kemper, "and we tried to stick with that notion, letting the audience feel like they were right there overhearing these gangsters and gunrunners. We shot it all on location around Boston, and there was a different location almost every day. We worked fast, and I don't think we spent more than a day on any location. And that was tough, packing up, setting up somewhere new every day, but that gave it a certain flavor of reality and spontaneity, grabbing scenes on the go. It kind of reflected the way these shifty characters lived."

Like Harry Graham in *Going Home,* Eddie Coyle was a sad-faced loser living in a present haunted by past mistakes, but here the criminal milieu, Coyle's world of omnipresent corruption, connected the character to the classic era of film noir and to Mitchum's cinematic past in a way that provided the film with a strong sense of tradition, of ritual. To those who knew and loved Mitchum's earlier work, Eddie Coyle was a middle-aged relative of outside-the-law protagonists like Jeff Bailey, Dan Milner, and the other noir stumblebums who tried to play both sides against the middle and came up dead or close to it. In an era of glamorous, "cool" antiheroes, Mitchum—who had invented the type—went in the opposite direction for Coyle. There was nothing glamorous about his rumpled, self-pitying, and not too bright Eddie, the actor's thorough characterization involving not only the assumption of a perfect blue-collar Boston accent but the willing of his body into the form of a plain-faced, craggy, doughy Irish-American. Mitchum said he owed it all to an effective "Eddie Coyle sort of haircut . . . short but not too short." In fact, he created the character—voice, gesture, body language, attitude—out of his usual mixture of instinct, imagination, and observation. During his first few days in Boston he soaked up the atmosphere, studied the fauna, going on the town with his tough-talking driver and other local fellows, hanging out with the production's contingent of Teamsters, some of whom, it was rumored, were not unfamiliar with the city's mob-related activities. Mitchum happily bent an elbow with some fellows he was assured were members in good standing of the notorious Bunker Hill Gang. "I think it's necessary for people to understand something about the humors of the criminal mentality," said Mitchum. According to the actor, George V. Higgins himself came to warn Peter Yates that Mitchum was hanging around with some very dangerous men, including a few the DA's office was in the process of trying to send to jail. "Well, fuck," said Mitchum, "there's hardly anyone you can talk to in Boston without—you know. Anyway, it's a two-way street, because the guys Higgins means are associating with a known criminal in talking to me."

As he worked and played on assorted Boston locations, the star was given close scrutiny by reporter Grover Lewis, on assignment for *Rolling Stone* magazine (the cover story no less, "The Last Celluloid Desperado," with a portrait of the stone-faced star complete with Eddie Coyle haircut). Times had certainly changed since the heyday of Hedda and *Photoplay* and the other more protective outlets for film studio publicity. Lewis mingled and recorded, in prime New Journalism style, bringing home a spirited portrait of Mitchum in the raw—funny, outrageous, erudite, opinionated, incoherent. After much excited, worshipful, or intimidated commentary by coworkers concerning Mitchum's legendary propensity for substance abuse, his violence, his allure to the female sex, his grand-scale movie star-ness, the man himself arrives and does nothing to disappoint, telling stories, rapping with reputed hoods, boozing, passing a hash pipe, giving away joints like calling cards, pissing with the door open, cavorting and apparently cohabiting with a pair of voluptuous blonde groupies, a stewardess and a Euro-accented photographer, known in the article as Girl A and Girl B (with replacement Girls C and D spotted just over the horizon). Tim Wallace was around to provide the journalist with supplementary anecdotal data, in typical good taste:

"Listen, you guys, I gotta tell this story on Bob here. He was ballin' this babe one time, see. He was in the saddle, see, and his nuts was swingin' back and forth in the air, see. And this babe's dog jumps up on the bed and takes his nuts in its mouth, see. *Big* sonofabitch . . . So I walk into the room by accident, see, and this dog has hold of Bob's nuts like a retriever would hold a bird. I couldn't help it—I started laughin'—"

Mitchum grins. "I told him, *don't laugh.*" I very slowly got, uh . . . disengaged. And I smacked that motherin' dog—*whap!*—clear across the room. I woulda shot it if I'd had a gun."

Also on hand, observing it all—the boozing, Girls A-B-C-D—

with philosophical tolerance and good cheer was Mitchum's obviously adoring daughter, Trina, now a beautiful twenty year old and described as an aspiring writer (it had become, after acting, the family profession, this aspiring writing). "When I was growing up, he wasn't around too much," she told Lewis. She recalled a childhood without regimentation, with much freedom, her mother, though, a great lady, a steadying influence. "She's stood by him through everything, and I guess she's put up with a lot and suffered a lot, but she keeps on going." Trina remembered years gone by, adventures with her "oddball" father—so others thought him—Sunday morning drives, buying hand puppets at Schwab's drugstore, being stopped by police for driving on the sidewalk, Dad not even aware he'd gone off the road. "Pretty embarrassing," said Trina, affectionately.

Though he was in only roughly one-quarter of the movie, Mitchum's peformance in *The Friends of Eddie Coyle* easily stole the show and earned the actor an assortment of rave notices. More than one of the reviewers digressed to express their notions of Mitchum as one of the most overlooked and undervalued film stars—but considering the often dismissive reviews he had received through the years, who was it they thought had done all the overlooking? Following in Pauline Kael's wake, Andrew Sarris, the other great film critic of the era, now weighed in with his own words of praise for an actor he said had muscled his way through the movies "with the professional dedication of a fighter who knows there is nothing outside the ring except an endless gutter." Recalling a distant memory of seeing the man for the first time in the "very charming" *West of the Pecos* in some Wild East grindhouse in New York City, Sarris mused that Mitchum's work had always been oddly subversive, slipping past the conventional critical radar. Sarris confessed that he had not viewed many of the actor's films, including some of his most interesting work, until long after they were dismissed and forgotten by the respectable tastemakers of the day. "I was always turning to someone or someone was turning to me, and saying *wasn't* he good? instead of *isn't* he good?" Sarris believed Mitchum's scandalous past—the pot bust, the jail term—and generally raffish image had had an insidious effect on his critical standing. "No one in places of high cultural authority took Mitchum very seriously." Nowadays, in the egalitarian environment of television, of endless Million Dollar Movie and Late Show broadcasts (as well as in the more esoteric realms of auteurist and cultist repertory screenings), people were belatedly coming to realize how many unusual and fascinating films—*The Night of the Hunter,* the still little-known *Out of the Past, Angel Face, The Wonderful Country,* and so on—Mitchum had made in his long and "subversive" career.

Mitchum followed *Eddie Coyle* with another unusual gangster film, this one as glamorous, exotic, and romantic as Coyle had been drab and realistic. *The Yakuza* referred to the organized crime gangs of Japan, their exploits popularly mythologized in hundreds of bloody, highly ritualized motion pictures. Leonard Schrader, an American teacher in Japan, had written stories of the Nipponese mobsters, and his film critic–aspiring screenwriter brother Paul had managed to see a number of Yakuza films in Little Tokyo moviehouses in California. Together they constructed an East-meets-West elegiac and violent story of a tough American detective, Harry Kilmer, once a soldier stationed in postwar Japan, returned to that country to rescue a friend's daughter from the local mafia. Between battles with the enemy gangs, Kilmer is reunited with his former mistress, Eiko, but this relationship is haunted by a humiliating secret—due to the dire circumstances after the war, Eiko's husband, Ken, was compelled to pose as her brother during her love affair with the American soldier. In the end, before his return to America, obligated to Ken in many ways, Kilmer unexpectedly fulfills a ritual self-sacrifice—the cutting off and presentation of a fingertip.

The highly unusual screenplay commanded a whopping three-hundred-thousand-dollar payment from Warner Bros., and Lee Marvin was offered the lead. The studio wanted to reteam Marvin with his *Dirty Dozen* director, Robert Aldrich. But Marvin dropped out after Warner refused to make his suggested script changes. Mitchum signed on, with director approval. He and Aldrich met in a bungalow at the Beverly Hills Hotel. For six hours they talked and drank, remembered the old days, Wild Bill Wellman, *G.I. Joe*, Greece, Greek girls. They told stories, insulted their peers, the works. "I really considered him my friend, and I admired him," said Aldrich. "I think he's a brilliant actor—a strange, convoluted guy." The day after their marathon bull session, Mitchum sent word that he didn't want Aldrich to direct *The Yakuza*. Sydney Pollack, a man not known for his work with tough guy actors or violent subject matter, came on board. Robert Towne, the hired gun who had helped to make *Villa Rides* all that it became, was put to work on a rewrite of the Schrader script. The company arrived in Japan in January 1974. A small press conference was held. Mitchum looked out at a gathering of Japanese journalists and said to them, "Remember Pearl Harbor."

The film's real coup was its casting of Takakura Ken (most likely the Schraders' hope from the get-go) as Mitchum's comrade and the secret husband of Eiko. Ken was a legendary film actor in Japan, the Bogart or perhaps the Mitchum of his country's gangster cinema. His tragic heroic aura, a distinctively dour charisma, was a perfect complement to Mitchum's own wonderfully sad, soulful performance. "Mitchum and Ken got along just great. I think they really respected each other," said Michael Moore, the film's assistant director. "Ken was a prince to work with, and he was a big help throughout the filming, whenever there were difficulties with locations or with local conflicts. A true gentleman, Ken Takakura. A wonderful man."

They filmed on locations in Tokyo and Kyoto, interiors in a Tokyo studio. The key American crew had to adjust to the surprisingly simple, almost primitive conditions of the Japanese soundstage. "It was a little strange at first," said Michael Moore. "No overhead structures for the lights or for the electricians to work off of. Everything was hung up with ropes and bamboo poles. But we had a local crew with us and they showed us how it all worked." They traveled to Kyoto on the bullet train. Pollack wanted to shoot on the actual moving train instead of faking it, so they took over a whole car and filmed Mitchum as the scenery streamed behind him.

In public, any time he wandered from the sets or took a walk,

Mitchum would recall, he was surrounded by chirping, giggling schoolgirls, bowing and huddling. Everywhere he'd hear them chanting, "*Please, Kirk Douglas-san, your autograph!*" He also met some of the less demure Japanese. As with *The Friends of Eddie Coyle*'s Boston hard cases, *The Yakuza* put Mitchum in contact with real-life local gangsters. They were acquaintances of someone or other with the production, sleekly groomed, sharkskin-suited fellows in wraparound shades. One man showed Mitchum his automatic pistol—it was ten years in prison if you were caught holding it. "If anyone gets in your way while you're in Japan," a thug calmly told him, "just let us know. We'll cut him down."

He had his fun on the locations. "He became very fond of Japanese sake," said Moore. He had his bad days. The studio publicist slipped a reporter into a dinner party in Kyoto one night and the actor erupted at the intrusion, the attempt to work him in his private time. The publicist said to relax; it was all part of being a star. Mitchum told him he didn't want to be a star anymore. "I want out. I really want out. Perhaps the only way they will believe me is if I pack my bags and get out of here tomorrow. . . . Greta Garbo did it. . . ." Mitchum began shouting and pounding his fists in the direction of the now disinvited reporter, who fled the restaurant. Mitchum said people didn't believe he didn't give a damn anymore. He said, "Cross my heart and hope to die, no, I don't give a damn!"

"He didn't raise hell many times on that show," said Michael Moore, "but when he did it was a good one. The furniture came out the windows of the hotel. The management had to be well paid off. Then when we were coming home, we were all at the airport together and Mitchum showed up with a framed picture he had bought, some Japanese scene. I swear you needed a van to move the thing, but he dragged it to the plane. He was loaded, and he wouldn't take no for an answer, dragged the thing onto the plane, Japan Airlines. I guess they were afraid to take it away from him. So they found someplace on board for it and we flew home."

"I found him to be like a very, very powerful and lazy horse," said Sydney Pollack of Robert Mitchum. "He wants to walk as slow as possible and wants to get away with doing as little as possible. You used to really have to push him. He won't offer the full emotional nature of a performance, at least he didn't for me, until you went after him a little bit." Still, Mitchum's performance was a grand one, a glorious tough/tender characterization, and he looked more purely movie star glamorous—the leonine presence, face of decaying beauty, broad shoulders caped in a camel's hair overcoat—than he had for years. The film suffered from the director's fondness for mushy, soft-focus visuals, but overall *The Yakuza* was a very entertaining and wonderfully exotic film.

If Bob had been reading his *Los Angeles Times* in late January 1974, he would have encountered news of an old friend, not heard from in ages. In a seedy stretch of Melrose Avenue in Hollywood, a nineteen-year-old transient named Roger B. Lebel had been stabbed to death. The suspected killer was an unstable drifter from Connecticut, a Bible salesman. Police investigating the murder found that Lebel's only known acquaintance in the neighborhood was a female minister in a small church on nearby Western Avenue, The Spiritual Mission, Inc., Laymen's Evangelist (SMILE). Her name was Lila Leeds. Now forty-eight years old, fuller of face, hair no longer blonde, she lived in a tiny court apartment on Melrose. Back in 1949, she had left California, banished from the state by the same judge who had sentenced her to sixty days behind bars. She had roamed around in the Midwest, working in nightclubs, getting married more than once, getting into trouble, going to jail. She'd gotten hooked on heroin. Once she'd been caught with the stuff on her while visiting her current husband in prison. Fifteen years an addict. In 1966, she had drifted back to Los Angeles, sick, penniless. One day she heard church bells ringing. It seemed like all the church bells in LA were ringing at once. She began to study religion, volunteered to help in the local missions. She did healings. For a time she sang and gave testimony of her deliverance at the Johnny Barton Miracle Crusade ("Come for your Miracle. . . . Come early, doors open at 1:00"), hosted by a man with the hair and sideburns of an Elvis Presley imitator. After so long a time as a bad girl, she believed she had finally been blessed, chosen to do good works for the Lord.

At the SMILE center in Hollywood she tried to offer help to drug addicts and others with problems. So many young kids came out there, said Lila Leeds, wanting to get into the movies and finding nothing but trouble.

*

In the spring, returned from Japan, Mitchum gets a call, a voice out of the past. It's Otto Preminger, in France, preparing an "international thriller" called *Rosebud* about a group of yachting debutantes kidnapped by Arab terrorists. Preminger needs a name actor for the sort-of lead, the role of the two-fisted government agent in pursuit of the terrorists. The part means two months' work on the Côte d'Azur and Corsica in summer. A tempting offer. They call each other friend now. Otto is like Henry Hathaway, a charming gentleman when he's not directing. Mitchum tries not to remember what Preminger is like when he is directing. He accepts the part.

In June Mitchum arrives in Juan les Pins. He is coaxed into attending a press conference. He is in fine form. Here, a sampling of his responses to reporters (questions immaterial):
  "You want to suck what?"
  "As long as it has tits. . . ."
  "Fuck you! I'm not here to sell your papers."

The company moves to Corsica. Bastia. Mitchum and his wife move into a deluxe hotel overlooking a palmy seashore. Up to now the filming has been a series of disappointments and minor disasters. The script doesn't play. Production values must be reduced or sacrificed altogether. Some of the actors do not, after all, speak coherent English. It's a mess. Some on the production believe—pray—that Mitchum's skill and charisma will turn things around.
  They don't. After two weeks on location, Mitchum has worked only three days. Bored, he shifts between smooth professionalism and strange, erratic behavior. Preminger has his own problems, has never been a hand-holder, and is oblivious to the star's growing rest-

lessness. Shooting at an old mill, Mitchum wanders over to meet some local farmers, who present him with a mason jar of *eau-de-vie*, a mightily potent fruit mash. He is pleased with the gift and samples it readily. A writer, Theodore Gershuny, is chronicling the making of *Rosebud* for a book and records the actor's antics as they try to film the scene. Mitchum and a group of raiders are lined up before the camera, studying a map. One of the actors cannot pronounce his line of dialogue. Mitchum is blithely mocking. The actor continues to screw up his line. "I should take out my dick and show him the map," says Mitchum. "Take out what?" Preminger says. "I should piss on his arm! Hahaha—" "Bob, we are rolling!" "I'd take out *your* dick, if I could find it. . . ." "Bob, please, there are ladies present!"

In the evening, in town, Mitchum is drinking tall glasses of *pastis* with droplets of water. He sits at a café and ruminates sullenly to a reporter, William Hall: "I'm trapped. It's an economic expedient, nothing more. I've no pride in my films. I don't like being a movie star. I don't like being owned. . . ." Later, the mood lightens, he scats to an appreciative audience. How he taught Gina Lollobrigida a new diet, "isometric farting." Tells about the time he was at Eleanor Roosevelt's joint and was trying on one of her nightgowns when Noel Coward comes in and starts kissing him on the hand and then FDR's old lady walks in on them. Someone asks where he's stashed his own wife. Mitchum says, "She's here somewhere. I'm expecting her to show up at some embarrassing moment—like when I'm in bed with a cop. . . ."

He can't sleep. Actor Cliff Gorman, in the hotel room below, hears Mitchum moving about all night. Preminger has scheduled two scenes to be shot at dawn: Mitchum, Cliff Gorman, and others scaling a wall, and a fight scene between Mitchum and French-Arab actor Amidou. A production assistant comes for him at 4 A.M. It is still pitch-dark when Mitchum arrives at the set. He enters the big catering tent where some members of the company are having coffee or breakfast. He shouts that he should not have been called so early and that a half hour had been wasted going to the wrong location. After getting no satisfactory response from the film's associate producer, Mitchum goes over to the big wooden pole in the center of the catering tent and in his best Samson imitation attempts to pull it down. The members of the crew go on drinking their coffee, thinking that if they ignore him, there is a chance the tent will not come down on their heads. Mitchum storms out, growling that he would make them pay for this, that Preminger would have to do fifty takes for every shot in the picture.

Outside, Mitchum spots Preminger supervising the preparation of the tracks for the camera.

Mitchum screams, with mocking accent, "Vy haff you gotten me out here at this fucking hour of ze night, Otto?"

"Bob, you have been drinking with the Corsicans," says Preminger.

"Yeah, that's what they got here. Ship in some Jews and I'll drink with them."

"You were drinking yesterday when we tried to film. It cannot go on like this."

"Just what are you trying to tell me, Otto?"

". . . cannot go on . . ."

"You're giving me my walking papers? Okay, let's shake hands and I'll be on my way, pal."

"I don't want to shake hands," Preminger says. "There is nothing to shake hands about."

"Right," Mitchum says. "That's it then. Bon voyage, buddy."

Mitchum turns around and heads back to his car and driver. On the ride back to the hotel he leans his head against the young female chauffeur, closes his eyes, and begins to snore.

At the hotel, Mitchum announces that he's been fired. He wakes Dorothy and tells her to start packing. The producer's camp claims that Mitchum wasn't fired, he quit. With insurers to think about, it would be costly to take the blame. Preminger is furious, convincing himself that Mitchum has been the source of his problems all along, even the ones before he hired him. Later in the morning there is a tense scene in the production office as Mitchum demands his first-class tickets home. A telephone is thrown around. Preminger has someone call the police.

"Fuck Preminger and the boat he sailed in on," says Mitchum. "The *Exodus!*"

Gershuny reports a conversation that evening between Mitchum and Israeli actor Josef Shiloah. Mitchum grabs Shiloah's hand. He says, "Kill me, brother. *Kill me!*" Mitchum is very sorry about what has happened. "If you are sorry," the Israeli says, "you must call Preminger because he is older." Mitchum says, "You Jew bastard, you stick with him." Shiloah says no, it is the right thing to do. Mitchum calls Preminger, but Preminger doesn't take the call. Shiloah says, "And I know is not a great star leaving. No! This is man with pain. He hurt to leave."

Mitchum and his wife board a flight to Madrid that night. No one from the *Rosebud* company sees them off.

Within days Preminger hires Peter O'Toole, who has not worked much for several years. Victor Buono calls Bob with the news. "That," says Mitchum, "is like replacing Ray Charles with Helen Keller."

Nearly sixty years old and fired for inappropriate behavior, drunk and disorderly, that was the way people were telling it. Nearly ready for Social Security and still Hollywood's reigning bad boy. Mitchum, back home, shrugged it off. Preminger was having one of his fits and the actor called his bluff, that was all. Then came *Jackpot*. He was entirely innocent this time. The picture, with Richard Burton costarring, was supposed to start rolling in Europe later that year. Mitchum said he wasn't leaving home till the check cleared his American bank. He called their bluff, too. The check never cleared, and while Burton—too drunk to know if he'd been paid or not—sat in his hotel room waiting to be carried to the set, the producers abandoned the production. But all some people in the business heard was that Mitchum was connected with another big mess. One careless mention in the press even suggested that he had been replaced on the picture, fired because of a poor performance. "He just wasn't coming across," said *Women's Wear Daily*. Did they mean across the Atlantic? Anyway, Mitchum was under a cloud. It was a funny time to start working on the last great film of his career.

Elliott Kastner had dreamed of making a movie from one of Raymond Chandler's private eye novels long before he ever started producing pictures. Raymond Chandler: the great bard of hard-boiled literature, whose tales of crime and detection in Southern California were both violent, convoluted mystery stories and poetic ruminations on the human condition, told in the voice of Chandler's ruefully wisecracking, philosophical, tough guy hero, knight errant of LA's mean streets, Philip Marlowe. Early on, the various screen rights had been unaffordable or slipped through his hands and went to other people. Kastner had settled for a Chandler pretender, Ross MacDonald, buying *The Moving Target* and making *Harper*, with Paul Newman as a smirking excuse for detective Lew Archer. By 1973, with many hits to his credit, the producer could make his dream come true. There was one major Chandler book unfilmed, *The Long Goodbye*. Kastner wanted to do it right. He hired Leigh Brackett for the script—she had done *The Big Sleep* for Bogart back in the '40s. And to play Philip Marlowe, Kastner wanted Robert Mitchum. United Artists said no. They wanted to go with somebody more *happening* and imposed that ace contemporary star Elliott Gould. Direction was entrusted to another *now* personage, Robert Altman, who proceeded to make a smug kind of anti-Chandler movie, with a stoned-looking, hippie-student-protester Philip Marlowe. It was a disaster, barely making it into a few theaters. But Kastner kept the faith. Two years later he was ready to make another Chandler, having purchased the rights to *Farewell, My Lovely* from the current owners. This time he got the man he wanted for the role of Raymond Chandler's urban knight.

To direct, Kastner and his team of producers hired Dick Richards, a former photographer for *Look* and *Life* magazines, a maker of television commercials, and now a feature film director with two pictures under his belt, *The Culpepper Cattle Company*, a Western, and *Rafferty and the Gold Dust Twins*, a seriocomic road picture, both of them unusual and often striking works. It was a time of many new, young directors in Hollywood, and Richards was by no means the least interesting. His first inspired decision was to make *Farewell, My Lovely* a period piece. Kastner had never considered anything but a contemporary setting for the production, like The *Long Goodbye,* like *Marlowe* with James Garner as the detective, like every other Chandler adaptation. The continuing value of the Marlowe stories was supposed to be all in the plot, the characters, the wisecracking dialogue. It took a certain sensibility in 1975 to begin to see works like the novels of Raymond Chandler or the '40s film noir as talismanic items from a mythic pop cultural past. Kastner agreed to Richards's choice, not out of any great interest in the poetic possibilities of an evocation of archaic forms and character types but in acknowledgment of the success of recent "historical" movies, the recreations of the '30s and '40s in such popular films as *The Godfather, Chinatown,* Bertolucci's voluptuous *The Conformist* set in Fascist Italy. For Dick Richards, though, the idea of returning this Philip Marlowe movie to the time of the novel's original writing and the heyday of the private eye movie was more than an attempt to ape *Chinatown*'s success or to parade some quaint old automobiles and retro-chic pinstriped suits and fedoras across the screen. Richards's film would be as much elegy as detective story. From the opening shot of a weary (fedoraed and pinstriped) Robert Mitchum bathed in the soft glow of red neon, and the opening line—"This past spring was the first that I'd felt tired and realized I was growing old"—*Farewell, My Lovely* was to be a consciously mythopoetic work, tribute to the shadow-haunted melodramas of the past and to a man who was among the last surviving links to that lost golden age, a movie star who had indeed grown old and done it on camera before our very eyes.

Richards worked on the script with David Zelag Goodman, leaving out relatively little from the novel but adding scenes, adding characters like Marlowe's newspaper vendor sidekick, the burned out jazzman, and his half-black son, underscoring the story's place in time with references to the war, to Joe DiMaggio, and slipping in various other bits of filigree that blended smoothly with Chandler's original text; switching the novel's sanitarium sequence to a more provocative brothel setting, giving the movie a chance to have *some* contemporary touches, a bit of sex and nudity in consideration of the box office. It was decided that there would be no studio work in the film. All locations, interiors and exteriors, were vintage properties, found mostly in the old neighborhoods, downtown, Hollywood, Echo Park, the old Wilshire shopping district. Some of the homes and buildings they would film in looked as if they hadn't changed so much as a light bulb since Ray Chandler rolled his first page into an Underwood. A shipboard sequence was to be shot with cast and crew crammed into a stateroom on the luxury liner *Queen Mary*, now a tourist hotel docked in Long Beach. Production designer Dean Tavoularis would recreate the period with authentic materials, enough '40s-era furnishings, evocative advertisements, peeling, sun-faded wallpaper, neon signage, and assorted gewgaws to fill all of LA's antiques and thrift stores, with enough left over for an entire East Hollywood flophouse or two. Cinematographer John Alonzo—interestingly, he had also filmed *Chinatown,* though in a completely different style—made a pact with director Richards that they would shoot everything as it would have been done in the '40s—no zooms, no Steadicams, no helicopter shots, no "Raindrops Keep Fallin'" musical interludes.

The wardrobe included many well-worn items off the racks of Western Costume. Marlowe's dark, pin-striped suit was one of a kind, no backup if anything happened to it. Originally made for Victor Mature at Fox, circa 1940, it still had Mature's name sewn inside. Richards loved it. Mitchum hated it.

"I won't wear this fucking thing in the picture," Mitchum said.

"Bob, it fits you," Richards said. "A little alteration. I love this suit!"

Mitchum said, "I'm not wearing this old fucking thing. . . . Victor Mature's farted it all up!"

He wore it. It became a running joke. "Every time he wanted to give me a hard time," said Dick Richards, "he'd bring up the suit. Only thing he wore throughout the film, never changes, one suit. He'd say to me, 'You son of a bitch, you got me wearing a farted-up suit, you cheap son of a bitch! It smells bad. . . . I'm in Victor Mature's old farted-up suit, goddamn it!'"

The role of femme fatale Velma went to Briton Charlotte

Rampling, fresh from wearing Nazi cap, suspenders, and not much else in the controversial *The Night Porter*. She would be styled for maximum slinkiness, made to resemble—and sound like—a jaded version of '40s-era Lauren Bacall. Moose Malloy, violent, lovelorn hulk in search of his lost Velma, would be played by a newcomer, a towering ex-boxer named Jack O'Halloran. Dick Richards had remembered him from a fight at the Garden in New York. O'Halloran was boxing George Foreman. "This was my memory: a gruesome guy fighting Foreman; he's hanging in there, a tough guy. I had pretty good seats, and the guy was bleeding everywhere. Kastner and his group of producers had somebody—he was seven feet tall, but he wasn't tough. I found this guy O'Halloran, and I paid for his airfare to come to California. Let Mitchum meet both guys. That's all I had to do. Jack and Mitchum hit it off. O'Halloran was a street-fighting kid from Philadelphia, claimed all sorts of things in his background. Talked tough, looked tough, and he was tough. You'd be afraid to meet this guy anywhere. The other guy looked soft. Mitchum said to me, 'Are you thinking the same way I am?' I said, 'Yeah.' Mitchum told Kastner to get O'Halloran or he wasn't doing the picture. He was that kind of guy. He meant it."

John Ireland, Mitchum's pal of more than thirty years—shared memories of shared starlets, reefers under the table at Lucey's, and all that—was cast as Detective Lieutenant Nulty. And for the tiny role of Velma's respectable elderly husband Judge Grayle, they hired a man better known for his writing than his acting, brilliant, accursed author of *The Killer Inside Me* and *The Getaway*, Jim Thompson. One of *Farewell*'s producers, Jerry Bick, was friendly with the novelist and sometime screenwriter, knew that he could use some money, and recommended him for the small part. Richards was familiar with Thompson's work and agreed to meet with the man. "I thought he was very sick. I felt he would be OK, but he was sick, gravely ill. But I wanted that kind of person for the part. And he was wonderful. Soft-spoken, quiet man. Very nice man, the kind, in those days, you would have said, here was a gentleman." Thompson and Mitchum, it turned out, had some history. Back in 1949, in his last days as a rewrite man with the *Los Angeles Mirror*, before being canned for drunkenness, Thompson had gone over to the court house, been among the crowd of reporters covering the actor's sentencing to prison.

"We had a couple of people that the director cast and we didn't know whether they were going to make it through the day," Mitchum said. "It is sort of a museum piece. All the subjects are all worn out—I certainly am."

Things began inauspiciously with a protest by the Screen Extras Guild. The company had hoped to save some money by using nonguild extras. "They may have been right about this, I don't know," said Dick Richards. "We were on a limited budget. Whatever, they were striking outside our location for not using them. Screaming, dogs barking. We couldn't record sound. They let us know they were going to do it every day, which I thought was not only illegal but not very nice. The producer had taken it upon himself to fight them. But Mitchum was very pro-union. He said he was not going to be in a movie where they didn't use proper extras. He let me know it immediately, in no uncertain terms. He was not proceeding until everything was straightened out. So that was it. They got it all straightened out the next day, and that was that." Mitchum was for the little guy, said Richards, and Mitchum hated the big guys, the producers. And *Farewell, My Lovely* had enough producers for half a dozen pictures. "He called them 'The Magnificent Seven.' One producer, I won't name names, Mitchum called him over. He said, 'Hey you. Two coffees, one with cream, one with sugar.' Pretended he was a messenger. 'That's how you treat these guys,' he said, 'these dummies.'"

"Bob was a very liberal guy," said Henry Lange, assistant director on *Farewell, My Lovely*. "He had no movie star airs, he was a real guy's guy, and the crew adored him. He would arrive on a given morning and he would talk to anybody. And he had an assistant, Reva, who came every day with something for the crew, nothing big, but something—watermelon, burritos, bags of pistachio nuts, whatever—and everybody was very grateful. Bob was the greatest guy. And he used to have lunch in his dressing room, a motor home, not like these block-long ones you have today but a little tiny motor home a family might drive to the woods for the weekend. And he would invite some of us to come have lunch. And he'd eat and tell stories. Back to the cowboy days and *G.I. Joe*. And he had a driver he would send out for a jug. He drank bourbon then. And he'd ask you in for a drink in the trailer. Very social, very pleasant. It was later in the day; it was never a problem.

"At one point a couple of the producers were questioning the bill I was putting in for Bob's liquor. And one said, 'We don't have to pay for this. What is this? It shouldn't go on our tab.' I'd been working on this show for a month and a half then, and I had gotten to know how Bob reacted pretty well. I said to the producer, 'Well, look, here's the deal. You're absolutely right, and Bob will be the first to agree with you. But if you tell him you don't want to pay this twelve-fifty or whatever it is for his whiskey, he'll say that you're right and he'll say that he's going to go right out and buy his own. There's a place he'll say he likes over in Long Beach or somewhere, and it will take him so long to get back to work that you'll regret you ever mentioned it.' So they reconsidered. Bob was of that school. He drinks. It was no secret. It was fine, never a problem.

"Bob had a great attitude. It was a business to him, he didn't take it too seriously. I remember we were shooting at the Harold Lloyd estate, scene of Mitchum and Charlotte Rampling walking down the hallway. I told him he could take a break, go back to his trailer, we were going to do a point-of-view shot of Mitchum's character looking at Charlotte as she walks ahead of him. We shot it and I go back to get him to do the reverse shot. I say, 'OK, we can use you, we're going to—' And he says, 'I know, I know, now we shoot her asshole's point-of-view of me.'" That was Mitchum—he could really zero in on the absurd aspects of what he was doing. I mean, the way he felt, he knew he wasn't curing cancer on this job."

*

"I have wonderful memories of him from that film," said Kate Murtagh, who played Amthor, fierce lesbian brothel owner in this version of *Farewell.* "He was one of the fellas. You would never know he was the star. Could have been one of the extras. Mixed with the crew and had a lot of fun with them. You don't see that very often, believe me. I remember they were setting up for the scenes in the brothel, and Mitchum was joking with the crew. He said, 'This is why I took this job, to work with these gorgeous women. So far all I've been around is you guys and your stinking armpits.' But he was very friendly, very considerate. I remember one of the girls who were working as extras in those scenes asked him if he would mind posing with her for a photo, a keepsake. He said, 'Why, of course.' And then he said, 'What about the other girls?' And he got somebody to take pictures, and he posed with each girl and got each girl a picture. He was lovely about it, like they were doing him a favor rather than the other way around.

"I had a scene where I had to hit him, and he hit me back. I had never been trained to do anything like this. It came his turn to punch me. I was standing in front of him, and he was seated. And I heard him say, 'She's a mighty brave lady to do this.' I said, 'I heard that. What did you mean by that?' He said, 'Kate, when one person's sitting and the other's standing, the natural thing is for the person standing to start leaning forward. I have this punch spaced out to miss you by just an inch. So if you lean forward an inch closer, I'll hit you and break your jaw.' So I do my line and take a deep breath and not lean any closer, and he missed me by an inch. And afterward he told me how he'd been knocked out cold doing bits like that. He told me he'd done movie fights with ex-prizefighters, and I said I guessed that was safer because they knew what they were doing. And he said, 'No, they were the worst, because they weren't so smart and always forgot to miss.'

"To me he seemed a very nice, gentle man. Very sweet. I'll give you an example. My first agent out here was Thelma White—she had been in the Ziegfeld Follies and a child star and became an agent. And I told her I would be working with Mitchum, and she remembered working with him at the very beginning of his career. So we were sitting around on the set one day and I said, 'Oh, I forgot, I have a hello for you from someone, Thelma White. Do you remember her?' And Mitchum's face broke out in this beautiful sad smile and he said, 'Oh my, Thelma White . . . She knew me . . . back when I used to be handsome.' It was such a sweet, poetic thing to say, don't you think?"

Director Dick Richards, it was said, liked to change things, rework scenes, rehearse on film, and shoot it again if he thought of something better. His methods created tensions with some of the crew, which undermined Mitchum's faith. At times Mitchum complained openly against the last-minute and after-the-last-minute changes. "Listen, Richards, you've got to get your act together," he'd say. "I didn't sign my name on the dotted line to have you change the script every five minutes. I have twelve lawyers outside in the parking lot, and they're ready to leap on you if you make me do anything I didn't sign for." And yet often enough Richards's improvisatory methods created terrific stuff, a nuanced, tactile, and spontaneous-seeming quality of real life amid all that '40s bric-a-brac. Mitchum's memorable scene with Sylvia Miles as the pathetic floozie Mrs. Florian, for example, was in large part an improvisation. The song the pair sing together—"Sunday" by Jule Styne—was chosen on the spot. Mitchum knew the words. They had no permission to use the song, just shot it and hoped they could get the rights. A beautiful scene, perfectly staged—you can hear the flies buzzing, feel the dust floating in the tatty living room, Miles blending the poignance and the awfulness of the aged vaudevillian, Mitchum observant, gently insidious—an entirely convincing demonstration of a detective's particular fact-gathering and people-burrowing skills in action. Indeed, throughout the film, in comparison with Bogart's glamorous, always self-assured Marlowe in *The Big Sleep*, Mitchum's characterization, in addition to its other unique qualities, was altogether the more believable for the role of a twenty-five-bucks-a-day-and-expenses Hollywood Boulevard private eye.*

*Dick Powell's turn at the role in 1944 was surprisingly smart but one-dimensional—the actor nailed the pulp in Chandler's creation but not the poetry. What Chandler would have thought of Mitchum—the toughest and seediest of the Marlowes—playing his hero is not known, but the author's personal choice for the part was Cary Grant.

As filming continued, the relationship between Mitchum and Richards appeared to suffer a growing deterioration (though Richards himself believed it was never less than a close and respectful collaboration). Mitchum nicknamed him "Itchy McGinnis" because of the way he was always nervously changing his mind. He mockingly fixated on Richards's background as a photographer, said he was making the picture one frame at a time. Told reporters the man yelled, "Cut!" when he meant, "Action!" and vice versa. Most of the complaints sounded like pandering to the griping crew. Certainly, Richards's carefully budgeted film, made under difficult, constricting conditions—with '70s LA ever ready to disrupt the period recreations—was a breakneck breeze compared with the ten-month tortures of *Ryan's Daughter.* "Toward the end," said Henry Lange, "Bob didn't like Dick. He got mad at him. Part of it was because Bob and Dick just weren't the same kind of guys. One morning, Bob's talking to the grips and Dick comes up to him and started talking about the scene and how there are various shades of gray he would like to see if he can bring in. And Bob says, 'You want to suck what?' And Dick sort of walked away. Another time Bob got a gun with blanks from the prop guy, and he and Dick were having a disagreement about something, actor-director things, and Mitchum wanted to get his attention, so he drew the gun and started firing off rounds, scared the hell out of him. Only Bob would do that.

"The classic night between Bob and Dick was the night of the Academy Awards. John Alonzo was up for the award, and we had a substitute cameraman, and it was a difficult night. We were shooting on a real boat, out at sea. It was raining terribly that night. It had taken six or seven hours just to get everything set up. Bob is supposed to pull a gun out of his trench coat. Dick had approved this trench coat months ago and Bob had kept complaining, 'I'm a forty-two, this is a forty-six!' Dick told him not to worry about it; it was fine. Now came the night when Mitchum is in the raincoat and he's supposed to pull his gun out. And he's had a few by now. And he can't get the gun out. There's too much coat. He's having a hilarious time not getting the gun out. He's acting like there's coat all over the place. And he proceeded to torment Dick Richards shamelessly for most of the night, enjoying the fact that he was going to prove that he'd been right about the coat being too big."

What the hell. However the two men got through the day, they achieved something wonderful together.

This would be Mitchum's *Ride the High Country,* his *True Grit,* his *Limelight,* the autumnal work, the one that acknowledged a hero grown old, the summing up that reflected upon all that had come before. Whether Mitchum appreciated it or not, Richards had the insight to see him as something other than a nearly sixty-year-old journeyman movie actor hanging on for a few more years as a leading man, to see him as a living legend with a movie past and a cultural presence that transcended *Farewell*'s whodunit text. It was Richards who chose to create out of Chandler's familiar detective story a meditative, memory-laden work and a showcase where Mitchum could achieve apotheosis. Critics were largely enthusiastic about the evocative reconstruction of the past, this homage to '40s melodrama (*film noir* still not a cliché of the American critical lexicon), and many were close to ecstatic about the wistful, wry, haunting, iconographic presence of Robert Mitchum as Philip Marlowe.

They said, as they had said previously—wrongly—about *The Sundowners. Home from the Hill,* and *Ryan's Daughter,* that *Farewell* was certain to garner Mitchum a Best Actor nomination, quite possibly even the statuette itself. It was what they did, wasn't it? Give one to the great veterans when they had made what seemed to be their career-capping, summing-up performance? But there was no award, not even a nomination.

It really was a return to the past. The filming of *Farewell, My Lovely* had taken Mitchum to derelict neighborhoods he had once known, to streets he had last walked a near lifetime ago. Past midnight on Sixth and Main, a stone's throw from the old Rescue Mission that had staked a hungry boy to a hot meal and a bed. Forty years and more had come and gone. Nothing much had changed. The winos and the drifters and the junkie hookers still roamed these streets as before. A few who could make it to their feet straggled over to check him out, gave him a toothless grin, as if recognizing an old friend. *My people*, Mitchum thought. He peeled off singles and five spots for each. They took the handout, and a cigarette, thanked him boisterously or mumbled incoherently, staggered away back to the shadows. An old cop watched him working. Man was way past retirement age. How long had he pounded this miserable beat on the graveyard shift? The old cop stared at him and after a while he came over, looked him up and down. He said, "So you're back."

Part five

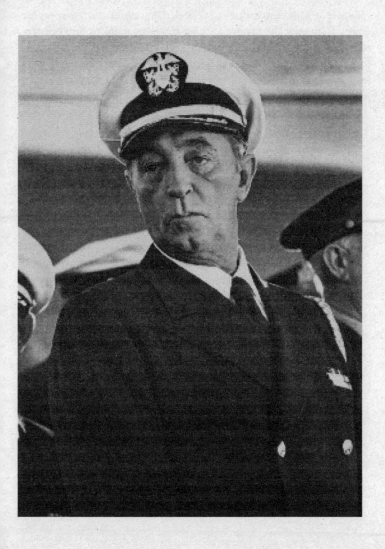

CHAPTER SIXTEEN

Big Sleep

In 1978, the Mitchums moved out of Los Angeles for the last time. They sold the house in Bel Air, sold the horse ranch in Atascadero, and purchased a two-bedroom, single-story with pool and Pacific view in the wealthy Santa Barbara community of Montecito a hundred miles to the north. It was a beautiful and pristine part of the world. The town was a mandated architectural imitation of a Mediterranean resort, and Montecito was considered lovely Santa Barbara's most attractive and exclusive enclave. It was an area where the abundance of old money, under the liberating influence of California sea and sunshine, could loosen its collar a bit, an area just formal and snooty enough for new money to *feel* like old if it so desired. "Dorothy wanted to take him away from the guys he knew, anybody that would take him out and get him schnockered," said an associate, speaking of the Mitchums' sudden and final exit from LA. "And I think she wanted to become a society matron." If this was the case, then one of these goals, anyway, was more or less achieved. Beverley Jackson, Santa Barbara's well-connected society columnist, who befriended the Mitchums, recalled, "There was a very definite social scene in Montecito in those days, and they became accepted into it. They rather quickly became part of the inner social crowd around here. Dorothy went on some of the better charity boards, and though Bob *hated* being paraded around, if it was a very good cause Dorothy would drag him and he'd sure do his duty. They were asked to a lot of charity functions; and they really did their part and it was appreciated. I mean, they were taken in as members of Burnham Wood Country Club who'd *never* taken in a movie star before...."

They were not to be entirely among new acquaintances. There was a small, growing colony of Hollywood expats, some of them old friends of the Mitchums, like Mandeville Canyon neighbors Richard Widmark and Olive Carey, widow of Harry Carey, Sr., who became a beloved den mother in the area, hosting down-home gatherings at her little place on the property of a well-to-do friend, Irma Kellogg, presiding like an affable Hawaiian queen in her big muumuus with a hibiscus behind one ear. "There was a little group of us that lived within a few blocks of each other in the village at that time," said Jack Elam. "In those days, even the biggest name movie star was not much more than a poor bum in Montecito. That's the town where the real money was. So nobody really paid much attention to any of those guys. There was Stu Whitman—he lived across the road from Bob, built a house on a vacant four-acre lot—and I lived down the street, and John Ireland lived another few blocks away. Dick Widmark lived at the other end, but he was in Connecticut a lot of the time. Jane Russell, she was married to a guy named John Peoples by then, and she lived down on the beach a few minutes away, moved off to Sedona, Arizona, then moved back. And it was a quiet little area. We'd all run into each other. There were a couple of restaurants, a café in the village, Café del Sol. You went there for coffee in the morning, and you'd usually run into Mitchum or Ireland, or Widmark would wander by; you'd sit and chew the fat a little. There were no tourists around, and the locals didn't even look at any of the movie folk. They didn't give a shit."

With a new house to be gotten out of, Mitchum went back to work. The period of uninterrupted acclaim and great roles—a three-picture parlay that began with *Eddie Coyle* and culminated in the actor's brilliant, defining performance as Philip Marlowe in *Farewell, My Lovely*—did not continue. Faye Dunaway had lobbied hard to have him cast as the world-weary television executive opposite her in *Network* and had finally convinced writer-producer Paddy Chayefsky, but director Sidney Lumet resisted—Mitchum wasn't sufficiently urban, he was trouble, whatever, he didn't want him—and the part went to William Holden. Instead of *Network*,

Mitchum's follow-up to *Farewell* would be *Midway*, a cheesy replay of the World War II battle in the Pacific (in ear-busting Sensurround) in which he portrayed Adm. "Bull" Halsey. For thirty years Mitchum had spoken of the day when he could become like Claude Rains or Lionel Barrymore, nabbing those tasty, scene-stealing supporting roles that were well paid and required only ten days' work. Hell, they didn't even have to be tasty. *Midway* became the movie that replaced *The Last Time I Saw Archie* as his publicly declared all-time favorite: the whole job was done in a single day, horizontally, in a hospital bed.

The Last Tycoon was more to the Claude Rains standard, ten days and a small but showy, carefully written part as a Louis B. Mayer–style movie mogul. *Tycoon* was a prestigious Sam Spiegel production based on F. Scott Fitzgerald's last, unfinished novel about brilliant, troubled Monroe Stahr, a production head in '30s Hollywood based on Irving Thalberg. The screenplay was by English playwright Harold Pinter, and Spiegel's *On the Waterfront* collaborator Elia Kazan had been hired to direct. The large cast was a mix of New and Old Hollywood: Robert DeNiro, Jack Nicholson, Ingrid Boulting, Theresa Russell, and Anjelica Huston mixing it up with actual veterans of the golden-age studio system, Mitchum, Tony Curtis, Ray Milland, Dana Andrews, and John Carradine. Off the set the players seemed to divide into generational camps, with the old-timers to be found kibbitzing together on the sidelines, swapping rollicking stories about the old days. Kazan devoted most of his efforts to DeNiro, whose complex Actors' Studio–trained approach to a role required high maintenance, and to newcomer Boulting—a Spiegel "discovery"—who simply needed all the help she could get. Mitchum respected DeNiro's talent, but he joined some of the others in their eye-rolling reaction to the New Yorker's all-consuming immersion in his role, his walking around in costume and character off camera as well as on. During lunch break DeNiro would often remain sitting in his office set, ruminating on the character he played. One afternoon Mitchum and Milland came back to the set after the break, and one or the other had finished a funny story and they both burst into hearty laughter. Suddenly the prop venetian blinds inside the office set shot open and the pair looked over to see DeNiro fiercely staring at the two of them having a great time. Mitchum whispered, "I hope Kid Monroe there doesn't dock our pay."

Milland would occasionally become miffed at the lack of attention Kazan showed to him in contrast to his work with DeNiro ("Ray gave everybody with hair a hard time," said Mitchum). He would run back to the other veterans irate with tidbits of the director's latest intriguing suggestions to his young star. For instance, wanting to give the character an air of distracted thoughtfulness, as if Monroe Stahr's brilliant mind was forever in two places at once, Kazan—Milland relayed—had told DeNiro to always be thinking about something entirely different while speaking his lines.

"Shit," said Mitchum, "I've been doing that for years!"

*

"It was a grim picture, and DeNiro felt the need to be quite somber," said assistant director Ron Wright. "We started using the term *grim up* to mean we had to get in the mood for the scenes. Well, when Mitchum got there, that blew apart. He was joking and he had a lot of fun. Not that he was disrespectful of Kazan or DeNiro. There was a very good mutual respect. And I think, actually, he raised Kazan's spirits. It was a relief to Kazan, working with the old-timers, the guys who didn't have to go off and go get their shit together before they could come to the set, or while they're *on* the set and everyone standing around waiting for them. Kazan brightened up because he didn't have to create an environment for Mitchum and Milland and these old pros, who could do just as good a job, but all they needed was to come in, say the words, and not trip over the furniture.

"Mitchum was fabulous. He kept the crew happy; he'd send his secretary downtown to bring back authentic Mexican food for everybody. He was a doll. He was also very good with helping some of the newer people, like Teresa Russell, who was called Teresa Pope then—Mitchum called her Tessy Poop." Playing Mitchum's daughter, Russell found it difficult to give out a convincingly startled laugh as required in one scene. After several aborted takes, Mitchum planted himself in front of the actress and when the camera turned he dropped his pants and raised his bare ass at her. Russell's reaction can be seen in the finished film.

Pinter's script was thoughtful but moribund. However, Sam Spiegel loved Pinter and had a lingering resentment of Kazan, whose authority had diminished since the *Waterfront* days. Spiegel seemed determined to keep Kazan in his place. The director was not permitted to change so much as a comma in the screenplay without a long conference call to England. (Not even the physical dimensions of the document could be altered; all copies of the script were made in the larger British format of Pinter's original.) No auteurist alchemy saved the day—the deadly script became the lifeless film. Even more of a disappointment than *Ryan's Daughter*, *The Last Tycoon* had been anticipated as the prestige film release of the year until its first screening. There were extraordinary moments scattered throughout, but most of it played like a picnic at a cemetery.

No prestige, real or anticipated, was attached to *Matilda*, a whimsy about a boxing kangaroo. Playing a Damon Runyon–Paul Gallico type of colorful sportswriter encouraging Elliott Gould as a boxing promoter, Mitchum's participation was brief. Though producer Al Ruddy had originally intended to use a real kangaroo for the boxing and other scenes, the animal proved lazy and scary and wasted miles of film, so he was replaced by an actor in a kangaroo suit named Gary Morgan. "They tried a few others for the part," said Morgan, "but I was the only one made that suit come alive." It was an imperfect creation, heavy, awkward—Morgan spent most of the production gasping for air, falling unconscious, and getting bloodied and knocked out by the real heavyweight boxers he went up against. "Yep, the same thing happened to me in my boxing scenes," Mitchum told him, consolingly, "but I don't remember wearing all that padding."

"Mitchum was great, such a cool guy," said Morgan. "The funny thing I remember, the first day we're on location working at Harrah's in Reno and they threw a kind of PR party at the hotel. It was one of these goodwill things, so the hotel executives and their wives could ogle the Hollywood stars up close. Everyone looked at it as a kind of an inconvenience, and no one expected Mitchum to even show up for this thing. But instead Mitchum was there early, sitting at the bar, holding court, entertaining everybody, and even after everybody left, Mitchum was still there until the bartender said, 'Last call,' and Mitchum says, 'Thank you very much,' and went to bed. But he was just a real cool guy, very nice to me, and we did all sorts of crazy promos for the movie, the *Tonight Show* and everything—I remember sitting with him there just before he went on the show with Johnny Carson, and an aid brought him a large tumbler glass of straight whiskey; and he just drank it down in a couple of gulps like a big glass of water. And I was always in the kangaroo suit hopping around with him and he'd just treat me like his kangaroo sidekick, didn't faze him in the least. And if somebody said, 'Who's this?' he'd say, 'Why, under that kangaroo hide beats the heart of Gary Morgan.' I just adored him. And he told stories nonstop, for every occasion. Somebody'd mention Angie Dickinson, for instance, and he'd tell about the time he was making some Western with Angie and they're sitting around on the location in their camp chairs waiting for the crew to get ready. And some cute girl slips over to Mitchum and says, 'Oh my, Bob Mitchum . . . I'd just really love to give you a blow job!' And he says, 'Well, that's a great offer, honey, but I see they're right now calling me back to work.' And according to Bob, he says to the girl, 'Well, gee, Angie's not doing anything, why don't you ask her?'

"That picture, *Matilda,* got scathing reviews, and I think it was because the press packet tried to pretend we used a real kangaroo in the thing. Then when the press saw the picture, it was like, 'What, are you kidding?' It pissed the critics off. So the reviews were like, 'Fuck you!'

"Anyway . . . Robert Mitchum? You couldn't get me to say anything but salt of the earth. I ran into him several years later. Lots of times, you're a little guy working with big stars, next time they see you they look right through you, don't have the time of day. Mitchum? I gave him a wave, it's years later; he grabbed me like I was a little brother, like it was old home week. . . . What a real cool guy he was."

After turning down the lead in *The French Connection* years before, largely because of a distaste for the role of a drug-busting hero, Mitchum now signed on to play an agent of the U.S. Drug Enforcement Agency in a far less promising project, *The Amsterdam Kill.* The film belonged to Hong Kong's Raymond Chow and Golden Harvest Productions and was to be directed by Robert Clouse, the American who had called the shots on Bruce Lee's most successful vehicle, *Enter the Dragon.* Shooting roamed from London to Amsterdam to Hong Kong, and Mitchum seemed to enjoy himself nowhere. He was sixty years old, and Clouse—who Mitchum said was deaf and had never before directed anyone without a black belt in karate—had him doing all his own stunts. "Look, if my knee goes, it's a three-month lunch," he told Clouse, to not much avail. His performance included jumping into the questionable, murky liquid that flowed in a Dutch canal. "They're filthy," he told Roderick Mann, "all those houseboats spewing out their garbage. And there I am, up to my neck in it . . . Can you see Elizabeth Taylor or Cary Grant in a canal? Or Victor Mature? Out of the question. He wouldn't even get on a horse unless it was bolted to the ground. But me, with my shining heart, in I go . . ." The company agreed to pay for his tetanus shot though, he claimed, not for a typhoid antidote as the sweating it induced might hold up production. He felt no more sanguine about his Amsterdam hotel and refused to shoot a scene on the front steps that he believed had been arranged as a blatant promotional payback to the owners of the place. "Me, who turned down $250,000 just to wash my hair on TV! No way, I said, you'll get me to plug this dump." And then there was the omnipresence, said the star, of dog shit, huge mounds of it lining the curbs: "They must have dogs six feet tall here."

Things proved still more unpleasant in Hong Kong. According to Robert Clouse, Mitchum was openly verbally abusive to the Golden Harvest personnel and Chinese crew. The sentiments were returned in kind. The atmosphere became so charged that Mitchum began harboring fears that the film company was planning to kill him. He had somehow convinced himself that Golden

Harvest was secretly holding extra insurance policies that would pay a fortune in the event of his death during production. Clouse himself believed there was an element of dangerous vengefulness in the way members of the Chinese contingent at dinner one night plied Mitchum with what some feared was a lethal portion of a devastatingly powerful local spirit. He was carried out of the restaurant and back to his hotel but ultimately took a fall on a bathroom floor and busted two ribs.

Once again a behind-the-scenes "making of" a documentary might have proved more entertaining than the actual confused, simple-minded feature itself.

Mitchum returned to the role of Philip Marlowe for the second and last time in a screen adaptation of Chandler's first novel, *The Big Sleep,* already filmed marvelously twenty-some years before as a studio-bound violent comedy of manners, directed by Howard Hawks and starring Humphrey Bogart. Producer Elliott Kastner, financed by Britain's Sir Lew Grade, offered the project to writer-director Michael Winner. Winner, a colorful, smart, and waspishly funny moviemaker, had begun his career as a social satirist chronicling the rise of "Swinging London" in several clever to brilliant films starring Oliver Reed. He then switched gears in the '70s to become a specialist in brisk and often lurid genre entertainments, many of them vehicles for Charles Bronson.

Though he had written a screenplay that was in fact more faithful to the original novel than Hawks's version, Michael Winner made the radical decision to transplant *The Big Sleep* to modern London. "It came about because it seemed to me the original film was so immensely well known," said Winner, "that to ape it in any way would be ridiculous. Furthermore, Raymond Chandler was a great Anglophile, and when I read the book I thought it was quite a bit like reading Oscar Wilde. I know this man's meant to be a famous American writer, but it's an immensely British style of writing. So much so that when Jimmy Stewart was sent the script, he said, 'I can't play General Sternwood because he's written as an Englishman.' I said, 'Jimmy, every word is Raymond Chandler's and he's a famous American writer.' But Jimmy was actually being quite bright. . . . So, I thought we'd try something completely different. And I saw it very much as a gavotte, that is, a lot of people dancing around each other in a very classical way."

By working at his usual brisk pace and carefully arranging the schedule, Winner was able to afford Mitchum a notably starry supporting cast, including Stewart, *Ryan's Daughter* mates Sarah Miles and John Mills, Oliver Reed, Joan Collins, Candy Clark, Edward Fox, and Richard Boone. "Mitchum was held in very high regard by the other actors. And I think he was an inducement for them to work in the picture. Just as when you do a picture with Marlon you know that more people will turn up. And also, I think they were all very good parts. Very sharp." Although the film was spruced up for the '70s with a few flashes of nudity and an array of agressively sexy dames, the modern Marlowe remained a surprisingly chaste fellow, leading Mitchum to voice some sardonic suspicions: "Marlowe throws Candy Clark out of his bed, resists the advances of Sarah Miles, and has pictures of himself all over his apartment. I kept expecting him to open a closet and find exotic black panty hose and rhinestone shoes and jazz."

Installed in a flat at Arlington House on a very posh street overlooking St. James Park and coutured for the film in the finest Savile Row suitings—nothing farted up by Vic Mature this go-round—Mitchum went to work, enjoying London as he always did, though there were the usual grousings and wisecracks to reporters or any audience he could muster. They were shooting in London, he said, "because it's the only place they can practice industrial slavery. Around eight or nine at night I'd say, 'Isn't it getting a little late?' 'Oh, weren't you informed,' they'd say, 'today is an extended day?' Turned out to be a day you worked until midnight." Twelve hours, fourteen hours a day he claimed to be on the job. "By the time I make the report out to the Screen Actors Guild, I will *own* Sir Lew Grade."

Everybody else had the Claude Rains roles this time. James Stewart as Sternwood, the rich, wheelchair-bound old man with the errant daughters, flew in from Los Angeles for a few days to shoot his two scenes. Though just seventy years old now, the great movie star appeared much older. "The picture was all about corpses," Mitchum told Donald Dewey, "but Jimmy looked deader than any of them." Stewart had a hearing and possible memory impairment and kept fumbling on one of his lines. "Every time he'd flub it, he'd look at me and apologize to me like he'd just committed some kind of atrocious crime. Damned embarrassing, I'll tell you. What the hell is Jimmy Stewart apologizing to *me* about?"

Joan Collins, playing the sexy, scheming bookshop clerk, Agnes, thought Mitchum one of the greatest actors she had ever worked with, but was initially terrified of being bruised or broken by him during their on-camera tussle. "He had to wrestle with me on the floor, fling me across the room onto a sofa, grab my hair, then throw me over his knee and spank me really hard while I wriggled around trying to dodge his slaps." Mitchum did all the action as required, but Collins found the whole thing a remarkably gentle and bruise-free experience. "Honey, I'm an actor," he told her afterwards, "and I know how to *play* rough. I've been doin' this stuff for about a hundred years so I'm not about to hurt an actress in a scene, 'specially not in *this* piece of crap."

The great casting coup for the British *Big Sleep,* besides Mitchum's return to the role, was Richard Boone playing trigger-man Lash Canino. Boone's Olympian charisma turned the small part into the most compelling villain Mitchum had gone up against since Robert Ryan—or Jane Greer. "In the evening Bob tended to drink," said Winner, "and, bless him, Dick Boone drank a bit." In fact, Boone, like Mitchum, was considered a world-class imbiber; and on the night they were to film their last violent encounter, both were feeling no pain. Staggering about the set and blasting away at each other, the two old pros had a high old time of it. Winner: "I did say, during the final shoot-out, 'This is like *The Gunfight at Alcoholics Anonymous.*' I mean, that was being a little cruel, but they were a bit stoked up there. But they were fine."

Mitchum and Sarah Miles—in the Lauren Bacall role—were happily reunited for the production. They had remained chums through the years, fostering continued speculation about their relationship; and as Miles's marriage to Robert Bolt had come undone, she would admit to having again been tempted by the American's sexual allure. But nothing came of it. Miles valued Mitchum's friendship all the more when he became one of only three showbiz acquaintances to immediately defend her during a horrible, scandalous crisis she had endured a few years earlier. Miles had somehow gotten entangled in a bizarre relationship with a *TIME* magazine reporter, David Whiting, who had seduced her and then managed to make himself a permanent fixture in her life. Although he was clearly unstable and beat her violently numerous times, Miles was incapable of doing whatever it took to get away from the man. Violently jealous, he bestowed beatings on several of her costars and friends as well—*including Mitchum*. The actor had arrived in London for a visit and left a message for Miles to call him. Mitchum had just concluded the purchase of some marijuana from a local connection and was closing the door to his flat when Whiting arrived in a maniacal fury, knocking Mitchum to the floor. "I caught his eye and there was death perching right in the corner of it," Mitchum told her. He clung to the floor in a ball while Whiting kicked him again and again, then grabbed his newly purchased pot stash and fled. It was the only time, Mitchum said, he had ever refused to fight back when attacked. "No way, man! Never fight when you see death in the eye."

Whiting followed Miles to the American West where she was shooting a film, and one night—after he had given her another beating, and she had revealed as much to costar Burt Reynolds and others—Whiting was found dead on her bathroom floor under mysterious circumstances. Miles felt that many of those close to her, including family members, believed she was complicit in the man's death—his murder no less—and Mitchum was among the shockingly few to offer support and prove a stalwart friend.

Mitchum had his own small scandals to engender during the course of *The Big Sleep*'s production, consorting with a luscious young Londoner, to the delight of Fleet Street's strenuous tabloids. "There was a whole thing in the paper about it," Michael Winner recalled. "I had interviewed a girl that afternoon because we had to do a book cover with some nudes on it, to be seen within the movie. And we took the photos ourselves. The girl was a nude model, and she came to see me to be a nude model for this. It was a one-hour modeling assignment, probably fifteen dollars. And by absolute, amazing coincidence I met Mitchum in the lobby of a theater that evening—he was seeing John Mills in a Terrence Rattigan play— and he turned up with this girl. And he hadn't met her through me. How he met her, I don't know. It was strange. There she was going to the theater with him. And this girl says, 'Hello.' She was perfectly pleasant. And she was his girlfriend, I think, during his stay. She sold her story to the English press, so I'm not telling a tale out of school. And then they all had a fight with some other girl outside his apartment. That was also in the papers here. Some other woman who was following him around, and they had a fight outside the apartment. I said, 'Bob, I hope it wasn't *inside* because we'll do you for the damage, you know!'"

Mitchum and Winner remained pals in the years ahead. "Well, Bob was two people, really. When he had a drink or two he was the mumbling raconteur or, if he had had enough, quite a rowdy fellow. But most of the time he was a very quiet person, read a great deal, read poetry, important books. He used to write poetry, rather proudly. I knew this chap very well. He was a very intellectual person. The great amount of time that I saw him he was very quiet, very sober, very dedicated. He was almost like the head of a midwestern university. And he wasn't doing this to impress me. Why should he? *Ha ha*—I went to Cambridge, you know!"

Winner would have been the first—well, perhaps not the first—to acknowledge that his *Big Sleep* did not surpass the achievement of the Bogart classic of the '40s. But the new one was jolly good fun, a spirited go at the material, and here and there, particularly in several ripely acted characterizations—by Boone, Collins, the always delightful Oliver Reed as a reptilian mobster—it actually was the superior of the revered Hawks version. However, many reviewers could not get beyond Winner's transatlantic relocation and desecrating contemporaneity. How things had changed in the few years since Dick Richards had thought to make *Farewell, My Lovely* into a period piece. Now every weatherman turned television movie critic was a Raymond Chandler purist.

*

Playwright John Guare had written an original scenario that was to be directed by his French friend Louis Malle. It was called *Atlantic City*, and it was the story of a seedy, aged hood in the New Jersey gambling resort who finds a last shot at riches and romance. Guare and Malle had thought of several actors for the part of the nostalgic old criminal, but when Robert Mitchum's name came up a light went off. "We both said, 'Of course!'" Guare recalled. "We thought he would be terrific. His age, his aura, the whole connection to film noir. It seemed perfect. We sent him the script, and Louis went out to California to see him. Mitchum met him at the door. Louis took one look and saw immediately that Mitchum had had a face-lift. There was not a wrinkle in sight. And he was quite open about it. He said yes, he had just had it done. He had read the script we sent him, he said he was very happy to be asked to do the part, but, he said, 'I'm only playing forty-five now.' Forty-five years old, in other words. And that was that. We got Burt Lancaster instead." Lancaster's performance in the role brought him critical acclaim and an Oscar nomination, among other honors.

Mitchum closed out the decade with two more jobs of work. *Breakthrough,* filmed in Austria, was a modest sequel to Peckinpah's WWII epic, *Cross of Iron,* with Mitchum as an American officer. Top billing went to Richard Burton, playing the German hero Sergeant Steiner. Burton's glamour was sadly depleted by now, and he looked like a bloated, strung-out tortoise inside his great steel army helmet. *Agency* was a Canadian thriller shot in Toronto in the winter of 1978–79, with Lee Majors as a funky adman foiling a plot to control public policy through subliminal messages, the plot hatched by evil, brilliant senior advertising executive Mitchum.

"He's a total outcast," the producer Robert Lantos gushed to a reporter. "Outside the Hollywood system. He has no agent, probably the only major star who doesn't, and you deal directly with him."

Mitchum pocketed five hundred thousand dollars for a dramatic but supporting part. Asked by the reporter if he ever got excited about any of his films, Mitchum responded with what was described as a "very long pause."

Valerie Perrine played the film's statuesque love interest—Lee's. She told Mitchum, "I've never been in a picture with guns." Mitchum told her, "I've never been in one without."

*

He started the new decade with an even worse movie, if that were possible: *Nightkill*. It was a James M. Cain-ish tale of a homicidal wife, with *Charlie's Angel* Jaclyn Smith starring as the murderess and Mitchum as a mysterious private eye on her trail. It was a gorilla picture all the way. So poor were the film's prospects that Avco-Embassy decided to sell it directly to television, and NBC promoted its December broadcast as the world premiere of a made-for-TV movie rather than as the world premiere of a not-good-enough-for-theaters movie.

Ironically, it was during this period—on December, 8, 1980—as his career seemed to have returned to the B picture murk whence it began, that Mitchum was honored with a Lifetime Achievement Award by the Los Angeles Film Critics association. He was the fifth recipient of the honor, following Allan Dwan, King Vidor, Orson Welles, and John Huston. "I would like to thank you all," said Mitchum, "for picking my name out of a hat."

Later that same month, his twenty-eight-year-old daughter, Trina, wed a California musician and composer named Scott Richardson. Trina had gone through a period as an aspiring writer, then as a burgeoning photographer. Now she was said to be interested in movie production work. Brothers Chris and James were still plugging away at their father's business. After more than twenty years as an actor,

Jim had never broken through to the big time and was reduced to working in mostly out-of-the-mainstream movies. Sometimes he tried to make his own breaks and got involved on the production side. One underfunded project called *King of the Mountain* fell apart after shooting began in New Mexico, and, according to John Mitchum, Robert had had to pay off bill collectors to the tune of eleven thousand dollars. Jim's most recent credits were unknown quantities called *Blackout* and *Toxic Monster*. "I wish I could tell you that Jim is a famous surgeon or even a box boy in the supermarket," his father uncharitably said to a reporter. "But I can't. He curses the stars and wonders why he wasn't singled out for eternal glory."

Chris, who drifted into acting when nothing else worked out, had gotten a number of jobs through sympathetic associates of his father's, Howard Hawks and John Wayne. An agent then found him a role in a film made in Spain, a thriller called *The Summertime Killer*. It would not get much play in the States, but the picture was a sizable hit throughout Europe, and its success led to other jobs there and in Asia, mostly in action and horror movies. Usually, he would say jokingly, he played a smiling, renegade CIA agent who kills hundreds of people. He went where the work was and moved the family to Spain for three years. In Hollywood they couldn't even spell it, but the name Chris Mitchum on a marquee meant good box office in Algeciras or Manila. In 1980, he returned to the United States hoping to try his luck again in Hollywood. "From 1980 to 1982, I didn't work at all," he told the *Los Angeles Times*. "That was one of the many times I bottomed out." It was rough, he said. He'd had an established price for his services in Europe, and in California no one wanted to pay it.

John Mitchum had continued to work in the business. He was a busy journeyman character actor with dozens of credits by now, his most prominent job to date the role of Det. Frank Di Georgio, supporting Clint Eastwood in *Dirty Harry* and two sequels. He seemed content with the career he had found for himself and was well liked by people in the business. His personal life, though, had for many years been beset by tragedy. Years before, his wife, Nancy, had been diagnosed with malignant exophthalmos, or Graves' disease. Bone surgery on her face had left her in a condition that made it difficult to keep her eyes from falling out of their sockets. She suffered for a decade with complications from the disease and then, in 1976, died from terminal, undiagnosed cancer. John was married for a third time, briefly and unhappily, and then once more, happily, to a stage actress named Bonnie Duff, brother Bob serving as best man at the outdoor ceremony.

The 1977 ABC broadcast of a multipart adaptation of Alex Haley's best-selling book *Roots* had met with enormous acclaim and an unprecedented viewership. It would prove to be the model for a new television format, the blockbuster miniseries—lengthy, sprawling, melodramatic pop literature transformed into lengthy, sprawling, et cetera, TV programming.

In 1980, the ABC network announced its intention of producing a thirty-five-million-dollar, sixteen-hour-long adaptation of Herman Wouk's novel *The Winds of War,* a thick, fictional account of world events between the German invasion of Poland in 1939 and the Japanese attack on the Hawaiian islands in 1941, the epic canvas centered around the globe-trotting family of U.S. Navy captain Victor "Pug" Henry. With his long-established skill as a storyteller, Wouk had written a compelling page-turner in which his primary characters—Pug, son Byron, daughter-in-law Natalie—managed to interact with every world leader from FDR to Stalin and/or experience every earth-shattering event—from Pearl Harbor to the Holocaust—of those tumultuous years. The tale had action, spectacle, suspense, adultery, heartbreak, history, and a moral lesson or two.

To make this, the costliest of all television programs, ABC and coproducer Paramount Television handed the creative reins to Dan Curtis, whose fame rested on the 1960s vampire soap opera *Dark Shadows* and several glossy prime-time TV movies, such as his 1973 version of *Dracula* with Jack Palance. Curtis was a rare figure among important television producers in that he directed his own projects. With the completion of the massive screenplay by Wouk himself, the plans for a vast production took shape, with filming to be done in six countries and hundreds of locations, from Hawaii to the wilds of Yugoslavia. There were nearly three hundred speaking roles to be cast, first and foremost that of the story's central character, the link to all the various threads in the sprawling epic. According to Wouk's description of Captain Henry, the role might have properly belonged to someone in the age range and bulldog shape of an Ed Asner, but Curtis and ABC saw the story's steadfast military hero and patriarch in more classical terms. The producer-director considered a long list of prominent names for the role, but after a luncheon with Robert Mitchum—granite face, tall, broad-shouldered, American as Mount Rushmore, a tough SOB with awesome presence—he knew he had found his man. Gary Nardino, the president of Paramount TV, gave him no argument. Said Nardino of Mitchum, "He's the only Gary Cooper still alive."

Through the years Mitchum had had nothing much good to say about the medium of television. It had always looked like too much work, too little pay, and the end result was a load of crap. But that was . . . then. He was sixty-three years old, and maybe he had worn out his welcome in features. The big pictures these days all seemed to be aimed at half-witted teenagers anyway, and he could not easily imagine himself dressed up in gold tights like a chorus boy for one of those Star-whatever outer space adventures or sitting around chewing the fat with a retarded-looking extraterrestrial. Advisers pleaded: This is going to be the biggest thing ABC has ever done. It will be the television event of the year. And they want you to star in it!

Dan Curtis called him for his answer.

Mitchum said, "How long?"

"About forty weeks."

"How much?"

"A million."

"Why not?"

*

Other principal roles went to Polly Bergen as Mrs. Pug, John Houseman as the Jewish scholar Aaron Jastrow, Briton Victoria Tennant as Pamela Tudsbury (Mitchum's love interest), Ralph Bellamy reprising his *Sunrise at Campobello* turn as Franklin Roosevelt, Ali MacGraw as the impetuous Natalie, and Jan-Michael Vincent (playing Mitchum's son for the second time) as Byron Henry, the latter two casting choices not made until long after the production had been under way. Shooting began in December, pleasantly enough, on the decks of the *Queen Mary* in Long Beach, filling in for the German liner *Bremen,* and then on the tennis court of a Hancock Park estate (where it was discovered that Mitchum, unlike Pug Henry, had never touched a racket in his life; a tennis-playing double for the star had to be found). After Christmas break they moved on to more rigorous locations in Yugoslavia, filling in for the Russian front; arrangements had been made to rent most of the Yugoslav army. Mitchum's departure for Europe coincided with his catching a strain of Thai flu, and he arrived in Zagreb with a 104-degree temperature. For over a week, he worked while shaking and shivering with fever. The weather was indeed Russian-front cold, nearly as frigid on some of the interior sets as it was in the forest. "Every toilet within four miles was frozen," said Mitchum. "Slivovitz kept me alive." Once Curtis interrupted a take to ask why Mitchum's suit appeared to be moistly shiny. The actor had sweated right through his shirt and jacket, and the sweat had beaded and frozen solid.

"Everyone could see how sick he was," said Victoria Tennant, who had come to be a great admirer and good pal of the actor. "But he kept working. He was the only actor the Yugoslavs recognized, and when he looked like he was going to drop, they were still after him for autographs."

The food Mitchum would recall as nothing but nightmarish variants of porridge. The thirty-five-million-dollar production was spending fifty bucks on catering, he said. Standard fare was a soup of barley and rainwater thick enough to plant a telephone pole in. On special occasions, he said, it would also contain a greasy hunk of congealed red mystery meat. After several weeks, the company's

Zagreb hotel became infested with a group of three dozen roistering Russian conventioneers who had apparently not bathed since the revolution. The group were omnipresent in the lobby, dining room, and elevators and gave off such a collective reek that some of the *Winds* people took to carrying face towels from their rooms to cover their mouths and nostrils against the nauseating smell. Mitchum and Jan-Michael Vincent had gone up in the elevator with a half-dozen of the reeking Russkies. "After we got out," Vincent recalled, "Mitchum held the door, whipped out a tube of Crazy Glue, and began squirting great quantities of it up one side of the elevator door and down the other. Then he waved good-bye to them and they nodded appreciatively, thinking he had fixed something. We learned later that it had taken the hotel servicemen six hours to get those Russians out of that elevator."

Mitchum was in Zagreb for two months, most of it, he would say, spent falling on his ass in the snow while trying to reach an outhouse. After one particularly debilitating day's shoot, he received a phone call from Bo Derek, who had wanted him to play her father in *Tarzan, the Ape Man,* shooting in sunny Sri Lanka and the Seychelles. Nearly in tears, he whimpered to Victoria Tennant that he could at that moment be headed for a warm beach somewhere to play with busty Bo. "Yes, and here you are with a freezing flat-chested English girl," said a possibly unsympathetic Tennant, "in the middle of fucking Yugoslavia."

At last Mitchum was given a break to go home and recuperate while the others labored on. A doctor told him he had been working all this time with a solid case of pneumonia. When he returned to Yugoslavia he brought with him crates of fresh California fruit to bestow on the grateful company. More weeks in Zagreb; then at last they moved on to more congenial locations in Italy, Austria, and England. Mitchum would be given periodic vacations throughout the year, but they never seemed long enough to recover. Despite the vast-sounding budget and a twelve-month shoot, they were, after all, trying to make the equivalent of nine feature films in that time. For all its opulence, *The Winds of War* still ended up being shot like any other television production, with corners cut wherever possible and speed always of the essence. They worked six days a week, late into the evening almost every night. The shooting schedule was so efficiently planned that they were forever filming sequences that were wildly out of continuity with the previous one and the next, requiring Mitchum to change constantly in and out of nearly one hundred different costumes and two dozen pairs of shoes, none worn long enough to be broken in ("My toes are still braided"). Just trying to find where they were in the script, shifting the pages, say, from Scene 19 to Scene 643 in the massive screenplay, could give you a double hernia. Mitchum had not had to work so fast on a picture since those seven-day wonders at Monogram. Throughout, he complained like a foulmouthed Job, but ABC publicist James Butler thought it was in large part an act and that he was having "a good time with his hard-times." Butler observed in the journal he kept that when no one was around to be entertained, the "other" Mitchum came out. "He is singing softly to himself much of the endless time between scenes. Country songs, usually. His voice is warm, low, spirited . . . it makes him enormously human and enormously likable."

Month after month, ferocious Dan Curtis never let up, keeping things on schedule, never intimidated by logistics that might have vanquished General Eisenhower. "He had shortened the lives of his players an aggregate total of two hundred and fifty years," said Mitchum. One day, while filming a marching batallion, Curtis reeled back, clutching his chest. Someone shouted, "Dan Curtis is having a heart attack!" Said Mitchum, "I have never seen so many smiles at one time in my life."

"Bob," said the director, "likes to kid."

Mitchum was a good soldier, the ultimate pro, Curtis called him, though when the director's attention turned away, and Bob considered himself abandoned "to the wolves," he would slip away to a pub and get drunk. "Then," said Mitchum, "he'd have to spend a day finding me."

Shooting was completed a year and one week after it began, with the filming of the attack on Pearl Harbor, staged at Port Heuneme, California, on December 7 to coincide with the fortieth anniversary of the actual event. Curtis shot it with typical efficiency, in one afternoon, using eight cameras, two takes. One of the ABC people gloat-ed, "It took *Tora, Tora, Tora* three months to do the same action!" Mitchum shrugged: "It took the Japanese fifteen minutes."

It had been a long, long job. Mitchum calculated that in the end, with the amount of time he had put in, his $1.25 million salary had worked out to about $2.40 an hour. "I could have done better pick-ing potatoes."

With his virginity now taken, and no feature film offer imminent, Mitchum accepted another job in television. His Santa Barbara neighbor Mel Ferrer was producing and had tossed the script on his driveway next to the morning paper. It was a straight, old-fashioned private detective mystery with an awful title, *So Little Cause for Caroline.* They soon changed it to something just as bad: *One Shoe Makes It Murder.* They shot it in the spring. The schedules were crazy, dawn to bedtime, everyone running around under pressure. OK, that's it for television, he said. It was a sloppy and sleepy B pic-ture, but Mitchum and costar Angie Dickinson made it something more than watchable—the senior citizen and the old broad were sexier together than most of the "hot" young couples Hollywood was offering.

Jason Miller's play *That Championship Season* had been an off and then on Broadway sensation, winning the Tony Award for Best Play and a Pulitzer Prize in 1972. It concerned the twenty-fifth anniver-sary get-together of an old high school basketball coach and his four former stars, that long ago "championship season" still the defining moment of their lives. In a time before delineations of American machismo and jock culture had become commonplace, Miller's work was found incisive and shocking with its dramatically charged exploration of the characters' emotional lives and the raw, obsceni-ty-filled dialogue reflecting their casual racism and misogyny. There had been plans to make a film of the play since its first season on the stage, but they had come to nothing. In the late '70s, a director (William Friedkin) and a full cast (including Nick Nolte and George C. Scott as the coach) had been assembled, but this, too, fell apart.

Miller himself bought back the screen rights and went peddling the property again, attaching himself as writer-director. Menahem Golan and Yoram Globus, two Israelis who had founded Cannon Films, were launching themselves as a Hollywood presence, bankrolling a slew of genre schlock films with stars like Stallone and Bronson while keeping an eye out for a few more distinguished projects as well. Jason Miller's prizewinner filled the bill.

A cast was assembled—Bruce Dern, Martin Sheen, Stacy Keach, and Paul Sorvino (a survivor from the original Broadway cast) as the forty-something former teammates. William Holden had agreed to play their once and forever coach but had cracked his skull open in a drunken fall and died, his body not found for days. Mitchum was offered the part and accepted. Filming began in Scranton, Pennsylvania, in July 1982, the writer having "opened up" his play to include two reels of street scenes, parades, crowds, an elephant, with extra work and bit parts for nearly the whole town, including Jason Miller's parents. There was a real sense of elation among the four younger actors, all of them convinced Miller had written them the best roles of their lives. "I've wanted to do this play since I saw it on Broadway," said Keach. "I'm so excited about the work that's been happening I'm getting superstitious. We're all pushing and challenging each other, just like on a team. . . ." Mitchum, of course, managed to contain his girlish delight. Had he seen the play? someone asked. "No. I don't go to movies or plays. I've seen only one movie in ten years. I was ankle-deep in popcorn and pot." As for his fellow performers, their enthusiasm and, in some cases, their competitiveness seemed at times a tad hard for him to take. "They walk back and forth and hyperventilate," he said. "This is like working with an English company; all these guys talk about is acting. I'm from the school where all we talked about was overtime and screwing."

"When I met him I was in awe of him," said Paul Sorvino. "And I think you're only in awe of someone who is mysterious, whom you can't read easily. In fact, we used that awe, all of us, in the movie."

The work for once was easy on the knees, Mitchum could say that much, requiring nothing more physical than the tossing of an imaginary basketball. But the part, this "pivotal blowhard" as he called him, took some finessing. Too much of the dialogue still smelled of "the boards," of theatricality. "He felt some passages in the screenplay were redundant," Miller told Donald Chase, "And he felt there were places where he could have a quicker attack on a line. . . . Since I hadn't in fact reduced the play's rhetoric as I wanted to, I followed his suggestions when I thought they applied." Miller's frequent use of sports references in the script and in his direction seemed to go over Mitchum's head. The actor confessed to knowing no more about basketball than he did about tennis. "I never saw a game in my life. Jason would take me aside and say, 'This is it, Bob, the last quarter.' I didn't know what the hell he was talking about."

There were times when the lines didn't come easily—rare for Mitchum, still ordinarily "Charley One Take" (per Dan Curtis) even after all these years. One important speech, a rallying lecture invoking the spirit of Theodore Roosevelt, eluded him time after time as the camera rolled. He would get so far, then feel it all come apart in his mouth, and he'd shake his head, cursing. It helped very little to have the film's financier, Golan, standing nearby in dismay. "Every time he says, 'Shit!' " Golan joked, "it costs me five thousand dollars."

The crowds that gathered on the Scranton streets and outside the houses and sets to watch the filming offered an object lesson in the difference between movie actors and movie legends. Keach, Dern, and the rest were glanced at by the Scranton citizenry with distant recognition or vague looks of interest. Mitchum, though, wandering into view, created an instant physical and verbal response, a chorus of whispers, bodies suddenly shifting forward, necks craning, at times the gawkers literally chanting his name while the old lion made his way, throwing them a smile or a wave or grumbling, "Oh, fuck," depending on the time of day.

Production concluded in California, at Zoetrope Studios in Los Angeles, where Robert's sixty-fifth birthday was celebrated with an on-set party and the appearance of a well-proportioned stripper with the birthday cake. Photos captured the fun, everyone crowded around, big gleeful grins, the stripper with her chest hovering before Mitchum, and on the face of the birthday boy a look of complete indifference.

*

The dynamism and contained intensity of Miller's play, a kind of macho group therapy session, did not survive its transfer to film. Broken up into an assortment of medium shots, it became just so much horseplay and shouting. As the coach, Mitchum looked wrong, too handsome, too stylish, badly in need of a pair of Archie Bunker trousers and an Eddie Coyle haircut, and he exuded a rakish, world-weary spirit equally inappropriate to the role of a fusty, Teddy Roosevelt–quoting old-timer who felt his life had been well spent yelling at high school boys. Under the proper circumstances Mitchum could easily have nailed the alien character—the evidence was there in Coyle, Preacher Powell, even Charles Shaughnessy—but neophyte director Miller didn't seem to know how to let him do it.

With that Tony and Pulitzer attached to Miller's work, Cannon dreamed that their *Championship Season* might be award worthy, too, and from the start of production treated the film to a major publicity campaign, bringing a number of reporters and photographers to the Scranton and Los Angeles sets, resulting in respectful coverage in many national publications, including a lengthy prerelease write-up in *Newsweek* magazine. Closer to the film's premiere, they also successfully fostered the "buzz" that Mitchum's performance was a strong candidate for the next Best Actor Oscar. In addition to their own efforts, Cannon happily piggybacked on ABC's massive efforts for Mitchum's other upcoming appearance in *The Winds of War,* now scheduled for a staggering eighteen hours of prime time in February 1983.

The film's world premiere and press party occurred on December 8. Mitchum had seemed docile and cooperative while on location in Pennsylvania and on the LA soundstage. The man who came to Manhattan for the *Championship* festivities was another fellow altogether.

Mitchum arrived from Montecito with Dorothy in tow. He was bored, drunk, belligerent, ill, coughing up a lung after every puff on his Pall Malls. He had been drinking for . . . no one could guess how long, how many days and nights. When the publicists reconnoitered with their star in his suite at the Waldorf Astoria and saw what condition and mood he was in, they rushed to cancel a battery of press interviews and hoped—prayed to God—that he would get a bit of rest and be in proper condition for the premiere and party that night.

No such luck.

Passing the clamoring photographers outside the movie theater, he sneered and admonished, "Am I a monkey? Are you going to throw peanuts at me? Isn't that what you do to monkeys, throw peanuts at them?"

The premiere party was at the Seventh Regiment Armory on Park Avenue, where the free seafood crepes and chocolate truffles had lured the likes of Pat Lawford, Gloria Steinem, Arlene Dahl, and Norman Mailer among a hundred or so others, with nearly as many select reporters and photogs allowed in to gape at their glamour and hearty appetites. Mitchum, clutching a scotch, wandered along the press gauntlet, tossing profane epithets, sticking his tongue out as the flashes lit. "Everybody is pushing me. Grabbing me," he complained. "Sticking their fingers in my face. Turn this way or this way. Everybody wants something." A girl of about fifteen years, in attendance with her parents, slipped up to ask for an autograph. "I loved your movie," she told him. "I thought you were wonderful." Mitchum grabbed the girl and twisted her arm up behind her back, then flung her back from where she had come. "I thought it was just a joke," she told an observing reporter. "He hurt me, but I didn't know what to say."

Flacks hovered nervously, smiling at the hooded eyes behind Mitchum's large, tinted glasses, telling him he was doing just fine, most cooperative. A publicist with an overdeveloped sense of sarcasm remarked that, after all, he'd been expecting Mitchum to do something really "wild," like break a chair over someone's head. "Is

that what you want? You want me to break chairs?" said Mitchum.
A female reporter from the *Chicago Tribune* was standing among
them, seeing all that had occurred and thinking of that psycho
preacher in—what was the damn movie with the fist tattoos of Hate
and Love?—and suddenly he grabbed her, his thick hand thrusting
inside the top of her blouse and taking hold of her breast. "I'll break
every fucking chair in the joint!" Mitchum hissed. The reporter
remembered turning color, shocked, but trying to "play it light,"
telling him, "Well, I've got the lead to my story." Mitchum's hand
slid from the breast and grabbed her arm and twisted it backward—
hard.

"You want a lead?" he said. "You want me to humiliate you? You
want me to destroy you right here? I can put you on the floor! I'll
break your arm!"

"You're hurting me," the woman cried. "What did I do?"

"You want ambulances here? Is that the story you want to write?
I'll give you that—gladly."

A group of celebrities wandered up. Mitchum greeted them, slipping his arm around the shoulder of the woman reporter, now near
tears.

"Gently . . ."

"Hell, I'm always gentle," Mitchum said.

Mitchum, Stacy Keach, Martin Sheen, and Jason Miller were herded
together for a group shot. The photographers moved in close, two
rows. There were no freelancers, none of the wilder breed of
paparazzi, just top assigned photographers from magazines and
newspapers, *Newsweek,* AP, the *Daily News.* One of these was
Yvonne Hemsey, a young woman on assignment for *TIME.* She had
met Mitchum and the rest months before, in Scranton. He had been
aloof but pleasant, cooperative. She had been in awe of him that day,
very polite, and he had done whatever she had asked. That night at
the Armory she heard from one of the flacks that Mitchum was acting a bit "edgy," but she went up to him with pleasant memories of
the Scranton visit and said hello. "You photographers," he told her,
"you're all royal pains in the ass," and walked away. Now she had

moved up in the group of men and one or two women positioning for the group pose. Someone came up with a basketball for the guys to hold, a prop, tie-in to the movie, The Coach and His Boys. Now Mitchum had the basketball in his hands.

"I was in the middle, wide-angle lens, four, five feet in front of him. Mitchum took the ball and threw it in my face. Straight at me. I'm not looking. I'm focusing to take a picture. Didn't expect it. I've got the camera, my glasses, right against my eye. I was stunned. The ball broke my glasses. The flash cut my skin. Everybody was shocked. I just remember shock. The photography all stopped. I don't remember if they moved him right away or what. Fellow photographers came around to make sure I was OK. And I remember the one that came over was Martin Sheen to see if I was all right. No one knew what to say, it was so off the wall.

"Then Menachem Golan came to me. He apologized, very upset. He said he would pay for the camera. He apologized profusely. He didn't even know what had happened. Then he took me over, he said it was a misunderstanding, let Mitchum apologize. Mitchum was back at his table, sitting with his wife. He was totally plastered. I remember seeing his eyes, and they were strange. And Golan brought me over and said, 'Bob, please apologize to the lady.' Mitchum refused. He looked up at me and said, "Fuck you. Go fuck yourself!" And Golan was more embarrassed than ever. And Mitchum's wife sat there, pretending nothing happened. She didn't even want to look me in the eye. At this point I really became furious. We moved away and I got my things to get out of there. Martin Sheen came up, he said, 'I'm so sorry he did this to you.' I was shocked, angry. I went and dropped the film at the lab, and I called my then boyfriend who was assignment editor at NBC. We called the media adviser at the police department. Then TIME magazine demanded an apology, and they never got it either. And that was it. I got an attorney."

Hemsey sued. Dozens of people were subpoenaed. Photographers, media people, the woman whose breast had been fondled and arm twisted. Corroborative photos were found, some from the event, some from other events before and after. "Pictures of him with drinks in his hand, totally out of it." Many months later, in her attorney's office in New York, Hemsey saw Robert Mitchum again, now with three lawyers surrounding him. "The person sitting there," said Hemsey, "it was almost like it was a different person. It was not the person who was at the party and threw the ball. He sat there quietly. He lied a lot, said someone had thrown the ball at him and he just threw it back, and so on, but he was very quiet, very polite."

Hemsey's lawyer told the press, "The time has come when Mitchum must learn that the public will not tolerate or condone unwarranted brute force, especially when directed at a woman by a man." Mitchum's attorneys made a settlement. Between that and the months of legal fees, the basketball toss had cost him his *Championship* salary and a portion of his *Winds of War* money, too.

The day after attending the New York premiere and party, Mitchum and his costars boarded a flight for Los Angeles, where they were scheduled to do it all over again for the West Coast. The first-class section of the TWA flight out of JFK was no-smoking, but Mitchum had lit up anyway. A businesswoman from New York, sitting one row ahead, suffered from various allergies and was not pleased with the gray clouds wafting her way. She turned around in her seat and explained that there was a smoking section in the rear of the plane. Mitchum jabbed out his cigarette. "I wonder which way's the no-farting section," he said. A little later, the allergic woman looked up to see Mitchum suddenly standing very close before her. Standing in the aisle he shifted around so that his back was to her, then bent way over, bracing himself on the back of a seat, and farted in her face. It was not just any fart, witnesses would recall in awe, but something long and deep and sonorous, like nothing they had ever heard before. It very nearly knocked the aircraft off course. Mitchum straightened up, turned, and made his way back to his seat.

The Winds of War was broadcast between February 6 and February 13. It was a television sensation. While some critics derided the clichéd melodrama and the middlebrow pretensions to Tolstoyan

grandeur, many heaped praise on the epic series, and the huge viewing audience was enthralled—by the grand scale, the sweeping narrative, the brilliant action scenes. Mitchum received for the most
part hostile reviews—they variously thought him miscast, too old,
too inert, too heavy, and too disinterested. There were remarkably
few sensitive to the rare and formidable presence and sense of grav-
ity he bestowed upon *Winds'* American hero. Noble, indomitable,
he moved through the story's eighteen hours of troubled waters like
a kind of human battleship. One solid supporter of Mitchum's work
turned out to be the author and scriptwriter. "Robert Mitchum rose
to the moment with brilliant professionalism and stunning authority," wrote Herman Wouk. "Authority was the key to Victor Henry
in my books, and authority, unchallengeable authority, was what
Robert Mitchum brought to the screen."

In the media blitz that surrounded the "landmark" broadcast, the
reviews were almost an afterthought. *The Winds of War* sparked the
most extensive, distinguished, and respectful publicity Mitchum
had ever received. In full navy whites, he took the cover of *TIME*
magazine, still a rare mark of distinction in those not yet pop-cul-
ture-saturated days. The cover of *TV Guide,* too. *People, Newsweek,*
and many more printed lengthy pieces covering the epic miniseries,
giving most of their copy over to the sixty-five-year-old star, one of
the last of the great Hollywood giants, they all agreed, descended
from the big screen pantheon to show the pygmies of television how
it was done.

In the midst of this nonstop idolatry came a bombshell. Of
course. Things had been too happy, too polite. The praise, the puff
pieces, all that talk about Robert Mitchum, the living national monument. It just wasn't . . . right.

In February, timed to coincide with the *Winds* broadcast, a six-
page profile was printed in *Esquire* magazine: "ROBERT MITCHUM
GIVES A RARE INTERVIEW" by a New York–based *TIME* reporter
named Barry Rehfeld. The interview had actually taken place the
previous August, while Mitchum was shooting the Cannon picture
in Los Angeles, and then on a second day up in Santa Barbara. At the
Montecito house, in the morning, Mitchum is relaxed and scatting,

some old jokes, some new ones: Duke's four-inch lifts, murdering Shelley Winters ("Best thing that ever happened to her"). For lunch they go to a local Mexican restaurant. The movie star orders some margaritas and food and takes in the scenery: a woman with a large rear end wiggles by. "Make a great hoop shot," Mitchum mutters. "Like in sodomy . . . Well, she has a rather commodious ass." Back to the house and he hits the tequila, continues riffing on his simple virtues. Works cheap, works quick, and doesn't have to commune with the white powder and a spoon like some of these guys today. He sounds off about the indignities of publicity. Why do it? Rehfeld asks him. The producers, the publicists force him into it, Mitchum says, suddenly getting a little . . . edgy. "Like Eichmann said, 'Ee's my job.'" He tells Rehfeld that he and some buddies wanted to go to Israel wearing big buttons: I like Eich. Then: "How do you say 'trust me' in Jewish? 'Fuck you.'"

Mitchum is warming up. More double shots of tequila. He talks about Vietnam, shares some of his "inside" skinny on the war, how it could have been over like that, how they could have bombed the dam at Haiphong, washed all of 'em out to sea. Rehfeld asks what about "moral principles"?

"You can design a moral principle for rape if you're so inclined."

"As Hitler did?" the interviewer asks.

"Hitler needed lebensraum."

"And the slaughter of six million Jews?"

"So the Jews say."

"So they say?"

"I don't know. People dispute that."

Mitchum changes subjects. Pres. Ronald Reagan's name comes up. Mitchum has known him for nearly forty years, he says, Ronnie the Eagle Scout. He's for him because he's an old pal but has no idea what he stands for. Never votes. It doesn't matter, he explains. He once met people in Europe, they told him how the future would go, and every word of it came true. The whole world—didn't Rehfeld understand?—was run by an international cartel of business. He tells him to investigate *that* story. "Why don't you try . . . if you want to *die* . . . You'll find out how powerful the cartel is."

He goes on: about international bankers, about the CIA, about Henry Ford and a "sneaky hebe" Hitler contributor named Ralph Beaver Strassburger. Dorothy enters the room and tells them to break it up. Mitchum keeps ranting. Dorothy tells him to *shut up.* A simmering Mitchum asks what exactly was Rehfeld planning to write about?

Dorothy gets the reporter out of the den while Mitchum, in the background, can be heard: "I guess I'm not the best interview in the world."

At least he hadn't lost his sense of humor.

A few moments in the living room with the calming Dorothy and then Rehfeld eagerly gets out of the house and into his car. He is about to start the engine when Mitchum suddenly appears framed in the window. He opens the door, looks down at the startled reporter, and hands him a Diet Sunkist orange soda and some napkins for the long ride home.

Though Mitchum's impolitic, bizarre, and contemptible comments would in fact have little effect on the generally idolatrous treatment he received for much of the rest of the year—salutes, tributes, a Robert Mitchum Day in Los Angeles hosted by the mayor—a small but persistent outcry followed him for months. The militant Jewish Defense League threw a press conference with Mitchum's photo—a portrait from *Esquire,* arms folded defiantly, in his finest Members' Only jacket—laid on top of a Nazi flag and a banner: "Is Pug Henry Really a Nazi?" The JDL's Irv Rubin, wearing a button that read "I Am a Zionist Hoodlum," accused Mitchum of being a Hitler sympathizer. He said they had hired a detective to find the actor's residence, and they would make a midnight demonstration. "If he doesn't apologize, we have to do everything in our power, legally of course, to get him to . . . but I can't be responsible for everything that happens in Mitchum's life."

Columnists requested a clarification of the actor's views. Mitchum resorted to a tried-and-true formula: denial and blaming the other guy. "I'm sorry there's such an unnecessary flap, but I guess there isn't a great deal I can do about it," said the actor. "I certainly did not plan to offend anyone, and I'm very sorry if I've upset or offended anyone." Mitchum claimed it was all a mistake, a put-on, a misinterpretation by the interviewer. Much of what was printed reflected Mitchum going into the character of the bigoted old coach he played in *That Championship Season,* he said. Rehfeld must have thought he was speaking for himself when he was actually quoting the intolerant character! Which sounded awfully like Mitchum's dismissal of the raucous Grover Lewis piece in *Rolling Stone* years before—*that* reporter, said the actor, had made it all up from one of George Higgins's novels.

Mitchum: "I occasionally say something outrageous so they'll say: he's not well, let's leave him alone." There were plenty of people familiar with Bob's penchant for harsh and shocking rhetoric when he was drinking, the references to "niggers" and "spics" and "hebe agents," the description of Kirk Douglas as a "bowlegged kike" and of David Selznick as "one of those wet-lipped, sybaritic Jews," and so on. It seemed a strange concept, a man voicing such coarse prejudices who did not himself believe them—or, as he would state for the record, who was constitutionally opposed to them but simply liked to talk a lot of bullshit, got a kick out of "pushing people's buttons," and so on. But that, old friends liked to say—and to hope, perhaps—was the case. "That guy," said columnist James Bacon, "would say or do anything to shock you. If he was bored, if he wanted to get a rise out of you—and he'd had a few? I don't think there was anything more to it."

Toni Cosentino, who knew him well beginning some years after the *Esquire* flap, said, "He was a strange guy, but he got a bad rap on one thing, that he's anti-Semitic. I have to tell you from my heart, that's not true. But he was a curmudgeon; he didn't like anybody at certain times. When he started drinking, he loved to be a contrarian. I don't give a shit what you're talking about. If tomorrow is Wednesday, when he's drunk Bob will argue that tomorrow is Thursday, for the fuck of it. People really didn't understand that about him. I must tell you, he really was not anti-Semitic. I've heard him say stuff and—if that stuff ever got out, Jesus Christ, it would be awful. He loved to look for trouble, he really did. I don't know what it was in him, but in his heart, no. I knew people that he really liked, and if they were Jewish, they were Jewish, it didn't matter to him. And he would say 'dago' this and that one's a 'mick,' but that's how people talked and I'm used to it. But you can't do that in this day and age of sensitivity. And I know names hurt. But what was awful was the questioning of the Holocaust. And he said to me, 'I didn't say it.' And we had conversations about that. Right after *Schindler's List* came out, and that movie devastated me. And I was talking to him about it, and he asked me my opinion about the sheer numbers of it. And I said, 'Bob, I don't know if the numbers are exaggerated, but it doesn't matter if there's an extra zero; if one person had to go through that, it's the same as six million.' And he said, 'You're absolutely right. I just don't like it when people define it with numbers because that really cheapens the whole thing.' And conspiracy theories? Oliver Stone asked him to do *JFK*. They came to him, will you do this part, that part. And I said, 'What do you think of that bullshit?' He said, 'I think it's bullshit.' He wasn't conspiratorially minded at all. I said, 'The only conspiracy was when you got busted for drugs, right?' And he laughed. 'Shit happens,' that was his philosophy."

"In thirty-odd years that I was with him," said Reva Frederick, "I never heard him express an interest or an opinion about politics or a politician. There were a couple of people that he knew personally, that he liked. But other than that he never said a word to indicate he was a Democrat, a Republican, a Socialist, or what have you. He told me more than once that he had never voted in his life; and on election days, when I would tell him I was going out to vote, he would just laugh and make fun of the whole thing."

"I knew him for a lot of years," said Reni Santoni. "And I never knew where that redneck, crackpot stuff came from. He was a cool guy, a doper, strictly live and let live. And then came this other stuff, out of nowhere. Vietnam—drown 'em all. The Watts riots—he said we had to put the whole lot of 'em in a camp, lock 'em up in there and that'll be it. Picking on Peter Falk, on *Anzio*, because he was a New York Jew. Dorothy asked him what they should give Trina for her birthday once and Bob says, 'Let's give her a Jew; she's got everything else.' And things like that, where you would go, 'Whoa, where did that come from?' Suddenly he would be in that mode. And I tried to think how he was out of a different era and how that's the way people related to people in his formative years, I guess. But I really couldn't tell you what motivated him. I look back now, after all the time I spent with him, and I have to admit that I could not get up in a room and say that I understood him or could say with a certainty that anything somebody might say about him was not possibly true—maybe with the single exception that if you said he was gay, I would be very surprised."

There was yet another bombshell to go off in what was supposed to have been Mitchum's time of triumph. In November 1981, Reva Frederick Youngstein suffered a stroke that required her to take a temporary leave of absence from the seventy-thousand-dollar-a-year job she had filled since 1948. She had been Robert's personal assistant, office manager, script reader, press liaison, studio liaison, confidante, dresser, baby-sitter, caterer, drink steward, and at some time or another provided any and all other services as needed, except for the one presumably supplied by his wife and a series of girlfriends. Four months later, in March 1982, her employment was terminated. Thirty-four years working for Robert, a virtual adjunct family member for much of that time, and she was out, without compensation. In Hollywood they read about the breakup in the trades and wondered what to make of it. Rumors and accusations that followed the firing pointed to an ugly rift. As the Mitchums told the story, Reva's absence led to Dorothy looking over the office records and business expenses and not liking what she found. But many close to them understood that Dorothy had long resented Reva's professional devotion to her boss. "I'm sure there was a tremendous amount of resentment," said Frederick. "Being so involved in a man's life and livelihood you're bound to find out things that not even his wife knows, and that becomes a very difficult thing for any wife to live with. No wife is going to accept that. They are always going to be *pissed off*. And I can understand that. I would know who would go where and do what with her husband,

and she would not know. You know part of her husband's private life that is not a part of their life together. That's where resentment really comes into play."

In March 1983, Reva's lawyers announced the filing of a $1.85 million lawsuit in Los Angeles Superior Court against her former employer, Robert Mitchum, and his wholly owned corporation, Talbot Productions. The suit charged that in addition to being wrongfully fired while recovering from "a severe and disabling stroke," Reva had been denied a promised $150,000 retirement benefit. No matter which way the facts fell, it was an unfortunate matter. Industry people, various strata of producers, publicists, and showbiz press, recalled how helpful and devoted Reva had been to Mitchum through the years, and how well she had covered for him or kept his feet out of the fire on numerous occasions. One Mitchum acquaintance remembered him once saying of her after she had left the room, and without further explanation, "That woman has kept me from going back to prison." (Another person remembered him saying almost exactly the same line about his wife; it may have been a job for more than one woman.) The Mitchums' friends, meanwhile, would hear the other side's version of events. "We saw Bob and Dorothy in Santa Barbara right after, and they felt they had been screwed," said Kathie Parrish. "I mean, bills for shoes, and Bob would say, 'I haven't bought a pair of shoes in twenty years. I take them from the pictures.' And first-night theater tickets. He said, 'I don't go to the theater. It makes my ass sore.'"

"I mean, what happened to Reva and Bob at the end . . . there was a mishmash and they got rid of her," said Anthony Caruso. "They were totally surprised at her actions. There was a big split-up, and she sued him. But she sure shouldn't have because they treated her like a daughter. Dorothy was very good to her."

The accusations increased in size with the passage of time. "Well, his version, though he would never talk in public," said an associate who knew Mitchum in his last years, "was that somehow they had gotten him to sign over the rights to his movies. He didn't own *Thunder Road* anymore. And all this money was gone. I said, 'If that happened, why didn't you call the cops? How come you didn't sue?'

Perhaps there were people who knew where all the bones were buried, and he just couldn't afford to make a fight."

"It was all dismissed by different lawyers," said Reva. "It all remained, I guess you'd call it, a void. Everybody just forgot everything, and everything was dismissed. And we never went further with anything. It was never a settlement or . . . anything. You go your way and I'll go my way is sort of how things came to a final decision. And that was the end of our association."

Mitchum appeared at the fifty-fifth annual Academy Awards presentation, paired off with Sigourney Weaver. There was the usual badinage, which Mitchum delivered with typical insouciance. The normally witty Weaver was reduced to the Margaret Dumont square's role on this occasion.

> Sigourney: I'm so honored tonight to be here with Mr.
> Mitchum and present the award for Best Supporting Actress.
> Mitchum: Is that what we're doing? (audience laughs) All right,
> we'll keep it shorter than *Winds of War*.

Winner Jessica Lange loped onstage for her prize, Mitchum offering a quite formal handshake.

Mitchum agreed to fill in for Burt Lancaster, after the actor underwent an emergency heart bypass operation, in a second Cannon Films production, *Maria's Lovers*, starring Nastassja Kinski, John Savage, and Keith Carradine. The film was set among a mostly Slavic community in rural Pennsylvania just after World War II, the story of a returning GI whose psychological problems render him impotent only with his new bride, Maria, who reluctantly finds romance elsewhere. Mitchum's role was that of the ex-soldier's lusty but dying immigrant father. *Maria's Lovers* was to be the first American-based work by the brilliant Russian filmmaker Andrei Konchalovsky. The son of well-known Russian poets (his father the composer of the Soviet national anthem), Konchalovsky had for many years written scripts for Andrei Tarkovsky before directing the acclaimed *Siberiade,* a prizewinner at the Cannes Film Festival. "I left Russia in 1979 and I was for three years unemployed, couldn't put anything together," Konchalovsky recalled. "When I came to Hollywood no one knew me, basically, except for Kinski. She was just coming up as star and she asked me if I would do something with her. I had this script, which I had planned to make in Europe with Adjani. Kinski was hot, so I got some clout, and finally Menahem Golan said, 'Set the story in America and we will do it.' But I thought it would not be right in truly American society, these characters, too emotional, so I put it in a Yugoslav enclave. We shot in Pennsylvania, Brownsville and other small town, near where Cimino shot *Deer Hunter.*

"Mitchum came aboard, Golan brought him in, and I found him wonderful person. Very intimidating at the beginning. You say, 'How are you, Mr. Mitchum?' He says, '*Worse!*' I think of him like Rachmaninoff, great Russian composer, very introverted in front of others, but when he accepts you as friend he is opening up. And I knew much about him, what was inside him, because I had had romance with Shirley MacLaine two years before and she told me about Mitchum quite a lot. She said he was very much a rebel, very left, his views were extreme left. She told me how he saw *himself.* That he was 'poet with an ax.' And this was beautiful metaphor of the person. I understood completely. It meant a very tender person who can be very cruel and relentless with his poetic substance. And at the second of our meetings, I decided to use this. I said, 'You are a poet with an ax.' And his eye had a flicker and he smiled. That was the beginning of good relationship.

"His humor was very dry, required close attention, especially for a foreigner. His humor was like a stone in the water, a few words, *boom, boom,* and everyone's supposed to laugh. It was a wonderful kind of American personality. He was like a wild animal. Reminded me of a lion. Always alone with himself, independent of everything. And to tame wild animal, director should be careful, and friendly. He can bite, he can claw you. And I pushed him further sometimes. I said, 'I want you to do more.' And once I wanted him to cry. He didn't want to, but he said, 'OK.' And we did a second take. 'But

Robert, you should cry here.' And he says, 'What the hell do you want? There's a tear in my eye!' It was very Irish cry, one tear, but he's supposed to be playing Yugoslav with a fountain of tears! But I couldn't make him do any more. It was beautiful, anyway.

"It was very common for Kerouac's generation, to feel the need to be an intellectual and at the same time a maverick, a tough guy. It is a pattern for a certain type of intellectual—drinking, fighting. Mitchum would start to drink during the second part of the day. And there were some times he had troubles. He went to the bar. I remember that he had a brawl there with some guys. Some confrontation. When he got drunk he could get—not mean, but sordid. Sordid. Once he fell and broke a rib. He said, 'I cannot shoot today; I broke a rib.' And he was in a lot of pain. I said, 'OK, we'll do it tomorrow. But please, no more of this!'

"He had, I think, a soft spot for Nastassja Kinski. She told me that he came once to her trailer, knocked the door and opened it, gave her little ivory elephant. Ivory elephant is an object of happiness. And she was so pleased. He gave it and walked away. I think romantically she excited him very much. But she was having a love affair with another actor, Vince Spano, and she had a baby from that. But I think that was reason why Mitchum never put the make on her.

"It was a very, very hot summer and it was very tough for him to work. He had terrible asthma or something in the lungs. But he never let it stop him. He was extremely professional and strong. The last day of shooting we had a drink after dinner. He looked at me and said, 'Andrei, I know I'll be seeing your name a lot. You're going to do well.' He said it like a blessing. It was nice to hear. I brought the movie to Santa Barbara. He watched, very proud, very happy. And he said after, 'You know, I *like* this film.' Said it very strange, like he was amazed. And he looked at me with a different attitude, with a new tenderness. It was our last meeting."

Another birthday. Sixty-six goddamn years old. Some days he hurt all over—back, chest, knees. He was going to call the stuntman's guild and ask for a pension. All those slips, dead falls, jumps, bashes in the eye from punch-drunk fighters. He had cataracts in his eyes.

The doctor saw tears in his lungs. The long, deep, unending smoker's cough was becoming as common as breathing these days. That was his greatest acting trick of the moment, doing the lines without coughing up his insides.

In October he received another tribute. Life Achievement Award of the American Theatre Arts. Who? He'd never heard of the fucking thing. But he put on his tuxedo and dropped by to check it out. The dinner cochairmen, Frank Sinatra and John Huston, couldn't make it. Frank sent a telegram, addressed to "Mother Mitchum": "It is a long overdue tribute. No one is more worthy." Huston spoke on a short piece of videotape: "The rest of us marvel at the extent of your contribution, its richness and its variety." Mitchum was given a framed letter from President Reagan: "Your career is outstanding. . . . Nancy and I were both glued to the TV set wondering what Pug Henry's next move would be." The president couldn't make it either. But Hal Linden and Paul Williams were there. Someone gave the honoree a computer portrait of himself in *Winds of War*. That was going to look good right next to his *Hoppy Serves a Writ* poster. The president of the Hollywood Chamber of Commerce got up and announced that one day in the near future Mitchum was going to have his name imprinted on the Hollywood Boulevard Walk of Fame. Mitchum said, "I thought it was already there."

He did one more for Golan-Globus at Cannon. This one they had set up to make back in the homeland, shooting in Tel Aviv and in the Occupied West Bank. It was a real lead this time, the title role: *The Ambassador*. Somehow or other the boys had managed to squeeze a tension-in-the–Middle East story out of an Elmore Leonard novel they owned, a novel that took place in Detroit. Mitchum's guy was an activist diplomat with a plan to bring the warring factions together even as he tries to handle a blackmail scheme involving in-flagrante footage of his wife and an Arab lover. Ellen Burstyn would play his straying wife, and Rock Hudson—just out of the hospital for a heart operation—took the supporting role of the ambassador's friend and problem solver. The film put

Mitchum back together with J. Lee Thompson, director of *Cape Fear*. Thompson had done a string of forgettable shoot-'em-ups in recent years, but this was a piece of material he liked, felt strongly about. A good, timely, important subject and a strong cast. The actors performed well. Mitchum made perfectly vivid and authentic-seeming the ambassador's peculiar combination of empathy and bullheadedness; and Burstyn was typically excellent, with some suprisingly sexy activities for the fifty-three-year-old actress, including a brief and perfectly creditable nude scene ("She liked doing it," Thompson recalled, "was all for it!"). There was a sense of excitement for some of the imported personnel, doing the story right where such things were actually happening. They were based in Tel Aviv, but there was much location shooting on the West Bank. At times there were whispered fears of terrorist attacks, and armed patrols were assigned to watch over them.

It was not a particularly happy production. "Rock Hudson was not in a good way," said Thompson. "It was a bad, small part, and it hadn't been cast before we began shooting. And then Menachem told me he was fetching Rock. It was a good move for the production; he was still quite a well-known name. But I felt terrible; it was such a nothing part. I tried to improve it a little. And he came and he obviously did it just for the money, and he couldn't wait to get away. I don't think that Mitchum cared for him, or he for Mitchum. And Rock was smoking away. Had just had quadruple bypass, and he just started up smoking again right in the hospital. He thought it was a good distraction. Poor Rock, he was not in a good way.

"And Bob, I'm afraid, his drinking by this time was a problem. It now started in the morning. There were amusing moments. He had a scene in bed with Ellen, supposedly at night, and they were both supposed to be sipping from drinks. And Ellen got his glass by mistake when she did the scene and found out that it had the real stuff in it. And she did not approve of drinking during the shooting, so it was quite a scene. She would get very angry at him, and he just looked like a small boy who was caught with his fingers in the jam. She was full of admiration for him as an actor, and she was a wonderful person, but she had a thing about drinking on the set. And this happened again, and she would smell it on his breath. . . . I had to cool her down on many occasions.

"He made a valiant attempt to stop during the shooting of *The Ambassador*. He would go days without even touching it. He was fighting it, and it was a fierce struggle for him. I had a sympathy. I could sympathize with what he was going through. Being an alcoholic myself, which I was, I could understand what was happening. It was quite painful to see. He made a valiant effort. I think he had come to a realization that it was finally getting the better of him."

Journalist Bart Mills talked to Mitchum and observed him at work on a number of productions in this period. "To me, beyond the inevitable depredations of age, he was now just sleepwalking through life. Going through the motions of living. Whether it was because he was a slave to alcohol or something deeper within him I can't say, but there was a huge impression of nihilism, of a near constant despair. He never voiced it except in the usual quotes, putting down the movie business, saying he was just in it for the money, hated working, all the usual stuff. But it ran deeper, I think. I just couldn't imagine living the way he did the last decade I saw him."

"Later on there, I think the work began to bore him," said Reni Santoni. "He knew he could do it and better than nearly anybody, and there was no challenge, no satisfaction perhaps. He made people intimidated, a lot of them who worked with him then. No one wanted to come up to the legend. He got it right on one take, and unless something had physically gone wrong, no one wanted to bother him to reshoot something. The directors didn't want to provoke him, I guess. And he liked it that way, but at the same time he felt like he was left out of something. He felt bad that no one wanted to try and direct him, and he'd see the interaction with other actors, and he'd say to me, 'I'd like to have some of that shit working for me, too.' And yet he was ambivalent. He knew he was cutting himself off and he did it anyway. He was doing this movie and the star, the actress, came up to him and asked him for some advice, a problem she was having about acting, about the process. And he said to me, 'You know, I knew how to help her. I had the answer, but

I didn't give it to her. I didn't feel like it.' And he felt bad about it. Strange story."

Santoni's long friendship with Mitchum began to fade at this time. "Getting loaded together had been certainly a factor in our relationship. I stopped drinking in '79. And once it was clear that we didn't get together to get loaded anymore, you know, there was an element missing. It was like the third member of a trio was missing. He never commented on it. I never felt that he was uncomfortable. When he came over he would bring his own bottle. It was '82–'83 we drifted apart. Looking back I can see that my stopping drinking was a factor."

"We'd had a lot of good times together," said another longtime Mitchum pal, Dobe Carey, "but what sort of spoiled our relationship was years ago when I quit drinking. And if you didn't drink you weren't going to stay too close to old Bob. I had had a great time for many years, but I felt I was going to lose my wife, my family, and I stopped for good. But if you told Bob you had stopped, well, he could never understand it. One time we were all in a car, it was that big Chili Cookoff out in the desert, sponsored by the guy that brought the London Bridge over. And we were riding out there, a bunch of us, and somebody said, 'How come you don't drink anymore, Dobe? You used to drink pretty good.' And Bob said, 'Because his dad was a big movie star. He had an inferiority complex.' And he had a whole psychological explanation for what made me drink and what made me stop. And it didn't have anything to do with that at all. In those days, it was all part of the everyday routine with most of us, a part of living. I missed it for a long time. But they used to say back in the old AA days, if your life became unmanageable because of alcohol . . . And I guess Bob never felt that his life was unmanageable. I know that Dorothy, when we would go up to my mother's place in Santa Barbara, she would come over and she would say, 'Oh, I wish Bob would stop drinking.' But maybe she was trying to make me feel better, I guess. I don't know."

There were days, even weeks, when he didn't touch a drop. He had stopped drinking a number of times, he would say to people.

Stopped just like that and no one noticed. So fuck 'em. They did notice the other times. "He would go drinking at a hotel near the house in Montecito," said a friend. "Do his happy hour thing. The bartenders would cringe, the waiters would cringe. He would just get ill-tempered, nasty. 'Where the fuck's my drink? What took you so fucking long!' This kind of thing." People remember the some-times vicious needling of family members, the need to get a rise out of somebody, relatives coming away in tears. There were embarrass-ing scenes in public—toppling over, passing out at dinner parties. Once, stepping before a gala audience and sliding to the floor unconscious. People gasped, thought he had dropped dead.

Reni Santoni: "Dorothy once said to me ... she knew I had stopped drinking for some time by then, ... she said, 'You know, we moved to Montecito for the spectacular sunsets. And now, with his drinking, we never notice them. . . .'"

Certain exigencies in American life in the '80s—namely, the neces-sity of dealing with a growing general population of drug users and addicts—had spawned a subculture of recovery and rehabilitation. Drunks and druggers who had once been left to a circumscribed destiny of premature physical decomposition and/or imprisonment were now offered a vast new hopeful menu of medical, spiritual, and philosophical methodologies for the treatment and cure of their problems—now more often sympathetically, less judgmentally, considered "diseases," just like German measles. This dependency-busting culture had found some of its first and most enthusiastic subscribers among wealthy and trend-conscious Californians.

Mitchum's increasingly unpredictable and destructive behavior finally so disturbed and frightened family members that, in May 1984, drastic measures were taken. He became the subject of an "intervention," a fashionable new method of making the addict con-front his wrongdoing face-to-face with his presumed loved ones. A sort of guerilla theater production, the participants surrounded Mitchum suddenly, forcing him to listen as one person after anoth-er read prepared statements regarding their anger, unhappiness, pain, fear. They opened old wounds and new. "They really sandbagged him," said a friend. "He said he felt just pathetic . . . devastated by the whole thing. And then they took him to Betty Ford. It was just terribly humiliating."

The Betty Ford Center in Rancho Mirage, in the desert near Palm Springs, had opened in October 1982 as a private clinic for the treatment of alcoholism and other drug dependencies. From the fact of its namesake and chief publicist—the wife of former president Gerald Ford, who had herself recovered from various addictions—and from the steady, much-publicized arrival of a series of celebrity patients in various states of duress, including Elizabeth Taylor and Peter Lawford, the center had come to be known as the "rehab of the stars," a glamorous spa for the famous and fucked up, and gossip columns wrote of its glittery clientele as they once had of the Mocambo and the Brown Derby.

It wasn't so glamorous, really. Patients were given a small room and required to make their beds in the morning and be up and out for breakfast at six, before the long day of counseling and therapy. "No hardship," Mitchum said, as they ran through the rules. "I made my bed all through the army." At Castaic, too, come to think of it.

It wasn't so easy, really. "He was not happy to be there," said Jean (not her real name), a therapeutic nurse at the center. "And he made it quite clear. One time we were getting him into the swimming pool with the other patients and he didn't want to go. So he peed into the pool in front of everyone."

"He said it was awful," an associate remembered. "He had a very hard time in the detox area, just cleaning it out of his system. . . . He hated it."

To the inquiring press Mitchum would reveal only indifference. "I stayed there until they were through with me," he said. "I don't know if it 'worked.' I don't understand that." Perhaps it had helped to "modify" his behavior a little. "I don't fall down so much." Anyway, he said, it was his wife's idea the whole thing; he'd done it for her.

A friend came to meet him on the day he was released from the center. They headed home by way of Los Angeles. Mitchum asked to stop at the Beverly Hilton Hotel. He went to the bar, put a ten-dollar bill down, and ordered a double scotch. The bartender poured it out. Mitchum threw it back, slid the ten over, said, "Fuck 'em all," and went back to the car, and they drove to Montecito.

He continued working. Now, well past retirement age, there was not so much talk about retiring. It was a different tune these days. What am I gonna do, he would say to associates, "stay home and roll my socks?" He did guest shots in theatrical features and leads in made-for-TV movies. Some great work, too: he was chilling, fascinating in *Killer in the Family*, playing Gary Tyson, a real-life kind of Pa Barker (or perhaps a Papa Max Cady) leading his brood on a crime spree through the Southwest. Rare for a network production, the ABC movie was uncompromisingly brutal, the scenes of violence like hammer blows to the head. It was the last entry in the actor's remarkable rogues' gallery. There was a final teaming of Mitchum with Deborah Kerr for an HBO cable movie filmed in Britain, *Reunion at Fairborough*, bittersweet tale of an old American ex-bomber pilot returning to his wartime haunt in England, finding a lost love and an unexpected granddaughter. The two had remained, in that showbusiness extended family way, warm but not close friends through the years. Deborah occasionally penned a note to him, always addressing it, "Dear Mr. Allison. . . ." In the cable movie, Kerr and Mitchum still had a certain ineffable rapport, but the evidence of time's levy since *Allison* was saddening.

A movie for CBS broadcast, *Promises to Keep*, also dealt with an old man stirring up the past. This time it was a possibly terminally ill ranch foreman who travels to California to look up the family he'd run out on three decades ago. Ex-wife and adult son are bitter but—as in the HBO movie—the old man sparks up a relationship with a young grandchild. It was the sort of touchy-feely, troubled-family drama television had come to specialize in. There was a casting gimmick: father, son, and grandson would be played by real-life equivalents in Robert, Chris, and a new addition to the performing dynasty, Chris's eighteen-year-old son, now called Bentley, a broad-faced blond with earrings and a Farrah Fawcett hairdo. To make the movie even more personal, they were going to shoot the thing in Bob's backyard, in and around the town of Santa Barbara.

It had been Chris's project. For two years he had been "developing" the script, and it had gone through a purported two dozen revisions. In the end, though, it was not the rather superficial teleplay but the "Mitchum clan" gimmick that sold the project to CBS. Perhaps, the network thought, audiences would be titillated by the intimations of a blending of fiction and real life in the story of distant, frustrated father-son relations. And perhaps they would be onto something. For a sequence showing the characters looking through a family album with snapshots of the fictional father and son in earlier, happier days, Chris claimed the only appropriate photos they could find of real-life father and son had been staged, taken by press and publicity photographers back in the '40s and '50s. "I thought, God, did we only get affection because there was a camera crew there?"

The press coverage told a story more poignant than the one being filmed. In putting the movie together, Chris admitted to the *New York Times*, he had hoped to make his father proud of him. "Whether he is or not, God knows; he'll never tell me. Until we did this picture together I never had any evidence he knew what I did for a living. We never discussed the fact that I was an actor. My father has never expressed an opinion one way or another about my doing anything. . . . My father didn't say to me nine times a day, like I do to my kids, 'I love you.' "

Reporters pressed for the warm and fuzzy angle, generations bouncing on each other's knee, sharing tales of the good times together, but it wasn't easy. The senior Mitchum did not do warm and fuzzy. He preferred hanging out with the crew, flirting with passing females (to a well-endowed production assistant in a souvenir Grand Canyon T-shirt he cracked, "Shouldn't that say Grand *Teton?*"). When pressed to comment on the enterprise they were presently shooting, Mitchum said, "I figured it provided my son with employment and his son with employment. It's cheaper than paying their room and board. . . . I don't have to watch it; that doesn't come with the contract."

If they wanted enthusiasm, they were going to have to hire somebody else's dad.

"He just won't open up," Chris said. "But I know my father loves me."

Two weeks after an article on "Three Generations of Mitchums" appeared in *People* magazine, Christopher fired off a letter to the editor decrying the "inaccurate and out-of-context quotes," creating "the image of a family of isolated individuals living in awe and fear of a patriarch. . . . [O]ur family remains as close as a family can be. My father's 46-year marriage should tell you something of the truth." Was it counterpropaganda or self-delusion? The fact was that separate stories and quotes quite similar in nature to the *People* piece appeared within days of each other in the *New York Times,* the *Los Angeles Times,* and elsewhere.

Promises to Keep received withering reviews. Critics called it "mawkish," "predictable," "trite," and "dull."

*

The performing Mitchums kept coming. Chris's beautiful twenty-year-old daughter, Carrie, was now acting. Robert went to see her perform in a play at the University of California at Santa Barbara. In the course of the drama Carrie removed her top. "Nice to see you with your clothes on," Mitchum told her backstage. She would hear that he had complimented her performance to other people. "But he told me nothing," she said. Soon she would find a degree of success acting on a daytime TV soap opera called *The Bold and the Beautiful.*

In April 1986, Mitchum was the honored guest at the Cognac Film Fest du Policier—a recently established festival devoted to the thriller, the gangster picture, le film noir. Mitchum had long been popular among cinephiles in France, a favorite of the intellectuals—Mitchum, *un vrai existentialiste*. The crowds were ecstatic. As the applause simmered down Mitchum told them, "You'd think I found a cure for cancer." The translator missed something, and the papers said: "Robert Mitchum has found a cure for cancer."

Five years after their triumphant broadcast of *The Winds of War*, ABC announced the start of production on a sequel. *War and Remembrance*, from Herman Wouk's own finale to the saga of Pug Henry and company, would be an even costlier, longer, and more ambitious miniseries—the narrative covering all of World War II from just after Pearl Harbor to the Axis defeat. Dan Curtis returned to the helm and began gathering his cast. Victoria Tennant, Polly Bergen, David Dukes, and many others reprised their roles from the earlier miniseries. Ali MacGraw, who had been in her early forties and playing twenty-nine at the time of *Winds*, was replaced as Natalie Jastrow Henry by Jane Seymour. John Gielgud took the role of Aaron Jastrow from a dying John Houseman. Hart Bochner replaced Jan-Michael Vincent as Byron Henry. As for Victor "Pug" Henry . . . critics had attacked the sixty-five-year-old Robert Mitchum with an ageist glee back in 1983. And now the actor was a septuagenarian. What would those critics have to say about a seventy-year-old—who, Curtis couldn't deny, was starting to look every day of it—a seventy-year-old winning World War II and in his spare time romancing the lovely young Ms. Tennant? Other names were considered: James Coburn, George C. Scott. In the end, Curtis just couldn't see the point—whatever they would gain in fewer wrinkles, in greater physical energy, they would be losing in stature, in audience identification, in mighty presence. It was like they used to say in those corny old movie trailers: Robert Mitchum *is* Pug Henry.

Mitchum met with Herman Wouk for a kind of refresher course in their shared creation. The key to it all, Wouk told the actor, was the man's sense of loyalty, of patriotism, keeping sight of the greater good (never mind about the adulterous affair with Pamela Tudsbury; even Eisenhower had a bit on the side). For Mitchum, the filming, especially by comparison with the awful memories of Yugoslavia on the other one, was relatively stress free. They shot in Hawaii; in Bremerton, Washington; in D.C.; Mobile, Alabama; and Pensacola, Florida. In consideration of Mitchum's age and health, his scenes were carefully scheduled, giving him a hiatus before each major location change. Kind of fun, Mitchum thought. Plenty of variety, new faces every day. You stand around in front of the camera, and one day they march in FDR and the next day you're working with Harry Truman or Eisenhower.

Dan Curtis's labors were considerably more taxing. Mitchum came to have enormous respect and great affection for the unwavering, fanatical filmmaker. He drove everyone crazy, but he did his homework, slaving like a determined schoolboy, and he knew what he wanted and he got it, whatever it took. The man really could have won World War II, Mitchum thought. Complete tunnel vision. They were in Hawaii, Curtis in a motorboat shouting orders; the boat sprang a leak, started to sink under him, and the director was still waving and screaming for his damned long shot. They were on the destroyer up in Bremerton harbor, tearing out of the harbor at eighteen knots, and Curtis shouts, "Hold it! Hold it. Do it again. . . . Back it up." Mitchum was standing near the ship's captain. The look on the man's face was worth his one-million-dollar salary. "It takes three miles to stop a destroyer, and Dan thinks it's like driving a Porsche. The captain said, 'I am going to be in my quarters, padlocked within. . . .'"

Mitchum returned to Santa Barbara in July with a month off before finishing up, three more weeks in D.C., Florida, and Alabama. While at home he got a call from John Huston. Mitchum's old pal, eighty-one years old now, suffered from emphysema, carried a tank of oxygen with him everywhere these days. Wheezing away into the phone, Johnny said he was about to start an acting job in Newport, Rhode Island, a picture his kid Danny was directing, *Mr. North.*

"I'm not in the best of shape, kid," Huston said. "Might need a favor. Don't want to let the boy down. Small part. Think you could take over for me, kid, if it comes to that?"

Mitchum knew he had to be in Washington on August 13, but he didn't hesitate. "Pencil me in, John. But we both know you'll do the damn thing yourself."

On July 28, hours before he was to start his acting job (he'd also cowritten the script), Huston had a severe attack of the lung disease and was rushed to Charlton Memorial Hospital in Fall River, -

Massachusetts. The doctors diagnosed pneumonia. Mitchum got word that he would have to do the favor after all. He arrived in Newport days later and went to the hospital to see Huston.

The old buccaneer looked like hell. He was tied up to a dozen tubes, his flesh purple where it had any color at all. Huston's eyes widened, and he greeted Mitchum with a weakened version of that signature crooked, rascally grin.

"Well, you suckered me," said Mitchum. "I can see by the look of you ya never had any intention of doing this picture."

"I hoaxed you, kid, you're right."

Huston had always told people that Mitchum was one of the few Hollywood stars he was really fond of, while Robert's enchantment with Huston—not to mention his imitations of him—had been a constant since the days and nights on Tobago. It figured they got along. They were much alike, with their lifelong disdain for the presumptuous and the pretentious, their contempt for Hollywood bullshit (as long as it wasn't their own), their shared fondness for losers and faraway places and women and liquor and for a good story about any of the same.

They could only make small talk now. Mitchum said the nurse was worried that Huston wasn't eating enough. There was some rude back-and-forth about the nurse and what she could try eating. Then the medical people returned, taking tests, reattaching Huston to his respirator. Out in the halls there were people hovering. One of John's girlfriends was crying. Mitchum said he didn't look so bad. "I'm telling you, they'll have to drive a stake through his heart."

He shot the small role of a crusty old millionaire under the direction of Danny Huston. It was supposed to be a sunny comedy, but it was shot on a death watch.

Huston died on August 28. By then Mitchum had left Rhode Island and returned to finish *War and Remembrance.*

It was bigger by far than *Winds*—longer, more expensive, more expansive, shot in a dozen countries, and involving a total of more than forty thousand paid extras. Dan Curtis's final cut ran a whopping thirty hours with commercials. ABC chose to further divide the

Winds sequel into two sections, the first broadcast throughout November 1988 and the concluding hours the following May. For all of its repeated descents into soap opera dramatics and Saturday cliff-hanger suspense, *War and Remembrance* was in many ways an astonishing achievement. TV had for so long been accepted as a medium for the intimate, the anecdotal, the superficial. Curtis, Wouk, and company had reinvented the wheel with the epic size and seriousness of purpose of their prime-time endeavor. Curtis's terrifying, apocalyptic staging of the Nazi death camp exterminations—the most explicit and detailed recreation of the Holocaust ever attempted—arguably placed *War and Remembrance* among the most powerful works in the history of American television. Once again, though, critics attacked Mitchum's participation with a cruel relish—they said he was calcified, near moribund. They said, "His acting days are over."

Mitchum filled in for another ailing actor in the fall of 1987, this time a guy he didn't know, Edward Woodward, the star of a CBS series called *The Equalizer.* While Woodward recovered from a heart attack, a two-part episode was put together featuring Mitchum as a mysterious superspy. It was a terrific appearance, Mitchum glamorous, tough, cool as hell. In another few years he would become involved with his own weekly series and it was a mess—a smart action show like this was the sort of thing he ought to have done.

Mitchum's daughter, Trina, had a friend in Los Angeles who worked on filmed bits for *Saturday Night Live,* the long-running comedy program that played on NBC. An invitation was procured for Dad to guest host an upcoming installment. With some reluctance he agreed. In California, Trina and her filmmaker friend put together a piece for the occasion, Robert reunited with Jane Greer in a film noir spoof shot in black-and-white. In the second week of November 1987, Mitchum flew to New York, accompanied by Toni Cosentino of Charter Management, for the required six days of bull sessions, publicity, and rehearsals with the regular cast before the live telecast on the night of November 14.

"Most of them were in awe of him," said Cosentino. "Phil Hartman was just the sweetest, and the whole staff were very good to him. And he was pleasant and everything went great."

The writers came up with a monologue and a series of sketches that played off Mitchum's public and cinematic personae—as the sardonic don't-give-a-shit hack movie actor not afraid to "jeopardize that 104th movie role" and as the golden-age icon in the *Out of the Past* filmed short and a *Farewell, My Lovely*-esque skit playing with the cliché of first-person, voice-over narration. Mitchum objected to nothing they threw at him, knew exactly where the laughs were supposed to be, and had his lines down in a way none of the cue-card-reading regulars could match. He rehearsed another sketch that was cut before airtime, the setting an old folks home for stuntmen and Mitchum a doddering Hollywood roughneck who'd fallen off one chuck wagon too many. "They had him on a walker, all kooky in the head," Cosentino recalled. "It was one of those *Saturday Night Live* sketches that was going to just lay there without a laugh. And I said, 'You know, we're doing this for you to look cool, why do this shit? Who the hell wants to see you in a walker?' And they cut it out, which was the only thing I insisted on."

Toward the end of the rehearsal period, Mitchum asked Phil Hartman, "So when do we start getting these things on tape?"

"You're kidding, right?" said Hartman. "It's done live. You know . . . Saturday Night . . . *Live?*"

Mitchum said, "Oh . . ."

On Saturday, a concerted effort was made to keep the host sober. "It was sort of like that movie *My Favorite Year*," said Cosentino. "We just had to keep liquor away from him and it went fine. It went great. Of course, when Dorothy got there at the end of the week we had to put a stop to having fun. And then they had the wrap party afterwards. And there were people came to be in the audience just to see Bob—Victoria Tennant from *Winds of War* was there and others. And everyone wanted him to be at the wrap party, but Mrs. Mitchum took him back to the hotel. She didn't want him to drink. She would be embarrassed when he would get so bombed. God forbid he would pop back a few with the *Saturday Night* crew."

Producer-writer Andrew Fenady put together a project to be shown on the USA cable network, *Jake Spanner, Private Eye,* based on a novel called *The Old Dick* by L. A. Morse, a breezy, hard-boiled mystery about "the world's oldest detective." George Burns lobbied for the part. "He was ninety-something years old, for chrissake," said Fenady. Fenady knew there was one perfect "old dick" and it was Robert Mitchum. Through John Mitchum, Fenady got the script to Robert. Fenady: "We talked on the phone. He said, 'Yeah, yeah, yeah, OK.' I said, 'Should I see what your agent has to say?' He said, 'Agents? Hell, those guys are just mail drops.' I said, 'I got to make the deal with somebody.' So he gave me the name of a guy named Mike Greenfield. Old Greeny. I knew him. So we talked. He said he thought it would be fine. He told me I ought to go over and meet him first. And he said, 'Look, the most important thing with Mitchum is he needs to have the right cameraman if you want him to do it.' I said, 'Who the hell is he, Greta Garbo?' And the agent explained this and that Mitchum needed. So I said, 'Well, if that's what it takes to get Mitchum, I'll do it.' I knew a damn good cameraman named Hector Figueroa and I asked him a favor, get me a compilation tape of his very best stuff he'd done. I got the damn thing, I found out where Mitchum was, and we met. And I said, 'I brought a tape. I understand you have certain requirements.' 'Well,' he said, 'I'd like to be paid.' I said, 'I understand you like to have approval of the cameraman. Have you got a tape machine I can play this—' He said, 'A tape machine? What the hell are you talking about? I'm not looking at any damn tapes!' I said, 'But Greenfield said—' "Greenfield must be full of shit. . . . If you like the cameraman, that's fine with me. Tell me when to show up and I'll do what I can. Oh, and can you find a good part for brother John in there somewhere?' Anyway, it worked out great."

While many of the people Mitchum worked with these days knew as much about his long career in the movies as he did about basketball—there were producers and directors on the scene startlingly ignorant of cinema history or anything else older than six months ago—Fenady was a film buff as well as a veteran and could recite Mitchum's hundred-plus credits backward. The first time he'd seen the actor in the flesh was nearly forty years ago, on the old forty-acres lot, Mitchum walking with Susan Hayward, shooting *The Lusty Men.* "The son of a bitch was all chest, his chest was two minutes ahead of him, and he was a good-looking bastard, loaded with sex appeal. Oh Christ, he looked like a movie star." Fenady made *Jake Spanner* a nostalgic wallow for Mitchum fans, securing footage from *Out of the Past* for a daydream sequence, filling the film with cameos by RKO vintage actresses and faded starlets like Terry Moore, Sheree North, and Stella Stevens, renting an old RKO soundstage, and generally referencing Mitchum's and the movies' days gone by. During casting, Robert suggested they consider giving another part to one of the family. Like he said, it beat paying their room and board. Fenady took the hint and picked a role that seemed good for Chris, but he was unavailable and Jim Mitchum was offered the part.

The director, Lee Katzin, recalled, "Everyone enjoyed working with Bob. He was terrifically professional and very funny. And very dirty, in the nicest sense of the word. He kept the crew in hysterics. There were many scenes where there would be voice-overs as in the old detective movies, Bob describing his thoughts or narrating the action on screen. And when we would do these, Bob would just improvise dialogue to cover, whatever came into his head. And he would do these monologues about his 'tallywhacker' and the size of his tallywhacker, where he was supposed to be doing this serious action under the voice-over—just for the amusement of the crew, and they were falling over. He was very funny."

"Bob was just fantastic," said Fenady. "Such a pro. And at the end we had a chase scene and he broke his goddamn ankle. And I said, 'That's it. Shit, we're in trouble. We'll have to shut down for a week before we can finish.' I went up to him, and he was turning blue from agony. I said, 'Bob, shall I close down the company?' He said, 'I'll let you know.' He started for home. He was quivering with pain. He stopped and said, 'I'll see you tomorrow.' I didn't see how. But he showed up. Still in great pain. He literally could not stand. But he was there. And we rewrote the scene so he could sit for most of it, but if he'd had to stand he would have stood. That was the kind of a man Robert Mitchum was. It was the last day of shooting, and we got it done.

"He was a marvelous man. And such an underestimated actor. They always talk about all the bad pictures he did. But I'll tell you something. Add 'em up. Nobody made as many *good* pictures as Mitchum did. He should have gotten all the awards many times over. Christ . . ."

Nineteen-ninety. He would be seventy-three in August. It was getting lonely out there. There were damn few men or women left alive who had been movie stars in 1944, let alone still busting their hump at it the way he was. And now, almost a half century in the business, he was all signed up to try something new. A TV series. A situation comedy. NBC had . . . what was the word . . . "green-lighted" the . . . what the fuck did they call that thing they had shot? Now he was —the *pilot,* that was the fucking—now he was gonna be the star of a situation comedy on network television. On NBC, Saturdays at 8 P.M. Seventy-two years old and he was going to be making like Bill Cosby, with the jokes and the double takes. The offer had come, a guy named Arnold Margolin had created the thing. It was a role tailor-made for him, they said: a cranky, homeless bum with a heart of gold. A family of orphans adopts him out of a packing crate in the city park, asks him to pose as their grandpa so they can all go on living together. Takes the job serious: pours their milk, looks at their report cards, even—this was a good one—uncovers the kid's stash and yells at him for smoking marijuana. It was all very sweet, good for the whole family, and timely too—bums were in the news all over the place these days, just like in 1933. If it was a hit, they said, and ran four, five years, he'd make more money than God.

In mid-1989, a pilot had been produced for NBC in a two-hour, TV-movie format. Screened for test audiences, that TV-movie turned out to have one of the highest test scores in NBC's history. As one associate of the show put it, "They could not *not* OK a series." In late November, NBC gave the go-ahead for *A Family for Joe* as a standard, taped-before-a-studio-audience, thirty-minute program, with its prime-time run scheduled to begin on March 24.

Mitchum's first day of work had been delayed. Ann Harriet Gunderson Mitchum Clancy Morris had died on February 2 at the age of ninety-six. She had been a strong presence in his life until the end, through all the years a valued sounding board and confidante, with her sharp mind and no-nonsense discernment. He would never get used to her being gone.

Arnold Margolin and associates recast most of the kid roles and hired a staff, including top-ranked sitcom director Alan Rafkin and a flock of writers. Among the latter were two young men, writing partners Phil Rosenthal and Oliver Goldstick, who had lately come from the New York theater to look for work in Hollywood. "It was our first real paying job in show business, and we grabbed it," said Rosenthal. "But to be honest, we had the same reaction everyone else did: *Robert Mitchum in a sitcom?* We thought the whole idea was dubious. Mitchum wasn't particularly known for his comedic skills."

"We were thinking of this guy from *Out of the Past*, and it just didn't add up," said Goldstick. "But we saw the pilot and now we thought, OK, they're going for a W. C. Fields kind of thing, where he's gruff and he hates kids, hates animals. The idea of this marginal Charles Bukowski alcoholic figure becoming stuck in a suburban household surrounded by kids and busybody schoolteachers . . . yeah, it started to sound like it might be funny after all."

During the days when the writing and production staff were coming together, Phil Rosenthal caught a broadcast of *The Night of the Hunter* and taped it, brought it in to show to the other staff writers and anyone else he thought might want to marvel at the guy they were going to be working with. Some of them, including one of the writers, laughed derisively at the film, at Mitchum's performance as Preacher Powell. "God, this is corny," somebody said.

Welcome to prime time.

"Mitchum came in for the first meeting," said Rosenthal, "and he was always very deadpan, completely straight-faced. You never knew when he was putting you on. That first day he brought a big book with him. He said, 'This is a book I treasure. It's about my favorite entertainer of all time. A man I truly admire.' It was the life story of Petomane. The—whatever it was, seventeenth, eighteenth-century French entertainer who farted on stage. The world-famous farter. He said, 'This man was a great artist. . . .'"

"Knew everything there was to know about Petomane," Oliver Goldstick confirmed. "Some people thought it was tongue-in-cheek. I swear to God I think it was legitimate. He loved that guy. He said, 'Farting . . . now that's the way to make a buck.'"

The show went into production, but from day one there was a sense of frustration, even hopelessness. "If they had used him as a natural curmudgeon as it was originally intended," said Phil Rosenthal, "that would have worked. But right away they—somebody, the network, some of the producers—began demanding a softened-up image, make him more likable, to the point where in the first shot on the first show he was wearing an apron and putting flowers on the table! So right away, they took his balls from him, and what was left?"

Goldstick: "We went to one of the producers, Bill D'Angelo, and complained. 'You're robbing him of his grit. This is a guy's been living on the street. He's arranging tulips in a vase. This guy would be eating the tulips!' But this was the time of these new family sitcoms, appealing to much younger audiences, and I think they decided that was going to be their audience. And whatever idiosyncracies were present in the pilot were already being jettisoned for this sort of avuncular, Mr. Belvedere kind of character. And Robert Mitchum was certainly the anti-Belvedere if there ever was one."

"The show was terrible," said director Alan Rafkin. "It got sappier and sappier, and Mitchum pretty much knew it; but he came to work like it was for an Academy Award winner, never complained or disparaged, and he took direction better than anyone I ever worked with and I've worked with about four million actors by now. He knew every line, and between takes he was a raconteur second to none."

Rosenthal: "He was always just 'Point me where you want me to go. I do my job; I go home.' There was only one time—and I thought this was interesting—where he questioned something that we wrote. There was some dialogue and it included a play on the speech from *Casablanca*. He runs into a woman he had an affair with long ago. And she's the kids' kindergarten teacher. And he has this speech after the one in *Casablanca*, something about 'of all the kindergartens in the world she had to walk into mine.' Well, he questioned it. It sounded odd to him. We told him it was a spoof on *Casablanca*. He said, 'What do you mean?' We said, 'of all the gin joints . . . Bogie in *Casablanca*.' He'd never seen it, never heard the line before. So we explained it, and then it was fine and he went and did it."

Goldstick: "The only person who didn't get along with Mitchum on that show was Juliette Lewis. There were some fireworks. He didn't like her, and I don't think she really cared for him. Why? I don't know. Within two weeks they both had their own wranglers, someone to watch each of them." Lewis hadn't wanted to do the show, according to Toni Cosentino. "And so she kind of made everybody suffer. But then she got into it. And Bob ended up liking her. And he saw her in a movie while they were working. And he saw that she could really act."

There was some concern that Mitchum would have trouble performing in front of the large studio audience that came to the tapings—he hadn't done a sustained piece of live theater in over four decades. Mitchum shrugged: "I've been working in front of a hundred crew guys for years, and they're the toughest audience there is." It was not a problem. Said Alan Rafkin, "He was introduced at the beginning, and they would applaud and scream and stomp their feet. He was very pleased by the reaction. Said they really seemed to like seeing him. And then he would go ahead and not even notice them." The problem with the audience was of a different sort. The network and the producers, busily trying to position the series as a kids' show, were distraught at the demographics of their live audiences. "The audience was practically all female," said Oliver Goldstick, "and most of them were old, from seventy-five to death.

They flipped for him. He was still the sexiest thing on earth to them, and I don't think they paid any attention to the kids in the show!"

Nine episodes of *A Family for Joe* were produced, after which NBC canceled the series. "He had known it wasn't going to last," said Alan Rafkin, "but never got angry or bitter or anything. There was a wrap party. He didn't stay very long. His manager said, 'I don't want him to hang around. You don't want to see that.' Meaning that if he had more than a couple of drinks . . . she didn't want us to see him other than the way we knew and loved him. He had never been anything but straight and sober on the set. So he had a drink or two, he was fine, and then she hustled him out of there. I was sad to see him go. I loved him to death, you know, and I had hoped we could have done this thing for a couple of years. Grown old together . . ."

*

On March 16, 1990, Bob and Dorothy celebrated their fiftieth wedding anniversary at L'Ermitage in Beverly Hills. "In its own way it was a very good marriage," said their Santa Barbara friend Beverley Jackson. "When all was said and done, he adored Dorothy. He would never have thought of leaving her, and he never did. She was his security blanket and his first love and his last love. And the same for her. And he may have had his affairs, but by heck it was his Dottie and he always came back. And she was a devoted wife and wonderful mother. But there were times when she was crushed, very hurt. And if Dorothy had had an affair he would have died. They were very puritanical people in their own way. Other women, European women, would have just accepted that their husbands had lovers. Deep down, Bob was very devoted to her. But it was part of his macho image. Listen, some people just have a bigger sex drive."

"I traveled with them a lot," a close associate reflected, "and it seemed like it was now more fond affection, brother-sister kind of thing. But then she would get horribly jealous, so there must have still been some sparks there. Dorothy thought everybody was screwing Bob. But most of Bob's screwing was mental, not physical. He was more into mental games with women than physical. Let's just say the last fifteen years of Bob's life he was impotent. He wanted that game, but he couldn't do anything about it. Dorothy thought this guy probably had a hard-on that reached from Santa Barbara to Los Angeles, and there was no way that was possible, as far as fucking women. That was long gone. He liked the chase—can I get a young girl to like me? But not follow through. Bob was the king of male chauvinist pigs and putting hands on people. And he was not above putting his hand on a tit or something. But for him, that was nothing."

They had remade *Out of the Past* a few years ago. *Against All Odds* they called it, with Jeff Bridges and Rachel Ward substituting for Mitchum and Greer. It was very pretty, nice Mexican scenery—sort of *Gidget Goes to Cozumel*. Jacques, Robert, and Jane had nothing to worry about. Now they were remaking *Cape Fear*. Robert DeNiro was playing Max Cady. Martin Scorsese was directing. They wanted Mitchum and Gregory Peck to do cameos. An *hommage*. Mitchum said no. Greg called him up, said, "C'mon, Bob, let's go do it for the guys." Part of the joke was, they switched personas. Mitchum was an upright deputy sheriff this time, Peck was Cady's sleazy lawyer. DeNiro was covered in tattoos, like somebody in a circus sideshow. It was a pleasant time with Scorsese. "Very humorous, quick, and efficient," Mitchum said. Scorsese, a cinephile, had seen all 103 of his pictures. "That beat me," said Mitchum. "I've seen about seven of 'em."

On January 18, 1991, Mitchum received the Cecil B. DeMille Award for "outstanding contribution to the entertainment field" by the Hollywood Foreign Press Association at their annual Golden Globe ceremony. The following month he was set to receive the D. W. Griffith Career Achievement Award from the National Board of Review in New York. When he learned that he was supposed to provide his own transport and accommodations, Mitchum told them to keep it. The board gave the award to Lauren Bacall instead. She lived in Manhattan and presumably only cost them cab fare.

Toni Cosentino of Charter Management was a diehard Republican and determinedly tried to bring Mitchum into the fold. "I'm the worst conservative, and I was a very big George Bush supporter, so I made him do all this stuff for the Bush campaign. I got him to go on the stump for a while. He wasn't very political, but he said he liked George Bush because, of course, he knew him when he was head of the CIA in Vietnam. And then he got an invitation to go to Bob Hope's house for a fund-raiser. And Bob says, 'Do you want to go?' And I say, 'Yes, yes!' So I got to go and it was fabulous. And I got to meet George Bush and everything. They were talking about Vietnam stuff and it was really neat, things that happened in Vietnam. It was so cool, stuff I didn't even know. It sounded like Bob sort of went into Cambodia, but he couldn't tell me. And I was just dying because it was so cool. . . ."

Mitchum's voice would ultimately ring out of the Republican Convention hall as narrator of the biographical/promotional film that played to the delegates and to television viewers before the candidate's arrival on the convention stage. Mitchum's anarchic, lawless (in Pauline Kael's phrase) profile, his criminal record and marijuana use were unremembered or wished away in the eagerness to foster this powerful association.* Bush had an image problem that dogged him—the wimp factor they called it—and his campaign people slavered at the prospect of Mitchum's testicular intonations ringing across the auditorium. He was the only John Wayne left.

Mitchum had always liked to call himself a plumber, and now finally he was doing jobs that were about as glamorous as fixing a stopped-up toilet. When Glenn Ford became ill with heart and circulatory problems, Mitchum signed for a recurring role on a Family Channel cable television series called *African Skies,* starring Catherine Bach, the cutoff jeans girl from *The Dukes of Hazard.* It was a kind of weekly cameo appearance as a blustery tycoon, fitted in among shots of

*Back in the '50s, President Eisenhower had refused to allow any Mitchum movie to be screened in the White House because of his association with drugs.

zebras and elephants. The show could have used a good boxing kangaroo. He appeared briefly in a wretched knockabout farce about lady firefighters called *Backfire*. It seemed intended for those who had found the *Police Academy* movies too subtle. Mitchum played a senile fire chief. He looked weirdly out of place among a swarm of smooth-fleshed, empty-headed youths, like Buster Keaton in those *Beach Party* movies in the '60s (in fact, he looked here very much like the aged Keaton, with the same collapsed face and eloquently vacant deadpan). But the damndest thing was, in the midst of even this awful movie, he was good, maintained his dignity, and for a couple of moments here and there he was hilarious.

Part of a package deal put together by the ICM agency, he went to South Africa to make a sexy mystery called *Woman of Desire,* starring a frequently naked Bo Derek. Jeff Fahey and Steven Bauer were the rival males, with lots of teeth and clenching eyebrows. Mitchum played a lawyer who acted more like a detective, stoically tracking down the facts after Fahey is accused of murder. Mitchum was seventy-five and creaking, but director Robert Ginty was a fellow actor and an admirer and presented Mitchum beautifully. He looked cool. He could still play that tough private investigator part like no one else. His underplaying and reality brought the melodrama back to earth whenever he was on-screen. "He was an old man," said Ginty, "but the whole sense of presence and charisma, the whole aura was still very much intact. He had that unique rhythm he gave to a scene, the way he said the lines, the way he moved. The same off camera. There was nothing uncomfortable or self-conscious about him. I would say he was the most comfortable guy in his body that I ever met in the movie business. No affectation, no curious behavior. Very casual. He got along with everybody, talked to anybody. He had found his niche in life. He loved the world of the set. The cameraderie, the adventure. He would come to the set when he wasn't working, just to hang out. Just liked being part of it. He said he couldn't retire. Didn't have the money. He'd lost most of it in various bad deals, and lots of people depended on him. But I think there was also that mind-set with some old pros, like with some musicians, they got to keep in the game; if they stop playing, they'll die."

They filmed in Capetown and Johannesburg. Because of the developing social crisis—the imploding of apartheid—it was considered dangerous to venture far from the hotels and foolhardy to go out at night. The Californians looked wide-eyed as the local whites, even young girls, showed off the firearms they carried for protection. Mitchum came to the set each day or sat at the bar talking to people—the crew, tourists, the barmen. Mitchum was very fond of Bo Derek, but the two liked to goad each other about one's bad and one's terribly good habits. She scolded him for his smoking, and Mitchum mocked her health food and exercise regimen. "Don't you want to die of *somethin'*?" he asked.

The mostly South African technical crew were not up to Hollywood standards ("It looked like a carpet commercial," Mitchum scoffed). The film also suffered from an imposed bogusness. As a practical measure, to forestall controversy, the producers had decided to use the Capetown and Jo'burg locations as an abstract setting—passing them off as someplace else—America, the Caribbean, Ruritania. It gave the whole thing an anonymity, an unfixed dimension. *Woman of Desire* skipped the theaters and went straight to home video and cable TV.

He purchased a property in Paradise Valley, Arizona, near Scottsdale. A nice spread, a place to go in the winter, a place to keep a few horses. Jim was often there. Some people got the idea the place was his.

In the summer of 1993, Mitchum signed on to play old man Clanton in *Tombstone,* a new telling of the Wyatt Earp story. His back gave out on him the first day in the saddle, and he had to quit. The doctor sent him home. Writer-director Kevin Jarre was distraught—Mitchum was a totem for this attempted revival of the grand scale Western. Rather than recast, he retired the role. Mitchum would come back to read the film's voice-over introduction. More than ever the voice seemed to have a value all its own. Ask George Bush. Though it was nurtured in Connecticut and Delaware, it had come to sound like the voice of the West, of frontier values, masculine values, the sound of when men were Men. In a time of quiche and oat bran, Mitchum with his basso grumble was the natural spokesman for the American Beef Council, the voice of big, strong, artery-clogged America. *"Beef! It's what's for dinner!"* It became his most identifiable line, his *"Top of the world, Ma."*

Bruce Weber, a noted commercial photographer, had made two films, documentaries, *Broken Noses* and *Let's Get Lost,* the latter a brilliant study of beatific, junkie jazz trumpeter Chet Baker. Weber was a connoisseur of cool and a chronicler of sultry masculine images, and Robert Mitchum was an all-time favorite icon. He showed him a tape of the Baker documentary, and Mitchum was impressed. He agreed to talk on camera for a similar sort of project. There was no money involved. Just for fun. A new audience to hear some old stories. They shot in Montecito and down in LA, in hotel rooms, bars. Weber found lush fashion models, leggy, pouty young things to drape around the star. Weber delighted in Mitchum's reaction to each new female on the scene, "his appreciation of all kinds of women: his sheer joy of looking them up and down, smiling, and just wondering." He loved Mitchum's old records and set up new recording sessions that he would shoot for the documentary. They went into a studio and Bob warbled some of his favorites: "Dream a Little Dream of Me," "When It's Sleepy Time Down South." He sang duets with Dr. John and Marianne Faithfull—he found the aging, smoky-voiced, blonde chanteuse very appealing. Weber would keep calling, every time he was in Los Angeles, to see if Bob was free for some more fun. It went on for years.

His lungs were shot. After nearly seventy years of treating them like an open-hearth furnace, the toll was now coming due. The doctors said emphysema. The lung tissues were torn, rotted away. The elasticity required to let them do their job was no longer present. Respiration—breathing—was going to become increasingly difficult and painful. He was told to quit smoking immediately. An artificial respirator and tanks of oxygen were ordered. Mitchum lit up another unfiltered Pall Mall and went on home.

They kept it a secret for a while. He was afraid it would end any chance of another job. And he didn't want the pity. And it was nobody's damn business. Finally, one of the tabloids printed an item. Mitchum was on oxygen, suffering from a fatal disease. "I didn't know about it," said Toni Cosentino. "I got a call from some paper asking me to confirm that Mitchum was ill, was on oxygen. I said, 'No way. Absolutely not.' But I called his brother. I said, 'Do you know anything about this?' He says, 'Emphysema. It's bad. He's got a couple of years.' I started crying and crying. When I talked to Bob I said, 'Why didn't you tell me?' He just took it very lightly, like it was nothing. I asked what about the oxygen. He said, 'I only need it to breathe.'"

He was offered a picture to be filmed in Europe. *The Sunset Boys* it was called, then *Waiting for Sunset*. A comedy tinged with nostalgia and sorrow, about old buddies, Americans and Europeans, fulfilling a pact, a series of difficult and sometimes outlandish last requests that take them to various locales from Germany to Norway. The project had a varied set of backers, from national film boards in Norway and Denmark to the Paul Mitchell salons and hair-care magnate John Paul DeJoria. "Alan Oberholzer came to me and we started this company called Yellow Cottage Productions, with the idea of doing something really good and really big," DeJoria recalled. "We had this fabulous script, and I had a couple of friends in the movie industry—Cliff Robertson was a real buddy, and Mitchum I had met, but it was his agent, Jack Gilardi, who was a very good friend. I drove up to Santa Barbara with Alan and had lunch with Robert at the Biltmore Hotel. A real cool old hotel, a class act. And we had lunch at the tables outside. They came for the drink order and Robert said, 'I'll have the usual.' So I said, 'I'll have whatever Robert's having.' Well, the usual, unbeknownst to me, was a huge vodka, straight up. I had no idea I would be getting this much booze! I started sipping it. And while I'm sipping away, Robert's done and orders another. And I knew that he had been ailing. Not on his death bed, but ailing. He spoke of his illness a little bit. And I couldn't keep myself from saying, 'Robert, you told me you'd been a little off and you're trying to get better. Should you be drinking so much? It can't be helping any.' And Robert's answer to me was, 'Look, I live a certain life. And nothing, no medical doctor, no priest, nobody is going to interfere with that.' He said, 'I'm not going to change what I like to do just to add on another three or five months or a year.' And he smiled and he seemed just totally confident in his conviction. And I thought, Wow, now that's a man. No compromises. Good for him."

Robert and Dorothy and Bob Stephens (the stuntman and actor who had taken on some of the jobs once fulfilled by Tim Wallace, who had passed away) flew to Oslo. Mitchum was tremendously jet-lagged on arrival, and when a female reporter sneaked onto the aircraft when it landed and began questioning him, he was tremendously pissed off. They were met by members of the production company, including Leidulv Risan, a top name in Norwegian film and television, who would be directing *Sunset*. A press conference had been arranged only hours after the plane landed. Mitchum sat with Cliff Robertson and their costars, Sweden's Erland Josephson and Norway's Espen Skjonberg. Mitchum felt like nodding off, but nearly all the questions were for him. "It was like no one else existed," Leidulv Risan recalled. "The Norwegian press, all the film critics, just looked at Mitchum like it was a visit from God himself."

They went straight to work the next day, shooting in Oslo for a week. Robert had written to his cousin that he and Dorothy were coming to Norway. There was a reunion in the town of Tonsberg, and nearly two dozen relatives showed up from all over Norway. "He came back and he spoke very proudly of his Norwegian heritage," said Risan. "Very proud memories of his grandfather, a fisherman, a sailor. He talked about how this was supposed to have been a helluva man. But, you know, he also spoke several times about his Indian background, and he was quite proud of that. He said that he was so strong physically . . . that it came from his Indian blood."

Risan's directions were very much in a European, theater-based style, an active, intimate relationship with the performer. On the second day of this close coaching, Mitchum turned to him stiffly and glared. "Are you . . . trying to direct me?"

The question seemed loaded with suspicion, but Risan could see no other way of answering. "Yes."

Mitchum glared harder, then shrugged. "Huh . . . No one's done that before," he said.

Risan wondered if he was missing something. "It's what I'm here for," he said.

"Oh yeah, yeah . . . you're right. It makes sense."

Risan: "He was very, very ill with emphysema. And I worried many times that he would be all right. And there was a scene where he had to do some running. And he said, 'You want to kill me?' I said, 'What choice is there? You have to run in the scene.' He said, 'OK, as long as I have no choice.' And thank God it went all right. But, you know, he had this illness and still he smoked so heavily, without filters, and I was told he had a drinking problem, and a couple of times he was drinking like hell, two or three times, but it was not really a problem. He threw one party, after his wife left to go back. He had a very good time."

Mitchum was aloof, closed off to him at first but Risan was a film scholar, knew the man's work, and persisted with questions about Hawks and Huston and the rest until the stories began to flow and Mitchum began to open up on a personal level. "I saw that he was actually a very tender, very nice man, and quite wise. I came to realize what an extremely intelligent man he was. He had such wide knowledge, down to general classical culture. He spoke of his love of classical music, he was very much into opera, and he was like an encyclopedia on this subject. His image and what he was inside were such very different things. He said that what he really wished he could have become was a writer. He loved words and stories. He talked about the writing of *Thunder Road* and the way he had plotted the story, and how they had made up most of *El Dorado* and other films, invented the dialogue. And toward the end of shooting we had some scene where the dialogue was very bad; I was not happy. And I finally said to him, 'Can't you try to sharpen the lines here? I don't think they're very good.' And he just right away on the set rewrote them and made it so much better. And there was only another week to go on the film, and I was very pissed with myself that I didn't ask him to do this with every scene. It was the opposite with Cliff Robertson, who tried to write new scenes, new dialogue for himself, hundreds of pages, and I would look at it and I would have to say, 'It's not what I'm looking for.' Sad to say. You see, it's very difficult to be a director!

"I sat with him during some nights and he was very revealing. He had some bitterness about things in his life. Disappointments in his personal life. He was pissed that he felt he had to keep working, even now when he was so very old. But, you know, he was also very funny and had a sweet nature most of the time, very joyful when he was at the bar and talking and drinking. And on the set, always singing. Once, I remember, we had a disaster with the catering. Everyone was dying for their lunch, all the actors. And the catering did not come with the food. And the line producer stepped up and gave a speech, said, 'I can tell you for a fact that this will never happen again!' And Mitchum starts singing: '*It seems to me I've heard that song before. . . .*'

"It didn't happen to be the best film ever made, but that wasn't his fault. He was a wonderful, interesting man."

People had been after Mitchum for years to write his autobiography. An agent in New York was the last to talk to him about it. Mitchum said, fine, why not, if they could get him Jackie Kennedy for his editor. The agent got back a few days later. Mrs. Onassis would be delighted to do the book with him. Mitchum had always been her favorite movie star, she said to the startled agent, had always reminded her very much of her own father. Appointments were made for Mitchum and Jackie to meet in New York after he finished his next job. Then Onassis was diagnosed with cancer and was not going to be editing any more books, and that was that.

*

Jim Jarmusch was a New York–based, independent filmmaker of modest-budgeted, absurdist comedies about lowlifes and bohemians in various states of anomie and alienation. He had a fondness for Old Hollywood hipster and rebel figures like Nick Ray and Sam Fuller, and Robert Mitchum was a hands-down favorite. Jarmusch was about to make a new film called *Dead Man*, a Western, though a decidedly unusual—postmodern, the film journals would call it—Western, sprinkled with surrealist gags, mysticism, and references to poet William Blake. Johnny Depp was the film's picaresque protagonist, wandering through an ever more inexplicable American frontier. The roaming nature of the story left room for a number of guest shots, and for the small part of Mr. Dickinson, a viciously crazy old rich man who sets a group of bounty hunters on Depp's trail, Jarmusch went after Mitchum. The actor agreed to meet him. Mitchum had never heard of the director or seen any of his work. Jarmusch recalled, "I went and met with him and spent one of the most bizarre and amazing afternoons of my life listening to him talk when I was really supposed to be telling him the story of the film. Instead, he told me some of the wildest shit I've ever heard."

Managing at last to get in a few sentences about *Dead Man,* Jarmusch left the script and departed. Days later he got a call. "Mr. Mitchum would be happy to accept this role." Like so many who had come before him, Jarmusch found Mitchum to be a fascinating and funny guy to work with. He didn't want background or motivation, no long thing, Jarmusch remembered. "He just wants to know that he's hitting the character the way that I want it to be and what he feels it is, and then you just take it from there."

One day while they were working, Jarmusch found the old actor staring into the distance. "Years ago," Mitchum said, keeping his eyes on the Western horizon, "I saved up a million dollars from acting . . . and I spent it on a horse farm in Tucson. Now when I go down there, I look at the place and realize my whole acting career adds up to a million dollars' worth of horseshit."

He did some more work. There was a cameo as movie director George Stevens in a film about James Dean's last days on earth. Robert's granddaughter Carrie played Dean's girlfriend Pier Angeli.

Better to think of *Dead Man* and ferocious old shotgun-wielding

Dickinson as the end of the line. A scene-stealing bad guy in the Old West, just the way it had all begun, fifty-three years ago.

*

It was getting bad. He needed the respirator within reach more often. His weight was dropping. There were days when a walk across the living room exhausted him. Doctors came around. They tried again to make him give up the cigarettes and the liquor.

In April 1996, he agreed to a request from the Turner Classic Movies cable channel—they wanted to sit him alongside his long-time dear friend and Montecito neighbor Jane Russell and make them chat about the good old days at RKO. Robert Osborne would be interviewing them. Osborne had gotten in Mitchum's good graces years before when the Los Angeles critics were handing him one of those lifetime achievement awards. Osborne had been properly ironic about the thing and read some of Mitchum's worst reviews through the years. Mitchum got a kick out of it. He and Jane flew to Atlanta—Turner headquarters—for the interview. For Osborne and the others there was a great deal of shock and despair at the sight of Robert Mitchum in very bad shape, wasted away, hooked up to his oxygen. In an Atlanta bar that night all those feelings vanished as Mitchum held court, telling uproarious stories between sips of vodka and oxygen. To Osborne's dismay, all that ebullience was gone the next day in front of the TV cameras, as a wan and slack-jawed Mitchum sat on a couch beside a vibrant, gray-haired Jane Russell. "Either because of illness or cantankerousness, he was about as pleasant to interview that day as Attila the Hun. Ask him anything and he'd retort with one- and two-word answers. 'Yes.' 'No.' 'Don't remember.' Only when I'd ask about people such as Marilyn Monroe and Howard Hughes . . . would he open up. Or when the names of certain directors or actors he didn't like would be mentioned. Then he'd talk." Russell, smart and charming, sat like a loving sister who'd seen all of brother Bob's mood swings a million times and paid them no mind. They broke for lunch and once again Mitchum became the delightful raconteur. Then back to the set and again he clammed up. For two hours the cameras turned—"It seemed like two years in Beirut," said Osborne—from which forty minutes of television were extracted.

In the spring of 1997, the doctors said lung cancer. They wanted to put him in the hospital, but Mitchum refused. The sickness attacked with brutal speed. Dorothy begged him to go for the radiation treatments that were prescribed. Reluctantly, he agreed. "I'm doing it for your mom," he told Trina.

*

His strength drained away; his body shriveled. The boy who had dreamed of becoming invisible now saw it happening in painful, daily increments. Was it really so, he had wondered aloud in better times, that the supreme value in a man is his continued existence? He had never been afraid of oblivion, a place—with any luck— where a man could get a good night's sleep at last. "What I need is a black void," he liked to say back then. "Black voids aren't too easy to come by these days. But someday I'll find one."

Word of Bob's worsening condition spread through the Hollywood community. People called, friends, associates, paying their respects, hoping the rumors were exaggerated. Jane Greer, whose fame remained inextricably tied to her work with Mitchum, and who had always been one of his most affectionate and loyal supporters, called the house at Montecito. "I talked to Dorothy. She said he was in really bad shape. I wanted to come up, she said don't. I called their neighbor, Jane Russell. Jane was always straightforward. She said, 'Don't come up here. He doesn't want you to see him. He looks awful. He's lost a lot of weight. He just doesn't want you to see him this way.' So I never went up. I never went back. I never saw him again."

There were others who had not been in touch in many years but treasured memories of the time they had spent together. Karen Sharpe, the pretty young ingenue in *Man with a Gun,* now married to Stanley Kramer for many years, had never forgotten Bob's kindness to a newcomer in the business. "I was a long time retired, but I was talking to a man who ran a film festival in Tennessee and he mentioned that Bob was very ill. It had been so long since I'd seen him. And I just picked up the phone and called. And he got on immediately. 'Bob, this is Karen Sharpe, do you remember me?' 'Yes, yes, of course,' he said, and he was very sweet. And you would not have known from the sound of him that he was ill. And it was only days before the end. We chatted for about ten minutes. I asked about Dorothy and I told him I had seen his brother not too long ago. Finally, I just got very sentimental and I said, 'You have to know, working with you was one of the great experiences of my life. It's so many years ago now, and time goes by and you never end up telling anybody how you feel or what they meant to you. You were just the dearest person to me, Bob.' And he just said softly, in that drawling way, 'Thank you, Karen.' I told him Stanley and I both sent our love and then we said good-bye."

Anthony Caruso, a friend for sixty years, had come up to Santa Barbara for a get-together just before things had gotten bad. They'd had dinner, gotten bombed, told the old stories, some of them so old you couldn't remember who they had happened to. "Remember that, Tone?" Bob would say encouragingly, wanting backup for some crazy tale, and Tony would say, "I remember, Bob," just like in the days back on Highland Avenue at El Rancho Broke-O. "I would call him after he got sick. He'd come on, 'Hey, Tone. . . .' I'd say, 'How you doing now?' And he'd say, 'Fair to middlin'.' I'd say, 'Come on, Bob, tell me how you're doing.' 'Fair to middlin'. I'm OK.' He wasn't somebody who could tell you if he wasn't feeling good. And knowing him, I didn't expect he would do that. And then I would tell him I was coming up to see him. And he said, 'Well, Tony, don't come up right now. Wait till I'm in a little better shape.' And then I heard he was doing worse and I told him I was coming. He said, 'Let me get back on my feet, Tone. Let's make it in a few days.' And then, you know . . . there weren't any more days."

A month before the end, Jane Russell saw him for the last time. Dorothy brought Robert over to Jane's and her husband John's house for a barbecue. "We all knew the end was near," said Russell. "Bob was so frail . . . But he was as witty and nonchalant about death as ever. He was a lovable smartmouth right to the end. We laughed, talked about the old times . . . He could always bring tears of laughter to your eyes."

Toni Cosentino, his business associate and friend for ten years, found herself unwilling to see Mitchum in his deteriorated condition. It hurt too much. She didn't want to think of him like that. It was bad enough even a year before. People would see him and call and say, "Oh, my God, he looks so awful." She couldn't stand the idea of someone who had been so strong and unflappable, now so helpless. "We talked on the phone. And he would leave messages on my machine. Sometimes he sounded down and sometimes he would leave really funny messages, or he would end it saying, 'Gotta go, my Ex-Lax is working.' Or, 'Gotta go, I hear the vultures circling.' And then, toward the end, they would be more abrupt. Just, 'OK, give me a call.' You could hear he was down.

"Father's Day, in June, I wrote him—which I never did—I wrote a little card and note for Father's Day, just telling him how much I missed him. He called, left a message thanking me for the card. I called him the day he died. Dorothy answered. I said, 'Mrs. Mitchum, could I talk to Bob?' She said he was sleeping. I said I would call back. She said to call back, but that he was very, very bad. I said, 'I guess I just wanted to let him know that somebody's sending something for him. They'd really like him to do it, a narration job.' They were always sending things like that for him. And Dorothy said, 'Good. He'll like to know that they still want him. . . .' And that was the last word I ever spoke to her."

*

"I was at brother Jack's house that night," said Julie Mitchum. "Jack and Bonnie had gone to bed about ten o'clock. I had a night-light on. I felt Bob leaving us. Felt him slipping away. We had always had ESP, the two of us. And I started to go with him. There is a line in the Faith, 'Thus far and no farther. . . .' Well, I heard those words come to me. 'Thus far and no farther.' And I had to come back. But I knew Bob was going away then. . . ."

That night, on the last day of June 1997, Robert Mitchum awoke, took a cigarette from the pack on the bedroom table, and lit it up. He drew the smoke of an unfiltered Pall Mall into what remained of his lungs. One for the road.

At five o'clock in the morning, Dorothy could no longer hear him breathing. She sat at the edge of the bed and took his hands in hers. Held his hands. Then she leaned closer and kissed him good-bye.

CHAPTER SEVENTEEN

Guys Like Me Last Forever

"I don't want to die."
Out of the Past.
"Neither do I, baby, but if I do . . . I want to die last."

He had very nearly pulled it off. Fifty-four years in the saddle. Worked to the day he couldn't breathe without help and kept working. The world media eulogized. He was a legend, screen immortal, the last of the great Hollywood tough guys. They quoted Scorsese: "Mitchum *was* film noir." Jarmusch: "There was and is no other screen presence like his: dangerous, strong but guarded . . . so damn cool." Photographer Bruce Weber said, "I would still like to believe that he is out there to help me fight battles with life, love, and friendship." Kirk Douglas, generously overlooking a half century of Mitchum's ribbing, was the first of his surviving peers to say a kind word. "Bob was a very talented actor with a unique style," he told the press. "I will miss him a lot." Writer Pete Hamill, then editor of the tabloid *New York Daily News,* the noirest of American newspapers, gave to the movie actor the entire front page for July 2, a rare and eloquent salute. The press raked over the colorful old scandals, eased away from the more troubling allegations. Printed the truths and fictions equitably, some things long ago disproven. Listed the filmography, fifty-four years' worth, the seemingly haphazard hundred-plus titles, many of them unknown entities to even the heartiest film buff. American Movie Classics and Turner Classic Movies, the U.S. cable television channels devoted to the older Hollywood product, put on marathon tributes within days of his passing. AMC's ran for twenty-four hours. Turner rebroadcast the 1996 interview session with the dying, ravaged, but still pugnacious star, host Robert Osborne thanklessly playing straight man, asking, "You don't have a favorite Robert Mitchum film?" Mitchum, one last time deadpanning, "*They don't pay you to see 'em.*"

Then Jane Russell, giving the question some thought: "I just like . . . *Robert Mitchum movies.*"

One day after Mitchum, Jimmy Stewart died. Pundits with a longer lead time got to ponder a supposed irony in this random apposition. Gone within twenty-four hours of each other, they were offered up as two ends of the spectrum of Hollywood icons, the cinema's finest representatives of daylight and darkness, the small-town guy and the man from the mean streets, the all-American optimist and the cynic, the pessimist, the outsider. But Stewart had his dark side, in film and in life, just as so many of Mitchum's antiheroes and lowlifes were possessed of nobility and self-sacrifice, and there were the many behind-the-scenes kindnesses and his professionalism and stuff that had never made good copy. What the hell. The thing was, the real point, what people were feeling, they were gone now and no one would replace them and no one would ever again make the kinds of films they had made. "The words 'legend,' 'hero' and 'myth' have echoed this week," wrote Maureen Dowd in the *New York Times.* "It is the end of something," wrote Chris Chase in the *Los Angeles Times.* "William Shakespeare said, 'The heavens themselves blaze forth the death of princes'—and these were princes."

Reading and thinking about the loss of Mitchum and Stewart in the first weeks of July, an extraordinary concluded chapter in America's cultural history seemed even more golden and more remote.

The body had been cremated and the remains returned to the family on Thursday, July 3. On the following Sunday morning, family members and one invited friend—Jane Russell—boarded a schooner belonging to a Santa Barbara neighbor, Fess Parker, a vintner and long-ago television's Davy Crockett. They sailed a half mile off the coast, in view of the Montecito house, and, as per Robert's request, his ashes were scattered into the wind and the water.

"Two or three days later," said Julie Mitchum, "I was having trouble with the tear ducts. The eyes were getting wet. And I don't believe in carrying on like that. So I tried to suppress it. And Bob came to me then. He nudged me and said, 'Annie . . . ,' which is what he always called me. I heard his voice. I heard him speak to me. We could hear each other like that all our lives. And we still do. And he said, 'Annie . . . come on, don't cry. I'm fine. I'm here with all the gang that made it before me.'"

Many in Los Angeles had expected there would be a memorial service, a remembrance where the people who knew him could come and say something. But there was nothing. Time went by and they never did have anything like that. Tony Caruso had understood that it was only family when they scattered the ashes. He had talked to Dorothy about a memorial, and she'd said they might or they might not. He guessed that might not was preferable.

But that was OK. He remembered him in his heart. A lot of years. He could still see that kid back in Long Beach. Quite a story. "He had his flaws; we all do. And that's it. I don't know what else I can tell you. He was my buddy and I loved him. And, man, he was good up there on that movie screen."

Sources

Interviews

Edward Anhalt
Ken Annakin
James Bacon
Mrs. Alva Barr
Gene Barry
Earl Bellamy
A. I. Bezzerides
Theodore Bikel
Budd Boetticher
Mrs. Layne Britton
Rock Brynner
Harry Carey, Jr.
Anthony (Tony) Caruso
Anthony Cerbone
Charles Champlin
John Davis Chandler
Frank Coghlan, Jr.
John Colicos
Barnaby Conrad
Stanley Cortez
John Paul DeJoria
Jeannette Dill
Phyllis Diller

Edward Dmytryk
Robert Donner
Jim Dougherty
Al Dowtin
Jack Elam
William Feeder
Andrew J. Fenady
Rhonda Fleming
Joe Franklin
Sam Fuller
John Gabriel
William S. Gilmore, Jr.
Robert Ginty
Oliver Goldstick
Leo Gordon
Ray Gosnell
Bert Granet
Margie Reagan Cate Green
Jane Greer
Paul Gregory
John Guare
Guy Hamilton
Jerry Hardin

Toni Cosentino Hayes
David Hedison
Paul Helmick
Edie Hemphill
Hope Holiday
Dave Holland
Mickey Hoyle
Red Hoyle
Kim Hunter
Beverley Jackson
Anne Jeffreys
Roy Jenson
Lee Katzin
Victor Kemper
Burt Kennedy
Sally Kirkland
Max Kleven
Howard Koch
Andrei Konchalovsky
Stanley Kramer
Buzz Kulik
Irv Kupcinet
Otto Lang
Henry Lange, Jr.
Marc Lawrence
Tom Lea
Lila Leeds
Perry Leiber, Jr.
Janet Leigh
Herbert Leonard
Mrs. Carey Loftin
Malachy McCourt
Roddy McDowall
Andrew V. McLaglen
Dina Merrill
Bart Mills

Lisa Mitchell
D. Michael Moore
Elliott Morgan
Gary Morgan
Terry Morse
Kate Murtagh
Ronald Neame
Alan Oberholzer
Margaret (Smith) O'Connor
Kathie Parrish
Virginia Paskey
Michael Pate
Robert Peters
Norm Peterson
Fred Pinkard
Jean Porter
Vincent Price
Henry Rackin
Alan Rafkin
Sheldon Reynolds
Dick Richards
Leidulv Risan
Allen Rivkin
Phil Rosenthal
Johnny Sands
Reni Santoni
Julie Mitchum Sater
Harry Schein
Doris Seibel
Walter Seltzer
Karen Sharpe
Jerome Siegel
Carolyn Sofia
Herb Speckman
J. Lee Thompson
Ingrid Thulin

Les Tremayne   Richard Wilson
Paul Valentine   Michael Winner
Emma Warner   Ron Wright
William Wellman, Jr.   Reva Frederick Youngstein

Books

Agee, James. *Agee on Film.* Boston: Beacon Press, 1962.

Arnold, Edwin T., and Eugene L. Miller, Jr. *The Films and Career of Robert Aldrich.* Knoxville: University of Tennessee Press, 1986.

Bacon, James. *Hollywood Is a Four Letter Town.* Chicago: Henry Regnery, 1976.

————. *Made in Hollywood.* Chicago: Contemporary Books, 1977.

Baker, Carroll. *Baby Doll.* New York: Arbor House, 1983.

Baxter, John. *The Cinema of Josef von Sternberg.* London: Zwemmer, 1971.

Belton, John. *Robert Mitchum.* New York: Pyramid, 1976.

Bennett, Patrick. *Rough and Rowdy Ways.* College Station: Texas A&M University Press, 1988.

Bergreen, Laurence. *James Agee.* New York: Dutton, 1984.

Bernstein, Matthew. *Walter Wanger: Hollywood Independent.* Berkeley: University of California Press, 1994.

Brady, John. *The Craft of the Screenwriter.* New York: Simon and Schuster, 1981.

Bragg, Melvyn. *Richard Burton: A Life.* Boston: Little, Brown, 1988.

Britton, Andrew. *Talking Films: Best of the Guardian Lectures.* London: Fourth Estate, 1992.

Broccoli, Cubby, and Donald Zec. *When the Snow Melts.* London: Macmillan, 1999.

Broughton, Frank, ed. *Time Out Interviews.* (Interview with Christ Petit and Chris Wicking, Interview with Chris Peachment and Geoff Andrew). London: Penguin, 1998.

Brown, Peter Harry, and Pat H. Broeske. *Howard Hughes: The Untold Story.* New York: Dutton, 1996.

Brownlow, Kevin. *David Lean.* New York: St. Martin's, 1997.

Brynner, Rock. *Yul: The Man Who Would Be King.* New York: Simon and Schuster, 1989.

Callow, Simon. *Charles Laughton: A Difficult Actor.* New York: Grove Press, 1988.

Canham, Kingsley. *Michael Curtiz/Raoul Walsh/Henry Hathaway.* London: Tantivy Press, 1973.

Castle, William. *Step Right Up!* New York: Putnam, 1976.

Caute, David. *Joseph Losey: A Revenge on Life.* London: Faber and Faber, 1994.

Ciment, Michel. *Conversations with Losey.* New York: Methuen, 1985.

Collins, Joan. *Second Act.* New York: St. Martin's, 1997.

Conrad, Barnaby. *Name Dropping.* San Francisco: Wild Coconuts, 1997.

Coursodon, Jean-Pierre, and Bertrand Tavernier. *50 Ans de Cinema Americain.* Paris: Nathan, 1995.

D'Antonio, Joanne. *Andrew Marton.* Metuchen, N.J.: Scarecrow Press, 1991.

Dewey, Donald. *James Stewart.* Atlanta: Turner, 1997.

Dmytryk, Edward. *It's a Hell of a Life But Not a Bad Living.* New York: Times Books, 1978.

Downing, David. *Robert Mitchum.* London: Comet, 1985.

Ebert, Roger. *A Kiss Is Still a Kiss.* New York: Andrews, McMeel and Parker, 1984.

Eells, George. *Robert Mitchum.* New York: Franklin Watts, 1984.

Eisenschitz, Bernard. *Nicholas Ray: An American Journey.* London: Faber and Faber, 1993.

Eyman, Scott. *Five American Cinematographers.* Metuchen, N.J.: Scarecrow Press, 1987.

Farber, Manny. *Negative Space.* New York: Praeger, 1971.

Farrow, Mia. *What Falls Away.* New York: Doubleday, 1997.

Finch, Christopher. *Linda Rosenkrantz. Gone Hollywood.* Garden City: Doubleday, 1979.

Fine, Marshall. *Bloody Sam: The Life and Films of Sam Peckinpah.* New York: Donald I. Fine, 1991.

Fleischer, Richard. *Just Tell Me When to Cry: A Memoir.* New York: Carroll and Graf, 1993.

Freedland, Michael. *Gregory Peck.* New York: William Morrow, 1980.

———. *Jack Lemmon.* New York: St. Martin's, 1985.

Frischauer, Willi. *Behind the Scenes of Otto Preminger.* New York: William Morrow, 1974.

Fuller, Graham. "Looking Like Nothing Much Matters." Chap. 15 in *Projections 7: Film-Makers in Film-Making,* edited by John Boorman and Walter Donahue. London: Faber and Faber, 1997.

Gardner, Ava. *Ava: My Story.* New York: Bantam, 1990.

Garnett, Tay. *Light Up Your Torches and Pull Up Your Tights.* New Rochelle: Arlington House, 1973.

Gershuny, Theodore. *Soon to Be a Major Motion Picture.* New York: Holt, Rinehart and Winston, 1980.

Giesler, Jerry, as told to Pete Martin. *The Jerry Giesler Story.* New York: Simon and Schuster, 1960.

Gish, Lillian, and Ann Pinchot. *The Movies, Mr. Griffith and Me.* Englewood Cliffs, N.J.: Prentice-Hall, 1969.

Granger, Stewart. *Sparks Fly Upward.* New York: Putnam, 1981.

Griggs, John. *The Films of Gregory Peck.* Secaucus, N.J.: Citadel Press, 1984.

Grobel, Lawrence. *The Hustons.* New York: Scribner's, 1989.

Grubb, Davis. *The Night of the Hunter.* New York: Harper and Row, 1953.

Guralnick, Peter. *Last Train to Memphis: The Rise of Elvis Presley.* New York: Little, Brown, 1994.

Hardy, Phil, ed. *Raoul Walsh.* Edinburgh: Edinburgh Film Festival, 1974.

Harris, Warren G. *Lucy and Desi.* New York: Simon and Schuster, 1991.

Harvey, James. *Romantic Comedy.* New York: Knopf, 1987.

Harvey, Stephen. *Directed by Vincente Minnelli.* New York: Harper and Row, 1989.

Higham, Charles. *Hollywood Cameramen.* Bloomington: Indiana University Press, 1970.

————. *Howard Hughes: The SecrXet Life.* New York: G. P. Putnam's, 1993.

————, and Joel Greenberg. *Hollywood in the Forties.* London: Zwemmer, 1968.

Huston, John. *An Open Book.* New York:x Knopf, 1980.

Jewell, Richard B., and Vernon Harbin. *The RKO Story.* London: Octopus Books, 1982.

Kael, Pauline. *Deeper into Movies.* Boston: Little, Brown, 1973.

Kaminsky, Stuart M. *Don Siegel: Director.* New York: Curtis, 1974.

Kelley, Kitty. *His Way.* New York: Bantam, 1986.

Knight, Vivienne. *Trevor Howard: A Gentleman and a Player.* New York: Beaufort Books, 1986

Kobal, John. *Rita Hayworth: The Time, the Place and the Woman.* New York: W. W. Norton, 1977.

Koszarski, Richard, ed. *Hollywood Directors: 1941–1976.* New York: Oxford University Press, 1977.

LaGuardia, Robert, and Gene Arceri. *Red: The Tempestuous Life of Susan Hayward.* New York: Macmillan, 1985.

Lambert, Gavin. *On Cukor.* New York: Capricorn Books, 1973.

Lanchester, Elsa. *Elsa Lanchester Herself.* New York: St. Martin's, 1983.

Lang, Otto. *A Bird of Passage.* Missoula, Mont.: Pictorial Histories Publishing, 1996.

Leaming, Barbara. *Rita Hayworth: If This Was Happiness.* New York: Viking, 1989.

LeRoy, Mervyn. *Take One.* New York: Hawthorn Books, 1974.

Linet, Beverly. *Ladd.* New York: Arbor House, 1979.

————. *Susan Hayward: Portrait of a Survivor.* New York: Atheneum, 1980.

Logan, Joshua. *Josh.* New York: Delacorte Press, 1976.

Loy, Myrna, and James Kotsilibas-Davis. *Myrna Loy—Being and Becoming.* New York: Knopf, 1987.

MacLaine, Shirley. *My Lucky Stars.* New York: Bantam, 1995.

Malcolm, Derek. *Robert Mitchum.* New York: Hippocrene, 1984.

Marshall, J. D. *Blueprint on Babylon.* Tempe, Ariz.: Phoenix House, 1978.

McBride, Joseph. *Hawks on Hawks.* Berkeley: University of California Press, 1982.

McCarthy, Todd. *Howard Hawks.* New York: Grove Press, 1997.

McCarthy, Todd, and Charles Flynn, eds. *Kings of the Bs.* New York: Dutton, 1975.

McCauley, Michael. *Jim Thompson: Sleep with the Devil.* New York: Mysterious Press, 1991.

McClelland, Doug. *Forties Film Talk.* Jefferson, N.C.: McFarland, 1992.

McCourt, Malachy. *A Monk Swimming.* New York: Hyperion, 1998.

McGilligan, Patrick. *George Cukor: A Double Life.* New York: St. Martin's, 1991.

McGilligan, Patrick, ed. *Backstory.* Berkeley: University of California Press, 1986.

———. *Backstory Two.* Berkeley: University of California Press, 1991.

McKern, Leo. *Just Resting.* London: Methuen, 1983.

Meredith, Burgess, *So Far, So Good.* Boston: Little, Brown. 1994.

Miles, Sarah. *Serves Me Right.* London: Macmillan, 1994.

Miller, Don. *B Movies.* New York: Curtis Books, 1973.

Mills, John. *Up in the Clouds, Gentlemen, Please.* New York: Ticknor and Fields, 1981.

Milne, Tom. *Losey on Losey.* New York: Doubleday, 1968.

Minnelli, Vincente, with Hector Arce. *I Remember It Well.* Garden City: Doubleday, 1974.

Mitchum, John. *Them Ornery Mitchum Boys.* Pacifica, Calif.: Creatures at Large Press, 1989.

Mitchum, Robert. "Problems on Producing." In *The Hollywood Reporter,* edited by Tichi Wilkerson and Marcia Borie. New York: Arlington House, 1984.

Moore, Dick. *Twinkle, Twinkle, Little Star.* New York: Harper and Row, 1984.

Mordden, Ethan. *The Hollywood Studios.* New York: Knopf, 1988.

Mosley, Leonard. *Zanuck.* Boston: Little, Brown, 1984.

Munn, Michael. *Trevor Howard: The Man and His Films.* Chelsea: Scarborough House, 1989.

Nash, Alanna. *Elvis Aaron Presley.* New York: HarperCollins, 1995.

Nevins, Francis M., Jr. *The Films of Hopalong Cassidy.* Waynesville, N.C.: World of Yesterday, 1988.

Olson, James S., and Randy Roberts. *John Wayne: American.* New York: Free Press, 1995.

Otash, Fred. *Investigation Hollywood!* Chicago: Henry Regnery, 1976.

Parrish, Robert. *Hollywood Doesn't Live Here Anymore.* Boston: Little, Brown, 1988.

Peary, Danny, ed. *Close Ups.* New York: Simon and Schuster, 1978.

Peters, Robert. *Love Poems for Robert Mitchum.* Saint John, Kans.: Chiron Review Press, 1992.

Polito, Robert. *Savage Art.* New York: Knopf, 1995.

Pratley, Gerald. *The Cinema of John Huston.* New York: A. S. Barnes, 1977.

Preminger, Otto. *Preminger.* New York: Doubleday, 1977.

Pyle, Ernie. *Brave Men.* New York: Henry Holt, 1944.

Rainsberger, Todd. *James Wong Howe Cinematographer.* San Diego: A. S. Barnes, 1981.

Roberson, Chuck, and Bodie Thoene. *The Fall Guy.* North Vancouver: Hancock House, 1980.

Roberts, Jerry. *Robert Mitchum: A Bio Bibliography.* Westport, Conn.: Greenwood, 1992.

Roeburt, John. *Get Me Giesler.* New York: Belmont, 1962.

Rothel, David. *Those Great Cowboy Sidekicks.* Metuchen, N.J.: Scarecrow Press, 1984.

Rubin, Benny. *Come Backstage with Me.* Bowling Green, Ohio: Bowling Green University Press, n.d.

Russell, Jane. *Jane Russell: An Autobiography.* New York: Franklin Watts, 1985.

Salter, James. *The Hunters.* New York: Harper and Brothers, 1956.

Sarris, Andrew. *Confessions of a Cultist.* New York: Simon and Schuster, 1970.

———. *The Films of Josef von Sternberg.* New York: Museum of Modern Art, 1966.

Schary, Dory. *Heyday.* Boston: Little, Brown, 1979.

Schickel, Richard. *The Men Who Made the Movies*. London: Elm Tree Books, 1977.

Schnayerson, Michael. *Irwin Shaw*. New York: G. P. Putnam's, 1989.

Schwartz, Nancy Lynn. *The Hollywood Writers War*. New York: Knopf, 1982.

Server, Lee. *Screenwriter: Words Become Pictures*. Pittstown, N.J.: Main Street Press, 1987.

Server, Lee, Ed Gorman, and Martin Greenberg, eds. *The Big Book of Noir*. New York: Carroll and Graf, 1998.

Sherman, Eric. *Directing the Film*. Los Angeles: Acrobat Books, 1988.

Shindler, Colin. *Hollywood Goes to War*. London: Routledge and Kegan Paul, 1979.

Siegel, Don. *A Siegel Film*. London: Faber and Faber, 1993.

Silver, Alain, and James Ursini. *Robert Aldrich: His Life and His Films*. New York: Limelight Editions, 1995.

Spada, James. *Shirley and Warren*. New York: Macmillan, 1985.

Spoto, Donald. *Stanley Kramer: Film Maker*. Los Angeles: Samuel French, 1990.

Sternberg, Josef von. *Fun in a Chinese Laundry*. New York: Macmillan, 1965.

Stewart, Donald Ogden. *By a Stroke of Luck!* New York: Paddington Press, 1975.

Stuart, Sandra Lee. *The Pink Palace*. New York: Pocket Books, 1979.

Suid, Lawrence. *Guts and Glory*. Reading, Mass.: Addison-Wesley, 1978.

Thomas, Bob. *Golden Boy: The Untold Story of William Holden*. New York: St. Martin's, 1983.

Thompson, Frank. *William A. Wellman*. Metuchen, N.J.: Scarecrow Press, 1983.

Thomson, David. *Showman: The Life of David O. Selznick*. New York: Knopf, 1992.

Tomkies, Mike. *The Robert Mitchum Story: "It Sure Beats Working."* Chicago: Henry Regnery, 1972.

Tosches, Nick. *Dino*. New York: Doubleday, 1992.

Troyan, Michael. *A Rose for Mrs. Miniver.* Lexington: University Press of Kentucky, 1999.

Truffaut, Francois. *The Films in my Life.* New York: Da Capo, 1994.

Uys, Errol Lincoln. *Riding the Rails.* New York: TV Books, 1999.

Wallis, Hal, and Charles Higham. *Starmaker.* New York: Berkley, 1981.

Walsh, Raoul. *Each Man in His Time.* New York: Farrar Straus and Giroux, 1974.

Wansell, Geoffrey. *Haunted Idol.* New York: William Morrow, 1984.

Wayne, Aissa. *John Wayne, My Father.* New York: Random House, 1991.

Wayne, Jane Ellen. *Ava's Men.* New York: St. Martin's, 1990.

Weddle, David. *If They Move . . . Kill 'Em.* New York: Grove, 1994.

Wellman, William A. *A Short Time for Insanity.* New York: Hawthorn Books, 1974.

Wenders, Wim, and Chris Sievernich. *Nick's Film/Lightning over Water.* Frankfurt: Zweitausendeins, 1981.

Widener, Don. *Lemmon.* New York: Macmillan, 1975.

Wilkie, Jane. *Confessions of an Ex-Fan Magazine Writer.* Garden City: Doubleday, 1981.

Willeford, Charles. *I Was Looking for a Street.* Woodstock, Vt.: Countryman, 1988.

Wills, Gary. *John Wayne's America.* New York: Simon and Schuster, 1997.

Wilson, Earl. *The Show Business Nobody Knows.* Chicago: Henry Regnery, 1971.

Winters, Shelley. *Shelley.* New York: Ballantine, 1981.

———. *Shelley II.* New York: Simon and Schuster, 1989.

Wolfe, Tom. *The Kandy-Kolored Tangerine-Flake Streamline Baby.* New York: Farrar, Straus and Giroux, 1965.

Zinnemann, Fred. *An Autobiography: A Life in Film.* New York: Scribner's, 1992.

Periodicals and Documents

"A Bare Starlet Puts Mitchum in Doghouse." *Los Angeles Daily News,* April 5, 1954.

"A Parfait Knight, That's Mitchum." United Press, January 22, 1955.

"A Totally Unpredictable Personality . . ." Chicago Tribune–N.Y. News Syndicate, November 24, 1963.

Abdu'l-Baha. "Tablets of the Divine Plan." N.p., n.d.

"Actor Mitchum Flips with Aid of Irishman." *Los Angeles Times,* August 5, 1959.

"Actor Robert Mitchum Phoned . . ." *TIME,* January 31, 1972.

"Actor, Wife Separate; Accord Hope Told." N. p., March 11, 1953.

"Actors: Waiting for a Poisoned Peanut." *TIME,* August 16, 1968.

"Actress Explains Half-Clad Pose with Mitchum." *Los Angeles Examiner,* April 6, 1954.

"Actress Freed of Vow to Sportsman." N.p., May 8, 1946.

"Agent Sues Mitchum on Pact." *Los Angeles Examiner,* June 2, 1959.

Ahier, Robert. "Mitchum Says Storm Scared His GI Army." *New York Sunday News,* November 12, 1961.

Albright, Dana, and Roberta Ostroff. "Robert Mitchum Raised Hell to the End." *Globe,* July 15, 1997.

Alleyne, Enid. "Oh Nights Are Too Short in Trinidad!" *Port-of-Spain Gazette,* May 20, 1956.

Alpert, Don. "Mitchum's Bad, Bad, Bad World." *Los Angeles Times,* December 19, 1965.

Anderson, Janette Hyem. "'I'll Go Anywhere for a Free Lunch.'" *Trail Dust,* Summer/Fall 1994.

Andrew, Geoff. "In Memoriam." *Time Out* (London), July 9, 1997.

Anthony, George. "Robert Mitchum Talks." *Entertainment Magazine,* February 1974.

Archerd, Army. "In True Mitchum Style . . ." *Variety,* July 2, 1997.

———. "Just for Variety." *Variety,* June 27, 1974; May 13, 1983; July 29, 1985; April 16, 1986; July 29, 1987; July 31, 1987; May 20, 1988; September 2, 1992; June 11, 1993.

Arkadin. "Losey on Location." *Sight and Sound,* Summer 1968.

"Arrest Scene." *Los Angeles Examiner,* September 2, 1949.

"Arrest Scene Draws Crowds." N.p., circa September 1948.

"Aussie High Court Gets Appeal on Mitchum Tax." *Variety,* April 21, 1965.

Austen, David. "Gunplay and Horses." *Films and Filming,* October 1968.

"Avant-Garde." *Esquire,* October 1971.

"Awards I." *Hollywood Reporter,* January 14, 1992.

Bacon, James. "Mark of Mitchum—Irish Will Long Remember Film Star." *Newark Sunday News,* October 9, 1960.

———. "Mitchum, Despite Himself, Making Bid for Oscar." *Los Angeles Herald-Examiner,* November 13, 1970.

———. "Retirement for Good." *Los Angeles Herald-Examiner,* June 5, 1970.

———. "Surprise Party Like RKO Reunion." *Los Angeles Herald-Examiner,* June 7, 1970.

"Bandido!" Press Kit, 1956.

"Barbara Walters, Star Reporter . . ." *Los Angeles Times,* April 13, 1983.

Barnes, Aleene. "Hankers for ze Cheeseburger." *Los Angeles Times,* June 13, 1956.

Battelle, Phyllis. "Mitchum Rich—but Honest." *Cleveland Plain Dealer,* April 4, 1965.

———. "The Bad and the Good." *Los Angeles Herald-Examiner,* March 9, 1968.

Beck, Marilyn. "Retired for Good Says Bob Mitchum." *Hollywood Citizen-News,* June 8, 1970.

Bennetts, Leslie. "3 Mitchums Starring in a New CBS Movie." *New York Times,* October 14, 1985.

Berg, Louis. "Foreign Intrigue's Wonder Boy." *This Week,* December 6, 1953.

Besas, Peter. "Mitchum Feted at Spanish Fest." *Variety,* September 14, 1993.

"Bob Goes Legit." *Movie,* circa 1946.

"Bob Mitchum Denied License to Race Hoss in New Mexico." *Variety,* December 24, 1965.

"Bob Mitchum Due in Court on Flee Rap." *Los Angeles Mirror,* December 4, 1953.

"Bob Mitchum Fired for Dunking Film Manager." *Hollywood Citizen-News,* January 12, 1955.

"Bob Mitchum Puzzles Cop." *Los Angeles Examiner,* December 3, 1953.

"Bob Mitchum Rides Shiny Bus to Farm." *Los Angeles Daily News,* February 16, 1949.

"Bob Mitchum, 3 Others Jailed After Dope Raid." *Los Angeles Daily News,* September 1, 1948.

"Bob's Not a Slob." *The Sun* (Sydney), December 22, 1959.

Bogdanovich, Peter. "Interview with Otto Preminger." *On Film,* 1971.

"Bond Posted for Mitchum in Traffic Case." *Los Angeles Times,* December 4, 1953.

"Bosomy Gina Raps Mitchum for 'Another Dame' Tag." *Los Angeles Herald Express,* November 2, 1955.

"Bouncing Around. . . ." N.p., January 21, 1975.

"Bouncing Back. . . ." *Women's Wear Daily,* January 24, 1975.

Bowers, Carolyn A. "Robert Mitchum: If Anyone Catches Me Acting . . ." *Stars and Stripes,* circa 1970.

"Break Up Party in Home of Lila Leeds." *Los Angeles Herald Express,* September 1, 1948.

"Bridgeporter on Radio." *Bridgeport Post,* July 29, 1945.

Brooks, Ed. "Jane Russell, Bob Mitchum Star in Newsmen's Interview." *New Orleans Times-Picayune,* September 23, 1952.

Buchwald, Art. "Europe's Lighter Side." *New York Herald Tribune,* April 15, 1954.

Burke, David. "Mitchum Is 'Bored Stiff.'" *Sydney Sun Herald,* October 11, 1959.

Byrne, Bridget. "Mitchum Blunt, Riotous." *Los Angeles Herald-Examiner,* October 18, 1970.

Carpenter, Daniel. "Mitchum Remembered." *Forbes FYI,* September 22, 1997.

Carroll, Harrison. "Bob Wants Dorothy to Reconcile, Join Him on Mexican Location." *Los Angeles Herald Express,* March 19, 1953.

————. "Mitchums Celebrate Anniversary at Ciro's but Fail to Reconcile." *Los Angeles Herald Express,* March 17, 1953.

Carter, Gene. "'Sleepy Eyes' Mitchum Can't Sleep." *National Enquirer,* July 20, 1958.

Castle, Ray. "Mitchum's Just Been Sittin' Since the Rain's Came to Cooma." *Sydney Daily Telegraph,* October 12, 1959.

————. "Movie Quest." *Sydney Daily Telegraph,* November 13, 1959.

————. "The Three Moods of Mr. Mitchum." *Sydney Daily Telegraph,* September 30, 1959.

"Celebs from U.S. to Receive Italian Award." *Hollywood Reporter,* June 21, 1988.

Champlin, Charles. "Mitchum: Hollywood's Enduring Bad Boy." *Los Angeles Times,* July 2, 1997.

————. "One Icon, Hard-boiled." *Los Angeles Times,* October 2, 1994.

"Chance to Leave Jail Makes Mitchum Sad." *Los Angeles Times,* February 16, 1949.

Chase, Chris. "Stewart, Mitchum: Defining America in Light and Dark." *Los Angeles Times,* July 6, 1997.

Chase, Donald. "That Mitchum Season." *Horizon,* January–February 1983.

Churchill, Reba and Bonnie. "Mitchum Sought for 'Wire' Epic." *Beverly Hills Newsfile,* January 20, 1954.

"Clarification." *Hollywood Reporter,* January 15, 1992.

Clooney, Nick. "Mitchum's Act Was Quiet Thunder." *Cincinnati Post,* July 4, 1997.

Coe, Jonathan. "They Spawned the Hollywood Monsters." *Observer* (London), July 6, 1997.

"Col. Bob Mitchum in Bar Brawl; GI Hospitalized." *Hollywood Citizen-News,* November 8, 1951.

"Conversation with Robert Mitchum, Dorothy Mitchum, Hedda Hopper . . ." Unedited conversation for subsequent Hopper article, circa March 1953.

"Crisis in Hollywood." *TIME,* September 13, 1948.

"Dancer Vicki Evans Arraigned as Fugitive in New York Court." *Los Angeles Times,* January 14, 1949.

Dangaard, Colin. "Mitchum Slams in As Marlowe the Eighth." *National Star,* May 27, 1975.

Darrach, Brad. "The Last of the Iron Assed Loners." *Penthouse,* September 1972.

"Daughter Born to Mitchum's Wife." *Hollywood Citizen-News,* March 3, 1952.

Davidson, Bill. "The Many Moods of Robert Mitchum." *Saturday Evening Post,* August 25, 1962.

Davis, Victor. "Robert Mitchum: After All Those Years, Still One of a Kind." *Chicago Tribune,* November 23, 1984.

"Death Notices." *Wall Street Journal,* July 10, 1997.

DeBona, Joe. "Our Bridgeport's Just a Memory for Mitchum." *Bridgeport Herald,* n.d.

De La Fuente, Anna Marie. "Mitchum Getting Lifetime Honor at San Sebastian." *Hollywood Reporter,* September 14, 1993.

Delehanty, Thornton. "He Prides Himself on His Failures." *New York Herald Tribune,* April 13, 1947.

"Despite Fans' OK on Mitchum, RKO and Biz Recognize a 'Problem.'" N.p., n.d.

DiMona, Joseph. "Last of the Tough Guys." *Family Weekly,* August 25, 1985.

Drew, Bernard. "Tough Mitchum Facade Hides a Poet." Tarrytown (N.Y.) *Daily News,* September 12, 1969.

"Driver Sues Mitchum." *Los Angeles Examiner,* June 15, 1954.

"Droolettes." Associated Press, n.d.

DuBrow, Rick. "Mitchum's a Solid Anchor in Time of 'Remembrance.'" *Los Angeles Herald-Examiner,* November 11, 1988.

"Dunking Row . . . Refused to Apologize in Dispute." N.p., January 12, 1955.

Ebert, Alan. "Robert Mitchum Hates Hollywood . . ." *In the Know,* December 1975.

Ebert, Roger. "Don't Give a Damn Mitchum." *New York Times,* September 14, 1969.

————. "Robert Mitchum: Bogart of the 90s." *US Magazine,* April 4, 1978.

Ellison, Bob. "Mitchum, First Hippie, Really a Pussycat." *Chicago Tribune,* September 14, 1969.

"Extortion Inquiry Takes New Turn." *Los Angeles Times,* September 24, 1949.

"Farewell My Lovely Son." *People,* June 7, 1976.

Fay, Bill, and Lila Leeds. "Narcotics Ruined Me." *Colliers,* July 26, 1952.

Fenady, Andrew J. "Robert Mitchum—The Ice Man." *Variety,* November 14, 1989.

Fields, Sidney. "The Mitchum Manner." *New York Daily News,* June 20, 1972.

"Film Actress on Mend After Drug Error." N.p., circa 1946.

"Filmlore Answer: . . ." *Hollywood Reporter,* October 26, 1983.

"Final Resting Place." *Los Angeles Times,* July 10, 1997.

"Fire Mitchum from Picture." United Press, circa January 1955.

"Fire Robert Mitchum, Who Then Interviews Press in Underwear." *Variety,* January 19, 1955.

Fletcher, Adele Whitely. "The Strange Case of Robert Mitchum." *Photoplay,* November 1948.

"'Foul!' Cries Woman." *New York Daily News,* December 10, 1982.

Freeman, David. "Robert Mitchum." *Los Angeles Magazine,* October 1995.

Fuller, Tyra. "Robert Mitchum Puts Aside Bad Man Roles for Hero Parts." N.p., circa 1946.

Gehman, Richard. "Star Who Hates Hollywood." *True Magazine,* October 1962.

"GI Actors 'Afraid of Sea,' Mitchum Says." *Los Angeles Times,* November 12, 1961.

"Giesler Maps Defense of Mitchum on Drug Charge." *Los Angeles Daily News,* September 9, 1948.

Gilmore, Eddy. "Black-Eyed Mitchum Is Meek." *New York Journal-American,* August 5, 1959.

Godbout, Oscar. "Mitchum: Doctor, Pastor, Newsman." *New York Times,* June 12, 1955.

Gold. "Book Review." *Variety,* May 9, 1984.

Goldman, Kevin. "Robert Mitchum Adds Class to Trash Bags." *Wall Street Journal,* July 26, 1995.

Graham, Sheilah. "Mitchum Brother Takes New Name." *Bridgeport Herald,* December 17, 1950.

———. "Mitchum Happy as Maryland Farmer." *Hollywood Citizen-News,* April 17, 1965.

———. "Robert Mitchum a Put-On Complainer?" *Hollywood Citizen-News,* August 21, 1969.

"Grand Jury Dope Inquiry Proposed in Mitchum Case." *Los Angeles Times,* September 3, 1948.

"Grand Jury Indicts Mitchum, 3 Friends." *Los Angeles Daily News,* September 8, 1948.

Greenspun, Roger. "A Movie That Might Have Been Merely Ridiculous." *New York Times,* November 17, 1968.

Grigsby, Wayne. "Man with the Golden Grunt." *Macleans,* February 19, 1979.

Grosh, Stacey Lane. "Dean Film to Debut in Wabash." *Chronicle Tribune,* September 9, 1997.

Gross, Linda. "Jane Greer: Out of Her Past." *Los Angeles Times,* March 4, 1984.

Haber, Joyce. "70 Films a Lot of Work for One Lazy Cowpoke." *Los Angeles Times,* March 23, 1969.

Hackett, George. "Legendary Bad Boy. . . ." *Newsweek,* February 6, 1984.

Hale, Wanda. "As Writer-Producer Reynolds Shoots First." *New York Daily News,* May 3, 1956.

———. "Mitchum of Maryland." *New York Daily News,* April, 26, 1965.

Hall, William. "Robert Mitchum: Poet with a Four-Letter Soul." *Playgirl,* November 1974.

Harris, Eleanor. "The Man with the Immoral Face." *Photoplay,* December 1945.

———. "This Man Mitchum." *The American Weekly.* October 30, 1955.

"Head East." *Los Angeles Times,* May 12, 1955.

Heffernon, Harold. "Writer Flays Studios for Condoning Moral Laxity That Led to Dope Scandal; Demands Housecleaning." *Indianapolis Star,* September 19, 1948.

Hettrick, Scott. "Fallen Stars' Dual Marathons." *Hollywood Reporter,* July 3, 1997.

Hickey, William. "After Robert Mitchum, They Broke the Mold." *Cleveland Plain Dealer,* January 20, 1983.

Higham, Charles. "Hollywood's New Wave of Writers." *New York Times,* September 29, 1974.

Hills, Gladwin. "Hollywood Denies Drug Use Is Wide." *New York Times,* September 3, 1948.

"Holiday for Mrs. Mitchum." *Sydney Morning Herald,* November 13, 1959.

"Hollywood 'Exposé' for Revenge Hinted." Newspaper story. N.p., n.d.

Honeycutt, Kirk. "Robert Mitchum Rolls Merrily On—Despite the Vehicles." *New York Times,* April 9, 1978.

Hopper, Hedda. "Bitter Realist, but a Clown, Too." Chicago Tribune–N.Y. News Syndicate, March 1961.

———. "Bob Mitchum: Horse Opera Past, Fillies in the Future." *Los Angeles Times,* November 24, 1963.

———. "He Says What He Thinks!" *Chicago Sunday Tribune,* June 28, 1953.

———. "Hollywood." *Los Angeles Daily News,* September 7, 1948.

———. "Jane Russell Likely as Mitchum Costar." *Los Angeles Times,* January 19, 1949.

———. "Mitchum Case Tough Blow to Hollywood." *Los Angeles Times,* September 7, 1948.

———. "Nothing Stops Bob!" *Chicago Sunday Tribune,* April 26, 1961.

———. "They're Pulling for Bob." *Chicago Sunday Tribune,* November 6, 1949.

"Hot Icon." *Rolling Stone,* May 14, 1992.

Howard, Anthony. "Heaven Knows, Mr. Allison Location Tobago." 20th Century-Fox publicity release, circa 1957.

Hoy, Michael J. "Robert Mitchum's Son Reveals: Secret of My Parents' 37-Year Marriage." *National Enquirer,* October 1977.

Hull, Bob. "TV Talk . . . Mitchum 'In' with Teenagers." *Los Angeles Herald-Examiner,* November 2, 1967.

Hyams, Joe. "Angler Robert Mitchum vs Work." *New York Herald Tribune,* April 30, 1959.

———. "This Is Hollywood." *New York Herald Tribune,* October 13, 1955.

"'I'm Ruined,' Says Mitchum After Marijuana Arrest." *Los Angeles Examiner,* September 2, 1948.

"In 1941, James Mitchum Was Born . . ." Magazine article. N.p., circa 1940s.

In Touch for Men Magazine. Magazine article, title, byline unknown. N.d.

"It Was a Sultry Night. . . ." *Time,* June 7, 1968.

"Jail Doors Open for Mitchum and Lila Leeds." *Los Angeles Times,* March 30, 1949.

"Jail Mitchum Halting Film." *Motion Picture Herald,* February 19, 1949.

Jameson, Sam. "Firsthand Report on the Eruption of Mt. Mitchum." *Los Angeles Times,* April 21, 1974.

"JDL Hassles Mitchum on Alleged Anti-Semitic Slurs in Esquire Story." *Variety,* March 9, 1983.

"Jockey in Marijuana Case Pleads Guilty." N.p., n.d.

Jones, Jack. "Ex-'Bad Girl' Turns to God." *Los Angeles Times,* January 31, 1974.

Jordan, Charles. "Robert Mitchum, the Nude Who Came to Dinner." *Confidential Magazine,* June 1955.

"Judge Refuses Mitchum Plea to Postpone Term." *Los Angeles Times,* February 12, 1949.

Kael, Pauline. "The Current Cinema." *New Yorker,* December 4, 1971.

Kasindorf, Martin. "How Now, Dick Daring?" *New York Times,* September 10, 1972.

Keller, Kevin. "Mitchum Joins Robertson as One of 'Boys.'" *Hollywood Reporter,* August 9, 1994.

Kennedy, Bill. "Mr. L.A." *Los Angeles Herald-Examiner,* June 28, 1968.

Kent, Rosemary. "Robert Mitchum: 'I'll Never Know Why I Do These Things.'" N.p., circa 1973.

Kilfeather, Frank. "Here Comes the Spanish Armada (Again). *Irish Times,* July 8, 1997.

King, Susan. "The Interview, Mitchum-Style." *Los Angeles Times,* April 1, 1990.

Klein, Andy. "Ol' Droopy Eyes Is Back." *L.A. Reader,* December 3, 1993.

Kramer, Stanley. "Into Surgery for 'Not as a Stranger.'" *Colliers,* February 4, 1955.

Kristal, Mark. "Has Robert Mitchum Been the Real Philip Marlowe All Along?" Los Angeles, August 1975.

Kupcinet, Irv. "Irv Kup." *Los Angeles Daily News,* October 1, 1948.

"Landlady's Lawyer Says Mitchum Has No Privacy." *Los Angeles Times,* January 28, 1949.

Lardine, Bob. "I've Had It with Films." *New York Sunday News,* December 13, 1970.

Lavin, Cheryl. "A Tough Night with a Tough Mitchum." *Chicago Tribune,* January 9, 1983.

Lawrenson, Helen. "The Man Who Never Got to Speak for National Youth Day." *Esquire,* May 1964.

LeBlanc, Jerry. "Mitchum Candid When Interviewed." *Newark Evening News,* October 12, 1968.

Leeds, Lila. "I Am a Hollywood Exile." N.p., n.d.

———. "Lila Leeds' Own Story." *New York Daily News,* January 15, 1950.

Lewin, David. "Revelations of a Sensual Rogue." *Photoplay,* June 1978.

Lewis, Grover. "The Last Celluloid Desperado." *Rolling Stone,* March 15, 1973.

Lieber, Perry. "Robert Mitchum Biography." RKO publicity release. February 12, 1946.

"Lila Leeds Hubby Put in Cooler as Holdup Suspect." *Los Angeles Examiner,* February 26, 1951.

"Lila Leeds Sued for Return of Betrothal Ring." *Los Angeles Examiner,* September 30, 1948.

"Liz Smith Passes on a. . . ." *Los Angeles Herald-Examiner,* October 3, 1987.

Lochte, Dick. "Just One More Hangover." *Los Angeles Free Press,* June 29 and July 6, 1973.

MacAdams, Lewis. "Robert Mitchum." *L.A. Weekly,* December 9-15, 1983.

MacPherson, Virginia. "Mitchum Upholds Reputation." United Press, January 10, 1951.

"Madrid Hails Mitchum." *Hollywood Reporter,* October 12, 1967.

Mann, Roderick. "I Gave Up Being Serious." *New York World-Telegram,* August 15, 1959.

———. "Mitchum—Down and Out in Amsterdam." *Los Angeles Times,* February 27, 1977.

———. "Mitchum: Out of Step with Style and Aplomb." *Los Angeles Times,* October 8, 1978.

Manners, Dorothy. "At Last He Is a Hero." *Los Angeles Herald-Examiner,* January 12, 1964.

———. "Jersey Eyeing Mitchum." *Los Angeles Herald-Examiner,* July 26, 1971.

"Marijuana Goes Up in Smoke; This Seized by Raiders." *Los Angeles Examiner,* n.d.

Marks, Audi. "Quiet Role for Tough-Guy Actor." *New York Newsday,* circa 1969.

Maslin, Janet. "Stewart, Mitchum and a Nation's Character." *New York Times,* July 13, 1997.

Masters, Dorothy. "Mitchum Has Word for Film-Making in Greece." *New York Sunday News,* August 3, 1958.

Mastronardi, Pete. "Bridgeport Born Bob Mitchum Penned Poems When a Boy Here." *Bridgeport Post,* September 5, 1948.

McAsh, Ian F. "Robert Mitchum the Dancing Bear Meets the Hawks." *Films Illustrated,* April 1979.

McBride, Joseph. ""Bob Mitchum Comments About Life and Work." *Variety,* May 16, 1977.

McCarthy, Todd. "L.A. Film Critics Give Award for Career's Work to Mitchum." *Variety,* October 9, 1980.

McWilliams, Michael. "Robert Mitchum: From Shadows to Slow, Quiet Fame." *Detroit News,* July 2, 1997.

"Meillon Stars Again." *Sydney Morning Herald TV Guide,* October 12, 1959.

Mendelsohn. "White Witch Doctor." 20th Century-Fox publicity release, 1953.

"Merrymaking in Montecito." *Los Angeles Times,* February 27, 1980.

Michelson, Herb. "Robert Mitchum Reminisces on Stage at S.F. Filmfest." *Variety,* May 5, 1983.

Michener, Charles. "Taking the Team Picture." *Newsweek,* August 9, 1982.

Mills, Bart. "'Big Sleep' Revives Mitchum as Marlowe." *Los Angeles Times,* October 23, 1977.

———. "Mitchum: Recalling a Warm, Cuddly Bear of a Man." *Outlook,* July 5, 1997.

Mills, Nancy. "Mitchums: All in the Family." *Los Angeles Times,* October 15, 1985.

"Mitchum and Pals to Plead in Court Next Wednesday." *Los Angeles Daily News,* September 21, 1948.

"Mitchum and Wife Parted." *Los Angeles Times,* March 12, 1953.

"Mitchum Answers Damage Claim Suit." *Los Angeles Mirror,* January 31, 1949.

"Mitchum Appears on Dope Charges." *Los Angeles Times,* September 9, 1948.

"Mitchum Asks Additional Time to Enter Plea." Newspaper story. N.p., n.d.

"Mitchum Back on Movie Lot." *Hollywood Citizen-News,* January 11, 1949.

"Mitchum Begins Behind-Bars Role." *Los Angeles Times,* February 11, 1949.

"Mitchum Denies He Labeled GIs Scared." *Los Angeles Times,* November 13, 1961.

"Mitchum Denies Kicking GI in Bar Row." *Los Angeles Examiner,* November 9, 1951.

"Mitchum Denies Nude Hamburger Act, Sues." *Los Angeles Herald Express,* May 9, 1955.

"Mitchum Denies Role of 'Nudeburger'; Sues." *Los Angeles Examiner,* May 10, 1955.

"'Mitchum Didn't Rap GI's: Zanuck." *Los Angeles Examiner,* November 12, 1961.

"Mitchum Drug Case Is Sent to Grand Jury." *Los Angeles Herald Tribune,* September 3, 1948.

"Mitchum Explains Film Firing." January 13, 1955. Newspaper story. N.p., n.d.

"Mitchum Fined $200." *Los Angeles Herald Express,* December 8, 1953.

"Mitchum Fired for Pushing Aid into Frisco Bay." Newspaper story. N.p., January 12, 1955.

"Mitchum Freed to Resume Career." *Los Angeles Times,* March 31, 1949.

"Mitchum Friend Faces New Charge." *Los Angeles Times,* January 27, 1949.

"Mitchum Gets 60-Day Jail Sentence." *Los Angeles Times,* February 10, 1949.

"Mitchum Gets Few Lines as Witness in Lawsuit." *Los Angeles Times,* December 23, 1949.

"Mitchum Goes to Jail Farm." *Los Angeles Examiner,* February 17, 1949.

"Mitchum Has New Chores on County's Honor Farm." *Los Angeles Times,* February 17, 1949.

"Mitchum Holds Hobo Instinct; Had Varied Jobs Before Films." Newspaper story. N.p., circa 1948.

"Mitchum in Court Today." *Los Angeles Examiner,* December 4, 1953.

"Mitchum in Dutch for Ditching Cop." *Los Angeles Mirror,* December 3, 1953.

"Mitchum in Homestretch, Back in Jail." *Los Angeles Daily News,* March 24, 1949.

"Mitchum in Trouble over Ticket." *Los Angeles Times,* December 3, 1953.

"Mitchum Incorporated Telefilm Prod. in Firm." *Variety*, November 24, 1953.

"Mitchum Indicted on 2 Drug Counts." *New York Herald Tribune*, September 8, 1948.

"Mitchum Indicted with Three Others." *Los Angeles Times*, September 8, 1948.

"Mitchum Indictments Will Be Sought Today." *Los Angeles Examiner*, September 7, 1948.

"Mitchum Is In Town." *Observer* (London), October 2, 1969.

"Mitchum Kicked Soldier, Says Brawl Witness." *Hollywood Citizen-News*, November 9, 1951.

"Mitchum Leaves: 'Cheesed Off.'" *Sydney Morning Herald*, December 18, 1959.

"Mitchum Loses Star Role in Film for Horseplay." *Los Angeles Times*, January 13, 1955.

"Mitchum May Get Prison on 'Evading Arrest' Charges." *Los Angeles Herald Express*, December 4, 1953.

"Mitchum Passes Up Grand Jury Hearing." *Hollywood Citizen-News*, September, 7, 1948.

"Mitchum Picked. . . ." *Los Angeles Times*, December 13, 1991.

"Mitchum Quits Farm for Jail." *Los Angeles Examiner*, March 25, 1949.

"Mitchum Returns from Outdoors to Serve Rest of Sentence in Jail." *Los Angles Times*, March 25, 1949.

"Mitchum Revealed: Not as a Stranger." Magazine article. N.p., n.d.

"Mitchum Roused Early to Scrub Prison Floors." United Press, February 10, 1949.

"Mitchum Says Jail Sure Cure for Insomnia." *Los Angeles Daily News*, February 17, 1949.

"Mitchum Seeks Stay for Film." *Los Angeles Examiner*, February 11, 1949.

"Mitchum Settles 'Marijuana Den' Damage Suit." *Los Angeles Times*, May 4, 1951.

"Mitchum Sounds Off On H'wood Acting . . . 'It's Humiliating.'" *Morning Telegraph*, circa 1961.

"Mitchum Sued for $50,200 in Auto Crash." *Los Angeles Times,* June 15, 1954.

"Mitchum Sued by Business Associate." *Los Angeles Herald-Examiner,* March 29, 1983.

"Mitchum Sues Magazine for $1,000,000." *Los Angles Times,* May 10, 1955.

"Mitchum Sues Film Actress." *Los Angeles Times,* January 19, 1949.

"Mitchum Suing Over Use of His Name in Ad." *Los Angeles Times,* January 19, 1949.

"Mitchum to Treasure 'Booby' Award." *Hollywood Citizen-News,* December 20, 1950.

"Mitchum 'Treasures' Award of 'Least Co-operative Actor.'" *Los Angeles Herald Express,* December 21, 1950.

"Mitchum Trial Held Up Due to Giesler Accident." *Los Angeles Times,* November 13, 1948.

"Mitchum vs Irisher—and the Jig Is Up!" United Press International, August 5, 1959.

"Mitchum Will Sing 'Man' Praises on TV." *Variety,* October 26, 1955.

"Mitchum Won't Go Before Jury." *Los Angeles Examiner,* September 5, 1948.

"Mitchum's Baby Makes Camera Debut." *Bridgeport Post,* August 31, 1952.

"Mitchum's Career Safe Despite Jail." *Los Angeles Times,* February 10, 1949.

"Mitchum's Pal Ford Gets 60 Days in Jail." *Los Angeles Times,* March 17, 1949.

"Mitchum's Son Injured When Hit by Auto." *Los Angeles Times,* April 29, 1949.

"Mitchum's View on Acting." *Long Beach Press-Telegram,* June 28, 1988.

Mitchum, Christopher. "Robert Mitchum" (letter to the editor). *People,* November 11, 1985.

Mitchum, Dorothy. "My Bob—Our Man Behind the Mask." *Photoplay,* December 1954.

"Mitchum, Girls Sued by House Owner." *Los Angeles Daily News*, October 26, 1948.

"Mitchum, Lila Leeds to Leave Jail Today." *Los Angeles Examiner*, March 30, 1949.

"Mitchum, Lila to Quit Jail for Vicki Trial." *Los Angeles Daily News*, February 15, 1949.

"Mitchum, Lila Won't Testify." *Los Angeles Examiner*, March 9, 1949.

"Mitchum, Lila, Ford Guilty." *Los Angeles Examiner*, January 11, 1949.

Mitchum, Robert. "Do I Get Another Chance?" *Photoplay*, May 1949.

———. "Mitchum's Mirror." United Artists, press release, 1956.

———. "Not So Tough Guy." *Memories*, Fall 1988.

———. "Robert Mitchum's Story." *New York Sunday News*, February 20, 1949.

"Mitchum, Three Others Indicted on Two Counts." *Los Angeles Exmainer*, September 8, 1948.

Modderno, Craig. "Mitchum the Marvel." *US*, June 19, 1980.

———. "The Tired Eyed Tough Guy Takes on Hollywood." *Oui*, February 1981.

"Modest." *Los Angeles Examiner*, n.d.

"Morning Report." *Los Angeles Times*, October 1, 1987.

Mosby, Aline. "New Way for Stars to Save." Newspaper story. N.p., n.d..

———. "Robert Mitchum Is Free Today." United Press, March 29, 1949.

"Mother Gets Subpoena for Trial of Mitchum." *Los Angeles Times*, January 1, 1949.

"Mother Ordered to Mitchum Trial." *Los Angeles Daily News*, January 1, 1949.

"Mrs. Mitchum Says She'll Stand By." *Los Angeles Times*, September 4, 1948.

Muir, Florabel. "What Now for Mitchum?" *Photoplay*, April 1949.

"Narcotic Arrest Smashes Film Career, Says Mitchum." Newspaper story. N.p., September 2, 1948.

Natale, Richard. "Screen Legend." *Variety,* July 2, 1997.

"NBC-TV Gives Go-Ahead to Mitchum Sitcom 'Joe.'" *Variety,* November 21, 1989.

Neigher, Harry. "Mitchum Vows to Win Wife Back Once Again." *Sunday Herald,* March 15, 1953.

"New Dope Arrests Due in Hollywood Cleanup." *Los Angeles Examiner,* September 2, 1948.

"News for Women." *Sydney Daily Telegraph,* November 13, 1959.

"Newsmakers." *Newsweek,* August 4, 1975.

"'Not Blotto,' Says Lila Leeds; Free on Bail." Newspaper story. N.p., June 8, 1949.

"Note from Bob Mitchum in Amsterdam." *Los Angeles Herald-Examiner,* November 12, 1976.

Obituary. *Los Angeles Times,* July 2, 1997.

Obituary. *New York Times,* July 2, 1997.

Obituary. Reuters, July 1, 1997.

"Of Skunks and Actors." N.p., circa 1954.

O'Hallaren, Bill. "He's the Only Gary Cooper Still Alive." *TV Guide,* January 29, 1983.

"On location in Japan. . . ." *TIME,* February 25, 1974.

"One Minute Interview: Robert Mitchum." N.p., circa 1975.

Oppenheimer, Peer J. "The Mellowing of a Hollywood Roughneck." *Family Weekly,* January 2, 1966.

Osborne, Robert. "Rambling Reporter." *Hollywood Reporter,* December 31, 1996; July 3, 1997.

"Our Own Mitchum in Best Role Yet." *Bridgeport Herald,* April 7, 1957.

Parsons, Louella O. "Hollywood's Determined Rebel." N.p., circa 1955.

———. "Mitchum Role Given Wayne." *Los Angeles Examiner,* January 17, 1955.

———. "Mitchum's Sister Marries." *Los Angeles Examiner,* February 8, 1960.

———. "Mitchum 'Sick' Executives Say." N.p., circa September 1948.

"Passing Judgment." *Los Angeles Herald-Examiner,* April 14, 1983.

"People." *Time,* July 15, 1985.

"Perrine, Majors, Mitchum Set for Roles in 'Agency.'" *Boxoffice,* November 20. 1978.

Poster, Tom, and Don Singleton. "Actor Threw $45M Ball." *New York Daily News,* January 28, 1984.

Prelutsky, Burt. "A Hindsight View of Robert Mitchum." *New York Post,* December 12, 1970.

————. "Bulgar Bob." *Los Angeles Times West Magazine,* December 6, 1970.

"Prize for Mitchum." *Hollywood Reporter,* December 3, 1991.

"Producers Hunt Sedate Sub for Gay Bob Mitchum." *Los Angeles Mirror,* January 12, 1955.

"Production Line." *Screen International,* September 16, 1994.

"Re Mitchum and Prem." Unsourced memo to studio from the set of Rosebud.

"Reagan Aids Tribute to Robert Mitchum." *Variety,* October 12, 1983.

Redelings, Lowell. "The Hollywood Scene: One Minute Interviews." *Hollywood Citizen-News,* January 23, 1953.

"Reel for Real." Title unknown, September 1957.

Rehfeld, Barry. "Robert Mitchum Gives a Rare Interview." *Esquire,* February 1963.

Rickey, Carrie. "A Seasoned Champion." *Village Voice,* December 21, 1982.

"Robert Mitchum." *Western Clippings,* September–October 1997.

"Robert Mitchum Faces Marijuana Count with Lila Leeds, Two Others." *Los Angeles Times,* September 1, 1948.

"Robert Mitchum in Bar Brawl, Soldier Winds Up in a Hospital." Newspaper story. N.p., n.d.

"Robert Mitchum Playing Journalist." *Hollywood Citizen-News,* July 24, 1967.

"Robert Mitchum Quits Movie After Row with Director Otto Preminger." Incomplete newspaper clipping. N.p., circa July 1974.

"Robert Mitchum Tells of $20 Dole by Agent." *Los Angeles Times,* February 5, 1948.

"Robert Mitchum, Bo Derek. . . ." *Screen International,* November 13, 1992.

"Robert Mitchum. . . ." *Screen International,* July 31, 1992.

Robertson, Nan. "On the Tumult in Tobago for 'Mr. Allison.'" *New York Times,* November 18, 1956.

Roura, Phil, and Tom Poster. "People." *New York Daily News,* May 8, 1984.

Ruark, Robert C. "Mitchum's Sins." *Los Angeles Times,* September 9, 1948.

Russell, Fred H. "Meet Robert Mitchum, Boy Who Made Good in Films." *Bridgeport Post,* January 14, 1945.

Sanders, Richard, and David Wallace. "Three Generations of Mitchums Wrestle with Some Real-Life Family Problems in a TV Movie." *People,* October 21, 1985.

Sarris, Andrew. ". . . and the Man Who Made It." *New York Times,* November 17, 1968.

———. "He Does Something Different." *Village Voice,* July 26, 1973.

Schallert, Edwin. "Kramer to Advertise in Mitchum's Defense." *Los Angeles Times,* January 18, 1955.

Scheuer, Philip K. "Critics? There's No Pleasing 'Em at All." *Los Angeles Times,* December 12, 1962.

———. "Films Regain Poetry in 'Voice in the Wind.'" *New York Times,* circa 1944.

———. "Foreign Intrigue Producer Finds Pot of Gold Abroad." *Los Angeles Times,* June 17, 1956.

Schmitt, Joan Dew. "On Becoming a Liberated Man." *You,* May 1971.

Schwager, Jeff. "The Past Rewritten." *Film Comment,* January/February 1991.

Scott, Adrian. "You Can't Do That." *Screen Writer,* August 1947.

Scott, John L. "Mitchum's Mobile Cabin Takes Him into Wilds He Really Loves." *Los Angeles Times,* August 24, 1952.

Scott, Vernon. "Bob Mitchum: Happy Rebel." *The Record,* March 12, 1975.

————. "Luncheon with Robert Mitchum." *Hollywood Citizen-News*, November 16, 1962.

————. "Mitchum Doesn't Pull His Punches." *Hollywood Citizen-News*, April 10, 1965.

————. "Movie Stars Live Everywhere These Days, but in Hollywood." *New York Morning Telegraph*, December 29, 1958.

————. "Young Mitchum Rising on Own." *Los Angeles Times*, January 10, 1976.

Scott, Walter. "Walter Scott." *Parade*, May 31, 1992.

Seligmann, Jean. "Two Chips Off Old Blocks." *Newsweek*, March 30, 1987.

"Series Debut for Mitchum." *Los Angeles Times*, November 21, 1989.

Seymore, James W. "Rough, Tough and Rowdy Robert Mitchum." *People*, February 14, 1983.

Sharp, Kathleen. "A Star in Spite of Himself." *Parade*, June 12, 1994.

Shearer, Lloyd. "Hollywood's Most Underrated Actor." *Bridgeport Post*, February 19, 1961.

Sheehan, Henry. "Mitchum's Appearance Belied His Dedication." *Orange County Register*, July 2, 1997.

"Short Takes." *Variety.* January 16 and July 29, 1992.

Skolsky, Sidney. "Hollywood Is My Beat." *New York Post*, May 4, 1952; July 17, 1955.

"Sleepy Eyes. . . ." *Women's Wear Daily*, July 1, 1974.

Smith, Alan, and Michael Glynn. "Robert Mitchum: Why He Refused Treatment to Save His Life." *The National Enquirer*, July 15, 1997.

Smith, Cecil. "Mitchum to Make TV Debut in ABC Film." *Los Angeles Times*, December 31, 1980.

"Snootful of Trouble." *Newsweek*, August 17, 1959.

"Social Cannibals." *Sydney Telegraph*, December 20, 1959.

Sofia, Carolyn. "Mitchum Heads 'Grass' Menagerie at MGM." *Chronicle*, November 5, 1970.

Somers, Alan. "3 Teenage Girls Tell Police: 'Robert Mitchum Hit Us . . . Tried to Turn Us On to Drugs.'" *Motion Picture*, December 1970.

"Son of Robert Mitchum Gets Film Contract." *Los Angeles Times,* May 6, 1961.

St. Johns, Elaine. "Robert Mitchum's Own Story." *Los Angeles Mirror,* February 17, 1949.

Stage & Cinema. Incomplete magazine article, title, author unknown, September 29, 1967.

"Star Brought His Camera." *Sydney Morning Herald,* September 30, 1959.

Starman, Ray. "Arthur Ripley." *Films in Review.*

"Still Active." *New York Times,* June 6, 1954.

Story, Judy. "Robert Mitchum." USO Public Relations Department, February 2, 1967.

"Strange Behavior in Chase." Newspaper story. N.p., circa December 3, 1953.

"Studios Won't Aid Mitchum at Trial; Grand Jury to Act." *Los Angeles Examiner,* September 3, 1948.

"Suit Against Mitchum Settled During Trial Recess." *Los Angeles Daily News,* May 3, 1951.

"Suit for $2500 Over Raid Case Names Mitchum." *Los Angeles Times,* October 27, 1948.

"Suit over Privacy Lost by Mitchum." *Los Angeles Times,* March 3, 1949.

Sullivan, Ed. "Little Old New York." *New York Daily News,* December 16, 1954.

Sun, Victoria. "Robert Mitchum, Actor with Tough-Guy Image, Dead At 79." Associated Press, July 2, 1997.

"Surprised." *Los Angeles Times,* September 2, 1948.

"Take It from Mitchum. . . ." *Los Angeles Herald-Examiner,* June 27, 1988.

Taylor, Frank. "Robert Mitchum, A Long Beach Original." *Southland Sunday,* November 29, 1970.

"That $ Sign 'Don't Hang It on Me.'" Australian newspaper story. N.p., circa 1959.

"The Big Sleep Has Opened Across the U.S.A." Scimitar Films (London) press release, n.d.

"The Love Scene They Tried to Cut." *Motion Picture,* June 1955.

"The New Pictures." *TIME*, August 13, 1956.

"The Shaggy Man . . . Guess Who?" *Sydney Sun-Herald*, November 29, 1959.

"Then They Saw More Simone." Associated Press, April 7, 1954.

"This Will Drive You In-Zane. . . ." *Variety*, June 29, 1993.

Thomas, Bob. "Mitchum Contends . . . on Nude Bathing." *Los Angeles Mirror*, October 18, 1955.

———. "Nobody Got Dunked, Mitchum Still Fired, Wayne Has Job." *Los Angeles Herald Express*, January 18, 1955.

Thomas, John D. "Down by Law." *Creative Loafing*, May 11, 1996.

Thompson, Douglas. "Mitchum Is Just Punchy About Pouchy Partner." *New York Post*, June 17, 1978.

Thompson, Howard. "Actress in Action." *New York Times*, December 26, 1954.

Thompson, Madeline. "Hollywood Miracle." *Motion Picture*, October 1945.

Thompson, Richard. "Robert Mitchum Is Better Than Dean Martin." *Scanlans*, April 1970.

Thompson, Thomas. "Robert Mitchum: Funky, Funny, Tender, Profane." *Cosmopolitan*, November 1976.

Trachtenberg, J. A. "Mitchum: New Season for an Old Pro." *Women's Wear Daily*, December 4, 1982.

"Trial Ordered for Mitchum." *Los Angeles Examiner*, September 30, 1948.

"Try to Save Mitchum by Dancer Revealed." *Los Angeles Times*, March 10, 1949.

Turner, George E. "Creating the Night of the Hunter." *American Cinematographer*, December 1982.

———. "Out of the Past." *American Cinematographer*, March 1984.

Tusher, Will. "ATA Puts on Lavish Mitchum Tribute." *Variety*, October 7, 1983.

Tusher, William. "How Chris Mitchum Suffered for Dad's Wild Ways." *Photoplay*, April 1973.

———. "My God, I'm Blind!" *Photoplay*, March 1971.

"Two Film Stars to Try TV." *New York Times*, December 13, 1980.

Tyler, Tim. "Hero-Bum Gets Knocked Down and Gets Up Without a Grunt." *San Francisco Examiner,* April 19, 1970.

———. "Will Success Spoil Robert Mitchum?" *Los Angeles Times West Magazine,* February 1, 1970.

Unger, Henry. "The JDL vs Robert Mitchum." *Los Angeles Herald-Examiner,* March 8, 1983.

"Valediction." *Hollywood Reporter,* July 10, 1997.

"Vicki Evans Weeps as Jury Chosen for Marijuana Trial." *Hollywood Citizen-News,* n.d.

"Vicki Loses Reefer Plea, Faces Trial with Mitchum." *Los Angeles Daily News,* October 8, 1948.

"Vicki to Return, 'Clear It All Up.'" *Los Angeles Mirror,* January 12, 1949.

"Waiting for a Poisoned Peanut." *Time,* August 16, 1968.

"Wanted List." *TV Guide,* December 23, 1989.

Ward, Robert. "Mr. Bad Taste and Trouble Himself Robert Mitchum." *Rolling Stone,* March 1, 1983.

Waterbury, Ruth. "He's Murder." *Photoplay,* April 1948.

———. "The Very Private Life of a Rebel Male." *Modern Screen,* March 1969.

Waters, Harry F. "ABC's High-Flying 'Winds.'" *Newsweek,* February 7, 1983.

Watts, Stephen. "Focus on Amour in a Stately Home." *New York Times,* June 26, 1960.

Webb, John M. "Robert Mitchum's Wife: My Tough Guy Husband Is Really a Sensitive Man Who Writes Poetry." *National Enquirer,* October 17, 1974.

Weber, Bruce. "Robert Mitchum." *Interview,* 1997.

"Weissmuller, Mitchum Boys Nabbed." *Los Angeles Mirror,* March 15, 1956.

"Whose Responsibility?" *St. Louis Globe-Democrat,* September 6, 1948.

"Why Can't Mitchum Behave?" *Movie,* circa 1954.

"Wife Defends Mitchum After Reconciliation; Asserts 'He's Sick Man.'" *Los Angeles Examiner,* September 4, 1948.

Wilkerson, W. R. "Radeviews." *Hollywood Reporter*, February 10, 1949.

Wilson, Earl. "Battling Bob." Syndicated column. January 19, 1971.

———. "Earl Wilson on Broadway." *New York Post*, July 8, 1967; June 24, 1972.

———. "It Happened Last Night." *New York Post*, June 20, 1969; January 12, 1971.

———. "Mitchum's Advice on Pot." *Los Angeles Herald-Examiner*, June 30, 1969.

———. "Quotable Mr. Mitchum." *Los Angeles Herald-Examiner*, January 19, 1971.

———. "Testimonial." *New York Post*, November 27, 1960.

Wilson, Jeff. "Robert Mitchum Dies in Sleep at Age 79." *Orange County Register*, July 2, 1997.

Winner, Karin. "Making Waves on the Queen Mary." *Women's Wear Daily*, April 29, 1975.

Winslow, Thyra Samter. "Mitchum–Free Style." *Photoplay*, September 1947.

Wolfsen. "Bob Mitchum, Who Looks Like a Beachcomber. . . ." 20th Century-Fox publicity release, circa 1957.

Wood, Andy. "After What My Wife Did . . . I Can't Go Home Again!" *Photoplay*, May 1968.

Wood, Robin. "The Shadow Worlds of Jacques Tourneur." *Film Comment*, Summer 1972.

Woodyard, Chris. "Mitchum Checks into Ford Center for the Cure." *Los Angeles Herald-Examiner*, May 8, 1984.

Wouk, Herman. "Robert Mitchum." *TV Guide*, August 2, 1997.

"Wrong Bottle, Says Lila Leeds." *Los Angeles Examiner*, March 9, 1948.

"Youngstein Files Suit vs Mitchum, Talbot Prods." *Hollywood Reporter*, April 1, 1983.

Yudain, Sidney. "Tip on Mitchum Pay Runs into Big Story." *Bridgeport Herald*, September 5, 1948.

Zec, Donald. "Mr. Robert Mitchum—Facing the World at 10:30 am." N.p., circa 1963.

In addition the following newspapers and magazines were examined for reviews of Robert Mitchum films between 1943 and 1997; The *New York Times*, The *Chicago Tribune*, The *Los Angeles Times*, The *New York Daily News*, *Time*, *Newsweek*, The *New Yorker*, The *Nation*, The *New Republic*, The *New York Herald Tribune*, *Variety*, The *Hollywood Reporter*.

Film/Video

The Frank Sinatra Show. January 10, 1958. ABC.
Saturday Night Live. November 14, 1987.
The RKO Story (aka: *Hollywood: The Golden Years*). 1987. BBC/RKO.
Robert Mitchum: The Reluctant Star. 1991. Cinemax.
Interview with Robert Mitchum, Jane Russell by Robert Osborne. Turner Classic Movies.
Interview with Robert Mitchum by Charles Champlin, Dave Holland. 1994.

Filmography

Robert Mitchum

Hoppy Serves a Writ. 1943. United Artists, Harry Sherman. Producer: Harry Sherman. Director: Lesley Selander. Screenplay: Michael Wilson. Players: William Boyd, Andy Clyde, Jay Kirby, Victor Jory, George Reeves, Roy Barcroft, Bob Mitchum.

Border Patrol. 1943. United Artists, Harry Sherman. Producer: Harry Sherman. Director: Lesley Selander. Screenplay: Michael Wilson. Players: William Boyd, Andy Clyde, Jay Kirby, Russell Simpson, George Reeves, Duncan Renaldo, Pierce Lyden, Bob Mitchum.

The Leather Burners. 1943. United Artists, Harry Sherman. Producer: Harry Sherman. Director: Joseph Henabery. Screenplay: Jo Pagano. Players: William Boyd, Andy Clyde, Jay Kirby, Victor Jory, George Reeves, Bob Mitchum.

The Human Comedy. 1943. MGM. Producer-Director: Clarence Brown. Screenplay: Howard Estabrook, William Ludwig. Players: Mickey Rooney, Frank Morgan, Fay Bainter, Van Johnson, James Craig, Donna Reed, Bob Mitchum.

Follow the Band. 1943. Universal. Producer: Paul Malvern. Director: Jean Yarbrough. Screenplay: Warren Wilson, Dorothy Bennett. Players: Eddie Quillan, Mary Beth Hughes, Leon Errol, Samuel S. Hinds, Bob Mitchum.

Colt Comrades. 1943. United Artists, Harry Sherman. Producer:

Harry Sherman. Director: Lesley Selander. Screenplay: Michael Wilson. Players: William Boyd, Andy Clyde, Jay Kirby, George Reeves, Douglas Fowley, Bob Mitchum.

We've Never Been Licked. 1943. Universal. Producer: Walter Wanger. Director: John Rawlins. Screenplay: Nick Grinde, Norman Reilly Raine. Players: Anne Gwynne, Richard Quine, Martha O'Driscoll, William Frawley, Mantan Moreland, Bob Mitchum.

Beyond the Last Frontier. 1943. Republic. Director: Howard Bretherton. Screenplay: John K. Butler, Morton Grant. Players: Eddie Dew, Smiley Burnette, Lorraine Miller, Bob Mitchum.

Bar 20. 1943. United Artists, Harry Sherman. Producer: Harry Sherman. Director: Lesley Selander. Screenplay: Norman Houston, Michael Wilson, Morton Grant. Players: William Boyd, Andy Clyde, George Reeves, Victor Jory, Dustine Farnum, Douglas Fowley, Bob Mitchum.

Doughboys in Ireland. 1943. Columbia. Producer: Jack Fier. Director: Lew Landers. Screenplay: Howard J. Green, Monte Brice. Players: Kenny Baker, Jeff Donnell, Bob Mitchum.

Aerial Gunner. 1943. Paramount. Producer: William Pine, William Thomas. Director: William Pine. Screenplay: Maxwell Shane. Players: Chester Morris, Richard Arlen, Jimmy Lydon, Billy Benedict, Bob Mitchum.

Corvette K-225. 1943. Universal. Producer: Howard Hawks. Director: Richard Rosson. Screenplay: John Rhodes Sturdey. Players: Randolph Scott. Ella Raines, James Brown, Barry Fitzgerald, Andy Devine, Charles McGraw, Robert Mitchum.

The Lone Star Trail. 1943. Universal. Director: Ray Taylor. Screenplay: Oliver Drake, Victor Halperin. Players: Johnny Mack Brown, Tex Ritter, Fuzzy Knight, Jennifer Holt, Bob Mitchum.

False Colors. 1943. United Artists, Harry Sherman. Producer: Harry Sherman. Director: George Archainbaud. Screenplay: Bennett Cohen. Players: William Boyd, Andy Clyde, Douglas Dumbrille, Jimmy Rogers, Bob Mitchum.

The Dancing Masters. 1943. 20th Century-Fox. Producer: Lee Marcus. Director: Mal St. Clair. Screenplay: Scott Darling.

Starring: Stan Laurel, Oliver Hardy, Trudy Marshall, Margaret Dumont, Bob Mitchum.

Riders of the Deadline. 1943. United Artists, Harry Sherman. Producer: Harry Sherman. Director: Lesley Selander. Screenplay: Bennett Cohen. Players: William Boyd, Andy Clyde, Jimmy Rogers, Bob Mitchum.

Gung Ho! 1943. Universal. Producer: Walter Wanger. Director: Ray Enright. Screenplay: Lucien Hubbard. Players: Randolph Scott, Alan Curtis, Noah Beery, Jr., Grace MacDonald, J. Carroll Naish, Bob Mitchum.

Minesweeper. 1943. Paramount. Producer: William Pine, William Thomas. Director: William Berke. Screenplay: Edward T. Lowe, Maxwell Shane. Players: Richard Arlen, Jean Parker, Russell Hayden, Guinn "Big Boy" Williams, Bob Mitchum.

Cry Havoc. 1943. MGM. Producer: Edwin Knopf. Director: Richard Thorpe. Screenplay: Paul Osborne. Players: Margaret Sullavan, Ann Sothern, Joan Blondell, Fay Bainter, Marsha Hunt, Ella Raines, Heather Angel, Frances Gifford, Diana Lewis, Victor Killian, Bob Mitchum.

Johnny Doesn't Live Here Anymore. 1944. Monogram, King Brothers. Producer: Maurice King. Director: Joe May. Screenplay: Philip Yordan, John Kafka. Players: Simone Simon, James Ellison, William Terry, Minna Gombell, Chick Chandler, Alan Dinehart, Grady Sutton, Rondo Hatton, Jerry Maren, Robert Mitchum.

When Strangers Marry. 1944. Monogram, King Brothers. Producer: Maurice King, Frank King. Director: William Castle. Screenplay: Philip Yordan, Dennis Cooper. Players: Kim Hunter, Dean Jagger, Robert Mitchum, Neil Hamilton, Lou Lubin, Dewey Robinson, Rhonda Fleming.

Thirty Seconds Over Tokyo. 1944. MGM. Producer: Sam Zimbalist. Director: Mervyn LeRoy. Screenplay: Dalton Trumbo from the book by Ted W. Lawson. Players: Spencer Tracy, Van Johnson, Robert Walker, Phyllis Thaxter, Robert Mitchum, Horace McNally, Donald Curtis, Louis Jean Heydt, Steve Brodie.

Mr. Winkle Goes to War. 1944. Columbia. Producer: Jack Moss.

Director: Alfred E. Green. Screenplay: Waldo Salt, Louis Solomon. Players: Edward G. Robinson, Ruth Warrick, Robert Armstrong, Ted Donaldson, Bob Haymes, Richard Gaines, Ann Shoemaker, Jeff Donnell, Hugh Beaumont, Robert Mitchum.

Girl Rush. 1944. RKO. Director: Gordon Douglas. Screenplay: Robert E. Kent. Players: Wally Brown, Alan Carney, Frances Langford, Vera Vague, Robert Mitchum.

Nevada. 1944. RKO. Producer: Herman Schlom. Director: Edward Killy. Screenplay: Norman Houston from the novel by Zane Grey. Players: Robert Mitchum, Anne Jeffreys, Guinn "Big Boy" Williams, Nancy Gates, Richard Martin.

West of the Pecos. 1945. RKO. Producer: Herman Schlom. Director: Edward Killy. Screenplay: Norman Houston from the novel by Zane Grey. Players: Robert Mitchum, Barbara Hale, Richard Martin, Thurston Hall, Russell Hopton, Bill Williams, Rita Corday.

The Story of G.I. Joe (aka *War Correspondent*). 1945. United Artists/Lester Cowan. Producer: David Hall. Director: William A. Wellman. Screenplay: Leopold Atlas, Guy Endore, Philip Stevenson from the book *Brave Men* by Ernie Pyle. Players: Burgess Meredith, Robert Mitchum, Freddie Steele, Jimmy Lloyd, Wally Cassell, Jack Reilly.

Till the End of Time. 1946. RKO. Producer: Dore Schary. Director: Edward Dmytryk. Screenplay: Allen Rivkin from the novel *They Dream of Home* by Niven Busch. Players: Dorothy McGuire, Guy Madison, Robert Mitchum, Bill Williams, Jean Porter, Tom Tully, William Gargan, Harry Von Zell, Johnny Sands.

Undercurrent. 1946. MGM. Producer: Pandro S. Berman. Director: Vincente Minnelli. Screenplay: Edward Chodorov. Players: Katharine Hepburn, Robert Taylor, Robert Mitchum, Edmund Gwenn, Marjorie Main, Jayne Meadows, Clinton Sundberg, Barbara Billingsley, Hank Worden.

The Locket. 1946. RKO. Producer: Bert Granet. Director: John Brahm. Screenplay: Sheridan Gibney. Players: Laraine Day, Brian Aherne, Robert Mitchum, Gene Raymond, Ricardo Cortez.

Pursued. 1947. Warner Bros. Producer: Milton Sperling. Director:

Raoul Walsh. Screenplay: Niven Busch. Players: Teresa Wright, Robert Mitchum, Judith Anderson, Dean Jagger, John Rodney, Harry Carey, Jr.

Crossfire. 1947. RKO. Producer: Adrian Scott. Director: Edward Dmytryk. Screenplay: John Paxton from the novel *The Brick Foxhole* by Richard Brooks. Players: Robert Young, Robert Mitchum, Robert Ryan, Gloria Grahame, Paul Kelly, Sam Levene, Steve Brodie, Jacqueline White, Lex Barker.

Desire Me. 1947. MGM. Producer: Arthur Hornblow, Jr. Director: (uncredited: George Cukor, Mervyn LeRoy, Victor Saville, Jack Conway). Screenplay: Marguerite Roberts, Zoe Akins from the novel *Karl and Anna* by Leonhard Frank. Players: Greer Garson, Robert Mitchum, Richard Hart, George Zucco, Florence Bates.

Out of the Past. 1947. RKO. Producer: Warren Duff, Robert Sparks. Director: Jacques Tourneur. Screenplay: Geoffrey Homes (psuedonym for Daniel Mainwaring) from his novel *Build My Gallows High* (uncredited additions by Frank Fenton, James M. Cain). Players: Robert Mitchum, Jane Greer, Kirk Douglas, Paul Valentine, Rhonda Fleming, Steve Brodie, Richard Webb, Virginia Huston, Dickie Moore.

Rachel and the Stranger. 1948. RKO. Producer: Richard H. Berger. Director: Norman Foster. Screenplay: Waldo Salt from stories by Howard Fast. Players: Loretta Young, William Holden, Robert Mitchum, Gary Gray.

Blood on the Moon. 1948. RKO. Producer: Theron Warth. Director: Robert Wise. Screenplay: Lillie Hayward from the novel *Gunman's Chance* by Luke Short. Players: Robert Mitchum, Barbara Bel Geddes, Robert Preston, Walter Brennan, Phyllis Thaxter, Frank Faylen, Harry Carey, Jr., Charles McGraw, Iron Eyes Cody.

The Red Pony. 1949. Republic. Producer: Charles K. Feldman. Director: Lewis Milestone. Screenplay: John Steinbeck from his novel. Players: Myrna Loy, Robert Mitchum, Louis Calhern, Shepperd Strudwick, Peter Miles, Beau Bridges.

The Big Steal. 1949. RKO. Producer: Jack J. Gross. Director: Don Siegel. Screenplay: Geoffrey Homes, Gerald Drayson Adams from a story by Richard Wormser. Players: Robert Mitchum, Jane Greer, William Bendix, Patric Knowles, Ramon Navarro, Don Alvarado, John Qualen.

Holiday Affair. 1949. RKO. Producer-Director: Don Hartman. Screenplay: Isobel Lennart from a story by John D. Weaver. Players: Robert Mitchum, Janet Leigh, Wendell Corey, Gordon Gebert.

Where Danger Lives. 1950. RKO. Producer: Irving Cummings, John Farrow. Director: John Farrow. Screenplay: Charles Bennett from a story by Leo Rosten. Players: Robert Mitchum, Faith Domergue, Claude Rains, Maureen O'Sullivan.

My Forbidden Past. 1951. RKO. Producer: Robert Sparks, Polan Banks. Director: Robert Stevenson. Screenplay: Marion Parsonnet from the novel *Carriage Entrance* by Polan Banks. Players: Robert Mitchum, Ava Gardner, Melvyn Douglas, Janis Carter, Lucille Watson.

His Kind of Woman. 1951. RKO. Producer: Howard Hughes, Robert Sparks, John Farrow. Director: John Farrow (uncredited: Richard Fleischer). Screenplay: Frank Fenton (uncredited: Earl Felton, Howard Hughes). Players: Robert Mitchum, Jane Russell, Vincent Price, Raymond Burr, Charles McGraw, Tim Holt, Jim Backus, Marjorie Reynolds, Anthony Caruso.

The Racket. 1951. RKO. Producer: Edmund Grainger, Howard Hughes. Director: John Cromwell (uncredited: Nicholas Ray). Screenplay: William Wister Haines, W. R. Burnett from the play by Bartlett Cormack. Players: Robert Mitchum, Robert Ryan, Lizabeth Scott, Ray Collins, Joyce MacKenzie, William Conrad, Virginia Huston, Les Tremayne.

Macao. 1952. RKO. Producer: Alex Gottlieb. Director: Josef von Sternberg (uncredited: Nicholas Ray). Screenplay: Bernard C. Schoenfeld, Stanley Rubin (uncredited: Walter Newman, Robert Mitchum, others). Players: Robert Mitchum, Jane Russell, William Bendix, Thomas Gomez, Gloria Grahame, Brad Dexter, Philip Ahn, Vladimir Sokoloff.

One Minute to Zero. 1952. RKO. Producer: Edmund Grainger. Director: Tay Garnett. Screenplay: Milton Krims, William Wister

Haines (uncredited: Andrew Solt). Players: Robert Mitchum, Ann Blythe, William Talman, Charles McGraw, Richard Egan, Edward Franz.

The Lusty Men. 1952. RKO. Producer: Jerry Wald, Norman Krasna. Director: Nicholas Ray (uncredited: Robert Parrish). Screenplay: Horace McCoy, David Dortort (Andrew Solt) from a story by Claude Stanush. Players: Susan Hayward, Robert Mitchum, Arthur Kennedy, Arthur Hunnicutt, Frank Faylen, Carol Nugent, Eleanor Todd, Maria Hart, Lorna Thayer, Burt Mustin, Chuck Roberson, John Mitchum.

Angel Face. 1952. RKO. Producer-Director: Otto Preminger. Screenplay: Frank Nugent, Oscar Millard from a story by Chester Erskine. Players: Robert Mitchum, Jean Simmons, Mona Freeman, Herbert Marshall, Leon Ames, Barbara O'Neil, Ken Tobey, Jim Backus.

White Witch Doctor. 1953. 20th Century-Fox. Producer: Otto Lang. Director: Henry Hathaway. Screenplay: Ivan Goff, Ben Roberts from the book by Louise A. Stinetorf. Players: Susan Hayward, Robert Mitchum, Walter Slezak, Timothy Carey, Mashood Ajala, Joseph Narcisse.

Second Chance. 1953. RKO. Producer: Sam Weisenthal, Edmund Grainger. Director: Rudolph Mate. Screenplay: Oscar Millard, Sydney Boehm from a story by D. M. Marshman. Players: Robert Mitchum, Linda Darnell, Jack Palance, Milburn Stone, Dan Seymour, Abel Fernandez, Rodolfo Hoyos, Jr.

She Couldn't Say No. 1954. RKO. Producer: Robert Sparks. Director: Lloyd Bacon. Screenplay: D. D. Beauchamp, William Powers, Richard Flournoy. Players: Robert Mitchum, Jean Simmons, Arthur Hunnicutt, Edgar Buchanan, Wallace Ford, Raymond Walburn, Eleanor Todd, Burt Mustin, Dabbs Greer, Pinky Tomlin.

River of No Return. 1954. 20th Century-Fox. Producer: Stanley Rubin. Director: Otto Preminger (uncredited: Jean Negulescu). Screenplay: Frank Fenton. Players: Robert Mitchum, Marilyn Monroe, Rory Calhoun, Tommy Rettig, Murvyn Vye, Douglas Spencer.

Track of the Cat. 1954. Warner Bros., Wayne-Fellows. Producer: Robert Fellows. Director: William A. Wellman. Screenplay: A. I. Bezzerides from the novel by Walter Van Tilburg Clark. Players: Robert Mitchum, Teresa Wright, Tab Hunter, Beulah Bondi, Diana Lynn, William Hopper, Carl Switzer.

Not as a Stranger. 1955. United Artists. Producer-Director: Stanley Kramer. Screenplay: Edward and Edna Anhalt from the novel by Morton Thompson. Players: Olivia DeHavilland, Robert Mitchum, Frank Sinatra, Gloria Grahame, Broderick Crawford, Charles Bickford, Myron McCormick, Lee Marvin, Lon Chaney, Jr.

The Night of the Hunter. 1955. United Artists. Producer: Paul Gregory. Director: Charles Laughton (uncredited: Robert Mitchum). Screenplay: James Agee (uncredited: Charles Laughton) from the novel by Davis Grubb. Players: Robert Mitchum, Shelley Winters, Lillian Gish, Billy Chapin, Sally Jane Bruce, Peter Graves, Evelyn Varden, James Gleason.

Man With the Gun. 1955. United Artists. Producer: Samuel Goldwyn, Jr. Director: Richard Wilson. Screenplay: N. B. Stone, Jr. Players: Robert Mitchum, Jan Sterling, Karen Sharpe, Henry Hull, Leo Gordon, Emile Meyer, John Lupton, Ted De Corsia, Angie Dickinson.

Foreign Intrigue. 1956. United Artists. Producer-Director-Writer: Sheldon Reynolds. Players: Robert Mitchum, Ingrid Tulean (Thulin), Genevieve Page, Frederick O'Brady.

Bandido!. 1956. United Artiists. Producer: Robert L. Jacks. Director: Richard Fleischer. Screenplay: Earl Felton. Players: Robert Mitchum, Gilbert Roland, Ursula Thiess, Zachary Scott, Rodolfo Acosta, Douglas Fowley.

Heaven Knows, Mr. Allison. 1957. 20th Century-Fox. Producer: Buddy Adler, Eugene Frenke. Director: John Huston. Screenplay: John Lee Mahin, John Huston from the novel by Charles Shaw. Players: Deborah Kerr, Robert Mitchum.

Fire Down Below. 1957. Columbia. Producer: Irving Allen, Albert R. Broccoli. Director: Robert Parrish. Screenplay: Irwin Shaw from the novel by Max Catto. Players: Rita Hayworth, Robert

Mitchum, Jack Lemmon, Herbert Lom, Bernard Lee, Anthony Newley, Bonar Colleano, Edric Connor.

The Enemy Below. 1957. 20th Century-Fox. Producer-Director: Dick Powell. Screenplay: Wendell Mayes from a story by Commander D. A. Rayner. Players: Robert Mitchum, Curt Jurgens, David Hedison, Theodore Bikel, Kurt Kreuger, Russell Collins, Doug McClure.

Thunder Road. 1958. United Artists, DRM. Producer: Robert Mitchum. Director: Arthur Ripley (uncredited: Robert Mitchum). Screenplay: James Atlee Phillips, Walter Wise from a story by Robert Mitchum. Songs: "The Ballad of Thunder Road" and "The Whippoorwill" by Robert Mitchum and Don Raye. Players: Robert Mitchum, Keely Smith, Gene Barry, Jacques Aubuchon, Jim Mitchum, Mitchell Ryan, Peter Breck, Jerry Hardin, Sandra Knight, Betsy Holt.

The Hunters. 1958. 20th Century-Fox. Producer-Director: Dick Powell. Screenplay: Wendell Mayes from the novel by James Salter. Players: Robert Mitchum, May Britt, Robert Wagner, Richard Egan, Lee Philips, John Gabriel.

The Angry Hills. 1959. MGM. Producer: Raymond Stross. Director: Robert Aldrich. Screenplay: A. I. Bezzerides from the novel by Leon Uris. Players: Robert Mitchum, Stanley Baker, Gia Scala, Elisabeth Mueller, Theodore Bikel, Sebastian Cabot, Leslie Philips, Donald Wolfit, Marius Goring, Kieron Moore, Jackie Lane.

The Wonderful Country. 1959. United Artists, DRM. Producer: Chester Erskin, Robert Mitchum. Director: Robert Parrish. Screenplay: Robert Ardrey (uncredited: Tom Lea) from the novel by Tom Lea. Players: Robert Mitchum, Julie London, Gary Merrill, Pedro Armendariz, Jack Oakie, Albert Dekker. Leroy "Satchel" Paige, Charles McGraw, Victor Mendoza, Anthony Caruso, Tom Lea, Chuck Roberson.

Home From the Hill. 1960. MGM. Producer: Edmund Grainger. Director: Vincente Minnelli. Screenplay: Irving Ravetch, Harriet Frank, Jr., from the novel by William Humphrey. Players: Robert Mitchum, Eleanor Parker, George Peppard, George Hamilton,

Everett Sloan, Luana Patten, Guinn "Big Boy" Williams, Denver Pyle, Burt Mustin, Anne Seymour, Constance Ford, Dub Taylor.

The Night Fighters (aka *A Terrible Beauty*). 1960. United Artists, DRM, Raymond Stross. Producer: Raymond Stross. Director: Tay Garnett. Screenplay: Robert Wright Campbell from the novel *A Terrible Beauty* by Arthur Roth. Players: Robert Mitchum, Anne Heywood, Dan O'Herlihy, Richard Harris, Cyril Cusack, Hilton Edwards.

The Grass Is Greener. 1960. Universal. Producer-Director: Stanley Donen. Screenplay: Hugh and Margaret Williams from their play. Players: Cary Grant, Deborah Kerr, Robert Mitchum, Jean Simmons.

The Sundowners. 1960. Warner Bros. Producer-Director: Fred Zinnemann. Screenplay: Isobel Lennart from the novel by Jon Cleary. Players: Deborah Kerr, Robert Mitchum, Peter Ustinov, Michael Anderson, Jr., Glynis Johns, Dina Merrill, Chips Rafferty.

The Last Time I Saw Archie. 1961. United Artists, Mark VII, Talbot. Producer-Director: Jack Webb. Screenplay: William Bowers. Players: Robert Mitchum, Jack Webb, Martha Hyer, France Nuyen, Joe Flynn, James Lydon, Louis Nye, Don Knotts, Richard Arlen, Harvey Lembeck, Robert Strauss, Howard McNear, Dick Cathcart.

Cape Fear. 1962. Universal, Melville, Talbot. Producer: Sy Bartlett (uncredited: Gregory Peck). Director: J. Lee Thompson. Screenplay: James R. Webb from the novel *The Executioners* by John D. MacDonald. Players: Gregory Peck, Robert Mitchum, Polly Bergen, Martin Balsam, Lori Martin, Telly Savalas, Jack Kruschen, Barrie Chase.

The Longest Day. 1962. 20th Century-Fox, Darryl F. Zanuck. Producer: Darryl F. Zanuck. Director: Andrew Marton, Ken Annakin, Bernhard Wicki. Screenplay: Cornelius Ryan from his book (uncredited: James Jones, Romain Gary). Players: John Wayne, Robert Mitchum, Henry Fonda, Robert Ryan, Richard Beymer, Richard Burton, Jeffrey Hunter, Robert Wagner, Peter Lawford, Richard Todd, Eddie Albert, Fabian, Red Buttons, Paul

Anka, Sal Mineo, Roddy McDowell, Irina Demich, Gert Frobe, Bourvil.

Two for the Seesaw. 1962. United Artists, Mirisch, Argyle/Talbot. Producer: Walter Mirisch. Director: Robert Wise. Screenplay: Isobel Lennart from the play by William Gibson. Players: Robert Mitchum, Shirley MacLaine, Elisabeth Fraser, Demond Ryan, Billy Gray.

The List of Adrian Messenger. 1963. Universal. Producer: Edward Lewis. Director: John Huston. Screenplay: Anthony Veiller from the novel by Philip MacDonald. Players: George C. Scott, Kirk Douglas, Dana Wynter, Clive Brook, Gladys Cooper, Herbert Marshall, Marcel Dalio, Tony Huston, John Huston, Robert Mitchum, Frank Sinatra, Tony Curtis, Burt Lancaster.

Rampage. 1963. Warner Bros., Talbot. Producer: William Fadiman. Director: Phil Karlson. Screenplay: Robert I. Holt, Marguerite Roberts from the novel by Allan Caillou. Players: Robert Mitchum, Jack Hawkins, Elsa Martinelli, Sabu.

Man in the Middle. 1964. 20th Century-Fox, Pennebaker, Talbot. Producer: Walter Seltzer. Director: Guy Hamilton. Screenplay: Keith Waterhouse from the novel *The Winston Affair* by Howard Fast. Players: Robert Mitchum, Trevor Howard, Barry Sullivan, France Nuyen, Keenan Wynn, Alexander Knox, Sam Wanamaker.

What a Way to Go! 1964. 20th Century-Fox. Producer: Arthur P. Jacobs. Director: J. Lee Thompson. Screenplay: Betty Comden and Adolph Green. Players: Shirley MacLaine, Dick Van Dyke, Dean Martin, Robert Mitchum, Paul Newman, Gene Kelly, Bob Cummings. Margaret Dumont, Army Archerd, Burt Mustin.

Mister Moses. 1965. United Artists, Frank Ross, Talbot. Producer: Frank Ross. Director: Ronald Neame. Screenplay: Charles Beaumont, Monja Danischewsky from a novel by Max Catto. Players: Robert Mitchum, Carroll Baker, Alexander Knox, Ian Bannen, Raymond St. Jacques.

The Way West. 1967. United Artists. Producer: Harold Hecht. Director: Andrew V. McLaglen. Screenplay: Ben Maddow, Mitch Lindemann from the novel by A. B. Guthrie, Jr., Players: Kirk

Douglas, Robert Mitchum, Richard Widmark, Lola Albright, Sally Field, Katherine Justice, Jack Elam, Michael Whitney, Stubby Kaye, Harry Carey, Jr., John Mitchum.

El Dorado. 1967. Paramount. Producer-Director: Howard Hawks. Screenplay: Leigh Brackett based on the novel *The Stars in Their Courses* by Harry Brown (and, uncredited, on the film *Rio Bravo*). Players: John Wayne, Robert Mitchum, James Caan, Arthur Hunnicutt, Charlene Holt, Paul Fix, Edward Asner, Michele Carey, Christopher George, Robert Donner, John Gabriel, Robert Rothwell, John Mitchum.

Anzio. 1968. Columbia, DeLaurentiis. Producer: Dino DeLaurentiis. Director: Edward Dmytryk. Screenplay: Harry A. L. Craig, Frank DeFelitta, Giuseppe Mangione from the novel by Wynford Vaughan-Thomas. Players: Robert Mitchum, Peter Falk, Arthur Kennedy, Robert Ryan, Earl Holliman, Reni Santoni, Arthur Franz.

Five Card Stud. 1968. Paramount, Hal Wallis. Producer: Hal Wallis. Director: Henry Hathaway. Screenplay: Marguerite Roberts. Players: Dean Martin, Robert Mitchum, Inger Stevens, Roddy McDowall, Katherine Justice, Yaphet Kotto, Roy Jenson.

Villa Rides. 1968. Paramount. Producer: Ted Richmond. Director: Buzz Kulik. Screenplay: Sam Peckinpah, Robert Towne. Players: Yul Brynner. Robert Mitchum, Charles Bronson, Herbert Lom, Grazia Buccella, Robert Viharo, Alexander Knox, John Ireland, Fernando Rey, Jill Ireland.

Secret Ceremony. 1968. Universal. Producer: John Heyman, Norman Priggen. Director: Joseph Losey. Screenplay: George Tabori. Players: Elizabeth Taylor, Mia Farrow, Robert Mitchum, Peggy Ashcroft, Pamela Brown, Robert Douglas.

Young Billy Young. 1969. United Artists. Producer: Max E. Youngstein. Director: Burt Kennedy. Writer: Burt Kennedy from the novel *Who Rides with Wyatt* by Will Henry. Players: Robert Mitchum, Angie Dickinson, Robert Walker, Jr., David Carradine, Jack Kelly, Paul Fix, John Anderson, Deana Martin, Rodolfo Acosta.

The Good Guys and the Bad Guys. 1969. Warner Bros. Producer:

Ronald M. Cohen, Dennis Shyrack. Director: Burt Kennedy. Screenplay: Ronald M. Cohen. Players: Robert Mitchum, George Kennedy, Martin Balsam, David Carradine, Lois Nettleton, Tina Louise, Douglas Fowley, John Davis Chandler, Marie Windsor, Dick Peabody.

Ryan's Daughter. 1970. MGM. Producer: Anthony Havelock-Allan. Director: David Lean. Screenplay: Robert Bolt. Players: Robert Mitchum, Sarah Miles, Trevor Howard, Christopher Jones, John Mills, Leo McKern, Barry Foster.

Going Home. 1971. MGM. Producer-Director: Herbert B. Leonard. Screenplay: Lawrence. B. Marcus. Players: Robert Mitchum, Jan-Michael Vincent, Brenda Vaccaro, Sally Kirkland, Jason Bernard, Lou Gilbert, Josh Mostel, Vicki Sue Robinson.

The Wrath of God. 1972. MGM. Producer: William S. Gilmore, Jr. Director: Ralph Nelson. Screenplay: Ralph Nelson from the novel by James Graham. Players: Robert Mitchum, Ken Hutcheson, Rita Hayworth, Frank Langella, Victor Buono, John Colicos, Gregory Sierra.

The Friends of Eddie Coyle. 1973. Paramount. Producer: Paul Monash. Director: Peter Yates. Screenplay: Paul Monash from the novel by George V. Higgins. Players: Robert Mitchum, Peter Boyle, Richard Jordan, Alex Rocco, Steven Keats, Joe Santos, Mitchell Ryan, Helena Carroll.

The Yakuza. 1975. Warner Bros. Producer-Director: Sydney Pollack. Screenplay: Paul Schrader, Robert Towne from a story by Leonard Schrader. Players: Robert Mitchum, Takakura Ken, Kishi Keiko, Brian Keith, Herb Edelman, Richard Jordan, James Shigeta.

Farewell, My Lovely. 1975. Avco Embassy. Producer: Elliott Kastner, Jerry Bick, Jerry Bruckheimer, George Pappas. Director: Dick Richards. Screenplay: David Zelag Goodman from the novel by Raymond Chandler. Players: Robert Mitchum, Charlotte Rampling, Jack O'Halloran, Sylvia Miles, John Ireland, Anthony Zerbe, Harry Dean Stanton, Kate Murtagh, Sylvester Stallone, Walter McGinn, Jim Thompson.

Midway. 1976. Universal. Producer: Walter Mirisch. Director: Jack

Smight. Screenplay: Donald S. Sanford. Players: Charlton Heston, Henry Fonda, Glenn Ford, James Coburn, Cliff Robertson, Robert Wagner, Toshiro Mifune, Robert Mitchum.

The Last Tycoon. 1976. Paramount. Producer: Sam Spiegel. Director: Elia Kazan. Screenplay: Harold Pinter from the novel by F. Scott Fitzgerald. Players: Robert DeNiro, Tony Curtis, Robert Mitchum, Jack Nicholson, Jeanne Moreau, Ray Milland, Ingrid Boulting, Dana Andrews, Theresa Russell, John Carradine, Anjelica Huston.

The Amsterdam Kill. 1977. Columbia, Golden Harvest. Producer: André Morgan, Raymond Chow. Director: Robert Clouse. Screenplay: Robert Clouse, Gregory Teifer. Players: Robert Mitchum, Bradford Dillman, Richard Egan, Leslie Nielsen, Keye Luke, Chan Sing, Stephen Leung.

The Big Sleep. 1978. United Artists, ITC. Producer: Elliott Kastner, Jerry Bick, Michael Winner. Director: Michael Winner. Screenplay: Michael Winner from the novel by Raymond Chandler. Players: Robert Mitchum, James Stewart, Sarah Miles, Richard Boone, Oliver Reed, Candy Clark, Joan Collins, John Mills, Edward Fox, Dudley Sutton, Diana Quick, John Justin, Harry Andrews, Richard Todd, James Donald.

Matilda. 1978. American-International. Producer: Albert S. Ruddy. Director: Daniel Mann. Screenplay: Albert S. Ruddy, Timothy Galfas from the novel by Paul Gallico. Players: Elliott Gould, Robert Mitchum, Harry Guardino, Clive Revill, Roy Clark, Lionel Stander, Art Metrano, Lenny Montana, Gary Morgan.

Breakthrough (aka *Steiner-Das Eiserne Kreuz 2*). 1978. Palladium, Rapid Film, Maverick Pictures. Producer: Wolf C. Hartwig. Director: Andrew V. McLaglen. Screenplay: Tony Williamson based on characters from the film *Cross of Iron*. Players: Richard Burton, Robert Mitchum, Rod Steiger, Michael Parks, Curt Jurgens.

Agency. 1979. Jensen Farley, Ambassador, RSL. Producer: Stephen J. Roth, Robert Lantos. Director: George Kaczender. Screenplay: Noel Hynd from a novel by Paul Gottlieb. Players: Robert

Mitchum, Lee Majors, Valerie Perrine, Alexandra Stewart, Saul Rubinek.

Nightkill. 1980. Avco Embassy. Producer: Richard Hellman, David Gil. Director: Ted Post. Screenplay: Joane Andre. Players: Jaclyn Smith, Robert Mitchum, James Franciscus, Mike Connors, Fritz Weaver, Sybil Danning. (Premiered on television: NBC.)

One Shoe Makes It Murder. CBS, Lorimar. Producer: Mel Ferrer. Director: William Hale. Sreenplay: Felix Culver from the novel *So Little Cause for Caroline* by Eric Bercovici. Players: Robert Mitchum, Angie Dickinson, Mel Ferrer, Howard Hesseman.(Television feature.)

That Championship Season. 1982. Cannon. Producer: Menahem Golan, Yoram Globus. Director: Jason Miller. Screenplay: Jason Miller from his play. Players: Bruce Dern, Stacy Keach, Robert Mitchum, Martin Sheen, Paul Sorvino.

The Winds of War. 1983. ABC, Paramount. Producer-Director: Dan Curtis. Screenplay: Herman Wouk from his novel. Players: Robert Mitchum, Ali MacGraw, Jan-Michael Vincent, Polly Bergen, Victoria Tennant, John Houseman, David Dukes, Topol, Peter Graves, Ralph Bellamy, Lisa Eilbacher, Ben Murphy, Jeremy Kemp. (Television miniseries.)

A Killer in the Family. 1983. ABC, Taft, Sunn Classics, Stan Margulies. Producer: Robert Aller. Director: Richard T. Heffron. Screenplay: Sue Grafton, Steven Humphrey, Robert Aller. Players: Robert Mitchum, James Spader, Lance Kerwin, Eric Stoltz, Salome Jens, Catherine Mary Stewart. (Television feature.)

Maria's Lovers. 1984. Cannon. Producer: Menahem Golan, Yoram Globus. Director: Andrei Konchalovsky. Screenplay: Andrei Konchalovsky, Gerard Brach, Marjorie David. Players: Nastassja Kinski, Robert Mitchum, John Savage, Keith Carradine, Anita Morris, Vincent Spano.

The Ambassador. 1984. Cannon. Producer: Menahem Golan, Yoram Globus. Director: J. Lee Thompson. Screenplay: Max Jack from the novel *52 Pick-Up* by Elmore Leonard. Players: Robert

Mitchum, Ellen Burstyn, Rock Hudson, Donald Pleasance, Fabio Testi.

The Hearst and Davies Affair. 1985. ABC. Producer-Director: David Lowell Rich. Screenplay: Alison Cross, David Solomon. Players: Robert Mitchum, Virginia Madsen, Fritz Weaver, Lorne Kennedy. (Television feature.)

Reunion at Fairborough. 1985. HBO, Columbia. Producer: William Hill, Alan King. Director: Herbert Wise. Screenplay: Albert Ruben. Players: Robert Mitchum, Deborah Kerr, Judi Trott, Red Buttons, Barry Morse. (Cable television feature.)

Promises to Keep. 1985. CBS. Producer: Sandra Harmon. Director: Noel Black. Screenplay: Phil Penningroth. Players: Robert Mitchum, Christopher Mitchum, Bentley Mitchum, Claire Bloom, Tess Harper, Jane Sibbett. (Television feature.)

North and South. 1985. ABC, David L. Wolper. Producer: Paul Freeman. Director: Richard T. Heffron. Screenplay: Douglas Heyes, Paul F. Edwards, Patricia Green, Kathleen Shelley from the novel by John Jakes. Players: Patrick Swayze, Kirstie Alley, David Carradine, Genie Francis, Lesley-Anne Down, Elizabeth Taylor, Robert Mitchum, Jean Simmons, Hal Holbrook, Johnny Cash, Gene Kelly, Morgan Fairchild, George Stanford Brown, Robert Guillaume, Forrest Whitaker, Ron O'Neal. (Television miniseries.)

Thompson's Last Run. 1986. CBS, Cypress Point, Phoenix Productions. Producer: Jennifer Faulstich. Director: Jerrold Freedman. Screenplay: John Carlen. Players: Robert Mitchum, Wilford Brimley, Susan Tyrrell, Kathleen York. (Television feature.)

The Equalizer: "Mission: McCall." 1987. CBS. Producer: Marc Laub, Daniel Lieberstein. Director: Alan Metzger. Screenplay: Ed Waters, Scott Shepherd. Players: Robert Mitchum, Robert Jordan, Robert Lansing, Frances Fisher, Edward Woodward. (Two hour-long episodes of dramatic television series.)

Mr. North. 1988. Samuel Goldwyn. Producer: Steven Haft, Skip Steloff, John Huston, Tom Shaw. Director: Danny Huston. Screenplay: John Huston, Janet Roach, James Costigan from the novel *Theophilus North* by Thornton Wilder. Players: Anthony Edwards, Robert Mitchum, Anjelica Huston, Lauren Bacall, Harry Dean Stanton.

Scrooged. 1988. Paramount. Producer: Richard Donner, Art Linson. Director: Richard Donner. Screenplay: Michael O'Donoghue, Mitch Glazer from the novella *A Christmas Carol* by Charles Dickens. Players: Bill Murray, Karen Allen, Robert Mitchum, John Glover, Carol Kane, David Johansen, Bobcat Goldthwaite.

War and Remembrance. 1988–89. ABC, Paramount. Producer: Barbara Steele, Dan Curtis. Director: Dan Curtis. Screenplay: Herman Wouk, Dan Curtis, Earl W. Wallace from the novel by Wouk. Players: Robert Mitchum, Jane Seymour, Victoria Tennant, Hart Bochner, Polly Bergen, John Gielgud, David Dukes, Sharon Stone, Sami Frey, John Rhys-Davies, Ian McShane, Ralph Bellamy. (Television miniseries.)

Brotherhood of the Rose. 1989. NBC. Producer-Director: Marvin J. Chomsky. Screenplay: Guy Waldron from the novel by David Morrell. Players: Robert Mitchum, Peter Strauss, Connie Sellecca, David Morse, James B. Sikking. (Television miniseries.)

Jake Spanner, Private Eye. 1990. USA Network. Producer: Andrew J. Fenady. Director: Lee H. Katzin. Screenplay: Andrew J. Fenady from the novel *The Old Dick* by L. A. Morse. Players: Robert Mitchum, Ernest Borgnine, John Mitchum, Jim Mitchum, Stella Stevens, Dick Van Patten, Edy Williams, Edie Adams, Terry Moore, Sheree North, Nita Talbot, Richard Yniguez, Kareem Abdul-Jabbar. (Cable television feature.)

Midnight Ride. 1990. Cannon. Producer: Joan Weidman. Director: Robert Bralver. Screenplay: Russel V. Manzatt, Robert Bralver. Players: Michael Dudikoff, Mark Hamill, Robert Mitchum.

Believed Violent. 1990. Candice Productions. Producer: Sergio Gobbi. Director: George Lautner. Screenplay: Sergio Gobbi, Gilles Lambert from a novel by James Hadley Chase. Players: Michael Brandon, Robert Mitchum, Sophie Duez, Francis Perrin, Mario Adorf.

A Family for Joe. 1990. NBC. Producer: Arnold Margolin, Sonny Grosso, Larry Jacobson, Richard Learman. Director: Jeffrey

Melman. Screenplay: Arnold Margolin. Players: Robert Mitchum. Maia Brewton, Jarrad Paul, Chris Furth, Jessica Player, Barbara Babcock, John Mitchum. (Television feature, pilot for series.)

A Family for Joe. 1990. NBC. Producer: Arnold Margolin, Sonny Grosso, Larry Jacobson, William P. D'Angelo, Byron Chudnow. Director: Alan Rafkin. Staff writers: Oliver Goldstick, Phil Rosenthal, others. Players: Robert Mitchum, Juliette Lewis, Ben Savage, David Lascher, Jessica Player, Barry Gordon, Leon the Dog. (Half-hour network television series.)

Cape Fear. 1991. Universal. Producer: Barbara DeFina, Kathleen Kennedy, Frank Marshall. Director: Martin Scorsese. Screenplay: Wesley Strick from the novel by John D. MacDonald and previous screen adaptation. Players: Robert DeNiro, Nick Nolte, Jessica Lange, Juliette Lewis, Joe Don Baker, Illeana Douglas, Gregory Peck, Robert Mitchum, Martin Balsam.

Waiting for the Wind. 1991. Envoy Productions. Producer: Jeffrey Zeitlin, Don Schroeder. Director: Don Schroeder. Screenplay: Douglas Lloyd McIntosh. Players: Robert Mitchum, Rhonda Fleming, Jameson Parker, Fred Pinkard. (Syndicated half-hour television drama.)

African Skies. 1992. Family Channel, Atlantis. Players: Catherine Bach, Robert Mitchum, Simon James. (Half-hour cable television series.)

Woman of Desire. 1993. Nu Image. Producer: Avi Lerner, Danny Lerner, Joanna Plafsky, Trevor Short. Director: Robert Ginty. Screenplay: Anthony Palmer. Players: Bo Derek, Jeff Fahey, Steven Bauer, Robert Mitchum.

Tombstone. 1993. Producer: Andrew Vajna. Director: George Cosmatos. Writer: Kevin Jarre. Players: Kurt Russell, Val Kilmer, Powers Booth, Charlton Heston, Robert Mitchum (narrator).

Backfire. 1994. Producer: J. Christian Ingvordsen. Director: A. Dean Bell. Screenplay: A. Dean Bell. Players: Kathy Ireland, Robert Mitchum, Telly Savalas, Mary McCormack, Shelly Winters, Josh Mosby.

Dead Man. 1995. Miramax. Producer: Karen Koch, Demetra

MacBride. Director: Jim Jarmusch. Screenplay: Jim Jarmusch. Players: Johnny Depp, Lance Henriksen, Gary Farmer, Mili Avital, Iggy Pop, Crispin Glover, Robert Mitchum.

Waiting for Sunset (aka *Pakten*). 1995. Norsk Film, Yellow Cottage. Producer: John Paul DeJoria, Allan Oberholzer, Gerd Haag, Nina Crone. Director: Leidulv Risan. Screenplay: Arthur Johansen, Leidulv Risan, Alan Oberholzer. Players: Robert Mitchum, Cliff Robertson, Erland Josephson, Espen Skjonberg, Hanna Schygulla, Nadja Tiller.

James Dean: Race with Destiny. 1997. Producer-Director: Mardi Rustam. Screenplay: Dan Sefton. Players: Casper Van Dien, Carrie Mitchum, Diane Ladd, Robert Mitchum.

Acknowledgments

The creation of the preceding pages has been made possible with the help of hundreds of individuals, friends and strangers alike, some contributing so generously and tirelessly that these few lines of appreciation in no way do them justice.

I thank the following for interviews, conversations, and correspondence (in some cases predating the official start of this project): James Bacon, Budd Boetticher, Mrs. L. Britton, Anthony Caruso, Phyllis Diller, Toni Cosentino Hayes, Beverly Jackson, Perry Leiber, Jr., Kathie Parrish, Henry Rackin, Reni Santoni, William Wellman, Jr., Gene Barry, Theodore Bikel, Harry Carey, Jr., John Davis Chandler, Frank Coghlan, Jr., John Colicos, Robert Donner, Jack Elam, Rhonda Fleming, John Gabriel, Robert Ginty, Leo Gordon, the eternally alluring Jane Greer, Jerry Hardin, Phil Hartman, David Hedison, Kim Hunter, Anne Jeffreys, Roy Jenson, Sally Kirkland, Lila Leeds, Janet Leigh, Pierce Lyden, Malachy McCourt, Roddy McDowall, Dina Merrill, Gary Morgan, Kate Murtagh, Michael Pate, Fred Pinkard, Jean Porter, Vincent Price, Johnny Sands, Karen Sharpe, Harry Dean Stanton, Ingrid Thulin, Les Tremayne, Paul Valentine (we'll always have Musso & Frank's), Edward Anhalt, old buddy A. I. Bezzerides, Rock Brynner, Barnaby Conrad, Sam Fuller, Oliver Goldstick, John Guare, Howard Koch, Tom Lea, Allen Rivkin, Phil Rosenthal, John Paul DeJoria, Andrew J. Fenady, William S. Gilmore, Jr., Bert Granet, Paul Gregory, Paul Helmick, Otto Lang, Alan Oberholzer, Walter Seltzer, Ken Annakin, Earl Bellamy, Edward Dmytryk, Guy Hamilton, Lee Katzin, Burt Kennedy, Andrei Konchalovsky, Stanley Kramer, Buzz Kulik,

Herbert Leonard, Andrew V. McLaglen, Ronald Neame, Alan Rafkin, Sheldon Reynolds, Dick Richards, Leidulv Risan, J. Lee Thompson, Robert Wise, Richard Wilson, Michael Winner, Anthony Cerbone, Stanley Cortez, Ray Gosnell, Victor Kemper, Max Kleven, Henry Lange, Jr., D. Michael Moore, Terry Morse, Jerome Siegel, Ron Wright, Charles Champlin, William Feeder, Joe Franklin, Irv Kupcinet, Bart Mills, Carolyn Sofia, Mrs. Alva Barr, Jeannette Dill, Jim Doughtery, Al Dowtin, Caroline Ferrera, Margie Reagan Cate Doherty Green, Edie Hemphill, Dave Holland (founding honcho of the Lone Pine Film Festival), Mickey Hoyle, Red Hoyle, Mrs. Carey Loftin, Elliott Morgan, Margaret O'Connor, Virginia Paskey, Norm Peterson, Harry Schein, Doris Siebel, Herb Speckman, Emma Warner. I also thank those persons who offered stories, information, and corroboration but preferred to do so off the record. Sad to say, some of the above have passed away since this work began.

Of all the many people who agreed to speak with me I must make special note of two women whose experiences and perspectives were particularly helpful in my attempt to tell Robert Mitchum's life story. First: Mitchum's personal assistant for more than thirty years, Reva Frederick Youngstein. She is as sharp, tough-minded, and all knowing today as she must have been in her boss's heyday. Though her relationship with Mitchum concluded unpleasantly, she was never other than fair and sympathetic in recollecting their time together—indeed, she would often correct for me rumors or printed stories that painted her old associate in a bad light.

Second: Robert's sister, Julie Mitchum Sater, who gave generously and prodigiously from her memories of a beloved brother during many hours of conversation. Intelligent, iconoclastic, and possessing a remarkable memory, she is a fascinating character in her own right.

More than one thousand documents and published works were consulted for this book. A collective thank-you to the numerous journalists and writers who chronicled—in some cases anonymously—my subject's life and career from the 1940s to his demise. Of particular value were the various columns, articles, or archived files of Hedda Hopper, Ruth Waterbury, Sidney Skolsky, Bob Thomas, William Tusher, Grover Lewis, Robert Ward, Helen Lawrenson, James Bacon, Army Archerd, Bart Mills, Bill Davidson, Andrew Sarris, and Pauline Kael. Of book-length works devoted to Mitchum, I have enjoyed and found most helpful the biographic efforts by Mike Tomkies and George Eells and bibliographic volume by Jerry Roberts. In a special category all its own is brother John Mitchum's wonderful, rollicking memoir.

My great appreciation and thanks to organizations and facilities who gave me access to the materials consulted: the Margaret Herrick Library of the Academy of Motion Picture Arts and Sciences, an invaluable institution, ditto the Special Collections department of the U.C.L.A., the New York Public Library (Lincoln Center), the British Film Institute, the Bridgeport Library, Felton High School, the Los Angeles Public Library, Victoria State Library, Melbourne (Australia), University of California Cinema Archives, Museum of Modern Art; the New York *Daily News,* the *Connecticut Post,* the *Pittsburgh Post-Gazette,* the *Asheville Citizen-Times,* the *Long Beach Press-Telegram,* the *Guardian* (Trinidad). More thanks for various services rendered: the Biltmore Hotel; the Otani Hotel; the Beverly Hills Hotel in Los Angeles; the Pacific Sands Motel in Santa Monica; the Ritz Carlton Huntington Hotel in Pasadena; the Queen Mary, Long Beach; the Dorchester Hotel, London; the Posada Tepozteco, Tepotzlan.

For assisting me in various important ways during the preparation of this book I want to thank writer Dean Server, researcher Dianne Kraft, all-around Hollywood expert Lisa Mitchell, and delightful actress and skilled producer Hope Holiday. To my valued friends Tedd and Pat Thomey who guided me through Long Beach, California's past and present, and the irascible and indestructible Marc Lawrence who got things kick started in Palm Springs when I would have preferred to do anything else—what can I say? Thank you, thank you.

More thanks to the many who gave aid and comfort when it was needed: Ed Gorman, Burks Hamner, Talmage Powell (pulp vet and my Asheville connection), George P. Pelecanos, Helen Smith, Carol Hardin, Sandy Silverman, Annie Nocenti, Janwillem van de Wetering, Arlene Hellerman, Dick Lochte, Deborah Deal, Neke Carson, Linda Danz, Julie Barker, Sal Ceravolo, Jorge Jaramillo, Alphagraphics, Bryan Cholfin, Tom Leigh, Alan Kaufman, Teresa Zarzycka.

At St. Martin's Press I am grateful to Cal Morgan who gave this project a home before himself flying the coop; and to my editor, Gordon Van Gelder, guiding the book over the pitfalls of publication with sympathy, discernment, and inspiration.

To my agent Roz Targ I send affection, admiration, and much thanks for your dedication and tender loving care.

To my mother my love and gratitude for everything, and to Terri, amiga and invaluable collaborator from day one: could not have done it without you—more later.

Throw in a tip of the hat to a theatre on Forty-second Street (was it the Lyric or the Brandt? *Requiescant in pace* in any case) where a kid, long ago, saw *Farewell, My Lovely* for a dollar and a quarter.

—L. SERVER
LServ500@aol.com

Index